THE LOEB CLASSICAL LIBRARY

FOUNDED BY JAMES LOEB, LL.D.

EDITED BY

G. P. GOOLD, PH.D.

FORMER EDITORS

†T. E. PAGE, C.H., LITT.D.   †E. CAPPS, PH.D., LL.D.

†W. H. D. ROUSE, LITT.D.   †L. A. POST, L.H.D.

†E. H. WARMINGTON, M.A., F.R.HIST.SOC.

PLUTARCH'S LIVES

VIII

100

PLUTARCH'S LIVES

WITH AN ENGLISH TRANSLATION BY
BERNADOTTE PERRIN

IN ELEVEN VOLUMES

VIII

SERTORIUS AND EUMENES
PHOCION AND CATO THE YOUNGER

CAMBRIDGE, MASSACHUSETTS
HARVARD UNIVERSITY PRESS

MCMLXXXIX

ISBN 0-674-99111-7

First printed 1919
Reprinted 1949, 1959, 1969, 1989

Printed in Great Britain by
St Edmundsbury Press Ltd, Bury St Edmunds, Suffolk

CONTENTS

PREFATORY NOTE

As in the preceding volumes of this series, agreement between the Sintenis (Teubner, 1873–1875) and Bekker (Tauchnitz, 1855-1857) editions of the *Parallel Lives* has been taken as the basis for the text. Any preference of one to the other, and any important departure from both, have been indicated. An abridged account of the manuscripts of Plutarch may be found in the Introduction to the first volume. None of the *Lives* presented in this volume are contained in the two oldest and best manuscripts—the Codex Sangermanensis (S^g) and the Codex Seitenstettensis (S), or in the excellent Paris manuscript No. 1676 (F^a). Their text therefore rests principally on the Paris manuscripts Nos. 1671, 1673, and 1674 (ACD). No attempt has been made, naturally, to furnish either a diplomatic text or a full critical apparatus. For these, the reader must be referred to the major edition of Sintenis (Leipzig, 1839–1846, 4 voll., 8vo), or to the rather inaccessible text of the *Lives* by Lindskog and Ziegler, in the Teubner

PREFATORY NOTE

Library of Greek and Latin texts (Vol. III., Fasc. I. was published in 1915). In the present edition, the reading which follows the colon in the brief critical notes is that of the Teubner Sintenis, and also, unless otherwise stated in the note, of the Tauchnitz Bekker.

All the standard translations of the *Lives* have been carefully compared and utilized, including those of the *Sertorius* and *Cato* by Professor Long.

B. PERRIN.

New Haven, Connecticut, U.S.A.
October, 1919.

ORDER OF THE PARALLEL LIVES IN THIS EDITION IN THE CHRONOLOGICAL SEQUENCE OF THE GREEK LIVES.

viii

THE TRADITIONAL ORDER OF THE PARALLEL LIVES.

(1) Theseus and Romulus.

(2) Lycurgus and Numa.

(3) Solon and Publicola.

(4) Themistocles and Camillus.

(5) Pericles and Fabius Maximus.

(6) Alcibiades and Coriolanus.

(7) Timoleon and Aemilius Paulus.

(8) Pelopidas and Marcellus.

(9) Aristides and Cato the Elder.

(10) Philopoemen and Flamininus.

(11) Pyrrhus and Caius Marius.

(12) Lysander and Sulla.

(13) Cimon and Lucullus.

(14) Nicias and Crassus.

(15) Sertorius and Eumenes.

(16) Agesilaüs and Pompey.

(17) Alexander and Julius Caesar.

(18) Phocion and Cato the Younger.

(19) Agis and Cleomenes, and Tiberius and Caius Gracchus.

(20) Demosthenes and Cicero.

(21) Demetrius and Antony.

(22) Dion and Brutus.

. . . .

(23) Artaxerxes.

(24) Aratus.

(25) Galba.

(26) Otho.

SERTORIUS

ΣΕΡΤΩΡΙΟΣ

I. Θαυμαστὸν μὲν ἴσως οὐκ ἔστιν, ἐν ἀπείρῳ
τῷ χρόνῳ τῆς τύχης ἄλλοτε ἄλλως ῥεούσης, ἐπὶ
ταὐτὰ συμπτώματα πολλάκις καταφέρεσθαι τὸ
αὐτόματον. εἴτε γὰρ οὐκ ἔστι τῶν ὑποκειμένων
ὡρισμένον τὸ πλῆθος, ἄφθονον ἔχει τῆς τῶν
ἀποτελουμένων ὁμοιότητος χορηγὸν ἡ τύχη τὴν
τῆς ὕλης εὐπορίαν, εἴτ᾽ ἔκ τινων ὡρισμένων
ἀριθμῷ συμπλέκεται τὰ πράγματα, πολλάκις
ἀνάγκη ταὐτὰ γίνεσθαι διὰ τῶν αὐτῶν περαινό-
2 μενα. ἐπεὶ δ᾽ ἀγαπῶντες ἔνιοι τὰ τοιαῦτα συνά-
γουσιν ἱστορίᾳ καὶ ἀκοῇ τῶν κατὰ τύχην γεγονότων ὅσα λογισμοῦ καὶ προνοίας ἔργοις ἔοικεν,
οἷον ὅτι δυεῖν Ἀττέων γενομένων ἐμφανῶν, τοῦ
μὲν Σύρου, τοῦ δὲ Ἀρκάδος, ἑκάτερος ὑπὸ συὸς
ἀπώλετο, δυεῖν δὲ Ἀκταιώνων, ὁ μὲν ὑπὸ τῶν
κυνῶν, ὁ δ᾽ ὑπὸ τῶν ἐραστῶν διεσπάσθη, δυεῖν δὲ
Σκηπιώνων, ὑφ᾽ οὗ μὲν ἐνικήθησαν Καρχηδόνιοι
πρότερον, ὑφ᾽ οὗ δὲ ὕστερον ἄρδην ἀνῃρέθησαν,
3 ἑάλω δὲ τὸ Ἴλιον ὑφ᾽ Ἡρακλέους διὰ τὰς Λαομέ-
δοντος ἵππους καὶ ὑπὸ Ἀγαμέμνονος διὰ τοῦ
δουρείου προσαγορευθέντος ἵππου, τρίτον δ᾽ ὑπὸ

---

[1] The story of a Lydian Attis who was killed by a wild
boar is told by Pausanias, vii. 17, 5; that of the Arcadian
Attis is unknown.

[2] The Actaeon, son of Aristaeus, who saw Artemis bathing,

2

SERTORIUS

I. It is perhaps not to be wondered at, since fortune is ever changing her course and time is infinite, that the same incidents should occur many times, spontaneously. For, if the multitude of elements is unlimited, fortune has in the abundance of her material an ample provider of coincidences; and if, on the other hand, there is a limited number of elements from which events are interwoven, the same things must happen many times, being brought to pass by the same agencies. Now, there are some who delight to collect, from reading and hearsay, such accidental happenings as look like works of calculation and forethought. They note, for example, that there were two celebrated persons called Attis, one a Syrian,[1] the other an Arcadian, and that both were killed by a wild boar; that there were two Actaeons, one of whom was torn in pieces by his dogs, the other by his lovers[2]; that there were two Scipios, by one of whom the Carthaginians were conquered in an earlier war, and by the other, in a later war, were destroyed root and branch; that Ilium was taken by Heracles on account of the horses of Laomedon, by Agamemnon by means of what is called the wooden

was changed by the goddess into a stag and devoured by his own dogs. An Actaeon, son of Melissus, was beloved by Archias of Corinth, who sought to take him away by violence. The friends of Actaeon resisted, and in the struggle Actaeon was torn to death (Plutarch, *Morals*, p. 772).

Χαριδήμου, ταῖς πύλαις ἵππου τινὸς ἐμπεσόντος
ἀποκλεῖσαι ταχὺ τῶν Ἰλιέων μὴ δυνηθέντων,
δυεῖν δὲ ὁμωνύμων τοῖς εὐωδεστάτοις φυτοῖς πόλεων, Ἴου καὶ Σμύρνης, τὸν ποιητὴν Ὅμηρον ἐν
4 ᾗ μὲν γενέσθαι λέγουσιν, ἐν ᾗ δὲ ἀποθανεῖν, φέρε
καὶ τοῦτο προσθῶμεν αὐτοῖς, ὅτι καὶ τῶν στρατηγῶν οἱ πολεμικώτατοι καὶ πλεῖστα δόλῳ κατερ-
γασάμενοι μετὰ δεινότητος ἑτερόφθαλμοι γεγό-
νασι, Φίλιππος, Ἀντίγονος, Ἀννίβας καὶ περὶ
οὗ τόδε τὸ σύγγραμμα Σερτώριος, ὃν Φιλίππου
μὲν ἄν τις ἀποφαίνοιτο σωφρονέστερον περὶ τὰς
γυναῖκας, Ἀντιγόνου δὲ πιστότερον περὶ φίλους,
5 Ἀννίβου δὲ ἡμερώτερον πρὸς πολεμίους, λειπό-
μενον δὲ συνέσει μὲν οὐδενὸς τούτων, τύχῃ δὲ
πάντων, ᾗ πολὺ τῶν ἐμφανῶν πολεμίων χαλε-
πωτέρᾳ περὶ πάντα χρησάμενος ἐπανίσωσεν
ἑαυτὸν ἐμπειρίᾳ μὲν τῇ Μετέλλου, τόλμῃ δὲ τῇ
Πομπηΐου, τύχῃ δὲ τῇ Σύλλα, δυνάμει δὲ τῇ
Ῥωμαίων, φυγὰς καὶ βαρβάρων ἔπηλυς ἄρχων
ἀντιταξάμενος.
6   Τούτῳ δὴ μάλιστα τῶν Ἑλλήνων τὸν Καρδιανὸν ὁμοιοῦμεν Εὐμένη· ἀμφότεροι γὰρ ἀρχικοὶ
καὶ σὺν δόλῳ πολεμικοί, καὶ τῆς μὲν αὐτῶν
ἀποξενωθέντες, ἡγησάμενοι δ᾽ ἀλλοδαπῶν, τύχῃ
δὲ χρησάμενοι βιαίῳ καὶ ἀδίκῳ περὶ τὴν τελευ-
τήν· ἐπιβουλευθέντες γὰρ ἀμφότεροι, μεθ᾽ ὧν
τοὺς πολεμίους ἐνίκων, ὑπὸ τούτων ἀνῃρέθησαν.

ΙΙ. Κοΐντῳ Σερτωρίῳ γένος ἦν οὐκ ἀσημότα-
τον ἐν πόλει Νούσσοις τῆς Σαβίνων· τραφεὶς δὲ

4

horse, and a third time by Charidemus, because a
horse fell in the gateway and prevented the Ilians
from closing the gate quickly enough; that there are
two cities which have the same name as the most
fragrant plants, Ios and Smyrna,[1] in one of which the
poet Homer is said to have been born, and in the
other to have died. I will therefore make this
addition to their collection. The most warlike of
generals, and those who achieved most by a mixture
of craft and ability, have been one-eyed men,—
Philip, Antigonus, Hannibal, and the subject of this
Life, Sertorius; of whom one might say that he was
more continent with women than Philip, more
faithful to his friends than Antigonus, more merciful
towards his enemies than Hannibal, and inferior to
none of them in understanding, though in fortune to
them all. Fortune he ever found harder to deal
with than his open foes, and yet he made himself
equal to the experience of Metellus, the daring of
Pompey, the fortune of Sulla, and the power of
Rome, though he was an exile and a stranger in
command of Barbarians.

With him we may best compare, among the Greeks,
Eumenes of Cardia. Both were born to command
and given to wars of stratagem; both were exiled
from their own countries, commanded foreign soldiers,
and in their deaths experienced a fortune that was
harsh and unjust; for both were the victims of plots,
and were slain by the very men with whom they
were conquering their foes.

II. Quintus Sertorius belonged to a family of some
prominence in Nussa,[2] a city of the Sabines. Having

---

[1] *Violet* and *Myrrh*.
[2] Nursia, in Latin writers, and in Amyot.

κοσμίως ὑπὸ μητρὶ χήρᾳ πατρὸς ὀρφανὸς ὑπερφυῶς δοκεῖ φιλομήτωρ γενέσθαι. ὄνομα τῆς μητρὸς Ῥέαν λέγουσιν. ἤσκητο μὲν οὖν καὶ περὶ δίκας ἱκανῶς, καί τινα καὶ δύναμιν ἐν τῇ πόλει μειράκιον ὢν ἀπὸ τοῦ λέγειν ἔσχεν· αἱ δὲ 569 περὶ τὰ στρατιωτικὰ λαμπρότητες αὐτοῦ καὶ κατορθώσεις ἐνταῦθα τὴν φιλοτιμίαν μετέστησαν.

III. Πρῶτον μὲν οὖν Κίμβρων καὶ Τευτόνων ἐμβεβληκότων εἰς Γαλατίαν στρατευόμενος ὑπὸ Καιπίωνι, κακῶς ἀγωνισαμένων τῶν Ῥωμαίων καὶ τροπῆς γενομένης ἀποβεβληκὼς τὸν ἵππον καὶ κατατετρωμένος τὸ σῶμα τὸν Ῥοδανὸν διεπέρασεν, αὐτῷ τε τῷ θώρακι καὶ θυρεῷ πρὸς ἐναντίον ῥεῦμα πολὺ νηχόμενος· οὕτω τὸ σῶμα ῥωμαλέον ἦν αὐτῷ καὶ διάπονον τῇ ἀσκήσει. 2 δεύτερον δὲ τῶν αὐτῶν ἐπερχομένων μυριάσι πολλαῖς καὶ δειναῖς ἀπειλαῖς, ὥστε καὶ τὸ μένειν ἄνδρα Ῥωμαῖον ἐν τάξει τότε καὶ τὸ πείθεσθαι τῷ στρατηγῷ μέγα ἔργον εἶναι, Μάριος μὲν ἡγεῖτο, Σερτώριος δὲ κατασκοπὴν ὑπέστη τῶν πολεμίων. ἐσθῆτι δὲ Κελτικῇ σκευασάμενος καὶ τὰ κοινότατα τῆς διαλέκτου πρὸς ἔντευξιν ἐπὶ καιροῦ παραλαβών, ἀναμίγνυται τοῖς βαρβάροις· καὶ τὰ μὲν ἰδών, τὰ δ' ἀκοῇ πυθόμενος τῶν ἐπειγόντων ἐπανῆλθε πρὸς Μάριον. τότε μὲν οὖν ἀριστείων ἔτυχεν· ἐν δὲ τῇ λοιπῇ στρατείᾳ πολλὰ καὶ συνέσεως ἔργα καὶ τόλμης ἀποδειξάμενος εἰς ὄνομα καὶ πίστιν ὑπὸ τοῦ στρατηγοῦ προήχθη. μετὰ δὲ τὸν Κίμβρων καὶ Τευτόνων πόλεμον ἐκπεμφθεὶς ὑπὸ Δειδίῳ στρατηγῷ χιλίαρχος ἐπὶ Ἰβηρίας ἐν τῇ πόλει Καστλῶνι

lost his father, he was properly reared by a widowed mother, of whom he appears to have been excessively fond. His mother's name, we are told, was Rhea. As a result of his training he was sufficiently versed in judicial procedure, and acquired some influence also at Rome from his eloquence, although a mere youth; but his brilliant successes in war turned his ambition in this direction.

III. To begin with, when the Cimbri and Teutones invaded Gaul,[1] he served under Caepio, and after the Romans had been defeated and put to flight, though he had lost his horse and had been wounded in the body, he made his way across the Rhone, swimming, shield and breastplate and all, against a strongly adverse current; so sturdy was his body and so inured to hardships by training. In the next place, when the same enemies were coming up with many myriads of men and dreadful threats,[2] so that for a Roman even to hold his post at such a time and obey his general was a great matter, while Marius was in command, Sertorius undertook to spy out the enemy. So, putting on a Celtic dress and acquiring the commonest expressions of that language for such conversation as might be necessary, he mingled with the Barbarians; and after seeing or hearing what was of importance, he came back to Marius. At the time, then, he received a prize for valour; and since, during the rest of the campaign, he performed many deeds which showed both judgement and daring, he was advanced by his general to positions of honour and trust. After the war with the Cimbri and Teutones, he was sent out as military tribune by Didius the praetor to Spain,[3] and spent the winter in Castulo, a

---

[1] In 105 b.c. [2] In 102 b.c.
[3] In 97 b.c. Didius was then pro-consul.

4 παρεχείμαζε τῆς Κελτιβήρων. ἐπεὶ δὲ τῶν
στρατιωτῶν ἐν ἀφθόνοις ὑβριζόντων καὶ τὰ
πολλὰ μεθυόντων καταφρονήσαντες οἱ βάρβαροι
μετεπέμψαντο νυκτὸς ἐπικουρίαν παρὰ τῶν
ἀστυγειτόνων Ὠριτανῶν καὶ κατ' οἰκίας ἐπιόντες
ἔκτεινον αὐτούς, ὑπεκδὺς ὁ Σερτώριος μετ' ὀλίγων
καὶ τοὺς ἐκπίπτοντας συναγαγὼν κύκλῳ τὴν
πόλιν περιῆλθε· καὶ καθ' ἃς οἱ βάρβαροι πύλας
ἔλαθον παρεισπεσόντες ἀνεῳγμένας εὑρών, οὐ
ταὐτὸν ἐκείνοις ἔπαθεν, ἀλλὰ φρουρὰς ἐπιστήσας
καὶ καταλαβὼν πανταχόθεν τὴν πόλιν ἔκτεινε
5 τοὺς ἐν ἡλικίᾳ πάντας. ὡς δὲ ἀνῃρέθησαν, ἐκέλευσε τοὺς στρατιώτας πάντας τὰ μὲν αὐτῶν
ὅπλα καὶ τὴν ἐσθῆτα καταθέσθαι, τοῖς δὲ τῶν
βαρβάρων ἐνσκευασαμένους ἔπεσθαι πρὸς τὴν
πόλιν ἐκείνην ἐξ ἧς ἀπεστάλησαν οἱ νύκτωρ
ἐπιπεσόντες αὐτοῖς. ψευσάμενος δὲ τῇ τῶν
ὅπλων ὄψει τοὺς βαρβάρους τάς τε πύλας ἀνεῳγμένας εὗρε καὶ πλῆθος ἀνθρώπων ἔλαβεν οἰο-
μένων ἀπαντᾶν εὖ πεπραχόσι φίλοις καὶ πολίταις. διὸ πλεῖστοι μὲν ὑπὸ τῶν Ῥωμαίων
ἐσφάττοντο περὶ τὰς πύλας, οἱ δὲ λοιποὶ παρα-
δόντες ἑαυτοὺς ἐπράθησαν.

IV. Ἐκ τούτου Σερτώριος ἐν τῇ Ἰβηρίᾳ διε-
βοήθη· καὶ ὅτε πρῶτον ἐπανῆκεν εἰς Ῥώμην,
ταμίας ἀποδείκνυται τῆς περὶ Πάδον Γαλατίας,
ἐν δέοντι. τοῦ γὰρ Μαρσικοῦ πολέμου συνιστα-
μένου, στρατιώτας τε προσταχθὲν αὐτῷ καταλέ-
γειν καὶ ὅπλα ποιεῖσθαι, σπουδὴν καὶ τάχος

city of the Celtiberians. Here the soldiers shook off all discipline in the midst of plenty, and were drunk most of the time, so that the Barbarians came to depise them, and one night sent for aid from their neighbours, the Oritanians, and falling upon the Romans in their quarters began to kill them. But Sertorius with a few others slipped out, and assembled the soldiers who were making their escape, and surrounded the city. He found the gate open by which the Barbarians had stolen in, but did not repeat their mistake; instead, he set a guard there, and then, taking possession of all quarters of the city, slew all the men who were of age to bear arms. Then, when the slaughter was ended, he ordered all his soldiers to lay aside their own armour and clothing, to array themselves in those of the Barbarians, and then to follow him to the city from which the men came who had fallen upon them in the night. Having thus deceived the Barbarians by means of the armour which they saw, he found the gate of the city open, and caught a multitude of men who supposed they were coming forth to meet a successful party of friends and fellow citizens. Therefore most of the inhabitants were slaughtered by the Romans at the gate; the rest surrendered and were sold into slavery.

IV. In consequence of this exploit the name of Sertorius was noised abroad in Spain; and as soon as he returned to Rome he was appointed quaestor of Cisalpine Gaul, and at a critical time. For the Marsic war[1] was threatening, and he was ordered to levy troops and procure arms; to which task he brought such earnestness and celerity, as compared with the

[1] Or Social War, 90–88 B.C.

9

προσθεὶς τῷ ἔργῳ παρὰ τὴν τῶν ἄλλων νέων
βραδυτῆτα καὶ μαλακίαν ἀνδρὸς ἐμπράκτως βιω-
2 σομένου δόξαν ἔσχεν. οὐ μὴν ὑφήκατο τῆς
στρατιωτικῆς τόλμης εἰς ἀξίωμα προεληλυθὼς
ἡγεμόνος, ἀλλὰ καὶ χειρὸς ἐπιδεικνύμενος ἔργα
θαυμαστὰ καὶ τὸ σῶμα τοῖς ἀγῶσιν ἀφειδῶς
ἐπιδιδούς, τῶν ὄψεων ἀπέβαλε τὴν ἑτέραν ἐκ-
κοπεῖσαν. ἐπὶ τούτῳ δὲ καὶ καλλωπιζόμενος
ἀεὶ διετέλει. τοὺς μὲν γὰρ ἄλλους οὐκ ἀεὶ τὰ
μαρτύρια τῶν ἀριστειῶν περιφέρειν, ἀλλὰ καὶ
ἀποτίθεσθαι στρεπτὰ καὶ δόρατα καὶ στεφάνους,
αὐτῷ δὲ τῆς ἀνδραγαθίας παραμένειν τὰ γνωρί-
σματα, τοὺς αὐτοὺς ἔχοντι τῆς ἀρετῆς ἅμα καὶ
3 τῆς συμφορᾶς θεατάς. ἀπέδωκε δὲ καὶ ὁ δῆμος
αὐτῷ τιμὴν πρέπουσαν. εἰσελθόντα γὰρ εἰς θέατρον ἐξεδέξαντό τε κρότῳ καὶ κατευφήμησαν, ὧν
οὐδὲ τοῖς πάνυ προήκουσιν ἡλικίᾳ τε καὶ δόξῃ
τυχεῖν ἦν ῥᾴδιον. δημαρχίαν μέντοι μετιὼν
Σύλλα καταστασιάσαντος αὐτὸν ἐξέπεσε· διὸ 570
4 καὶ δοκεῖ γενέσθαι μισοσύλλας. ἐπεὶ δὲ Μάριος
μὲν ὑπὸ Σύλλα κρατηθεὶς ἔφευγε, Σύλλας δὲ
Μιθριδάτῃ πολεμήσων ἀπῆρε, τῶν δὲ ὑπάτων
Ὀκτάβιος μὲν ἐπὶ τῆς Σύλλα προαιρέσεως ἔμενε,
Κίννας δὲ νεωτερίζων ὑποφερομένην ἀνεκαλεῖτο
τὴν Μαρίου στάσιν, τούτῳ προσένειμεν αὐτὸν ὁ
Σερτώριος, ἄλλως τε καὶ τὸν Ὀκτάβιον ὁρῶν
αὐτὸν μὲν ἀμβλύτερον ὄντα, τοῖς δὲ Μαρίου
5 φίλοις ἀπιστοῦντα. γενομένης δὲ τοῖς ὑπάτοις

10

slowness and indolence of the other young men, that he got the reputation of a man whose life would be one of great achievement. However, he did not remit the activities of a daring soldier after he had advanced to the dignity of a commander, but displayed astonishing deeds of prowess and exposed his person unsparingly in battle, in consequence of which he got a blow that cost him one of his eyes. But on this he actually prided himself at all times. Others, he said, could not always carry about with them the evidences of their brave deeds, but must lay aside their necklaces, spears, and wreaths; in his own case, on the contrary, the marks of his bravery remained with him, and when men saw what he had lost, they saw at the same time a proof of his valour. The people also paid him fitting honours. For, when he came into the theatre, they received him with clapping of hands and shouts of welcome, testimonials which even those who were far advanced in years and honours could not easily obtain. Notwithstanding this, when he stood for the tribuneship, Sulla formed a party against him, and he lost the election; for which reason, apparently, he became an opponent of Sulla. And so when Marius was overwhelmed by Sulla and went into exile,[1] and Sulla had set out to wage war against Mithridates,[2] and one of the consuls, Octavius, adhered to the party of Sulla, while the other, Cinna, who aimed at a revolution, tried to revive the drooping faction of Marius, Sertorius attached himself to Cinna, especially as he saw that Octavius was rather sluggish himself and distrustful of the friends of Marius. A great battle was fought in the

[1] In 88 B.C.
[2] In 87 B.C. Cf. the *Marius*, xli. 1.

ἐν ἀγορᾷ μάχης μεγάλης Ὀκτάβιος μὲν ἐκράτησε,
Κίννας δὲ καὶ Σερτώριος οὐ πολλῷ ἐλάττους τῶν
μυρίων ἀποβαλόντες ἔφυγον· καὶ τῶν περὶ τὴν
Ἰταλίαν ἔτι διεσπαρμένων στρατοπέδων προσα-
γόμενοι τὰ πλεῖστα πειθοῖ ταχὺ κατέστησαν
ἀξιόμαχοι τοῖς περὶ τὸν Ὀκτάβιον.

V. Μαρίου δὲ καταπλεύσαντος ἐκ Λιβύης καὶ
τῷ Κίννᾳ προστιθέντος ἑαυτὸν ὡς ἰδιώτην ὑπάτῳ,
τοῖς μὲν ἄλλοις ἐδόκει δέχεσθαι, Σερτώριος δὲ
ἀπηγόρευεν, εἴτε τὸν Κίνναν ἧττον οἰόμενος ἑαυτῷ προσέξειν ἀνδρὸς ἡγεμονικωτέρου παρόντος,
εἴτε τὴν βαρύτητα τοῦ Μαρίου δεδοικώς, μὴ
πάντα τὰ πράγματα συγχέῃ θυμῷ μέτρον οὐκ
ἔχοντι, πέρα δίκης ἐν τῷ κρατεῖν προερχόμενος.
2 ἔλεγεν οὖν μικρὸν εἶναι τὸ ὑπολειπόμενον ἔργον
αὐτοῖς ἤδη κρατοῦσι, δεξαμένων δὲ τὸν Μάριον
τὸ σύμπαν οἴσεσθαι τῆς δόξης ἐκεῖνον καὶ τῆς
δυνάμεως, χαλεπὸν ὄντα πρὸς κοινωνίαν ἀρχῆς
καὶ ἄπιστον. εἰπόντος δὲ τοῦ Κίννα ταῦτα μὲν
ὀρθῶς ὑπολογίζεσθαι τὸν Σερτώριον, αἰδεῖσθαι
δὲ καὶ διαπορεῖν ὅπως ἀπώσεται τὸν Μάριον
αὐτὸς ἐπὶ κοινωνίᾳ πραγμάτων κεκληκώς, ὑπο-
3 λαβὼν ὁ Σερτώριος εἶπεν· "Ἀλλ' ἐγὼ μὲν αὐτὸν
ἀφ' ἑαυτοῦ Μάριον ἥκειν νομίζων εἰς Ἰταλίαν τὸ
συμφέρον ἐσκόπουν· σοὶ δὲ τὴν ἀρχὴν οὐδὲ βουλεύεσθαι καλῶς εἶχεν ἥκοντος ὃν αὐτὸς ἐλθεῖν
ἠξίωσας, ἀλλὰ χρῆσθαι καὶ δέχεσθαι, τῆς πί-

forum between the consuls, in which Octavius was victorious, and Cinna and Sertorius took to flight, after losing almost ten thousand men; and then, winning over to their side most of the troops still scattered about Italy, they soon made themselves able to cope with Octavius.[1]

V. And when Marius sailed home from Libya [2] and was proposing to serve under Cinna as a private citizen under a consul, the rest thought that his offer should be accepted, but Sertorius declared against it, either because he thought that Cinna would pay less attention to him when a man of greater military experience was at hand, or because he was afraid of the harshness of Marius, and feared that he would throw everything into confusion by a passion which knew no limits, and exceed the bounds of justice in the hour of victory. Accordingly, he said that little remained for them to do, now that they were already victorious, and that if they received Marius he would appropriate to himself all the glory and the power, since he found it hard to share authority and was not to be trusted. Cinna replied that these considerations of Sertorius were sound, but that for his part he had perplexing scruples about rejecting Marius after having himself invited him to join their cause. To this Sertorius answered: "Indeed, I for my part thought that Marius was come of his own accord into Italy, and so I was trying to discover what was advantageous in the matter; but in thy case it was not well to deliberate at all after the arrival of one whom thou thyself didst ask to come; nay, thou shouldst have received and employed him,

---

[1] In 87 B.C. Cf. the *Marius*, xli. 1.
[2] Cf. the *Marius*, xli. 2 ff.

στεως μηδενὶ λογισμῷ χώραν διδούσης." οὕτως
μεταπέμπεται τὸν Μάριον Κίννας· καὶ τριχῇ τῆς
δυνάμεως διανεμηθείσης ἦρχον οἱ τρεῖς.

4   Διαπολεμηθέντος δὲ τοῦ πολέμου καὶ τῶν περὶ
τὸν Κίνναν καὶ Μάριον ἐμφορουμένων ὕβρεώς τε
καὶ πικρίας ἁπάσης, ὥστε χρυσὸν ἀποδεῖξαι
Ῥωμαίοις τὰ τοῦ πολέμου κακά, Σερτώριος λέγεται μόνος οὔτε ἀποκτεῖναί τινα πρὸς ὀργὴν
οὔτε ἐνυβρίσαι κρατῶν, ἀλλὰ καὶ τῷ Μαρίῳ
δυσχεραίνειν καὶ τὸν Κίνναν ἐντυγχάνων ἰδίᾳ καὶ
5 δεόμενος μετριώτερον ποιεῖν. τέλος δὲ τῶν δού-
λων, οὓς Μάριος συμμάχους μὲν ἐν τῷ πολέμῳ
δορυφόρους δὲ τῆς τυραννίδος ἔχων ἰσχυροὺς καὶ
πλουσίους ἐποίησε, τὰ μὲν ἐκείνου διδόντος καὶ
κελεύοντος, τὰ δὲ καὶ βίᾳ παρανομούντων εἰς τοὺς
δεσπότας, σφαττόντων μὲν αὐτούς, ταῖς δὲ δεσ-
ποίναις πλησιαζόντων καὶ βιαζομένων τοὺς παῖδας, οὐκ ἀνασχετὰ ποιούμενος ὁ Σερτώριος ἅπαντας ἐν ταὐτῷ στρατοπεδεύοντας κατηκόντισεν,
οὐκ ἐλάττους τετρακισχιλίων ὄντας.

VI. Ἐπεὶ δὲ Μάριος μὲν ἐτελεύτησε καὶ Κίννας ἀνῃρέθη μικρὸν ὕστερον, ὁ δὲ νεανίας Μάριος
ἄκοντος αὐτοῦ παρὰ τοὺς νόμους ὑπατείαν ἔλαβε,
Κάρβωνες δὲ καὶ Νωρβανοὶ καὶ Σκηπίωνες ἐπι-
όντι Σύλλᾳ κακῶς ἐπολέμουν, καὶ τὰ μὲν ἀνανδρίᾳ
καὶ μαλακίᾳ τῶν στρατηγῶν ἐφθείρετο, τὰ δὲ οἱ
2 προδιδόντες ἀπώλλυσαν, ἔργον δὲ οὐδὲν ἦν αὐτοῦ
παρόντος τοῖς πράγμασι μοχθηρῶς ὑποφερομέ-
νοις διὰ τὸ χεῖρον φρονεῖν τοὺς μᾶλλον δυναμέ-

---

[1] That is, when the party of Sulla and the senate ceased to
resist and Rome had surrendered.
[2] Cf. the *Marius*, xliv. 6.   [3] In 86 B.C.

since a pledge leaves room for no discussion." So
Cinna sent for Marius, the army was divided into
three parts, and the three men held command.

When the war had been brought to an end,[1] Cinna
and Marius were filled with insolence and all bitter-
ness, and made the evils of war appear as gold to the
Romans; Sertorius alone, as we are told, neither
killed any one to gratify his anger, nor waxed inso-
lent with victory, but actually rebuked Marius, and
by private interviews and entreaties made Cinna
more moderate. And finally, there were the slaves
whom Marius had used as allies during the war and as
body-guards of his tyranny. They had thus become
powerful and rich, partly by the permission and under
the orders of Marius, and partly through their lawless
and violent treatment of their masters, whom they
would slay, and then lie with their masters' wives,
and outrage their masters' children. Such a state
of things Sertorius felt to be unendurable, and therefore when the slaves were all encamped together he
had them shot down with javelins, and they were as
many as four thousand in number.[2]

VI. But presently Marius died;[3] and shortly afterwards Cinna was murdered;[4] and the younger Marius,
against the wishes of Sertorius and contrary to the
laws, assumed the consulship;[5] and such men as
Carbo, Norbanus, and Scipio were unsuccessfully opposing Sulla's advance upon Rome; and the cause of
the popular party was being ruined and lost, partly
through the cowardice and weakness of its generals,
and partly by treachery; and there was no reason
why Sertorius should remain to see matters go from
bad to worse owing to the inferior judgement of those

[4] In 84 b.c. Cf. the *Pompey*, chapter v.   [5] In 82 b.c.

νους, τέλος δὲ Σύλλας Σκηπίωνι παραστρατοπε-
δεύσας καὶ φιλοφρονούμενος, ὡς εἰρήνης ἐσομένης,
διέφθειρε τὸ στράτευμα, καὶ ταῦτα προλέγων
Σκηπίωνι καὶ διδάσκων Σερτώριος οὐκ ἔπειθε,
παντάπασιν ἀπογνοὺς τὴν πόλιν ὥρμησεν εἰς
Ἰβηρίαν, ὡς, εἰ φθάσει τὴν ἐκεῖ κρατυνάμενος
ἀρχήν, καταφυγὴ τοῖς πταίουσιν ἐνταῦθα τῶν 571
φίλων ἐσόμενος.

3   Χειμῶσι δὲ χαλεποῖς χρησάμενος ἐν χωρίοις
ὀρεινοῖς ὑπὸ βαρβάρων ἐπράττετο τέλη καὶ
μισθοὺς τοῦ παρελθεῖν τὴν ὁδόν. ἀγανακτούν-
των δὲ τῶν σὺν αὐτῷ, καὶ δεινολογουμένων εἰ
Ῥωμαίων ἀνθύπατος τέλη καταβαλεῖ βαρβάροις
ὀλέθροις, μικρὰ φροντίσας τοῦ δοκοῦντος αἰσχροῦ,
καὶ καιρὸν ὠνεῖσθαι φήσας, οὗ σπανιώτερον οὐδὲν ἀνδρὶ μεγάλων ἐφιεμένῳ, τοὺς μὲν βαρβάρους
ἐθεράπευσε χρήμασι, τὴν δ' Ἰβηρίαν ἐπειχθεὶς
4   κατέσχε. παραλαβὼν δὲ ἔθνη πλήθει μὲν καὶ
ἡλικίᾳ ἀκμάζοντα, πλεονεξίᾳ δὲ καὶ ὕβρει τῶν
πεμπομένων ἑκάστοτε στρατηγῶν πρὸς ὅλην
κακῶς διακείμενα τὴν ἡγεμονίαν, ἀνελάμβανεν
ὁμιλίᾳ τε τοὺς δυνατοὺς καὶ φόρων ἀνέσει τοὺς
πολλούς. μάλιστα δὲ τῶν ἐπισταθμιῶν ἀπαλ-
λάξας ἠγαπήθη· τοὺς γὰρ στρατιώτας ἠνάγκαζεν
ἐν τοῖς προαστείοις χειμάδια πήγνυσθαι, πρῶτος
5   αὐτὸς οὕτω κατασκηνῶν. οὐ μὴν ἐπὶ τῇ τῶν
βαρβάρων εὐνοίᾳ τὸ πᾶν ἐποιήσατο, Ῥωμαίων δὲ

who had superior power. And finally, Sulla encamped near Scipio and made friendly overtures, assuming that peace was to be made, and proceeded to corrupt his army.[1] Sertorius warned Scipio of this plainly, but could not persuade him. At last, therefore, altogether despairing of the city, he set out for Spain, in order that, in case he should succeed in firmly establishing his power there, he might afford a refuge to those of his friends who were worsted at Rome.

After encountering grievous storms in mountainous regions, he was asked by the Barbarians to pay them tribute and purchase his passage. His companions were indignant, and considered it a terrible thing for a Roman pro-consul to render tribute to pestilent Barbarians; but Sertorius made light of what they thought a disgrace, and with the remark that he was purchasing time, than which nothing is more precious to a man bent on great achievements, he pacified the Barbarians with money, and then hastened on and took possession of Spain. He found its peoples strong in numbers and in fighting men, and since the rapacity and insolence of the Roman officials sent thither from time to time had made them hostile to the empire in all its aspects, he tried to win them over, the chiefs by his personal intercourse with them, the masses by a remission of taxes. His greatest popularity, however, was won by ridding them of the necessity of furnishing quarters for soldiers; for he compelled his soldiers to build their winter-quarters in the suburbs of the cities, and he himself was first to pitch his tent there. However, he did not rely wholly on the goodwill of the Barbarians, but he armed all the

----

[1] Cf. the *Sulla*, xxviii, 1-3.

17

τῶν αὐτόθι μετοικούντων τοὺς ἐν ἡλικίᾳ καθοπλίσας, μηχανάς τε παντοδαπὰς καὶ ναυπηγίας τριήρων ὑποβαλόμενος, διὰ χειρὸς εἶχε τὰς πόλεις, ἥμερος μὲν ὢν ἐν ταῖς εἰρηνικαῖς χρείαις, φοβερὸς δὲ τῇ παρασκευῇ κατὰ τῶν πολεμίων φαινόμενος.

VII. Ὡς δὲ Σύλλαν μὲν ἐπυνθάνετο τῆς Ῥώμης κρατεῖν, ἔρρειν δὲ τὴν Μαρίου καὶ Κάρβωνος στάσιν, αὐτίκα προσδοκῶν στρατιὰν διαπολεμήσουσαν αὐτῷ μεθ' ἡγεμόνος ἀφίξεσθαι φράγνυται τὰ Πυρηναῖα ὄρη διὰ Ἰουλίου Σαλινάτορος ἑξακισχιλίους ὁπλίτας ἔχοντος. καὶ μετ' οὐ πολὺ Γάϊος Ἄννιος ἐκπεμφθεὶς ὑπὸ Σύλλα καὶ τὸν Ἰούλιον ἀπρόσμαχον ὁρῶν ἐν ἀπόρῳ καθῆστο 2 παρὰ ταῖς ὑπωρείαις. Καλπουρνίου δέ τινος ἐπίκλησιν Λαναρίου δολοφονήσαντος τὸν Ἰούλιον καὶ τῶν στρατιωτῶν τὰ ἄκρα τῆς Πυρήνης ἐκλιπόντων, ὑπερβαλὼν Ἄννιος ἐπῄει χειρὶ μεγάλῃ τοὺς ἐμποδὼν ἀνιστάς. Σερτώριος δὲ οὐκ ὢν ἀξιόμαχος μετὰ τρισχιλίων εἰς Καρχηδόνα τὴν νέαν καταφυγών, κἀκεῖθεν ἐπιβὰς τῶν νεῶν καὶ διαπεράσας τὸ πέλαγος, Λιβύῃ κατὰ τὴν Μαυ-3 ρουσίαν προσέσχεν. ἀφυλάκτοις δὲ τοῖς στρατιώταις ὑδρευομένοις τῶν βαρβάρων ἐπιπεσόντων, συχνοὺς ἀποβαλὼν αὖθις εἰς Ἰβηρίαν ἀπέπλει· καὶ ταύτης μὲν ἀποκρούεται, Κιλισσῶν δὲ λῃστρίδων αὐτῷ προσγενομένων Πιτυούσσῃ νήσῳ προσέβαλε, καὶ ἀπέβη τὴν παρ' Ἀννίου φρουρὰν βιασάμενος. Ἄννιος δὲ μετ' οὐ πολὺ παρῆν ναυσί

Roman settlers of the country who were of military age, and by undertaking the construction of all sorts of engines of war and the building of triremes, kept the cities well in hand, being mild in the affairs of peace, but showing himself formidable by the preparations which he made against his enemies.

VII. When he learned that Sulla was master of Rome,[1] and that the party of Marius and Carbo was on the way to ruin, he expected that an army with a commander would come at once to fight the issue out with him. He therefore sent Julius Salinator with six thousand men-at-arms to bar the passage of the Pyrenees. And not long afterwards Caius Annius was sent out by Sulla, and seeing that Julius could not be assailed, he knew not what to do, and sat idly down at the base of the mountains. But a certain Calpurnius, surnamed Lanarius, treacherously killed Julius, whose soldiers then abandoned the heights of the Pyrenees; whereupon Annius crossed over and advanced with a large force, routing all opposition. Sertorius, not being able to cope with him, took refuge with three thousand men in New Carthage; there he embarked his forces, crossed the sea, and landed in the country of the Maurusii, in Africa. But while his soldiers were getting water and were off their guard, the Barbarians fell upon them, and after losing many men, Sertorius sailed back again to Spain. From this shore too he was repulsed, but after being joined by some Cilician piratical vessels he attacked the island of Pityussa, overpowered the guard which Annius had set there, and effected a landing. After a short time, however, Annius came

---

[1] In 82 B.C.

τε πολλαῖς καὶ πεντακισχιλίοις ὁπλίταις, πρὸς
ὃν ἐπεχείρησε μὲν διαναυμαχεῖν, καίπερ ἐλαφροῖς
καὶ πρὸς τάχος, οὐ πρὸς ἀλκήν, πεποιημένοις
4 σκάφεσι χρώμενος, ζεφύρῳ δὲ λαμπρῷ τοῦ πελά-
γους ἀνισταμένου καὶ τὰ πολλὰ τῶν τοῦ Σερτωρίου πλοίων ὑπὸ κουφότητος πλάγια ταῖς
ῥαχίαις περιβάλλοντος, αὐτὸς ὀλίγαις ναυσὶ τῆς
μὲν θαλάσσης ὑπὸ τοῦ χειμῶνος εἰργόμενος, τῆς
δὲ γῆς ὑπὸ τῶν πολεμίων, ἡμέρας δέκα σαλεύων
πρὸς ἐναντίον κῦμα καὶ κλύδωνα τραχὺν ἐπιπό-
νως διεκαρτέρησεν.

VIII. Ἐνδόντος δὲ τοῦ πνεύματος φερόμενος
νήσοις τισὶν ἐναυλίζεται σπόρασιν ἀνύδροις· κἀκεῖθεν ἄρας καὶ διεκβαλὼν τὸν Γαδειραῖον πορθ-
μὸν ἐν δεξιᾷ τοῖς ἐκτὸς ἐπιβάλλει τῆς Ἰβηρίας,
μικρὸν ὑπὲρ τῶν τοῦ Βαίτιος ἐκβολῶν, ὃς εἰς τὴν
Ἀτλαντικὴν ἐκφερόμενος θάλατταν ὄνομα τῇ
περὶ αὑτὸν Ἰβηρίᾳ παρέσχεν.

2 Ἐνταῦθα ναῦταί τινες ἐντυγχάνουσιν αὐτῷ
νέον ἐκ τῶν Ἀτλαντικῶν νήσων ἀναπεπλευκότες,
αἳ δύο μὲν εἰσὶ λεπτῷ παντάπασι πορθμῷ διαι-
ρούμεναι, μυρίους δ' ἀπέχουσι Λιβύης σταδίους
καὶ ὀνομάζονται Μακάρων. ὄμβροις δὲ χρώμεναι 572
μετρίοις σπανίως, τὰ δὲ πλεῖστα πνεύμασι μαλα-
κοῖς καὶ δροσοβόλοις, οὐ μόνον ἀροῦν καὶ φυτεύειν
παρέχουσιν ἀγαθὴν καὶ πίονα χώραν, ἀλλὰ καὶ
καρπὸν αὐτοφυῆ φέρουσιν ἀποχρῶντα πλήθει καὶ
γλυκύτητι βόσκειν ἄνευ πόνων καὶ πραγματείας
3 σχολάζοντα δῆμον. ἀὴρ δὲ ἄλυπος ὡρῶν τε κρά-

with numerous ships and five thousand men-at-arms,
and with him Sertorius attempted to fight a decisive
naval battle, although the vessels which he had were
light and built for speed rather than for fighting.
But the sea ran high with a strong west wind, and
the greater part of the vessels of Sertorius, owing to
their lightness, were driven aslant upon the rocky
shore, while he himself, with a few ships, excluded
from the open sea by the storm, and from the land
by the enemy, was tossed about for ten days in a
battle with adverse waves and fierce surges, and
with difficulty held his own.

VIII. But the wind subsided and he was borne
along to certain scattered and waterless islands, where
he spent the night; then, setting out from there, and
passing through the strait of Cadiz, he kept the
outer coast of Spain on the right and landed a little
above the mouths of the river Baetis, which empties
into the Atlantic sea and has given its name to the
adjacent parts of Spain.

Here he fell in with some sailors who had recently
come back from the Atlantic Islands.[1] These are
two in number, separated by a very narrow strait;
they are ten thousand furlongs distant from Africa,
and are called the Islands of the Blest. They enjoy
moderate rains at long intervals, and winds which for
the most part are soft and precipitate dews, so that
the islands not only have a rich soil which is excellent
for plowing and planting, but also produce a natural
fruit that is plentiful and wholesome enough to feed,
without toil or trouble, a leisured folk. Moreover, an

---

[1] Perhaps Madeira and Porto Santo, though these are forty
miles apart. Features of the Canary Islands have doubtless
crept into the description.

σει καὶ μεταβολῆς μετριοτητι κατέχει τὰς νήσους. οἱ μὲν γὰρ ἐνθένδε τῆς γῆς ἀποπνέοντες ἔξω βορέαι καὶ ἀπηλιῶται διὰ μῆκος ἐκπεσόντες εἰς τόπον ἀχανῆ διασπείρονται καὶ προαπολείπουσι, πελάγιοι δὲ περιρρέοντες ἀργέσται καὶ ζέφυροι βληχροὺς μὲν ὑετοὺς καὶ σποράδας ἐκ θαλάττης ἐπάγοντες, τὰ δὲ πολλὰ νοτεραῖς αἰθρίαις ἐπιψύχοντες ἡσυχῇ τρέφουσιν, ὥστε μέχρι τῶν βαρβάρων διῖχθαι πίστιν ἰσχυρὰν αὐτόθι τὸ Ἠλύσιον εἶναι πεδίον καὶ τὴν τῶν εὐδαιμόνων οἴκησιν, ἣν Ὅμηρος ὕμνησε.

IX. Ταῦθ᾽ ὁ Σερτώριος ἀκούσας ἔρωτα θαυμαστὸν ἔσχεν οἰκῆσαι τὰς νήσους καὶ ζῆν ἐν ἡσυχίᾳ, τυραννίδος ἀπαλλαγεὶς καὶ πολέμων ἀπαύστων. αἰσθόμενοι δὲ οἱ Κίλικες, οὐθὲν εἰρήνης δεόμενοι καὶ σχολῆς, ἀλλὰ πλούτου καὶ λαφύρων, εἰς Λιβύην ἀπέπλευσαν, Ἄσκαλιν τὸν Ἴφθα κατά-
2 ξοντες ἐπὶ τὴν Μαυρουσίων βασιλείαν. οὐ μὴν ἀπέκαμεν ὁ Σερτώριος, ἀλλὰ τοῖς πρὸς τὸν Ἄσκαλιν διαπολεμοῦσιν ἔγνω βοηθεῖν, ὡς οἱ σὺν αὐτῷ καινήν τινα λαβόντες ἐλπίδων ἀρχὴν καὶ πράξεων ἑτέρων ὑπόθεσιν μὴ διαλυθεῖεν ὑπὸ τῆς ἀπορίας. ἀσμένοις δὲ τοῖς Μαυρουσίοις ἀφικόμενος εἴχετο ἔργου, καὶ καταμαχεσάμενος τὸν
3 Ἄσκαλιν ἐπολιόρκει. Σύλλα δὲ Πακκιανὸν ἐκπέμψαντος βοηθῆσαι τοῖς περὶ τὸν Ἄσκαλιν μετὰ δυνάμεως, συμβαλὼν ὁ Σερτώριος τὸν μὲν Πακκιανὸν ἀπέκτεινε, τὴν δὲ στρατιὰν κρατήσας

air that is salubrious, owing to the climate and the moderate changes in the seasons, prevails on the islands. For the north and east winds which blow out from our part of the world plunge into fathomless space, and, owing to the distance, dissipate themselves and lose their power before they reach the islands; while the south and west winds that envelope the islands from the sea sometimes bring in their train soft and intermittent showers, but for the most part cool them with moist breezes and gently nourish the soil. Therefore a firm belief has made its way, even to the Barbarians, that here is the Elysian Field and the abode of the blessed, of which Homer sang.[1]

IX. When Sertorius heard this tale, he was seized with an amazing desire to dwell in the islands and live in quiet, freed from tyranny and wars that would never end. The Cilicians, however, who did not want peace or leisure, but wealth and spoils, when they were aware of his desire, sailed away to Africa, to restore Ascalis the son of Iphtha to the throne of Maurusia. Nevertheless Sertorius did not despair, but resolved to go to the aid of those who were fighting against Ascalis, in order that his followers might get some fresh ground for hope and occasion for new enterprise, and so might remain together in spite of their difficulties. The Maurusians were glad to have him come, and he set himself to work, defeated Ascalis in battle, and laid siege to him. Moreover, when Sulla sent out Paccianus with an army to give aid to Ascalis, Sertorius joined battle with Paccianus and slew him, won over his soldiers after their defeat,

---

[1] *Odyssey*, iv. 563–568.

προσηγάγετο, καὶ τὴν Τίγγιν, εἰς ἣν ὁ Ἄσκαλις
συνέφυγε μετὰ τῶν ἀδελφῶν, ἐξεπολιόρκησεν.

Ἐνταῦθα τὸν Ἀνταῖον οἱ Λίβυες ἱστοροῦσι
κεῖσθαι· καὶ τὸν τάφον αὐτοῦ Σερτώριος διέ-
σκαψε τοῖς βαρβάροις ἀπιστῶν διὰ μέγεθος.
ἐντυχὼν δὲ τῷ σώματι πηχῶν ἑξήκοντα μῆκος,
ὥς φασι, κατεπλάγη, καὶ σφάγιον ἐντεμὼν συνέ-
χωσε τὸ μνῆμα, καὶ τὴν περὶ αὐτοῦ τιμήν τε καὶ
4 φήμην συνηύξησε. Τιγγῖται δὲ μυθολογοῦσιν
Ἀνταίου τελευτήσαντος τὴν γυναῖκα Τίγγην
Ἡρακλεῖ συνελθεῖν, Σόφακα δ' ἐξ αὐτῶν γενόμενον βασιλεῦσαι τῆς χώρας καὶ πόλιν ἐπώνυμον
τῆς μητρὸς ἀποδεῖξαι, Σόφακος δὲ παῖδα γενέσθαι
Διόδωρον, ᾧ πολλὰ τῶν Λιβυκῶν ἐθνῶν ὑπήκουσεν Ἑλληνικὸν ἔχοντι στράτευμα τῶν αὐτόθι
κατῳκισμένων ὑφ' Ἡρακλέους Ὀλβιανῶν καὶ
5 Μυκηναίων. ἀλλὰ ταῦτα μὲν ἀνακείσθω τῇ
Ἰόβα χάριτι, τοῦ πάντων ἱστορικωτάτου βασι-
λέων· ἐκείνου γὰρ ἱστοροῦσι τοὺς προγόνους
Διοδώρου καὶ Σόφακος ἀπογόνους εἶναι.

Σερτώριος δὲ πάντων ἐγκρατὴς γενόμενος τοὺς
δεηθέντας αὐτοῦ καὶ πιστεύσαντας οὐκ ἠδίκησεν,
ἀλλὰ καὶ χρήματα καὶ πόλεις καὶ τὴν ἀρχὴν
ἀπέδωκεν αὐτοῖς, ὅσα καλῶς εἶχε δεξάμενος διδόντων.

X. Ἐντεῦθεν ὅποι χρὴ τραπέσθαι βουλευό-
μενον ἐκάλουν Λυσιτανοὶ πρέσβεις πέμψαντες
ἐφ' ἡγεμονία, πάντως μὲν ἄρχοντος ἀξίωμα μέγα
καὶ ἐμπειρίαν ἔχοντος δεόμενοι πρὸς τὸν ἀπὸ

and forced to a surrender the city of Tingis,
into which Ascalis and his brethen had fled for
refuge.

In this city the Libyans say that Antaeus is buried;
and Sertorius had his tomb dug open, the great size
of which made him disbelieve the Barbarians. But
when he came upon the body and found it to be sixty
cubits long, as they tell us, he was dumbfounded, and
after performing a sacrifice filled up the tomb again,
and joined in magnifying its traditions and honours.
Now, the people of Tingis have a myth that after the
death of Antaeus, his wife, Tinga, consorted with
Heracles, and that Sophax was the fruit of this union,
who became king of the country and named a city
which he founded after his mother; also that Sophax
had a son, Diodorus, to whom many of the Libyan
peoples became subject, since he had a Greek army
composed of the Olbians and Mycenaeans who
were settled in those parts by Heracles. But this
tale must be ascribed to a desire to gratify Juba, of
all kings the most devoted to historical enquiry; for
his ancestors are said to have been descendants of
Sophax and Diodorus.

Sertorius, then, having made himself master of the
whole country, did no wrong to those who were his
suppliants and put their trust in him, but restored to
them both property and cities and government,
receiving only what was right and fair in free gifts
from them.

X. As he was deliberating whither to turn his
efforts next, the Lusitanians sent ambassadors and
invited him to be their leader. They were altogether
lacking in a commander of great reputation and experience as they faced the terror of the Roman arms,

Ῥωμαιων φόβον, ἐκείνῳ δὲ πιστεύοντες αὑτοὺς
μόνῳ πυνθανόμενοι παρὰ τῶν συγγεγονότων τὸ
2 ἦθος αὐτοῦ. λέγεται δὲ[1] ὁ Σερτώριος οὔτε ὑφ'
ἡδονῆς οὔτε ὑπὸ δέους εὐάλωτος γενέσθαι, φύσει
δὲ ἀνέκπληκτος ὢν παρὰ τὰ δεινὰ καὶ μέτριος εὐτυχίαν ἐνεγκεῖν· καὶ πρὸς μὲν εὐθυμαχίαν οὐδενὸς
ἀτολμότερος τῶν καθ' ἑαυτὸν ἡγεμόνων, ὅσα δὲ
κλωπείας ἐν πολέμοις ἔργα καὶ πλεονεξίας περὶ
τόπους ἐχυροὺς καὶ διαβάσεις τάχους δεομένας
ἀπάτης τε καὶ ψευδῶν ἐν δέοντι, σοφιστὴς δεινό- 573
3 τατος. ἐν δὲ ταῖς τιμαῖς τῶν ἀνδραγαθημάτων
δαψιλὴς φαινόμενος, περὶ τὰς τιμωρίας ἐμετρίαζε
τῶν ἁμαρτημάτων. καίτοι δοκεῖ περὶ τὸν ἔσχατον αὐτοῦ βίον ὠμότητος καὶ βαρυθυμίας τὸ περὶ
τοὺς ὁμήρους πραχθὲν ἔργον ἐπιδεῖξαι τὴν φύσιν
οὐκ οὖσαν ἥμερον, ἀλλ' ἐπαμπεχομένην λογισμῷ
4 διὰ τὴν ἀνάγκην. ἐμοὶ δὲ ἀρετὴν μὲν εἰλικρινῆ καὶ
κατὰ λόγον συνεστῶσαν οὐκ ἄν ποτε δοκεῖ τύχη
τις ἐκστῆσαι πρὸς τοὐναντίον, ἄλλως δὲ προαιρέ-
σεις καὶ φύσεις χρηστὰς ὑπὸ συμφορῶν μεγάλων
παρ' ἀξίαν κακωθείσας οὐκ ἀδύνατον τῷ δαίμονι
συμμεταβαλεῖν τὸ ἦθος. ὃ καὶ Σερτώριον οἶμαι
παθεῖν ἤδη τῆς τύχης αὐτὸν ἐπιλειπούσης, ἐκτρα-
χυνόμενον ὑπὸ τῶν πραγμάτων γινομένων πονηρῶν πρὸς τοὺς ἀδικοῦντας.

XI. Οὐ μὴν ἀλλὰ τότε γε τῶν Λυσιτανῶν
καλούντων ἀπῆρεν ἐκ Λιβύης. καὶ τούτους συνέ-
ταττεν εὐθὺς αὐτοκράτωρ στρατηγός, καὶ τὴν
ἐγγὺς Ἰβηρίαν ὑπήκοον ἐποιεῖτο, τῶν πλείστων

---

[1] δὲ Coraës and Bekker read γὰρ with one (inferior)
MS.

and they entrusted themselves to him, and to him alone, when they learned about his character from those who had been with him. And it is said that Sertorius was no easy victim either of pleasure or of fear, but that he was naturally unterrified in the face of danger, and bore prosperity with moderation ; in straightforward fighting he was as bold as any commander of his time, while in all military activities demanding stealth and the power to seize an advantage in securing strong positions or in crossing rivers, where speed, deceit, and, if necessary, falsehood are required, he was an expert of the highest ability. Moreover, while he showed himself generous in rewarding deeds of valour, he used moderation in punishing transgressions. And yet, in the last part of his life, the savage and vindictive treatment which he bestowed upon his hostages[1] would seem to show that his mildness was not natural to him, but was worn as a garment, from calculation, as necessity required. In my opinion, however, a virtue that is sincere and based upon reason can never by any fortune be converted into its opposite, although it is true that excellent principles and natures, when impaired by great and undeserved calamities, may possibly change their character as the guiding genius changes. And this, I think, was the case with Sertorius when fortune at last began to forsake him ; as his cause grew hopeless he became harsh toward those who did him wrong.

XI. However, at the time of which I speak he set out from Africa on the invitation of the Lusitanians. These he proceeded to organize at once, acting as their general with full powers, and he brought the neighbouring parts of Spain into subjection. Most

---

[1] See chapter xxv. 4.

ἑκουσίως προστιθεμένων, μάλιστα μὲν διὰ τὸ
πρᾷον αὐτοῦ καὶ δραστήριον, ἔστι δὲ ἃ καὶ σοφι-
στικῶς αὐτὸς εἰς ἀπάτην καὶ κήλησιν ἐμηχανᾶτο.
καὶ πρῶτόν γε πάντων τὸ περὶ τὴν ἔλαφον. ἦν
δὲ τοιόνδε.

2   Σπανὸς ἀνὴρ δημότης τῶν ἐπὶ χώρας βιούντων
ἐλάφῳ νεοτόκῳ φευγούσῃ κυνηγέτας ἐπιτυχὼν
αὐτῆς μὲν ἀπελείφθη, τὴν δὲ νεβρόν, ἐκπλαγεὶς
τῇ καινότητι τῆς χρόας (λευκὴ γὰρ ἦν πᾶσα),
λαμβάνει διώξας. κατὰ τύχην δὲ Σερτωρίου τοῖς
τόποις ἐναυλισαμένου, καὶ πᾶν ὅ τις ἐξ ἄγρας ἢ
γεωργίας ἥκοι κομίζων δῶρον ἀσμένως δεχομένου,
καὶ φιλοφρόνως ἀμειβομένου τοὺς θεραπεύοντας,
3 ἐγχειρίζει φέρων αὐτῷ τὴν νεβρόν. ὁ δὲ δεξάμενος αὐτίκα μὲν ἥσθη μετρίως· χρόνῳ δὲ
ποιησάμενος τιθασὸν οὕτω καὶ φιλάνθρωπον
ὥστε καὶ καλοῦντος ἀκούειν, καὶ βαδίζοντί ποι
παρακολουθεῖν, ὄχλου τε καὶ θορύβου παντὸς
ἀνέχεσθαι στρατιωτικοῦ, κατὰ μικρὸν ἐξεθείαζε
φάσκων Ἀρτέμιδος δῶρον τὴν ἔλαφον εἶναι, καὶ
πολλὰ τῶν ἀδήλων ἐπεφήμιζεν αὐτῷ δηλοῦν,
γινώσκων εὐάλωτον εἰς δεισιδαιμονίαν εἶναι φύσει
4 τὸ βαρβαρικόν. ὁ δὲ καὶ προσετεχνᾶτο τοιάδε·
γνοὺς γὰρ ἂν κρύφα τοὺς πολεμίους ἐμβεβληκό-
τας ποι τῆς ὑπ᾽ αὐτὸν χώρας ἢ πόλιν ἀφιστάντας,
προσεποιεῖτο τὴν ἔλαφον αὐτῷ κατὰ τοὺς ὕπνους
διειλέχθαι, κελεύουσαν ἐν ἑτοίμῳ τὰς δυνάμεις
ἔχειν. αὖθις δὲ νίκην τινὰ τῶν ἑαυτοῦ στρατη-

of the people joined him of their own accord, owing chiefly to his mildness and efficiency ; but sometimes he also betook himself to cunning devices of his own for deceiving and charming them. The chief one of these, certainly, was the device of the doe, which was as follows.

Spanus, a plebeian who lived in the country, came upon a doe which had newly yeaned and was trying to escape the hunters. The mother he could not overtake, but the fawn—and he was struck with its unusual colour, for it was entirely white—he pursued and caught. And since, as it chanced, Sertorius had taken up his quarters in that region, and gladly received everything in the way of game or produce that was brought him as a gift, and made kindly returns to those who did him such favours, Spanus brought the fawn and gave it to him. Sertorius accepted it, and at the moment felt only the ordinary pleasure in a gift ; but in time, after he had made the animal so tame and gentle that it obeyed his call, accompanied him on his walks, and did not mind the crowds and all the uproar of camp life, he gradually tried to give the doe a religious importance by declaring that she was a gift of Diana, and solemnly alleged that she revealed many hidden things to him, knowing that the Barbarians were naturally an easy prey to superstition. He also added such devices as these. Whenever he had secret intelligence that the enemy had made an incursion into the territory which he commanded, or were trying to bring a city to revolt from him, he would pretend that the doe had conversed with him in his dreams, bidding him hold his forces in readiness. Again, when he got tidings of some victory won by his generals, he would hide the

γῶν ἀκούσας τὸν μὲν ἄγγελον ἔκρυπτε, τὴν δὲ
ἔλαφον ἐστεφανωμένην ἐπ᾽ εὐαγγελίοις προῆγεν,
εὐθυμεῖσθαι παρακαλῶν καὶ τοῖς θεοῖς θύειν ὡς
ἀγαθόν τι πευσομένους.

XII. Οὕτω δὲ χειροήθεις ποιησάμενος αὐτοὺς
ἐχρῆτο πρὸς ἅπαντα μετριωτέροις, οὐχ ὑπ᾽ ἀνδρὸς ἀλλοδαποῦ λογισμῶν, ἀλλ᾽ ὑπὸ θεοῦ στρατηγεῖσθαι πειθομένοις, ἅμα καὶ τῶν πραγμάτων
ἐπιμαρτυρούντων τῷ παρὰ λόγον τὴν δύναμιν
2 αὐξάνεσθαι. δισχιλίοις γὰρ ἑξακοσίοις οὓς
ὠνόμαζε Ῥωμαίους, συμμίκτοις δὲ ἑπτακοσίοις
Λιβύων εἰς Λυσιτανίαν αὐτῷ συνδιαβᾶσι πελτα-
στὰς τετρακισχιλίους Λυσιτανῶν καὶ ἱππεῖς
ἑπτακοσίους προσλαβὼν ἐπολέμει τέτταρσι Ῥωμαίων στρατηγοῖς, ὑφ᾽ οἷς ἦσαν πεζῶν μὲν δώδεκα μυριάδες, ἱππεῖς δὲ ἑξακισχίλιοι, τοξόται δὲ
καὶ σφενδονῆται δισχίλιοι, πόλεις δὲ ἀναρίθμητοι
τὸ πλῆθος, αὐτὸς εἴκοσι τὰς πάσας ἐν ἀρχῇ
3 κεκτημένος. ἀλλ᾽ ὅμως ἀσθενὴς οὕτω καὶ μικρὸς
ἀρξάμενος οὐ μόνον ἐθνῶν ἐκράτησε μεγάλων καὶ
πόλεις εἷλε πολλάς, ἀλλὰ καὶ τῶν ἀντιστρατή-
γων Κότταν μὲν ἐν τῷ περὶ τὴν Μελλαρίαν
πορθμῷ κατεναυμάχησε, Φουφίδιον δὲ τὸν ἄρχοντα τῆς Βαιτικῆς περὶ τὸν Βαῖτιν ἐτρέψατο 574
δισχιλίους ἀποκτείνας Ῥωμαίων, Δομέτιον δὲ
Λεύκιον[1] ἀνθύπατον ὄντα τῆς ἑτέρας Ἰβηρίας
4 διὰ τοῦ ταμίου καταγωνισάμενος, καὶ Θωράνιον,
ἄλλον ἡγεμόνα τῶν ὑπὸ Μετέλλου πεμφθέντων
μετὰ δυνάμεως, ἀνεῖλεν, αὐτόν τε τὸν Μέτελλον,

---

[1] Λεύκιον the conjecture of Sint.[2], after Amyot, for the MS.
καὶ Λούσιον; Reiske, followed by Sint.[1] and Bekker, read
Καλουίσιον.

messenger, and bring forth the doe wearing garlands
for the receipt of glad tidings, exhorting his men to
be of good cheer and to sacrifice to the gods, assured
that they were to learn of some good fortune.

XII. By these devices he made the people tractable,
and so found them more serviceable for all his plans;
they believed that they were led, not by the mortal
wisdom of a foreigner, but by a god. At the same
time events also brought witness to this belief by
reason of the extraordinary growth of the power of
Sertorius. For with the twenty-six hundred men
whom he called Romans, and a motley band of seven
hundred Libyans who crossed over into Lusitania with
him, to whom he added four thousand Lusitanian
targeteers and seven hundred horsemen, he waged
war with four Roman generals, under whom were a
hundred and twenty thousand footmen, six thousand
horsemen, two thousand bowmen and slingers, and
an untold number of cities, while he himself had
at first only twenty all told. But nevertheless, from
so weak and slender a beginning, he not only subdued great nations and took many cities, but was also
victorious over the generals sent against him: Cotta
he defeated in a sea-fight in the straits near Mellaria;
Fufidius, the governor of Baetica, he routed on the
banks of the Baetis with the slaughter of two
thousand Roman soldiers; Lucius Domitius, who was
pro-consul of the other Spain,[1] was defeated at the
hands of his quaestor; Thoranius, another of the
commanders sent out by Metellus with an army, he
slew; and on Metellus himself, the greatest Roman

---

[1] Spain was divided into two provinces, Hispania Citerior
(*Hither*) and Hispania Ulterior (*Further*), or Eastern and
Western Spain. Fufidius was pro-consul of Western Spain.

ἄνδρα Ῥωμαίων ἐν τοῖς τότε μέγιστον καὶ δοκιμώτατον, οὐκ ὀλίγοις σφάλμασι περιβαλὼν εἰς
τοσαύτην ἀπορίαν κατέστησεν ὥστε Λεύκιον μὲν
Μάλλιον ἐκ τῆς περὶ Ναρβῶνα Γαλατίας ἐλθεῖν
αὐτῷ βοηθόν, Πομπήϊον δὲ Μάγνον ἐκ Ῥώμης
κατὰ τάχος ἀποσταλῆναι μετὰ δυνάμεως.

5   Οὐ γὰρ εἶχεν ὁ Μέτελλος ὅ τι χρήσαιτο προσ-
πολεμῶν ἀνδρὶ τολμητῇ πάσης ἐξαναδυομένῳ
φανερᾶς μάχης, πᾶσαν δὲ μεταβαλλομένῳ μεταβολὴν εὐσταλείᾳ καὶ κουφότητι τῆς Ἰβηρικῆς
στρατιᾶς, αὐτὸς ὁπλιτικῶν καὶ νομίμων ἀσκητὴς
γεγονὼς ἀγώνων καὶ στρατηγὸς ἐμβριθοῦς καὶ
μονίμου φάλαγγος, ὥσασθαι μὲν εἰς χεῖρας
ἐλθόντας πολεμίους καὶ καταβαλεῖν ἄριστα
γεγυμνασμένης, ὀρειβατεῖν δὲ καὶ συνηρτῆσθαι
διώξεσι καὶ φυγαῖς ἀπαύστοις ἀνθρώπων ὑπη-
νεμίων καὶ λιμὸν ἀνέχεσθαι καὶ δίαιταν ἄπυρον
καὶ ἄσκηνον, ὥσπερ ἐκεῖνοι, μὴ δυναμένης.

XIII. Ἔτι δὲ αὐτὸς μὲν ἤδη πρεσβύτερος ἦν
καί τι καὶ πρὸς ἀνειμένην ἤδη καὶ τρυφερὰν δίαιταν ἐκ πολλῶν ἀγώνων καὶ μεγάλων ἐνδεδωκώς,
τῷ δὲ Σερτωρίῳ συνειστήκει πνεύματος ἀκμαίου
γέμοντι καὶ κατεσκευασμένον ἔχοντι θαυμασίως
2   τὸ σῶμα ῥώμῃ καὶ τάχει καὶ λιτότητι. μέθης
μὲν γὰρ οὐδὲ ῥᾳθυμῶν ἥπτετο, πόνους δὲ μεγά-
λους καὶ μακρὰς ὁδοιπορίας καὶ συνεχεῖς ἀγρυπνίας ὀλίγοις εἴθιστο καὶ φαύλοις ἀρκούμενος
σιτίοις διαφέρειν, πλάνοις δὲ χρώμενος ἀεὶ καὶ
κυνηγεσίοις ὁπότε σχολάζοι, πάσης διεκδύσεως

of the time and held in highest repute, he inflicted many defeats and reduced him to so great straits that Lucius Manlius came from Gallia Narbonensis to help him, and Pompey the Great was hurriedly dispatched from Rome with an army.

For Metellus was at his wits' end. He was carrying on war with a man of daring who evaded every kind of open fighting, and who made all manner of shifts and changes, owing to the light equipment and agility of his Iberian soldiers; whereas he himself had been trained in regular contests of heavy-armed troops, and was wont to command a ponderous and immobile phalanx,[1] which, for repelling and over-powering an enemy at close quarters, was most excellently trained, but for climbing mountains, for dealing with the incessant pursuits and flights of men as light as the winds, and for enduring hunger and a life without fire or tent, as their enemies did, it was worthless.

XIII. Besides this, Metellus was now getting on in years, and was somewhat inclined also, by this time, to an easy and luxurious mode of life after his many and great contests; whereas his opponent, Sertorius, was full of mature vigour, and had a body which was wonderfully constituted for strength, speed, and plain living. For in excessive drinking he would not indulge even in his hours of ease, and he was wont to endure great toils, long marches, and continuous wakefulness, content with meagre and indifferent food; moreover, since he was always wandering about or hunting when he had leisure for it, he obtained an acquaintance with every way

---

[1] Cf. the *Pompey*, xvii. 2.

φεύγοντι καὶ διώκοντι κυκλώσεως ἀβάτων τε καὶ
βασίμων τόπων ἐμπειρίαν προσειλήφει. διὸ τῷ
μὲν εἰργομένῳ μάχης ὅσα νικώμενοι πάσχουσιν
ἄνθρωποι βλάπτεσθαι συνέβαινεν, ὁ δὲ τῷ φεύ-
3 γειν εἶχε τὰ τῶν διωκόντων. καὶ γὰρ ὑδρείας
ἀπέκοπτε καὶ σιτολογίας εἶργε, καὶ προϊόντι μὲν
ἐκποδὼν ἦν, ἐκίνει δὲ ἱδρυνθέντα, πολιορκοῦντι
δὲ ἄλλους ἐπιφαινόμενος ἀντεπολιόρκει ταῖς τῶν
ἀναγκαίων ἀπορίαις, ὥστε τοὺς στρατιώτας
ἀπαγορεύειν, καὶ τοῦ Σερτωρίου μονομαχῆσαι
προκαλουμένου τὸν Μέτελλον, βοᾶν καὶ κελεύειν
μάχεσθαι στρατηγῷ στρατηγῷ καὶ Ῥωμαῖον
4 Ῥωμαίῳ, ἀναδυόμενον δὲ χλευάζειν. ὁ δὲ τούτων μέν, εὖ ποιῶν, κατεγέλα· στρατηγοῦ γάρ,
ὡς ἔφη Θεόφραστος, δεῖ θάνατον ἀποθνήσκειν τὸν
στρατηγόν, οὐ πελταστοῦ τοῦ τυχόντος. ὁρῶν δὲ
τοὺς Λαγγοβρίτας οὐ μικρὰ τῷ Σερτωρίῳ συλ-
λαμβανομένους, δίψῃ δὲ ὄντας εὐαλώτους (ἐν
γὰρ ἦν αὐτοῖς φρέαρ ἐν τῇ πόλει, τῶν δ' ἐν τοῖς
προαστείοις καὶ παρὰ τὰ τείχη ναμάτων ὁ πο-
λιορκῶν ἐπικρατεῖν ἔμελλεν), ἧκεν ἐπὶ τὴν πόλιν
ὡς ἡμέραις δυσὶ συναιρήσων τὴν πολιορκίαν,
ὕδατος οὐκ ὄντος. διὸ καὶ πέντε ἡμερῶν ἐπιφέρεσθαι σιτία μόνον προείρητο τοῖς στρατιώταις.
5 ὁ Σερτώριος δ' ὀξέως βοηθήσας ἐκέλευσε δισχιλίους ἀσκοὺς ὕδατος ἐμπλῆσαι, καθ' ἕκαστον ἀσκὸν
ἀργύριον συχνὸν τάξας. καὶ πολλῶν μὲν Ἰβήρων, πολλῶν δὲ Μαυρουσίων ὑφισταμένων τὸ
ἔργον, ἐπιλεξάμενος ἄνδρας εὐρώστους ἅμα καὶ

of escape for a fugitive, or of surrounding an enemy under pursuit, in places both accessible and inaccessible. The result was, therefore, that Metellus, by being kept from fighting, suffered all the harm which visits men who are defeated; while Sertorius, by flying, had the advantages of men who pursue. For he would cut off his opponent's supply of water and prevent his foraging; if the Romans advanced, he would get out of their way, and if they settled down in camp, he would harass them; if they besieged a place, he would come up and put them under siege in their turn by depriving them of supplies. At last the Roman soldiers were in despair, and when Sertorius challenged Metellus to single combat, they cried aloud and bade him fight, general with general, and Roman with Roman, and when he declined, they mocked at him. But Metellus laughed at all this, and he was right; for a general, as Theophrastus says, should die the death of a general, not that of a common targeteer. Then, seeing that the Langobritae were giving no slight assistance to Sertorius, and that their city could easily be taken for lack of water (since they had but one well in the city, and the streams in the suburbs and along the walls would be in the power of any besieger), Metellus came against the city, intending to complete the siege in two days, since there was no water there. On this account, too, he had given orders to his soldiers to take along provisions for only five days. But Sertorius quickly came to the rescue and ordered two thousand skins to be filled with water, offering for each skin a considerable sum of money. Many Iberians and many Maurusians volunteered for the work, and after selecting men who were both sturdy and swift of foot, he sent them

ποδώκεις ἔπεμψε διὰ τῆς ὀρεινῆς, κελεύσας, ὅταν
παραδῶσι τοὺς ἀσκοὺς τοῖς ἐν τῇ πόλει, τὸν
ἄχρηστον ὑπεξαγαγεῖν ὄχλον, ὅπως ἐξαρκῇ τοῖς
6 ἀμυνομένοις τὸ ποτόν. ἐκπύστου δὲ τούτου γενομένου πρὸς τὸν Μέτελλον, ἤχθετο μὲν ἤδη τὰ
ἐπιτήδεια τῶν στρατιωτῶν ὑπαναλωκότων, ἐξέ- 575
πεμψε δὲ ἐπὶ σιτολογίαν Ἀκύϊνον ἑξακισχιλίων
ἡγούμενον. αἰσθόμενος δὲ ὁ Σερτώριος καὶ προ-
λοχίσας τὴν ὁδὸν ἐπανερχομένῳ τῷ Ἀκύϊνῳ
τρισχιλίους ἄνδρας ἔκ τινος συσκίου χαράδρας
ἐπανίστησιν, αὐτὸς δὲ κατὰ στόμα προσβαλὼν
τρέπεται, καὶ τοὺς μὲν διαφθείρει, τοὺς δὲ λαμβάνει ζῶντας. Ἀκύϊνον δὲ μετὰ τῶν ὅπλων καὶ
τὸν ἵππον ἀποβεβληκότα δεξάμενος Μέτελλος
αἰσχρῶς ἀπῄει, πολλὰ χλευαζόμενος ὑπὸ τῶν
Ἰβήρων.

XIV. Ἔκ τε δὴ τούτων θαυμαζόμενος ἠγαπᾶτο
παρὰ τοῖς βαρβάροις ὁ Σερτώριος, καὶ ὅτι Ῥω-
μαϊκοῖς ὁπλισμοῖς καὶ τάξεσι καὶ συνθήμασιν
ἀφαιρῶν τὸ μανικὸν καὶ θηριῶδες αὐτῶν τῆς
ἀλκῆς ἀντὶ λῃστηρίου μεγάλου στρατὸν ἐποιεῖτο
2 τὴν δύναμιν. ἔτι δ' ἀργύρῳ χρώμενος ἀφειδῶς
καὶ χρυσῷ κράνη τε κατεκόσμει καὶ θυρεοὺς
αὐτῶν διεποίκιλλε, καὶ χλαμύσιν ἀνθιναῖς καὶ
χιτῶσι χρῆσθαι διδάσκων καὶ χορηγῶν εἰς ταῦτα
καὶ συμφιλοκαλῶν ἐδημαγώγει. μάλιστα δὲ
εἷλεν αὐτοὺς τὰ τῶν παίδων. τοὺς γὰρ εὐγε-
νεστάτους ἀπὸ τῶν ἐθνῶν συναγαγὼν εἰς Ὄσκαν,
πόλιν μεγάλην, διδασκάλους ἐπιστήσας Ἕλλη-

by a route through the mountains, with orders that
when they had delivered the skins to the people in the
city, they should secretly convey away the unservice-
able mass of the population, in order that the water
might suffice for the actual defenders of the city.
When Metellus learned that this had been done, he
was annoyed, since his soldiers had already consumed
their provisions, and sent out Aquinus, at the head
of six thousand men, to forage. But Sertorius learned
of this and set an ambush of three thousand men in
the road by which Aquinus was to return. These
sallied forth from a shady ravine and attacked Aquinus
in the rear, while Sertorius himself assailed him in
front, routed him, slew some of his men, and took
some of them prisoners. Aquinus, after losing both
his armour and his horse, got back to Metellus, who
then retired disgracefully, much flouted by the
Iberians.

XIV. In consequence of these successes Sertorius
was admired and loved by the Barbarians, and
especially because by introducing Roman arms and
formations and signals he did away with their frenzied
and furious displays of courage, and converted their
forces into an army, instead of a huge band of robbers.
Still further, he used gold and silver without stint for
the decoration of their helmets and the ornamen-
tation of their shields, and by teaching them to
wear flowered cloaks and tunics, and furnishing them
with the means to do this, and sharing their love
of beautiful array, he won the hearts of all. But
most of all were they captivated by what he did with
their boys. Those of the highest birth, namely, he
collected together from the various peoples, at Osca,
a large city, and set over them teachers of Greek and

νικῶν τε καὶ Ῥωμαϊκῶν μαθημάτων ἔργῳ μὲν
ἐξωμηρεύσατο, λόγῳ δὲ ἐπαίδευεν, ὡς ἀνδράσι
γενομένοις πολιτείας τε μεταδώσων καὶ ἀρχῆς.
3 οἱ δὲ πατέρες ἥδοντο θαυμαστῶς τοὺς παῖδας ἐν
περιπορφύροις ὁρῶντες μάλα κοσμίως φοιτῶντας
εἰς τὰ διδασκαλεῖα, καὶ τὸν Σερτώριον ὑπὲρ
αὐτῶν μισθοὺς τελοῦντα, καὶ πολλάκις ἀποδείξεις
λαμβάνοντα, καὶ γέρα τοῖς ἀξίοις νέμοντα, καὶ
τὰ χρυσᾶ περιδέραια δωρούμενον ἃ Ῥωμαῖοι
4 βούλλας καλοῦσιν. ἔθους δ' ὄντος Ἰβηρικοῦ τοὺς
περὶ τὸν ἄρχοντα τεταγμένους συναποθνήσκειν
αὐτῷ πεσόντι, καὶ τοῦτο τῶν ἐκεῖ βαρβάρων
κατάσπεισιν ὀνομαζόντων, τοῖς μὲν ἄλλοις ἡγεμόσιν ὀλίγοι τῶν ὑπασπιστῶν καὶ τῶν ἑταίρων,
Σερτωρίῳ δὲ πολλαὶ μυριάδες ἀνθρώπων κατε-
5 σπεικότων ἑαυτοὺς ἠκολούθουν. λέγεται δὲ πρός
τινι πόλει τροπῆς γενομένης καὶ τῶν πολεμίων
ἐπικειμένων τοὺς Ἴβηρας ἀμελήσαντας αὑτῶν
τὸν Σερτώριον σῴζειν καὶ τοῖς ὤμοις ἐπαραμένους
ἄλλους πρὸ ἄλλων ἀνακουφίσαι πρὸς τὰ τείχη,
γενομένου δ' ἐν ἀσφαλεῖ τοῦ ἄρχοντος, οὕτω
τρέπεσθαι πρὸς φυγὴν ἕκαστον αὐτῶν.

XV. Οὐ μόνον δὲ τοῖς Ἴβηρσιν ἦν ποθεινός,
ἀλλὰ καὶ τοῖς ἐξ Ἰταλίας στρατευομένοις. Περπέννα γοῦν Οὐέντωνος ἀπὸ τῆς αὐτῆς Σερτωρίῳ
στάσεως εἰς Ἰβηρίαν παραγενομένου μετὰ χρημάτων πολλῶν καὶ μεγάλης δυνάμεως, ἰδίᾳ δὲ
καθ' ἑαυτὸν ἐγνωκότος πολεμεῖν πρὸς τὸν Μέτελλον, ἐδυσχέραινον οἱ στρατιῶται, καὶ πολὺς ἦν
τοῦ Σερτωρίου λόγος ἐν τῷ στρατοπέδῳ, τὸν
Περπένναν ἀνιῶν εὐγενείᾳ καὶ πλούτῳ τετυφω-
2 μένον. οὐ μὴν ἀλλ' ἐπεὶ Πομπήϊος ἠγγέλλετο

Roman learning; thus in reality he made hostages of
them, while ostensibly he was educating them, with
the assurance that when they became men he would
give them a share in administration and authority.
So the fathers were wonderfully pleased to see their
sons, in purple-bordered togas, very decorously going
to their schools, and Sertorius paying their fees for
them, holding frequent examinations, distributing
prizes to the deserving, and presenting them with the
golden necklaces which the Romans call "bullae."
It was the custom among the Iberians for those who
were stationed about their leader to die with him if
he fell, and the Barbarians in those parts call this a
"consecration." Now, the other commanders had few
such shield-bearers and companions, but Sertorius was
attended by many thousands of men who had thus
consecrated themselves to death. And we are told
that when his army had been defeated at a certain
city and the enemy were pressing upon them, the
Iberians, careless of themselves, rescued Sertorius,
and taking him on their shoulders one after another,
carried him to the walls, and only when their leader
was in safety, did they betake themselves to flight,
each man for himself.

XV. And not only were the Iberians eager to
serve under him, but also the soldiers who came
from Italy. At any rate, when Perpenna Vento,
who belonged to the same party as Sertorius, came
to Spain with much money and a large force, and
was determined to wage war on his own account
against Metellus, his soldiers were displeased, and
there was much talk in the camp about Sertorius, to
the annoyance of Perpenna, who was puffed up over
his high birth and his wealth. However, when word

τὴν Πυρήνην ὑπερβάλλων, ἀναλαβόντες οἱ στρατιῶται τὰ ὅπλα καὶ τὰ σημεῖα τῶν τάξεων
ἀναρπάσαντες κατεβόησαν τοῦ Περπέννα, κελεύοντες ὡς τὸν Σερτώριον ἄγειν αὐτούς· εἰ δὲ μή,
καταλιπόντες ἐκεῖνον ἠπείλουν αὐτοὶ βαδιεῖσθαι
πρὸς ἄνδρα σώζεσθαι καὶ σώζειν δυνάμενον.
συγχωρήσας δὲ ὁ Περπέννας ἤγαγεν αὐτούς, καὶ
συνέμιξε τῷ Σερτωρίῳ πεντήκοντα καὶ τρεῖς
ἔχων σπείρας.

XVI. Σερτώριος δέ, τῶν ἐντὸς Ἴβηρος αὐτῷ
ποταμοῦ πάντων ὁμοῦ τι προστιθεμένων, πλήθει
μὲν ἦν μέγας· ἐπέρρεον γὰρ ἀεὶ καὶ συνεφέροντο
πανταχόθεν πρὸς αὐτόν· ἀταξίᾳ δὲ βαρβαρικῇ
καὶ θρασύτητι ταραττόμενος ἐπιχειρεῖν τοῖς πολεμίοις βοώντων καὶ τὴν τριβὴν δυσανασχετούντων
2 ἐπειρᾶτο παραμυθεῖσθαι διὰ λόγων. ὡς δὲ ἑώρα
χαλεπαίνοντας καὶ βιαζομένους ἀκαίρως, προήκατο καὶ περιεῖδε συμπλεκομένους τοῖς πολεμίοις 576
ἐν οἷς οὐ παντελῶς συντριβέντας, ἀλλὰ πληγὰς
λαβόντας ἤλπιζε πρὸς τὰ λοιπὰ κατηκόους μᾶλλον ἕξειν. ὧν δὲ εἴκαζε γενομένων, ἐπιβοηθήσας
ἀνέλαβέ τε φεύγοντας αὐτοὺς καὶ κατέστησεν
3 ἀσφαλῶς εἰς τὸ στρατόπεδον. βουλόμενος δὲ καὶ
τὴν ἀθυμίαν ἀφελεῖν, μεθ᾽ ἡμέρας ὀλίγας πάνδη-
μον ἐκκλησίαν ἀθροίσας ἵππους εἰσήγαγε δύο,
τὸν μὲν ἀσθενῆ τελέως καὶ πρεσβύτερον ἤδη, τὸν
δὲ ἕτερον εὐμεγέθη μὲν αὐτὸν καὶ ἰσχυρόν, θαυμαστὴν δὲ πυκνότητι καὶ κάλλει τριχῶν οὐρὰν
ἔχοντα. παρειστήκει δὲ τῷ μὲν ἀσθενεῖ μέγας

40

came that Pompey was crossing the Pyrenees, the soldiers caught up their arms and snatched up their standards and made an outcry against Perpenna, ordering him to lead them to Sertorius, and threatening, if he did not, to abandon him and go by themselves to a man who was able to save himself and save those under him. So Perpenna yielded and led them off, and joined Sertorius with fifty-three cohorts.

XVI. Sertorius, then, since all the peoples within the river Ebro were unitedly taking up his cause, had an army of great numbers, for men were all the while coming to him in streams from every quarter; but he was troubled by their barbaric lack of discipline and their overconfidence, since they called loudly upon him to attack the enemy and were impatient at his delay, and he therefore tried to pacify them by arguments. But when he saw that they were impatient and inclined to force their wishes upon him unseasonably, he let them take their way and permitted them to have an engagement with the enemy in which he hoped that they would not be altogether crushed, but would be severely handled, and so made more obedient for the future. Matters turning out as he expected, he came to their aid, gave them refuge in their flight, and brought them safely back to their camp. And now he wished to take away their dejection. So after a few days he called a general assembly and introduced before it two horses, one utterly weak and already quite old, the other large-sized and strong, with a tail that was astonishing for the thickness and beauty of its hair. By the side of the feeble horse stood a

ἀνὴρ καὶ ῥωμαλέος, τῷ δὲ ἰσχυρῷ μικρὸς ἕτερος
καὶ τὴν ὄψιν εὐκαταφρόνητος. σημείου δὲ δο-
θέντος αὐτοῖς ὁ μὲν ἰσχυρὸς ἀμφοτέραις ταῖς
χερσὶ τοῦ ἵππου τὴν κέρκον ὡς ἀπορρήξων εἷλκε
βίᾳ πρὸς αὑτόν, ὁ δὲ ἀσθενὴς τοῦ ἰσχυροῦ κατὰ
4 μίαν τῶν τριχῶν ἐξέτιλλεν. ἐπεὶ δὲ ὁ μὲν
οὐκ ὀλίγα πράγματα μάτην ἑαυτῷ καὶ πολὺν
γέλωτα τοῖς θεωμένοις παρασχὼν ἀπεῖπεν, ὁ δὲ
ἀσθενὴς ἀκαρεὶ καὶ σὺν οὐδενὶ πόνῳ ψιλὴν τριχῶν ἀπέδειξε τὴν οὐράν, ἀναστὰς ὁ Σερτώριος,
"Ὁρᾶτε," εἶπεν, "ἄνδρες σύμμαχοι, τὴν ἐπιμονὴν
ἀνυσιμωτέραν τῆς βίας οὖσαν, καὶ πολλὰ τῶν
ἀθρόως ἀλήπτων ἐνδιδόντα τῷ κατὰ μικρόν.
5 ἄμαχον γὰρ τὸ ἐνδελεχές, ᾧ πᾶσαν ἐπιὼν ὁ χρόνος
αἱρεῖ καὶ κατεργάζεται δύναμιν, εὐμενὴς ὢν σύμ-
μαχος τοῖς δεχομένοις λογισμῷ τὸν καιρὸν αὐτοῦ,
τοῖς δὲ ἀκαίρως ἐπειγομένοις πολεμιώτατος."
τοιαῦτα μὲν ὁ Σερτώριος ἑκάστοτε πλέκων
παραμύθια τοῖς βαρβάροις διεπαιδαγώγει τὸν
καιρόν.

XVII. Οὐδενὸς δὲ ἧττον αὐτοῦ τῶν πολεμικῶν
ἔργων ἐθαυμάσθη τὸ περὶ τοὺς λεγομένους Χαρα-
κιτανούς. εἰσὶ δὲ δῆμος ὑπὲρ τὸν Ταγώνιον
ποταμόν, οὐκ ἄστεσιν οὐδὲ κώμαις ἐνοικοῦντες,
ἀλλὰ λόφος ἐστὶν εὐμεγέθης καὶ ὑψηλὸς ἄντρα
καὶ κοιλώματα πετρῶν βλέποντα πρὸς βορέαν
περιέχων. ἡ δ' ὑποκειμένη πᾶσα χώρα πηλὸν
ἀργιλώδη καὶ γῆν ὑπὸ χαυνότητος εὔθρυπτον

man who was tall and robust, and by the side of
the powerful horse another man, small and of a con-
temptible appearance. At a signal given them, the
strong man seized the tail of his horse with both
hands and tried to pull it towards him with all his
might, as though he would tear it off; but the weak
man began to pluck out the hairs in the tail of the
strong horse one by one. The strong man gave himself no end of trouble to no purpose, made the
spectators laugh a good deal, and then gave up his
attempt; but the weak man, in a trice and with no
trouble, stripped his horse's tail of its hair. Then
Sertorius rose up and said: "Ye see, men of my
allies, that perseverance is more efficacious than
violence, and that many things which cannot be
mastered when they stand together yield when one
masters them little by little. For irresistible is the
force of continuity, by virtue of which advancing Time
subdues and captures every power; and Time is a
kindly ally for all who act as diligent attendants
upon opportunity, but a most bitter enemy for all
who urge matters on unseasonably."[1] By contriving from time to time such exhortations for the
Barbarians, Sertorius taught them to watch for their
opportunities.

XVII. But of all his military exploits that which
he performed in dealing with the people called
Characitani is admired as much as any. They are a
people beyond the river Tagonius, and they do not
dwell in cities or villages, but on a large and lofty
hill containing caves and hollows in the cliffs which
look towards the north. The whole country at the
base of the hill abounds in white clay and a soil that

[1] The story is told also in Valerius Maximus, vii. 3, 6.

43

ἀναδίδωσιν, οὔτε τοὺς ἐπιβαίνοντας ἀνέχεσθαι
καρτερᾶν, καὶ μικρὸν ἁψαμένων, ὥσπερ ἄσβεστον
2 ἢ τέφραν, ἐπὶ πολὺ διαχεομένην. τῶν οὖν βαρβάρων, ὁσάκις φόβῳ πολέμου καταδύντες εἰς τὰ
σπήλαια καὶ τὴν λείαν εἴσω συναγαγόντες ἀτρε-
μοῖεν, ὄντων ἀλήπτων ὑπὸ βίας, τὸν δὲ Σερτώριον
τότε διακεκριμένον ἀπὸ τοῦ Μετέλλου καὶ κατα-
στρατοπεδεύσαντα παρὰ τὸν λόφον ὑπερφρονούν-
των ὡς κεκρατημένον, εἴτε ὑπ᾽ ὀργῆς ἐκεῖνος εἴτε
μὴ δοκεῖν φεύγειν βουλόμενος ἅμ᾽ ἡμέρᾳ προσε-
3 λάσας κατεσκέπτετο τὸν τόπον. οὐδαμόθεν δὲ
προσβολὴν ἔχοντος, ἄλλως ἀλύων καὶ κεναῖς
χρώμενος ἀπειλαῖς ὁρᾷ τῆς γῆς ἐκείνης κονιορτὸν
ἄνω πολὺν ὑπὸ πνεύματος ἐπ᾽ αὐτοὺς φερόμενον.
τέτραπται μὲν γάρ, ὡς ἔφην, τὰ σπήλαια πρὸς
βορέαν, ὁ δὲ ἀπὸ τῆς ἄρκτου πνέων[1] ἄνεμος,
Καικίαν ἔνιοι καλοῦσιν, ἐπέχει μάλιστα καὶ
πλεῖστός ἐστι τῶν ἐκεῖ πνευμάτων, ἐξ ὑγρῶν
πεδίων καὶ νιφοβόλων συμφυσώμενος ὀρῶν· τότε
δὲ καὶ θέρους ἀκμάζοντος ἰσχύων καὶ τρεφόμενος
τῇ τῶν ὑπαρκτίων ἀνέσει πάγων ἥδιστος ἐπέπνει
καὶ κατεῖχεν αὐτούς τε καὶ βοτὰ δι᾽ ἡμέρας ἀνα-
4 ψύχων. ταῦτα δὴ συλλογιζόμενος ὁ Σερτώριος
καὶ παρὰ τῶν ἐγχωρίων ἀκούων, ἐκέλευσε τοὺς
στρατιώτας τῆς ἀραιᾶς καὶ τεφρώδους γῆς ἐκείνης
ἀποσπῶντας καὶ παραφέροντας καταντικρὺ τοῦ
λόφου θῖνα ποιεῖν, ἣν οἱ βάρβαροι χώματος ἐπ᾽
αὐτοὺς εἶναι κατασκευὴν ὑπονοοῦντες ἐχλεύαζον.
5 τότε μὲν οὖν ἐργασαμένους τοὺς στρατιώτας ἄχρι

---

[1] πνέων Van Herwerden : ῥέων.

is porous and crumbly; it is not firm enough to bear the tread of man, and spreads far about if only slightly stirred, like unslaked lime or ashes. These Barbarians, then, whenever they were afraid of war, would hide themselves in their caves, take all their plunder in with them, and keep quiet, for they could not be taken by force; and at the time of which I speak, when Sertorius had retired before Metellus and encamped at the base of their hill, they thought scornfully of him as a vanquished man, and he, either out of anger, or because he did not wish to be thought a fugitive, at break of day rode up to the place and inspected it. There was no attacking it anywhere, but as he was wandering about to no purpose and indulging in empty threats, he saw that dust from the soil which I have described was being carried up against the Barbarians in great quantities by the wind. For the caves, as I have said, faced the north, and the wind which blows from that quarter (some call it Caecias) is the most prevalent and the strongest of the winds in that country, being a confluent of winds from watery plains and snow-covered mountains; and at this time particularly, which was the height of summer, it was strong, was fed by the melting snows of northern regions, and blew most delightfully with continual refreshment for man and beast all day. So, reflecting on these things and getting information about them from the natives of the country, Sertorius ordered his soldiers to take some of the loose and ashy soil that I have described, carry it directly opposite the hill, and make a heap of it there. This the Barbarians conjectured to be a mound raised for assaulting them, and jeered at their enemy. On that day, then, the soldiers of Sertorius worked until night, and were

45

νυκτὸς ἀπήγαγεν· ἅμα δ' ἡμέρᾳ πρῶτον μὲν αὔρα
μαλακὴ προαπέπνει διακινοῦσα τῆς συμπεφορη-
μένης γῆς τὸ λειότατον ὥσπερ ἄχνην σκιδνάμενον,
ἔπειτα σοβαροῦ τοῦ Καικίου πρὸς τὸν ἥλιον ἐκ-
χεομένου καὶ τῶν λόφων κονιωμένων ἐπιστάντες
οἱ στρατιῶται τόν τε χοῦν ἀνέτρεπον διὰ βάθους   577
καὶ τὸν σπίλον ἔκοπτον, ἔνιοι δὲ καὶ τοὺς ἵππους
ἄνω καὶ κάτω διεξήλασαν ἀνιστάντες τὸ χαύνωμα
6 καὶ τῇ πνοῇ μετέωρον παραδιδόντες. ἡ δ' ὑπο-
λαμβάνουσα πᾶν τὸ θρυπτόμενον καὶ κινούμενον
ἄνω προσέβαλλε τοῖς οἰκήμασι τῶν βαρβάρων,
κατὰ θύρας δεχομένοις τὸν Καικίαν. οἱ δέ, ἅτε
δὴ τῶν σπηλαίων μίαν ἐκείνην ἀναπνοὴν ἐχόντων
ᾗ τὸ πνεῦμα προσέπιπτε, ταχὺ μὲν ἀπεσκοτοῦντο
τὰς ὄψεις, ταχὺ δ' ἀνεπίμπλαντο πνιγώδους
ἄσθματος, τραχὺν ἀέρα καὶ πολλῇ κόνει συμ-
7 πεφυρμένον ἕλκοντες. ὅθεν ἡμέρας δύο μόλις
ἀνασχόμενοι τῇ τρίτῃ παρέδωκαν ἑαυτούς, οὐ
τοσοῦτον Σερτωρίῳ δυνάμεως ὅσον δόξης προσ-
θέντες, ὡς τὰ δι' ὅπλων ἀνάλωτα σοφίᾳ κατεργα-
σαμένῳ.

XVIII. Μέχρι μὲν οὖν τοῖς περὶ Μέτελλον
ἐπολέμει, τὰ πλεῖστα κατευτυχεῖν ἐδόκει, γήρᾳ
καὶ φυσικῇ βραδυτῆτι τοῦ Μετέλλου πρὸς ἄνδρα
τολμητὴν καὶ λῃστρικῆς μᾶλλον ἢ στρατιωτικῆς
ἡγούμενον δυνάμεως οὐκ ἀναφέροντος· ἐπεὶ δὲ καὶ
Πομπηΐῳ τὴν Πυρήνην ὑπερβαλόντι παραστρατο-
πεδεύσας, καὶ πᾶσαν ἅμα μὲν διδούς, ἅμα δὲ
λαμβάνων στρατηγικῶν παλαισμάτων πεῖραν,
ἀντιτεχνώμενός τε καὶ φυλαττόμενος πλεῖον εἶχε,
κομιδῇ διεβοήθη μέχρι Ῥώμης ὡς δεινότατος ὢν

then led back to camp. But when the next day came,
at first a gentle breeze arose, stirring up the lightest
portions of the gathered soil and scattering them like
chaff; then, when Caecias was blowing strong with the
mounting of the sun and covering the hills with dust,
the soldiers came and stirred up the mound of earth
to the bottom and broke up the lumps, while some
actually drove their horses back and forth through it,
throwing up the loosened earth and giving it to the
wind to carry. Then the wind caught up all the
earth thus broken and stirred and threw it up against
the dwellings of the Barbarians, which opened so as
to admit Caecias. And the Barbarians, since their
caves had no other inlet for air than that against
which the wind was dashing, were quickly blinded,
and quickly choked, too, as they tried to inhale an
air that was harsh and mingled with great quantities
of dust. Therefore, after holding out with difficulty
for two days, on the third day they surrendered, thereby adding not so much to the power as to the fame
of Sertorius, since by his skill he had subdued what
could not be taken by arms.

XVIII. Well, then, as long as he carried on the
war with Metellus as his antagonist, he was thought
to be successful for the most part because, owing to
great age and natural slowness, Metellus could not
cope with a man who was bold and headed a force
composed of robbers rather than soldiers; but when
Pompey also crossed the Pyrenees and became his
antagonist,[1] and each of them had offered and
accepted every test of a general's powers, and
Sertorius had the advantage in counter-planning and
watchfulness, then indeed it was noised abroad as far

[1] In 76 B.C.

πόλεμον μεταχειρίσασθαι τῶν τότε στρατηγῶν.
2 οὐ γάρ τι μικρὸν ἦν τὸ Πομπηΐου κλέος, ἀλλ'
ἤνθει τότε μάλιστα πρὸς δόξαν ἐκ τῶν περὶ
Σύλλαν ἀνδραγαθημάτων, ἐφ' οἷς καὶ Μάγνος ὑπ'
αὐτοῦ, τουτέστι μέγας, ἐπωνομάσθη τιμῶν τε
θριαμβικῶν οὔπω γενειῶν ἔτυχεν. ὅθεν καὶ
πολλαὶ τῶν ὑπὸ Σερτωρίῳ πόλεων ἀποβλέψασαι
πρὸς αὐτὸν ὁρμὴν μεταβολῆς ἔσχον, εἶτα ἐπαύ-
σαντο, τοῦ περὶ Λαύρωνα πάθους παρὰ πᾶσαν
ἐλπίδα συμβάντος.
3   Σερτωρίου γὰρ πολιορκοῦντος αὐτοὺς ἧκε Πομπήϊος πανστρατιᾷ βοηθήσων· εἶτα ὁ μὲν λόφον
εὖ δοκοῦντα πεφυκέναι κατὰ τῆς πόλεως προ-
ληψόμενος, ὁ δὲ τοῦτο κωλύσων ἠπείγετο. τοῦ
δὲ Σερτωρίου φθάσαντος ἐπιστήσας τὸν στρατὸν
ὁ Πομπήϊος ἔχαιρε τῇ συντυχίᾳ, νομίζων ἐν μέσῳ
τῆς πόλεως καὶ τῆς αὐτοῦ στρατιᾶς ἀπειλῆφθαι
τὸν Σερτώριον· καὶ πρὸς τοὺς Λαυρωνίτας εἰσέ-
πεμψε θαρρεῖν κελεύων καὶ καθῆσθαι περὶ τὰ
4 τείχη θεωμένους πολιορκούμενον Σερτώριον. ἐκεῖνος δ' ἀκούσας ἐγέλασε, καὶ τὸν Σύλλα μαθητὴν
(οὕτω γὰρ τὸν Πομπήϊον ἐπισκώπτων προση-
γόρευεν) αὐτὸς ἔφη διδάξειν ὅτι δεῖ τὸν στρατηγὸν
κατόπιν μᾶλλον ἢ κατὰ πρόσωπον βλέπειν.
ταῦτα δὲ λέγων ἅμα τοῖς πολιορκουμένοις ἐπε-
δείκνυεν ἑξακισχιλίους ὁπλίτας ὑπ' αὐτοῦ κατα-
λελειμμένους ἐπὶ τοῦ προτέρου χάρακος, ὅθεν
ὁρμηθεὶς κατειλήφει τὸν λόφον, ὅπως ἐπὶ σφᾶς
48

as Rome that he was the ablest general of his time in
the conduct of a war. For the fame of Pompey was by
no means inconsiderable, nay, at this time his reputation was in most vigorous flower in consequence of the
valiant deeds which he performed in the cause of Sulla,
deeds for which he was given the surname of
"Magnus" (that is, *Great*) by Sulla, and received the
honours of a triumph while he was still beardless.
Therefore, too, many of the cities which were subject
to Sertorius turned their eyes towards Pompey and felt
inclined to change their allegiance; they ceased to do
this, however, after the disaster at Lauron, which
happened contrary to all expectation.

For Sertorius was besieging that city, and Pompey
came to its assistance with all his forces. Now
there was a hill which was thought to afford a
good command of the city, and this hill Sertorius
strove to seize in advance, while Pompey sought to
prevent him. But Sertorius got there first, whereupon Pompey, taking position with his army, was
delighted with the way things had turned out,
believing that Sertorius was caught between the city
and his adversary's forces; he also sent a messenger
in to the people of Lauron bidding them be of good
cheer and take seats along their walls for the spectacle
of Sertorius undergoing siege. When Sertorius heard
of this, he gave a laugh, and said that to Sulla's pupil
(for thus he was wont to style Pompey in jest) he
himself would give a lesson, namely, that a general
must look behind him rather than in front of him.
As he said this, he pointed out to his beleaguered
troops six thousand men-at-arms whom he had left
behind at their former camp, from which he had sallied
forth to seize the hill; these, in case Pompey moved

49

τρεπομένῳ τῷ Πομπηΐῳ κατὰ νώτου προσπέσοιεν.
5 ὁ δὴ καὶ Πομπήϊος ὀψὲ μάλα συμφρονήσας ἐπιχειρεῖν μὲν οὐκ ἐθάρρει κύκλωσιν δεδοικώς, ἀπολιπεῖν δὲ ᾐσχύνετο κινδυνεύοντας ἀνθρώπους,
παρὼν δὲ καὶ καθήμενος ἠναγκάζετο ὁρᾶν ἀπολ-
λυμένους· ἀπέγνωσαν γὰρ αὑτοὺς οἱ βάρβαροι
6 καὶ τῷ Σερτωρίῳ παρέδωκαν. ὁ δὲ τῶν μὲν σωμάτων ἐφείσατο καὶ πάντας ἀφῆκε, τὴν δὲ πόλιν
κατέπρησεν, οὐχ ὑπ' ὀργῆς οὐδ' ὠμότητος, ἐλά-
χιστα γὰρ δοκεῖ θυμῷ χαρίσασθαι τῶν στρατηγῶν οὗτος ἀνήρ, ἀλλ' ἐπ' αἰσχύνῃ καὶ κατηφείᾳ
τῶν τεθαυμακότων Πομπήϊον, ἵνα ᾖ λόγος ἐν τοῖς
βαρβάροις ὅτι παρὼν ἐγγὺς καὶ μονονοῦ θερμαι-
νόμενος τῷ πυρὶ τῶν συμμάχων οὐ προσήμυνεν.

XIX. Ἧτται μὲν οὖν τῷ Σερτωρίῳ πλείονες
συνέβαινον, αὐτὸν μὲν ἀήττητον ἀεὶ φυλάττοντι 578
καὶ τοὺς καθ' αὑτόν, θραυομένῳ δὲ περὶ τοὺς
ἄλλους ἡγεμόνας· ἐκ δὲ ὧν ἐπηνωρθοῦτο τὰς
ἥττας μᾶλλον ἐθαυμάζετο νικώντων τῶν ἀντι-
στρατήγων, οἷον ἐν τῇ περὶ Σούκρωνι μάχῃ πρὸς
Πομπήϊον, καὶ πάλιν ἐν τῇ περὶ Τουρίαν [1] πρός
2 τε τοῦτον ὁμοῦ καὶ Μέτελλον. ἡ μὲν οὖν περὶ
Σούκρωνι μάχη λέγεται γενέσθαι τοῦ Πομπηΐου
κατεπείξαντος, ὡς μὴ μετάσχοι τῆς νίκης Μέτελλος. ὁ δὲ Σερτώριος ἐβούλετο μὲν τῷ Πομπηΐῳ,
πρὶν ἐπελθεῖν τὸν Μέτελλον, διαγωνίσασθαι,
παραγαγὼν δὲ ἑσπέρας ἤδη συνέβαλεν, οἰόμενος
ξένοις οὖσι καὶ ἀπείροις τῶν χωρίων τοῖς πολεμίοις τὸ σκότος ἔσεσθαι καὶ φεύγουσιν ἐμπόδιον

---

[1] Τουρίαν Sintenis[2], after Ukert; Sintenis[1], Coraës and
Bekker have Τουττίαν. The MSS. reading is uncertain.

against the occupants of the hill, were to fall upon
his rear. Pompey also became aware of this all too
late, and did not venture to attack Sertorius for fear
of being surrounded, but he was ashamed to go away
and leave the people of the city in their peril, and so
was compelled to sit there quietly and see them
ruined; for the Barbarians gave up all hope and
surrendered to Sertorius. Sertorius spared their
lives and let them all go, but he burned down their
city,[1] not because he was angry or cruel, for he
appears to have given way to passion less than any
other general, but to put to shame and confusion the
admirers of Pompey, in order that it might be said
among the Barbarians that though he was near at hand
and all but warming himself at the flames of an allied
city, he did not come to its relief.

XIX. It is true that Sertorius suffered several
defeats, and yet he always kept himself and his own
forces undefeated, and got his crushing blows where
other generals than he were in command; and from
the way in which he repaired his defeats he was more
admired than the victorious generals opposed to him,
as, for instance, in the battle on the Sucro against
Pompey, and, again, in the battle near Turia against
both Pompey and Metellus. Now, the battle on the
Sucro[2] is said to have been precipitated by Pompey,
in order that Metellus might not share in the victory.
Sertorius, too, wished to fight the issue out with
Pompey before Metellus came up, and therefore
drew out his forces when evening was already at
hand, and began the engagement, thinking that,
since his enemies were strangers and unacquainted
with the region, darkness would be a hindrance to

---

[1] Cf. the *Pompey*, xviii. 3.
[2] Cf. the *Pompey*, chapter xix.

3 καὶ διώκουσι. γενομένης δὲ τῆς μάχης ἐν χερσὶν
ἔτυχε μὲν οὐ πρὸς Πομπήϊον αὐτός, ἀλλὰ πρὸς
Ἀφράνιον ἐν ἀρχῇ συνεστηκὼς ἔχοντα τὸ ἀρι-
στερόν, αὐτὸς ἐπὶ τοῦ δεξιοῦ τεταγμένος. ἀκούσας
δὲ τῷ Πομπηΐῳ τοὺς συνεστῶτας ὑποχωρεῖν
ἐγκειμένῳ καὶ κρατεῖσθαι, τὸ μὲν δεξιὸν ἐπ'
ἄλλοις ἐποιήσατο στρατηγοῖς, πρὸς δὲ ἐκεῖνο τὸ
4 νικώμενον αὐτὸς ἐβοήθρόμει. καὶ τοὺς μὲν ἤδη
τρεπομένους τοὺς δὲ ἔτι μένοντας ἐν τάξει συναγαγὼν καὶ ἀναθαρρύνας, ἐξ ὑπαρχῆς ἐνέβαλε τῷ
Πομπηΐῳ διώκοντι, καὶ φυγὴν ἐποιήσατο πολλήν,
ὅτε καὶ Πομπήϊος ἐγγὺς ἐλθὼν ἀποθανεῖν καὶ
τραυματισθεὶς παραλόγως διέφυγεν. οἱ γὰρ μετὰ
Σερτωρίου Λίβυες, ὡς ἔλαβον αὐτοῦ τὸν ἵππον
χρυσῷ κεκοσμημένον καὶ φαλάρων ἀνάπλεων πολυτελῶν, ἐν τῷ διανέμεσθαι καὶ διαφέρεσθαι πρὸς
5 ἀλλήλους προήκαντο τὴν δίωξιν. Ἀφράνιος δὲ
τοὺς ἀνθεστῶτας πρὸς αὐτὸν ἅμα τῷ Σερτώριον
ἀπελθεῖν ἐπὶ θάτερα βοηθοῦντα τρεψάμενος εἰς τὸ
στρατόπεδον κατήραξε· καὶ συνεισπεσὼν ἐπόρθει
σκότους ἤδη ὄντος, μήτε τὴν Πομπηΐου φυγὴν
εἰδὼς μήτε τοὺς στρατιώτας τῆς ἁρπαγῆς ἐπισχεῖν
δυνάμενος. ἐν τούτῳ δὲ Σερτώριος ἀνέστρεψε τὸ
καθ' αὑτὸν νενικηκώς· καὶ τοῖς Ἀφρανίου δι'
ἀταξίαν ταρασσομένοις ἐπιπεσὼν πολλοὺς διέ-
6 φθειρε. πρωῒ δὲ αὖθις ἐξοπλισθεὶς ἐπὶ μάχην
κατέβαινεν, εἶτα Μέτελλον αἰσθόμενος ἐγγὺς
εἶναι λύσας τὴν τάξιν ἀνέζευξεν, εἰπών· "Ἀλλ'
ἔγωγε τὸν παῖδα τοῦτον, εἰ μὴ παρῆν ἡ γραῦς

them either in flight or in pursuit. When the fighting was at close quarters, it happened that Sertorius was not himself engaged with Pompey at first, but with Afranius, who commanded Pompey's left, while Sertorius himself was stationed on the right. Hearing, however, that those of his men who were engaged with Pompey were yielding before his onset and being worsted, he put his right wing in command of other generals, and hastened himself to the help of the wing that was suffering defeat. Those of his men who were already in retreat he rallied, those who were still keeping their ranks he encouraged, then charged anew upon Pompey, who was pursuing, and put his men to a great rout, in which Pompey also came near being killed, was actually wounded, and had a marvellous escape. For the Libyans with Sertorius, after getting Pompey's horse, which had golden decorations and was covered with costly trappings, were so busy distributing the booty and quarrelling with one another over it, that they neglected the pursuit. Afranius, however, as soon as Sertorius had gone off to the other wing with aid and succour, routed his opponents and drove them headlong into their camp; and dashing in with the fugitives, it being now dark, he began to plunder, knowing nothing of Pompey's flight and having no power to keep his soldiers from their pillaging. But meanwhile Sertorius came back from his victory on the other wing, and falling upon the straggling and confused soldiers of Afranius, slew great numbers of them. In the morning, moreover, he armed his troops and came out for battle; then, learning that Metellus was near, he broke up his array and decamped, saying: "But as for this boy, if that old

ἐκείνῃ, πληγαῖς ἂν νουθετήσας εἰς Ῥώμην ἀπε-
στάλκειν."

XX. Ἠθύμει δὲ δεινῶς διὰ τὸ μηδαμοῦ φανερὰν
τὴν ἔλαφον ἐκείνην εἶναι· μηχανῆς γὰρ ἐπὶ τοὺς
βαρβάρους ἐστέρητο θαυμαστῆς, τότε δὴ μάλιστα
παραμυθίας δεομένους. εἶτα μέντοι νυκτὸς ἄλλως πλανώμενοί τινες ἐπιτυγχάνουσιν αὐτῇ, καὶ
2 γνωρίσαντες ἀπὸ τῆς χρόας λαμβάνουσιν. ἀκούσας δὲ ὁ Σερτώριος ἐκείνοις μὲν ὡμολόγησεν, ἂν
μηδενὶ φράσωσι, χρήματα πολλὰ δώσειν, ἀπο-
κρύψας δὲ τὴν ἔλαφον καὶ διαλιπὼν ὀλίγας
ἡμέρας προῄει μάλα φαιδρὸς ἀπ' ὄψεως ἐπὶ τὸ
βῆμα, διηγούμενος τοῖς ἡγεμόσι τῶν βαρβάρων
ὡς ἀγαθόν τι μέγα τοῦ θεοῦ προμηνύοντος αὐτῷ
κατὰ τοὺς ὕπνους· εἶτα ἀναβὰς ἐπὶ τὸ βῆμα τοῖς
3 ἐντυγχάνουσιν ἐχρημάτιζεν. ἡ δὲ ἔλαφος ὑπὸ
τῶν φυλαττόντων αὐτὴν ἐγγὺς ἀφεθεῖσα καὶ
κατιδοῦσα τὸν Σερτώριον ἐχώρει δρόμῳ περιχαρὴς
πρὸς τὸ βῆμα, καὶ παραστᾶσα τὴν κεφαλὴν
ἐπέθηκε ταῖς γόνασιν αὐτοῦ καὶ τῷ στόματι τῆς
δεξιᾶς ἔψαυεν, εἰθισμένη καὶ πρότερον τοῦτο
ποιεῖν. ἀντιφιλοφρονουμένου δὲ τοῦ Σερτωρίου
πιθανῶς καί τι καὶ δακρύσαντος, ἔκπληξις εἶχε
τοὺς παρόντας τὸ πρῶτον, εἶτα κρότῳ καὶ βοῇ
τὸν Σερτώριον ὡς δαιμόνιον ἄνδρα καὶ θεοῖς φίλον
οἴκαδε προπέμψαντες ἐν εὐθυμίαις καὶ χρησταῖς
ἐλπίσιν ἦσαν.

XXI. Ἐν δὲ τοῖς τῶν Σαγουντίνων πεδίοις εἰς
τὰς ἐσχάτας ἀπορίας κατακεκλεικὼς τοὺς πολεμίους, ἠναγκάσθη συμβαλεῖν αὐτοῖς καταβαίνου- 579
σιν ἐφ' ἁρπαγὴν καὶ σιτολογίαν. ἠγωνίσθη δὲ
λαμπρῶς παρ' ἀμφοτέρων. καὶ Μέμμιος μὲν ὁ

54

woman had not come up, I should have given him a sound beating and sent him back to Rome."

XX. He was now greatly disheartened because that doe of his[1] was nowhere to be found; for he was thus deprived of a wonderful contrivance for influencing the Barbarians, who at this time particularly stood in need of encouragement. Soon, however, some men who were roaming about at night on other errands came upon the doe, recognized her by her colour, and caught her. When Sertorius heard of it he promised to give the men a large sum of money if they would tell no one of the capture, and after concealing the doe and allowing several days to pass, he came forth with a glad countenance and proceeded to the tribunal, telling the leaders of the Barbarians that the Deity was foretelling him in his dreams some great good fortune. Then he ascended the tribunal and began to deal with the applicants. And now the doe was released by her keepers at a point close by, spied Sertorius, and bounded joyfully towards the tribunal, and standing by his side put her head in his lap and licked his hand, as she had been wont to do before. Sertorius returned her caresses appropriately and even shed a few tears, whereupon the bystanders were struck with amazement at first, and then, convinced that Sertorius was a marvellous man and dear to the gods, escorted him with shouts and clapping of hands to his home, and were full of confidence and good hopes.

XXI. In the plains of Saguntum, after he had reduced his enemies to the greatest straits, he was forced to give them battle when they came out for plunder and forage. Both sides fought splendidly. Memmius, the most capable of Pompey's generals,

[1] Cf. chapter xi.

τῶν ὑπὸ Πομπηΐῳ στρατηγῶν ἡγεμονικώτατος
ἐν τῷ καρτερωτάτῳ τῆς μάχης ἔπεσεν, ἐκράτει
δὲ Σερτώριος καὶ φόνῳ πολλῷ τῶν ἔτι συνεστώ-
2 των ἐωθεῖτο πρὸς αὐτὸν Μέτελλον. ὁ δὲ παρ'
ἡλικίαν ὑποστὰς καὶ περιφανῶς ἀγωνιζόμενος
παίεται δόρατι. τοῦτο τοὺς μὲν ἰδόντας τῶν
Ῥωμαίων, τοὺς δὲ ἀκούσαντας αἰδὼς ἔσχεν ἐγ-
καταλιπεῖν τὸν ἡγεμόνα, καὶ θυμὸς ἅμα πρὸς
τοὺς πολεμίους παρέστη. προθέμενοι δὲ τοὺς
θυρεοὺς καὶ συνεξενεγκόντες εὐρώστως ἐξωθοῦσι
3 τοὺς Ἴβηρας· καὶ γενομένης οὕτω παλιντρόπου
τῆς νίκης, ὁ Σερτώριος ἐκείνοις τε φυγὰς ἀδεεῖς
μηχανώμενος καὶ τεχνάζων ἑτέραν αὐτῷ δύναμιν
συνελθεῖν ἐφ' ἡσυχίας, εἰς πόλιν ὀρεινὴν καὶ
καρτερὰν ἀναφυγὼν ἐφράγνυτο τὰ τείχη καὶ τὰς
πύλας ὠχυροῦτο, πάντα μᾶλλον ἢ πολιορκίαν
4 ὑπομένειν διανοούμενος. ἀλλ' ἐξηπάτα τοὺς πο-
λεμίους· ἐκείνῳ γὰρ προσκαθεζόμενοι καὶ τὸ
χωρίον οὐ χαλεπῶς λήψεσθαι προσδοκῶντες,
τούς τε φεύγοντας τῶν βαρβάρων προΐεντο καὶ
τῆς ἀθροιζομένης αὖθις τῷ Σερτωρίῳ δυνάμεως
ἠμέλησαν. ἠθροίζετο δέ, πέμψαντος ἡγεμόνας
ἐπὶ τὰς πόλεις αὐτοῦ, καὶ κελεύοντος ὅταν ἤδη
πολλοὺς ἔχωσιν, ἄγγελον ἀποστεῖλαι πρὸς αὐτόν.
5 ἐπεὶ δὲ ἀπέστειλαν, σὺν οὐδενὶ πόνῳ διεκπαισά-
μενος τοὺς πολεμίους συνέμιξε τοῖς ἑαυτοῦ· καὶ
πάλιν ἐπῄει πολὺς γεγονὼς καὶ περιέκοπτεν
αὐτῶν τὴν μὲν ἀπὸ τῆς γῆς εὐπορίαν ἐνέδραις καὶ
κυκλώσεσι καὶ τῷ πανταχόσε φοιτᾶν ὀξὺς ἐπιών,

fell in the thickest of the battle, and Sertorius was carrying all before him, and, with great slaughter of the enemy who still held together, was forcing his way towards Metellus himself. Then Metellus, who was holding his ground with a vigour that belied his years, and fighting gloriously, was struck by a spear. All the Romans who saw or heard of this were seized with shame at the thought of deserting their commander, and at the same time were filled with rage against the enemy. So, after they had covered Metellus with their shields and carried him out of danger, they stoutly drove the Iberians back. Victory had now changed sides, and therefore Sertorius, contriving a safe retreat for his men and devising the quiet assembly of another force for himself, took refuge in a strong city among the mountains, and there began to repair the walls and strengthen the gates, although his purpose was anything rather than to stand a siege. But he completely deceived his enemies; for they sat down to invest him and expected to take the place without difficulty, and thus suffered the Barbarians who were in flight to escape, and took no heed of the force that was being collected anew for Sertorius. And collected it was, after Sertorius had sent officers to the cities, with orders that as soon as they had a large body of troops, they should send a messenger to him. Then, when the cities sent their messengers, he cut his way through the enemy with no trouble and effected a junction with his new troops; and so once more he advanced upon the enemy with large reinforcements and began to cut off their land supplies by means of ambuscades, flank movements, and swift marches in

τὰ δ' ἐκ θαλάττης λῃστρικοῖς σκάφεσι κατέχων
τὴν παραλίαν, ὥστε ἠναγκάσθησαν οἱ στρατηγοὶ
διαλυθέντες ὁ μὲν εἰς Γαλατίαν ἀπελθεῖν, Πομπήϊος δὲ περὶ Βακκαίους διαχειμάσαι μοχθηρῶς
ὑπὸ ἀχρηματίας, γράφων πρὸς τὴν σύγκλητον
ὡς ἀπάξει τὸν στρατόν, εἰ μὴ πέμποιεν ἀργύριον
αὐτῷ· καταναλωκέναι γὰρ ἤδη τὰ αὑτοῦ προ-
6 πολεμῶν τῆς Ἰταλίας. καὶ πολὺς ἦν οὗτος ἐν
Ῥώμῃ λόγος, ὡς Πομπηΐου πρότερος εἰς Ἰταλίαν
ἀφίξοιτο Σερτώριος· εἰς τοσοῦτον τοὺς πρώτους
καὶ δυνατωτάτους τῶν τότε στρατηγῶν ἡ Σερτωρίου δεινότης κατέστησεν.

XXII. Ἐδήλωσε δὲ καὶ Μέτελλος ἐκπεπληγ-
μένος τὸν ἄνδρα καὶ μέγαν ἡγούμενος. ἐπεκήρυξε
γάρ, εἴ τις αὐτὸν ἀνέλοι Ῥωμαῖος, ἑκατὸν ἀργυρίου τάλαντα δώσειν καὶ πλέθρα δισμύρια γῆς·
εἰ δὲ φυγάς, κάθοδον εἰς Ῥώμην, ὡς ἀπογνώσει
φανερᾶς ἀμύνης ὠνούμενος τὸν ἄνδρα διὰ προδο-
2 σίας. ἔτι δὲ νικήσας ποτὲ μάχῃ τὸν Σερτώριον
οὕτως ἐπήρθη καὶ τὴν εὐτυχίαν ἠγάπησεν ὥστε
αὐτοκράτωρ ἀναγορευθῆναι, θυσίαις δ' αὐτὸν αἱ
πόλεις ἐπιφοιτῶντα καὶ βωμοῖς ἐδέχοντο. λέγεται δὲ καὶ στεφάνων ἀναδέσεις προσίεσθαι καὶ
δείπνων σοβαρωτέρων ὑποδοχάς, ἐν οἷς ἐσθῆτα
θριαμβικὴν ἔχων ἔπινε, καὶ Νῖκαι πεποιημέναι δι'
ὀργάνων ἐπιδρόμων χρύσεα τρόπαια καὶ στεφάνους διαφέρουσαι κατήγοντο, καὶ χοροὶ παίδων
καὶ γυναικῶν ἐπινικίους ὕμνους ᾖδον εἰς αὐτόν.
3 ἐφ' οἷς εἰκότως ἦν καταγέλαστος, εἰ δραπέτην

every direction, and their maritime supplies by be-
setting the coast with piratical craft; so that the
Roman generals were compelled to separate, Metellus
retiring into Gaul, and Pompey spending the winter
among the Vaccaei. Here he suffered much from
lack of supplies, and wrote to the senate that he
would bring his army home unless they sent him
money, since he had already exhausted his own re-
sources in his war for the defence of Italy.[1] Indeed,
this story was prevalent in Rome, that Sertorius
would come back to Italy before Pompey did. To
such straits were the first and ablest generals of the
time reduced by the skill of Sertorius.

XXII. And Metellus also made it clear that he
was afraid of Sertorius and considered him a great
leader. For he made proclamation that to any
Roman who should kill Sertorius he would give a
hundred talents of silver and twenty thousand acres
of land, and to any exile, freedom to return to Rome;
implying his despair of openly defeating the man by
this attempt to purchase his betrayal. Moreover,
after a victory which he once won over Sertorius he
was so elated and delighted with his success that his
soldiers saluted him as Imperator and the cities
celebrated his visits to them with altars and sacrifices.
Nay, it is said that he suffered wreaths to be bound
upon his head and accepted invitations to stately
banquets, at which he wore a triumphal robe as he
drank his wine, while Victories, made to move by
machinery, descended and distributed golden trophies
and wreaths, and choirs of boys and women sang hymns
of victory in his praise. For this it was natural that
men should laugh at him, since, while calling

---

[1] Cf. the *Pompey*, xx. 1.

Σύλλα καὶ λείψανον τῆς Κάρβωνος φυγῆς ἀπο-
καλῶν τὸν Σερτώριον οὕτω κεχαύνωται καὶ περιχαρὴς γέγονεν, ὑποχωρήσαντος αὐτοῦ περιγενό-
μενος.

Μεγαλοφροσύνης δὲ τοῦ Σερτωρίου πρῶτον μὲν
τὸ τοὺς φεύγοντας ἀπὸ Ῥώμης βουλευτὰς καὶ
παρ᾽ αὐτῷ διατρίβοντας σύγκλητον ἀναγορεῦσαι,
4 ταμίας τε καὶ στρατηγοὺς ἐξ ἐκείνων ἀποδεικνύ-
ναι, καὶ πάντα τοῖς πατρίοις νόμοις τὰ τοιαῦτα
κοσμεῖν· ἔπειτα τὸ χρώμενον ὅπλοις καὶ χρήμασι καὶ πόλεσι ταῖς Ἰβήρων μηδ᾽ ἄχρι λόγου
τῆς ἄκρας ἐξουσίας ὑφίεσθαι πρὸς αὐτούς, Ῥω-   580
μαίους δὲ καθιστάναι στρατηγοὺς καὶ ἄρχοντας
αὐτῶν, ὡς Ῥωμαίοις ἀνακτώμενον τὴν ἐλευθερίαν,
5 οὐκ ἐκείνους αὔξοντα κατὰ Ῥωμαίων. καὶ γὰρ
ἦν ἀνὴρ φιλόπατρις καὶ πολὺν ἔχων ἵμερον τοῦ
κατελθεῖν· ἀλλὰ δυσπραγῶν μὲν ἠνδραγάθει καὶ
ταπεινὸν οὐδὲν ἔπραττε πρὸς τοὺς πολεμίους, ἐν
δὲ ταῖς νίκαις διεπέμπετο πρὸς Μέτελλον καὶ
πρὸς Πομπήιον ἕτοιμος ὢν τὰ ὅπλα καταθέσθαι
καὶ βιοῦν ἰδιώτης καθόδου τυχών· μᾶλλον γὰρ
ἐθέλειν ἀσημότατος ἐν Ῥώμῃ πολίτης ἢ φεύγων
τὴν ἑαυτοῦ πάντων ὁμοῦ τῶν ἄλλων αὐτοκράτωρ
ἀναγορεύεσθαι.

6   Λέγεται δὲ οὐχ ἥκιστα τῆς πατρίδος ἐπιθυμεῖν
διὰ τὴν μητέρα, τραφεὶς ὀρφανὸς ὑπ᾽ αὐτῇ καὶ τὸ
σύμπαν ἀνακείμενος ἐκείνῃ. καλούντων δὲ τῶν
περὶ τὴν Ἰβηρίαν φίλων αὐτὸν ἐφ᾽ ἡγεμονίᾳ,

Sertorius a runaway slave of Sulla and a remnant of the routed party of Carbo, he was so puffed up with pride and overjoyed merely because he had won an advantage over Sertorius and Sertorius had retired before him.

But the magnanimity of Sertorius showed itself, firstly, in his giving the name of senate to the senators who fled from Rome and joined his cause, appointing quaestors and praetors from their number, and making all such arrangements in accordance with the customs of his country ; and, secondly, in his using the arms, wealth, and cities of the Iberians without even pretending to yield to the Iberians themselves a portion of the supreme power, but selecting Roman generals and commanders over them, feeling that he was recovering freedom for the Romans, and not strengthening the inhabitants against the Romans. For he was a man who loved his country and had a strong desire to return home from exile. And yet in his misfortunes he played a brave man's part and would not humble himself at all before his enemies ; while as a victor he would send to Metellus and Pompey expressing his readiness to lay down his arms and lead the life of a private citizen if he could get the privilege of returning home, since, as he said, he preferred to live in Rome as her meanest citizen rather than to live in exile from his country and be called supreme ruler of all the rest of the world together.

We are told that his desire for his native country was due in large measure to his attachment to his mother, by whom he was reared after his father's death, and to whom he was entirely devoted.[1] When his friends in Spain were inviting him to take the

----

[1] Cf. chapter ii. 1.

πυθόμενος τὴν τελευτὴν τῆς μητρὸς ὀλίγον ἐδέ-
ησεν ὑπὸ λύπης προέσθαι τὸν βίον. ἑπτὰ γὰρ
ἡμέρας οὔτε σύνθημα δοὺς οὔτε ὀφθείς τινι τῶν
φίλων ἔκειτο, καὶ μόλις οἱ συστράτηγοι καὶ ὁμό-
τιμοι τὴν σκηνὴν περιστάντες ἠνάγκασαν αὐτὸν
προελθόντα τοῖς στρατιώταις ἐντυχεῖν καὶ τῶν
7 πραγμάτων εὖ φερομένων ἀντιλαμβάνεσθαι. διὸ
καὶ πολλοῖς ἔδοξεν ἥμερος ἀνὴρ φύσει γεγονὼς
καὶ πρὸς ἡσυχίαν ἔχων ἐπιεικῶς δι᾽ αἰτίας παρὰ
γνώμην ταῖς στρατηγικαῖς ἀρχαῖς χρῆσθαι, καὶ
μὴ τυγχάνων ἀδείας, ἀλλὰ συνελαυνόμενος ὑπὸ
τῶν ἐχθρῶν εἰς τὰ ὅπλα φρουρὰν ἀναγκαίαν τοῦ
σώματος περιβάλλεσθαι τὸν πόλεμον.

XXIII. Ἦν δὲ καὶ τὰ πρὸς Μιθριδάτην αὐτοῦ
πολιτεύματα μεγαλοφροσύνης. ἐπεὶ γὰρ ἐκ τοῦ
κατὰ Σύλλαν σφάλματος ὁ Μιθριδάτης ὥσπερ
εἰς πάλαισμα δεύτερον ἀνιστάμενος αὖθις ἐπεχείρησε τῇ Ἀσίᾳ, μέγα δὲ ἤδη τὸ Σερτωρίου κλέος
ἐφοίτα πανταχόσε καὶ τῶν περὶ αὐτοῦ λόγων
ὥσπερ φορτίων ξενικῶν οἱ πλέοντες ἀπὸ τῆς
2 ἑσπέρας ἀναπεπλήκεσαν τὸν Πόντον, ὥρμητο
διαπρεσβεύεσθαι πρὸς αὐτόν, ἐπηρμένος μάλιστα
ταῖς τῶν κολάκων ἀλαζονείαις, οἳ τὸν μὲν Σερτώριον Ἀννίβᾳ, τὸν δὲ Μιθριδάτην Πύρρῳ παρεικά-
ζοντες οὐκ ἂν ἔφασαν Ῥωμαίους πρὸς τηλικαύτας
ὁμοῦ φύσεις τε καὶ δυνάμεις ἐπιχειρουμένους
διχόθεν ἀντισχεῖν, τοῦ δεινοτάτου στρατηγοῦ τῷ
3 μεγίστῳ τῶν βασιλέων προσγενομένου. πέμπει
δὴ πρέσβεις ὁ Μιθριδάτης εἰς Ἰβηρίαν γράμ-

leadership there, he learned of the death of his
mother, and almost died of grief. For seven days
he lay prostrate in his tent without giving out a
watchword or being seen by any of his friends, and
it was only with difficulty that his fellow-generals
and the men of like rank with him who surrounded
his tent could force him to come forth and meet the
soldiers and take part in their enterprises, which
were moving on well. Therefore many people were
led to think that he was a man of gentle temper
and naturally disposed to a quiet life, but was
practically forced against his wishes into the career
of a soldier, where, not achieving safety, but being
driven by his enemies to have recourse to arms,
he encompassed himself with war as a necessary
protection to his person.

XXIII. His negotiations with Mithridates also
gave proof of his magnanimity. For Mithridates,
after the fall which Sulla gave him, rose up, as it
were, for another wrestling bout and tried once more
to get the province of Asia into his power. At this
time, too, the fame of Sertorius was already great
and was travelling every whither, and sailors from
the west had filled the kingdom of Pontus full of
the tales about him, like so many foreign wares.
Mithridates was therefore eager to send an embassy to him, and was incited thereto most of all by
the foolish exaggerations of his flatterers. These
likened Sertorius to Hannibal and Mithridates to
Pyrrhus, and declared that the Romans, attacked
on both sides, could not hold out against two such
natures and forces combined, when the ablest of
generals was in alliance with the greatest of kings.
So Mithridates sent envoys to Iberia carrying letters

63

ματα Σερτωρίῳ καὶ λόγους κομίζοντας, δι' ὧν
αὐτὸς μὲν ἐπηγγέλλετο χρήματα καὶ ναῦς παρέ-
ξειν εἰς τὸν πόλεμον, ὑπ' ἐκείνου δὲ ἠξίου τὴν
Ἀσίαν αὐτῷ βεβαιοῦσθαι πᾶσαν, ἧς ὑπεχώρησε
Ῥωμαίοις κατὰ τὰς πρὸς Σύλλαν γενομένας συν-
4 θήκας. ἀθροίσαντος δὲ Σερτωρίου βουλήν, ἣν
σύγκλητον ὠνόμαζε, καὶ τῶν ἄλλων δέχεσθαι τὰς
προκλήσεις καὶ ἀγαπᾶν κελευόντων (ὄνομα γὰρ
καὶ γράμμα κενὸν αἰτουμένους περὶ τῶν οὐκ
ὄντων ἐπ' αὐτοῖς, ἀντὶ τούτων λαμβάνειν ὧν
μάλιστα δεόμενοι τυγχάνουσιν), οὐκ ἠνέσχετο ὁ
Σερτώριος, ἀλλὰ Βιθυνίαν μὲν ἔφη καὶ Καππαδοκίαν λαμβάνοντι Μιθριδάτῃ μὴ φθονεῖν, ἔθνη
βασιλευόμενα καὶ μηδὲν προσήκοντα Ῥωμαίοις,
5 ἣν δὲ τῷ δικαιοτάτῳ τρόπῳ Ῥωμαίων κεκτημέ-
νων ἐπαρχίαν ἀφελόμενος καὶ κατασχὼν πολεμῶν μὲν ἐξέπεσεν ὑπὸ Φιμβρίου, σπενδόμενος δὲ
πρὸς Σύλλαν ἀφῆκε, ταύτην οὐκ ἔφη περιόψεσθαι
πάλιν ὑπ' ἐκείνῳ γενομένην· δεῖν γὰρ αὔξεσθαι
τὴν πόλιν ὑπ' αὐτοῦ κρατοῦντος, οὐκ ἐλαττώσει
τῶν ἐκείνης κρατεῖν αὐτόν· γενναίῳ γὰρ ἀνδρὶ
μετὰ τοῦ καλοῦ νικᾶν αἱρετόν, αἰσχρῶς δὲ οὐδὲ
σῴζεσθαι.

XXIV. Ταῦτα ἀπαγγελθέντα Μιθριδάτης διὰ 581
θάμβους ἐποιεῖτο· καὶ λέγεται μὲν εἰπεῖν πρὸς
τοὺς φίλους· "Τί δῆτα προστάξει Σερτώριος ἐν
Παλατίῳ καθεζόμενος, εἰ νῦν εἰς τὴν Ἀτλαντικὴν
ἐξεωσμένος θάλασσαν ὅρους ἡμῶν τῇ βασιλείᾳ
τίθησι καὶ πειρωμένοις Ἀσίας ἀπειλεῖ πόλεμον;"

and oral propositions to Sertorius, the purport of which was that Mithridates for his part promised to furnish money and ships for the war, but demanded that Sertorius confirm him in the possession of the whole of Asia, which he had yielded to the Romans by virtue of the treaties made with Sulla. Sertorius assembled a council, which he called a senate, and here the rest urged him to accept the king's proposals and be well content with them; for they were asked to grant a name and an empty title to what was not in their possession, and would receive therefor that of which they stood most in need. Sertorius, however, would not consent to this. He said he had no objection to Mithridates taking Bithynia and Cappadocia, countries used to kings and of no concern whatever to the Romans; but a province which Mithridates had taken away and held when it belonged in the justest manner to the Romans, from which he had been driven by Fimbria in war, and which he had renounced by treaty with Sulla,—this province Sertorius said he would not suffer to become the king's again; for the Roman state must be increased by his exercise of power, and he must not exercise power at the expense of the state. For to a man of noble spirit victory is to be desired if it comes with honour, but with shame not even life itself.

XXIV. When this was reported to Mithridates he acted like one amazed; and we are told that he said to his friends: "What terms, pray, will Sertorius impose when he is seated on the Palatine, if now, after he has been driven forth to the Atlantic sea, he sets bounds to our kingdom and threatens us with war if

2 οὐ μὴν ἀλλὰ γίνονταί γε συνθῆκαι καὶ ὅρκοι,
Καππαδοκίαν καὶ Βιθυνίαν ἔχειν Μιθριδάτηι
Σερτωρίου στρατηγὸν αὐτῷ καὶ στρατιώτας πέμποντος, Σερτώριον δὲ παρὰ Μιθριδάτου λαβεῖν
3 τρισχίλια τάλαντα καὶ τεσσαράκοντα ναῦς. πέμ-
πεται δὲ καὶ στρατηγὸς εἰς Ἀσίαν ὑπὸ Σερτωρίου τῶν ἀπὸ βουλῆς πεφευγότων πρὸς αὐτὸν
Μάρκος Μάριος, ᾧ συνεξελὼν τινὰς πόλεις τῶν
Ἀσιάδων ὁ Μιθριδάτης εἰσελαύνοντι μετὰ ῥά-
βδων καὶ πελέκεων αὐτὸς εἵπετο δευτέραν τάξιν
4 καὶ σχῆμα θεραπεύοντος ἑκουσίως ἀνειληφώς. ὁ
δὲ τὰς μὲν ἠλευθέρου, ταῖς δὲ ἀτέλειαν γράφων
χάριτι Σερτωρίου κατήγγελεν, ὥστε τὴν Ἀσίαν
αὖθις ἐνοχλουμένην μὲν ὑπὸ τῶν τελωνῶν, βα-
ρυνομένην δὲ ταῖς πλεονεξίαις καὶ ὑπερηφανίαις
τῶν ἐπισκήνων, ἀναπτοηθῆναι πρὸς τὴν ἐλπίδα
καὶ ποθεῖν τὴν προσδοκωμένην μεταβολὴν τῆς
ἡγεμονίας.

XXV. Ἐν δ' Ἰβηρίᾳ τῶν περὶ Σερτώριον συγκλητικῶν καὶ ἰσοτίμων, ὡς πρῶτον εἰς ἀντίπαλον
ἐλπίδα κατέστησαν, ἐπανέντος τοῦ φόβου, φθό-
νος ἥπτετο καὶ ζῆλος ἀνόητος τῆς ἐκείνου δυνάμεως. ἐνῆγε δὲ Περπέννας δι' εὐγένειαν ἐπαιρό-
μενος φρονήματι κενῷ πρὸς τὴν ἡγεμονίαν, καὶ
λόγους μοχθηροὺς διεδίδου κρύφα τοῖς ἐπιτηδεί-
2 οις· "Τίς ἄρα πονηρὸς ἡμᾶς ὑπολαβὼν ἐκ κακῶν
εἰς χείρονα φέρει δαίμων, οἳ Σύλλᾳ μὲν ὁμοῦ τι
συμπάσης ἄρχοντι γῆς καὶ θαλάττης ποιεῖν τὸ
προσταττόμενον οὐκ ἠξιοῦμεν οἴκοι μένοντες,
δεῦρο δὲ φθαρέντες ὡς ἐλεύθεροι βιωσόμενοι

we try to get Asia?" However, a treaty was actually
made and ratified with oaths. Mithridates was to
have Cappadocia and Bithynia, Sertorius sending him
a general and soldiers, while Sertorius was to receive
from Mithridates three thousand talents and forty
ships. Accordingly, a general was sent to Asia by
Sertorius by the senators who had taken refuge
with him, Marcus Marius.[1] He was assisted by
Mithridates in the capture of certain cities of Asia, and
when he entered them with fasces and axes, Mithridates would follow him in person, voluntarily assuming
second rank and the position of a vassal. Marius gave
some of the cities their freedom, and wrote to others
announcing their exemption from taxation by grace
of Sertorius, so that Asia, which was once more
harassed by the revenue-farmers and oppressed by
the rapacity and arrogance of the soldiers quartered
there, was all of a flutter with new hopes and yearned
for the expected change of supremacy.

XXV. But in Spain, as soon as the senators and
men of equal rank about Sertorius felt confident that
they were a match for their enemies and dismissed
their fears, they were seized with envy and foolish
jealousy of their leader. They were encouraged in
these feelings by Perpenna, whose high birth filled
him with vain aspirations for the chief command, and
he would hold malevolent discourses in secret among
his associates: "What evil genius, pray, has seized
us and is hurrying us from bad to worse? We would
not consent to remain at home and do the bidding of
Sulla when he was lord of all the earth and sea together, but we came to this land of destruction with
the idea of living like freemen, and are now

---

[1] Cf. the *Lucullus*, viii. 5.

δουλεύομεν ἑκουσίως τὴν Σερτωρίου δορυφο-
ροῦντες φυγήν, ὄνομα χλευαζόμενον ὑπὸ τῶν ἀκου-
όντων, σύγκλητος, ὄντες, ὕβρεις δὲ καὶ προσ-
τάγματα καὶ πόνους οὐκ ἐλάττονας Ἰβήρων καὶ
3 Λυσιτανῶν ὑπομένοντες·" τοιούτων ἀναπιμπλά-
μενοι λόγων οἱ πολλοὶ φανερῶς μὲν οὐκ ἀφί-
σταντο, δεδοικότες αὐτοῦ τὴν δύναμιν, κρύφα δὲ
τάς τε πράξεις ἐλυμαίνοντο, καὶ τοὺς βαρβάρους
ἐκάκουν κολάζοντες πικρῶς καὶ δασμολογοῦντες,
ὡς Σερτωρίου κελεύοντος. ἐξ ὧν ἀποστάσεις
4 ἐγίνοντο καὶ ταραχαὶ περὶ τὰς πόλεις. οἱ δὲ
πεμπόμενοι ταῦτα θεραπεύειν καὶ ἀποπραΰνειν
ἐπανήρχοντο πλείονας ἐξειργασμένοι πολέμους
καὶ τὰς ὑπαρχούσας ηὐξηκότες ἀπειθείας, ὥστε
τὸν Σερτώριον ἐκ τῆς προτέρας ἐπιεικείας καὶ
πραότητος μεταβαλόντα περὶ τοὺς ἐν Ὄσκῃ
τρεφομένους παρανομῆσαι παῖδας τῶν Ἰβήρων,
τοὺς μὲν ἀνελόντα, τοὺς δὲ ἀποδόμενον.

XXVI. Ὁ δ' οὖν Περπέννας πλείονας ἐνωμό-
τους ἔχων πρὸς τὴν ἐπίθεσιν προσάγεται καὶ
Μάλλιον, ἕνα τῶν ἐφ' ἡγεμονίας. οὗτος ἐρῶν
τινος τῶν ἐν ὥρᾳ μειρακίου καὶ φιλοφρονούμενος
πρὸς αὐτὸ φράζει τὴν ἐπιβουλήν, κελεύων ἀμελή-
σαντα τῶν ἄλλων ἐραστῶν αὐτῷ μόνῳ προσέχειν
ὡς ἐντὸς ἡμερῶν ὀλίγων μεγάλῳ γενησομένῳ. τὸ
δὲ μειράκιον ἑτέρῳ τινὶ τῶν ἐραστῶν Αὐφιδίῳ
2 μᾶλλον προσπεπονθὸς ἐκφέρει τὸν λόγον. ἀκούσας δὲ ὁ Αὐφίδιος ἐξεπλάγη· καὶ γὰρ αὐτὸς
μετεῖχε τῆς ἐπὶ Σερτώριον συνωμοσίας, οὐ μέντοι
τὸν Μάλλιον ἐγίνωσκε μετέχοντα. Περπένναν
δὲ καὶ Γρακῖνον καί τινας ἄλλους, ὧν αὐτὸς ᾔδει

voluntarily slaves in the body-guard ot Sertorius the exile, being a senate, a name jeered at by all who hear it, and submitting to no lesser insults, injunctions, and toils than Iberians and Lusitanians." Most of his hearers, their minds infected with such sentiments as these, did not, indeed, openly desert Sertorius, because they were in fear of his power; but they secretly tried to vitiate his enterprises, and abused the Barbarians with severe punishments and exactions, on the plea that Sertorius thus ordered. Consequently there were revolts and disturbances among the cities. And those who were sent to assuage and cure these disorders brought more wars to pass before they returned, and increased the existing insubordination, so that Sertorius laid aside his former clemency and mildness and wrought injustice upon the sons of the Iberians who were being educated at Osca,[1] killing some, and selling others into slavery.

XXVI. Perpenna, accordingly, having now more accomplices in his attempt upon Sertorius, brought into their number Manlius also, one of those in high command. This Manlius was enamoured of a beautiful boy, and as a mark of his affection for him told him of the conspiracy, bidding him neglect his other lovers and devote himself to him alone, since within a few days he was to be a great personage. But the boy carried the tale to another one of his lovers, Aufidius, to whom he was more devoted. And Aufidius, on hearing the story, was astounded; for though he himself was a party to the conspiracy against Sertorius, he did not know that Manlius was. But since the boy mentioned by name Perpenna, Gracinus, and sundry others of those whom Aufidius knew to

[1] Cf. chapter xiv. 2 f.

69

συνωμοτῶν, ὀνομάζοντος τοῦ μειρακίου, διαταρα-
χθεὶς πρὸς ἐκεῖνον μὲν ἐξεφλαύριζε τὸν λόγον,
καὶ παρεκάλει τοῦ Μαλλίου καταφρονεῖν ὡς
κενοῦ καὶ ἀλαζόνος, αὐτὸς δὲ πρὸς τὸν Περπένναν
πορευθεὶς καὶ φράσας τὴν ὀξύτητα τοῦ καιροῦ
3 καὶ τὸν κίνδυνον ἐκέλευσεν ἐπιχειρεῖν. οἱ δὲ
ἐπείθοντο, καὶ παρασκευάσαντες ἄνθρωπον γράμματα κομίζοντα τῷ Σερτωρίῳ προσήγαγον. ἐδή- 58
λου δὲ τὰ γράμματα νίκην τινὸς τῶν ὑπ' αὐτῷ
στρατηγῶν καὶ φόνον πολὺν τῶν πολεμίων. ἐφ'
οἷς τοῦ Σερτωρίου περιχαροῦς ὄντος καὶ θύοντος
εὐαγγέλια, Περπέννας ἑστίασιν αὐτῷ καὶ τοῖς
παροῦσι φίλοις (οὗτοι δὲ ἦσαν ἐκ τῆς συνωμοσίας) ἐπηγγέλλετο, καὶ πολλὰ λιπαρήσας ἔπεισεν
ἐλθεῖν.
4   Ἀεὶ μὲν οὖν τὰ μετὰ Σερτωρίου δεῖπνα πολλὴν εἶχεν αἰδῶ καὶ κόσμον, οὔτε ὁρᾶν τι τῶν
αἰσχρῶν οὔτε ἀκούειν ὑπομένοντος, ἀλλὰ καὶ
τοὺς συνόντας εὐτάκτοις καὶ ἀνυβρίστοις παι-
διαῖς χρῆσθαι καὶ φιλοφροσύναις ἐθίζοντος· τότε
δέ, τοῦ πότου μεσοῦντος, ἀρχὴν ἀψιμαχίας ζητοῦν-
τες ἀναφανδὸν ἀκολάστοις ἐχρῶντο ῥήμασι, καὶ
πολλὰ προσποιούμενοι μεθύειν ἠσέλγαινον ὡς
5 παροξυνοῦντες ἐκεῖνον. ὁ δὲ εἴτε δυσχεραίνων
τὴν ἀκοσμίαν, εἴτε τὴν διάνοιαν αὐτῶν τῇ θρασύτητι τῆς λαλιᾶς καὶ τῇ παρὰ τὸ εἰωθὸς ὀλιγωρίᾳ
συμφρονήσας, μετέβαλε τὸ σχῆμα τῆς κλισίας,
ὕπτιον ἀνεὶς ἑαυτόν, ὡς οὔτε προσέχων οὔτε
κατακούων. ἐπεὶ δὲ ὁ Περπέννας φιάλην τινὰ
λαβὼν ἀκράτου μεταξὺ πίνων ἀφῆκεν ἐκ τῶν
χειρῶν καὶ ψόφον ἐποίησεν, ὅπερ ἦν αὐτοῖς σύμ-

be among the conspirators, Aufidius was confounded, and after making light of the story to the boy and exhorting him to despise Manlius as an empty braggart, he himself went to Perpenna, told him of the sharpness of the crisis and of their peril, and urged him to attempt the deed. The conspirators were persuaded, and after providing a man to act as the bearer of letters, they introduced him to Sertorius. His letters made known a victory of one of the generals serving under Sertorius, and a great slaughter of the enemy. At this Sertorius was overjoyed and offered a sacrifice of glad tidings, during which Perpenna proposed a banquet for him and his friends who were present (and these were of the conspiracy), and after much entreaty persuaded him to come.

Now, the suppers at which Sertorius was present were always marked by restraint and decorum, since he would not consent to see or hear anything that was disgraceful, but held his associates to the practice of indulging only in mirth and merriment that was decorous and restrained. On this occasion, however, when the drinking was well under way, the guests, seeking occasion for a quarrel, openly indulged in dissolute language, and, pretending to be drunk, committed many indecencies, with the hope of angering Sertorius. But he, either because he was vexed at their disorderly conduct, or because he had become aware of their purpose from the boldness of their talk and their unwonted contempt for his wishes, changed his posture on the couch and threw himself upon his back, as though he neither heard nor regarded them. But when Perpenna, after taking a cup of wine in his hands, dropped it as he was drinking and made a clatter with it, which was

βολον, Ἀντώνιος ὑπερκατακείμενος παίει τῷ
6 ξίφει τὸν Σερτώριον. ἀναστρέψαντος δὲ πρὸς
τὴν πληγὴν ἐκείνου καὶ συνεξανισταμένου, περιπεσὼν εἰς τὸ στῆθος κατέλαβε τὰς χεῖρας ἀμφοτέρας, ὥστε μηδὲ ἀμυνόμενον πολλῶν παιόντων
ἀποθανεῖν.

XXVII. Οἱ μὲν οὖν πλεῖστοι τῶν Ἰβήρων
εὐθὺς ᾤχοντο καὶ παρέδωκαν ἑαυτοὺς ἐπιπρε-
σβευσάμενοι τοῖς περὶ Πομπήϊον καὶ Μέτελλ ν·
τοὺς δὲ συμμείναντας ὁ Περπέννας ἀναλαβὼν
ἐπεχείρει τι πράττειν. χρησάμενος δὲ ταῖς Σερτωρίου παρασκευαῖς ὅσον ἐνασχημονῆσαι καὶ
φανερὸς γενέσθαι μήτε ἄρχειν μήτε ἄρχεσθαι
2 πεφυκώς, Πομπηΐῳ προσέβαλε· καὶ ταχὺ συν-
τριβεὶς ὑπ' αὐτοῦ καὶ γενόμενος αἰχμάλωτος οὐδὲ
τὴν ἐσχάτην ὑπέμεινε συμφορὰν ἡγεμονικῶς,
ἀλλὰ τῶν Σερτωρίου γραμμάτων κύριος γεγονὼς
ὑπισχνεῖτο Πομπηΐῳ δείξειν ὑπατικῶν ἀνδρῶν
καὶ μέγιστον ἐν Ῥώμῃ δυναμένων αὐτογράφους
ἐπιστολάς, καλούντων Σερτώριον εἰς Ἰταλίαν,
ὡς πολλῶν ποθούντων τὰ παρόντα κινῆσαι καὶ
3 μεταβαλεῖν τὴν πολιτείαν. ἔργον οὖν ὁ Πομπήϊος οὐ νέας φρενός, ἀλλ' εὖ μάλα βεβηκυίας καὶ
κατηρτυμένης ἐργασάμενος μεγάλων ἀπήλλαξε
τὴν Ῥώμην φόβων καὶ νεωτερισμῶν. τὰς μὲν
γὰρ ἐπιστολὰς ἐκείνας καὶ τὰ γράμματα τοῦ
Σερτωρίου συναγαγὼν ἅπαντα κατέκαυσεν οὔτε
αὐτὸς ἀναγνοὺς [1] οὔτε ἐάσας ἕτερον· αὐτὸν δὲ τὸν
Περπένναν κατὰ τάχος ἀνεῖλε, φοβηθεὶς μὴ τῶν
ὀνομάτων ἐξενεχθέντων πρός τινας ἀποστάσεις
καὶ ταραχαὶ γένωνται.

---

[1] αὐτὸς ἀναγνοὺς Naber : ἀναγνούς.

their signal, Antonius, who reclined above Sertorius on the couch, smote him with his sword. Sertorius turned at the blow and would have risen with his assailant, but Antonius fell upon his chest and seized both his hands, so that he could make no defence even, and died from the blows of many.

XXVII. Well, then, most of the Iberians immediately went away, sent ambassadors to Pompey and Metellus, and delivered themselves up to them; but those who remained Perpenna took under his command and attempted to do something. After using the materials provided by Sertorius just enough to cut a sorry figure and make it clear that he was fitted by nature neither to command nor to obey, he attacked Pompey; and having been quickly crushed by him and taken prisoner, he did not even endure this extreme misfortune as a leader should, but, being in possession of the papers of Sertorius, he promised to show Pompey autograph letters from men of consular rank and of the highest influence in Rome, in which they invited Sertorius to come to Italy, assuring him that there were many there who desired eagerly to stir up a revolution and change the constitution. Pompey, then, did not act in this emergency like a young man, but like one whose understanding was right well matured and disciplined, and so freed Rome from revolutionary terrors. For he got together those letters and all the papers of Sertorius and burned them, without reading them himself or suffering anyone else to do so; and Perpenna himself he speedily put to death, through fear that seditions and disturbances might arise if the names of the correspondents of Sertorius were communicated to anybody.[1]

[1] Cf. the *Pompey*, xx. 4.

4   Τῶν δὲ τῷ Περπέννᾳ συνομοσαμένων οἱ μὲν
ἐπὶ Πομπήϊον ἀναχθέντες διεφθάρησαν, οἱ δὲ
φεύγοντες εἰς Λιβύην ὑπὸ Μαυρουσίων κατη-
κοντίσθησαν. διέφυγε δ' οὐδεὶς πλὴν Αὐφίδιος
ὁ τοῦ Μαλλίου ἀντεραστής· οὗτος δὲ ἢ λαθὼν ἢ
παραμεληθεὶς ἔν τινι βαρβάρῳ κώμῃ πενόμενος
καὶ μισούμενος κατεγήρασεν.

Of Perpenna's fellow conspirators, some were brought to Pompey and put to death, others fled to Africa and fell victims to the spears of the Maurusians. Not one escaped, except Aufidius, the rival of Manlius; he, either because men did not notice him or because they did not heed him, came to old age in a barbarian village, a poor and hated man.

EUMENES

ΕΥΜΕΝΗΣ

I. Εὐμένη δὲ τὸν Καρδιανὸν ἱστορεῖ Δοῦρις 58:
πατρὸς μὲν ἁμαξεύοντος ἐν Χερρονήσῳ διὰ πενίαν
γενέσθαι, τραφῆναι δὲ ἐλευθερίως ἐν γράμμασι
καὶ περὶ παλαίστραν· ἔτι δὲ παιδὸς ὄντος αὐτοῦ
Φίλιππον παρεπιδημοῦντα καὶ σχολὴν ἄγοντα
τὰ τῶν Καρδιανῶν θεάσασθαι παγκράτια μειρα-
κίων καὶ παλαίσματα παίδων, ἐν οἷς εὐημερή-
σαντα τὸν Εὐμένη καὶ φανέντα συνετὸν καὶ ἀν-
δρεῖον ἀρέσαι τῷ Φιλίππῳ καὶ ἀναληφθῆναι.
2 δοκοῦσι δὲ εἰκότα λέγειν μᾶλλον οἱ διὰ ξενίαν καὶ
φιλίαν πατρῴαν τὸν Εὐμένη λέγοντες ὑπὸ τοῦ
Φιλίππου προαχθῆναι. μετὰ δὲ τὴν ἐκείνου
τελευτὴν οὔτε συνέσει τινὸς οὔτε πίστει λείπεσθαι δοκῶν τῶν περὶ Ἀλέξανδρον ἐκαλεῖτο μὲν
ἀρχιγραμματεύς, τιμῆς δὲ ὥσπερ οἱ μάλιστα
φίλοι καὶ συνήθεις ἐτύγχανεν, ὥστε καὶ στρατηγὸς ἀποσταλῆναι κατὰ τὴν Ἰνδικὴν ἐφ' ἑαυτοῦ
μετὰ δυνάμεως, καὶ τὴν Περδίκκου παραλαβεῖν
ἱππαρχίαν, ὅτε Περδίκκας, ἀποθανόντος Ἡφαι-
3 στίωνος, εἰς τὴν ἐκείνου προῆλθε τάξιν. διὸ καὶ
Νεοπτολέμου τοῦ ἀρχιυπασπιστοῦ μετὰ τὴν

EUMENES

I. EUMENES of Cardia, according to Duris, was the son of a man whom poverty drove to be a waggoner, in the Thracian Chersonesus, but received a liberal education in literature and athletics. While he was still a boy, Duris says further, Philip, who was sojourning in the place and had an hour of leisure, came to see the young men and boys of Cardia exercising in the pancratium[1] and in wrestling, among whom Eumenes had such success and gave such proofs of intelligence and bravery that he pleased Philip and was taken into his following. But in my opinion those historians tell a more probable story who say that a tie of guest-friendship with his father led Philip to give advancement to Eumenes. After Philip's death Eumenes was thought to be inferior to none of Alexander's followers in sagacity and fidelity, and though he had only the title of chief secretary, he was held in as much honour as the king's principal friends and intimates, so that on the Indian expedition he was actually sent out as general with a force under his own orders,[2] and received the command in the cavalry which Perdiccas had held, when Perdiccas, after Hephaestion's death, was advanced to that officer's position. Therefore when Neoptolemus, the commander of the Shield-bearers, after Alexander's

---

[1] A mixture of wrestling and boxing.
[2] Cf. Arrian, *Anab.* v. 24, 6 f.

Ἀλεξάνδρου τελευτὴν λέγοντος ὡς αὐτὸς μὲν
ἀσπίδα καὶ λόγχην, Εὐμένης δὲ γραφεῖον ἔχων
καὶ πινακίδιον ἠκολούθει, κατεγέλων οἱ Μακεδόνες, μετὰ τῶν ἄλλων καλῶν τὸν Εὐμένη καὶ τῆς
κατὰ τὸν γάμον οἰκειότητος ὑπὸ τοῦ βασιλέως
εἰδότες ἀξιωθέντα. Βαρσίνην γὰρ τὴν Ἀρταβάζου πρώτην ἐν Ἀσίᾳ γνοὺς ὁ Ἀλέξανδρος, ἐξ ἧς
υἱὸν ἔσχεν Ἡρακλέα, τῶν ταύτης ἀδελφῶν Πτο-
λεμαίῳ μὲν Ἀπάμαν, Εὐμένει δὲ Βαρσίνην ἐξέδωκεν, ὅτε καὶ τὰς ἄλλας Περσίδας διένειμε καὶ
συνῴκισε τοῖς ἑταίροις.

II. Οὐ μὴν ἀλλὰ καὶ προσέκρουσε πολλάκις
Ἀλεξάνδρῳ, καὶ παρεκινδύνευσε δι' Ἡφαιστίωνα.
πρῶτον μὲν γὰρ Εὐίῳ τῷ αὐλητῇ τοῦ Ἡφαιστίωνος οἰκίαν κατανείμαντος ἦν οἱ παῖδες ἔτυχον
τῷ Εὐμένει προκατειληφότες, ἐλθὼν ὑπὸ ὀργῆς
πρὸς τὸν Ἀλέξανδρον ὁ Εὐμένης ἐβόα μετὰ Μέν-
τορος ὡς αὐλεῖν εἴη κράτιστον ἢ τραγῳδεῖν τὰ
ὅπλα ῥίψαντας ἐκ τῶν χειρῶν, ὥστε Ἀλέξανδρον
αὐτῷ συναγανακτεῖν καὶ λοιδορεῖσθαι τῷ Ἡφαι-
2 στίωνι. ταχὺ μέντοι μεταπεσὼν αὖθις εἶχε τὸν
Εὐμένη δι' ὀργῆς, ὡς ὕβρει μᾶλλον πρὸς ἑαυτὸν ἢ
παρρησίᾳ πρὸς Ἡφαιστίωνα χρησάμενον.

Ἔπειτα Νέαρχον ἐκπέμπων μετὰ νεῶν ἐπὶ τὴν
ἔξω θάλασσαν ᾔτει χρήματα τοὺς φίλους· οὐ γὰρ
ἦν ἐν τῷ βασιλείῳ. τοῦ δ' Εὐμένους αἰτηθέντος
μὲν τριακόσια τάλαντα, δόντος δὲ ἑκατὸν μόνα,
καὶ ταῦτα γλίσχρως καὶ μόλις αὐτῷ συνειλέχθαι

death, said that he had followed the king with shield and spear, but Eumenes with pen and paper, the Macedonians laughed him to scorn; they knew that, besides his other honours, Eumenes had been deemed worthy by the king of relationship in marriage. For Barsiné the daughter of Artabazus, the first woman whom Alexander knew in Asia, and by whom he had a son, Heracles, had two sisters; of these Alexander gave one, Apama, to Ptolemy, and the other, also called Barsiné,[1] to Eumenes. This was at the time when he distributed the other Persian women as consorts among his companions.[2]

II. However, Eumenes was often in collision with Alexander, and he got himself into danger through Hephaestion. In the first place, for instance, when Hephaestion assigned to Euius the flute-player the quarters which his servants had already taken up for Eumenes, Eumenes, accompanied by Mentor, came in a passion to Alexander and cried out that it was best for him to throw away his arms and be a flute-player or a tragic actor. The immediate result was that Alexander shared his indignation and heaped abuse upon Hephaestion. Soon, however, he changed his mind and was angry with Eumenes, feeling that he had indulged in insolence towards himself more than in bold words against Hephaestion.

Again, when Alexander was sending out Nearchus with a fleet to explore the outer sea, he asked money of his friends, since the royal treasury was empty. Eumenes was asked for three hundred talents, but gave only a hundred, and said that even these had been slowly and with difficulty collected for him by

[1] In Arrian, *Anab.* vii. 4, 6, the names of the sisters are Artacama and Artonis, respectively.

[2] Cf. the *Alexander*, lxx. 2.

διὰ τῶν ἐπιτρόπων φάσκοντος, οὐδὲν ἐγκαλέσας
οὐδὲ δεξάμενος ἐκέλευσε τοὺς παῖδας κρύφα τῇ
σκηνῇ τοῦ Εὐμένους πῦρ ἐνεῖναι, βουλόμενος ἐκ-
κομιζομένων τῶν χρημάτων λαβεῖν ἐπ᾽ αὐτοφώρῳ
3 ψευδόμενον. ἔφθη δὲ ἡ σκηνὴ καταφλεχθεῖσα,
καὶ μετενόησε τῶν γραμμάτων διαφθαρέντων ὁ
Ἀλέξανδρος. τὸ δὲ συγχυθὲν χρυσίον καὶ ἀργύριον ὑπὸ τοῦ πυρὸς ἀνευρέθη πλεῖον ἢ χιλίων
ταλάντων. ἔλαβε δὲ οὐδέν, ἀλλὰ καὶ γράψας
τοῖς πανταχοῦ σατράπαις καὶ στρατηγοῖς ἀντί-
γραφα τῶν διεφθαρμένων ἀποστέλλειν πάντα 58
παραλαμβάνειν ἐκέλευσε τὸν Εὐμένη.

4 Πάλιν δὲ περὶ δωρεᾶς τινος εἰς διαφορὰν καταστὰς πρὸς τὸν Ἡφαιστίωνα, καὶ πολλὰ μὲν
ἀκούσας κακῶς, πολλὰ δὲ εἰπών, τότε μὲν οὐκ
ἔλαττον ἔσχε· μετ᾽ ὀλίγον δὲ τελευτήσαντος
Ἡφαιστίωνος περιπαθῶν ὁ βασιλεὺς καὶ πᾶσιν
οὓς ἐδόκει ζῶντι μὲν ἐκείνῳ φθονεῖν ἐπιχαίρειν δὲ
τεθνηκότι τραχέως ὁμιλῶν καὶ χαλεπὸς ὤν, μάλιστα τὸν Εὐμένη δι᾽ ὑποψίας εἶχε, καὶ προύφερε
5 πολλάκις τὰς διαφορὰς καὶ λοιδορίας ἐκείνας. ὁ
δὲ πανοῦργος ὢν καὶ πιθανὸς ἐπεχείρησεν οἷς
ἀπώλλυτο σώζειν ἑαυτόν. κατέφυγε γὰρ εἰς τὴν
πρὸς Ἡφαιστίωνα φιλοτιμίαν Ἀλεξάνδρου καὶ
χάριν, ὑφηγούμενός τε τιμὰς αἳ μάλιστα κοσμεῖν
ἔμελλον τὸν τεθνηκότα, καὶ χρήματα τελῶν εἰς
τὴν τοῦ τάφου κατασκευὴν ἀφειδῶς καὶ προθύμως.

his stewards. Alexander made no reproaches, nor
did he take the money, but ordered his servants
secretly to set fire to the tent of Eumenes, wishing
to take its owner in a manifest lie when the treasure
was carried out of it. But before that could be done
the tent was consumed, and the destruction of his
papers made Alexander repent him of his orders.
Still, the gold and silver that was melted down by
the fire was found to be more than a thousand talents'
worth. Alexander took none of it, however, but
actually wrote to his satraps and generals everywhere
to send copies of the documents that had been
destroyed, and ordered Eumenes to take them all in
charge.

And still again, Eumenes had a quarrel with
Hephaestion about a certain gift, and much abusive
language passed between them. At the time, indeed,
Eumenes was no less in favour than before; but a
little while afterwards Hephaestion died, and the
king, in his bitter sorrow, dealt harshly and was
severe with all who, as he thought, had been jealous
of his favourite while he lived and now rejoiced
at his death. Eumenes, in particular, he suspected
of such feelings, and often reproached him for his
former quarrels with Hephaestion and his abusive
language towards him. But Eumenes, who was wily
and persuasive, tried to make what threatened his
ruin conduce to his salvation. He sought refuge,
namely, in Alexander's ardent gratitude towards
Hephaestion, suggesting honours which were most
likely to adorn the memory of the deceased, and
contributing money for the construction of his tomb
lavishly and readily.

III. Ἀποθανόντος δὲ Ἀλεξάνδρου καὶ τῆς φάλαγγος διεστώσης πρὸς τοὺς ἑταίρους, τῇ μὲν γνώμῃ τούτοις προσένειμεν ἑαυτὸν ὁ Εὐμένης, τῷ δὲ λόγῳ κοινός τις ἦν πρὸς ἀμφοτέρους καὶ ἰδιώτης, ὡς οὐδὲν αὐτῷ προσῆκον ξένῳ ὄντι πολυπραγμονεῖν ἐν ταῖς[1] Μακεδόνων διαφοραῖς. καὶ τῶν ἄλλων ἑταίρων ἐκ Βαβυλῶνος ἀνασκευασαμένων αὐτὸς ὑπολειφθεὶς ἐν τῇ πόλει κατεπράϋνε πολλοὺς τῶν πεζῶν καὶ πρὸς τὰς διαλύσεις ἡδί-
2 ους ἐποίησεν. ἐπεὶ δὲ ἀναμιχθέντες ἀλλήλοις οἱ στρατηγοὶ καὶ καταστάντες ἐκ τῶν πρώτων ταραχῶν διενέμοντο σατραπείας καὶ στρατηγίας, Εὐμένης λαμβάνει Καππαδοκίαν καὶ Παφλαγονίαν καὶ τὴν ὑποκειμένην τῇ Ποντικῇ θαλάττῃ μέχρι Τραπεζοῦντος, οὔπω τότε Μακεδόνων οὖσαν, Ἀριαράθης γὰρ αὐτῆς ἐβασίλευεν, ἀλλ᾽ ἔδει Λεοννάτου καὶ Ἀντίγονον χειρὶ μεγάλῃ τὸν Εὐμένη κατάγοντας ἀποδεῖξαι τῆς χώρας σατράπην.
3 Ἀντίγονος μὲν οὖν οὐ προσέσχε τοῖς γραφεῖσιν ὑπὸ Περδίκκου, μετέωρος ὢν ἤδη καὶ περιφρονῶν ἁπάντων, Λεοννάτος δὲ κατέβη μὲν ἄνωθεν εἰς Φρυγίαν ἀναδεξόμενος Εὐμένει τὴν στρατείαν· Ἑκαταίου δὲ τοῦ Καρδιανῶν τυράννου συμμίξαν-

---

[1] ἐν ταῖς Bekker, after Coraës: ταῖς.

---

[1] June 13, 323 B.C.
[2] The quarrel was over the succession to Alexander's throne. The officers, supported by the cavalry, proposed that the crown be reserved for the child of Roxana by

III. When Alexander was dead[1] and a quarrel had arisen between the Macedonian men-at-arms and his principal officers, or companions,[2] Eumenes sided with the latter in his opinions, but in what he said he was a kind of common friend to both and held himself aloof from the quarrel, on the ground that it was no business of his, since he was a stranger, to meddle in disputes of Macedonians. Moreover, when the rest of the principal officers had withdrawn from Babylon, he remained behind in the city and mollified many of the men-at-arms and made them more disposed towards a settlement of the quarrel. And when the officers, having conferred with one another, brought their first tumultuous proceedings to an end, and were distributing satrapies and commands, Eumenes received Cappadocia, Paphlagonia, and the southern coast of the Euxine sea as far as Trapezus. It is true that at the time this territory was not yet subject to the Macedonians, for Ariarathes held royal sway over it; but Leonnatus and Antigonus, with a great army, were to conduct Eumenes thither and declare him satrap of the country.

Now, Antigonus paid no heed to the edicts of Perdiccas, being already lifted up in his ambitions and scorning all his associates; but Leonnatus came down from the interior into Phrygia in order to undertake the expedition in behalf of Eumenes. Here, however, Hecataeus the tyrant of Cardia joined him and be-

---

Alexander, if it should be a son, and that Perdiccas should be regent in the meantime; the infantry demanded that Arrhidaeus, the bastard brother of Alexander, should at once be proclaimed king. In the end a compromise was effected, and Perdiccas became chief in command under Arrhidaeus, with whom Alexander's son, when born, was to be joint king. Cf. the *Alexander*, lxxvii. 5.

τος αὐτῷ καὶ δεομένου βοηθεῖν μᾶλλον Ἀντιπάτρῳ
καὶ Μακεδόνων τοῖς ἐν Λαμίᾳ πολιορκουμένοις,
ὥρμητο διαβαίνειν καὶ τὸν Εὐμένη παρεκάλει καὶ
4 διήλαττε πρὸς τὸν Ἑκαταῖον. ἦν γὰρ αὐτοῖς
πατρική τις ἐκ πολιτικῶν διαφορῶν ὑποψία πρὸς
ἀλλήλους· καὶ πολλάκις ὁ Εὐμένης ἐγεγόνει φανερὸς κατηγορῶν τοῦ Ἑκαταίου τυραννοῦντος καὶ
παρακαλῶν Ἀλέξανδρον ἀποδοῦναι τοῖς Καρδια-
νοῖς τὴν ἐλευθερίαν. διὸ καὶ τότε τοῦ Εὐμένους
παραιτουμένου τὴν ἐπὶ τοὺς Ἕλληνας στρατείαν,
καὶ δεδιέναι φάσκοντος Ἀντίπατρον, μήπως
Ἑκαταίῳ χαριζόμενος καὶ πάλαι μισῶν αὐτὸν
ἀνέλῃ, πιστεύσας ὁ Λεοννάτος οὐδὲν ὧν ἐφρόνει
5 πρὸς αὐτὸν ἀπεκρύψατο. λόγος μὲν γὰρ ἦν ἡ
βοήθεια καὶ πρόφασις, ἐγνώκει δὲ διαβὰς εὐθὺς
ἀντιποιεῖσθαι Μακεδονίας· καί τινας ἐπιστολὰς
ἔδειξε Κλεοπάτρας μεταπεμπομένης αὐτὸν εἰς
Πέλλαν ὡς γαμησομένης. ὁ δ᾽ Εὐμένης, εἴτε τὸν
Ἀντίπατρον δεδοικὼς εἴτε τὸν Λεοννάτου ἔμπληκτον ὄντα καὶ φορᾶς μεστὸν ἀβεβαίου καὶ ὀξείας
ἀπογνούς, νύκτωρ ἀνέζευξε τὴν ἑαυτοῦ λαβὼν
ἀποσκευήν. εἶχε δὲ τριακοσίους μὲν ἱππεῖς, δια-
κοσίους δὲ τῶν παίδων ὁπλοφόρους, ἐν δὲ χρυσοῖς
6 εἰς ἀργυρίου λόγον τάλαντα πεντακισχίλια. φυγὼν δὲ οὕτως πρὸς Περδίκκαν καὶ τὰ Λεοννάτου
βουλεύματα κατειπὼν εὐθὺς μὲν ἴσχυε μέγα παρ᾽
αὐτῷ καὶ τοῦ συνεδρίου μετεῖχεν, ὀλίγον δὲ ὕστερον εἰς Καππαδοκίαν κατήχθη μετὰ δυνάμεως,

---

[1] On the death of Alexander the Greeks had revolted from
Macedonia, and had driven Antipater and his army into
Lamia, a city of southern Thessaly.

[2] The sister of Alexander, widow, since 326 B.C., of the

sought him to go rather to the assistance of Antipater
and the Macedonians besieged in Lamia.[1] Leonnatus
therefore determined to cross over to Greece, invited Eumenes to go with him, and tried to reconcile
him with Hecataeus. For they had a hereditary distrust of one another arising from political differences ;
and frequently Eumenes had been known to denounce
Hecataeus when a tyrant and to exhort Alexander
to restore its freedom to Cardia. Therefore at this
time also Eumenes declined to go on the expedition
against the Greeks, saying he was afraid that Antipater, who had long hated him, would kill him to
please Hecataeus. Then Leonnatus took him into his
confidence and revealed to him all his purposes.
Assistance to Antipater, namely, was what he alleged
as a pretext for his expedition, but he really meant,
as soon as he had crossed into Europe, to lay claim
to Macedonia ; and he showed certain letters from
Cleopatra [2] in which she invited him to come to Pella
and promised to marry him. But Eumenes, either
because he was afraid of Antipater, or because he
despaired of Leonnatus as a capricious man full of
uncertain and rash impulses, took his own equipment
and decamped by night.[3] And he had three hundred
horsemen, two hundred armed camp-followers, and in
gold what would amount to five thousand talents of
money. With this equipment he fled to Perdiccas, and
by telling him of the designs of Leonnatus at once
enjoyed great influence with him and was made a
member of his council. Moreover, a little while after
he was conducted into Cappadocia with an army

king of Epeirus. No less than six of Alexander's generals
sought her hand in marriage.

[3] According to Nepos (*Eumenes*, ii. 4), Leonnatus, failing
to persuade Eumenes, tried to kill him.

αὐτοῦ Περδίκκου παρόντος καὶ στρατηγοῦντος. 585
Ἀριαράθου δὲ ληφθέντος αἰχμαλώτου καὶ τῆς
χώρας ὑποχειρίου γενομένης ἀποδείκνυται σατρά-
7 πης. καὶ τὰς μὲν πόλεις τοῖς ἑαυτοῦ φίλοις
παρέδωκε, καὶ φρουράρχους ἐγκατέστησε καὶ δικαστὰς ἀπέλιπε καὶ διοικητὰς οὓς ἐβούλετο, τοῦ
Περδίκκου μηδὲν ἐν τούτοις πολυπραγμονοῦντος,
αὐτὸς δὲ συνανέζευξεν ἐκεῖνόν τε θεραπεύων καὶ
τῶν βασιλέων ἀπολείπεσθαι μὴ βουλόμενος.

IV. Οὐ μὴν ἀλλ' ὁ Περδίκκας ἐφ' ἃ μὲν ὥρμητο
πιστεύων δι' αὑτοῦ προσάξεσθαι, τὰ δὲ ὑπολειπό-
μενα δεῖσθαι δραστηρίου τε καὶ πιστοῦ φύλακος
οἰόμενος, ἀπέπεμψεν ἐκ Κιλικίας τὸν Εὐμένη,
λόγῳ μὲν ἐπὶ τὴν ἑαυτοῦ σατραπείαν, ἔργῳ δὲ
τὴν ὅμορον Ἀρμενίαν τεταραγμένην ὑπὸ Νεοπτο-
2 λέμου διὰ χειρὸς ἕξοντα. τοῦτον μὲν οὖν ὁ Εὐμένης, καίπερ ὄγκῳ τινὶ καὶ φρονήματι κενῷ
διεφθαρμένον, ἐπειρᾶτο ταῖς ὁμιλίαις κατέχειν·
αὐτὸς δὲ τὴν φάλαγγα τῶν Μακεδόνων ἐπηρμένην
καὶ θρασεῖαν εὑρών, ὥσπερ ἀντίταγμα κατεσκεύ-
αζεν αὐτῇ δύναμιν ἱππικήν, τῶν μὲν ἐγχωρίων
τοῖς ἱππεύειν δυναμένοις ἀνεισφορίας διδοὺς καὶ
3 ἀτελείας, τῶν δὲ περὶ αὐτὸν οἷς μάλιστα ἐπίστευεν
ὠνητοὺς διανέμων ἵππους, φιλοτιμίαις τε καὶ δω-
ρεαῖς τὰ φρονήματα παροξύνων καὶ τὰ σώματα
κινήσεσι καὶ μελέταις διαπονῶν, ὥστε τοὺς μὲν
ἐκπλαγῆναι, τοὺς δὲ θαρρῆσαι τῶν Μακεδόνων,
ὁρῶντας ὀλίγῳ χρόνῳ περὶ αὐτὸν ἠθροισμένους

---

[1] Arrhidaeus and the infant son of Alexander, both under
the guardianship of Perdiccas. Eumenes thus ranged himself with the legitimists.

which Perdiccas commanded in person. There Aria-rathes was taken prisoner, the country was brought into subjection, and Eumenes was proclaimed satrap. He entrusted the cities of the country to his own friends, appointed commanders of garrisons, left behind him such judges and administrators as he wished, Perdiccas not at all interfering in these matters, and then marched away with Perdiccas, de-siring to pay court to that general, and not wishing to be separated from the kings.[1]

IV. However, Perdiccas felt confident of carrying out his projects by himself, and thought that the country they had left behind them needed an efficient and faithful guardian, and therefore sent Eumenes back from Cilicia, ostensibly to his own satrapy, but really to reduce to obedience the adjacent country of Armenia, which had been thrown into confusion by Neoptolemus.[2] Accordingly, although Neoptolemus was a victim of ostentation and empty pride, Eumenes tried to constrain him by personal intercourse ; then, finding that the Macedonian men-at-arms were con-ceited and bold, he raised a force of cavalry as a counterpoise to them, by offering the natives of the country who were able to serve as horsemen immunity from contributions and tributes, and by distributing horses that he had bought among those of his followers in whom he placed most confidence ; the spirits of these men, too, he incited by honours and gifts, and developed their bodies by exercise and discipline; so that a part of the Macedonians were amazed, and a part emboldened, when they saw that in a short time

[2] One of the principal officers of Alexander, to whom Armenia had been assigned as a province. Cf. chapter i. 3.

ἱππεῖς οὐκ ἐλάττους ἑξακισχιλιων καὶ τριακο-
σιων.

V. Ἐπεὶ δὲ Κρατερὸς καὶ Ἀντίπατρος τῶν
Ἑλλήνων περιγενόμενοι διέβαινον εἰς Ἀσίαν τὴν
Περδίκκου καταλύσοντες ἀρχήν, καὶ προσηγγέλ-
λοντο μέλλοντες ἐμβαλεῖν εἰς Καππαδοκίαν, ὁ
Περδίκκας αὐτὸς ἐπὶ Πτολεμαῖον στρατεύων ἀπέδειξε τὸν Εὐμένη τῶν ἐν Ἀρμενίᾳ καὶ Καππα-
2 δοκίᾳ δυνάμεων αὐτοκράτορα στρατηγόν· καὶ
περὶ τούτων ἐπιστολὰς ἔπεμψεν, Ἀλκέταν μὲν
καὶ Νεοπτόλεμον Εὐμένει προσέχειν κελεύσας,
Εὐμένη δὲ χρῆσθαι τοῖς πράγμασιν ὅπως αὐτὸς
ἔγνωκεν. Ἀλκέτας μὲν οὖν ἄντικρυς ἀπείπατο
τὴν στρατείαν, ὡς τῶν ὑπ' αὐτῷ Μακεδόνων
Ἀντιπάτρῳ μὲν αἰδουμένων μάχεσθαι, Κρατερὸν
δὲ καὶ δέχεσθαι δι' εὔνοιαν ἑτοίμων ὄντων· Νεοπτόλεμος δὲ βουλεύων μὲν ἐπ' Εὐμένει προδοσίαν
οὐκ ἔλαθε, καλούμενος δὲ οὐχ ὑπήκουεν, ἀλλὰ
3 παρέταττε τὴν δύναμιν. ἔνθα πρῶτον ὁ Εὐμένης
ἀπέλαυσε τῆς ἑαυτοῦ προνοίας καὶ παρασκευῆς·
ἡττώμενος γὰρ ἤδη κατὰ τὸ πεζὸν ἐτρέψατο τοῖς
ἱππεῦσι τὸν Νεοπτόλεμον καὶ τὴν ἀποσκευὴν
ἔλαβεν αὐτοῦ, καὶ τῇ φάλαγγι διεσπαρμένῃ περὶ
τὴν δίωξιν ἄθρους ἐπελάσας ἠνάγκασε τὰ ὅπλα
θέσθαι καὶ δόντας καὶ λαβόντας ὅρκους αὐτῷ
συστρατεύειν.

4 Ὁ μὲν οὖν Νεοπτόλεμος ὀλίγους τινὰς συναγαγὼν ἐκ τῆς τροπῆς ἔφυγε πρὸς Κρατερὸν καὶ

---

[1] One of the ablest of Alexander's officers, who, in the
division of the empire that followed Alexander's death, was
made ruler, in common with Antipater, of Macedonia and
Greece.

he had assembled about him no fewer than sixty-three hundred horsemen.

V. And when Craterus[1] and Antipater, after overpowering the Greeks,[2] were crossing into Asia[3] to overthrow the power of Perdiccas, and were reported to be planning an invasion of Cappadocia, Perdiccas, who was himself heading an expedition against Ptolemy,[4] appointed Eumenes commander of the forces in Armenia and Cappadocia with plenary powers. He also sent letters on the subject, in which he commanded Alcetas[5] and Neoptolemus to look to Eumenes for orders, and Eumenes to manage matters as he thought best. Alcetas, then, flatly refused to serve in the campaign, on the ground that the Macedonians under him were ashamed to fight Antipater, and were so well disposed to Craterus that they were ready to receive him with open arms. Neoptolemus, however, plotting treachery against Eumenes, was detected, and when he was summoned would not obey, but drew up his forces in battle array. Here first did Eumenes reap the fruit of his forethought and preparation; for when his infantry had already been defeated, he routed Neoptolemus with his cavalry, and captured his baggage, and when the men-at-arms of Neoptolemus were scattered in pursuit of their enemies, charged upon them with his entire body of horse and compelled them to lay down their arms and make oath with him to serve under him.

Neoptolemus, then, collected a few of his men from the rout and fled to Craterus and Antipater.

[2] In the battle of Crannon, Aug. 7, 322, which put an end to the revolt of the Greeks and the war called the "Lamian" war.   [3] In 321 B.C.

[4] Now governor of Egypt.   [5] A brother of Perdiccas.

Ἀντίπατρον. παρ᾽ ἐκείνων δὲ ἀπέσταλτο πρε-
σβεία πρὸς Εὐμένη παρακαλοῦσα μεταθέσθαι
πρὸς αὐτούς, καρπούμενον μὲν ἃς εἶχε σατραπείας, προσλαβόντα δὲ στρατιὰν καὶ χώραν παρ᾽
αὐτῶν, Ἀντιπάτρῳ μὲν ἀντ᾽ ἐχθροῦ φίλον γενόμενον, Κρατερῷ δὲ μὴ γενόμενον ἐκ φίλου πολέ-
5 μιον. ταῦτα ὁ Εὐμένης ἀκούσας Ἀντιπάτρῳ μὲν
οὐκ ἂν ἔφη παλαιὸς ὢν ἐχθρὸς νῦν γενέσθαι φίλος,
ὅτε αὐτὸν ὁρᾷ τοῖς φίλοις ὡς ἐχθροῖς χρώμενον,
Κρατερὸν δὲ Περδίκκᾳ διαλλάττειν ἕτοιμος εἶναι
καὶ συνάγειν ἐπὶ τοῖς ἴσοις καὶ δικαίοις· ἄρχοντος
δὲ πλεονεξίας τῷ ἀδικουμένῳ βοηθήσειν μέχρι ἂν
ἐμπνέῃ, καὶ μᾶλλον τὸ σῶμα καὶ τὸν βίον ἢ τὴν
πίστιν προήσεσθαι.

VI. Οἱ μὲν οὖν περὶ τὸν Ἀντίπατρον πυθόμενοι
ταῦτα κατὰ σχολὴν ἐβουλεύοντο περὶ τῶν ὅλων,
ὁ Νεοπτόλεμος δὲ μετὰ τὴν φυγὴν ἀφικόμενος   586
πρὸς αὐτοὺς τήν τε μάχην ἀπήγγελλε καὶ παρεκάλει βοηθεῖν, μάλιστα μὲν ἀμφοτέρους, πάντως
δὲ Κρατερόν· ποθεῖσθαι γὰρ ὑπερφυῶς ἐκεῖνον
ὑπὸ τῶν Μακεδόνων, κἂν μόνον ἴδωσι τὴν καυσίαν
αὐτοῦ καὶ τὴν φωνὴν ἀκούσωσι, μετὰ τῶν ὅπλων
2 ἥξειν φερομένους. καὶ γὰρ ἦν ὄντως ὄνομα τοῦ
Κρατεροῦ μέγα, καὶ μετὰ τὴν Ἀλεξάνδρου τελευτὴν τοῦτον ἐπόθησαν οἱ πολλοί, μνημονεύοντες
ὅτι καὶ πρὸς Ἀλέξανδρον ὑπὲρ αὐτῶν ἀνεδέξατο
πολλάκις ἀπεχθείας πολλάς, ὑποφερομένου πρὸς
τὸν Περσικὸν ζῆλον ἀντιλαμβανόμενος, καὶ τοῖς
πατρίοις ἀμύνων διὰ τρυφὴν καὶ ὄγκον ἤδη περιυ-
βριζομένοις.

3   Τότε δ᾽ οὖν ὁ Κρατερὸς τὸν μὲν Ἀντίπατρον

92

But they had already sent an embassy to Eumenes inviting him to come over to their side; he would enjoy possession of his present satrapies, would receive additional troops and territory from them, would become a friend to Antipater instead of an enemy, and would not become an enemy to Craterus instead of a friend. On hearing this proposition Eumenes replied that he had been Antipater's enemy from of old and could not now become his friend, when he saw him treating his friends as enemies, but that he was ready to reconcile Craterus with Perdiccas and bring the two together on just and equal terms; if, however, either undertook to overreach the other he would give aid to the injured party as long as he had breath, and would rather lose his life than his honour.

VI. Craterus and Antipater, then, after getting this answer, were taking deliberate counsel about the whole situation, when Neoptolemus came to them after his flight, told them about the battle he had lost, and urged them to come to his aid, both of them if possible, but at any rate Craterus; for the Macedonians longed for him exceedingly, and if they should only see his cap and hear his voice, they would come to him with a rush, arms and all. And indeed the name of Craterus was really great among them, and after the death of Alexander most of them had longed for him as their commander. They remembered that he had many times incurred the strong displeasure of Alexander himself in their behalf, by opposing his gradually increasing desire to adopt Persian customs, and by defending the manners of their country, which, thanks to the spread of luxury and pomp, were already being treated with contempt.

At the time of which I speak, then, Craterus sent

93

εἰς Κιλικίαν ἀπέστειλεν, αὐτὸς δὲ τῆς δυνάμεως
ἀναλαβὼν πολὺ μέρος ἐπὶ τὸν Εὐμένη μετὰ τοῦ
Νεοπτολέμου προῆγεν, οἰόμενος οὐ προσδεχομένῳ
καὶ μετὰ πρόσφατον νίκην ἐν ἀταξίᾳ καὶ περὶ
πότους ἔχοντι τὴν δύναμιν ἐπιπεσεῖσθαι. τὸ μὲν
οὖν προαισθέσθαι τὴν ἔφοδον αὐτοῦ τὸν Εὐμένη
καὶ προπαρασκευάσασθαι νηφούσης ἄν τις ἡγεμο-
4 νίας, οὐ μὴν ἄκρας θείη δεινότητος· τὸ δὲ μὴ
μόνον τοὺς πολεμίους ἃ μὴ καλῶς εἶχεν αἰσθέσθαι
διαφυγεῖν, ἀλλὰ καὶ τοὺς μετ' αὐτοῦ στρατευο-
μένους ἀγνοοῦντας ᾧ μαχοῦνται προενσεῖσαι τῷ
Κρατερῷ καὶ ἀποκρύψαι τὸν ἀντιστράτηγον, ἴδιον
δοκεῖ τούτου τοῦ ἡγεμόνος ἔργον γενέσθαι. διέ-
δωκε μὲν οὖν λόγον ὡς Νεοπτόλεμος αὖθις ἐπίοι
καὶ Πίγρης, ἔχοντες ἱππεῖς καὶ Καππαδοκῶν καὶ
Παφλαγόνων. νυκτὸς δὲ ἀναζεῦξαι βουλόμενος,
5 εἶτα καταδαρθὼν ὄψιν εἶδεν ἀλλόκοτον. ἐδόκει
γὰρ ὁρᾶν Ἀλεξάνδρους δύο παρασκευαζομένους
ἀλλήλοις μάχεσθαι, μιᾶς ἑκάτερον ἡγούμενον φά-
λαγγος· εἶτα τῷ μὲν τὴν Ἀθηνᾶν, τῷ δὲ τὴν
Δήμητραν βοηθοῦσαν ἐλθεῖν, γενομένου δὲ ἀγῶνος ἰσχυροῦ κρατηθῆναι τὸν μετὰ τῆς Ἀθηνᾶς,
τῷ δὲ νικῶντι σταχύων δρεπομένην τὴν Δήμητραν
συμπλέκειν στέφανον.
6 Αὐτόθεν μὲν οὖν τὴν ὄψιν εἴκαζεν εἶναι πρὸς
αὑτοῦ, μαχομένου περὶ γῆς ἀρίστης καὶ τότε
πολὺν καὶ καλὸν ἐχούσης ἐν κάλυκι στάχυν·
ἅπασα γὰρ κατέσπαστο καὶ παρεῖχεν εἰρήνη

---

[1] Antipater, Craterus and Ptolemy had declared war
against Perdiccas. The destruction of Perdiccas' ally, Eumenes, was a side issue. Perdiccas, taking with him Arrhidaeus and Roxana and her infant son, had already invaded

Antipater into Cilicia,[1] while he himself with a large part of the forces advanced with Neoptolemus against Eumenes. He thought that he should fall upon him when he was off his guard, and when, after their recent victory, his soldiers were in revelry and disorder. Now, that Eumenes should learn beforehand of his approach and get himself ready for it in advance, one might consider a mark of sober generalship, though not of superlative ability; but that he should keep his enemies from getting any knowledge that would work him harm, and, besides this, that he should hurl his soldiers upon Craterus before they knew with whom they were fighting, and conceal from them the name of the opposing general, seems to me to have been an exploit peculiar to this commander. He gave out word, then, that Neoptolemus was once more coming against him, with Pigres, and that they had a force of Paphlagonian and Cappadocian cavalry. One night he was planning to decamp and then fell asleep and had a strange vision. He dreamed, namely, that he saw two Alexanders ready to give each other battle, each at the head of a phalanx; then Athena came to help the one, and Demeter the other, and after a fierce struggle the one who had Athena for a helper was beaten, and Demeter, culling ears of grain, wove them into a wreath for the victor.

At once, then, he conjectured that the vision was in his favour, since he was fighting for a country that was most fertile and had at that time an abundance of fine young grain in the ear; for the land had everywhere been sown and bespoke a time of peace,

Egypt in an attempt to destroy Ptolemy. Antipater was hastening to the aid of Ptolemy.

πρέπουσαν ὄψιν, ἀμφιλαφῶς τῶν πεδίων κομών-
των· μᾶλλον δὲ ἐπερρώσθη πυθόμενος σύνθημα
τοῖς πολεμίοις Ἀθηνᾶν καὶ Ἀλέξανδρον εἶναι.
Δήμητραν δὴ καὶ αὐτὸς ἐδίδου σύνθημα καὶ
Ἀλέξανδρον, ἀναδεῖσθαί τε πάντας ἐκέλευε καὶ
καταστέφειν τὰ ὅπλα τῶν σταχύων λαμβάνοντας.
7 ὁρμήσας δὲ πολλάκις ἐξαγορεῦσαι καὶ φράσαι
τοῖς περὶ αὐτὸν ἡγεμόσι καὶ στρατηγοῖς πρὸς
ὃν ἔμελλεν ὁ ἀγὼν ἔσεσθαι, καὶ μὴ μόνος ἐν αὑτῷ
θέμενος ἀποκρύψαι καὶ κατασχεῖν ἀπόρρητον
οὕτως ἀναγκαῖον, ὅμως ἐνέμεινε τοῖς λογισμοῖς
καὶ διεπίστευσε τῇ γνώμῃ τὸν κίνδυνον.

VII. Ἀντέταξε δὲ Κρατερῷ Μακεδόνων μὲν
οὐδένα, δύο δὲ ἱππαρχίας ξενικάς, ὧν Φαρνάβαζος
ὁ Ἀρταβάζου καὶ Φοῖνιξ ὁ Τενέδιος ἡγοῦντο,
διακελευσάμενος ὀφθέντων τῶν πολεμίων ἐλαύνειν
κατὰ τάχος καὶ συμπλέκεσθαι, μὴ διδόντας ἀνα-
στροφὴν μηδὲ φωνήν, μηδὲ κήρυκα πεμπόμενον
προσιεμένους. ἐδεδίει γὰρ ἰσχυρῶς τοὺς Μακεδόνας, μὴ γνωρίσαντες τὸν Κρατερὸν οἴχωνται
2 μεταβαλόμενοι πρὸς ἐκεῖνον. αὐτὸς δὲ τοὺς
ἐρρωμενεστάτους ἵππεῖς τριακοσίους εἰς ἄγημα
συντάξας καὶ παρελάσας ἐπὶ τὸ δεξιὸν ἔμελλε
τοῖς περὶ Νεοπτόλεμον ἐπιχειρεῖν. ὡς δὲ τὸν ἐν
μέσῳ λόφον ὑπερβαλόντες ὤφθησαν ὀξεῖαν καὶ
μεθ᾽ ὁρμῆς σφοδροτέρας ποιούμενοι τὴν ἔφοδον,
ἐκπλαγεὶς ὁ Κρατερὸς καὶ πολλὰ λοιδορήσας τὸν
Νεοπτόλεμον ὡς ἐξηπατημένος ὑπ᾽ αὐτοῦ περὶ
τῆς τῶν Μακεδόνων μεταβολῆς, ἐγκελευσάμενος 587
ἀνδραγαθεῖν τοῖς περὶ αὐτὸν ἡγεμόσιν ἀντεξή-
λασε.

3   Γενομένης δὲ τῆς πρώτης ϲυρράξεως βαρείας

now that its plains were covered with a luxuriant growth ; and he was all the more strengthened in his belief when he learned that the enemy's watchword was " Athena and Alexander." Accordingly, he too gave out a watchword, namely, " Demeter and Alexander," and ordered all his men to crown themselves and wreathe their arms with ears of grain. But though he often felt an impulse to speak out and tell his principal officers who it was against whom their struggle was to be, and not to keep hidden away in his own breast alone a secret so important, nevertheless he abode by his first resolution and made his judgment surety for the peril.

VII. However, he arrayed against Craterus not a single Macedonian, but two troops of foreign horse commanded by Pharnabazus the son of Artabazus and Phoenix of Tenedos, who had strict orders to charge at full speed when the enemy came into view and engage them at close quarters, without giving them a chance to withdraw or say anything, and without receiving any herald they might send. For he had strong fears that his Macedonians, if they recognized Craterus, would go over to him. He himself, with a division of his best horsemen, three hundred in number, rode along to the right wing, where he purposed to attack Neoptolemus. When the forces of Eumenes had crossed the intervening hill and were seen coming on to the attack with a swift and impetuous dash, Craterus was dumbfounded and heaped much abuse upon Neoptolemus for having deceived him about the Macedonians changing sides ; but he exhorted his officers to act like brave men, and charged upon the enemy.

The first collision was severe, the spears were

καὶ τῶν δοράτων ταχὺ συντριβέντων, τοῦ δὲ
ἀγῶνος ἐν τοῖς ξίφεσιν ὄντος, οὐ καταισχύνας ὁ
Κρατερὸς τὸν Ἀλέξανδρον, ἀλλὰ πολλοὺς μὲν
καταβαλών, πολλάκις δὲ τρεψάμενος τοὺς ἀντι-
τεταγμένους, τέλος δὲ πληγεὶς ὑπὸ Θρᾳκὸς ἐκ
πλαγίων προσελάσαντος ἀπερρύη τοῦ ἵππου.
4 πεσόντα δὲ αὐτὸν οἱ μὲν ἄλλοι παρήλασαν ἀγνο-
οῦντες, Γοργίας δὲ τῶν Εὐμένους στρατηγῶν ἔγνω
τε καὶ καταβὰς περιέστησε φρουρὰν τῷ σώματι
κακῶς ἤδη διακειμένου καὶ δυσθανατοῦντος. ἐν
τούτῳ δὲ καὶ Νεοπτόλεμος Εὐμένει συνήρχετο.
μισοῦντες γὰρ ἀλλήλους πάλαι καὶ δι' ὀργῆς
ἔχοντες ἐν μὲν δυσὶν ἀναστροφαῖς οὐ κατεῖδον,
ἐν δὲ τῇ τρίτῃ γνωρίσαντες εὐθὺς ἤλαυνον,
5 σπασάμενοι τὰ ἐγχειρίδια καὶ βοῶντες. τῶν δ'
ἵππων ἐξ ἐναντίας βίᾳ συμπεσόντων ὥσπερ
τριήρων, τὰς ἡνίας ἀφέντες ἀλλήλων ἐπεδρά-
ξαντο ταῖς χερσί, τά τε κράνη περισπῶντες καὶ
περιρρηγνύντες ἐκ τῶν ἐπωμίδων τοὺς θώρακας.
πρὸς δὲ τὸν σπαραγμὸν ὑπεκδραμόντων ἅμα τῶν
ἵππων, ἀπορρυέντες εἰς γῆν καὶ περιπεσόντες
6 ἀλλήλοις ἐν λαβαῖς ἦσαν καὶ διεπάλαιον. εἶτα ὁ
μὲν Εὐμένης τοῦ Νεοπτολέμου προεξανισταμένου
τὴν ἰγνύαν ὑπέκοψεν αὐτὸς εἰς ὀρθὸν φθάσας
καταστῆναι, ὁ δὲ Νεοπτόλεμος εἰς θάτερον ἐρεισά-
μενος γόνυ, θάτερον δὲ πεπηρωμένος, ἠμύνετο
μὲν εὐρώστως κάτωθεν, οὐ θανασίμους δὲ πληγὰς
ὑποφέρων, πληγεὶς δὲ παρὰ τὸν τράχηλον ἔπεσε
7 καὶ παρείθη. τοῦ δὲ Εὐμένους δι' ὀργὴν καὶ
μῖσος παλαιὸν τά τε ὅπλα περισπῶντος αὐτοῦ

quickly shattered, and the fighting was done with the swords. Here Craterus did not disgrace Alexander, but slew many foes, and frequently routed the opposing arrays. At last, however, he was wounded by a Thracian who attacked him from the side, and fell from his horse. As he lay prostrate there all his enemies rode past him, not knowing who he was, except Gorgias, one of the officers of Eumenes; he recognized him, dismounted from his horse, and stood guard over his body, for he was now in an evil plight and struggling with death. In the meantime Neoptolemus also was engaged with Eumenes. They had long hated one another with a deadly hatred, but in two onsets neither had caught sight of the other; in the third, however, they recognized each other, and at once drew their swords and with loud cries rode to the attack. Their horses dashed together with the violence of colliding triremes, and dropping the reins they clutched one another with their hands, each trying to tear off the other's helmet and strip the breastplate from his shoulders. While they were struggling, their horses ran from under them and they fell to the ground, where they closed with one another and wrestled for the mastery. Then Eumenes, as Neoptolemus sought to rise first, gave him an undercut in the ham, and himself got to his feet before his adversary did; but Neoptolemus, supporting himself on one knee, and wounded in the other, defended himself vigorously from underneath. He could not, however, inflict fatal wounds, but was himself wounded in the neck, fell to the ground, and lay there prostrate. His sword, however, he still retained, and while Eumenes, transported with rage and ancient hatred, was stripping off his armour and

καὶ κακῶς λέγοντος, ἔτι τὸ ξίφος ἔχων ἔλαθεν
ὑπὸ τὸν θώρακα τρώσας, ᾗ παρέψαυσε τοῦ
βουβῶνος ἀποβάς. ἡ δὲ πληγὴ μᾶλλον ἐφόβησεν
ἢ ἔβλαψε τὸν Εὐμένη, δι' ἀσθένειαν ἀμυδρὰ
γενομένη.

Σκυλεύσας δὲ τὸν νεκρὸν εἶχε μὲν χαλεπῶς
ὑπὸ τραυμάτων μηροὺς καὶ βραχίονας διακεκομ-
μένος, ὅμως δὲ ἀναβληθεὶς ἐπὶ τὸν ἵππον ἐδίωκε
πρὸς θάτερον κέρας, ὡς ἔτι συνεστώτων τῶν
8 πολεμίων. πυθόμενος δὲ τὴν Κρατεροῦ τελευτὴν
καὶ προσελάσας, ὡς εἶδεν ἐμπνέοντα καὶ συνιέντα,
καταβὰς ἀπεδάκρυσε καὶ τὴν δεξιὰν ἐνέβαλε, καὶ
πολλὰ μὲν ἐλοιδόρησε τὸν Νεοπτόλεμον, πολλὰ
δὲ ἐκεῖνον μὲν ᾠκτίσατο τῆς τύχης, αὑτὸν δὲ τῆς
ἀνάγκης, δι' ἣν ἀνδρὶ φίλῳ καὶ συνήθει ταῦτα
πεισόμενος ἢ δράσων συνηνέχθη.

VIII. Ταύτην τὴν μάχην Εὐμένης ἡμέραις δέκα
σχεδόν τι μετὰ τὴν προτέραν ἐνίκησε· καὶ δόξῃ
μὲν ἤρθη μέγας ἀπ' αὐτῆς, ὡς τὰ μὲν σοφίᾳ, τὰ
δὲ ἀνδρείᾳ κατειργασμένος, φθόνον δὲ πολὺν ἔσχε
καὶ μῖσος ὁμαλῶς παρά τε τοῖς συμμάχοις καὶ
τοῖς πολεμίοις, ὡς ἔπηλυς ἀνὴρ καὶ ξένος ὅπλοις
καὶ χερσὶ τῶν Μακεδόνων τὸν πρῶτον αὐτῶν καὶ
2 δοκιμώτατον ἀνῃρηκώς. ἀλλ' εἰ μὲν ἔφθη Περδίκκας πυθόμενος τὴν Κρατεροῦ τελευτήν, οὐκ
ἂν ἄλλος ἐπρώτευσε Μακεδόνων· νυνὶ δὲ ἀνῃρη-
μένου Περδίκκου κατὰ στάσιν ἐν Αἰγύπτῳ δυσὶν
ἡμέραις πρότερον ἧκεν οὗτος ὁ περὶ τῆς μάχης

reviling him, Neoptolemus surprised him with a wound under the breastplate, where it reaches the groin. But the blow gave Eumenes more fright than harm, since lack of strength made it feeble.

After stripping the dead body, weak as he was from wounds received in legs and arms, Eumenes nevertheless had himself put upon his horse and hastened to the other wing, supposing that the enemy were still resisting. But when he learned of the fate of Craterus and had ridden up to where he lay, and saw that he was still alive and conscious, he dismounted, wept bitterly, clasped his hand, and had many words of abuse for Neoptolemus, and many words of pity for Craterus in his evil fortune, and for himself in the necessity which had brought him into a conflict with a friend and comrade, where he must do or suffer this harm.[1]

VIII. This battle was won by Eumenes about ten days after the former.[2] It lifted his reputation high, and he was thought to have accomplished his task alike with wisdom and bravery ; but it got him much envy and hatred as well among his allies as among his enemies. They felt that he, an alien and a stranger, had used the arms and might of the Macedonians for slaying the foremost and most approved of them. Now, if Perdiccas could have learned in time of the death of Craterus, no one else would have had chief place among Macedonians ; but as it was, he was slain in a mutiny of his soldiers in Egypt[3] two days before this report of the battle

---

[1] According to Nepos (*Eumenes*, iv. 4), Eumenes gave Craterus worthy funeral rites, and sent his remains to his wife and children in Macedonia.

[2] Cf. chapter v. 3.   [3] See the note on chapter vi. 3.

λόγος εἰς τὸ στρατόπεδον, καὶ πρὸς ὀργὴν εὐθὺς
οἱ Μακεδόνες θάνατον τοῦ Εὐμένους κατέγνωσαν.
ἀπεδείχθη δὲ τοῦ πολέμου τοῦ πρὸς αὐτὸν ᾿Αντί-
γονος μετὰ ᾿Αντιπάτρου στρατηγός.

3 ᾿Επεὶ δὲ Εὐμένης τοῖς βασιλικοῖς ἱπποφορβίοις
περὶ τὴν ῎Ιδην νεμομένοις ἐπιτυχὼν καὶ λαβὼν
ἵππους ὅσων ἔχρῃζε τοῖς ἐπιμεληταῖς τὴν γραφὴν
ἔπεμψε, λέγεται γελάσαι τὸν ᾿Αντίπατρον καὶ
εἰπεῖν ὅτι θαυμάζει τὸν Εὐμένη τῆς προνοίας,
ἐλπίζοντα λόγον αὐτοῖς ἀποδώσειν τῶν βασιλι-
4 κῶν ἢ λήψεσθαι παρ᾿ αὐτῶν. περὶ δὲ τὰς Σάρδεις
ἐβούλετο μὲν ἱπποκρατῶν ὁ Εὐμένης τοῖς Λυδοῖς
ἐναγωνίσασθαι πεδίοις, ἅμα καὶ τῇ Κλεοπάτρᾳ 588
τὴν δύναμιν ἐπιδεῖξαι φιλοτιμούμενος· αὐτῆς δὲ
ἐκείνης δεηθείσης (ἐφοβεῖτο γὰρ αἰτίαν τινὰ
λαβεῖν ὑπὸ τῶν περὶ τὸν ᾿Αντίπατρον) ἐξήλασεν
εἰς τὴν ἄνω Φρυγίαν καὶ διεχείμαζεν ἐν Κελαιναῖς·
ὅπου τῶν μὲν περὶ τὸν ᾿Αλκέταν καὶ Πολέμωνα
καὶ Δόκιμον ὑπὲρ ἡγεμονίας διαφιλοτιμουμένων
πρὸς αὐτόν, "Τοῦτο ἦν," ἔφη, "τὸ λεγόμενον,
5 ᾿Ολέθρου δ᾿ οὐθεὶς λόγος.'" τοῖς δὲ στρατιώταις
ὑποσχόμενος ἐν τρισὶν ἡμέραις τὸν μισθὸν ἀποδώσειν ἐπίπρασκεν αὐτοῖς τὰς κατὰ τὴν χώραν
ἐπαύλεις καὶ τετραπυργίας σωμάτων καὶ βοσκη-
μάτων γεμούσας. ὁ δὲ πριάμενος ἡγεμὼν τάγ-
ματος ἢ ξεναγὸς ὄργανα καὶ μηχανὰς τοῦ Εὐμένους
παρέχοντος ἐξεπολιόρκει· καὶ πρὸς τὸν ὀφειλό-
μενον μισθὸν οἱ στρατιῶται διενέμοντο τῶν
6 ἁλισκομένων ἕκαστον. ἐκ δὴ τούτου πάλιν ὁ
Εὐμένης ἠγαπᾶτο· καί ποτε γραμμάτων ἐν τῷ
στρατοπέδῳ φανέντων ἃ διέρριψαν οἱ τῶν πολε-

came to his camp, and his Macedonians, in a rage, at once condemned Eumenes to death. Moreover, Antigonus was appointed to conduct the war against him, in conjunction with Antipater.

When Eumenes fell in with the royal herds of horse that were pasturing about Mount Ida, he took as many horses as he wanted and sent a written statement of the number to the overseers. At this, we are told, Antipater laughed and said that he admired Eumenes for his forethought, since he evidently expected to give an account of the royal properties to them, or to receive one from them. Because he was superior in cavalry, Eumenes wished to give battle in the plains of Lydia about Sardis, and at the same time he was ambitious to make a display of his forces before Cleopatra[1]; but at the request of that princess, who was afraid to give Antipater any cause for complaint, he marched away into upper Phrygia and wintered at Celaenae. Here Alcetas, Polemon, and Docimus strove emulously with him for the chief command, whereupon he said: "This bears out the saying, 'Of perdition no account is made.'" Moreover, having promised to give his soldiers their pay within three days, he sold them the homesteads and castles about the country, which were full of slaves and flocks. Then every captain in the phalanx or commander of mercenaries who had bought a place was supplied by Eumenes with implements and engines of war and took it by siege; and thus every soldier received the pay that was due him, in a distribution of the captured properties. In consequence of this, Eumenes was again in high favour; and once when letters were found in his camp which the leaders of the enemy

---

[1] See the note on chapter iii. 5.

μίων ἡγεμόνες, ἑκατὸν τάλαντα καὶ τιμὰς διδόντες
τῷ κτείναντι τὸν Εὐμένη, σφόδρα παρωξύνθησαν
οἱ Μακεδόνες, καὶ δόγμα ποιοῦνται χιλίους τῶν
ἡγεμονικῶν περὶ αὐτὸν ἀεὶ δορυφοροῦντας εἶναι
καὶ φυλάττειν ἐν περιόδῳ καὶ παρανυκτερεύειν.

7 οἱ δὲ ἐπείθοντο, καὶ τιμὰς ἠγάπων παρ' αὐτοῦ
λαμβάνοντες ἃς οἱ φίλοι παρὰ τῶν βασιλέων.
ἐξῆν γὰρ Εὐμένει καὶ καυσίας ἁλουργεῖς καὶ
χλαμύδας διανέμειν, ἥτις ἦν δωρεὰ βασιλικωτάτη
παρὰ Μακεδόσι.

IX. Τὸ μὲν οὖν εὐτυχεῖν καὶ τοὺς φύσει
μικροὺς συνεπικουφίζει τοῖς φρονήμασιν, ὥστε
φαίνεσθαί τι μέγεθος περὶ αὐτοὺς καὶ ὄγκον
ἐκ πραγμάτων ὑπερεχόντων ἀποβλεπομένους·
ὁ δὲ ἀληθῶς μεγαλόφρων καὶ βέβαιος ἐν τοῖς
σφάλμασι μᾶλλον καὶ ταῖς δυσημερίαις ἀναφέρων
2 γίνεται κατάδηλος, ὥσπερ Εὐμένης. πρῶτον
μὲν γὰρ ἐν Ὀρκυνίοις τῆς Καππαδοκίας ἡττηθεὶς
ὑπὸ Ἀντιγόνου διὰ προδοσίας καὶ διωκόμενος οὐ
παρῆκε τὸν προδότην ἐκ τῆς φυγῆς διαπεσεῖν
πρὸς τοὺς πολεμίους, ἀλλὰ συλλαβὼν ἐκρέμασε.
φεύγων δὲ τὴν ἐναντίαν ὁδὸν τοῖς διώκουσι μετέβαλε λαθών, καὶ παραλλάξας, ὡς ἦλθεν ἐπὶ τὸν
τόπον οὗ τὴν μάχην συνέβη γενέσθαι, κατε-
στρατοπέδευσε, καὶ συναγαγὼν τοὺς νεκροὺς καὶ
τῶν ἐν κύκλῳ κωμῶν τὰ θυρώματα κατασχίσας
ἔκαυσεν ἰδίᾳ μὲν ἡγεμόνας, ἰδίᾳ δὲ τοὺς πολλούς,
καὶ πολυάνδρια χώσας ἀπῆλθεν, ὥστε καὶ τὸν

---

[1] Early in 320 B.C.
[2] Antigonus had corrupted Apollonides, commander of a
division of cavalry under Eumenes, and he went over to the

had caused to be scattered there, wherein they offered a hundred talents and honours to any one who should kill Eumenes, his Macedonians were highly incensed and made a decree that a thousand of the leading soldiers should serve him continually as a body-guard, watching over him when he went abroad and spending the night at his door. These carried out the decree, and were delighted to receive from Eumenes such honours as kings bestow upon their friends. For he was empowered to distribute purple caps and military cloaks, and this was a special gift of royalty among Macedonians.

IX. Now, prosperity lifts even men of inferior natures to higher thoughts, so that they appear to be invested with a certain greatness and majesty as they look down from their lofty state; but the truly magnanimous and constant soul reveals itself rather in its behaviour under disasters and misfortunes. And so it was with Eumenes. For, to begin with, he was defeated by Antigonus[1] at Orcynii in Cappadocia through treachery,[2] and yet, though in flight, he did not suffer the traitor to make his escape out of the rout to the enemy, but seized and hanged him. Then, taking the opposite route in his flight to that of his pursuers, he changed his course before they knew it, and, passing along by them, came to the place where the battle had been fought. Here he encamped, collected the bodies of the dead, and burned them on pyres made from the doors of the neighbouring villages, which he had split into billets. He burned the bodies of the officers on one pyre, those of the common soldiers on another, heaped great mounds of earth over the ashes, and

enemy in the midst of the battle, with his division. Cf. Diodorus, xviii. 40, 5–8.

'Αντίγονον ὕστερον ἐπελθόντα θαυμάζειν τὸ θάρσος αὐτοῦ καὶ τὴν εὐστάθειαν.

3 Ἔπειτα ταῖς ἀποσκευαῖς τοῦ 'Αντιγόνου περιπεσών, καὶ λαβεῖν ῥᾳδίως δυνάμενος πολλὰ μὲν ἐλεύθερα σώματα, πολλὴν δὲ θεραπείαν καὶ πλοῦτον ἐκ πολέμων τοσούτων καὶ λεηλασιῶν ἠθροισμένον, ἔδεισε μὴ καταπλησθέντες ὠφελείας καὶ λαφύρων οἱ σὺν αὐτῷ βαρεῖς γένωνται πρὸς τὴν φυγήν, καὶ μαλακώτεροι τὰς πλάνας ὑπομένειν καὶ τὸν χρόνον, ἐν ᾧ μάλιστα τοῦ πολέμου τὰς ἐλπίδας εἶχεν, ὡς ἀποστρέψων τὸν 'Αντί-
4 γονον. ἐπεὶ δὲ ἄντικρυς χαλεπὸν ἦν ἀποτρέπειν Μακεδόνας χρημάτων ἐν ἐφικτῷ παρόντων, ἐκέλευσε θεραπεύσαντας αὐτοὺς καὶ τοῖς ἵπποις χιλὸν ἐμβαλόντας οὕτω βαδίζειν ἐπὶ τοὺς πολεμίους. αὐτὸς δὲ πέμπει κρύφα πρὸς τὸν ἐπὶ τῆς ἀποσκευῆς τῶν πολεμίων Μένανδρον, ὡς κηδόμενος αὐτοῦ φίλου γεγονότος καὶ συνήθους, φυλάξασθαι παραινῶν καὶ ἀναχωρῆσαι τὴν ταχίστην ἐκ τῶν ἐπιδρόμων καὶ ταπεινῶν πρὸς τὴν ἐγγὺς ὑπώρειαν ἄφιππον οὖσαν καὶ κυκλώ-
5 σεις οὐκ ἔχουσαν. τοῦ δὲ Μενάνδρου ταχὺ συμφρονήσαντος τὸν κίνδυνον καὶ ἀνασκευασαμένου, κατασκόπους ἔπεμπεν ὁ Εὐμένης φανερῶς, καὶ 589 παρήγγειλε τοῖς στρατιώταις ὁπλίζεσθαι καὶ τοὺς ἵππους ἐγχαλινοῦν ὡς προσάξων τοῖς πολεμίοις. τῶν δὲ κατασκόπων ἀπαγγειλάντων ὅτι παντάπασιν ὁ Μένανδρος ἄληπτος εἴη καταπεφευγὼς εἰς τόπους χαλεπούς, ἄχθεσθαι προσποιούμενος ὁ Εὐμένης ἀπῆγε τὴν στρατιάν.
6 λέγεται δέ, τοῦ Μενάνδρου ταῦτα μαρτυρήσαντος πρὸς τὸν 'Αντίγονον, καὶ τῶν Μακεδόνων ἐπαι-

departed, so that even Antigonus, when he came up later, admired his boldness and constancy.

Again, when he came upon the baggage of Antigonus, and could easily have captured many free-men, many slaves, and wealth amassed from so many wars and plunderings, he was afraid that his men, if loaded down with booty and spoils, would become too heavy for flight, and too luxurious to endure wander-ings and lapse of time. In lapse of time, however, he placed his chief hopes for ending the war, feeling that he could thus cause Antigonus to turn back. But since it was quite a difficult matter to deflect his Mace-donians from good things which were within their reach, he ordered them to refresh themselves and bait their horses before advancing upon the enemy. He himself, however, sent a secret message to Menander, who was in charge of the enemy's baggage, implying that he was concerned for him as an old time friend and comrade, and advising him to be on his guard and withdraw as quickly as possible from his low-lying and accessible position to the foot-hills near by, which could not be reached by cavalry or surrounded. Menander speedily comprehended his peril and decamped, and then Eumenes openly sent out scouts and ordered his soldiers to arm themselves and bridle their horses, as he was going to lead them against the enemy. But when the scouts brought word that Menander was altogether safe from capture now that he had taken refuge in a difficult region, Eumenes pretended to be vexed, and led his forces away. And it is said that when Menander bore witness of these things to Antigonus, and the Macedonians began to praise Eumenes and felt more

νούντων τὸν Εὐμένη καὶ φιλανθρωπότερον δια-
τεθέντων, ὅτι καὶ παῖδας αὐτῶν ἀνδραποδίσασθαι
καὶ γυναῖκας αἰσχῦναι παρὸν ἐφείσατο καὶ παρῆκεν, "'Αλλ' ἐκεῖνός γε," φάναι τὸν 'Αντίγονον,
"οὐχ ὑμῶν, ὦ μακάριοι, κηδόμενος παρῆκεν, ἀλλ'
αὑτῷ φεύγοντι δεδιὼς περιθεῖναι πέδας τοσαύ-
τας."

X. Ἐκ τούτου πλανώμενος ὁ Εὐμένης καὶ
ὑποφεύγων ἔπεισε τοὺς πολλοὺς τῶν στρατιωτῶν
ἀπελθεῖν, εἴτε κηδόμενος αὐτῶν εἴτε ἐφέλκεσθαι
μὴ βουλόμενος ἐλάττονας μὲν τοῦ μάχεσθαι,
πλείονας δὲ τοῦ λανθάνειν ὄντας. καταφυγὼν
δὲ εἰς Νῶρα, χωρίον ἐν μεθορίῳ Λυκαονίας καὶ
Καππαδοκίας, μετὰ πεντακοσίων ἱππέων καὶ
διακοσίων ὁπλιτῶν, κἀντεῦθεν αὖθις, ὅσοι τῶν
φίλων ἐδεήθησαν ἀφεθῆναι τοῦ χωρίου τὴν χαλεπότητα καὶ τῆς διαίτης τὴν ἀνάγκην οὐ φέροντες,
πάντας ἀσπασάμενος καὶ φιλοφρονηθεὶς ἀπέ-
2 πεμψεν. ὡς δὲ ἐπελθὼν ὁ 'Αντίγονος εἰς λόγους
αὐτὸν ἐκάλει πρὸ τῆς πολιορκίας, ἀπεκρίνατο
πολλοὺς εἶναι τοὺς 'Αντιγόνου φίλους καὶ μετὰ
'Αντίγονον ἡγεμόνας, ὧν δὲ αὐτὸς προπολεμεῖ μηδένα λείπεσθαι μετ' αὐτόν· ὁμήρους δὲ πέμπειν
ἐκέλευσεν, εἰ χρῄζει διὰ λόγων αὐτῷ γενέσθαι.
τοῦ δὲ 'Αντιγόνου κελεύοντος ὡς κρείττονι λαλεῖν,
"Οὐδένα," εἶπεν, "ἐμαυτοῦ κρείττονα νομίζω,
3 μέχρι ἂν ὦ τοῦ ξίφους κύριος." ὅμως δὲ πέμψαντος τοῦ 'Αντιγόνου τὸν ἀδελφιδοῦν Πτολε-

kindly towards him, because, when it was in his power to enslave their children and outrage their wives, he had spared them and let them go, Antigonus said : " Nay, my good men, that fellow did not let them go out of regard for you, but because he was afraid to put such fetters on himself in his flight."

X. After this, as he wandered about and sought to elude his enemies, Eumenes persuaded most of his soldiers to leave him,[1] either out of regard for them, or because he was unwilling to trail after him a body of men too small to give battle, and too large to escape the enemy's notice. Moreover, after he had taken refuge in Nora, a stronghold on the confines of Lycaonia and Cappadocia, with five hundred horsemen and two hundred men-at-arms, even there again, whatsoever friends asked to be dismissed because they could not endure the asperities of the place and the constraint in diet, all these he sent away, after bestowing upon them tokens of affection and kindness. And when Antigonus came up and invited him to a conference before the siege began, he replied that the friends of Antigonus and officers to succeed Antigonus in command were many, whereas those in whose behalf he was fighting had no one left to command them after him; and he bade Antigonus to send hostages if he wanted to have a conference with him. Moreover, when Antigonus demanded to be addressed by him as a superior, Eumenes replied : " I regard no man as my superior so long as I am master of my sword." Nevertheless, after Antigonus had sent his nephew Ptolemy

[1] Many deserted to Antigonus, according to Diodorus (xviii. 41, 1).

μαῖον εἰς τὸ χωρίον, ὥσπερ ἠξίωσεν ὁ Εὐμένης,
κατέβη, καὶ περιβαλόντες ἀλλήλους ἠσπάσαντο
φιλικῶς καὶ οἰκείως, ἅτε δὴ ἀλλήλοις κεχρημένοι
πολλὰ καὶ συνήθεις γεγονότες. λόγων δὲ γενομένων πολλῶν καὶ τοῦ Εὐμένους οὐχ ὑπὲρ ἀσφαλείας μεμνημένου καὶ διαλύσεως, ἀλλὰ καὶ τὰς
σατραπείας ἀξιοῦντος αὐτῷ βεβαιοῦσθαι καὶ τὰς
δωρεὰς ἀποδίδοσθαι, θαῦμα τοὺς παρόντας εἶχε
4 τὸ φρόνημα καὶ τὴν εὐτολμίαν ἀγαμένους. ἅμα
δὲ πολλοὶ συνέτρεχον τῶν Μακεδόνων ἰδεῖν ὅστις
ἐστὶ τὸν Εὐμένη ποθοῦντες· οὐ γὰρ ἑτέρου λόγος
ἦν τοσοῦτος ἐν τῷ στρατῷ μετὰ τὴν τοῦ Κρατεροῦ τελευτήν. δείσας δὲ ὁ Ἀντίγονος ὑπὲρ
αὐτοῦ, μή τι πάθῃ βίαιον, πρῶτον μὲν ἀπηγόρευε
μὴ προσιέναι βοῶν, καὶ τοῖς λίθοις ἔβαλλε τοὺς
ἐπιφερομένους, τέλος δὲ ταῖς χερσὶ τὸν Εὐμένη
περιβαλὼν καὶ τὸν ὄχλον ἀπερύκων τοῖς δορυ-
φόροις μόλις εἰς τὸ ἀσφαλὲς ἀποκατέστησε.

XI. Τοὐντεῦθεν ὁ μὲν περιτειχίσας τὰ Νῶρα
καὶ φρουρὰν καταλιπὼν ἀνέζευξεν· Εὐμένης δὲ
πολιορκούμενος ἐγκρατῶς, τοῦ χωρίου σῖτον καὶ
ὕδωρ ἄφθονον καὶ ἅλας καὶ ἄλλο μηδὲν ἔχοντος
ἐδώδιμον μηδὲ ἥδυσμα πρὸς τὸν σῖτον, ἐκ τῶν
παρόντων ὅμως κατεσκεύαζε τοῖς συνοῦσιν ἱλαρὰν
τὴν δίαιταν, ἐν μέρει τε παραλαμβάνων πάντας
ἐπὶ τὴν αὑτοῦ τράπεζαν, καὶ τὸ συσσίτιον ὁμιλίᾳ
2 χάριν ἐχούσῃ καὶ φιλοφροσύνην ἐφηδύνων. ἦν
δὲ καὶ τὸ εἶδος ἡδύς, οὐ πολεμικῷ καὶ τετριμμένῳ
δι' ὅπλων ἐοικώς, ἀλλὰ γλαφυρὸς καὶ νεοπρεπής,
καὶ πᾶν τὸ σῶμα διηρθρωμένος ὡς ὑπὸ τέχνης
ἀκριβῶς τοῖς μέλεσι θαυμαστὴν συμμετρίαν ἔχου-

into the fortress, as Eumenes had demanded, Eumenes went down to meet him, and they embraced one another with greetings of friendship and affection, since they had formerly been close associates and intimate companions. A long conference was held, in which Eumenes made no mention of his own safety or of peace, but actually demanded that he should be confirmed in the possession of his satrapies, and that what was his by gift should be restored to him. At this the bystanders were amazed, and they admired his lofty spirit and confidence. But meanwhile many of the Macedonians came running together in their eagerness to see what sort of a man Eumenes was; for no one else had been so much talked about in the army since the death of Craterus. Then Antigonus, afraid that Eumenes might suffer some violence, first loudly forbade the soldiers to approach, and pelted with stones those who were hurrying up, but finally threw his arms about Eumenes and, keeping off the throng with his bodyguards, with much ado removed him to a place of safety.

XI. After this, Antigonus built a wall round Nora, left troops to guard it, and retired; Eumenes, however, although closely besieged in a stronghold which had grain, water in abundance, and salt, but no other edible, not even a relish to go with the grain, nevertheless, with what he had, managed to render the life of his associates cheerful, inviting them all by turns to his own table, and seasoning the meal thus shared with conversation which had charm and friendliness. For he had a pleasant face, not like that of a war-worn veteran, but delicate and youthful, and all his body had, as it were, artistic proportions, with limbs of astonishing symmetry ; and

σιν, εἰπεῖν δὲ οὐ δεινός, αἱμύλος δὲ καὶ πιθανός, ὡς ἐκ τῶν ἐπιστολῶν συμβάλλειν ἐστίν.

3 Ἐπεὶ δὲ τοὺς σὺν αὐτῷ πολιορκουμένους ἡ στενοχωρία μάλιστα πάντων ἔβλαπτεν, ἐν οἰκή- 590 μασι μικροῖς καὶ τόπῳ δυοῖν σταδίοιν ἔχοντι τὴν περίμετρον ἀναστρεφομένους, τροφὴν δὲ ἀγυμνά- στους μὲν αὐτοὺς λαμβάνοντας, ἀργοῖς δὲ τοῖς ἵπποις προσφέροντας, οὐ μόνον τὸν ἄλυν αὐτῶν ὑπὸ τῆς ἀπραξίας μαραινομένων ἀπαλλάξαι βουλόμενος, ἀλλὰ καὶ πρὸς φυγήν, εἰ παραπέσοι

4 καιρός, ἀμῶς γέ πως ἠσκημένοις χρήσασθαι, τοῖς μὲν ἀνθρώποις οἶκον, ὃς ἦν μέγιστος ἐν τῷ χωρίῳ, δεκατεσσάρων πηχῶν τὸ μῆκος, ἀπέδειξε περίπα- τον, κατὰ μικρὸν ἐπιτείνειν τὴν κίνησιν κελεύων, τῶν δ' ἵππων ἕκαστον ῥυτῆρσι μεγάλοις εἰς τὴν ὀροφὴν ἀναδεδεμένοις ὑποζώσας ἐκ τῶν περὶ τὸν αὐχένα μερῶν ἐμετεώριζε καὶ παρήγειρε διὰ τροχιλίας, ὥστε τοῖς μὲν ὀπισθίοις σκέλεσιν ἐπὶ τῆς γῆς ἐρείδεσθαι, τοῖς δὲ ἐμπροσθίοις ποσὶν

5 ἀκρωνύχους ἐπιψαύειν. οὕτω δ' ἀνηρτημένους οἱ ἱπποκόμοι παρεστῶτες ἅμα ταῖς τε κραυγαῖς καὶ ταῖς μάστιξιν ἐπηρέθιζον· οἱ δὲ πιμπλάμενοι θυμοῦ καὶ ὀργῆς τοῖς μὲν ὀπισθίοις ἐνήλλοντο καὶ διεσκίρτων σκέλεσι, τοῖς δὲ μετεώροις ἐφιέ- μενοι στηρίσασθαι καὶ κροτοῦντες τὸ ἔδαφος κατετείνοντο πᾶν τὸ σῶμα καὶ πολὺν ἠφίεσαν ἱδρῶτα καὶ σταλαγμόν, οὔτε πρὸς τάχος οὔτε πρὸς ῥώμην γυμναζόμενοι κακῶς. τὰς δὲ κριθὰς ἐνέβαλλον αὐτοῖς ἐπτισμένας, ἵνα κατεργάζωνται θᾶττον καὶ πέττωσι βέλτιον.

XII. Ἤδη δὲ τῆς πολιορκίας χρόνον λαμ-

though he was not a powerful speaker, still he was
insinuating and persuasive, as one may gather from
his letters.

But most of all detrimental to his forces thus besieged was their narrow quarters, since their movements were confined to small houses and a place only
two furlongs in circumference, so that neither men
nor horses could get exercise before eating or being
fed. Therefore, wishing to remove the weakness and
languor with which their inactivity afflicted them,
and, more than that, to have them somehow or other
in training for flight, if opportunity should offer, he
assigned the men a house, the largest in the place,
fourteen cubits long, as a place to walk, ordering
them little by little to increase their pace. And as
for the horses, he had them all girt round the neck
with great straps fastened to the roof, and raised
them partly up into the air by means of pulleys, so
that, while with their hind legs they rested firmly upon
the ground, they just touched it with the tips of their
fore hoofs. Then, while they were thus suspended,
the grooms would stand at their sides and stir them
up with shouts and strokes of the goad ; and the
horses, full of rage and fury, would dance and leap
about on their hind legs, while with their swinging
fore feet they would strike the ground and try to get
a footing there, thus exerting their whole bodies and
covering themselves with sweat and foam,—no bad
exercise either for speed or strength.[1] Then their
barley would be thrown to them boiled, that they
might the sooner dispatch and the better digest it.

XII. But presently, as the siege dragged along,

[1] This device of Eumenes is described also in Diodorus,
xviii. 42, 3 f., and in Nepos, *Eumenes*, v. 4 f.

βανούσης Ἀντίγονος τεθνηκέναι πυνθανόμενος
Ἀντίπατρον ἐν Μακεδονίᾳ, καὶ τεταράχθαι τὰ
πράγματα Κασάνδρου καὶ Πολυσπέρχοντος διαφερομένων, οὐδὲν ἔτι μικρὸν ἐλπίζων, ἀλλὰ τῇ
γνώμῃ τὴν ὅλην περιβαλλόμενος ἡγεμονίαν, ἐβούλετο τὸν Εὐμένη φίλον ἔχειν καὶ συνεργὸν ἐπὶ
τὰς πράξεις. διὸ πέμψας Ἱερώνυμον ἐσπένδετο
τῷ Εὐμένει, προτείνας ὅρκον, ὃν ὁ Εὐμένης διορ-
θώσας ἐπέτρεψεν ἐπικρῖναι τοῖς πολιορκοῦσιν
2 αὐτὸν Μακεδόσι, πότερος εἴη δικαιότερος. Ἀντίγονος μὲν γὰρ ἀφοσιώσεως ἕνεκεν ἐν ἀρχῇ τῶν
βασιλέων ἐπιμνησθεὶς τὸν λοιπὸν ὅρκον εἰς ἑαυτὸν ὥρκιζεν, Εὐμένης δὲ πρώτην μὲν ἐνέγραψε
τοῖς ὅρκοις Ὀλυμπιάδα μετὰ τῶν βασιλέων,
ἔπειτα ὤμνυεν οὐκ Ἀντιγόνῳ μόνον εὐνοήσειν
οὐδ᾽ ἐκείνῳ τὸν αὐτὸν ἐχθρὸν ἕξειν καὶ φίλον,
ἀλλὰ καὶ Ὀλυμπιάδι καὶ τοῖς βασιλεῦσιν. ὧν
δικαιοτέρων φανέντων, οἱ Μακεδόνες ταῦτα ὀρκί-
σαντες τὸν Εὐμένη τὴν πολιορκίαν ἔλυσαν, καὶ
πρὸς τὸν Ἀντίγονον ἀπέστελλον, ὅπως καὶ αὐτὸς
ἀποδῷ τῷ Εὐμένει τὸν ὅρκον.

3 Ἐν τούτῳ δὲ Εὐμένης ὅσους εἶχεν ἐν Νώροις
τῶν Καππαδοκῶν ὁμήρους ἀπεδίδου, λαμβάνων
ἵππους καὶ ὑποζύγια καὶ σκηνὰς παρὰ τῶν
κομιζομένων, καὶ συνῆγε τῶν στρατιωτῶν ὅσοι
διασπαρέντες ἀπὸ τῆς φυγῆς ἐπλανῶντο κατὰ
τὴν χώραν, ὥστε περὶ αὐτὸν ἱππεῖς ὀλίγῳ τῶν
χιλίων ἀποδέοντας γενέσθαι, μεθ᾽ ὧν ἐξελάσας

---

[1] In 320 B.C. After the death of Perdiccas the supreme
regency devolved upon Antipater, and he retired into Macedonia with the two kings. On his death he left the regency

114

Antigonus learned that Antipater had died in Macedonia,[1] and that matters were in confusion owing to the dissension between Cassander and Polysperchon. He therefore cherished no longer an inferior hope, but embraced the whole empire in his scheme, and desired to have Eumenes as friend and helper in his undertakings. Accordingly, he sent Hieronymus to make a treaty with Eumenes, and proposed an oath for him to take. This oath Eumenes corrected and then submitted it to the Macedonians who were besieging him, requesting them to decide which was the juster form. Antigonus, namely, for form's sake, had mentioned the kings[2] at the beginning of the oath, and then had made the rest of it refer to himself; but Eumenes wrote at the head of the oath the names of Olympias and the kings,[2] and proposed to swear fealty, not to Antigonus alone, but also to Olympias and the kings, and to have the same enemies and friends as they. This was thought to be more just, and the Macedonians accordingly administered this oath to Eumenes, raised the siege, and sent to Antigonus, that he too, on his part, might take the oath to Eumenes.

Meanwhile, however, Eumenes gave back all the Cappadocian hostages whom he was holding in Nora, and received from those who came for them horses, beasts of burden, and tents. He also collected all the soldiers who had become scattered by his flight and were now wandering about the country, so that he had a force of almost a thousand horsemen. With

to Polysperchon, a distinguished officer of Alexander, to the exclusion of his own son Cassander.

[2] See the notes on chapter iii. 1 and 7. Olympias was the queen-mother, the widow of Philip, mother of Alexander.

ἔφυγεν, ὀρθῶς φοβηθεὶς τὸν Ἀντίγονον. οὐ γὰρ
μόνον ἐκεῖνον ἐκέλευσε πολιορκεῖν αὖθις περιτει-
χίσαντας, ἀλλὰ καὶ τοῖς Μακεδόσι πικρῶς ἀντέ-
γραψε δεξαμένοις τοῦ ὅρκου τὴν διόρθωσιν.

XIII. Φεύγοντι δὲ Εὐμένει γράμματα κομί-
ζεται παρὰ τῶν ἐν Μακεδονίᾳ τὴν Ἀντιγόνου
δεδοικότων αὔξησιν, Ὀλυμπιάδος μὲν παρακα-
λούσης ἐλθόντα τὸ Ἀλεξάνδρου παιδίον παραλαβεῖν καὶ τρέφειν ὡς ἐπιβουλευόμενον, Πολυσπέρχοντος δὲ καὶ Φιλίππου τοῦ βασιλέως
κελευόντων Ἀντιγόνῳ πολεμεῖν τῆς ἐν Καππαδοκίᾳ δυνάμεως ἄρχοντα, καὶ τῶν ἐν Κουΐνδοις
χρημάτων πεντακόσια μὲν τάλαντα λαβεῖν εἰς
τὴν τῶν ἰδίων ἐπανόρθωσιν, εἰς δὲ τὸν πόλεμον
2 ὁπόσοις βούλεται χρῆσθαι. περὶ δὲ τούτων καὶ
Ἀντιγένει καὶ Τευτάμῳ τοῖς τῶν ἀργυρασπίδων
ἡγουμένοις ἐγεγράφεισαν. ἐπεὶ δὲ λαβόντες 591
ἐκεῖνοι τὰ γράμματα τῷ μὲν λόγῳ φιλανθρώπως
ἐδέξαντο τὸν Εὐμένη, φθόνου δὲ καὶ φιλονεικίας
ἐφαίνοντο μεστοί, δευτερεύειν ἀπαξιοῦντες ἐκείνῳ,
τὸν μὲν φθόνον ὁ Εὐμένης ἐθεράπευε τῷ τὰ
3 χρήματα μὴ λαβεῖν ὡς οὐδὲν δεόμενος, ταῖς δὲ
φιλονεικίαις καὶ φιλαρχίαις αὐτῶν μήτε ἡγεῖσθαι δυναμένων μήτε ἕπεσθαι βουλομένων ἐπῆγε
δεισιδαιμονίαν.

Ἔφη γὰρ Ἀλέξανδρον αὐτῷ κατὰ τοὺς ὕπνους
φανῆναι, καὶ δεῖξαί τινα σκηνὴν κατεσκευασμέ-
νην βασιλικῶς καὶ θρόνον ἐν αὐτῇ κείμενον· εἶτα
εἰπεῖν ὡς ἐνταῦθα συνεδρεύουσιν αὐτοῖς καὶ
χρηματίζουσιν αὐτὸς παρέσται καὶ συνεφάψεται

---

[1] Philip Arrhidaeus (see the note on chapter iii. 1).

these he set out in flight, being rightly in fear of
Antigonus. For Antigonus not only ordered his
Macedonians to wall him in again and besiege him,
but also wrote back bitter reproaches to them for
accepting the correction of the oath.

XIII. While Eumenes was in flight, letters were
brought to him from those in Macedonia who feared
the growing power of Antigonus. Olympias invited
him to come and take charge of Alexander's little son
and rear him, feeling that plots were laid against his
life; Polysperchon and Philip[1] the king ordered him,
as commander of the forces in Cappadocia, to wage
war upon Antigonus, to take five hundred talents of
the treasure at Quinda[2] in reparation of his own
losses, and to use as much of it as he wished for the
war. They had also written concerning these matters
to Antigenes and Teutamus, the commanders of the
Silver-shields. These men, on receiving their letters,
ostensibly treated Eumenes with friendliness, but
were plainly full of envy and contentiousness, dis-
daining to be second to him. Eumenes therefore
allayed their envy by not taking the money, alleging
that he had no need of it; while upon their love of
contention and love of command, seeing that they
were as unable to lead as they were unwilling to
follow, he brought superstition to bear.

He said, namely, that Alexander had appeared to
him in a dream, had shown him a tent arrayed in
royal fashion with a throne standing in it, and had
then said that if they held their councils and
transacted their business there, he himself would be

---

[2] Or Cyinda, better known as Anazarbus, a stronghold in
Cilicia, whither Antigenes and Teutamus had brought the
royal treasure from Susa.

βουλῆς τε πάσης καὶ πράξεως ἀρχομένοις ἀπ'
αὐτοῦ. ταῦτα ῥαδίως ἔπεισε τὸν Ἀντιγένη καὶ
τὸν Τεύταμον, οὔτε ἐκείνων βαδίζειν βουλομένων
πρὸς αὐτόν, οὔτε αὐτὸς ἀξιῶν ἐπὶ θύραις ἑτέρων
4 ὁρᾶσθαι. καὶ τιθέντες οὕτω σκηνὴν βασιλικὴν
καὶ θρόνον Ἀλεξάνδρῳ καταπεφημισμένον ἐκεῖ
συνεπορεύοντο βουλευόμενοι περὶ τῶν μεγίστων.

Ἐπεὶ δὲ προϊοῦσιν αὐτοῖς εἰς τὴν ἄνω χώραν ὁ
Πευκέστας μετὰ τῶν ἄλλων σατραπῶν ἀπήντησε
φίλος ὢν καὶ συνεμίξαντο τὰς δυνάμεις, πλήθει
μὲν ὅπλων καὶ λαμπρότητι παρασκευῆς ἐπέρ-
ρωσαν τοὺς Μακεδόνας, αὐτοὶ δὲ ἀνάγωγοι ταῖς
ἐξουσίαις καὶ μαλακοὶ ταῖς διαίταις γεγονότες
5 μετὰ τὴν Ἀλεξάνδρου τελευτήν, καὶ φρονήματα
τυραννικὰ καὶ τεθραμμένα βαρβαρικαῖς ἀλαζονείαις ἐπὶ ταὐτὸ συνενεγκάμενοι, πρὸς μὲν ἀλλήλους
βαρεῖς ἦσαν καὶ δυσάρμοστοι, τοὺς δὲ Μακεδόνας
κολακεύοντες ἐκκεχυμένως καὶ καταχορηγοῦντες
εἰς δεῖπνα καὶ θυσίας ὀλίγου χρόνου τὸ στρατόπεδον ἀσωτίας πανηγυριζούσης καταγώγιον
ἐποίησαν καὶ δημαγωγούμενον ἐπὶ αἱρέσει
στρατηγῶν ὄχλον, ὥσπερ ἐν ταῖς δημοκρατίαις.
6 αἰσθόμενος δὲ ὁ Εὐμένης αὐτοὺς ἀλλήλων μὲν
καταφρονοῦντας, αὐτὸν δὲ φοβουμένους καὶ
παραφυλάττοντας ἀνελεῖν, εἰ γένοιτο καιρός,
ἐσκήψατο χρημάτων δεῖσθαι καὶ συνεδανείσατο
τάλαντα πολλὰ παρὰ τῶν μάλιστα μισούντων
αὐτόν, ἵνα καὶ πιστεύωσι καὶ ἀπέχωνται περὶ

---

[1] In 317 B.C., against Antigonus, who was in Mesopotamia.
He had received the satrapy of Susiana.
[2] One of the most distinguished officers of Alexander,

present and would assist them in every plan and
enterprise which they undertook in his name.
Eumenes easily convinced Antigenes and Teutamus
that this was true. They were unwilling to go to
him, and he himself thought it undignified to be seen
at the doors of others. So they erected a royal tent,
and a throne in it which they dedicated to Alexander,
and there they met for deliberation on matters of
highest importance.

And now, as they advanced into the interior of the
country,[1] Peucestas,[2] who was a friend of Eumenes,
met them with the other satraps, and they joined
their forces, so that the number of their men and the
splendour of their equipment raised the spirits of the
Macedonians. But the leaders themselves had been
made unmanageable by their exercise of power, and
effeminate by their mode of life, after the death of
Alexander, and they brought into collision spirits
that were tyrannical and fed on barbaric arrogance,
so that they were harsh towards one another and
hard to reconcile. Moreover, by flattering the
Macedonian soldiery extravagantly and lavishing
money upon them for banquets and sacrifices, in a
short time they made the camp a hostelry of festal
prodigality, and the army a mob to be cajoled into
the election of its generals, as in a democracy.
Eumenes, however, perceiving that, while they
despised one another, they feared him and were on
the watch for an opportunity to kill him, pretended
to be in need of money, and got together many
talents by borrowing from those who hated him most,
in order that they might put confidence in him and
refrain from killing him out of regard for the money

who had been made satrap of Persia during Alexander's
lifetime.

τῶν δανείων ἀγωνιῶντες· ὥστε συνέβη τὸν ἀλλό-
τριον πλοῦτον αὐτῷ φύλακα τοῦ σώματος ἔχειν,
καὶ τῶν ἄλλων ἐπὶ σωτηρίᾳ διδόντων, μόνον ἐκ
τοῦ λαβεῖν κτήσασθαι τὴν ἀσφάλειαν.

XIV. Οὐ μὴν ἀλλ' οἱ Μακεδόνες ἀδείας μὲν
οὔσης ἐφθείροντο πρὸς τοὺς διδόντας, καὶ τὰς
ἐκείνων θύρας ἐθεράπευον, δορυφορουμένων καὶ
στρατηγιώντων· ἐπεὶ δὲ Ἀντίγονος αὐτοῖς παρε-
στρατοπέδευσε μετὰ πολλῆς δυνάμεως καὶ τὰ
πράγματα φωνὴν ἀφιέντα τὸν ἀληθινὸν ἐκάλει
στρατηγόν, οὐ μόνον οἱ στρατευόμενοι τῷ Εὐμένει προσεῖχον, ἀλλὰ καὶ τῶν ἐν εἰρήνῃ καὶ
τρυφῇ μεγάλων ἐκείνων ἕκαστος ἐνέδωκε καὶ
παρεῖχεν ἑαυτὸν σιωπῇ τὴν δοθεῖσαν φυλάττοντα
2 τάξιν. καὶ γάρ τοι περὶ τὸν Πασιτίγριν ποταμὸν
ἐπιχειρήσαντα διαβαίνειν τὸν Ἀντίγονον οἱ μὲν
ἄλλοι παραφυλάττοντες οὐδὲ ᾔσθοντο, μόνος δὲ
Εὐμένης ὑπέστη, καὶ συνάψας μάχην πολλοὺς
μὲν κατέβαλε καὶ νεκρῶν ἐνέπλησε τὸ ῥεῖθρον,
ἔλαβε δὲ τετρακισχιλίους αἰχμαλώτους. μάλιστα δὲ οἱ Μακεδόνες περὶ τὴν συμβᾶσαν ἀρ-
ρωστίαν αὐτῷ καταφανεῖς ἐγένοντο τοὺς μὲν
ἄλλους ἑστιᾶν λαμπρῶς καὶ πανηγυρίζειν, ἄρχειν
δὲ καὶ πολεμεῖν δυνατὸν ἡγούμενοι μόνον ἐκεῖνον.
3 ὁ μὲν γὰρ Πευκέστας ἐν τῇ Περσίδι λαμπρῶς
αὐτοὺς ἑστιάσας καὶ κατ' ἄνδρα διαδοὺς ἱερεῖον
εἰς θυσίαν ἤλπιζεν εἶναι μέγιστος· ὀλίγαις δὲ
ὕστερον ἡμέραις τῶν στρατιωτῶν ἐπὶ τοὺς πολεμίους βαδιζόντων, ἐτύγχανεν ὁ Εὐμένης ἐκ νόσου
τινὸς ἐπισφαλοῦς ἐν φορείῳ κομιζόμενος ἔξω τοῦ
στρατεύματος ἐν ἡσυχίᾳ διὰ τὰς ἀγρυπνίας.

they had lent him. The consequence was that the wealth of others was his body-guard, and that, whereas men generally preserve their lives by giving, he alone won safety by receiving.

XIV. The Macedonians, however, while there was no danger, continued to take gifts from their corrupters, and hung about the doors of these men, who now had body-guards and wanted to be generals. But when Antigonus encamped near them with a large force and the situation called aloud for a real general, not only did the common soldiers attach themselves to Eumenes, but also those who were great only when peace and luxury prevailed, every man of them, gave in to him and consented without a murmur to hold the post which he gave them. And, indeed, when Antigonus tried to cross the river Pasitigris, none of the other commanders who were watching his movements was even aware of it, but Eumenes, and he alone, withstood him, joined battle with him, slew many of his men and filled the stream with dead bodies, and took four thousand prisoners. But most of all in connection with the sickness that befell him did the Macedonians make it clear that they considered the others able to feast them splendidly and hold high festival, but him alone capable of wielding command and waging war. For Peucestas, having feasted them splendidly in Persis, and having given every man a victim for sacrifice, was expecting to be chief in command; and a few days afterwards, as the soldiers were marching against the enemy, it chanced that Eumenes, in consequence of a dangerous illness, was being carried along in a litter outside the ranks, where it was quiet and his sleep would not be broken. But after they had

μικρὸν δὲ προελθοῦσιν αὐτοῖς ἄφνω λόφους τινὰς 59:
ὑπερβάλλοντες ἐξεφάνησαν οἱ πολέμιοι, κατα-
4 βαίνοντες εἰς τὸ πεδίον. ὡς οὖν αἵ τε τῶν χρυ-
σῶν ὅπλων αὐγαὶ πρὸς τὸν ἥλιον ἐξέλαμψαν ἀπὸ
τῶν ἄκρων τοῦ ἀγήματος ἐν τάξει πορευομένων,
καὶ τῶν θηρίων τοὺς πύργους ἄνω καὶ τὰς πορ-
φύρας εἶδον, ὅσπερ ἦν αὐτοῖς κόσμος εἰς μάχην
ἀγομένοις, ἐπιστήσαντες οἱ πρῶτοι τὴν πορείαν
ἐβόων Εὐμένη καλεῖν αὐτοῖς, οὐ γὰρ ἂν προελθεῖν
ἐκείνου μὴ στρατηγοῦντος, καὶ τὰ ὅπλα πρὸς τὴν
γῆν ἐρείσαντες ἀλλήλοις μένειν διεκελεύοντο, καὶ
τοῖς ἡγεμόσιν ἡσυχίαν ἔχειν, καὶ χωρὶς Εὐμένους
μὴ μάχεσθαι μηδὲ κινδυνεύειν πρὸς τοὺς πολεμί-
5 ους. ἀκούσας δὲ ὁ Εὐμένης ἧκε πρὸς αὐτοὺς
δρόμῳ τοὺς κομίζοντας ἐπιταχύνας, καὶ τοῦ
φορείου τὰς ἑκατέρωθεν αὐλαίας ἀνακαλύψας
προὔτεινε τὴν δεξιὰν γεγηθώς. οἱ δὲ ὡς εἶδον,
εὐθὺς ἀσπασάμενοι Μακεδονιστὶ τῇ φωνῇ τάς τε
ἀσπίδας ἀνείλοντο καὶ ταῖς σαρίσαις ἐπιδουπή-
σαντες ἠλάλαξαν, προκαλούμενοι τοὺς πολεμίους
ὡς τοῦ ἡγεμόνος αὐτοῖς παρόντος.

XV. Ἀντίγονος δὲ παρὰ τῶν ἁλισκομένων
ἀκούων τὸν Εὐμένη νοσεῖν καὶ κομίζεσθαι κακῶς
διακείμενον, οὐ μέγα ἔργον ἡγεῖτο συντρῖψαι
τοὺς ἄλλους ἐκείνου νοσοῦντος. διὸ καὶ σπεύ-
2 δων ἐπὶ τὴν μάχην προσῆγεν. ὡς δὲ τῶν πολεμίων εἰς τάξιν καθισταμένων παρελάσας κατεῖδε
τὸ σχῆμα καὶ τὴν διακόσμησιν, ἐκπλαγεὶς ἐπέστη
πλείω χρόνον· εἶτα ὤφθη τὸ φορεῖον ἀπὸ θατέ-
ρου κέρως ἐπὶ θάτερον διαφερόμενον. γελάσας
οὖν ὁ Ἀντίγονος, ὥσπερ εἰώθει, μέγα, καὶ πρὸς

advanced a little way, suddenly the enemy were seen passing over some hills and descending into the plain. The gleams of their golden armour in the sun flashed down from the heights as they marched along in close formation, and on the backs of the elephants the towers and purple trappings were seen, which was their array when going into battle. Accordingly, the foremost Macedonians halted in their march and called with loud cries for Eumenes, declaring that they would not go forward unless he was in command of them ; and grounding their arms they passed word to one another to wait, and to their leaders to keep still, and without Eumenes not to give battle or run any hazard even with the enemy. When Eumenes heard of this, he quickened the pace of his bearers to a run and came to them, and lifting up the curtains of his litter on either side, stretched forth his hand in delight. And when the soldiers saw him, they hailed him at once in their Macedonian speech, caught up their shields, beat upon them with their spears, and raised their battle-cry, challenging the enemy to fight in the assurance that their leader was at hand.

XV. Now Antigonus, hearing from his prisoners that Eumenes was sick and in such wretched plight as to be borne along in a litter, thought it no great task to crush the other commanders if Eumenes was sick. He therefore hastened to lead his army to battle. But when, as the enemy were forming in battle order, he had ridden past their lines and observed their shape and disposition, he was amazed, and paused for some time ; then the litter was seen as it was carried from one wing to the other. At this, Antigonus gave a loud laugh, as was his wont,

τοὺς φίλους εἰπών, "Τοῦτο ἦν τὸ φορεῖον, ὡς
ἔοικε, τὸ ἀντιπαραταττόμενον ἡμῖν," εὐθὺς ἀπῆγε
τὴν δύναμιν ὀπίσω καὶ κατεστρατοπέδευσεν.

3   Οἱ δὲ μικρὸν ἀναπνεύσαντες αὖθις ἐδημαγω-
γοῦντο, καὶ τοῖς ἡγεμόσιν ἐντρυφῶντες σχεδὸν
ὅλην εἰς τὰ χειμάδια κατενείμαντο τὴν Γαβηνῶν,
ὥστε τοὺς ἐσχάτους τῶν πρώτων ἀποσκηνοῦν
ὁμοῦ τι χιλίους σταδίους. ταῦτα γνοὺς ὁ Ἀντίγονος ὥρμησεν ἐξαίφνης ἐπ' αὐτοὺς ὑποστρέψας
χαλεπὴν ὁδὸν καὶ ἄνυδρον, σύντομον δὲ καὶ
βραχεῖαν, ἐλπίζων, εἰ διεσπαρμένοις ἐπιπέσοι
περὶ τὰ χειμάδια, μηδ' ἂν συνελθεῖν ἔτι τὸ πλῆθος ῥᾳδίως εἰς τὸ αὐτὸ τοῖς στρατηγοῖς. ἐμβα-
λόντι δὲ εἰς γῆν ἀοίκητον αὐτῷ πνεύματά τε
δεινὰ καὶ κρύη μεγάλα διελυμαίνετο τὴν πορείαν
4 ἐνοχλουμένου τοῦ στρατεύματος. ἦν οὖν ἀναγ-
καία βοήθεια πυρὰ πολλὰ καίειν· ὅθεν οὐκ ἔλαθε
τοὺς πολεμίους, ἀλλὰ τῶν βαρβάρων οἱ τὰ
βλέποντα πρὸς τὴν ἀοίκητον ὄρη νεμόμενοι
θαυμάσαντες τὸ τῶν πυρῶν πλῆθος ἔπεμψαν
ἱππαστρίαις καμήλοις ἀγγέλους πρὸς Πευκέσταν.
ὁ δὲ ὡς ἤκουσεν, αὐτός τε παντάπασιν ἔκφρων
ὑπὸ δέους γενόμενος καὶ τοὺς ἄλλους ὁρῶν ὁμοίως
ἔχοντας ὥρμητο φεύγειν, ἀναστήσας τοὺς καθ'
ὁδὸν ὄντας αὐτοῖς μάλιστα τῶν στρατιωτῶν·
5 Εὐμένης δὲ τὴν ταραχὴν ἀφῄρει καὶ τὸν φόβον,
ὑπισχνούμενος ἐπιστήσειν τῶν πολεμίων τὸ
τάχος, ὥστε τρισὶν ὕστερον ἡμέραις ἢ προσδο-
κῶνται παραγενέσθαι. πεισθέντων δὲ αὐτῶν
ἅμα μὲν ἀγγέλους περιέπεμπε τὰς δυνάμεις ἐκ

and after saying to his friends, "This litter, it would seem, is what is arrayed against us," immediately retired with his forces and pitched his camp.[1]

But the Macedonians opposed to him, after getting a little respite, once more acted liked a capricious mob, and, mocking at their leaders, distributed themselves in winter quarters over almost the whole of Gabene, so that the rear was separated from the van by almost a thousand furlongs. When Antigonus became aware of this, he set out suddenly against them, taking this time a road that was difficult and without water, but direct and short, hoping that, in case he fell upon them when they were scattered about in their winter quarters, it would no longer be easy for the mass of them to join their generals. But after he had entered an uninhabited country, dire winds and severe frosts gave trouble to his army and impeded their march. The only help, therefore, was to burn many fires, and this was what revealed his presence to the enemy. For the Barbarians living on the mountains which overlooked the uninhabited tract, amazed at the number of fires, sent messengers on dromedaries to Peucestas. And he, when he heard the news, being himself quite out of his mind with fear and seeing that the other officers were in a like state, set out to fly, after rousing up those of their soldiers especially who were quartered along the route. But Eumenes tried to put a stop to their confusion and panic fear, by promising so to check the speed of the enemy that they would come up three days later than they were expected. And when his hearers were persuaded, he sent round

[1] These events are more fully and very differently described by Diodorus (xix. 24-32).

τῶν χειμαδίων καὶ τοὺς ἄλλους ἀθροίζεσθαι κατὰ
τάχος κελεύων, ἅμα δὲ αὐτὸς ἐξιππασάμενος
μετὰ τῶν ἄλλων ἡγεμόνων, καὶ τόπον ἐξ ἀπόπτου
καταφανῆ τοῖς ὁδεύουσι τὴν ἔρημον περιβαλό-
μενος καὶ διαμετρήσας, ἐκέλευε πυρὰ πολλὰ
καίειν ἐν διαστήμασιν, ὥσπερ οἱ στρατοπεδεύ-
6 οντες. γενομένου δὲ τούτου καὶ τῶν πυρῶν τοῖς
περὶ ᾿Αντίγονον ἐκ τῆς ὀρεινῆς καταφανέντων,
ἄχθος ἔσχε καὶ δυσθυμία τὸν ᾿Αντίγονον, οἰόμενον
ᾐσθημένους ἔκπαλαι τοὺς πολεμίους ἀπαντᾶν.
ἵν᾿ οὖν μὴ κατάκοπος καὶ τετρυμένος ἐκ πορείας
ἀναγκάζηται μάχεσθαι πρὸς ἀνθρώπους ἑτοίμους
καὶ καλῶς κεχειμακότας, προέμενος τὴν σύντομον 593
ἦγε διὰ κωμῶν καὶ πόλεων, καθ᾿ ἡσυχίαν ἀνα-
7 λαμβάνων τὸ στράτευμα. μηδενὸς δὲ ἐμποδὼν
ὄντος, ὥσπερ εἴωθεν ἀντικαθημένων πολεμίων,
τῶν δὲ περιχώρων λεγόντων στράτευμα μηδὲν
ὦφθαι, πυρῶν δὲ κεκαυμένων μεστὸν εἶναι τὸν
τόπον, ᾔσθετο κατεστρατηγημένος ὑπὸ Εὐμένους,
καὶ βαρέως φέρων προσῆγεν ὡς φανερᾷ μάχῃ
κριθησόμενος.

XVI. Ἐν τούτῳ δὲ τῆς δυνάμεως περὶ τὸν
Εὐμένη τὸ πλεῖστον ἠθροισμένον ἐθαύμαζε τὴν
σύνεσιν αὐτοῦ, καὶ μόνον ἐκέλευεν ἄρχειν· ἐφ᾿
ᾧ λυπούμενοι καὶ φθονοῦντες οἱ τῶν ἀργυρασπίδων ἡγεμόνες, ᾿Αντιγένης καὶ Τεύταμος, ἐπεβού-
λευον αὐτῷ, καὶ τοὺς πλείστους τῶν τε σατραπῶν
καὶ τῶν στρατηγῶν συναγαγόντες ἐβουλεύοντο
πότε χρὴ καὶ πῶς τὸν Εὐμένη διαφθεῖραι.
2 συνδόξαν δὲ πᾶσιν ἀποχρήσασθαι πρὸς τὴν
μάχην αὐτῷ, μετὰ δὲ τὴν μάχην εὐθὺς ἀνελεῖν

messengers with orders that the forces in winter quarters and elsewhere should assemble with all speed; at the same time, too, he himself rode forth with the other commanders, took possession of a place which could be seen at a distance by such as traversed the desert, measured it off, and ordered many fires to be made at intervals, as in an encampment. This was done, and when Antigonus saw these fires on the mountains, he was distressed and disheartened, supposing that his enemies had long been aware of his approach and were coming to meet him. In order, therefore, that he might not be forced to fight, when his men were worn and weary from their march, against those who had spent a comfortable winter and were ready for the conflict, he forsook the direct road and led his army through villages and cities, taking time to refresh it. But when no one tried to obstruct his progress, the thing which usually happens when enemies are facing one another, and when the people round about said they had seen no army, but that the place was full of lighted fires, Antigonus perceived that he had been outgeneraled by Eumenes, and in deep resentment led his forces forward to try the issue in open battle.

XVI. But meanwhile most of the forces with Eumenes had assembled, and, admiring his sagacity, demanded that he should be sole commander. At this, Antigenes and Teutamus, the leaders of the Silver-shields, were filled with vexation and jealousy, so that they plotted against the life of Eumenes, and, assembling most of the satraps and generals, deliberated when and how they might put him out of the way. They were unanimous in the decision to make every use of him in the ensuing battle, and after the battle

Εὔδαμος ὁ τῶν ἐλεφάντων ἡγεμὼν καὶ Φαίδιμος
ἐξαγγέλλουσι κρύφα τῷ Εὐμένει τὰ δεδογμένα,
δι᾽ εὔνοιαν μὲν οὐδεμίαν ἢ χάριν, εὐλαβούμενοι
δὲ μὴ τῶν χρημάτων, ἃ δεδανείκεσαν αὐτῷ,
στερηθῶσιν. Εὐμένης δὲ τούτους μὲν ἐπῄνεσεν,
εἰς δὲ τὴν σκηνὴν ἀπελθὼν καὶ πρὸς τοὺς φίλους
εἰπὼν ὡς ἐν πανηγύρει θηρίων ἀναστρέφοιτο,
διαθήκας ἔγραψε καὶ τὰ γραμματεῖα κατέσχισε
καὶ διέφθειρεν, οὐ βουλόμενος αὐτοῦ τελευτήσαντος ἐκ τῶν ἀπορρήτων αἰτίας καὶ συκοφαντήματα
3 τοῖς γράψασι γενέσθαι. ταῦτα διοικησάμενος
ἐβουλεύετο τὴν νίκην παρεῖναι τοῖς ἐναντίοις, ἢ
φυγὼν διὰ Μηδίας καὶ Ἀρμενίας ἐμβαλεῖν εἰς
Καππαδοκίαν. οὐδὲν δὲ κυρώσας τῶν φίλων
παρόντων, ἀλλ᾽ ἐπὶ πολλὰ τῇ γνώμῃ πολυτρόπῳ
παρὰ τὰς τύχας οὔσῃ κινήσας αὑτόν, ἐξέταττε
τὴν δύναμιν, τοὺς μὲν Ἕλληνας καὶ τοὺς βαρβάρους παρορμῶν, ὑπὸ δὲ τῆς φάλαγγος καὶ τῶν
ἀργυρασπίδων αὐτὸς παρακαλούμενος θαρρεῖν,
4 ὡς οὐ δεξομένων τῶν πολεμίων. καὶ γὰρ ἦσαν
οἱ πρεσβύτατοι τῶν περὶ Φίλιππον καὶ Ἀλέξανδρον, ὥσπερ ἀθληταὶ πολέμων ἀήττητοι καὶ
ἄπτωτες εἰς ἐκεῖνο χρόνου, πολλοὶ μὲν ἑβδομή-
κοντα ἔτη γεγονότες, νεώτερος δὲ οὐδεὶς ἑξη-
κονταετοῦς. διὸ καὶ τοῖς περὶ τὸν Ἀντίγονον
ἐπιόντες ἐβόων· "Ἐπὶ τοὺς πατέρας ἁμαρτάνετε,
ὦ κακαὶ κεφαλαί·" καὶ μετ᾽ ὀργῆς ἐμπεσόντες
ὅλην ὁμοῦ τὴν φάλαγγα συνέτριψαν, οὐδενὸς
ὑποστάντος αὐτούς, τῶν δὲ πλείστων ἐν χερσὶ
διαφθαρέντων.

to kill him at once. But Eudamus, the master of the elephants, and Phaedimus, secretly brought word to Eumenes of this decision; not that they were moved by any goodwill or kindness, but because they were anxious not to lose the money they had lent him.[1] These men Eumenes commended, and then went off to his tent, where he said to his friends that he was living in a great herd of wild beasts. Then he made his will, and tore up and destroyed his papers; he did not wish that after his death, in consequence of the secrets contained in these documents, accusations and calumnies should be brought against his correspondents. After this business had been finished, he deliberated whether to give over the victory to the enemy, or to take flight through Media and Armenia and invade Cappadocia. He came to no decision while his friends were with him, but after considering many expedients with a mind which was as versatile as his fortunes were changeable, he proceeded to draw up his forces, urging on the Greeks and the Barbarians, and himself exhorted by the phalanx and the Silver-shields to be of good courage, since, as they felt sure, the enemy would not withstand their attack. And indeed they were the oldest soldiers of Philip and Alexander, war's athletes as it were, without a defeat or a fall up to that time, many of them now seventy years old, and not a man younger than sixty. And so, when they charged upon the forces of Antigonus, they shouted: "It is against your fathers that ye sin, ye miscreants;" and falling upon them in a rage they crushed their whole phalanx at once, not a man withstanding them, and most of their opponents being cut to pieces at close quarters.

---

[1] Cf. chapter xiii. 6.

5   Ταύτῃ μὲν οὖν ὁ Ἀντίγονος ἡττᾶτο κατὰ
κράτος, τοῖς δ' ἱππεῦσιν ἐπεκράτει· τοῦ δὲ Πευ-
κέστου παντάπασιν ἐκλελυμένως καὶ ἀγεννῶς
ἀγωνισαμένου καὶ τὴν ἀποσκευὴν ἔλαβε πᾶσαν,
αὐτῷ τε νήφοντι χρησάμενος παρὰ τὰ δεινὰ καὶ
6   τοῦ τόπου συνεργοῦντος. ἀχανὲς γὰρ ἦν τὸ
πεδίον, οὔτε βαθύτερον οὔτε ἀπόκροτον καὶ
στερεόν, ἀλλὰ θινῶδες καὶ μεστὸν ἁλμυρίδος
αὐχμηρᾶς, ἣ τοσούτων μὲν ἵππων τοσούτων δὲ
ἀνθρώπων ξαινομένη δρόμοις ὑπὸ τὸν τῆς μάχης
καιρὸν ἐξήνθει κόνιν ὥσπερ ἄσβεστον, ἀπολευ-
καίνουσαν τὸν ἀέρα καὶ τὰς ὄψεις διαθολοῦσαν.
ᾗ καὶ ῥᾴδιον λαθὼν ὁ Ἀντίγονος τῆς ἀποσκευῆς
τῶν πολεμίων ἐκράτησε.

XVII. Παυσαμένης δὲ τῆς μάχης εὐθὺς οἱ
περὶ τὸν Τεύταμον ἐπρεσβεύοντο περὶ τῆς ἀποσκευῆς. Ἀντιγόνου δὲ καὶ ταύτην ἀποδώσειν
ὑπισχνουμένου τοῖς ἀργυράσπισι καὶ τἆλλα
χρήσεσθαι φιλανθρώπως, εἰ παραλάβοι τὸν
Εὐμένη, βούλευμα δεινὸν οἱ ἀργυράσπιδες ἐβου-
λεύσαντο, ἐγχειρίσαι ζῶντα τοῖς πολεμίοις τὸν
2   ἄνδρα. καὶ πρῶτον μὲν ἀνυπόπτως προσεπέλα-
ζον αὐτῷ καὶ παρεφύλαττον, οἱ μὲν ἀποδυρόμενοι
περὶ τῆς ἀποσκευῆς, οἱ δὲ θαρρεῖν ὡς νενικηκότα
κελεύοντες, οἱ δὲ τῶν ἄλλων ἡγεμόνων κατη-
γοροῦντες. ἔπειτα προσπεσόντες ἐξήρπασαν τὸ   594
ἐγχειρίδιον αὐτοῦ καὶ τῇ ζώνῃ τὰς χεῖρας ἀπο-
στρέψαντες ἔδησαν. ἐπεὶ δὲ ὑπὸ Ἀντιγόνου
Νικάνωρ ἐπέμφθη παραληψόμενος αὐτόν, ἐδεῖτο
λόγου τυχεῖν ἀγόμενος διὰ τῶν Μακεδόνων, οὐκ
εἰς δέησιν ἢ παραίτησιν, ἀλλ' ὡς περὶ τῶν ἐκείνοις
συμφερόντων διαλεξόμενος.

At this point, then, Antigonus was defeated over-whelmingly, but with his cavalry he got the upper hand; for Peucestas fought in a way that was altogether lax and ignoble, and Antigonus captured all the baggage. He was a man who kept cool in the presence of danger, and he was aided by the ground. For the plain were they fought was vast, and its soil was neither deep nor trodden hard, but sandy and full of a dry and saline substance, which, loosened up by the trampling of so many horses and men during the battle, issued forth in a dust like lime, and this made the air all white and obscured the vision. Therefore it was easy for Antigonus to capture the enemy's baggage unobserved.

XVII. After the battle was over, Teutamus at once sent an embassy to treat for the baggage. And when Antigonus promised not only to give this back to the Silver-shields but also to treat them kindly in other ways, provided they would deliver up Eumenes to him, the Silver-shields formed a dire design to put the man alive into the hands of his enemies. So, to begin with, they drew near him, without awakening his suspicions, and kept him in ward, some making complaints about their baggage, others bidding him to be of good courage, since he was victorious, and others still denouncing the other commanders. Then they fell upon him, snatched his sword away from him, and tied his hands fast with his girdle. And when Nicanor had been sent by Antigonus to receive him and he was being led along through the Macedonians, he begged for leave to speak to them, not with a view to supplication or entreaty, but in order to set forth what was for their advantage.

3 Γενομένης δὲ σιωπῆς ἐν ὑψηλῷ τινι καταστὰς
καὶ τὰς χεῖρας δεδεμένας προτείνας, "Ποῖον,"
εἶπεν, "ὦ κάκιστοι Μακεδόνων, τρόπαιον Ἀντίγονος ἐθελήσας ἂν ἔστησε καθ᾽ ὑμῶν, οἷον ὑμεῖς
καθ᾽ αὑτῶν ἀνίστατε τὸν στρατηγὸν αἰχμάλωτον
ἐκδιδόντες; οὐκ ἄρα δεινὸν ἦν κρατοῦντας ὑμᾶς
ἧτταν ἐξομολογεῖσθαι διὰ τὰς ἀποσκευάς, ὡς ἐν
τοῖς χρήμασιν, οὐκ ἐν τοῖς ὅπλοις τοῦ κρατεῖν
ὄντος, ἀλλὰ καὶ τὸν ἡγεμόνα πέμπετε λύτρον τῆς
4 ἀποσκευῆς. ἐγὼ μὲν οὖν ἀήττητος ἄγομαι, νικῶν
τοὺς πολεμίους, ὑπὸ τῶν συμμάχων ἀπολλύμενος·
ὑμεῖς δέ, πρὸς Διὸς στρατίου καὶ θεῶν ὁρκίων,
ἐνταῦθά με δι᾽ αὑτῶν κτείνατε. πάντως κἀκεῖ
κτεινόμενος ὑμέτερον ἔργον εἰμί. μέμψεται δὲ
οὐδὲν Ἀντίγονος· νεκροῦ γὰρ Εὐμένους δεῖται καὶ
οὐ ζῶντος. εἰ δὲ φείδεσθε τῶν χειρῶν, ἀρκέσει
5 τῶν ἐμῶν ἡ ἑτέρα λυθεῖσα πρᾶξαι τὸ ἔργον. εἰ δὲ
οὐ πιστεύετέ μοι ξίφος, ὑπορρίψατε τοῖς θηρίοις
δεδεμένον. καὶ ταῦτα πράξαντας ὑμᾶς ἀφίημι τῆς
ἐπ᾽ ἐμοὶ δίκης ὡς ἄνδρας ὁσιωτάτους καὶ δικαιο-
τάτους περὶ τὸν αὑτῶν στρατηγὸν γενομένους."

XVIII. Ταῦτα τοῦ Εὐμένους λέγοντος τὸ μὲν
ἄλλο πλῆθος ἄχθει κατείχετο καὶ κλαυθμὸς ἦν,
οἱ δὲ ἀργυράσπιδες ἄγειν ἐβόων καὶ μὴ φλυα-
ροῦντι προσέχειν· οὐ γὰρ εἶναι δεινὸν εἰ Χερρονησίτης ὄλεθρος οἰμώξεται μυρίοις γυμνάσας
πολέμοις Μακεδόνας, ἀλλ᾽ εἰ τῶν Ἀλεξάνδρου
καὶ Φιλίππου στρατιωτῶν οἱ κράτιστοι τοσαῦτα

Silence was made, and standing on an eminence he stretched forth his hands, bound as they were, and said: "What trophy, O ye basest of Macedonians, could Antigonus have so much desired to set up over your defeat, as this which ye yourselves are now erecting by delivering up your general as a prisoner? It is not a dreadful thing, then, that in the hour of your victory ye should acknowledge yourselves defeated for the sake of your baggage, implying that victory lies in your possessions and not in your arms, but ye must also send your leader as a ransom for that baggage. As for me, then, ye lead me away undefeated, a victor over my enemies, a victim of my fellow-soldiers; but as for you, by Zeus the god of armies and by the gods who hallow oaths, I bid you slay me here with your own hands. Even should I be slain yonder, it will be wholly your work. Nor will Antigonus find any fault; for he wants a dead and not a living Eumenes. And if ye would spare your own hands, one of mine, if released, will suffice to do the business. And if ye cannot trust me with a sword, cast me under the feet of your elephants, all bound as I am. If ye do this, I will absolve you from your guilt towards me, holding that ye have shown yourselves most just and righteous in your dealings with your own general."

XVIII. As Eumenes said this, the rest of the throng was overwhelmed with sorrow, and some wept, but the Silver-shields shouted to lead him along and pay no attention to his babbling; for it was not so dreadful a thing, they said, that a pest from the Chersonesus should come to grief for having harassed Macedonians with infinite wars, as that the best of the soldiers of Philip and Alexander,

καμόντες ἐν γήρᾳ στέρονται τῶν ἐπάθλων καὶ
τροφὴν παρ' ἑτέρων λαμβάνουσιν, αἱ δὲ γυναῖκες
αὐτῶν ἤδη τρίτην νύκτα τοῖς πολεμίοις συγκα-
θεύδουσιν. ἅμα δὲ ἦγον αὐτὸν ἐπιταχύνοντες.

2 Ἀντίγονος δὲ δείσας τὸν ὄχλον (ἀπελείφθη γὰρ
οὐδεὶς ἐν τῷ στρατοπέδῳ) δέκα τοὺς κρατιστεύ-
οντας ἐλέφαντας ἐξέπεμψε καὶ λογχοφόρους
συχνοὺς Μήδους καὶ Παρθυαίους διακρουσο-
μένους τὸ πλῆθος. εἶτ' αὐτὸς μὲν ἰδεῖν οὐχ ὑπέμεινε τὸν Εὐμένη διὰ τὴν προγεγενημένην φιλίαν
καὶ συνήθειαν, πυνθανομένων δὲ τῶν παρειληφό-
των τὸ σῶμα πῶς φυλάξουσιν, "Οὕτως," εἶπεν,
3 "ὡς ἐλέφαντα ἢ ὡς λέοντα." μετὰ μικρὸν δὲ
συμπαθὴς γενόμενος τῶν τε δεσμῶν τοὺς βαρεῖς
ἐκέλευσεν ἀφελεῖν καὶ παῖδα παραδέξασθαι τῶν
συνήθων, ὅπως ἀλείψαιτο, καὶ τῶν φίλων ἐφῆκε
τῷ βουλομένῳ συνδιημερεύειν καὶ κομίζειν τὰ
ἐπιτήδεια. βουλευόμενος δὲ περὶ αὐτοῦ πλείονας
ἡμέρας προσίετο καὶ λόγους καὶ ὑποσχέσεις,
Νεάρχου τε τοῦ Κρητὸς καὶ Δημητρίου τοῦ υἱοῦ
φιλοτιμουμένων τὸν Εὐμένη σῶσαι, τῶν δὲ ἄλλων
ὁμοῦ τι πάντων ἐνισταμένων καὶ κελευόντων ἀναιρεῖν.

4 Λέγεται δὲ τὸν Εὐμένη τοῦ φυλάσσοντος αὐτὸν Ὀνομάρχου πυθέσθαι τί δήποτε Ἀντίγονος
ἐχθρὸν ἄνδρα καὶ πολέμιον λαβὼν ὑποχείριον
οὔτε ἀποκτίννυσι ταχέως οὔτε εὐγενῶς ἀφίησι·
τοῦ δὲ Ὀνομάρχου πρὸς ὕβριν εἰπόντος ὡς οὐ
νῦν, ἀλλ' ἐπὶ τῆς μάχης ἔδει πρὸς θάνατον ἔχειν
εὐθαρσῶς, "Ναὶ μὰ τὸν Δία," φάναι τὸν Εὐμένη,
"καὶ τότε εἶχον· ἐροῦ δὲ τοὺς εἰς χεῖρας ἐλθόν-
ας· ἀλλ' οὐδενὶ κρείττονι προστυχὼν οἶδα." καὶ

after all their toils, should in their old age be robbed of their rewards and get their support from others, and that their wives should be spending the third night now in the arms of their enemies. At the same time they led him along at a quickened pace.

But Antigonus, fearing their multitude (since no one had been left behind in the camp), sent out ten of his strongest elephants and a great number of Median and Parthian spearmen to drive away the throng. He himself could not endure to see Eumenes, by reason of their former intimate friendship, and when those who had received him asked how they should guard his person, he said: " Just as ye would an elephant or a lion." But after a little while he became compassionate and ordered the keepers to remove the prisoner's heavy fetters and admit one of his personal servants to anoint him, and permitted any one of his friends who wished to spend the day with him and bring him what he needed. Then he deliberated many days what to do with him, and considered various arguments and suggestions, Demetrius his son and Nearchus the Cretan being eager to save the life of Eumenes, while the rest, almost all of them, were insistent in urging that he be put to death.

We are told, also, that Eumenes asked his keeper, Onomarchus, why in the world Antigonus, now that he had got a hated enemy in his hands, neither killed him speedily nor generously set him free; and when Onomarchus insolently told him it was not now, but on the field of battle, that he should have faced death boldly, " Yea, by Zeus," said Eumenes, " then, too, I did so; ask the men who fought with me; I know that none I met was a

τὸν Ὀνόμαρχον, "Οὐκοῦν ἐπεὶ νῦν," φάναι, "τὸν κρείττονα εὕρηκας, τί οὐκ ἀναμένεις τὸν ἐκείνου καιρόν;"

XIX. Ὡς δ' οὖν ἔδοξε τῷ Ἀντιγόνῳ τὸν Εὐμένη κτείνειν, ἐκέλευσεν αὐτοῦ τὴν τροφὴν ἀφελεῖν. καὶ δύο μὲν ἡμέρας ἢ τρεῖς ἄσιτος οὕτω προσήγετο πρὸς τὴν τελευτήν. αἰφνίδιον δὲ ἀναζυγῆς γενομένης εἰσπέμψαντες ἄνθρωπον ἀποσφάττουσιν αὐτόν. τὸ δὲ σῶμα τοῖς φίλοις παραδοὺς ὁ Ἀντίγονος ἐπέτρεψε καῦσαι καὶ τὰ λείψανα συνθέντας εἰς ἀργυρᾶν ὑδρίαν κομίζειν, ἀποδοθησόμενα τῇ γυναικὶ καὶ τοῖς παισίν.

2 Οὕτω δὲ ἀποθανόντος Εὐμένους οὐκ ἐπ' ἄλλῳ τινὶ τὴν τιμωρίαν ἐποιήσατο τῶν προδόντων αὐτὸν ἡγεμόνων καὶ στρατιωτῶν τὸ δαιμόνιον, ἀλλ' αὐτὸς Ἀντίγονος προβαλλόμενος ὡς ἀσεβεῖς καὶ θηριώδεις τοὺς ἀργυράσπιδας παρέδωκε Σιβυρτίῳ τῷ διοικοῦντι τὴν Ἀραχωσίαν, πάντα τρόπον ἐκτρῖψαι καὶ καταφθεῖραι κελεύσας, ὅπως μηδεὶς αὐτῶν εἰς Μακεδονίαν ἄπεισι μηδὲ ὄψεται τὴν Ἑλληνικὴν θάλατταν.

ΣΕΡΤΩΡΙΟΥ ΚΑΙ ΕΥΜΕΝΟΥΣ ΣΥΓΚΡΙΣΙΣ

I. Ταῦτα ἔστιν ἃ περὶ Εὐμένους καὶ Σερτωρίου μνήμης ἄξια παρειλήφαμεν. ἐν δὲ τῇ συγκρίσει κοινὸν μὲν ἀμφοτέροις ὑπάρχει τὸ ξένους καὶ ἀλλοδαποὺς καὶ φυγάδας ὄντας ἐθνῶν τε παντο-

---

[1] According to Nepos (*Eumenes*, xii. 4), Eumenes was

better man." "Well, then," said Onomarchus, "since now thou hast found thy better, why canst thou not bide his time?"

XIX. When, then, Antigonus had decided to kill Eumenes, he gave orders to deprive him of food. And so, after two or three days of fasting, the prisoner began to draw nigh his end. But camp was suddenly broken and a man was sent to dispatch him.[1] His body, however, was delivered to his friends by Antigonus, who permitted them to burn it and collect the ashes and place them in a silver urn, that they might be returned to his wife and children.

Eumenes thus slain, on no other man than Antigonus did Heaven devolve the punishment of the soldiers and commanders who betrayed him, but he himself, regarding the Silver-shields as impious and bestial men, put them into the service of Sibyrtius the governor of Arachosia, ordering him to wear them out and destroy them in every possible way, that not a man of them might ever return to Macedonia or behold the Grecian sea.

COMPARISON OF SERTORIUS AND EUMENES

I. Such are the memorable things in the careers of Eumenes and Sertorius which have come down to us. And now, as we compare the men, we find this common to both, that although they were strangers, aliens, and exiles, they were continually

strangled by his keepers, without the knowledge of Antigonus.

δαπῶν καὶ στρατευμάτων μαχίμων τε καὶ μεγάλων[1] ἡγουμένους διατελεῖν, ἴδιον δὲ Σερτωρίῳ μὲν
τὸ παρὰ πάντων τῶν συμμάχων δεδομένην ἔχειν
διὰ τὸ ἀξίωμα τὴν ἀρχήν, Εὐμένει δὲ τὸ πολλῶν
διαφερομένων περὶ τῆς ἡγεμονίας πρὸς αὐτὸν ἐκ
τῶν πράξεων λαμβάνειν τὸ πρωτεῖον· καὶ τῷ μὲν
ἄρχεσθαι βουλόμενοι δικαίως εἵποντο, τῷ δὲ ἄρχειν μὴ δυνάμενοι πρὸς τὸ συμφέρον ὑπήκουον.
2 καὶ γὰρ ὁ μὲν Ἰβήρων καὶ Λυσιτανῶν Ῥωμαῖος,
ὁ δὲ Χερρονησίτης Μακεδόνων ἦρχεν, ὧν οἱ μὲν
ἔκπαλαι Ῥωμαίοις ἐδούλευον, οἱ δὲ τότε πάντας
ἀνθρώπους ἐδουλοῦντο. καὶ Σερτώριος μὲν ἀπὸ
βουλῆς καὶ στρατηγίας θαυμαζόμενος, Εὐμένης
δὲ διὰ τὴν γραμματείαν καταφρονούμενος ἐφ'
ἡγεμονίαν προῆλθεν. οὐ μόνον τοίνυν ἐλάττοσι
πρὸς τὴν ἀρχὴν ἀφορμαῖς, ἀλλὰ καὶ μείζοσι πρὸς
3 τὴν αὔξησιν ἐχρήσατο κωλύμασιν Εὐμένης. καὶ
γὰρ ἄντικρυς τοὺς ἐνισταμένους καὶ κρύφα τοὺς
ἐπιβουλεύοντας εἶχε πολλούς, οὐχ ὥσπερ τῷ
ἑτέρῳ φανερῶς μὲν οὐδείς, λάθρα δὲ ὕστερον καὶ
ὀλίγοι τῶν συμμάχων ἐπανέστησαν. διὸ τῷ μὲν
ἦν πέρας τοῦ κινδυνεύειν τὸ νικᾶν τοὺς πολεμίους,
τῷ δὲ ἐκ τοῦ νικᾶν ὁ κίνδυνος ὑπὸ τῶν φθονούντων.

II. Τὰ μὲν οὖν κατὰ τὴν στρατηγίαν ἐφάμιλλα
καὶ παράλληλα· τῷ δὲ ἄλλῳ τρόπῳ φιλοπόλεμος
μὲν ὁ Εὐμένης καὶ φιλόνεικος, ἡσυχίας δὲ καὶ
πραότητος οἰκεῖος ὁ Σερτώριος. ὁ μὲν γάρ, ἀσφα-

---

[1] μεγάλων with Bekker : μεγάλων δυνάμεων.

in command of all sorts of peoples and of armies that were large and warlike; but it was peculiar to Sertorius that he held a command which was given him by all his confederates because of his reputation, and to Eumenes that many contended with him for the leadership, and yet he took the highest place in consequence of his achievements. Furthermore, the one was followed by those who wished to be under a just command; while the other was obeyed by those who were incapable of command and sought their own advantage. For the one, a Roman, commanded Iberians and Lusitanians, who had long been in subjection to Rome; the other, a Chersonesian, commanded Macedonians, who at that time were holding the whole world in subjection. Besides, Sertorius rose to leadership when a career in senate and field had brought him admiration; but Eumenes when his post as secretary had brought him contempt. Eumenes, therefore, not only had fewer advantages at the outset, but also greater hindrances as he advanced in his career. For there were many who directly opposed him and secretly plotted against him; whereas Sertorius was openly opposed by no one, and secretly only in the latter part of his career, when a few of his confederates rose up against him. For this reason Sertorius could put an end to his peril by a victory over his enemies; while Eumenes, in consequence of his victories, was in peril at the hands of those who envied him.

II. In their capacities as commanders, then, they were very much alike; but in their general dispositions Eumenes was fond of war and fond of strife, while Sertorius was a lover of peace and tranquillity. For the one, though it was in his power to

λῶς καὶ μετὰ τιμῆς βιοῦν ἐξὸν ἐκποδὼν γενομένῳ
τοῖς πρώτοις, μαχόμενος καὶ κινδυνεύων διετέ-
λεσε, τῷ δὲ οὐδὲν δεομένῳ πραγμάτων ὑπὲρ αὐτῆς
τῆς τοῦ σώματος ἀσφαλείας πρὸς οὐκ ἐῶντας
2 εἰρήνην ἄγειν ἦν ὁ πόλεμος. Εὐμένει μὲν γὰρ
Ἀντίγονος ἐκστάντι τῶν ὑπὲρ τοῦ πρωτεύειν
ἀγώνων ἡδέως ἂν ἐχρῆτο τὴν μετ' αὐτὸν ἀγα-
πῶντι τάξιν, Σερτωρίῳ δὲ οἱ περὶ Πομπήιον οὐδὲ
ζῆν ἀπραγμόνως ἐπέτρεπον. διὸ τῷ μὲν ἑκοντὶ
συνέβαινε πολεμεῖν ἐπ' ἀρχῇ, τῷ δὲ ἀκουσίως
3 ἄρχειν διὰ τὸ πολεμεῖσθαι. φιλοπόλεμος μὲν
οὖν ὁ τῆς ἀσφαλείας τὴν πλεονεξίαν προτιμῶν,
πολεμικὸς δὲ ὁ τῷ πολέμῳ κτώμενος τὴν ἀσφάλειαν.

Καὶ μὴν θανεῖν γε συνέβη τῷ μὲν οὐ προαισθο-
μένῳ, τῷ δὲ καὶ προσδεχομένῳ τὴν τελευτήν, ὧν
τὸ μὲν ἐπιεικείας, φίλοις γὰρ ἐδόκει πιστεύειν, τὸ
δὲ ἀσθενείας, βουλόμενος γὰρ φυγεῖν συνελήφθη.
4 καὶ τοῦ μὲν οὐ κατῄσχυνε τὸν βίον ὁ θάνατος,
πάσχοντος ὑπὸ τῶν συμμάχων ἃ τῶν πολεμίων
αὐτὸν οὐδεὶς ἐποίησεν· ὁ δὲ φεύγειν μὲν πρὸ 596
αἰχμαλωσίας μὴ δυνηθείς, ζῆν δὲ μετ' αἰχμαλω-
σίαν βουληθείς, οὔτε ἐφυλάξατο καλῶς τὴν τελευτὴν οὔθ' ὑπέμεινεν, ἀλλὰ προσλιπαρῶν καὶ
δεόμενος τοῦ σώματος μόνου κρατεῖν δοκοῦντα τὸν
πολέμιον καὶ τῆς ψυχῆς αὐτοῦ κύριον ἐποίησεν.

live in safety and with honour if he kept out of the way of the leading Macedonians, was continually fighting them at the risk of his life; whereas the other, though he craved no participation in affairs, had to wage war for his very life against those who would not suffer him to be at peace. For if Eumenes had stood aside from the struggles for the primacy and been satisfied with the second place, Antigonus would gladly have given him that; whereas Sertorius could not get permission from Pompey to live, even though in retirement. Therefore the one was ever waging war of his own accord for the sake of power; while the other held power against his wishes because war was waged upon him. Now, that man is fond of war who sets greed above safety; but that man is warlike who by war wins safety.

And further, the one met his death when he had no anticipation of it, the other when he was expecting the end. In the one case, death resulted from the man's goodness of heart, since he appeared to trust his friends; in the other, from weakness, since he wished to fly, but was arrested. Moreover, death brought no stain upon the life of Sertorius, since he suffered at the hands of confederates what none of his enemies could inflict upon him; Eumenes, however, who was unable to fly before being taken prisoner, but was willing to live after being taken prisoner, neither took good precautions against death, nor faced it well, but by supplicating and entreating the foe who was known to have power over his body only, he made him lord and master of his spirit also.

PHOCION

ΦΩΚΙΩΝ

I. Δημάδης ὁ ῥήτωρ ἰσχύων μὲν ἐν ταῖς Ἀθήναις διὰ τὸ πρὸς χάριν πολιτεύεσθαι Μακεδόνων καὶ Ἀντιπάτρου, πολλὰ δὲ γράφειν καὶ λέγειν ἀναγκαζόμενος παρὰ τὸ ἀξίωμα τῆς πόλεως καὶ τὸ ἦθος, ἔλεγε συγγνώμης ἄξιος εἶναι πολιτευόμενος τὰ ναυάγια τῆς πόλεως. τοῦτο δὲ εἰ καὶ τῷ ῥήτορι θρασύτερον εἴρηται, δόξειεν ἂν ἀληθὲς εἶναι μετενεχθὲν ἐπὶ τὴν Φωκίωνος πολιτείαν. 2 Δημάδης μὲν γὰρ αὐτὸς ἦν ναυάγιον τῆς πόλεως, οὕτως ἀσελγῶς βιώσας καὶ πολιτευσάμενος ὥστε Ἀντίπατρον εἰπεῖν ἐπ' αὐτοῦ, γέροντος ἤδη γεγονότος, ὅτι καθάπερ ἱερείου διαπεπραγμένου γλῶσσα καὶ κοιλία μόνον ἀπολείπεται· τὴν δὲ Φωκίωνος ἀρετήν, ὥσπερ ἀνταγωνιστῇ βαρεῖ καὶ βιαίῳ καιρῷ συλλαχοῦσαν, αἱ τύχαι τῆς Ἑλλάδος ἀμαυρὰν καὶ ἀλαμπῆ πρὸς δόξαν ἐποίησαν. 3 οὐ γὰρ Σοφοκλεῖ γε προσεκτέον ἀσθενῆ ποιοῦντι 742 τὴν ἀρετὴν ἐν οἷς φησιν·[1]

Ἀλλ' οὐ γάρ, ὦναξ, οὐδ' ὃς ἂν βλάστῃ μένει
νοῦς τοῖς κακῶς πράξασιν, ἀλλ' ἐξίσταται·

τοσοῦτον δὲ τῇ τύχῃ δοτέον ἀντιταττομένη πρὸς τοὺς ἀγαθοὺς ἄνδρας ἰσχύειν, ὅσον ἀντὶ τῆς ἀξίας τιμῆς καὶ χάριτος ἐνίοις ψόγους πονηροὺς καὶ

---

[1] *Antigone*, 563 f. (οὐ γάρ ποτ', ὦναξ, κτλ.).

144

PHOCION

I. Demades the orator, who was powerful at Athens because he conducted affairs so as to please Antipater and the Macedonians, and was forced to propose and favour many measures which were at variance with the dignity and character of the city, used to say that he was excusable because he was in command of a shipwrecked state. This may have been too hardy an utterance for the orator, but it would seem to be true when transferred to the administration of Phocion. Demades, indeed, was himself but wreckage of the state, since his life and administration were so outrageous that Antipater said of him, when he was now grown old, that he was like a victim when the sacrifice was over—nothing left but tongue and guts. But the fame of Phocion's virtue, which may be said to have found an antagonist in a grievous and violent time, the fortunes of Greece rendered obscure and dim. Surely we must not follow Sophocles in making virtue weak, as when he says :—

"Indeed, O King, what reason nature may have given
    Abides not with the unfortunate, but goes astray";

yet thus much power must be granted to Fortune in her conflicts with good men : instead of the honour and gratitude which are their due, she brings base

διαβολὰς ἐπιφέρουσαν τὴν πίστιν ἀσθενεστέραν
ποιεῖν τῆς ἀρετῆς.

ΙΙ. Καίτοι δοκοῦσιν οἱ δῆμοι μᾶλλον εἰς τοὺς
ἀγαθοὺς ἐξυβρίζειν ὅταν εὐτυχῶσιν, ὑπὸ πραγμάτων μεγάλων καὶ δυνάμεως ἐπαιρόμενοι· συμ-
βαίνει δὲ τοὐναντίον. αἱ γὰρ συμφοραὶ πικρὰ
μὲν τὰ ἤθη καὶ μικρόλυπα καὶ ἀκροσφαλῆ πρὸς
ὀργὰς ποιοῦσι, δύσκολον δὲ τὴν ἀκοὴν καὶ τρα-
χεῖαν, ὑπὸ παντὸς λόγου καὶ ῥήματος τόνον
ἔχοντος ἐνοχλουμένην· ὁ δὲ ἐπιτιμῶν τοῖς ἐξα-
μαρτανομένοις ἐξονειδίζειν τὰ δυστυχήματα
2 δοκεῖ, καὶ καταφρονεῖν ὁ παρρησιαζόμενος. καὶ
καθάπερ τὸ μέλι λυπεῖ τὰ τετρωμένα καὶ ἡλκω-
μένα μέρη τοῦ σώματος, οὕτως πολλάκις οἱ
ἀληθινοὶ καὶ νοῦν ἔχοντες λόγοι δάκνουσι καὶ
παροξύνουσι τοὺς κακῶς πράττοντας, ἐὰν μὴ
προσηνεῖς ὦσι καὶ συνείκοντες, ὥσπερ ἀμέλει τὸ
ἡδὺ "μενοεικὲς" ὁ ποιητὴς κέκληκεν, ὡς τῷ
ἡδομένῳ τῆς ψυχῆς ὑπεῖκον καὶ μὴ μαχόμενον
3 μηδ' ἀντιτυποῦν. καὶ γὰρ ὄμμα φλεγμαῖνον
ἥδιστα τοῖς σκιεροῖς καὶ ἀλαμπέσιν ἐνδιατρίβει
χρώμασι, τὰ δὲ αὐγὴν ἔχοντα καὶ φῶς ἀποστρέ-
φεται, καὶ πόλις ἐν τύχαις ἀβουλήτοις γενομένη
ψοφοδεὲς καὶ τρυφερόν ἐστι δι' ἀσθένειαν ἀνέχεσθαι παρρησίας, ὅτε μάλιστα δεῖται, τῶν πραγμάτων ἀναφορὰν ἁμαρτήματος οὐκ ἐχόντων.
διὸ πάντῃ σφαλερὸν ἡ τοιαύτη πολιτεία· συν-

censure and calumny upon some, and so weakens
the world's confidence in their virtue.

II. And yet it is commonly held that a people is
more apt to wreak its insolence upon good men
when it is prosperous, being then lifted up by
grandeur and power; but the reverse is often the
case. For calamities make men's dispositions bitter,
irritable, and prone to wrath, so that no one can say
anything to please or soften them, but they are annoyed by every speech or word that has vigour. He
who censures them for their transgressions is thought
to abuse them for their misfortunes, and he who is
outspoken with them, to despise them. And just as
honey irritates wounded and ulcerated parts of the
body, so often words of truth and soberness sting
and exasperate those who are in an evil plight,
unless uttered with kindness and complaisance; and
therefore, doubtless, the poet calls that which is
pleasant "menoeikes," on the ground that it *yields*
to that part of the *soul* which experiences pleasure,
and does not fight with it or resist it.[1] An eye that
is inflamed dwells most gratefully on colours which
are dark and lustreless, but shuns those which are
radiant and bright; and so a city that has fallen
on unfavourable fortunes is made by its weakness
too sensitive and delicate to endure frank speaking,
and that at a time when it needs it most of all, since
the situation allows no chance of retrieving the mistakes that have been made. Therefore the conduct
of affairs in such a city is altogether dangerous; for

As often, Plutarch's etymology is amiably wrong.
Homer uses " μενοεικές " as a stock epithet of good things in
such abundance as to be *spirit-suiting*, or *satisfying*.

ἀπόλλυσι γὰρ τὸν πρὸς χάριν λέγοντα καὶ προ-
απόλλυσι τὸν μὴ χαριζόμενον.

4 Ὥσπερ οὖν τὸν ἥλιον οἱ μαθηματικοὶ λέγουσι
μήτε τὴν αὐτὴν τῷ οὐρανῷ φερόμενον φορὰν μήτε
ἄντικρυς ἐναντίαν καὶ ἀντιβατικήν, ἀλλὰ λοξῷ
καὶ παρεγκεκλιμένῳ πορείας σχήματι χρώμενον
ὑγρὰν καὶ εὐκαμπῆ καὶ περιελιττομένην ἕλικα
ποιεῖν, ᾗ σώζεται πάντα καὶ λαμβάνει τὴν
ἀρίστην κρᾶσιν, οὕτως ἄρα τῆς πολιτείας ὁ μὲν
ὄρθιος ἄγαν καὶ πρὸς ἅπαντα τοῖς δημοσίοις [1]
ἀντιβαίνων τόνος ἀπηνὴς καὶ σκληρός, ὥσπερ αὖ
πάλιν ἐπισφαλὲς καὶ κάταντες τὸ συνεφελκό-
μενον οἷς ἁμαρτάνουσιν οἱ πολλοὶ καὶ συνεπιρ-
5 ρέπον, ἡ δὲ ἀνθυπείκουσα πειθομένοις καὶ διδοῦσα
τὸ πρὸς χάριν, εἶτα ἀπαιτοῦσα τὸ συμφέρον ἐπι-
στασία καὶ κυβέρνησις ἀνθρώπων πολλὰ πράως
καὶ χρησίμως ὑπουργούντων, εἰ μὴ πάντα δε-
σποτικῶς καὶ βιαίως ἄγοιντο, σωτήριος, ἐργώδης
δὲ καὶ χαλεπὴ καὶ τὸ σεμνὸν ἔχουσα τῷ ἐπιεικεῖ
δύσμικτον· ἐὰν δὲ μιχθῇ, τοῦτό ἐστιν ἡ πάντων
μὲν ῥυθμῶν, πασῶν δὲ ἁρμονιῶν ἐμμελεστάτη καὶ
μουσικωτάτη κρᾶσις, ᾗ καὶ τὸν κόσμον ὁ θεὸς
λέγεται διοικεῖν, οὐ βιαζόμενος, ἀλλὰ πειθοῖ καὶ
λόγῳ παράγων τὴν ἀνάγκην.

III. Ταῦτα δὲ καὶ Κάτωνι τῷ νέῳ συνέβη.
καὶ γὰρ οὗτος οὐ πιθανὸν ἔσχεν οὐδὲ προσφιλὲς
ὄχλῳ τὸ ἦθος, οὐδὲ ἤνθησεν ἐν τῇ πολιτείᾳ πρὸς

1 δημοσίοις Bekker has δήμοις, after Coraës.

148

she brings to ruin with herself the man who speaks but to win her favour, and she brings to ruin before herself the man who will not court her favour.

Now, the sun, as mathematicians tell us, has neither the same motion as the heavens, nor one that is directly opposite and contrary, but takes a slanting course with a slight inclination,[1] and describes a winding spiral of soft and gentle curves, thus preserving all things and giving them the best temperature. And so in the administration of a city, the course which is too straight, and opposed in all things to the popular desires, is harsh and cruel, just as, on the other hand, it is highly dangerous to tolerate or yield perforce to the mistakes of the populace. But that wise guidance and government of men which yields to them in return for their obedience and grants them what will please them, and then demands from them in payment what will advantage the state,—and men will give docile and profitable service in many ways, provided they are not treated despotically and harshly all the time,—conduces to safety, although it is laborious and difficult and must have that mixture of austerity and reasonableness which is so hard to attain. But if the mixture be attained, that is the most concordant and musical blending of all rhythms and all harmonies ; and this is the way, we are told, in which God regulates the universe, not using compulsion, but making persuasion and reason introduce that which must be.

III. These principles found an illustration in Cato the Younger also. For his manners were not winning, nor pleasing to the populace, nor was he eminent in

---

[1] *i.e.* to the plane of the ecliptic.

χάριν· ἀλλ' ὁ μὲν Κικέρων φησὶν αὐτὸν ὥσπερ
ἐν τῇ Πλάτωνος πολιτείᾳ καὶ οὐκ ἐν τῇ Ῥωμύλου
πολιτευόμενον ὑποστάθμη τῆς ὑπατείας ἐκπεσεῖν,
ἐμοὶ δὲ ταὐτὸ δοκεῖ παθεῖν τοῖς μὴ καθ' ὥραν
2 ἐκφανεῖσι καρποῖς. ὡς γὰρ ἐκείνους ἡδέως ὁρῶντες καὶ θαυμάζοντες οὐ χρῶνται, οὕτως ἡ Κάτωνος ἀρχαιοτροπία διὰ χρόνων πολλῶν ἐπιγενομένη
βίοις διεφθορόσι καὶ πονηροῖς ἔθεσι δόξαν μὲν
εἶχε μεγάλην καὶ κλέος, οὐκ ἐνήρμοσε δὲ ταῖς
χρείαις διὰ βάρος καὶ μέγεθος τῆς ἀρετῆς ἀσύμ-
3 μετρον τοῖς καθεστῶσι καιροῖς. καὶ γὰρ αὐτὸς
οὐ κεκλιμένης μὲν ἤδη τῆς πατρίδος, ὥσπερ ὁ
Φωκίων, πολὺν δὲ χειμῶνα καὶ σάλον ἐχούσης,
ὅσον ἱστίων καὶ κάλων ἐπιλαβέσθαι καὶ παρα-
στῆναι τοῖς πλέον δυναμένοις πολιτευσάμενος,
οἰάκων δὲ καὶ κυβερνήσεως ἀπωσθείς, ὅμως μέγαν
ἀγῶνα τῇ τύχῃ περιέστησεν. εἷλε μὲν γὰρ καὶ
κατέβαλε τὴν πολιτείαν δι' ἄλλους, μόλις δὲ καὶ
βραδέως καὶ χρόνῳ πολλῷ καὶ παρὰ μικρὸν
ἐλθοῦσαν περιγενέσθαι διὰ Κάτωνα καὶ τὴν
4 Κάτωνος ἀρετήν· ᾗ παραβάλλομεν τὴν Φωκίωνος, οὐ κατὰ κοινὰς ὁμοιότητας, ὡς ἀγαθῶν καὶ
πολιτικῶν ἀνδρῶν· ἔστι γὰρ ἀμέλει καὶ ἀνδρείας
διαφορὰ πρὸς ἀνδρείαν, ὡς τῆς Ἀλκιβιάδου πρὸς
τὴν Ἐπαμεινώνδου, καὶ φρονήσεως πρὸς φρόνη-

743

---

[1] Cicero, ad Att. ii. 1, 8, where, however, there is no
allusion to Cato's loss of the consulship. Dicit enim

his public career for popularity. Indeed, Cicero says it was because he acted as if he lived in Plato's commonwealth, and not among the dregs of Romulus, that he was defeated when he stood for the consulship;[1] but I think he fared just as fruits do which make their appearance out of season. For, as we look upon these with delight and admiration, but do not use them, so the old-fashioned character of Cato, which, after a long lapse of time, made its appearance among lives that were corrupted and customs that were debased, enjoyed great repute and fame, but was not suited to the needs of men because of the weight and grandeur of its virtue, which were out of all proportion to the immediate times. For his native city was not already prostrate, like that of Phocion, but struggling with great tempest and surge, and though he could only serve her by putting hand to sails and ropes and by supporting men of greater influence, but was repulsed from ruddersweeps and pilotage, he nevertheless gave Fortune a hard contest. She did, indeed, seize and overthrow the commonwealth by means of other men, but with difficulty, slowly, after a long time, and when it had almost won the day through Cato and the virtue of Cato. And with this virtue we compare that of Phocion, though not for their general resemblances, but on the ground that both were good men and devoted to the state. For there is surely a difference between the bravery of one man and that of another, as, for instance, between that of Alcibiades and that of Epaminondas; between the wisdom of one man and that of another, as,

---

[1] tamquam in Platonis πολιτείᾳ, non tamquam in Romuli faece, sententiam.

PLUTARCH'S LIVES

σιν, ὡς τῆς Θεμιστοκλέους πρὸς τὴν Ἀριστείδου,
καὶ δικαιοσύνης πρὸς δικαιοσύνην, ὡς τῆς Νομᾶ
5 πρὸς τὴν Ἀγησιλάου. τούτων δὲ τῶν ἀνδρῶν αἱ
ἀρεταὶ μέχρι τῶν τελευταίων καὶ ἀτόμων διαφορῶν ἕνα χαρακτῆρα καὶ μορφὴν καὶ χρῶμα
κοινὸν ἤθους ἐγκεκραμένον ἐκφέρουσιν, ὥσπερ
ἴσῳ μέτρῳ μεμιγμένου πρὸς τὸ αὐστηρὸν τοῦ
φιλανθρώπου καὶ πρὸς τὸ ἀσφαλὲς τοῦ ἀνδρείου,
καὶ τῆς ὑπὲρ ἄλλων μὲν κηδεμονίας, ὑπὲρ αὑτῶν
δὲ ἀφοβίας, καὶ πρὸς μὲν τὸ αἰσχρὸν εὐλαβείας,
πρὸς δὲ τὸ δίκαιον εὐτονίας συνηρμοσμένης
ὁμοίως· ὥστε λεπτοῦ πάνυ λόγου δεῖσθαι καθάπερ ὀργάνου πρὸς διάκρισιν καὶ ἀνεύρεσιν τῶν
διαφερόντων.

IV. Τὸ μὲν οὖν Κάτωνος ὡμολόγηται γένος ἐκ
λαμπρῶν ὑπάρχειν, ὡς λεχθήσεται· Φωκίωνα δὲ
τεκμαίρομαι μὴ παντάπασιν εἶναι γένους ἀτίμου
καὶ καταπεπτωκότος. εἰ γὰρ ἦν, ὥς φησιν Ἰδο-
μενεύς, δοιδυκοποιοῦ πατρός, οὐκ ἂν ἐν τῷ λόγῳ
Γλαύκιππος ὁ Ὑπερείδου μυρία συνειλοχὼς καὶ
εἰρηκὼς κατ' αὐτοῦ κακὰ τὴν δυσγένειαν παρῆκεν, οὐδ' ἂν οὕτως ἐλευθερίου βίου καὶ σώφρονος
παιδείας μετέσχεν ὥστε τῆς Πλάτωνος ἔτι μειράκιον ὤν, ὕστερον δὲ τῆς Ξενοκράτους διατριβῆς,
ἐν Ἀκαδημείᾳ μετασχεῖν, καὶ τῶν ἀρίστων ἐξ
2 ἀρχῆς ἐπιτηδευμάτων ζηλωτὴς γενέσθαι. Φωκίωνα γὰρ οὔτε γελάσαντά τις οὔτε κλαύσαντα
ῥᾳδίως Ἀθηναίων εἶδεν, οὐδ' ἐν βαλανείῳ δημοσι-
εύοντι λουσάμενον, ὡς ἱστόρηκε Δοῦρις, οὐδὲ
ἐκτὸς ἔχοντα τὴν χεῖρα τῆς περιβολῆς, ὅτε τύχοι
περιβεβλημένος. ἐπεὶ κατά γε τὴν χώραν καὶ

between that of Themistocles and that of Aristides; between the justice of one man and that of another, as, between that of Numa and that of Agesilaüs. But the virtues of these men, even down to their ultimate and minute differences, show that their natures had one and the same stamp, shape, and general colour; they were an equal blend, so to speak, of severity and kindness, of caution and bravery, of solicitude for others and fearlessness for themselves, of the careful avoidance of baseness and, in like degree, the eager pursuit of justice. Therefore we shall need a very subtle instrument of reasoning, as it were, for the discovery and determination of their differences.

IV. That Cato's lineage, then, was illustrious, is generally admitted, as will be said later; but Phocion's, as I judge, was not altogether ignoble or lowly. For had he been the son of a pestle-maker, as Idomeneus says, then Glaucippus the son of Hypereides, in the speech wherein he collected countless evil things to say against him, would not have omitted his mean birth; nor would Phocion have lived on so high a plane or enjoyed so sound an education as to have been a pupil of Plato when he was still a stripling, and later a pupil of Xenocrates, in the Academy, and to have cultivated the noblest behaviour from the very beginning. For hardly any Athenian ever saw Phocion in laughter or in tears, or making use of a public bath, as Duris tells us, or holding his hand outside his cloak,—when he wore a cloak. Since in the country, at least, and on his

τὰς στρατείας ἀνυπόδητος ἀεὶ καὶ γυμνὸς ἐβάδιζεν, εἰ μὴ ψῦχος ὑπερβάλλον εἴη καὶ δυσκαρ-
τέρητον, ὥστε καὶ παίζοντας ἤδη τοὺς στρατευο-
μένους σύμβολον μεγάλου ποιεῖσθαι χειμῶνος
ἐνδεδυμένον Φωκίωνα.

V. Τῷ δὲ ἤθει προσηνέστατος ὢν καὶ φιλαν-
θρωπότατος ἀπὸ τοῦ προσώπου δυσξύμβολος
ἐφαίνετο καὶ σκυθρωπός, ὥστε μὴ ῥᾳδίως ἄν τινα
μόνον ἐντυχεῖν αὐτῷ τῶν ἀσυνήθων. διὸ καὶ
Χάρητί ποτε πρὸς τὰς ὀφρῦς αὐτοῦ λέγοντι τῶν
Ἀθηναίων ἐπιγελώντων, " Οὐδέν," εἶπεν, " αὕτη
ὑμᾶς λελύπηκεν ἡ ὀφρύς· ὁ δὲ τούτων γέλως
2 πολλὰ κλαῦσαι τὴν πόλιν πεποίηκεν." ὁμοίως
δέ πως τοῦ Φωκίωνος καὶ ὁ λόγος ἦν ἐπὶ χρη-
στοῖς εὐτυχήμασι καὶ διανοήμασι σωτήριος,
προστακτικὴν τινα καὶ αὐστηρὰν καὶ ἀνήδυντον
ἔχων βραχυλογίαν. ὡς γὰρ ὁ Ζήνων ἔλεγεν ὅτι
δεῖ τὸν φιλόσοφον εἰς νοῦν ἀποβάπτοντα προφέ-
ρεσθαι τὴν λέξιν, οὕτως ὁ Φωκίωνος λόγος πλεῖστον ἐν ἐλαχίστῃ λέξει νοῦν εἶχε. καὶ πρὸς
τοῦτο ἔοικεν ἀπιδὼν ὁ Σφήττιος Πολύευκτος
εἰπεῖν ὅτι ῥήτωρ μὲν ἄριστος εἴη Δημοσθένης,
3 εἰπεῖν δὲ δεινότατος ὁ Φωκίων. ὡς γὰρ ἡ τοῦ
νομίσματος ἀξία πλείστην ἐν ὄγκῳ βραχυτάτῳ
δύναμιν ἔχει, οὕτω λόγου δεινότης ἐδόκει πολλὰ
σημαίνειν ἀπ' ὀλίγων. καὶ μέντοι καὶ αὐτόν
ποτε τὸν Φωκίωνά φασι πληρουμένου τοῦ θεά-
τρου περιπατεῖν ὑπὸ σκηνὴν αὐτὸν ὄντα πρὸς 744
ἑαυτῷ τὴν διάνοιαν· εἰπόντος δέ τινος τῶν φίλων,
" Σκεπτομένῳ, Φωκίων, ἔοικας," " Ναὶ μὰ τὸν
Δία," φάναι, " σκέπτομαι εἴ τι δύναμαι τοῦ λόγου ἀφελεῖν ὃν μέλλω λέγειν πρὸς Ἀθηναίους."

campaigns, he always walked without shoes or outer garment, unless the cold was excessive and hard to bear, so that presently his soldiers used to say in jest that it was a sign of severe winter when Phocion wore a cloak.

V. Though his nature was most gentle and most kind, his countenance made him seem forbidding and sullen, so that hardly any one of those who were not on intimate terms cared to converse with him alone. Therefore, when Chares once made the Athenians laugh by speaking of Phocion's frowning brows, "No harm," said Phocion, "has come to you from this brow of mine; but these men's laughter has cost the city many a tear." And in like manner Phocion's language, also, was salutary in its excellent inventions and happy conceits, although it had a brevity which was rather imperious, severe, and unpleasant. For, as Zeno used to say that a philosopher should immerse his words in meaning before he utters them, so Phocion's language had most meaning in fewest words. And this is probably what Polyeuctus the Sphettian had in mind when he said that Demosthenes was a most excellent orator, but Phocion a most powerful speaker. For, as a valuable coin has greatest worth in smallest bulk, so effective speech would seem to indicate much with few words. Indeed, it is said that once upon a time, when the theatre was filling up with people, Phocion himself was walking about behind the scenes lost in thought, and that when one of his friends remarked: "You seem to be considering, Phocion," he replied: "Yes, indeed, I am considering whether I can shorten the speech which I am to deliver to the Athenians." And

155

4 ὁ δὲ Δημοσθένης τῶν μὲν ἄλλων κατεφρόνει πολὺ ῥητόρων, ἀνισταμένου δὲ Φωκίωνος εἰώθει λέγειν ἀτρέμα πρὸς τοὺς φίλους, "Ἡ τῶν ἐμῶν λόγων κοπὶς πάρεστιν." ἀλλὰ τοῦτο μὲν ἴσως πρὸς τὸ ἦθος ἀνοιστέον· ἐπεὶ καὶ ῥῆμα καὶ νεῦμα μόνον ἀνδρὸς ἀγαθοῦ μυρίοις ἐνθυμήμασι καὶ περιόδοις ἀντίρροπον ἔχει πίστιν.

VI. Νέος δὲ ὢν Χαβρίᾳ προσέμιξεν ἑαυτὸν τῷ στρατηγῷ καὶ παρείπετο, πολλὰ μὲν εἰς ἐμπειρίαν τῶν πολεμικῶν ὠφελούμενος, ἔστι δὲ ἐν οἷς ἐπανορθούμενος τὴν ἐκείνου φύσιν ἀνώμαλον οὖσαν καὶ ἄκρατον. νωθρὸς γὰρ ὢν ὁ Χαβρίας καὶ δυσκίνητος ἄλλως ἐν αὐτοῖς τοῖς ἀγῶσιν ὤργα καὶ διεπυροῦτο τῷ θυμῷ καὶ συνεξέπιπτε τοῖς θρασυτάτοις παραβολώτερον, ὥσπερ ἀμέλει καὶ κατέστρεψε τὸν βίον ἐν Χίῳ πρῶτος εἰσελάσας τῇ τριήρει καὶ βιαζόμενος πρὸς τὴν ἀπό-
2 βασιν. ἀσφαλὴς οὖν ἅμα καὶ δραστήριος ὁ Φωκίων φαινόμενος τήν τε μέλλησιν ἀνεθέρμαινε τοῦ Χαβρίου, καὶ πάλιν ἀφῄρει τὴν ἄκαιρον ὀξύτητα τῆς ὁρμῆς. ὅθεν εὐμενὴς ὢν ὁ Χαβρίας καὶ χρηστός, ἠγάπα καὶ προῆγεν αὐτὸν ἐπὶ πράξεις καὶ ἡγεμονίας, γνώριμον ποιῶν τοῖς Ἕλλησι, καὶ τὰ πλείστης ἄξια σπουδῆς ἐκείνῳ χρώμενος. κἀκ τῆς περὶ Νάξον ναυμαχίας ὄνομα καὶ δόξαν οὐ μικρὰν Φωκίωνι περιεποίησε· τοῦ γὰρ εὐωνύμου κέρως ἀπέδωκεν αὐτῷ τὴν ἡγεμονίαν, καθ' ὃ καὶ τὴν μάχην ὀξεῖαν εἶχεν ὁ ἀγὼν καὶ κρίσιν
3 ἐποίησε ταχεῖαν. πρώτην οὖν ἐκείνην ναυμαχίαν

---

[1] Cf. the *Demosthenes*, x. 2.

Demosthenes, who held the other orators in great contempt, when Phocion rose to speak, was wont to say quietly to his friends: " Here comes the pruning-knife of my speeches." [1] But perhaps this must be referred to Phocion's character ; since a word or a nod merely from a good man is of more convincing weight than any number of elaborate periods.

VI. When he was a young man, Phocion attached himself to Chabrias the general as a close follower. profiting much thereby in military experience, and sometimes also rectifying that general's temperament, which was uneven and violent. For though Chabrias was sluggish and hard to move at other times, in actual battle his spirit was excited and all on fire, and he would rush on with the boldest at too great a hazard, just as, without doubt, he actually threw away his life at Chios [2] by being the first to drive his trireme to shore and trying to force a landing. So then Phocion, who showed himself at once safe and active, would put ardour into Chabrias when he delayed, and again would take away the unseasonable intensity of his efforts. Wherefore Chabrias, who was a good-natured and worthy man, made much of him and advanced him to enterprises and commands, making him known to the Greeks, and employing him in most affairs of moment. Especially in the sea-fight off Naxos [3] he conferred no little name and fame upon Phocion ; for he gave him command of the left wing, and here the battle raged hotly and the issue was speedily decided. Accordingly, as this was the first sea-fight which the

[2] In 357 B.C.   Chios, Rhodes, and Byzantium had revolted from Athens.

[3] In 376 B.C.   The Athenians defeated the Lacedaemonian fleet and regained the mastery of the sea.

ἡ πόλις αὐτὴ δι' αὐτῆς ἀγωνισαμένη τοῖς Ἕλλησι
μετὰ τὴν ἅλωσιν, καὶ κατατυχοῦσα, τόν τε Χαβρίαν ὑπερηγάπησε καὶ τοῦ Φωκίωνος ὡς ἀνδρὸς
ἡγεμονικοῦ λόγον ἔσχεν. ἐνίκων δὲ μεγάλοις
μυστηρίοις· καὶ παρεῖχεν οἰνοχόημα Χαβρίας
Ἀθηναίοις καθ' ἕκαστον ἐνιαυτὸν τῇ ἕκτῃ ἐπὶ
δέκα τοῦ Βοηδρομιῶνος.

VII. Ἐκ τούτου λέγεται πέμποντος αὐτὸν ἐπὶ
τὰς νησιωτικὰς συντάξεις τοῦ Χαβρίου καὶ ναῦς
εἴκοσι διδόντος εἰπεῖν, εἰ μὲν ὡς πολεμήσων πέμ-
ποιτο, μείζονος δεῖν δυνάμεως, εἰ δὲ ὡς πρὸς
συμμάχους, ἀρκεῖν ναῦν μίαν· καὶ πλεύσαντα τῇ
αὑτοῦ τριήρει καὶ διαλεχθέντα ταῖς πόλεσι καὶ
συγγενόμενον τοῖς ἄρχουσιν ἐπιεικῶς καὶ ἀφελῶς
καταπλεῦσαι μετὰ πολλῶν νεῶν, ἃς ἀπέστειλαν
οἱ σύμμαχοι τὰ χρήματα τοῖς Ἀθηναίοις κομι-
2 ζούσας. οὐ μόνον δὲ ζῶντα τὸν Χαβρίαν θεραπεύων διετέλει καὶ τιμῶν, ἀλλὰ καὶ τελευτήσαντος
αὐτοῦ τῶν προσηκόντων καλῶς ἐπεμελεῖτο, καὶ
τὸν παῖδα Κτήσιππον ἐβούλετο μὲν ἄνδρα ποιεῖν
ἀγαθόν, ἔμπληκτον δὲ ὁρῶν καὶ ἀνάγωγον ὅμως
οὐκ ἀπεῖπεν ἐπανορθούμενος καὶ ἀποκρύπτων τὰ
αἴσχη. πλὴν ἅπαξ λέγεται, παρενοχλοῦντος ἐν
στρατείᾳ τινὶ τοῦ νεανίσκου καὶ κόπτοντος αὐτὸν
ἐρωτήμασιν ἀκαίροις καὶ συμβουλίαις οἷον ἐπαν-
ορθουμένου καὶ παραστρατηγοῦντος, εἰπεῖν·
"Ὦ Χαβρία, Χαβρία, μεγάλην γέ σοι χάριν
ἐκτίνω τῆς φιλίας ὑπομένων σου τὸν υἱόν."

Athenians had fought with the Greeks on their own account since the capture of their city,[1] and as it had succeeded, they made exceeding much of Chabrias, and came to look upon Phocion as a man fit for command. They won the victory during the celebration of the great mysteries; and therefore Chabrias used to furnish the Athenians with wine for the festival every year on the sixteenth of the month Boëdromion.

VII. Afterwards, we are told, when Chabrias sent him to get their contributions from the islanders and offered him twenty ships, Phocion said that if he was sent to wage war, he needed a larger force, but if to confer with allies, one ship was enough; and after sailing out with his own trireme and discussing matters with the cities and dealing with the magistrates considerately and in a straightforward manner, he returned with many ships, which the allies sent off with money for the Athenians. And not only while Chabrias was alive did Phocion continue to show him attention and honour, but also after his death he took good care of his relatives, and especially of his son Ctesippus, whom he wished to make a good man; and although he saw that the youth was capricious and intractable, he nevertheless persisted in correcting and covering up his disgraceful conduct. Once, however, we are told, when the young man was troublesome to him on an expedition, and plied him with unseasonable questions and advice, like one making corrections and sharing in the command, he cried: "O Chabrias, Chabrias, surely I make thee a large return for thy friendship in enduring thy son."

---

[1] At the close of the Peloponnesian war (404 B.C.).

3 Ὁρῶν δὲ τοὺς τὰ κοινὰ πράσσοντας τότε διῃ-
ρημένους ὥσπερ ἀπὸ κλήρου τὸ στρατήγιον καὶ
τὸ βῆμα, καὶ τοὺς μὲν λέγοντας ἐν τῷ δήμῳ καὶ
γράφοντας μόνον, ὧν Εὔβουλος ἦν καὶ Ἀριστοφῶν
καὶ Δημοσθένης καὶ Λυκοῦργος καὶ Ὑπερείδης,
Διοπείθην δὲ καὶ Μενεσθέα καὶ Λεωσθένην καὶ
Χάρητα τῷ στρατηγεῖν καὶ πολεμεῖν αὔξοντας
ἑαυτούς, ἐβούλετο τὴν Περικλέους καὶ Ἀριστείδου καὶ Σόλωνος πολιτείαν ὥσπερ ὁλόκληρον
καὶ διηρμοσμένην ἐν ἀμφοῖν ἀναλαβεῖν καὶ ἀποδοῦναι. καὶ γὰρ τῶν ἀνδρῶν ἐκείνων ἕκαστος 745
ἐφαίνετο κατὰ τὸν Ἀρχίλοχον,[1]

Ἀμφότερον, θεράπων μὲν Ἐνναλίοιο θεοῖο,
καὶ Μουσέων ἐρατὸν δῶρον ἐπιστάμενος·

καὶ τὴν θεὸν ἑώρα πολεμικήν τε ἅμα καὶ πολιτι-
κὴν οὖσαν καὶ προσαγορευομένην.

VIII. Οὕτω δὲ συντάξας ἑαυτὸν ἐπολιτεύετο
μὲν ἀεὶ πρὸς εἰρήνην καὶ ἡσυχίαν, ἐστρατήγησε
δὲ πλείστας οὐ μόνον τῶν καθ᾽ ἑαυτόν, ἀλλὰ καὶ
τῶν πρὸ αὐτοῦ στρατηγίας, οὐ παραγγέλλων οὐδὲ
μετιών, ἀλλ᾽ οὐδὲ φεύγων οὐδὲ ἀποδιδράσκων τῆς
πόλεως καλούσης. ὁμολογεῖται γὰρ ὅτι πέντε
καὶ τεσσαράκοντα στρατηγίας ἔλαβεν οὐδ᾽ ἅπαξ
ἀρχαιρεσίοις παρατυχών, ἀλλ᾽ ἀπόντα μεταπεμ-
2 πομένων αὐτὸν ἀεὶ καὶ χειροτονούντων, ὥστε
θαυμάζειν τοὺς οὐκ εὖ φρονοῦντας τὸν δῆμον ὅτι,
πλεῖστα τοῦ Φωκίωνος ἀντικρούοντος αὐτῷ καὶ
μηδὲν εἰπόντος πώποτε μηδὲ πράξαντος πρὸς
χάριν, ὥσπερ ἀξιοῦσι τοὺς βασιλεῖς τοῖς κόλαξι

[1] Bergk, Poet. Lyr. Graeci, ii.⁴, p. 383 (εἰμὶ δ᾽ ἐγὼ θεράπων
. . . ἐρατόν).

He saw that the public men of his day had distributed among themselves as if by lot the work of the general and the orator. Some of them merely spoke before the people and introduced measures,— men like Eubulus, Aristophon, Demosthenes, Lycurgus, and Hypereides; while such men as Diopeithes, Menestheus, Leosthenes, and Chabrias advanced themselves by holding the office of general and waging war. He therefore wished to resume and restore the public service rendered by Pericles, Aristides, and Solon, which was equally apportioned in both fields of action. For each of those men showed himself to be, in the words of Archilochus,

"As well a squire of Enyalius god of war,
    As versed in the lovely Muses' gifts."

He also saw that the goddess Athena was a goddess of war as well as of statecraft, and was so addressed.

VIII. Having taken this stand, his civil policies were always in favour of peace and quiet; and yet he held the office of general more frequently than any man, and I speak not only of the men of his own time, but also of those who came before him. He did not seek the office or canvass for it; nor, on the other hand, did he flee or run away when his city called him. It is generally admitted, indeed, that he held the office of general forty-five times, although he was not even once present at the election, but was always absent when the people summoned and chose him. Therefore men of little understanding are amazed at the conduct of the Athenian people. For Phocion opposed them more than anybody else, and never said or did anything to win their favour; and yet, just as kings are

χρῆσθαι μετὰ τὸ κατὰ χειρὸς ὕδωρ, ἐχρῆτο οὗτος
τοῖς μὲν κομψοτέροις καὶ ἱλαροῖς ἐν παιδιᾶς μέρει
δημαγωγοῖς, ἐπὶ δὲ τὰς ἀρχὰς ἀεὶ νήφων καὶ
σπουδάζων τὸν αὐστηρότατον καὶ φρονιμώτατον
ἐκάλει τῶν πολιτῶν καὶ μόνον ἢ μᾶλλον ταῖς
βουλήσεσιν αὐτοῦ καὶ ὁρμαῖς ἀντιτασσόμενον.
3 χρησμοῦ μὲν γὰρ ἐκ Δελφῶν ἀναγνωσθέντος ὅτι,
τῶν ἄλλων Ἀθηναίων ὁμοφρονούντων, εἷς ἀνὴρ
ἐναντία φρονοίη τῇ πόλει, παρελθὼν ὁ Φωκίων
ἀμελεῖν ἐκέλευσεν, ὡς αὐτὸς ὢν ὁ ζητούμενος·
μόνῳ γὰρ αὐτῷ μηδὲν ἀρέσκειν τῶν πραττομένων.
ἐπεὶ δὲ λέγων ποτὲ γνώμην πρὸς τὸν δῆμον εὐ-
δοκίμει καὶ πάντας ὁμαλῶς ἑώρα τὸν λόγον ἀπο-
δεχομένους, ἐπιστραφεὶς πρὸς τοὺς φίλους εἶπεν·
" Οὐ δή πού τι κακὸν λέγων ἐμαυτὸν λέληθα; "

IX. Πρὸς δὲ θυσίαν τινὰ τῶν Ἀθηναίων αἰ-
τούντων ἐπιδόσεις, καὶ τῶν ἄλλων ἐπιδιδόντων,
κληθεὶς πολλάκις ἔφη· " Τούτους αἰτεῖτε τοὺς
πλουσίους· ἐγὼ δὲ αἰσχυνοίμην ἄν, εἰ τούτῳ μὴ
ἀποδιδοὺς ὑμῖν ἐπιδοίην," δείξας Καλλικλέα τὸν
δανειστήν. ὡς δ' οὐκ ἐπαύοντο κεκραγότες καὶ
2 καταβοῶντες, λόγον εἶπεν αὐτοῖς τοῦτον· " Ἀνὴρ
δειλὸς ἐπὶ πόλεμον ἐξῄει, φθεγξαμένων δὲ κορά-
κων τὰ ὅπλα θεὶς ἡσύχαζεν· εἶτα ἀναλαβὼν
αὖθις ἐξῄει, καὶ φθεγγομένων πάλιν ὑπέστη, καὶ
τέλος εἶπεν· ' Ὑμεῖς κεκράξεσθε μὲν μέγιστον ὡς

supposed to listen to their flatterers after dinner has begun, so the Athenians made use of their more elegant and sprightly leaders by way of diversion, but when they wanted a commander they were always sober and serious, and called upon the severest and most sensible citizen, one who alone, or more than the rest, arrayed himself against their desires and impulses. Indeed, when an oracle from Delphi was read out in the assembly, declaring that when the rest of the Athenians were of like mind, one man had a mind at variance with the city, Phocion came forward and bade them seek no further, since he himself was the man in question; for there was no one but he who disliked everything they did. And when, as he was once delivering an opinion to the people, he met with their approval, and saw that all alike accepted his argument, he turned to his friends and said : "Can it possibly be that I am making a bad argument without knowing it ? "

IX. The Athenians were once asking contributions[1] for a public sacrifice, and the rest were contributing, but Phocion, after being many times asked to give, said : "Ask from these rich men; for I should be ashamed to make a contribution to you before I have paid my debt to this man here," pointing to Callicles the money-lender. And once when his audience would not cease shouting and crying him down, he told them this fable. "A coward was going forth to war, but when some ravens croaked, he laid down his arms and kept quiet; then he picked them up and was going forth again, and when the ravens croaked once more, he stopped, and said at last : 'You may croak with all

[1] Cf. the *Alcibiades*, x. 1.

δυνατόν, ἐμοῦ δὲ οὐ γεύσεσθε.'" πάλιν δέ ποτε
τῶν Ἀθηναίων ἐξαγαγεῖν αὐτὸν ἐπὶ τοὺς πολεμίους κελευόντων, ὡς δ᾽ οὐκ ἐβούλετο, δειλὸν καὶ
ἄνανδρον ἀποκαλούντων, "Οὔτε ὑμεῖς," εἶπεν,
"ἐμὲ δύνασθε ποιῆσαι θαρσαλέον οὔτε ἐγὼ ὑμᾶς
3 δειλούς. οὐ μὴν ἀλλ᾽ ἴσμεν ἀλλήλους." ἐν δὲ
καιροῖς ἐπισφαλέσι τραχυνομένου τοῦ δήμου
πρὸς αὐτὸν σφόδρα καὶ τῆς στρατηγίας εὐθύνας
ἀπαιτοῦντος, "Σωθείητε," εἶπεν, "ὦ μακάριοι,
πρῶτον." ἐπεὶ δὲ πολεμοῦντες μὲν ἦσαν ταπεινοὶ
καὶ περιδεεῖς, γενομένης δὲ εἰρήνης ἐθρασύνοντο
καὶ κατεβόων τοῦ Φωκίωνος ὡς ἀφῃρημένου τὴν
νίκην αὐτῶν, "Εὐτυχεῖτε," εἶπεν, "ἔχοντες
στρατηγὸν εἰδότα ὑμᾶς· ἐπεὶ πάλαι ἂν ἀπωλώ-
4 λειτε." τοῖς δὲ Βοιωτοῖς οὐ βουλομένων αὐτῶν
δικάζεσθαι περὶ τῆς χώρας, ἀλλὰ πολεμεῖν,
συνεβούλευε διὰ τῶν λόγων, ἐν οἷς εἰσι κρείττους,
μὴ διὰ τῶν ὅπλων, ἐν οἷς εἰσιν ἥττους, μάχεσθαι.
λέγοντα δὲ αὐτὸν οὐ προσιεμένων οὐδὲ ὑπομενόν-
των ἀκούειν, "Ἐμέ," εἶπεν, "ὑμεῖς ἃ μὴ βούλομαι ποιεῖν βιάσασθαι δύνασθε, λέγειν δὲ ἃ μὴ
5 δεῖ παρὰ γνώμην οὐκ ἀναγκάσετε." τῶν δὲ
ἀντιπολιτευομένων αὐτῷ ῥητόρων Δημοσθένους
μὲν εἰπόντος, "Ἀποκτενοῦσί σε Ἀθηναῖοι, Φω- 746
κίων, ἂν μανῶσιν," εἶπε· "Σὲ δέ, ἂν σωφρονῶσι·"
Πολύευκτον δὲ τὸν Σφήττιον ὁρῶν ἐν καύματι
συμβουλεύοντα τοῖς Ἀθηναίοις πολεμεῖν πρὸς
Φίλιππον, εἶτα ὑπ᾽ ἄσθματος πολλοῦ καὶ ἱδρῶ-
τος, ἅτε δὴ καὶ ὑπέρπαχυν ὄντα, πολλάκις ἐπιρ-

your might, but you shall not get a taste of me.'"
And at another time, when the Athenians urged him
to lead forth against the enemy, and called him an
unmanly coward because he did not wish to do so,
he said: "Ye cannot make me bold, nor can I make
you cowards. However, we know one another."
And again, in a time of peril, when the people were
behaving very harshly towards him and demanding
that he render up accounts of his generalship, "My
good friends," said he, "make sure of your safety
first." Again, when they had been humble and
timorous during a war, but then, after peace had
been made, were getting bold and denouncing
Phocion on the ground that he had robbed them
of the victory, "Ye are fortunate," said he, "in
having a general who knows you; since otherwise
ye had long ago perished." Once, too, when the
people were unwilling to adjudicate with the Boeotians a question of territory, but wanted to go to
war about it, he counselled them to fight with words,
in which they were superior, and not with arms, in
which they were inferior. Again, when he was
speaking and they would not heed or even consent
to hear him, he said: "Ye can force me to act
against my wishes, but ye shall not compel me to
speak against my judgement." And when Demosthenes, one of the orators in opposition to him, said
to him, "The Athenians will kill thee, Phocion,
should they go crazy," he replied: "But they will
kill thee, should they come to their senses." Again,
when he saw Polyeuctus the Sphettian, on a hot
day, counselling the Athenians to go to war with
Philip, and then, from much panting and sweating,
since he was really very corpulent, frequently gulp-

ροφοῦντα τοῦ ὕδατος "Ἄξιον," ἔφη, "τούτῳ
πιστεύσαντας ὑμᾶς ψηφίσασθαι τὸν πόλεμον, ὃν
τί οἴεσθε ποιήσειν ἐν τῷ θώρακι καὶ τῇ ἀσπίδι,
τῶν πολεμίων ἐγγὺς ὄντων, ὅτε λέγων πρὸς ὑμᾶς
6 ἃ ἔσκεπται κινδυνεύει πνιγῆναι;" τοῦ δὲ Λυκούρ-
γου πολλὰ βλάσφημα πρὸς αὐτὸν εἰπόντος ἐν
ἐκκλησίᾳ, καὶ πρὸς ἅπασιν ὅτι, δέκα τῶν πολιτῶν ἐξαιτοῦντος Ἀλεξάνδρου, συνεβούλευεν ἐκ-
δοῦναι, εἶπε· "Πολλὰ ἐγὼ συμβεβούλευκα καλὰ
καὶ συμφέροντα τούτοις, ἀλλ' οὐ πείθονταί μοι."

X. Ἦν δέ τις Ἀρχιβιάδης ἐπικαλούμενος
Λακωνιστής, πώγωνά τε καθειμένος ὑπερφυῆ
μεγέθει καὶ τρίβωνα φορῶν ἀεὶ καὶ σκυθρωπάζων·
τοῦτον ἐν βουλῇ θορυβούμενος ὁ Φωκίων ἐπεκαλεῖτο τῷ λόγῳ μάρτυν ἅμα καὶ βοηθόν. ὡς δὲ
ἀναστὰς ἐκεῖνος ἃ πρὸς χάριν ἦν τοῖς Ἀθηναίοις
συνεβούλευεν, ἁψάμενος αὐτοῦ τῶν γενείων· "Ὦ
Ἀρχιβιάδη," εἶπε, "τί οὖν οὐκ ἀπεκείρω;"
2 Ἀριστογείτονος δὲ τοῦ συκοφάντου πολεμικοῦ
μὲν ὄντος ἐν ταῖς ἐκκλησίαις καὶ παροξύνοντος
ἐπὶ τὰς πράξεις τὸν δῆμον, ἐν δὲ τῷ καταλόγῳ
προσελθόντος ἐπὶ βακτηρίᾳ τὼ σκέλη καταδε-
δεμένου, πόρρωθεν αὐτὸν ἀπὸ τοῦ βήματος ἰδὼν
ὁ Φωκίων ἀνέκραγε· "Γράφε καὶ Ἀριστογείτονα
χωλὸν καὶ πονηρόν." ὥστε θαυμάζειν ὅπως καὶ
ὁπόθεν τραχὺς οὕτως ἀνὴρ καὶ σκυθρωπὸς ἐκτή-
σατο τὴν τοῦ χρηστοῦ προσηγορίαν.

3 Ἔστι δέ, οἶμαι, χαλεπόν, οὐ μὴν ἀδύνατον,

ing down water, Phocion said : "It is meet that ye should be persuaded by this man to go to war ; for what do ye think he would do under breastplate and shield, when the enemy were near, if, in making you a premeditated speech, he is in danger of choking to death?" At another time Lycurgus heaped much abuse upon him in the assembly, and above all because, when Alexander demanded ten of the citizens of Athens,[1] Phocion counselled their surrender ; Phocion, however, merely said : "I have given this people much good and profitable counsel, but they will not listen to me."

X. There was a certain Archibiades, nicknamed Laconistes, because, in imitation of the Spartans, he let his beard grow to an extravagant size, always wore a short cloak, and had a scowl on his face. Phocion was once stormily interrupted in the council, and called upon this man for testimony and support in what he said. But when the man rose up and gave such counsel as was pleasing to the Athenians, Phocion seized him by the beard and said : "O Archibiades, why, then, didst thou not shave thyself?" Again, when Aristogeiton the public informer, who was always warlike in the assemblies and tried to urge the people on to action, came to the place of muster leaning on a staff and with both legs bandaged, Phocion spied him from the tribunal when he was afar off, and cried out : "Put down Aristogeiton, too, as lame and worthless." So that one might wonder how and why a man so harsh and stern got the surname of The Good.

But though it is difficult, it is not impossible, I

[1] Cf. chapter xvii. 2 f.

ὥσπερ οἶνον, καὶ ἄνθρωπον τὸν αὐτὸν ἡδὺν ἅμα
καὶ αὐστηρὸν εἶναι· καθάπερ ἕτεροι πάλιν, φαινό-
μενοι γλυκεῖς, ἀηδέστατοι τοῖς χρωμένοις εἰσὶ
καὶ βλαβερώτατοι. καίτοι φασὶν Ὑπερείδην
ποτὲ εἰπεῖν πρὸς τὸν δῆμον, "Ἄνδρες Ἀθηναῖοι,
μὴ σκοπεῖτε μόνον εἰ πικρός, ἀλλ᾽ εἰ προῖκά εἰμι
πικρός," ὥσπερ τῇ πλεονεξίᾳ μόνον ἐπαχθεῖς καὶ
λυπηροὺς ὄντας, οὐχὶ μᾶλλον, ὅσοι πρὸς ὕβριν
καὶ φθόνον ἢ ὀργὴν ἢ φιλονεικίαν τινὰ χρῶνται
τῷ δύνασθαι, τούτους δεδιότων καὶ προβαλλομέ-
4 νων τῶν πολλῶν. Φωκίων τοίνυν ἔχθρα μὲν
οὐδένα τῶν πολιτῶν κακῶς ἐποίησεν, οὐδὲ ἐνόμιζεν ἐχθρόν· ἀλλ᾽ ὅσον ἔδει μόνον τῶν ἐνισταμένων οἷς ἔπραττεν ὑπὲρ τῆς πατρίδος κατεξανα-
στῆναι τραχὺς ὢν καὶ δυσεκβίαστος καὶ ἀπαραί-
τητος, εἰς τὸν ἄλλον βίον εὐμενῆ πᾶσι καὶ κοινὸν
καὶ φιλάνθρωπον ἑαυτὸν παρεῖχεν, ὥστε καὶ
πταίσασι βοηθεῖν καὶ κινδυνεύουσι συνεξετάζε-
5 σθαι τοῖς διαφόροις. ἐγκαλούντων δὲ τῶν φίλων
ὅτι πονηρῷ τινι κρινομένῳ συνεῖπε, τοὺς χρη-
στοὺς ἔφη μὴ δεῖσθαι βοηθείας. Ἀριστογείτονος
δὲ τοῦ συκοφάντου μετὰ τὴν καταδίκην πέμψαντος καὶ δεηθέντος ἐλθεῖν πρὸς αὐτόν, ὑπακούσας
ἐβάδιζεν εἰς τὸ δεσμωτήριον· οὐκ ἐώντων δὲ τῶν
φίλων, "Ἐάσατε," εἶπεν, "ὦ μακάριοι· ποῦ γὰρ
ἄν τις ἥδιον Ἀριστογείτονι συμβάλοι;"

XI. Καὶ μὴν οἵ γε σύμμαχοι καὶ οἱ νησιῶται
τοὺς Ἀθήνηθεν ἀποστόλους ἑτέρου μὲν ἐκπλέον-
τος στρατηγοῦ πολεμίους νομίζοντες ἐφράγνυντο

think, for the same man, like the same wine, to be at once pleasant and austere; just as others, on the contrary, appear to be sweet, but are most unpleasant to those who use them, and most injurious. And yet we are told that Hypereides once said to the people: "Do not ask, men of Athens, merely whether I am bitter, but whether I am paid for being bitter," as if the multitude were led by their avarice to fear and attack those only who are troublesome and vexatious, and not rather all who use their power to gratify their insolence or envy or wrath or contentiousness. Phocion, then, wrought no injury to any one of his fellow citizens out of enmity, nor did he regard any one of them as his enemy; but he was harsh, obstinate, and inexorable only so far as was necessary to struggle successfully against those who opposed his efforts in behalf of the country, and in other relations of life showed himself well-disposed to all, accessible, and humane, so that he even gave aid to his adversaries when they were in trouble or in danger of being brought to account. When his friends chided him for pleading the cause of some worthless man, he said that good men needed no aid. Again, when Aristogeiton the public informer, who was under condemnation, sent and asked him to come to him, he obeyed the summons and set out for the prison; and when his friends sought to prevent him, he said: "Let me go, my good men; for where could one take greater pleasure in meeting Aristogeiton?"

XI. And certainly the allies and the islanders regarded envoys from Athens under the conduct of any other general as enemies, barricading their

τείχη καὶ λιμένας ἀπεχώννυσαν καὶ κατεκόμιζον
ἀπὸ τῆς χώρας εἰς τὰς πόλεις βοσκήματα καὶ
ἀνδράποδα καὶ γυναῖκας καὶ παῖδας· εἰ δὲ Φωκίων
ἡγοῖτο, πόρρω ναυσὶν ἰδίαις ἀπαντῶντες ἐστε-
φανωμένοι καὶ χαίροντες ὡς αὑτοὺς κατῆγον.

XII. Παραδυομένου δὲ εἰς τὴν Εὔβοιαν τοῦ
Φιλίππου καὶ δύναμιν ἐκ Μακεδονίας διαβιβά-
ζοντος καὶ τὰς πόλεις οἰκειουμένου διὰ τυράννων,
Πλουτάρχου δὲ τοῦ Ἐρετριέως καλοῦντος τοὺς 747
Ἀθηναίους καὶ δεομένου τὴν νῆσον ἐξελέσθαι
καταλαμβανομένην ὑπὸ τοῦ Μακεδόνος, ἀπεστάλη στρατηγὸς ὁ Φωκίων ἔχων δύναμιν οὐ πολλήν,
ὡς τῶν ἐκεῖ συστησομένων ἑτοίμως πρὸς αὐτόν.
2 εὑρὼν δὲ προδοτῶν ἅπαντα μεστὰ καὶ νοσοῦντα
καὶ διορωρυγμένα δωροδοκίαις εἰς κίνδυνον μέγαν
κατέστη· καί τινα λόφον χαράδρᾳ βαθείᾳ τῶν
περὶ τὰς Ταμύνας ἐπιπέδων ἀποκρυπτόμενον
καταλαβὼν συνεῖχεν ἐν τούτῳ καὶ συνεκράτει τὸ
3 μαχιμώτατον τῆς δυνάμεως. τῶν δὲ ἀτάκτων
καὶ λάλων καὶ πονηρῶν διαδιδρασκόντων ἐκ τοῦ
στρατοπέδου καὶ ἀποχωρούντων ἐκέλευσεν ἀμελεῖν τοὺς ἡγεμόνας· καὶ γὰρ ἐνταῦθα δυσχρή-
στους ὑπὸ ἀταξίας ἔσεσθαι καὶ βλαβεροὺς τοῖς
μαχομένοις, κἀκεῖ τοιαῦτα συνειδότας αὑτοῖς
ἧττον αὐτοῦ καταβοήσεσθαι καὶ μὴ πάνυ συκο-
φαντήσειν.

XIII. Ὡς δὲ ἐπῄεσαν οἱ πολέμιοι, κελεύσας ἐν
τοῖς ὅπλοις ἀτρεμεῖν ἄχρι ἂν αὐτὸς σφαγιάσηται,
πλείω διέτριβε χρόνον ἢ δυσιερῶν ἢ βουλόμενος
ἐγγυτέρω τοὺς πολεμίους ἐπισπάσασθαι. διὸ
πρῶτον μὲν ὁ Πλούταρχος οἰόμενος ἀποδειλιᾶν

gates, obstructing their harbours, and bringing into their cities from the country their herds, slaves, women and children; but whenever Phocion was the leader, they went far out to meet him in their own ships, wearing garlands and rejoicing, and conducted him to their homes themselves.

XII. When Philip was stealing into Euboea and bringing a force across from Macedonia and making the cities his own by means of tyrants, and when Plutarch the Eretrian called upon the Athenians and begged them to rescue the island from its occupation by the Macedonian, Phocion was sent out as general with a small force,[1] in the belief that the people of the island would rally readily to his aid. But he found the whole island full of traitors, disaffected, and honeycombed with bribery, and was therefore in a position of great peril. So he took possession of a crest of ground which was separated by a deep ravine from the plains about Tamynae, and on this assembled and held together the best fighting men of his force. To the disorderly and worthless triflers who ran away from the camp and made their way home he bade his officers give no heed, for in the camp their lack of discipline would make them useless and harmful to the fighting men, while at home their accusing consciences would make them less liable to cry down their commander, and would keep them entirely from malicious accusations.

XIII. When the enemy came up against him, he ordered his men to remain quietly under arms until he should have finished sacrificing, and then waited a considerable time, either because the omens were bad, or because he wished to draw the enemy nearer. Therefore, to begin with, Plutarch, who

[1] In 350 b.c.

καὶ κατοκνεῖν ἐκεῖνον ἐξέδραμε μετὰ τῶν ξένων·
ἔπειτα τοῦτον ἰδόντες οἱ ἱππεῖς οὐκ ἐκαρτέρησαν,
ἀλλ' ἤλαυνον εὐθὺς εἰς τοὺς πολεμίους ἀσύντα-
κτοι καὶ σποράδες ἐκ τοῦ στρατοπέδου προσφερό-
2 μενοι. νικωμένων δὲ τῶν πρώτων ἅπαντες ἐσκε-
δάσθησαν καὶ ὁ Πλούταρχος ἔφυγε· καὶ τῷ
χάρακι προσμίξαντες ἔνιοι τῶν πολεμίων ἐκκό-
πτειν ἐπειρῶντο καὶ διασπᾶν ὡς ἁπάντων κεκρα-
τηκότες. ἐν τούτῳ δὲ τῶν ἱερῶν γενομένων, τοὺς
μὲν εὐθὺς ἐκ τοῦ στρατοπέδου προσπεσόντες οἱ
Ἀθηναῖοι τρέπουσι καὶ καταβάλλουσι τοὺς
πλείστους περὶ τοῖς ἐρύμασι φεύγοντας, ὁ δὲ
Φωκίων τὴν μὲν φάλαγγα προσέταξεν ἐφεδρεύειν
ἀναλαμβάνουσαν ἅμα καὶ προσδεχομένην τοὺς
ἐν τῇ φυγῇ πρότερον διασπαρέντας, αὐτὸς δὲ
τοὺς ἐπιλέκτους ἔχων ἐνέβαλε τοῖς πολεμίοις.
3 καὶ μάχης καρτερᾶς γενομένης πάντες μὲν ἐκθύ-
μως ἠγωνίσαντο καὶ ἀφειδῶς, Θάλλος δὲ ὁ Κινέου
καὶ Γλαῦκος ὁ Πολυμήδους περὶ αὐτὸν τεταγμένοι τὸν στρατηγὸν ἠρίστευσαν. οὐ μὴν ἀλλὰ καὶ
Κλεοφάνης ἄξιον πλείστου παρέσχεν ἑαυτὸν ἐν
ἐκείνῃ τῇ μάχῃ. τοὺς γὰρ ἱππεῖς ἀνακαλούμενος
ἐκ τῆς τροπῆς καὶ βοῶν καὶ διακελευόμενος κιν-
δυνεύοντι τῷ στρατηγῷ βοηθεῖν, ἐποίησεν ἀνα-
στρέψαντας ἐπιρρῶσαι τὸ νίκημα τῶν ὁπλιτῶν.
4 Ἐκ τούτου τόν τε Πλούταρχον ἐξέβαλεν ἐκ
τῆς Ἐρετρίας, καὶ Ζάρητρα φρούριον ἑλὼν ἐπι-
καιρότατον, ᾗ μάλιστα συνελαύνεται τὸ πλάτος
εἰς βραχὺ διάζωμα τῆς νήσου σφιγγομένης ἑκατέρωθεν ταῖς θαλάσσαις, ὅσους ἔλαβεν αἰχμαλώτους Ἕλληνας ἀφῆκε, φοβηθεὶς τοὺς ῥήτορας
τῶν Ἀθηναίων, μὴ πρὸς ὀργήν τι βιάσωνται τὸν
δῆμον ἀγνωμονῆσαι περὶ αὐτούς.

thought that Phocion's delay was due to cowardice, sallied forth with his mercenaries. Next, the horsemen, catching sight of Plutarch, could not restrain themselves, but rode at once into the enemy, hurrying out of the camp in a disorderly and scattered fashion. The foremost of them were conquered, and then all of them dispersed and Plutarch took to flight, while some of the enemy gained the ramparts and tried to cut them away and destroy them, supposing themselves to be entirely victorious. But at this point the sacrifices were completed, and the Athenians, bursting out of their camp, routed their assailants and slew most of them as they fled among the entrenchments. Then Phocion ordered his phalanx to halt for the reception and support of the troops which had been scattered in the previous flight, while he himself with his picked men fell upon the main body of the enemy. A fierce battle ensued, in which all the Athenians fought with spirit and gallantry; but Thallus the son of Cineas and Glaucus the son of Polymedes, whose post was at their general's side, bore away the palm. However, Cleophanes also did most valuable service in that battle. For, by calling back the cavalry from their flight and exhorting them with loud cries to succour their general in his peril, he made them turn back and confirm the victory of the men-at-arms.

After this, Phocion expelled Plutarch from Eretria, took possession of Zaretra, a fortress most advantageously situated where the island is reduced to its narrowest width by the sea, which hems it in on both sides, and released all the Greeks whom he had taken prisoners. For he was afraid that the orators at Athens might drive the people, in some fit of anger, to treat them with cruelty.

173

XIV. Ἐπεὶ δὲ ταῦτα διαπραξάμενος ἀπέπλευσεν ὁ Φωκίων, ταχὺ μὲν ἐπόθησαν οἱ σύμμαχοι τὴν χρηστότητα καὶ δικαιοσύνην αὐτοῦ, ταχὺ δὲ ἔγνωσαν οἱ Ἀθηναῖοι τὴν ἐμπειρίαν καὶ ῥώμην τοῦ ἀνδρός. ὁ γὰρ μετ᾿ ἐκεῖνον ἐλθὼν ἐπὶ τὰ πράγματα Μολοσσὸς οὕτως ἐπολέμησεν ὥστε καὶ ζῶν αὐτὸς ὑποχείριος γενέσθαι τοῖς πολεμίοις.

2 ἐπεὶ δὲ μεγάλα ταῖς ἐλπίσι περινοῶν ὁ Φίλιππος εἰς Ἑλλήσποντον ἦλθε μετὰ πάσης τῆς δυνάμεως, ὡς Χερρόνησον ἐν ταὐτῷ καὶ Πέρινθον ἕξων καὶ Βυζάντιον, ὡρμημένων δὲ τῶν Ἀθηναίων βοηθεῖν οἱ ῥήτορες ἠγωνίσαντο τὸν Χάρητα στρατηγὸν ἀποσταλῆναι, καὶ πλεύσας ἐκεῖνος οὐδὲν ἄξιον τῆς δυνάμεως ἔπραττεν, οὐδὲ αἱ πόλεις ἐδέχοντο τὸν στόλον, ἀλλ᾿ ὕποπτος ὢν πᾶσιν ἐπλανᾶτο χρηματιζόμενος ἀπὸ τῶν συμμάχων καὶ κατα-

3 φρονούμενος ὑπὸ τῶν πολεμίων, ὁ δὲ δῆμος ὑπὸ τῶν ῥητόρων παροξυνόμενος ἠγανάκτει καὶ μετενόει τοῖς Βυζαντίοις πέμψας τὴν βοήθειαν, ἀναστὰς ὁ Φωκίων εἶπεν ὅτι δεῖ μὴ τοῖς ἀπιστοῦσιν ὀργίζεσθαι τῶν συμμάχων, ἀλλὰ τοῖς ἀπιστουμένοις τῶν στρατηγῶν· "Οὗτοι γὰρ ὑμᾶς ποιοῦσι φοβεροὺς καὶ τοῖς χωρὶς ὑμῶν σώζεσθαι μὴ δυναμένοις."

Κινηθεὶς οὖν ὁ δῆμος ὑπὸ τοῦ λόγου καὶ μεταπεσὼν ἐκέλευεν αὐτὸν ἐκεῖνον ἑτέραν προσλαβόντα δύναμιν βοηθεῖν τοῖς συμμάχοις εἰς τὸν Ἑλλήσποντον· ὃ μεγίστην ῥοπὴν ἐποίησε πρὸς

174

XIV. After these things had been accomplished, Phocion sailed back home, and then the allies speedily felt the absence of his probity and justice, and speedily did the Athenians recognize the experience and vigour which had been shown by him. For his successor in command, Molossus, conducted the war in such a way as actually to fall alive into the hands of the enemy. And now Philip, cherishing great anticipations, went to the Hellespont with all his forces,[1] expecting to get the Chersonesus, and at the same time Perinthus and Byzantium, into his power. The Athenians were eager to give aid to their allies, but their orators strove successfully to have Chares sent out as commander, and he, after sailing thither, did nothing worthy of the force under his orders, nor would the cities even receive his armament into their harbours. On the contrary, he was held in suspicion by all of them, and wandered about exacting money from the allies and despised by the enemy, so that the people of Athens, instigated by their orators, were incensed at him, and repented of having sent aid to the Byzantians. Then Phocion rose in the assembly and declared that they must not be angry at their allies who showed distrust, but at their generals who were distrusted; "For these," said he, "make you to be feared even by those who can be saved only by your help."

Accordingly, moved by his words, the people changed their minds again and ordered him to take another force and go himself to the help of their allies on the Hellespont;[2] a commission which contributed more than anything else to the salvation of

---

[1] In 340 B.C.   [2] In 339 B.C.

4 τὸ σωθῆναι τὸ Βυζάντιον. ἦν μὲν γὰρ ἤδη
μεγάλη δόξα τοῦ Φωκίωνος· ἐπεὶ δὲ καὶ Λέων,[1]
ἀνὴρ Βυζαντίων πρῶτος ἀρετῇ καὶ τῷ Φωκίωνι
γεγονὼς ἐν Ἀκαδημείᾳ συνήθης, ἀνεδέξατο τὴν
πίστιν ὑπὲρ αὐτοῦ πρὸς τὴν πόλιν, οὐκ εἴασαν
ἔξω στρατοπεδεῦσαι βουλόμενον, ἀλλ᾽ ἀνοίξαντες
τὰς πύλας ἐδέξαντο καὶ κατέμιξαν ἑαυτοῖς τοὺς
Ἀθηναίους, οὐ μόνον ἀνεγκλήτους ταῖς διαίταις
καὶ σώφρονας, ἀλλὰ καὶ προθυμοτάτους ἐν τοῖς
5 ἀγῶσι διὰ τὴν πίστιν γενομένους. οὕτω μὲν ὁ
Φίλιππος ἐξέπεσε τοῦ Ἑλλησπόντου τότε καὶ
κατεφρονήθη, δοκῶν ἄμαχός τις εἶναι καὶ ἀναντα-
γώνιστος, ὁ δὲ Φωκίων καὶ ναῦς τινας εἷλεν
αὐτοῦ καὶ φρουρουμένας πόλεις ἀνέλαβε, καὶ
πολλαχόθι τῆς χώρας ἀποβάσεις ποιούμενος
ἐπόρθει καὶ κατέτρεχε, μέχρι οὗ τραύματα λαβὼν
ὑπὸ τῶν προσβοηθούντων ἀπέπλευσε.

XV. Τῶν δὲ Μεγαρέων ἐπικαλουμένων κρύφα,
φοβούμενος ὁ Φωκίων τοὺς Βοιωτοὺς μὴ προαισ-
θόμενοι φθάσωσι τὴν βοήθειαν, ἐκκλησίαν συνή-
γαγεν ἕωθεν, καὶ προσαγγείλας τὰ παρὰ τῶν
Μεγαρέων τοῖς Ἀθηναίοις, ὡς ἐπεψηφίσαντο, τῇ
σάλπιγγι σημήνας εὐθὺς ἀπὸ τῆς ἐκκλησίας
2 ἦγεν αὐτοὺς τὰ ὅπλα λαβόντας. δεξαμένων δὲ
τῶν Μεγαρέων προθύμως τήν τε Νίσαιαν ἐτεί-
χισε, καὶ διὰ μέσου σκέλη δύο πρὸς τὸ ἐπίνειον

---

[1] καὶ Λέων Sintenis' correction of the MSS. Κλέων ; Bekker
has Λέων, the correction of Wachsmuth.

[1] See the *Nicias*, xxii. 3.

Byzantium. For already Phocion was held in high
repute there ; and when Leon [1] also, a man who was
first among the Byzantians for virtue, and had been
a familiar companion of Phocion in the Academy,
went surety for him with the city, they would not
suffer him to go into camp outside the city, as he
wished, but threw open their gates and received the
Athenians into close companionship with themselves.
This mark of confidence caused the Athenians to be
not only discreet and blameless in their general
conduct, but also most spirited in the struggles for
the city's defence. In this way Philip was expelled
from the Hellespont at this time and brought into
contempt, although men had thought there was no
fighting or contending with him at all; moreover,
Phocion captured some of his ships and recovered
cities which he had garrisoned. He also landed in
many parts of Philip's territory and plundered and
overran it, until he was wounded by those who
rallied to its defence, and sailed back home.

XV. The people of Megara once made a secret
appeal to Athens for help,[2] and Phocion, fearing
that the Boeotians might get early knowledge of
the appeal and anticipate Athens in sending help,
called an assembly early in the morning and announced to the Athenians the message received from
Megara. Then, as soon as the requisite decree had
been passed, he ordered the trumpeter to give the
signal and led them, under arms, directly from the
assembly. The Megarians received him eagerly, and
he enclosed Nisaea [3] with a wall, built two long walls

[2] Against a faction in the city which would have delivered
it into the power of Philip. The date of these events is uncertain (perhaps 344–343 B.C.).

[3] The sea-port of Megara, about a mile away.

ἀπὸ τοῦ ἄστεος ἐνέβαλε, καὶ συνῆψε τῇ θαλάττῃ
τὴν πόλιν, ὥστε τῶν κατὰ γῆν πολεμίων ὀλίγον
ἤδη φροντίζουσαν ἐξηρτῆσθαι τῶν Ἀθηναίων.

XVI. Ἤδη δὲ πρὸς Φίλιππον ἐκπεπολεμωμέ-
νων παντάπασι, καὶ στρατηγῶν αὐτοῦ μὴ παρόντος ἑτέρων ἐπὶ τὸν πόλεμον ᾑρημένων, ὡς κατέ-
πλευσεν ἀπὸ τῶν νήσων, πρῶτον μὲν ἔπειθε τὸν
δῆμον εἰρηνικῶς ἔχοντος τοῦ Φιλίππου καὶ φοβουμένου τὸν κίνδυνον ἰσχυρῶς δέχεσθαι τὰς
2 διαλύσεις· καί τινος ἀντικρούσαντος αὐτῷ τῶν
εἰωθότων κυλινδεῖσθαι περὶ τὴν Ἡλιαίαν καὶ
συκοφαντεῖν, καὶ εἰπόντος, "Σὺ δὲ τολμᾷς, ὦ
Φωκίων, ἀποτρέπειν Ἀθηναίους ἤδη τὰ ὅπλα
διὰ χειρῶν ἔχοντας;" "Ἔγωγε," εἶπε, "καὶ ταῦτα
εἰδὼς ὅτι πολέμου μὲν ὄντος ἐγὼ σοῦ, εἰρήνης δὲ
γενομένης σὺ ἐμοῦ ἄρξεις." ὡς δ' οὐκ ἔπειθεν,
ἀλλ' ὁ Δημοσθένης ἐκράτει κελεύων ὡς πορρωτάτω τῆς Ἀττικῆς θέσθαι μάχην τοὺς Ἀθηναίους,
"Ὦ τᾶν," ἔφη, "μὴ ποῦ μαχώμεθα σκοπῶμεν,
3 ἀλλὰ πῶς νικήσωμεν. οὕτω γὰρ ἔσται μακρὰν
ὁ πόλεμος, ἡττωμένοις δὲ πᾶν ἀεὶ δεινὸν ἐγγὺς
πάρεστι." γενομένης δὲ τῆς ἥττης[1] καὶ τῶν
θορυβοποιῶν καὶ νεωτεριστῶν ἐν ἄστει[2] τὸν
Χαρίδημον ἑλκόντων ἐπὶ τὸ βῆμα καὶ στρατηγεῖν
ἀξιούντων, ἐφοβήθησαν οἱ βέλτιστοι· καὶ τὴν ἐξ
Ἀρείου πάγου βουλὴν ἔχοντες ἐν τῷ δήμῳ δεό-

---

[1] τῆς ἥττης Bekker, with CF^a : ἥττης.
[2] ἐν ἄστει Coraës and Bekker have τῶν ἐν ἄστει, after
Stephanus.

down to the sea-port from Megara, and thus united the city with the sea, so that she need now pay little heed to enemies on land and could be in close connection with Athens by sea.

XVI. Presently[1] the relations between Athens and Philip were altogether hostile, and, in Phocion's absence, other generals were chosen to conduct the war. But when Phocion returned with his fleet from the islands, to begin with, he tried to persuade the people, since Philip was peaceably inclined and greatly feared the peril of war, to accept the terms of settlement which he offered. And when one of those who haunted the law-courts in the capacity of public informer opposed him, and said, " Canst thou dare, O Phocion, to divert the Athenians from war when they are already under arms ? " " I can," said he, "and that, too, though I know that while there is war thou wilt be under my orders, but when peace has been made I shall be under thine." When, however, he could not prevail, but Demosthenes carried the day and was urging the Athenians to join battle with Philip as far from Attica as possible, " My good Sir," said Phocion, " let us not ask where we can fight, but how we shall be victorious. For in that case the war will be at a long remove ; but wherever men are defeated every terror is close at hand." But when the defeat came,[2] and the turbulent and revolutionary spirits in the city dragged Charidemus to the tribunal and demanded that he be made general, the best citizens were filled with fear ; and with the aid of the council of the Areiopagus in the assembly, by dint of entreaties and tears,

[1] In 340 B.C.

[2] In 338 B.C., at Chaeroneia, where Philip defeated the allied Greeks and put an end to their independence.

μενοι καὶ δακρύοντες μόλις ἔπεισαν ἐπιτρέψαι
τῷ Φωκίωνι τὴν πόλιν.

4 Ὁ δὲ τὴν μὲν ἄλλην τοῦ Φιλίππου πολιτείαν
καὶ φιλανθρωπίαν ᾤετο δεῖν προσδέχεσθαι· Δημάδου δὲ γράψαντος ὅπως ἡ πόλις μετέχοι τῆς
κοινῆς εἰρήνης καὶ τοῦ συνεδρίου τοῖς Ἕλλησιν,
οὐκ εἴα πρὸ τοῦ γνῶναι τίνα Φίλιππος αὐτῷ
5 γενέσθαι παρὰ τῶν Ἑλλήνων ἀξιώσει· κρατηθεὶς 74⁹
δὲ τῇ γνώμῃ διὰ τὸν καιρόν, ὡς εὐθὺς ἑώρα τοὺς
Ἀθηναίους μεταμελομένους, ὅτι καὶ τριήρεις ἔδει
παρέχειν τῷ Φιλίππῳ καὶ ἱππεῖς, "Ταῦτα,"
ἔφη, "φοβούμενος ἠναντιούμην· ἐπεὶ δὲ συνέ-
θεσθε, δεῖ μὴ βαρέως φέρειν μηδὲ ἀθυμεῖν, μεμνη-
μένους ὅτι καὶ οἱ πρόγονοι ποτὲ μὲν ἄρχοντες,
ποτὲ δὲ ἀρχόμενοι, καλῶς δὲ ἀμφότερα ταῦτα
ποιοῦντες καὶ τὴν πόλιν ἔσωσαν καὶ τοὺς Ἕλ-
6 ληνας." Φιλίππου δὲ ἀποθανόντος εὐαγγέλια
θύειν τὸν δῆμον οὐκ εἴα· καὶ γὰρ ἀγεννὲς εἶναι
ἐπιχαίρειν, καὶ τὴν ἐν Χαιρωνείᾳ παραταξαμένην
πρὸς αὐτοὺς δύναμιν ἑνὶ σώματι μόνον ἐλάττω
γενέσθαι.

XVII. Δημοσθένους δὲ λοιδοροῦντος τὸν Ἀλέξανδρον ἤδη προσάγοντα ταῖς Θήβαις ἔφη·

"Σχέτλιε, τίπτ' ἐθέλεις ἐρεθιζέμεν ἄγριον ἄνδρα

καὶ δόξης μεγάλης ὀρεγόμενον; ἢ βούλει πυρκαϊᾶς
τηλικαύτης οὔσης ἐγγὺς ῥιπίσαι¹ τὴν πόλιν;

¹ ῥιπίσαι Bryan's correction of the MSS. ῥῖψαι (to hurl),
which Coraës and Bekker retain.

¹ The congress of Greek states summoned by Philip to
meet at Corinth. It voted for war against Persia under the
leadership of Philip.

they persuaded them at last to entrust the city to the guidance of Phocion.

In general, Phocion thought that the policy and kindly overtures of Philip should be accepted by the Athenians; but when Demades brought in a motion that the city should participate with the Greeks in the common peace and in the congress,[1] Phocion would not favour it before they found out what demands Philip was going to make upon the Greeks. His opinion did not prevail, owing to the crisis, and yet as soon as he saw that the Athenians were repenting of their course, because they were required to furnish Philip with triremes and horsemen, "This is what I feared," said he, "when I opposed your action; but since you agreed upon it, you must not repine or be dejected, remembering that our ancestors also were sometimes in command, and sometimes under command, but by doing well in both these positions saved both their city and the Greeks." And on the death of Philip,[2] he was opposed to the people's offering sacrifices of glad tidings; for it was an ignoble thing, he said, to rejoice thereat, and the force which had been arrayed against them at Chaeroneia was diminished by only one person.

XVII. Again, when Demosthenes was heaping abuse upon Alexander, who was already advancing against Thebes, Phocion said: "'Rash one, why dost thou seek to provoke a man who is savage,'[3] and is reaching out after great glory? Canst thou wish, when so great a conflagration is near, to fan the city into flame? But I, who am bearing

[2] In 336 B.C. See the *Demosthenes*, chapter xxii.

[3] *Odyssey*, ix. 494, Odysseus, to a companion, of Polyphemus the Cyclops.

ἀλλ' ἡμεῖς οὐδὲ βουλομένοις ἀπολέσθαι τούτοις
ἐπιτρέψομεν, οἱ διὰ τοῦτο στρατηγεῖν ὑπομέ-
2 νοντες." ὡς δὲ ἀπωλώλεισαν αἱ Θῆβαι καὶ ὁ
Ἀλέξανδρος ἐξητεῖτο τοὺς περὶ Δημοσθένην καὶ
Λυκοῦργον καὶ Ὑπερείδην καὶ Χαρίδημον, ἡ δὲ
ἐκκλησία πρὸς ἐκεῖνον ἀπέβλεπεν, ὀνομαστὶ
πολλάκις καλούμενος ἀνέστη· καὶ τῶν φίλων
ἕνα παραστησάμενος, ᾧ μάλιστα χρώμενος διετέλει καὶ πιστεύων καὶ ἀγαπῶν, "Εἰς τοιαῦτα,"
ἔφη, "τὴν πόλιν οὗτοι παραγηόχασιν ὥστ' ἔγωγε,
κἂν Νικοκλέα τις τοῦτον ἐξαιτῇ, διδόναι κελεύσω.
3 τὸ μὲν γὰρ αὐτὸς ὑπὲρ ὑμῶν ἁπάντων ἀποθανεῖν
εὐτυχίαν ἂν ἐμαυτοῦ θείμην. ἐλεῶ δέ," εἶπεν,
"ἄνδρες Ἀθηναῖοι, καὶ τοὺς ἐκ Θηβῶν δεῦρο
πεφευγότας, ἀρκεῖ δὲ τὰς Θήβας κλαίειν τοῖς
Ἕλλησι. διὸ βέλτιόν ἐστιν ὑπὲρ ἀμφοῖν πείθειν
καὶ παραιτεῖσθαι τοὺς κρατοῦντας ἢ μάχεσθαι."
4 Τὸ μὲν οὖν πρῶτον ψήφισμα λέγεται τὸν
Ἀλέξανδρον, ὡς ἔλαβε, ῥῖψαι καὶ φυγεῖν ἀπο-
στραφέντα τοὺς πρέσβεις· τὸ δὲ δεύτερον ἐδέξατο, κομισθὲν ὑπὸ Φωκίωνος, τῶν πρεσβυτέρων
ἀκούων ὅτι καὶ Φίλιππος ἐθαύμαζε τὸν ἄνδρα
τοῦτον· καὶ οὐ μόνον τὴν ἔντευξιν ὑπέμεινεν αὐτοῦ καὶ τὴν δέησιν, ἀλλὰ καὶ συμβουλεύοντος
ἤκουσε. συνεβούλευε δ' ὁ Φωκίων, εἰ μὲν ἡσυχίας ὀρέγεται, θέσθαι τὸν πόλεμον· εἰ δὲ δόξης,
μεταθέσθαι, πρὸς τοὺς βαρβάρους ἀπὸ τῶν Ἑλ-
5 λήνων τραπόμενον. καὶ πολλὰ καὶ πρὸς τὴν

the burdens of command with this object in view, will not suffer these fellow citizens of mine to perish even if that is their desire." And when Thebes had been destroyed[1] and Alexander was demanding the surrender of Demosthenes, Lycurgus, Hypereides, Charidemus, and others, and the assembly turned their eyes upon Phocion and called upon him many times by name, he rose up, and drawing to his side one of his friends, whom he always cherished, trusted, and loved most of all, he said: "These men have brought the city to such a pass that I, for my part, even if this Nicocles should be demanded, would urge you to give him up. For if I might die myself in behalf of you all, I should deem it a piece of good fortune for me. And I feel pity," said he, "men of Athens, for those also who have fled hither from Thebes; but it is enough that the Greeks should have the fate of Thebes to mourn. Therefore it is better to supplicate and try to persuade the victors for both you and them, and not to fight."

Well, then, we are told that when Alexander got the first decree which the Athenians passed, he cast it from him and ran with averted face from the envoys; the second, however, he accepted, because it was brought by Phocion, and because he heard from the older Macedonians that Philip also used to admire this man. And he not only consented to meet Phocion and hear his petition, but actually listened to his counsels. And Phocion counselled him, if he sought quiet, to make an end of the war; but if glory, to transfer the war, and turn his arms away from Greece against the Barbarians. And

[1] In 335 B.C.

Ἀλεξάνδρου φύσιν καὶ βούλησιν εὐστόχως εἰπὼν
οὕτω μετέβαλε καὶ κατεπράϋνεν αὐτὸν ὥστε
εἰπεῖν ὅπως προσέξουσι τὸν νοῦν Ἀθηναῖοι τοῖς
πράγμασιν, ὡς, εἴ τι γένοιτο περὶ αὐτόν, ἐκείνοις
ἄρχειν προσῆκον. ἰδίᾳ δὲ τὸν Φωκίωνα ποιησάμενος αὐτοῦ φίλον καὶ ξένον, εἰς τοσαύτην ἔθετο
6 τιμὴν ὅσην εἶχον ὀλίγοι τῶν ἀεὶ συνόντων. ὁ
γοῦν Δοῦρις εἴρηκεν ὡς μέγας γενόμενος καὶ
Δαρείου κρατήσας ἀφεῖλε τῶν ἐπιστολῶν τὸ
χαίρειν πλὴν ἐν ὅσαις ἔγραφε Φωκίωνι· τοῦτον
δὲ μόνον, ὥσπερ Ἀντίπατρον, μετὰ τοῦ χαίρειν
προσηγόρευε. τοῦτο δὲ καὶ Χάρης ἱστόρηκε.

XVIII. Τὸ μέντοι περὶ τῶν χρημάτων ὁμολο-
γούμενόν ἐστιν, ὅτι δωρεὰν αὐτῷ κατέπεμψεν
ἑκατὸν τάλαντα. τούτων κομισθέντων εἰς Ἀθήνας, ἠρώτησεν ὁ Φωκίων τοὺς φέροντας τί δή
ποτε πολλῶν ὄντων Ἀθηναίων αὐτῷ μόνῳ τοσαῦτα δίδωσιν Ἀλέξανδρος. εἰπόντων δὲ ἐκείνων,
"Ὅτι σὲ κρίνει μόνον ἄνδρα καλὸν καὶ ἀγαθόν,"
"Οὐκοῦν," εἶπεν ὁ Φωκίων, "ἐασάτω με καὶ
2 δοκεῖν ἀεὶ καὶ εἶναι τοιοῦτον." ὡς δὲ ἀκολου-
θήσαντες εἰς οἶκον αὐτῷ πολλὴν ἑώρων εὐτέλειαν,
τὴν μὲν γυναῖκα μάττουσαν, ὁ δὲ Φωκίων αὐτὸς
ἀνιμήσας ὕδωρ ἐκ τοῦ φρέατος ἀπενίπτετο τοὺς
πόδας, ἔτι μᾶλλον ἐνέκειντο καὶ ἠγανάκτουν, 750
δεινὸν εἶναι λέγοντες εἰ φίλος ὢν τοῦ βασιλέως

---

[1] Cf. the *Alexander*, xiii. 2.

by saying many things that suited well with Alexander's nature and desires he so far changed and softened his feelings that he advised the Athenians to give close attention to their affairs, since, if anything should happen to him, the leadership of Greece would properly fall to them.[1] In private, too, he made Phocion his friend and guest, and showed him greater honour than most of his constant associates enjoyed. At any rate, Duris writes that after Alexander had become great and had conquered Dareius, he dropped from his letters the word of salutation, "chairein," except whenever he was writing to Phocion; him alone, like Antipater, he used to address with the word "chairein." This is the testimony of Chares also.

XVIII. The story about the money, indeed, is generally admitted, namely, that Alexander sent him a present of a hundred talents.[2] When this was brought to Athens, Phocion asked the bearers why in the world, when there were so many Athenians, Alexander offered such a sum to him alone. They replied: "Because Alexander judges that thou alone art a man of honour and worth." "In that case," said Phocion, "let him suffer me to be and be thought such always." But when the messengers accompanied him to his home and saw there a great simplicity,—his wife kneading bread, while Phocion with his own hands drew water from the well and washed his feet,—they were indignant, and pressed the money upon him still more urgently, declaring it an intolerable thing that he, though a friend of

[2] The talent was equivalent to about £235, or $1,200, with four or five times the purchasing power of modern money.

οὕτω διαιτήσεται πονηρῶς. ἰδὼν οὖν ὁ Φωκίων
πένητα πρεσβύτην ἐν τριβωνίῳ ῥυπαρῷ πορευόμενον, ἠρώτησεν εἰ τούτου χείρονα νομίζουσιν
3 αὐτόν. εὐφημεῖν δὲ ἐκείνων δεομένων, " Καὶ μὴν
οὗτος," εἶπεν, " ἀπ' ἐλαττόνων ἐμοῦ ζῇ καὶ ἀρκεῖ-
ται. τὸ δὲ ὅλον ἢ μὴ χρώμενος," ἔφη, " μάτην
ἔξω τοσοῦτον χρυσίον, ἢ χρώμενος ἐμαυτὸν ἅμα
κἀκεῖνον διαβαλῶ πρὸς τὴν πόλιν." οὕτω μὲν
ἐπανῆλθε πάλιν τὰ χρήματα ἐξ Ἀθηνῶν, ἐπιδεί-
ξαντα τοῖς Ἕλλησι πλουσιώτερον τοῦ διδόντος
4 τοσαῦτα τὸν μὴ δεόμενον. ἐπεὶ δὲ Ἀλέξανδρος
ἠγανάκτησε καὶ πάλιν ἔγραψε τῷ Φωκίωνι φίλους μὴ νομίζειν τοὺς μηδὲν αὐτοῦ δεομένους,
χρήματα μὲν οὐδ' ὡς Φωκίων ἔλαβεν, ἀφεθῆναι
δὲ ἠξίωσε τὸν σοφιστὴν Ἐχεκρατίδην καὶ τὸν
Ἴμβριον Ἀθηνόδωρον καὶ Ῥοδίους δύο, Δημά-
ρατον καὶ Σπάρτωνα, συνειλημμένους ἐπ' αἰτίαις
5 τισὶ καὶ καθειργμένους ἐν Σάρδεσι. τούτους μὲν
οὖν εὐθὺς ἀπέλυσεν ὁ Ἀλέξανδρος, Κρατερὸν δὲ
ἀποστέλλων εἰς Μακεδονίαν ἐκέλευσε τεττάρων
πόλεων ἐν Ἀσίᾳ, Κίου, Γεργίθου, Μυλάσων,
Ἐλαίας, μίαν, ἣν ἂν αἱρῆται, παραδοῦναι τῷ
Φωκίωνι, διατεινάμενος ἔτι μᾶλλον ὡς χαλεπανεῖ
μὴ λαβόντος. ἀλλ' οὔτε Φωκίων ἔλαβεν, ὅ τε
Ἀλέξανδρος ταχέως ἀπέθανεν. ἡ δὲ οἰκία τοῦ
Φωκίωνος ἔτι νῦν ἐν Μελίτῃ δείκνυται, χαλκαῖς
λεπίσι κεκοσμημένη, τὰ δὲ ἄλλα λιτὴ καὶ
ἀφελής.

---

[1] In 324 B.C., when Craterus was commissioned to lead the
veteran soldiers of Alexander back to Macedonia. See the
Alexander, chapter lxxi.

the king, should live in such poverty. Phocion, accordingly, seeing a poor old man walking the street in a dirty cloak, asked them if they considered him inferior to this man. "Heaven forbid!" they cried. "And yet this man," said Phocion, "has less to live upon than I, and finds it sufficient. And, in a word," said he, "if I make no use of this great sum of money, it will do me no good to have it; or, if I use it, I shall bring myself, and the king as well, under the calumnies of the citizens." So the treasure went back again from Athens, after it had showed the Greeks that the man who did not want so great a sum was richer than the man who offered it. Alexander was vexed and wrote back to Phocion that he could not regard as his friends those who wanted nothing of him. But not even then would Phocion take the money; he did, however, ask for the release of Echecratides the sophist, Athenodorus of Imbros, and two men of Rhodes, Demaratus and Sparton, who had been arrested upon sundry charges and imprisoned in Sardis. These men, then, Alexander set free at once, and at a later time,[1] when he sent Craterus back into Macedonia, he ordered him to turn over to Phocion the revenues from whichever one of four cities in Asia he might select,—either Cius, Gergithus, Mylasa, or Elaea,—insisting still more strongly than before that he would be angry if Phocion did not take them. But Phocion would not take them, and very soon Alexander died. And even to the present day Phocion's house is pointed out in Melité,[2] adorned with bronze disks, but otherwise plain and simple.

[2] A deme, or ward, in the S.W. part of Athens. See the *Themistocles*, xxii. 2.

XIX. Τῶν δὲ γυναικῶν ἃς ἔγημε, περὶ τῆς προτέρας οὐθὲν ἱστορεῖται, πλὴν ὅτι Κηφισόδοτος ἦν ὁ πλάστης ἀδελφὸς αὐτῆς, τῆς δὲ δευτέρας οὐκ ἐλάττων ἐπὶ σωφροσύνῃ καὶ ἀφελείᾳ λόγος ἦν παρὰ τοῖς Ἀθηναίοις ἢ Φωκίωνος ἐπὶ
2 χρηστότητι. καί ποτε θεωμένων καινοὺς τραγῳδοὺς Ἀθηναίων, ὁ μὲν τραγῳδὸς εἰσιέναι μέλλων βασιλίδος πρόσωπον ᾔτει κεκοσμημένας πολλὰς ὀπαδοὺς πολυτελῶς τὸν χορηγόν· καὶ μὴ παρέχοντος ἠγανάκτει καὶ κατεῖχε τὸ θέατρον οὐ βουλόμενος προελθεῖν. ὁ δὲ χορηγὸς Μελάνθιος ὠθῶν αὐτὸν εἰς τὸ μέσον ἐβόα· "Τὴν Φωκίωνος οὐχ ὁρᾷς γυναῖκα προϊοῦσαν ἀεὶ μετὰ μιᾶς θεραπαινίδος, ἀλλ' ἀλαζονεύῃ καὶ διαφθείρεις τὴν
3 γυναικωνῖτιν;" ἐξακούστου δὲ τῆς φωνῆς γενομένης ἐδέξατο κρότῳ πολλῷ καὶ θορύβῳ τὸ θέατρον. αὐτὴ δὲ ἡ γυνή, ξένης τινὸς Ἰωνικῆς ἐπιδειξαμένης χρυσοῦν καὶ λιθοκόλλητον κόσμον ἐν πλοκίοις καὶ περιδεραίοις, "Ἐμοὶ δέ," ἔφη, "κόσμος ἐστὶ Φωκίων εἰκοστὸν ἔτος ἤδη στρατηγῶν Ἀθηναίων."

XX. Φώκῳ δὲ τῷ υἱῷ βουλομένῳ ἀγωνίσασθαι Παναθηναίοις ἀποβάτην ἐφῆκεν,[1] οὐχὶ τῆς νίκης ὀρεγόμενος, ἀλλ' ὅπως ἐπιμεληθεὶς καὶ ἀσκήσας τὸ σῶμα βελτίων ἔσοιτο· καὶ γὰρ ἦν ἄλλως φιλοπότης καὶ ἄτακτος ὁ νεανίσκος. νικήσαντος δὲ καὶ πολλῶν αἰτουμένων ἑστιᾶσαι τὰ νικητήρια, τοὺς ἄλλους Φωκίων παραιτησάμενος ἑνὶ τὴν
2 φιλοτιμίαν ταύτην συνεχώρησεν. ὡς δὲ ἐλθὼν ἐπὶ τὸ δεῖπνον ἄλλην τε σοβαρὰν ἑώρα παρα-

---

[1] Φώκῳ . . . βουλομένῳ . . . ἐφῆκεν with Coraës, Sintenis[2], and Bekker, after Fᵃ: Φῶκον . . . βουλόμενον . . . ἀφῆκεν.

XIX. As for his wives, nothing is told us about the first, except that she was a sister of Cephisodotus the sculptor; but the reputation which the second had among the Athenians for sobriety and simplicity was not less than that of Phocion for probity. And once when the Athenians were witnessing an exhibition of new tragedies, the actor who was to take the part of a queen asked the choregus to furnish him with a great number of attendant women in expensive array; and when he could not get them, he was indignant, and kept the audience waiting by his refusal to come out. But the choregus, Melanthius, pushed him before the spectators, crying: "Dost thou not see that Phocion's wife always goes out with one maid-servant? Thy vanity will be the undoing of our women-folk." His words were plainly heard by the audience, and were received with tumultuous applause. And this very wife, when an Ionian woman who was her guest displayed ornaments of gold and precious stones worked into collars and necklaces, said: "My ornament is Phocion, who is now for the twentieth year a general of Athens."

XX. When Phocus his son wished to compete at the Panathenaic festival as a vaulting rider of horses, Phocion permitted it, not because he was ambitious for the victory, but in order that care and training of the body might make his son a better man; for in general the youth was fond of wine and irregular in his habits. The youth was victorious, and many asked him to their houses for the victor's banquet; but Phocion declined the other invitations and granted the coveted honour to one host only. And when he went to the banquet and saw the general

σκευὴν καὶ ποδανιπτῆρας οἴνου δι' ἀρωμάτων
προσφερομένους τοῖς εἰσιοῦσι, καλέσας τὸν υἱόν,
" Οὐ παύσεις," ἔφη, " τὸν ἑταῖρον, ὦ Φῶκε, δια-
φθείροντά σου τὴν νίκην;" βουλόμενος δὲ καὶ
καθόλου μεταστῆσαι τὸ μειράκιον ἐκ τῆς διαίτης
ἐκείνης, ἀπήγαγεν εἰς Λακεδαίμονα καὶ κατέμιξε
τοῖς ἀγομένοις τὴν λεγομένην ἀγωγὴν νεανίσκοις.
3 καὶ τοῦτο τοὺς Ἀθηναίους ἐλύπησεν, ὡς ὑπερ-
ορῶντος καὶ ὑπερφρονοῦντος τὰ οἰκεῖα τοῦ Φωκίωνος. εἰπόντος δὲ τοῦ Δημάδου πρὸς αὐτόν, " Τί
οὐ πείθομεν, ὦ Φωκίων, Ἀθηναίους τὴν Λακω-
νικὴν προσδέξασθαι πολιτείαν; ἐὰν γὰρ σὺ κε-   75
λεύῃς, ἐγὼ γράφειν καὶ λέγειν ἔτοιμός εἰμι,"
" Πάνυ γοῦν," ἔφη, " πρέψειεν ἄν σοι μύρου
τοσοῦτον ὄζοντι καὶ χλανίδα τοιαύτην φοροῦντι
συμβουλεύειν Ἀθηναίοις περὶ φιλιτίων καὶ τὸν
Λυκοῦργον ἐπαινεῖν."

XXI. Γράψαντος δὲ τοῦ Ἀλεξάνδρου περὶ
τριήρων, ὅπως ἀποστείλωσιν αὐτῷ, καὶ τῶν ῥητόρων ἐνισταμένων, τῆς δὲ βουλῆς τὸν Φωκίωνα
λέγειν κελευούσης, " Λέγω τοίνυν ὑμῖν," εἶπεν,
" ἢ τοῖς ὅπλοις κρατεῖν ἢ τοῖς κρατοῦσι φίλους
εἶναι." πρὸς δὲ Πυθέαν ἀρχόμενον τότε πρῶτον
ἐντυγχάνειν Ἀθηναίοις, ἤδη δὲ λάλον ὄντα καὶ
θρασύν, " Οὐ σιωπήσεις," ἔφη, " καὶ ταῦτα νεώ-
2 νητος ὢν τῷ δήμῳ;" ἐπεὶ δὲ Ἅρπαλος μετὰ
χρημάτων πολλῶν ἀποδρὰς Ἀλέξανδρον ἐκ τῆς
Ἀσίας τῇ Ἀττικῇ προσέβαλε, καὶ τῶν εἰωθότων

magnificence of the preparations, and particularly the foot-basins of spiced wine that were brought to the guests as they entered, he called his son and said : "Phocus, do not let thy companion ruin thy victory." Moreover, wishing to remove the young man entirely from that style of living, he took him off to Sparta and put him among the youths who were following the course of discipline called "agoge." [1] This vexed the Athenians, who thought that Phocion despised and looked down upon the native customs. And once Demades said to him : "Phocion, why shouldn't we try to persuade the Athenians to adopt the Spartan polity ? For if thou sayest the word, I am ready to introduce and support the requisite law." But Phocion replied : "Indeed it would very well become thee, with so strong a scent of ointment upon thee, and wearing such a mantle as thine, to recommend to the Athenians the public mess-halls of the Spartans, and to extol Lycurgus."

XXI. When Alexander wrote asking the Athenians to send him triremes, and the orators opposed the request, and the council bade Phocion speak upon the matter, "I tell you, then," he said, "either to be superior in arms or to be friends with those who are superior." To Pytheas, who at that time was just beginning to address the Athenians, but was already loquacious and bold, Phocion said : "Hold thy peace, thou who art but a newly bought slave of the people !" And when Harpalus, who had run away from Alexander out of Asia with great sums of money, landed in Attica,[2] and those who

---

[1] See the *Agesilaüs*, i. 1.
[2] See the *Demosthenes*, chapter xxv.

ἀπὸ τοῦ βήματος χρηματίζεσθαι δρόμος ἦν καὶ
ἄμιλλα φθειρομένων πρὸς αὑτόν, τούτοις μὲν ἀπὸ
πολλῶν μικρὰ δελεάζων προήκατο καὶ διέρριψε,
τῷ δὲ Φωκίωνι προσέπεμψε διδοὺς ἑπτακόσια
τάλαντα, καὶ τἆλλα πάντα, καὶ μετὰ πάντων
3 ἑαυτὸν ἐκείνῳ¹ μόνῳ παρακατατιθέμενος. ἀποκριναμένου δὲ τραχέως τοῦ Φωκίωνος οἰμώξεσθαι
τὸν Ἅρπαλον, εἰ μὴ παύσεται διαφθείρων τὴν
πόλιν, τότε μὲν συσταλεὶς ἀπέστη, μετ᾽ ὀλίγον δὲ
βουλευομένων Ἀθηναίων ἑώρα τοὺς μὲν εἰλη-
φότας τὰ χρήματα παρ᾽ αὐτοῦ μεταβαλλομένους
καὶ κατηγοροῦντας, ἵνα μὴ φανεροὶ γένωνται,
Φωκίωνα δὲ τὸν μηδὲν λαβόντα μετὰ τοῦ κοινοῦ
συμφέροντος ἅμα καὶ τὴν ἐκείνου σωτηρίαν ἔν
4 τινι λόγῳ τιθέμενον. πάλιν οὖν ἐνεχθεὶς ἐπὶ τὸ
θεραπεύειν ἐκεῖνον, αὐτὸν μὲν ὡς ἔρυμα πανταχόθεν ἀνάλωτον ὑπὸ τοῦ χρυσίου περιοδεύων
ἑώρα, Χαρικλέα δὲ τὸν γαμβρὸν αὐτοῦ ποιησάμενος συνήθη καὶ φίλον, ἀνέπλησε δόξης πονηρᾶς,
πάντα πιστεύων καὶ πάντα χρώμενος ἐκείνῳ.

XXII. Καὶ δὴ καὶ Πυθονίκης τῆς ἑταίρας ἀπο-
θανούσης, ἣν εἶχεν ὁ Ἅρπαλος ἐρῶν καὶ θυγα-
τρίου πατὴρ ἐξ αὐτῆς γεγόνει, μνημεῖον ἀπὸ
χρημάτων πολλῶν ἐπιτελέσαι θελήσας προσέ-
2 ταξε τῷ Χαρικλεῖ τὴν ἐπιμέλειαν. οὖσαν δὲ τὴν
ὑπουργίαν ταύτην ἀγεννῆ προσκατῄσχυνεν ὁ
τάφος συντελεσθείς. διαμένει γὰρ ἔτι νῦν ἐν

_____
¹ ἐκείνῳ with Coraës and Bekker : ἐπ᾽ ἐκείνῳ.

were wont to make merchandise of their influence
as orators came running to him at breakneck speed,
to these men he dropped and scattered small mor-
sels of his wealth by way of bait; but he sent to
Phocion and offered him seven hundred talents,
and everything else that he had, and put himself
with all his possessions at the sole disposition
of Phocion. But Phocion answered sharply that
Harpalus would rue it if he did not cease trying
to corrupt the city, and for the time being the
traitor was abashed and desisted from his efforts.
After a little, however, when the Athenians were
deliberating upon his case, he found that those who
had taken money from him were changing sides and
denouncing him, that they might not be discovered;
while Phocion, who would take nothing, was now
giving some consideration to the safety of Harpalus
as well as to the public interests. Again, therefore,
he was led to pay court to Phocion, but after all his
efforts to bribe him found that he was impregnable
on all sides like a fortress. Of Charicles, however,
Phocion's son-in-law, Harpalus made an intimate
associate and friend, trusting him in everything and
using him in everything, and thus covered him with
infamy.

XXII. For instance, on the death of Pythonicé
the courtesan, who was the passionately loved mistress of Harpalus and had borne him a daughter,
Harpalus resolved to build her a very expensive
monument, and committed the care of the work to
Charicles. This service was an ignoble one in itself,
but it acquired additional disgrace from the completed tomb. For this is still to be seen in Hermus,

Ἕρμει,[1] ᾗ βαδίζομεν ἐξ ἄστεος εἰς Ἐλευσῖνα,
μηδὲν ἔχων τῶν τριάκοντα ταλάντων ἄξιον, ὅσα
τῷ Ἁρπάλῳ λογισθῆναί φασιν εἰς τὸ ἔργον ὑπὸ
τοῦ Χαρικλέους. καὶ μέντοι καὶ τελευτήσαντος
αὐτοῦ τὸ παιδάριον ὑπὸ τοῦ Χαρικλέους καὶ τοῦ
Φωκίωνος ἀναληφθὲν ἐτύγχανε πάσης ἐπιμελείας.
3 κρινομένου μέντοι τοῦ Χαρικλέους ἐπὶ τοῖς Ἁρ-
παλείοις, καὶ δεομένου βοηθεῖν αὐτῷ τὸν Φωκίωνα
καὶ συνεισελθεῖν εἰς τὸ δικαστήριον, οὐκ ἠθέ-
λησεν, εἰπών· "Ἐγώ σε, ὦ Χάρικλεις, ἐπὶ πᾶσι
τοῖς δικαίοις γαμβρὸν ἐποιησάμην."

Πρώτου δὲ Ἀθηναίοις Ἀσκληπιάδου τοῦ Ἱπ-
πάρχου τεθνάναι προσαγγείλαντος Ἀλέξανδρον,
ὁ μὲν Δημάδης ἐκέλευε μὴ προσέχειν· πάλαι γὰρ
ἂν ὅλην ὄζειν νεκροῦ τὴν οἰκουμένην· ὁ δὲ Φωκίων
ἐπηρμένον ὁρῶν πρὸς τὸ νεωτερίζειν τὸν δῆμον
4 ἐπειρᾶτο παρηγορεῖν καὶ κατέχειν. ἀναπηδώντων
δὲ πολλῶν ἐπὶ τὸ βῆμα, καὶ βοώντων ἀληθῆ
τὸν Ἀσκληπιάδην ἀπαγγέλλειν καὶ τεθνάναι τὸν
Ἀλέξανδρον, "Οὐκοῦν," εἶπεν, "εἰ σήμερον τέ-
θνηκε, καὶ αὔριον ἔσται καὶ εἰς τρίτην τεθνηκώς,
ὥστε ἡμᾶς ἐν ἡσυχίᾳ βουλεύσασθαι, μᾶλλον δὲ[2]
μετὰ ἀσφαλείας."

XXIII. Ὡς δὲ φέρων ἐνέσεισεν ὁ Λεωσθένης
τὴν πόλιν εἰς τὸν Λαμιακὸν[3] πόλεμον, καὶ τοῦ
Φωκίωνος δυσχεραίνοντος ἠρώτα καταγελῶν τί

---

[1] Ἕρμει Bekker, after Coraës: Ἑρμείῳ.
[2] δὲ Bekker, after Coraës, corrects to καί.
[3] Λαμιακὸν Coraës and Bekker, after Xylander: Ἑλληνικόν.

---

[1] See Pausanias, i. 37, 5, with Frazer's notes. Pausanias
speaks of it as "the best worth seeing of all ancient Greek
tombs."

on the road from Athens to Eleusis, and it has nothing worthy of the large sum of thirty talents which Charicles is said to have charged Harpalus for the work.[1] And yet after the death of Harpalus himself,[2] his daughter was taken up by Charicles and Phocion and educated with every care. However, when Charicles was brought to trial for his dealings with Harpalus, and begged Phocion to help him and go with him into the court-room, Phocion refused, saying: "I made thee my son-in-law, Charicles, for none but just purposes."

Asclepiades the son of Hipparchus was the first one to bring to the Athenians the tidings that Alexander was dead. Thereupon Demades urged them to pay no heed to the report, since, had it been true, the whole earth would long ago have been filled with the stench of the body. But Phocion, who saw that the people were bent on revolution, tried to dissuade them and restrain them. And when many of them sprang towards the bema, and shouted that the tidings brought by Asclepiades were true and that Alexander was dead, "Well, then," said Phocion, "if he is dead to-day, he will be dead to-morrow and the day after. Therefore we can deliberate in quiet, and with greater safety."

XXIII. Leosthenes, who had plunged the city into the Lamian war[3] much to Phocion's displeasure, once asked him derisively what good he had done

---

[2] Antipater demanded his surrender by the Athenians, and Harpalus fled to Crete, where he was assassinated.

[3] 323–322 B.C. So named because the confederate Greeks held Antipater and his forces for some time besieged in Lamia, a city of S.E. Thessaly (§ 4).

πεποίηκεν ἀγαθὸν τὴν πόλιν ἔτη τοσαῦτα στρατηγῶν, "Οὐ μικρόν," ἔφη, "τὸ τοὺς πολίτας ἐν
2 τοῖς ἰδίοις μνήμασι θάπτεσθαι." πολλὰ δὲ θρα- 752
συνομένου καὶ κομπάζοντος ἐν τῷ δήμῳ τοῦ Λεωσθένους, ὁ Φωκίων, "Οἱ λόγοι σου," εἶπεν, "ὦ
μειράκιον, ἐοίκασι κυπαρίττοις· μεγάλοι γὰρ
ὄντες καὶ ὑψηλοὶ καρποὺς οὐ φέρουσιν." ὡς δὲ
ἐπαναστὰς ὁ Ὑπερείδης ἠρώτησε, "Πότε οὖν, ὦ
Φωκίων, συμβουλεύσεις πολεμεῖν Ἀθηναίοις;"
"Ὅταν," εἶπε, "τοὺς μὲν νέους ἴδω τὴν τάξιν
βουλομένους φυλάττειν, τοὺς δὲ πλουσίους εἰσφέρειν, τοὺς δὲ ῥήτορας ἀπέχεσθαι τοῦ κλέπτειν τὰ
δημόσια."

3   Θαυμαζόντων δὲ πολλῶν τὴν ὑπὸ τοῦ Λεωσθένους συνηγμένην δύναμιν, καὶ τοῦ Φωκίωνος
πυνθανομένων πῶς τι[1] παρεσκευάσθαι δοκοῦσιν αὐτῷ, "Καλῶς," ἔφη, "πρὸς τὸ στάδιον· τὸν
δὲ δόλιχον τοῦ πολέμου φοβοῦμαι, μήτε χρήματα
τῆς πόλεως ἕτερα μήτε ναῦς μήτε ὁπλίτας ἐχού-
4 σης." ἐμαρτύρει δὲ αὐτῷ καὶ τὰ ἔργα. πρῶτον
μὲν γὰρ ὁ Λεωσθένης λαμπρὸς ἤρθη ταῖς πράξεσι,
τῶν τε Βοιωτῶν μάχῃ κρατήσας καὶ τὸν Ἀντίπατρον εἰς Λάμιαν συνελάσας· ὅτε καὶ φασι τὴν
μὲν πόλιν ἐλπίδος[2] μεγάλης γενομένην ἑορτάζειν
εὐαγγέλια συνεχῶς καὶ θύειν τοῖς θεοῖς, τὸν δὲ
Φωκίωνα πρὸς τοὺς ἐλέγχειν αὐτὸν οἰομένους,
καὶ πυνθανομένους εἰ ταῦτα οὐκ ἂν ἤθελεν αὐτῷ
πεπρᾶχθαι, "Πάνυ μὲν οὖν," ἔφη, "βεβουλεῦσθαι δὲ ἐκεῖνα." καὶ πάλιν ἄλλων ἐπ᾽ ἄλλοις
εὐαγγελίων γραφομένων καὶ φερομένων ἀπὸ

<hr />

[1] πῶς τι Bekker, after Coraës, corrects to πῶς.
[2] ἐλπίδος Bekker, after Coraës, corrects to ἐπ᾽ ἐλπίδος.

the city during the many years in which he had
been general. "No slight good," said Phocion, "in
that its citizens are buried in their own sepulchres."
Again, when Leosthenes was talking very boldly
and boastfully in the assembly, Phocion said : "Thy
speeches, young man, are like cypress-trees, which
are large and towering, but bear no fruit." And
when Hypereides confronted him with the question,
"When, then, O Phocion, wilt thou counsel the
Athenians to go to war?" "Whenever," said
Phocion, "I see the young men willing to hold their
places in the ranks, the rich to make contributions,
and the orators to keep their thievish hands away
from the public moneys."

When many were admiring the force got together
by Leosthenes, and were asking Phocion what he
thought of the city's preparations, "They are good,"
said he, "for the short course;[1] but it is the long
course which I fear in the war, since the city has no
other moneys, or ships, or men-at-arms." And
events justified his fear. For at first Leosthenes
achieved brilliant successes, conquering the Boeotians
in battle, and driving Antipater into Lamia. Then,
too, they say that the city came to cherish high
hopes, and was continuously holding festivals
and making sacrifices of glad tidings. Phocion,
however, when men thought to convict him of error
and asked him if he would not have been glad to
have performed these exploits, replied : "By all
means; but I am glad to have given the advice
I did." And again, when glad tidings came in
quick succession by letter and messenger from the

---

[1] The short course in the foot-races was straight away, the
length of the stadium ; the long course was ten times back
and forth.

στρατοπέδου, "Πότε ἄρα," φάναι, "παυσόμεθα νικῶντες;"

XXIV. Ἐπεὶ δὲ τοῦ Λεωσθένους ἀποθανόντος οἱ φοβούμενοι τὸν Φωκίωνα, μὴ στρατηγὸς ἐκπεμφθεὶς καταλύσῃ τὸν πόλεμον, ἄνθρωπόν τινα τῶν οὐκ ἐπιφανῶν ἐν ἐκκλησίᾳ παρεσκεύασαν ἀναστάντα λέγειν ὅτι φίλος ὢν τοῦ Φωκίωνος καὶ συμπεφοιτηκὼς παραινεῖ φείδεσθαι τοῦ ἀνδρὸς καὶ φυλάσσειν, ὡς ἄλλον ὅμοιον οὐκ ἔχοντας, ἐκπέμπειν δὲ Ἀντίφιλον ἐπὶ τὸ στράτευμα, καὶ ταῦτα τοῖς Ἀθηναίοις συνεδόκει, παρελθὼν ὁ Φωκίων ἔλεγε μήτε συμπεφοιτηκέναι ποτὲ τῷ ἀνθρώπῳ μήτε ἄλλως γεγονέναι γνώριμος ἢ συνή- 2 θης· "'Ἀλλὰ νῦν," εἶπεν, "ἀπὸ τῆς σήμερον ἡμέρας καὶ φίλον σε ποιοῦμαι καὶ οἰκεῖον· ἃ γὰρ ἦν ἐμοὶ συμφέροντα συμβεβούλευκας."

Ὡρμημένων δὲ τῶν Ἀθηναίων ἐπὶ τοὺς Βοιωτοὺς στρατεύειν πρῶτον μὲν ἀντεῖχε· καὶ τῶν φίλων λεγόντων ὡς ἀποθανεῖται προσκρούων τοῖς Ἀθηναίοις, "'Ἀδίκως," εἶπεν, "ἂν ποιῶ τὸ συμ- 3 φέρον· ἂν δὲ παραβαίνω, δικαίως." ἐπεὶ δὲ ὁρῶν οὐκ ἀνιέντας, ἀλλὰ βοῶντας, ἐκέλευσε τὸν κήρυκα ἀνειπεῖν Ἀθηναίων τοὺς ἄχρι ἑξήκοντα ἐτῶν ἀφ' ἥβης πέντε ἡμερῶν σιτία λαβόντας εὐθὺς ἀκολουθεῖν ἀπὸ τῆς ἐκκλησίας, θορύβου πολλοῦ γενομένου καὶ τῶν πρεσβυτέρων βοώντων καὶ ἀναπηδώντων, "Οὐδέν," ἔφη, "δεινόν· ἐγὼ γὰρ ὁ στρατηγὸς ὀγδοηκοστὸν ἔχων ἔτος ἔσομαι μεθ' ὑμῶν." καὶ τότε μὲν οὕτως κατέπαυσεν αὐτοὺς καὶ μετέβαλε.

camp, " When, pray," said he, " will our victories cease ? "

XXIV. But Leosthenes was killed, and then those who feared that Phocion, if he were sent out as general, would put a stop to the war, arranged with a certain obscure person to rise in the assembly and say that he was a friend and intimate associate of Phocion, and therefore advised the people to spare him and keep him in reserve, since they had none other like him, and to send out Antiphilus to the army. This course was approved by the Athenians, whereupon Phocion came forward and said that he had never been intimately associated with the person, nor in any way familiar or acquainted with him ; " But now," said he, " from this very day I make thee a friend and close companion, for thou hast counselled what was for my advantage."

Again, when the Athenians were bent on making an expedition against the Boeotians, at first he opposed it ; and when his friends told him that he would be put to death by the Athenians if he offended them, " That will be unjust," said he, " if I act for their advantage ; but if I play them false, it will be just." Afterwards, however, seeing that they would not desist, but continued their clamour, he ordered the herald to make proclamation that every man in Athens under sixty years of age should take provisions for five days and follow him at once from the assembly. Thereupon a great tumult arose, the elderly men leaping to their feet and shouting their dissent. " It is no hardship," said Phocion, " for I who am to be your general am in my eightieth year." For the time being this checked them and changed their purpose.

XXV. Πορθουμένης δε τῆς παραλίας ὑπὸ Μικίωνος συχνοῖς Μακεδόσι καὶ μισθοφόροις ἀποβεβηκότος εἰς Ῥαμνοῦντα καὶ κατατρέχοντος τὴν χώραν, ἐξήγαγε τοὺς Ἀθηναίους ἐπ᾿ αὐτόν. ὡς δὲ προστρέχοντες ἀλλαχόθεν ἄλλος διεστρατήγουν καὶ συνεβούλευον αὐτοῦ τὸν λόφον καταλαβεῖν, ἐκεῖ περιπέμψαι τοὺς ἱππέας, ἐνταῦθα παρεμβαλεῖν, "Ὦ Ἡράκλεις," εἶπεν, "ὡς πολλοὺς ὁρῶ στρατηγούς, ὀλίγους δὲ στρατιώτας."
2 ἐπεὶ δὲ παρατάξαντος αὐτοῦ τοὺς ὁπλίτας εἰς πολὺ πρὸ τῶν ἄλλων προῆλθεν, εἶτα δείσας ἀντιστάντος ἀνδρὸς πολεμίου πάλιν εἰς τὴν τάξιν ἀνεχώρησεν, "Ὦ μειράκιον," εἶπεν, "οὐκ αἰδῇ δύο τάξεις ἀπολελοιπώς, ἣν ἐτάχθης ὑπὸ τοῦ στρατηγοῦ καὶ πάλιν ἐφ᾿ ἣν σεαυτὸν ἔταξας;" ἐμβαλὼν δὲ τοῖς πολεμίοις καὶ κατὰ κράτος τρεψά- 753
μενος, αὐτόν τε τὸν Μικίωνα καὶ πολλοὺς ἄλλους
3 ἀπέκτεινε. τὸ δὲ Ἑλληνικὸν ἐν Θετταλίᾳ στράτευμα, συμμίξαντος Ἀντιπάτρῳ Λεοννάτου καὶ τῶν ἐξ Ἀσίας Μακεδόνων, ἐνίκα μαχόμενον· καὶ Λεοννάτος ἔπεσεν, ἡγουμένου τῆς μὲν φάλαγγος Ἀντιφίλου, τῶν δὲ ἱππέων τοῦ Θεσσαλοῦ Μένωνος.

XXVI. Ὀλίγῳ δὲ ὕστερον χρόνῳ Κρατεροῦ διαβάντος ἐξ Ἀσίας μετὰ πολλῆς δυνάμεως καὶ γενομένης πάλιν ἐν Κραννῶνι παρατάξεως, ἡττήθησαν μὲν οἱ Ἕλληνες οὔτε μεγάλην ἧτταν οὔτε πολλῶν πεσόντων, ἀπειθείᾳ δὲ πρὸς τοὺς ἄρχοντας ἐπιεικεῖς καὶ νέους ὄντας, καὶ ἅμα τὰς πό-

XXV. However, when their sea-coast was being devastated by Micion, who landed at Rhamnus with a horde of Macedonians and mercenaries and over-ran the adjacent territory, Phocion led the Athenians out against him. And as they marched, men would run up to their general from all sides and show him what to do. He was advised to seize a hill here, to send his horsemen around thither, or to make his attack upon the enemy there. "O Heracles," said Phocion, "how many generals I see, and how few soldiers!" Again, after he had drawn up his men-at-arms, one of them went out far in advance of the rest, and then was stricken with fear when an enemy advanced to meet him, and went back again to his post. "Shame on thee, young man," said Phocion, "for having abandoned two posts, the one which was given thee by thy general, and the one which thou didst give thyself." However, he attacked the enemy, routed them utterly, and slew Micion himself together with many others. The Greek army in Thessaly, also, al-though Leonnatus and his Macedonians from Asia had joined Antipater, was victorious in battle, and Leonnatus fell; the Greek men-at-arms were led by Antiphilus, their cavalry by Menon the Thessalian.

XXVI. But a short time afterwards Craterus crossed from Asia with a large force,[1] and there was another pitched battle at Crannon. Here the Greeks were defeated. Their defeat was not severe, nor did many of them fall, but owing to their lack of obedience to their commanders, who were young and soft-hearted, and because at the same time

---

[1] Cf. chapter xviii. 5.

λεις αὐτῶν πειρῶντος ᾿Αντιπάτρου, διαρρυέντες
2 αἴσχιστα προήκαντο τὴν ἐλευθερίαν. εὐθὺς οὖν
ἐπὶ τὰς ᾿Αθήνας ἄγοντος τοῦ ᾿Αντιπάτρου τὴν
δύναμιν οἱ μὲν περὶ Δημοσθένην καὶ Ὑπερείδην
ἀπηλλάγησαν ἐκ τῆς πόλεως, Δημάδης δέ, μηθὲν
μέρος ὧν ὤφειλε χρημάτων ἐπὶ ταῖς καταδίκαις
ἐκτῖσαι τῇ πόλει δυνάμενος (ἡλώκει γὰρ ἑπτὰ
γραφὰς παρανόμων καὶ γεγονὼς ἄτιμος ἐξείρ-
γετο τοῦ λέγειν), ἄδειαν εὑρόμενος τότε, γράφει
ψήφισμα ἐκπέμπειν[1] πρὸς ᾿Αντίπατρον ὑπὲρ
3 εἰρήνης πρέσβεις αὐτοκράτορας. φοβουμένου δὲ
τοῦ δήμου καὶ καλοῦντος Φωκίωνα, καὶ μόνῳ
πιστεύειν ἐκείνῳ λέγοντος, "᾿Αλλ᾿ εἴγε ἐπιστευό-
μην," εἶπεν, "ἐγὼ συμβουλεύων ὑμῖν, οὐκ ἂν νῦν
ἐβουλευόμεθα περὶ πραγμάτων τοιούτων." οὕτω
δὲ τοῦ ψηφίσματος ἐπικυρωθέντος ἀπεστάλη
πρὸς ᾿Αντίπατρον ἐν τῇ Καδμείᾳ στρατοπεδεύ-
οντα καὶ παρασκευαζόμενον εὐθὺς εἰς τὴν ᾿Αττι-
κὴν βαδίζειν. καὶ τοῦτο πρῶτον ᾔτει, τὸ μένοντα
4 κατὰ χώραν ποιήσασθαι τὰς διαλύσεις. τοῦ δὲ
Κρατεροῦ λέγοντος ὡς οὐ δίκαια πείθει Φωκίων
ἡμᾶς, τὴν τῶν συμμάχων καὶ φίλων καθημένους
χώραν κακῶς ποιεῖν δυναμένους ἐκ τῆς τῶν
πολεμίων ὠφελεῖσθαι, λαβόμενος αὐτοῦ τῆς δεξιᾶς
ὁ ᾿Αντίπατρος, "Δοτέον," εἶπε, "Φωκίωνι ταύτην
τὴν χάριν." περὶ δὲ τῶν ἄλλων ἐκέλευεν αὐτοῖς
ἐπιτρέπειν τοὺς ᾿Αθηναίους, ὥσπερ ἐν Λαμίᾳ
Λεωσθένης ἐκεῖνον.

[1] ἐκπέμπειν with Doehner; the MSS. have καὶ πέμπει, which
Bekker retains: πέμπειν, after Coraës.

Antipater made tempting overtures to their several cities, their army melted away and most shamefully abandoned the cause of freedom. At once, therefore, Antipater led his forces against Athens, and Demosthenes and Hypereides left the city. Demades, however, though he was unable to pay any portion of the fines which had been imposed upon him by the city (he had been seven times convicted of introducing illegal measures, had lost his civic rights, and was therefore debarred from speaking in the assembly), obtained immunity at this time, and brought in a bill for sending to Antipater ambassadors plenipotentiary to treat for peace. But the people were fearful, and called upon Phocion, declaring that he was the only man whom they could trust. "But if I had been trusted," said he, "when I gave you counsel, we should not now be deliberating on such matters." And when the bill had thus been passed, he was sent off to Antipater, who was encamped in the Cadmeia,[1] and was making preparations to march into Attica at once. And this was the first request that Phocion made, namely, that Antipater should remain where he was and make the treaty. And when Craterus declared that it was not fair in Phocion to try to persuade them to remain in the territory of their friends and allies and ravage it, when they had it in their power to get booty from that of their enemies, Antipater took him by the hand and said : "We must grant Phocion this favour." But as for the other terms of the peace, he ordered the Athenians to leave them to the conquerors, just as, at Lamia, he had been ordered to do by Leosthenes.

---

[1] The citadel of Thebes.

XXVII. Ὡς οὖν ἐπανῆλθεν ὁ Φωκίων εἰς τὸ ἄστυ καὶ τοῖς Ἀθηναίοις ταῦτα ἔδοξεν ὑπ' ἀνάγκης, αὖθις εἰς Θήβας ἐβάδιζε μετὰ τῶν ἄλλων πρέσβεων, Ξενοκράτην τὸν φιλόσοφον τῶν Ἀθηναίων προσελομένων. τοσοῦτον γὰρ ἦν ἀξίωμα τῆς ἀρετῆς τοῦ Ξενοκράτους καὶ δόξα καὶ λόγος παρὰ πᾶσιν ὥστε οἴεσθαι μήτε ὕβριν εἶναι μήτε ὠμότητα μήτε θυμὸν ἐν ἀνθρωπίνῃ ψυχῇ φυόμενον, ᾧ Ξενοκράτους μόνον ὀφθέντος οὐκ ἂν αἰδοῦς

2 τι καὶ τιμῆς ἐγγένοιτο πρὸς αὐτόν. ἀπέβη δὲ τοὐναντίον ἀγνωμοσύνῃ τινὶ καὶ μισαγαθίᾳ τοῦ Ἀντιπάτρου. πρῶτον μὲν γὰρ οὐκ ἠσπάσατο τὸν Ξενοκράτην τοὺς ἄλλους δεξιωσάμενος· ἐφ' ᾧ φασιν εἰπεῖν ἐκεῖνον ὡς Ἀντίπατρος καλῶς ποιεῖ μόνον αὐτὸν αἰσχυνόμενος ἐφ' οἷς ἀγνωμονεῖν μέλλει πρὸς τὴν πόλιν· ἔπειτα λέγειν ἀρξάμενον οὐχ ὑπομένων, ἀλλ' ἀντικρούων καὶ δυσκολαίνων

3 ἐποίησεν ἀποσιωπῆσαι. τῶν δὲ περὶ τὸν Φωκίωνα διαλεχθέντων ἀπεκρίνατο φιλίαν ἔσεσθαι τοῖς Ἀθηναίοις καὶ συμμαχίαν ἐκδοῦσι μὲν τοὺς περὶ Δημοσθένην καὶ Ὑπερείδην, πολιτευομένοις δὲ τὴν πάτριον ἀπὸ τιμήματος [1] πολιτείαν, δεξαμένοις δὲ φρουρὰν εἰς τὴν Μουνυχίαν, ἔτι δὲ χρήματα τοῦ πολέμου καὶ ζημίαν προσεκτίσασιν.

4 Οἱ μὲν οὖν ἄλλοι πρέσβεις ἠγάπησαν ὡς φιλανθρώπους τὰς διαλύσεις, πλὴν τοῦ Ξενοκράτους· ἔφη γὰρ ὡς μὲν δούλοις μετρίως κεχρῆσθαι

---

[1] ἀπὸ τιμήματος Coraës and Bekker, with most MSS.: ἀπὸ τιμημάτων.

XXVII. Accordingly, Phocion returned to Athens with these demands, and the Athenians acceded to them, under the necessity that was upon them. Then Phocion went once more to Thebes, with the other ambassadors, to whom the Athenians had added Xenocrates the philosopher. For so high an estimate was set upon the virtue of Xenocrates, and so great was his reputation and fame in the eyes of all, that it was supposed the human heart could harbour no insolence or cruelty or wrath which the mere sight of the man would not infuse with reverence and a desire to do him honour. But the result in this case was the opposite, owing to a certain ruthlessness and hatred of goodness in Antipater. For, in the first place, he would not salute Xenocrates, although he greeted the other ambassadors; at which Xenocrates is said to have remarked: "Antipater does well to feel shame before me alone of his ruthless designs against our city." And again, when the philosopher began to speak, Antipater would not listen to him, but angrily contradicted him and forced him into silence. But when Phocion had made his plea, Antipater replied that the Athenians could be his friends and allies on condition that they delivered up Demosthenes and Hypereides, reverted to their earlier constitution with its basis of property qualification, received a garrison into Munychia,[1] and, in addition, paid the costs of the war and a fine.

The rest of the ambassadors were satisfied with these terms and considered them humane, with the exception of Xenocrates, who said that Antipater dealt with them moderately if he held them to be

---

[1] The acropolis of Peiraeus.

τὸν Ἀντίπατρον, ὡς δὲ ἐλευθέροις βαρέως. τοῦ
δὲ Φωκίωνος παραιτουμένου τὴν φρουρὰν καὶ
δεομένου λέγεται τὸν Ἀντίπατρον εἰπεῖν "Ὦ
Φωκίων, ἡμεῖς πάντα σοι χαρίζεσθαι βουλόμεθα 75
5 πλὴν τῶν καὶ σὲ ἀπολούντων καὶ ἡμᾶς." οἱ δὲ
οὐχ οὕτως φασίν, ἀλλὰ ἐρωτῆσαι τὸν Ἀντίπατρον εἰ τὴν φρουρὰν ἀνέντος αὐτοῦ τοῖς Ἀθηναίοις ὁ Φωκίων ἐγγυᾶται τὴν πόλιν ἐμμενεῖν τῇ
εἰρήνῃ καὶ μηθὲν πολυπραγμονήσειν· σιωπῶντος
δὲ ἐκείνου καὶ διαμέλλοντος, ἀναπηδήσαντα Καλλιμέδοντα τὸν Κάραβον, ἄνδρα θρασὺν καὶ μισό-
δημον, εἰπεῖν· "Ἐὰν δὲ οὗτος, ὦ Ἀντίπατρε,
φλυαρῇ, σὺ πιστεύσεις καὶ οὐ πράξεις ἃ διέ-
γνωκας;"

XXVIII. Οὕτω μὲν ἐδέξαντο φρουρὰν Μακεδόνων Ἀθηναῖοι καὶ Μένυλλον ἡγεμόνα, τῶν
ἐπιεικῶν τινα καὶ τοῦ Φωκίωνος ἐπιτηδείων.
ἐφάνη δὲ ὑπερήφανον τὸ πρόσταγμα, καὶ μᾶλλον
ἐξουσίας ὕβρει χρωμένης ἐπίδειξις ἢ πραγμάτων
ἕνεκα γιγνομένη κατάληψις. οὐ μικρὸν δὲ τῷ
πάθει προσέθηκεν ὁ καιρός. εἰκάδι γὰρ ἡ φρουρὰ Βοηδρομιῶνος εἰσήχθη, μυστηρίων ὄντων, ᾗ
τὸν Ἴακχον ἐξ ἄστεος Ἐλευσῖνάδε πέμπουσιν,
ὥστε τῆς τελετῆς συγχυθείσης ἀναλογίζεσθαι
τοὺς πολλοὺς καὶ τὰ πρεσβύτερα τῶν θείων καὶ
2 τὰ πρόσφατα. πάλαι μὲν γὰρ ἐν τοῖς ἀρίστοις[1]
εὐτυχήμασι τὰς μυστικὰς ὄψεις καὶ φωνὰς παρα-

---

[1] ἀρίστοις Bekker adopts G. Hermann's conjecture of
ἀπίστοις (incredible).

slaves, but severely if he held them to be freemen. Phocion, however, besought Antipater to spare them the garrison, to which Antipater, as we are told, replied : "O Phocion, we wish to gratify thee in all things, except those which will ruin thee and us." But some tell a different story, and say that Antipater asked whether, in case he indulged the Athenians in the matter of the garrison, Phocion would go surety that his city would abide by the peace and stir up no trouble ; and that when Phocion was silent and delayed his answer, Callimedon, surnamed Carabus,[1] an arrogant man and a hater of democracy, sprang to his feet and cried : " But even if the fellow should prate such nonsense, Antipater, wilt thou trust him and give up what thou hast planned to do ? "

XXVIII. Thus the Athenians were obliged to receive a Macedonian garrison, which was under the command of Menyllus, an equitable man and a friend of Phocion. But the measure was held to be an arrogant one, and rather a display of power which delighted in insolence than an occupation due to stress of circumstance. And it came at a time which added not a little to the distress of the people. For the garrison was introduced on the twentieth of the month Boëdromion, while the celebration of the mysteries was in progress, on the day when the god Iacchus is conducted from the city to Eleusis, so that the disturbance of the sacred rite led most men to reflect upon the attitude of the heavenly powers in earlier times and at the present day. For of old the mystic shapes and voices were vouchsafed to them in the midst of their most glorious successes,

[1] *Stag-beetle.*

γενέσθαι σὺν ἐκπλήξει καὶ θάμβει τῶν πολεμίων,
νῦν δὲ τοῖς αὐτοῖς ἱεροῖς τὰ δυσχερέστατα πάθη
τῆς Ἑλλάδος ἐπισκοπεῖν τοὺς θεούς, καὶ καθυ-
βρίζεσθαι τὸν ἁγιώτατον τοῦ χρόνου καὶ ἥδιστον
αὐτοῖς, ἐπώνυμον τῶν μεγίστων κακῶν γενόμενον.
πρότερον μὲν οὖν ὀλίγοις ἔτεσι χρησμὸν ἐξή-
νεγκαν αἱ Δωδωνίδες τῇ πόλει " τὰ ἀκρωτήρια
τῆς Ἀρτέμιδος φυλάσσειν," ὅπως ἄλλοι μὴ λά-
3 βωσι· τότε δὲ περὶ τὰς ἡμέρας ἐκείνας αἱ ταινίαι
μέν, αἷς περιελίττουσι τὰς μυστικὰς κοίτας,
βαπτόμεναι θάψινον ἀντὶ φοινικοῦ χρῶμα καὶ
νεκρῶδες ἀνήνεγκαν· ὃ δὲ μεῖζον ἦν, τὰ παραβα-
πτόμενα τῶν ἰδιωτικῶν πάντα τὸ προσῆκον ἄνθος
ἔσχε. μύστην δὲ λούοντα χοιρίδιον ἐν Κανθάρῳ
λιμένι κῆτος συνέλαβε καὶ τὰ κάτω μέρη τοῦ
σώματος ἄχρι τῆς κοιλίας κατέπιε, προδεικνύντος
αὐτοῖς τοῦ θεοῦ προφανῶς ὅτι τῶν κάτω καὶ
πρὸς θαλάσσῃ στερηθέντες τὴν ἄνω πόλιν διαφυ-
λάξουσιν.

4 Ἡ μὲν οὖν φρουρὰ διὰ Μένυλλον οὐδὲν ἠνίασε
τοὺς ἀνθρώπους· τῶν δὲ ἀποψηφισθέντων τοῦ
πολιτεύματος διὰ πενίαν ὑπὲρ μυρίους καὶ δισχιλίους γενομένων οἵ τε μένοντες ἐδόκουν σχέτλια
καὶ ἄτιμα πάσχειν, οἵ τε διὰ τοῦτο τὴν πόλιν
ἐκλιπόντες καὶ μεταστάντες εἰς Θρᾴκην, Ἀντιπά-

---

[1] See the *Themistocles*, xv. 1.
[2] Artemis was the patron goddess of Munychia.

and brought consternation and affright upon their enemies; [1] but now, while the same sacred ceremonies were in progress, the gods looked down with indifference upon the most grievous woes of Hellas, and the profanation of the season which had been most sweet and holy in their eyes made it for the future give its name to their greatest evils. Indeed, a few years before this the Athenians had received an oracle from Dodona bidding them "guard the summits of Artemis," [2] that strangers might not seize them; and now, during the days of the festival, when the fillets with which they entwine the mystic chests were dyed, instead of purple they showed a sallow and deathly colour, and, what was more significant still, all the articles for common use which were dyed along with the fillets took the natural hue. Moreover, as a mystic initiate was washing a pig [3] in the harbour of Cantharus,[4] a great fish seized the man and devoured the lower parts of his body as far as the belly, by which Heaven clearly indicated to them in advance that they would be deprived of the lower parts of the city which adjoined the sea, but would retain the upper city.

Now, the garrison, owing to the influence of Menyllus, did no harm to the inhabitants; but the citizens who were deprived of their franchise because of their poverty numbered more than twelve thousand, and those of them who remained at home appeared to be suffering grievous and undeserved wrongs, while those who on this account forsook the city and migrated to Thrace, where Antipater

[3] An offering for Demeter, the chief divinity of the mysteries.

[4] Part of the harbour of Peiraeus.

τρου γῆν καὶ πόλιν αὐτοῖς παρασχόντος, ἐκπεπολιορκημένοις ἐῴκεσαν.

XXIX. Ὁ δὲ Δημοσθένους ἐν Καλαυρίᾳ καὶ Ὑπερείδου πρὸς Κλεωναῖς θάνατος, περὶ ὧν ἐν ἄλλοις γέγραπται, μονονοὺκ ἔρωτα καὶ πόθον Ἀθηναίοις Ἀλεξάνδρου καὶ Φιλίππου παρίστη. καὶ τοῦτο[1] ὅπερ ὕστερον, ἀναιρεθέντος Ἀντιγόνου καὶ τῶν ἀνελόντων ἐκεῖνον ἀρξαμένων βιάζεσθαι καὶ λυπεῖν τοὺς ἀνθρώπους, ἀνὴρ ἄγροικος ἐν Φρυγίᾳ χωρίον ὀρύττων πυθομένου τινός, "Τί ποιεῖς;" στενάξας, "Ἀντίγονον," εἶπε, "ζητῶ."
2 τοῦτο[1] πολλοῖς ἐπῄει λέγειν διαμνημονεύουσι τὸν ἐκείνων τῶν βασιλέων θυμόν, ὡς τὸ μέγα καὶ γενναῖον εὐπαραίτητον εἶχον, οὐχ ὥσπερ Ἀντίπατρος ἰδιώτου προσώπῳ καὶ φαυλότητι χλαμυδίου καὶ διαίτης εὐτελείᾳ κατειρωνευόμενος τὴν ἐξουσίαν ἐπαχθέστερος ἦν τοῖς πάσχουσι κακῶς
3 δεσπότης καὶ τύραννος. ὅμως δ' οὖν ὁ Φωκίων καὶ φυγῆς ἀπήλλαξε πολλοὺς δεηθεὶς τοῦ Ἀντιπάτρου, καὶ φεύγουσι διεπράξατο μὴ καθάπερ οἱ λοιποὶ τῶν μεθισταμένων ὑπὲρ τὰ Κεραύνια ὄρη καὶ τὸν Ταίναρον ἐκπεσεῖν τῆς Ἑλλάδος, ἀλλὰ ἐν Πελοποννήσῳ κατοικεῖν, ὧν καὶ Ἁγνωνίδης ἦν ὁ
4 συκοφάντης. ἐπιμελόμενος δὲ τῶν κατὰ τὴν πόλιν πράως καὶ νομίμως τοὺς μὲν ἀστείους καὶ 75 χαρίεντας ἐν ταῖς ἀρχαῖς ἀεὶ συνεῖχε, τοὺς δὲ πολυπράγμονας καὶ νεωτεριστάς, αὐτῷ τῷ μὴ

[1] τοῦτο retained in both places by Bekker; the first is deleted by Coraës, after Reiske; the second is corrected to τότε by Sintenis².

furnished them with land and a city, were like men driven from a captured city.

XXIX. Moreover, the death of Demosthenes in Calauria, and that of Hypereides at Cleonae, about which I have written elsewhere,[1] made the Athenians yearn almost passionately for Philip and Alexander. At a later time, after Antigonus had been slain,[2] and those who slew him began to oppress and vex the people, a peasant in Phrygia who was digging on his farm was asked by someone what he was doing, and answered: "I am looking for Antigonus." So now many were moved to speak, as they called to mind how the greatness and generosity of those illustrious kings made their wrath easy to appease; whereas Antipater, although he tried to conceal his power under the mask of a common man of mean attire and simple mode of life, was really a more burdensome tyrant and master to those who were in trouble. But nevertheless Phocion successfully pleaded with Antipater for the exemption of many from exile, and for those who went into exile he obtained the privilege of residing in Peloponnesus, instead of being driven out of Hellas beyond the Ceraunian mountains and the promontory of Taenarum like other men in banishment. Of this number was Hagnonides the public informer. Furthermore, by managing the affairs of the city with mildness and according to the laws, he kept the men of education and culture always in office, while the busybodies and innovators, who withered into insignificance from the very fact that they held no office and

---

[1] See the *Demosthenes*, chapters xxviii.–xxx.

[2] Antigonus was defeated by Seleucus and Lysimachus at Ipsus, in Phrygia, in 301 B.C., and fell in the battle.

ἄρχειν μηδὲ θορυβεῖν ἀπομαραινομένους, ἐδίδαξε
φιλοχωρεῖν καὶ ἀγαπᾶν γεωργοῦντας. ὁρῶν δὲ
τὸν Ξενοκράτην τελοῦντα τὸ μετοίκιον ἐβούλετο
γράψαι πολίτην· ὁ δὲ ἀπεῖπε, φήσας οὐκ ἂν
μετασχεῖν ταύτης τῆς πολιτείας περὶ ἧς ἐπρέ-
σβευεν ἵνα μὴ γένηται.

XXX. Τοῦ δὲ Μενύλλου δωρεὰν αὐτῷ καὶ
χρήματα διδόντος, ἀπεκρίνατο μήτ᾽ ἐκεῖνον Ἀλεξάνδρου βελτίονα εἶναι μήτε κρείττονα τὴν αἰτίαν
ἐφ᾽ ᾗ λήψεται νῦν ὁ τότε μὴ δεξάμενος. ἀλλὰ
Φώκῳ γε τῷ παιδὶ λαβεῖν δεομένου τοῦ Μενύλλου, "Φώκῳ μέν," εἶπεν, "ἐὰν μὲν σωφρονῇ
μεταβαλόμενος, ἀρκέσει τὰ τοῦ πατρός· ὡς δ᾽
ἔχει νῦν, οὐδὲν ἱκανόν ἐστιν." Ἀντιπάτρῳ δὲ
τραχύτερον ἀπεκρίνατο βουλομένῳ τι γενέσθαι
δι᾽ αὐτοῦ τῶν μὴ πρεπόντων· "Οὐ δύναται γάρ,"
εἶπεν, "Ἀντίπατρος ἅμα μοι καὶ φίλῳ καὶ
2 κόλακι χρῆσθαι." τὸν δὲ Ἀντίπατρον αὐτὸν
εἰπεῖν λέγουσιν ὡς δυεῖν αὐτῷ φίλων Ἀθήνησιν
ὄντων, Φωκίωνος καὶ Δημάδου, τὸν μὲν λαβεῖν
οὐ πέπεικε, τὸν δὲ διδοὺς οὐκ ἐμπέπληκε. καὶ
μέντοι Φωκίων μὲν ὡς ἀρετὴν ἐπεδείκνυτο τὴν
πενίαν, ἐν ᾗ τοσαυτάκις Ἀθηναίων στρατηγήσας
καὶ βασιλεῦσι φίλοις χρησάμενος ἐγκατεγήρασε,
Δημάδης δὲ τῷ πλούτῳ καὶ παρανομῶν ἐκαλλω-
3 πίζετο. νόμου γὰρ ὄντος Ἀθήνησι τότε μὴ
χορεύειν ξένον ἢ χιλίας ἀποτίνειν τὸν χορηγόν,
ἅπαντας εἰσαγαγὼν ξένους τοὺς χορεύοντας

raised no uproars, were taught by him to be fond of home and to delight in tilling the soil. When he saw that Xenocrates paid the resident alien tax, he offered to enrol him as a citizen; but the philosopher refused, saying that he could not take part in an administration for the prevention of which he had served on an embassy.[1]

XXX. When Menyllus offered Phocion a gift of money, he replied that neither was Menyllus better than Alexander,[2] nor was there any stronger reason why the man who would not accept it then should take it now. Menyllus, however, begged him to take the money for his son Phocus at least, whereupon Phocion said: "For Phocus, should he be converted to sobriety of life, his patrimony will be enough; but as he is now, nothing is sufficient." Again, when Antipater desired him to do something that was not seemly, he gave him a sharper answer, saying: "Antipater cannot have from me the services of friend and flatterer at once." And Antipater himself once said, as we are told, that he had two friends at Athens, Phocion and Demades; one he could never persuade to take anything, the other he could never satisfy with his gifts. And verily Phocion displayed as a virtue the poverty in which, though he had been so many times a general of Athens and had enjoyed the friendship of kings, he had come to old age; whereas Demades made a great parade of his wealth, even though he was violating the laws to do so. For instance, there was a law of Athens at this time forbidding a choregus to have a foreigner in his chorus, under penalty of a thousand drachmas; but Demades presented a chorus of a hundred members

[1] Cf. chapter xxvii.   [2] Cf. chapter xviii.

ἑκατὸν ὄντας ἅμα καὶ τὴν ζημίαν ἀνὰ χιλίας
ὑπὲρ ἑκάστου εἰσήνεγκεν εἰς τὸ θέατρον. Δημέᾳ
δὲ τῷ υἱῷ νύμφην ἀγόμενος, " Ἐμοῦ μέν," εἶπεν,
" ὦ παῖ, τὴν σὴν μητέρα γαμοῦντος οὐδὲ ὁ γείτων
ᾔσθετο· τοῖς δὲ σοῖς γάμοις καὶ βασιλεῖς καὶ
δυνάσται συγχορηγοῦσιν."

4 Ἐνοχλούντων δὲ τῷ Φωκίωνι τῶν Ἀθηναίων
ὅπως ἀπαλλάξῃ τὴν φρουρὰν πείσας τὸν Ἀντίπατρον, εἴτε μὴ προσδοκῶν πείσειν εἴτε μᾶλλον
ὁρῶν σωφρονοῦντα τὸν δῆμον καὶ πολιτευόμενον
εὐτάκτως διὰ τὸν φόβον, ἐκείνην μὲν ἀεὶ διωθεῖτο
τὴν πρεσβείαν, τὰ δὲ χρήματα μὴ πράττειν, ἀλλὰ
μέλλειν καὶ ἀναβάλλεσθαι τὸν Ἀντίπατρον
ἔπεισε. μεταβάντες οὖν Δημάδην παρεκάλουν.
5 ὁ δὲ προθύμως ὑπέστη καὶ τὸν υἱὸν ἔχων ἀπῆρεν
εἰς Μακεδονίαν, ὑπὸ δαίμονός τινος, ὡς ἔοικεν,
εἰς τοῦτο καιροῦ κομισθεὶς ἐν ᾧ κατείχετο μὲν
Ἀντίπατρος ἤδη νόσῳ, Κάσανδρος δὲ τῶν πραγμάτων ἐγκρατὴς γεγονὼς εὗρεν ἐπιστολὴν Δημάδου γεγραμμένην πρὸς Ἀντίγονον εἰς Ἀσίαν,
παρακαλοῦντος αὐτὸν ἐπιφανῆναι τοῖς περὶ τὴν
Ἑλλάδα καὶ Μακεδονίαν, ἐκ παλαιοῦ καὶ σαπροῦ
κρεμαμένοις στήμονος, τὸν Ἀντίπατρον οὕτω
6 σκώψαντος. ὡς οὖν εἶδεν αὐτὸν ἀφιγμένον ὁ
Κάσανδρος, συνέλαβε, καὶ πρῶτα μὲν τὸν υἱὸν
ἐγγὺς προσαγαγὼν ἀπέσφαξεν, ὥστε καταδέξα-
σθαι τοῖς κόλποις τὸ αἷμα τὸν πατέρα καὶ κατα-
πλησθῆναι τοῦ φόνου, μετὰ ταῦτα δὲ εἰς ἀχαρι-
στίαν αὐτὸν καὶ προδοσίαν πολλὰ λοιδορήσας
καὶ καθυβρίσας ἀπέκτεινεν.

all of whom were foreigners, and at the same time brought into the theatre his fine of a thousand drachmas for each one of them. Again, when he was bringing home a wife for his son Demeas, he said to him: "When I married thy mother, my son, not even a neighbour noticed it; but to thy nuptials kings and potentates are contributing."

When the Athenians importuned Phocion to go and persuade Antipater to remove the garrison, whether it was because he despaired of persuading him, or because he saw that the people were more sensible and conducted public affairs with more decorum when they were thus under the influence of fear, he continually rejected that mission; he did, however, persuade Antipater not to exact the moneys due from the city, but to delay, and postpone their payment. The people, accordingly, transferred their importunities to Demades. He readily undertook the mission, and taking his son with him set out for Macedonia. He arrived there, as some heavenly power, doubtless, would have it, precisely at the time when Antipater was already afflicted with sickness, and when Cassander, who had assumed control of affairs, had found a letter which Demades had written to Antigonus in Asia, beseeching him to present himself suddenly in Greece and Macedonia, which hung by an old and rotten thread, as he facetiously called Antipater. When, therefore, Cassander saw Demades after his arrival, he arrested him, and first slaughtered his son, whom he had brought so near that the folds of his father's robe caught the blood of his murder and were filled with it, and then, after heaping much insult and abuse upon him for his ingratitude and treachery, slew the father too.

XXXI. Ἐπεὶ δὲ Ἀντίπατρος ἀποδείξας Πολυσπέρχοντα στρατηγόν, Κάσανδρον δὲ χιλίαρχον, ἐξέλιπεν, εὐθὺς διαναστὰς ὁ Κάσανδρος καὶ προκαταλαμβάνων τὰ πράγματα πέμπει κατὰ τάχος Νικάνορα τῷ Μενύλλῳ διάδοχον τῆς φρουραρχίας, πρὶν ἔκδηλον τὸν Ἀντιπάτρου θάνατον γενέσθαι κελεύσας τὴν Μουνυχίαν παρα-

2 λαβεῖν. γενομένου δὲ τούτου, καὶ μεθ' ἡμέρας ὀλίγας πυθομένων τῶν Ἀθηναίων ὅτι τέθνηκεν ὁ Ἀντίπατρος, ἐν αἰτίαις ὁ Φωκίων ἦν καὶ κακῶς ἤκουεν ὡς προαισθόμενος καὶ κατασιωπήσας χάριτι τοῦ Νικάνορος. ὁ δὲ τούτων μὲν οὐκ ἐφρόντιζεν, ἐντυγχάνων δὲ τῷ Νικάνορι καὶ διαλεγόμενος εἴς τε τἆλλα τοῖς Ἀθηναίοις πρᾷον αὐτὸν καὶ κεχαρισμένον παρεῖχε, καὶ φιλοτιμίας τινὰς ἔπεισε καὶ δαπάνας ὑποστῆναι γενόμενον ἀγωνοθέτην. 756

XXXII. Ἐν τούτῳ δὲ καὶ Πολυσπέρχων, τὴν τοῦ βασιλέως ἐπιμέλειαν ἔχων ὑφ' ἑαυτῷ καὶ καταπολιτευόμενος τὸν Κάσανδρον, ἔπεμψεν ἐπιστολὴν τοῖς ἐν ἄστει γεγραμμένην, ὡς τοῦ βασιλέως ἀποδιδόντος αὐτοῖς τὴν δημοκρατίαν καὶ πολιτεύεσθαι κατὰ τὰ πάτρια πάντας Ἀθη-

2 ναίους κελεύοντος. ἦν δὲ τοῦτο κατὰ τοῦ Φωκίωνος ἐπιβουλή. συσκευαζόμενος γὰρ εἰς ἑαυτόν, ὡς μικρὸν ὕστερον ἔδειξε τοῖς ἔργοις, ὁ Πολυσπέρχων τὴν πόλιν, οὐδὲν ἤλπιζε περαίνειν μὴ τοῦ Φωκίωνος ἐκπεσόντος· ἐκπεσεῖσθαι δὲ ἐκεῖνον

---

[1] Not to be taken in its literal meaning of *commander of a thousand*, but in the general sense of *lieutenant-general*, second in command. Antipater vainly sought to deprive his son of the succession.

XXXI. And when Antipater died, after appointing Polysperchon general-in-chief, and Cassander chiliarch,[1] Cassander at once became rebellious, promptly took the government into his own hands, and sent Nicanor with all speed to relieve Menyllus from the command of the garrison at Athens, bidding him take over Munychia before Antipater's death became known. This was done, and when, after a few days, the Athenians learned that Antipater was dead,[2] they blamed Phocion severely, alleging that he had known about it before and had held his peace as a favour to Nicanor. Phocion, however, paid no heed to these charges, but by interviews and discussions with Nicanor rendered him in general mild and gracious to the Athenians, and, in particular, persuaded him to undertake sundry expensive exhibitions as director of games.

XXXII. In the meantime, too, Polysperchon, who had the king[3] in his own personal charge and was seeking to thwart the schemes of Cassander, sent a letter to the citizens of Athens, announcing that the king restored to them their democracy and ordered that all Athenians should take part in the administration of the city according to their earlier polity. This was a plot against Phocion. For Polysperchon was scheming (as he plainly showed a little later) to dispose the city in his own interests, and had no hope of succeeding unless Phocion was banished; he was sure, however, that Phocion would be banished if the

---

[2] In 319 B.C.

[3] The imbecile Philip Arrhidaeus, half-brother of Alexander. The other king, the little son of Alexander by Roxana, was in Epeirus with Olympias, the mother of Alexander. See the *Eumenes*, iii. 1 and 7, with the notes.

ἅμα τῶν ἀπεψηφισμένων ἐπιχυθέντων τῇ πολιτείᾳ καὶ πάλιν τὸ βῆμα δημαγωγῶν κατασχόντων
καὶ συκοφαντῶν.

3 Ὑποκινουμένων δὲ πρὸς ταῦτα τῶν Ἀθηναίων,
βουλόμενος ἐντυχεῖν αὐτοῖς ὁ Νικάνωρ, ἐν Πειραιεῖ βουλῆς γενομένης, παρῆλθε, τῷ Φωκίωνι
ἐμπιστεύσας τὸ σῶμα. Δερκύλλου δὲ τοῦ ἐπὶ
τῆς χώρας στρατηγοῦ συλλαβεῖν αὐτὸν ἐπιχει-
ρήσαντος, ἐκεῖνος μὲν προαισθόμενος ἐξεπήδησε,
καὶ φανερὸς ἦν εὐθὺς ἀμυνούμενος τὴν πόλιν, ὁ
δὲ Φωκίων ἐπὶ τῷ προέσθαι τὸν ἄνδρα καὶ μὴ
κατασχεῖν ἐγκαλούμενος ἔφη πιστεύειν μὲν τῷ
Νικάνορι καὶ μηδὲν ἀπ᾽ αὐτοῦ προσδοκᾶν δεινόν·
εἰ δὲ μή, μᾶλλον ἐθέλειν ἀδικούμενος ἢ ἀδικῶν
4 φανερὸς γενέσθαι. τοῦτο δὲ ὑπὲρ αὐτοῦ μὲν ἄν
τινι σκοποῦντι δοκοίη καλοκαγαθικῶς λελέχθαι
καὶ γενναίως· ὁ δὲ εἰς πατρίδος ἀποκινδυνεύων
σωτηρίαν, καὶ ταῦτα στρατηγὸς καὶ ἄρχων, οὐκ
οἶδα μὴ μεῖζόν τι παραβαίνει καὶ πρεσβύτερον
τὸ πρὸς τοὺς πολίτας δίκαιον. οὐδὲ γὰρ ἐκεῖνο
ἔστιν εἰπεῖν, ὅτι φοβούμενος μὲν εἰς πόλεμον
ἐμβαλεῖν τὴν πόλιν ὁ Φωκίων ἀπέσχετο τοῦ
Νικάνορος, ἄλλως δὲ προὐβάλλετο τὴν πίστιν
καὶ τὸ δίκαιον, ὅπως αἰδούμενος ἐκεῖνος ἡσυχίαν
5 ἄγῃ καὶ μηδὲν ἀδικῇ τοὺς Ἀθηναίους· ἀλλ᾽ ὄντως
ἔοικεν ἰσχυρά τις αὐτῷ περὶ τοῦ Νικάνορος ἐγ-
γενέσθαι πίστις, ὅν γε πολλῶν προδιαβαλλόντων

disfranchised citizens overwhelmed the administration, and the tribunal was again at the mercy of demagogues and public informers.

Since the Athenians were somewhat stirred by these communications, Nicanor wished to address them,[1] and after a council had been convened in Peiraeus, he came before it, relying upon Phocion for the safety of his person. But Dercyllus, the Athenian general in command of the district, made an attempt to arrest him, whereupon Nicanor, who became aware of the attempt in time, dashed away, and was clearly about to inflict speedy punishment upon the city. Phocion, however, when assailed for letting Nicanor go and not detaining him, said that he had confidence in Nicanor and expected no evil at his hands; but in any case, he would rather be found suffering wrong than doing wrong. Now, such an utterance as this might seem honourable and noble in one who had regard to his own interests alone; but he who endangers his country's safety, and that, too, when he is her commanding general, transgresses, I suspect, a larger and more venerable obligation of justice towards his fellow citizens. For it cannot even be said that it was the fear of plunging the city into war which made Phocion refrain from seizing Nicanor, but that he sought to excuse himself on other grounds by protestations of good faith and justice, in order that Nicanor might respect these obligations and keep the peace and do the Athenians no wrong; nay, it would seem that he really had too strong a confidence in Nicanor. For though many gave warning against that officer and

---

[1] Nicanor, acting in the interests of Cassander, wished to expose to the Athenians the designs of Polysperchon.

καὶ κατηγορούντων ἐπιτίθεσθαι τῷ Πειραιεῖ καὶ
διαβιβάζειν εἰς Σαλαμῖνα ξένους καὶ διαφθείρειν
τινὰς τῶν ἐν Πειραιεῖ κατοικούντων, οὐ προσήκατο τὸν λόγον οὐδ' ἐπίστευσεν, ἀλλὰ καὶ Φιλο-
μήλου τοῦ Λαμπτρέως ψήφισμα γράψαντος
Ἀθηναίους ἅπαντας ἐν τοῖς ὅπλοις εἶναι καὶ τῷ
στρατηγῷ Φωκίωνι προσέχειν, ἠμέλησεν, ἄχρι
οὗ προσάγων ὁ Νικάνωρ ἐκ τῆς Μουνυχίας τὰ
ὅπλα τὸν Πειραιᾶ περιετάφρευσε.

XXXIII. Πραττομένων δὲ τούτων ὁ μὲν Φωκίων ἐθορυβεῖτο καὶ κατεφρονεῖτο τοὺς Ἀθηναίους
ἐξάγειν βουλόμενος, Ἀλέξανδρος δὲ ὁ Πολυσπέρχοντος υἱὸς ἧκε μετὰ δυνάμεως, λόγῳ μὲν ἐπὶ τὸν
Νικάνορα τοῖς ἐν ἄστει βοηθήσων, ἔργῳ δὲ τὴν
πόλιν, εἰ δύναιτο, καταληψόμενος αὐτὴν ἑαυτῇ
2 περιπετῆ γενομένην. οἵ τε γὰρ φυγάδες αὐτῷ
συνεισβαλόντες εὐθὺς ἦσαν ἐν ἄστει, καὶ τῶν
ξένων ἅμα καὶ τῶν ἀτίμων πρὸς αὐτοὺς εἰσδρα-
μόντων ἐκκλησία παμμιγὴς ἠθροίσθη καὶ ἄτακτος, ἐν ᾗ τὸν Φωκίωνα τῆς ἀρχῆς ἀπολύσαντες
ἑτέρους εἵλοντο στρατηγούς. εἰ δὲ μὴ συνιὼν εἰς
λόγους ὁ Ἀλέξανδρος τῷ Νικάνορι μόνος παρὰ
τὸ τεῖχος ὤφθη, καὶ τοῦτο ποιοῦντες πολλάκις
ὑποψίαν τοῖς Ἀθηναίοις παρέσχον, οὐκ ἂν ἡ
3 πόλις διέφυγε τὸν κίνδυνον. ἐπεὶ δὲ Ἁγνωνίδης
ὁ ῥήτωρ εὐθὺς ἐπεφύετο τοῖς περὶ τὸν Φωκίωνα
καὶ κατηγόρει προδοσίας, οἱ μὲν περὶ Καλλιμέδοντα καὶ Χαρικλέα φοβηθέντες ἀπῆλθον ἐκ τῆς
πόλεως, ὁ δὲ Φωκίων καὶ μετ' αὐτοῦ τῶν φίλων

757

accused him of hostile designs against the Peiraeus, in that he was sending mercenaries across to Salamis, and tampering with some of the residents in Peiraeus, Phocion would not give heed to the story nor believe it at all. Indeed, even after Philomelus of Lamptrae brought in a decree that all Athenians should stand under arms and await orders from Phocion their general, he paid no attention to the matter, until Nicanor led his troops forth from Munychia and began to run trenches around the Peiraeus.

XXXIII. In this state of affairs, Phocion, who now wished to lead the Athenians forth to battle, was stormed at and held in derision, and Alexander the son of Polysperchon came with an armed force. His ostensible design was to bring aid to the citizens against Nicanor, but he really wished to seize the city, if he could, now that she was ruinously divided against herself. For the exiles who had burst into the country with him were at once in the city, strangers and disfranchised citizens ran in to join them, and a motley and turbulent assembly was gathered together, in which Phocion was deposed from his command and other generals were chosen. And had not Alexander been seen in close conference with Nicanor near the walls, and had not their interview, which was often repeated, rendered the Athenians suspicious, the city would not have escaped its peril. Moreover, Hagnonides the orator[1] at once assailed Phocion and denounced him as a traitor, whereupon Callimedon and Charicles[2] took fright and left the city, while Phocion, and with him those

---

[1] The same as the public informer of xxix. 3.

[2] Prominent partisans of Antipater, who had transferred their allegiance to Cassander, the son of Antipater, rather than to Polysperchon, the successor of Antipater.

οἱ παραμείναντες ᾤχοντο πρὸς Πολυσπέρχοντα.
καὶ συνεξῆλθον αὐτοῖς χάριτι τοῦ Φωκίωνος ὁ
Πλαταιεὺς Σόλων καὶ Δείναρχος ὁ Κορίνθιος,
ἐπιτήδειοι τοῦ Πολυσπέρχοντος εἶναι δοκοῦντες
4 καὶ συνήθεις. ἀρρωστίᾳ δὲ χρησαμένου τοῦ
Δεινάρχου συχνὰς ἡμέρας ἐν Ἐλατείᾳ διέτριψαν,
ἐν αἷς Ἁγνωνίδου πείσαντος, Ἀρχεστράτου δὲ τὸ
ψήφισμα γράψαντος, ἔπεμπε πρεσβείαν ὁ δῆμος
κατηγορήσουσαν τοῦ Φωκίωνος. ἅμα δὲ καὶ
συνέμιξαν ἀμφότεροι τῷ Πολυσπέρχοντι μετὰ
τοῦ βασιλέως πορευομένῳ περὶ κώμην τινὰ τῆς
Φωκίδος, Φαρύγας, κειμένην ὑπὸ τὸ Ἀκρούριον
ὄρος, ὃ νῦν Γαλάτην καλοῦσιν.

5 Ἐνταῦθα δὴ θεὶς ὁ Πολυσπέρχων τὸν χρυσοῦν
οὐρανίσκον, καὶ καθίσας ὑπ' αὐτῷ τὸν βασιλέα
καὶ τοὺς φίλους, τὸν μὲν Δείναρχον εὐθὺς ἐκ
προόδου λαβεῖν ἐκέλευσε καὶ στρεβλώσαντας
ἀποκτεῖναι, τοῖς δὲ Ἀθηναίοις ἀπέδωκε λόγον.
ὡς δὲ θόρυβον καὶ κραυγὴν ἐποίουν ἀντικατη-
γοροῦντες ἀλλήλων ἐν τῷ συνεδρίῳ, καὶ προσελθὼν ὁ Ἁγνωνίδης εἶπεν, "Ἅπαντας ἡμᾶς εἰς
μίαν ἐμβαλόντες γαλεάγραν Ἀθηναίοις ἀναπέμ-
6 ψατε λόγον ὑφέξοντας," ὁ μὲν βασιλεὺς ἐγέ-
λασεν, οἱ δὲ περιεστῶτες τῷ συνεδρίῳ Μακεδόνες
καὶ ξένοι σχολὴν ἄγοντες ἐπεθύμουν ἀκούειν, καὶ
τοὺς πρέσβεις παρεκάλουν ἀπὸ νεύματος ἐνταῦθα
ποιεῖσθαι τὴν κατηγορίαν. ἦν δὲ οὐδὲν ἴσον,
ἀλλὰ τῷ μὲν Φωκίωνι πολλάκις ἀντέκρουσεν ὁ
Πολυσπέρχων λέγοντι, μέχρι οὗ τῇ βακτηρίᾳ

of his friends who remained faithful, set out to go to Polysperchon. There went forth with them also, out of regard for Phocion, Solon of Plataea and Deinarchus of Corinth,[1] who were reputed to be intimate friends of Polysperchon. But Deinarchus fell sick, and the party therefore tarried many days in Elateia, during which time the people of Athens, in accordance with a decree brought in by Archestratus and supported by Hagnonides, sent an embassy to denounce Phocion. Both the parties fell in with Polysperchon at the same time, as he was marching with the king near Pharygae, a village of Phocis lying at the foot of Mount Acrurium, which is now called Galata.

Here, then, Polysperchon, after setting up the golden canopy and seating beneath it the king and his friends, as soon as Deinarchus came forward, ordered him to be seized, tortured, and put to death,[2] and then gave audience to the Athenians. But they raised a tumultuous shouting with their denunciations of one another in the council, and at last Hagnonides came forward and said: "Throw us all into one cage and send us back to Athens to render an account." At this, the king burst out laughing; but the Macedonians and foreigners who were gathered about the council, having nothing else to do, were eager to listen, and nodded to the ambassadors to make their denunciation there. But there was no fairness in the conduct of the case, since, when Phocion tried to speak, he was frequently interrupted by Polysperchon, and at last, smiting the ground with

---

[1] Antipater's chief agent in Peloponnesus.

[2] In order to maintain himself in power, Polysperchon was forced to treat Antipater's friends as his own enemies.

πατάξας τὴν γῆν ἀπέστη καὶ κατεσιώπησεν.
7 Ἡγήμονος δὲ φήσαντος ὅτι μάρτυς αὐτῷ τῆς πρὸς
τὸν δῆμον εὐνοίας Πολυσπέρχων ἐστί, καὶ τοῦ
Πολυσπέρχοντος ἀποκριναμένου πρὸς ὀργήν,
" Παῦσαί μου πρὸς τὸν βασιλέα καταψευδό-
μενος," ἀναπηδήσας ὁ βασιλεὺς ὥρμησε λόγχῃ
τὸν Ἡγήμονα πατάξαι. ταχὺ δὲ τοῦ Πολυσπέρχοντος περιλαβόντος αὐτὸν οὕτω διελύθη τὸ
συνέδριον.

XXXIV. Τὸν δὲ Φωκίωνα καὶ τοὺς μετ᾽ αὐτοῦ
φυλακῆς περιεχούσης, ὅσοι τῶν ἑταίρων ἔτυχον
οὐκ ἐγγὺς ἑστῶτες, ὡς τοῦτο εἶδον, ἐγκαλυψά-
μενοι καὶ διαφυγόντες ἐσώθησαν. ἐκείνους δὲ
Κλεῖτος εἰς Ἀθήνας ἀνῆγε λόγῳ μὲν κριθησομέ-
2 νους, ἔργῳ δὲ ἀποθανεῖν κατακεκριμένους. καὶ
προσῆν τὸ σχῆμα τῇ κομιδῇ λυπηρόν, ἐφ᾽
ἁμάξαις κομιζομένων αὐτῶν διὰ τοῦ Κεραμεικοῦ
πρὸς τὸ θέατρον· ἐκεῖ γὰρ αὐτοὺς προσαγαγὼν ὁ
Κλεῖτος συνεῖχεν, ἄχρι οὗ τὴν ἐκκλησίαν ἐπλή-
ρωσαν οἱ ἄρχοντες, οὐ δοῦλον, οὐ ξένον, οὐκ
ἄτιμον ἀποκρίναντες, ἀλλὰ πᾶσι καὶ πάσαις
ἀναπεπταμένον τὸ βῆμα καὶ τὸ θέατρον παρα-
3 σχόντες. ἐπεὶ δὲ ἥ τ᾽ ἐπιστολὴ τοῦ βασιλέως
ἀνεγνώσθη, λέγοντος αὐτῷ μὲν ἐγνῶσθαι προδό-
τας γεγονέναι τοὺς ἄνδρας, ἐκείνοις δὲ διδόναι
τὴν κρίσιν ἐλευθέροις τε δὴ καὶ αὐτονόμοις οὖσι,
καὶ τοὺς ἄνδρας ὁ Κλεῖτος εἰσήγαγεν, οἱ μὲν
βέλτιστοι τῶν πολιτῶν ὀφθέντος τοῦ Φωκίωνος
ἐνεκαλύψαντο καὶ κάτω κύψαντες ἐδάκρυον, εἷς

his staff, he retired and held his peace. Moreover, when Hegemon[1] said that Polysperchon could bear witness to his good will towards the people, and Polysperchon replied in wrath, "Cease telling lies against me in the presence of the king," the king sprang to his feet and would have smitten Hegemon with a spear. But Polysperchon quickly threw his arms about the king, and thus the council was dissolved.

XXXIV. A guard was now placed about Phocion and his associates, and at sight of this all of his friends who were standing at some remove covered up their faces and sought safety in flight. Phocion and his party, however, were taken back to Athens by Cleitus, ostensibly to be tried, but really under sentence of death. And besides, the manner of their return to the city was shameful, for they were carried on waggons through the Cerameicus to the theatre. For thither Cleitus brought them and there he kept them, until the magistrates had made up an assembly, from which they excluded neither slave, foreigner, nor disfranchised person, but allowed all alike, both men and women, free access to theatre and tribunal. After the letter of the king had been read aloud, in which he said that according to his judgement the men were traitors, but that their fellow citizens, who were freemen and self-governing, should pronounce sentence upon them, Cleitus led the men in. Then the best of the citizens, at sight of Phocion, covered their faces, bent their heads, and wept. One of them, however, rose up

---

[1] One of Phocion's party, and, like him, under accusation of treachery, *i.e.* of favouring Cassander rather than Polysperchon.

δὲ ἀναστὰς ἐτόλμησεν εἰπεῖν ὅτι, τηλικαύτην
κρίσιν ἐγκεχειρικότος τῷ δήμῳ τοῦ βασιλέως,
καλῶς ἔχει τοὺς δούλους καὶ τοὺς ξένους ἀπελ-
4 θεῖν ἐκ τῆς ἐκκλησίας. οὐκ ἀνασχομένων δὲ τῶν
πολλῶν, ἀλλ' ἀνακραγόντων βάλλειν τοὺς ὀλι-
γαρχικοὺς καὶ μισοδήμους, ἄλλος μὲν οὐδεὶς
ὑπὲρ τοῦ Φωκίωνος ἐπεχείρησεν εἰπεῖν, αὐτὸς δὲ
χαλεπῶς καὶ μόλις ἐξακουσθεὶς, "Πότερον,"
εἶπεν, "ἀδίκως ἢ δικαίως ἀποκτεῖναι βούλεσθε
ἡμᾶς;" ἀποκριναμένων δέ τινων ὅτι δικαίως, 758
"Καὶ τοῦτο," ἔφη, "πῶς γνώσεσθε μὴ ἀκούσαν-
5 τες;" ἐπεὶ δὲ οὐθὲν μᾶλλον ἤκουον, ἐγγυτέρω
προσελθών, "Ἐγὼ μέν," εἶπεν, "ἀδικεῖν ὁμο-
λογῶ, καὶ θανάτου τιμῶμαι τὰ πεπολιτευμένα
ἐμαυτῷ· τούτους δέ, ἄνδρες Ἀθηναῖοι, διὰ τί
ἀποκτενεῖτε μηδὲν ἀδικοῦντας;" ἀποκριναμένων
δὲ πολλῶν, "Ὅτι σοὶ φίλοι εἰσίν," ὁ μὲν Φωκίων ἀποστὰς ἡσυχίαν ἦγεν, ὁ δὲ Ἀγνωνίδης
ψήφισμα γεγραμμένον ἔχων ἀνέγνω, καθ' ὃ τὸν
δῆμον ἔδει χειροτονεῖν περὶ τῶν ἀνδρῶν εἰ δοκοῦσιν ἀδικεῖν, τοὺς δὲ ἄνδρας, ἂν καταχειροτονη-
θῶσιν, ἀποθνήσκειν.

XXXV. Ἀναγνωσθέντος δὲ τοῦ ψηφίσματος
ἠξίουν τινὲς προσγράφειν ὅπως καὶ στρεβλωθεὶς
Φωκίων ἀποθάνοι, καὶ τὸν τροχὸν εἰσφέρειν καὶ
τοὺς ὑπηρέτας καλεῖν προσέταττον. ὁ δὲ Ἀγνωνίδης καὶ τὸν Κλεῖτον ὁρῶν δυσχεραίνοντα καὶ
τὸ πρᾶγμα βαρβαρικὸν εἶναι καὶ μιαρὸν ἡγούμενος, "Ὅταν," ἔφη, "Καλλιμέδοντα τὸν μαστι-

---

[1] In cases where the penalty was not fixed by law, the
accuser proposed a penalty, and the accused had the right to

and had the courage to say that, since the king had put a case of such importance into the hands of the people, it were well that slaves and foreigners should leave the assembly. This the multitude would not tolerate, but cried out to stone the oligarchs and haters of the people. Therefore no one else undertook to speak in behalf of Phocion, but he himself, with great difficulty, at last made himself heard, saying: "Do ye wish to put us to death unjustly or justly?" And when some answered, "Justly," he said: "And how will ye determine this without hearing me?" But they were not a whit more willing to hear him, and therefore, drawing nearer, he said: "I admit my own guilt, and I assign death as the penalty[1] for my political conduct; but these men with me, men of Athens, are not guilty at all, and why will ye put them to death?" "Because they are thy friends," answered many, whereat Phocion retired and held his peace. But Hagnonides read aloud an edict which he had prepared, in accordance with which the people were to vote by show of hands whether they thought the men to be guilty, and the men, if the show of hands was against them, were to be put to death.

XXXV. After the edict had been read aloud, some demanded an additional clause providing that Phocion should be tortured before he was put to death, and insisted that the rack should be brought in and the executioners summoned. But Hagnonides, who saw that Cleitus was displeased at this, and considered the measure abominable and barbarous, said: "Whenever we catch that rascally Callimedon, men of Athens,

propose a counter-penalty. The court then chose between the two penalties. Phocion waived all the advantage of this right, as Socrates, in a different way, had done.

227

γίαν λάβωμεν, ὦ ἄνδρες Ἀθηναῖοι, στρεβλώσο-
μεν· περὶ δὲ Φωκίωνος οὐδὲν ἐγὼ γράφω τοιοῦ-
2 τον." ἐνταῦθα τῶν ἐπιεικῶν τις ὑπεφώνησεν·
"'Ορθῶς γε σὺ ποιῶν· ἂν γὰρ Φωκίωνα βασανί-
σωμεν, σὲ τί ποιήσομεν;" ἐπικυρωθέντος δὲ τοῦ
ψηφίσματος καὶ τῆς χειροτονίας ἀποδοθείσης,
οὐδεὶς καθήμενος, ἀλλὰ πάντες ἐξαναστάντες, οἱ
δὲ πλεῖστοι καὶ στεφανωσάμενοι, κατεχειροτό-
νησαν αὐτῶν θάνατον. ἦσαν δὲ σὺν τῷ Φωκίωνι
Νικοκλῆς, Θούδιππος, Ἡγήμων, Πυθοκλῆς· Δημητρίου δὲ τοῦ Φαληρέως καὶ Καλλιμέδοντος καὶ
Χαρικλέους καί τινων ἄλλων ἀπόντων κατεψη-
φίσθη θάνατος.

XXXVI. Ὡς οὖν διαλύσαντες τὴν ἐκκλησίαν
ἦγον εἰς τὸ δεσμωτήριον τοὺς ἄνδρας, οἱ μὲν
ἄλλοι, περιπλεκομένων τῶν φίλων αὐτοῖς καὶ
οἰκείων, ὀδυρόμενοι καὶ καταθρηνοῦντες ἐβάδιζον,
τὸ δὲ Φωκίωνος πρόσωπον οἷον ὅτε στρατηγῶν
ἀπ' ἐκκλησίας προὐπέμπετο βλέποντες, ἐθαύ-
μαζον τὴν ἀπάθειαν καὶ μεγαλοψυχίαν τοῦ
2 ἀνδρός. οἱ δὲ ἐχθροὶ κακῶς ἔλεγον παρατρέχον-
τες· εἷς δὲ καὶ προσέπτυσεν ἐξεναντίας προσελθών. ὅτε καὶ τὸν Φωκίωνα λέγεται βλέψαντα
πρὸς τοὺς ἄρχοντας εἰπεῖν· "Οὐ παύσει τις
ἀσχημονοῦντα τοῦτον;" ἐπεὶ δὲ Θούδιππος ἐν
τῷ δεσμωτηρίῳ γενόμενος καὶ τὸ κώνειον ὁρῶν
τριβόμενον ἠγανάκτει καὶ κατέκλαιε τὴν συμφοράν, ὡς οὐ προσηκόντως τῷ Φωκίωνι συναπολ-
λύμενος, "Εἶτα οὐκ ἀγαπᾷς," εἶπεν, "ὅτι μετὰ
3 Φωκίωνος ἀποθνήσκεις;" ἐρομένου δέ τινος τῶν
φίλων εἴ τι πρὸς Φῶκον λέγει τὸν υἱόν, "Πάνυ

we will put him to the torture ; but I cannot make
any such motion in the case of Phocion." Here some
decent fellow called out in response : " Right thou
art ; for if we should torture Phocion, what would
be left for us to do to thee ? " So the form of the
edict was approved, and when the show of hands
was taken, no one keeping his seat, but all rising to
their feet, and most of them wreathing themselves
with garlands, they condemned the men to death.
Now, there were with Phocion, Nicocles, Thudippus,
Hegemon, and Pythocles ; and Demetrius of Phalerum, Callimedon, Charicles, and sundry others,
were condemned to death *in absentiâ*.

XXXVI. When, accordingly, the assembly had
been dissolved and the men were being led to the
prison, the rest of them, as their friends and relatives clung about them, walked along lamenting and
shedding tears ; but the countenance of Phocion was
the same as it used to be when he was escorted
from the assembly as general, and when men saw it,
they were amazed at the man's calmness and at his
grandeur of spirit. His enemies, however, ran along
by his side and reviled him ; and one of them actually came up and spat in his face. At this, as we are
told, Phocion looked towards the magistrates and
said : " Will not someone stop this fellow's unseemly
behaviour ? " Again, when Thudippus, on entering
the prison and seeing the executioner bruising the
hemlock, grew angry and bewailed his hard fate,
declaring it not fitting that he should perish with
Phocion, " Is it no satisfaction to thee, then," said
Phocion, " that thou art put to death in company
with Phocion ? " And when one of his friends
asked him if he had any message for his son Phocus,

μὲν οὖν," ἔφη· "λέγω μὴ μνησικακεῖν Ἀθηναίοις." τοῦ δὲ Νικοκλέους, ὃς ἦν αὐτῷ πιστότατος
τῶν φίλων, παρακαλοῦντος ὅπως αὐτὸν ἐάσῃ τὸ
φάρμακον πιεῖν πρότερον, "Βαρὺ μέν," εἶπεν,
"ὦ Νικόκλεις, ἐμοὶ τὸ αἴτημα καὶ λυπηρόν, ἐπεὶ
δὲ οὐδὲ ἄλλο οὐδέποτέ σοι παρὰ τὸν βίον οὐδὲν
4 ἠχαρίστησα, καὶ τοῦτο συγχωρῶ." πεπωκότων
δὲ ἤδη πάντων τὸ φάρμακον ἐπέλιπε, καὶ ὁ δημό-
σιος οὐκ ἔφη τρίψειν ἕτερον, εἰ μὴ λάβοι δώδεκα
δραχμάς, ὅσου τὴν ὁλκὴν ὠνεῖται. χρόνου δὲ
γενομένου καὶ διατριβῆς ὁ Φωκίων καλέσας τινὰ
τῶν φίλων, καὶ εἰπὼν εἰ μηδὲ ἀποθανεῖν Ἀθήνησι
δωρεάν ἐστιν, ἐκέλευσε τῷ ἀνθρώπῳ δοῦναι τὸ
κερμάτιον.

XXXVII. Ἦν δὲ ἡμέρα μηνὸς Μουνυχιῶνος
ἐνάτη ἐπὶ δέκα, καὶ τῷ Διῒ τὴν πομπὴν πέμποντες
οἱ ἱππεῖς παρεξῄεσαν· ὧν οἱ μὲν ἀφείλοντο τοὺς
στεφάνους, οἱ δὲ πρὸς τὰς θύρας δεδακρυμένοι
τῆς εἱρκτῆς ἀπέβλεψαν. ἐφάνη δὲ τοῖς μὴ
παντάπασιν ὠμοῖς καὶ διεφθαρμένοις ὑπ' ὀργῆς
καὶ φθόνου τὴν ψυχήν, ἀνοσιώτατον γεγονέναι τὸ
μηδ' ἐπισχεῖν τὴν ἡμέραν ἐκείνην, μηδὲ καθαρεῦ-
2 σαι δημοσίου φόνου τὴν πόλιν ἑορτάζουσαν. οὐ
μὴν ἀλλ' ὥσπερ ἐνδεέστερον ἠγωνισμένοις τοῖς
ἐχθροῖς ἔδοξε καὶ τὸ σῶμα τοῦ Φωκίωνος ἐξορί- 75
σαι καὶ μηδὲ πῦρ ἐναῦσαι μηδένα πρὸς τὴν
ταφὴν Ἀθηναίων. διὸ φίλος μὲν οὐδεὶς ἐτόλμησεν
ἅψασθαι τοῦ σώματος, Κωνωπίων δέ τις, ὑπουρ-
γεῖν εἰθισμένος τὰ τοιαῦτα μισθοῦ, κομισθέντα

"Certainly," said he; "my message is that he
cherish no resentment against the Athenians."
Again, when Nicocles, his most faithful friend,
begged the privilege of drinking the drug first,
"O Nicocles," he said, "thy request is grievous to
me and painful; but since I have never in all my
life denied thee any other favour, I grant thee this
one also." But when all the rest had drunk of it,
the drug ran short, and the executioner refused to
bruise another portion unless he were paid twelve
drachmas, which was the price of the weight required. However, after a delay of some length,
Phocion called one of his friends, and, asking if a
man could not even die at Athens without paying
for the privilege, bade him give the executioner his
money.

XXXVII. It was the nineteenth day of the month
Munychion,[1] and the horsemen conducting the pro-
cession in honour of Zeus were passing by the prison.
Some of them took off their garlands, and others
gazed at the door of the prison with tears in their
eyes. And it was thought by all those whose souls
were not wholly savage and debauched by rage and
jealousy, that an impious thing had been done in not
waiting over that day, and so keeping the city pure
from a public execution when it was holding festival.
However, his enemies, as if their triumph were in-
complete, got a decree passed that the body of
Phocion should be carried beyond the boundary of
the country, and that no Athenian should light a
fire for his obsequies. Therefore no friend of his
ventured to touch his body, but a certain Conopion,
who was wont to perform such services for hire,

1 Early in May, 318 B.C.

τὸν νεκρὸν ὑπὲρ τὴν Ἐλευσῖνα, πῦρ λαβὼν ἐκ
3 τῆς Μεγαρικῆς, ἔκαυσεν. ἡ δὲ γυνὴ παροῦσα
μετὰ τῶν θεραπαινίδων ἔχωσε μὲν αὐτόθι χῶμα
κενὸν καὶ κατέσπεισεν, ἐνθεμένη δὲ τῷ κόλπῳ τὰ
ὀστᾶ καὶ κομίσασα νύκτωρ εἰς τὴν οἰκίαν κατώ-
ρυξε παρὰ τὴν ἑστίαν, εἰποῦσα· "Σοί, ὦ φίλη
ἑστία, παρακατατίθεμαι ταῦτα ἀνδρὸς ἀγαθοῦ
λείψανα· σὺ δὲ αὐτὰ τοῖς πατρῴοις ἀπόδος
ἠρίοις, ὅταν Ἀθηναῖοι σωφρονήσωσι."

XXXVIII. Καὶ μέντοι χρόνου βραχέος δια-
γενομένου, καὶ τῶν πραγμάτων διδασκόντων οἷον
ἐπιστάτην καὶ φύλακα σωφροσύνης καὶ δικαιοσύνης ὁ δῆμος ἀπώλεσεν, ἀνδριάντα μὲν αὐτοῦ
χαλκοῦν ἀνέστησαν, ἔθαψαν δὲ δημοσίοις τέλεσι
τὰ ὀστᾶ. τῶν δὲ κατηγόρων Ἀγνωνίδην μὲν αὐτοὶ
θάνατον καταχειροτονήσαντες ἀπέκτειναν, Ἐπί-
κουρον δὲ καὶ Δημόφιλον ἀποδράντας ἐκ τῆς πόλεως ἀνευρὼν ὁ τοῦ Φωκίωνος υἱὸς ἐτιμωρήσατο.
2 Τοῦτον οὔτε τἄλλα σπουδαῖον ἄνδρα γενέσθαι
φασί, καὶ παιδίσκης ἐρῶντα παρὰ πορνοβοσκῷ
τρεφομένης κατὰ τύχην Θεοδώρῳ τῷ ἀθέῳ παραγενέσθαι λόγον ἐν Λυκείῳ διαλεγομένῳ τοιοῦτον·
"Εἰ τὸ φίλον λύσασθαι μὴ αἰσχρόν ἐστιν, οὐδὲ
τὸ φίλην ὁμοίως· εἰ δὲ μὴ τὸ ἑταῖρον, οὐδὲ τὸ
ἑταίραν·" θέμενον οὖν ἑαυτῷ πρὸς τὴν ἐπιθυμίαν
τὸν λόγον ὡς εὖ ἔχοντα, λύσασθαι τὴν ἑταίραν.

Ἀλλὰ τὰ μὲν περὶ Φωκίωνα πραχθέντα τῶν
περὶ Σωκράτην πάλιν ἀνέμνησε τοὺς Ἕλληνας,
ὡς ὁμοιοτάτης ἐκείνῃ τῆς ἁμαρτίας ταύτης καὶ
δυστυχίας τῇ πόλει γενομένης.

---

[1] Cf. chapter xix.

carried the body beyond Eleusis, took fire from the Megarian territory, and burned it. The wife of Phocion,[1] however, who was present with her maid-servants, heaped up a cenotaph on the spot and poured libations upon it; then, putting the bones in her bosom and carrying them by night to her dwelling, she buried them by the hearth, saying: "To thee, dear Hearth, I entrust these remains of a noble man; but do thou restore them to the sepulchre of his fathers, when the Athenians shall have come to their senses."

XXXVIII. And indeed, after a short time had passed, and when the course of events was teaching them what a patron and guardian of moderation and justice the people had lost, they set up a statue of him in bronze, and gave his bones a public burial. Moreover, as regards his accusers, the people themselves condemned Hagnonides and put him to death; while Epicurus and Demophilus, who had run away from the city, were found out by Phocion's son and visited with his vengeance.

This son of Phocion,[2] we are told, turned out to be a man of no worth in general, and once, being enamoured of a girl who was kept in a brothel, chanced to hear Theodorus the Atheist discourse in the Lyceium as follows: "If there is no disgrace in ransoming a man beloved, the same is true of a woman loved; what is true of a comrade, is true also of a mistress." Accordingly, his passion leading him to think the argument sound, he ransomed his mistress.

But Phocion's fate reminded the Greeks anew of that of Socrates;[3] they felt that the sin and misfortune of Athens were alike in both cases.

[2] Cf. chapters xx. and xxx. 1.　　[3] In 399 B.C.

CATO THE YOUNGER

ΚΑΤΩΝ

I. Κάτωνι δὲ τὸ μὲν γένος ἀρχὴν ἐπιφανείας
ἔλαβε καὶ δόξης ἀπὸ τοῦ προπάππου Κάτωνος,
ἀνδρὸς ἐν δόξῃ καὶ δυνάμει μάλιστα Ῥωμαίων
γενομένου δι' ἀρετήν, ὡς ἐν τοῖς περὶ ἐκείνου
γέγραπται, κατελείφθη δὲ γονέων ὀρφανὸς μετ'
ἀδελφοῦ Καιπίωνος [1] καὶ Πορκίας ἀδελφῆς. ἦν
δὲ καὶ Σερβιλία Κάτωνος ὁμομήτριος ἀδελφή.
καὶ πάντες οὗτοι παρὰ Λιβίῳ Δρούσῳ τροφὴν
καὶ δίαιταν εἶχον, θείῳ μὲν ὄντι πρὸς [2] μητρός,
ἄγοντι δὲ τὴν πολιτείαν τότε· καὶ γὰρ εἰπεῖν
δεινότατος ἦν, καὶ τἆλλα σώφρων ἀνὴρ ἐν τοῖς
μάλιστα, καὶ φρονήματος οὐδενὶ Ῥωμαίων
ὑφιέμενος.

2   Λέγεται δὲ Κάτων εὐθὺς ἐκ παιδίου τῇ τε
φωνῇ καὶ τῷ προσώπῳ καὶ ταῖς περὶ τὰς παιδιὰς
διατριβαῖς ἦθος ὑποφαίνειν ἄτρεπτον καὶ ἀπαθὲς
καὶ βέβαιον ἐν πᾶσιν. ἰσχύν τε γὰρ εἶχον
αὐτοῦ παρ' ἡλικίαν τελεσιουργὸν αἱ ὁρμαί, καὶ
τοῖς κολακεύουσι τραχὺς ὢν καὶ προσάντης, ἔτι
μᾶλλον ἐκράτει τῶν ἐκφοβούντων. ἦν δὲ καὶ
πρὸς γέλωτα κομιδῇ δυσκίνητος, ἄχρι μειδιά-
ματος σπανίως τῷ προσώπῳ διαχεόμενος, καὶ
πρὸς ὀργὴν οὐ ταχὺς οὐδὲ ὀλισθηρός, ὀργισθεὶς
δὲ δυσπαραίτητος.

---

[1] Καιπίωνος with Coraës and Bekker : Καπίωνος.
[2] πρὸς with Coraës and Bekker, after Xylander : τῆς.

236

CATO THE YOUNGER

I. CATO's family got its first lustre and fame from his great-grandfather Cato (a man whose virtue gained him the greatest reputation and influence among the Romans, as has been written in his Life), but the death of both parents left him an orphan, together with his brother Caepio and his sister Porcia. Cato had also a half-sister, Servilia, the daughter of his mother.[1] All these children were brought up in the home of Livius Drusus, their uncle on the mother's side, who at that time was a leader in the conduct of public affairs; for he was a most powerful speaker, in general a man of the greatest discretion, and yielded to no Roman in dignity of purpose.

We are told that from his very childhood Cato displayed, in speech, in countenance, and in his childish sports, a nature that was inflexible, imperturbable, and altogether steadfast. He set out to accomplish his purposes with a vigour beyond his years, and while he was harsh and repellent to those who would flatter him, he was still more masterful towards those who tried to frighten him. It was altogether difficult to make him laugh, although once in a while he relaxed his features so far as to smile; and he was not quickly nor easily moved to anger, though once angered he was inexorable.

[1] By her second husband, Q. Servilius Caepio, who was also the father of Cato's half-brother Caepio.

3 Ὡς οὖν εἰς τὸ μανθάνειν ἧκε, νωθρὸς ἦν ἀναλαβεῖν καὶ βραδύς, ἀναλαβὼν δὲ κάτοχος καὶ μνημονικός. ὃ δὴ καὶ πέφυκεν ἄλλως, τοὺς μὲν εὐφυεῖς ἀναμνηστικοὺς μᾶλλον εἶναι, μνημονικοὺς δὲ τοὺς μετὰ πόνου καὶ πραγματείας παραδεχομένους· γίνεται γὰρ οἷον ἔγκαυμα τῆς ψυχῆς τῶν

4 μαθημάτων ἕκαστον. ἔοικε δὲ καὶ τὸ δύσπειστον τῷ Κάτωνι ποιεῖν ἐργωδεστέραν τὴν μάθησιν· πάσχειν γάρ τι τὸ μανθάνειν ἀτεχνῶς ἐστι, καὶ τὸ πείθεσθαι ταχὺ τοῖς ἧττον ἀντέχειν δυναμένοις συμβέβηκε. διὸ πείθονται μᾶλλον νέοι γερόντων καὶ νοσοῦντες ὑγιαινόντων, καὶ ὅλως ἐν οἷς τὸ ἀποροῦν ἀσθενέστατόν ἐστι, ῥᾷστον τὸ

5 προστιθέμενον. τῷ μέντοι παιδαγωγῷ τὸν Κάτωνα πείθεσθαι μὲν λέγουσι καὶ ποιεῖν ἅπαν τὸ προσταττόμενον, ἑκάστου δὲ τὴν αἰτίαν ἀπαιτεῖν καὶ τὸ διὰ τί πυνθάνεσθαι. καὶ γὰρ ἦν χαρίεις ὁ παιδαγωγὸς αὐτοῦ καὶ λόγον ἔχων τοῦ κονδύλου προχειρότερον, ὄνομα Σαρπηδών.

II. Ἔτι δὲ παιδὸς τοῦ Κάτωνος ὄντος ἔπραττον οἱ σύμμαχοι τῶν Ῥωμαίων ὅπως μεθέξουσι τῆς ἐν Ῥώμῃ πολιτείας· καί τις Πομπαίδιος Σίλλων, ἀνὴρ πολεμικὸς καὶ μέγιστον ἔχων ἀξίωμα, τοῦ δὲ Δρούσου φίλος, κατέλυσε παρ' αὐτῷ πλείονας ἡμέρας, ἐν αἷς γεγονὼς τοῖς παιδίοις συνήθης, "Ἄγε," εἶπεν, "ὅπως ὑπὲρ ἡμῶν δεήσεσθε τοῦ θείου συναγωνίσασθαι περὶ τῆς πολι-

2 τείας." ὁ μὲν οὖν Καιπίων διαμειδιάσας ἐπέ-

760

When, accordingly, he came to study, he was sluggish of comprehension and slow, but what he comprehended he held fast in his memory. And this is generally the way of nature: those who are well endowed are more apt to recall things to mind, but those retain things in their memory who acquire them with toil and trouble;[1] for everything they learn becomes branded, as it were, upon their minds. It would appear, too, that Cato's reluctance to be persuaded made his learning anything more laborious. For, to learn is simply to allow something to be done to you, and to be quickly persuaded is natural for those who are less able to offer resistance. Therefore young men are more easily persuaded than old men, and sick folk, than those who are well, and, in a word, where the power to raise objections is weakest, the act of submission is easiest. However, we are told that Cato was obedient to his tutor, and did everything that was enjoined upon him, although in each case he demanded the reason and wanted to know the why and wherefore. And, indeed, his tutor was a man of culture, and more ready to reason with a pupil than to thrash him. His name was Sarpedon.

II. While Cato was still a boy, the Italian allies of the Romans were making efforts to obtain Roman citizenship. One of their number, Pompaedius Silo,[2] a man of experience in war and of the highest position, was a friend of Drusus, and lodged at his house for several days. During this time he became familiar with the children, and said to them once: "Come, beg your uncle to help us in our struggle for citizenship." Caepio, accordingly, consented with a

---

[1] Cf. Aristotle, *De Mem.* i. 1, 2, 24.

[2] Erroneously called Publius Silo in the *Marius*, xxxiii. 2.

νευσε, τοῦ δὲ Κάτωνος οὐδὲν ἀποκριναμένου καὶ
βλέποντος εἰς τοὺς ξένους ἀτενὲς καὶ βλοσυρόν,
ὁ Πομπαίδιος, "Σὺ δέ," εἶπεν, "ἡμῖν, ὦ νεανία,
τί λέγεις; οὐχ οἷος εἶ τοῖς ξένοις συλλαμβάνε-
3 σθαι πρὸς τὸν θεῖον, ὥσπερ ὁ ἀδελφός;" μὴ φθεγ-
γομένου δὲ τοῦ Κάτωνος, ἀλλὰ τῇ σιωπῇ καὶ τῷ
προσώπῳ δοκοῦντος ἀπολέγεσθαι τὴν δέησιν,
ἀράμενος αὐτὸν ὁ Πομπαίδιος ὑπὲρ θυρίδος ὡς
ἀφήσων ὁμολογεῖν ἐκέλευεν ἢ ῥίψειν ἔφασκεν,
ἅμα τῇ τε φωνῇ τραχυτέρᾳ χρώμενος καὶ ταῖς
χερσὶν ἀπηρτημένον τὸ σῶμα πολλάκις ὑπὲρ τῆς
4 θυρίδος κραδαίνων. ἐπεὶ δὲ πολὺν χρόνον οὕτω
διεκαρτέρησεν ὁ Κάτων ἀνέκπληκτος καὶ ἀδεής,
καταθέμενος αὐτὸν Πομπαίδιος ἡσυχῇ πρὸς τοὺς
φίλους εἶπεν· "Οἷον εὐτύχημα τῆς Ἰταλίας ὅτι
παῖς οὗτός ἐστιν· εἰ δὲ ἀνὴρ ἦν, μίαν οὐκ ἂν οἶμαι
ψῆφον ἡμῖν ἐν τῷ δήμῳ γίνεσθαι."

5 Πάλιν δὲ συγγενοῦς τινος ἐν γενεθλίοις καλέ-
σαντος ἐπὶ δεῖπνον ἄλλους τε παῖδας καὶ τοὺς
περὶ Κάτωνα, σχολὴν ἄγοντες ἔν τινι μέρει τῆς
οἰκίας ἔπαιζον αὐτοὶ καθ᾽ ἑαυτοὺς ἀναμεμιγμένοι
νεώτεροι καὶ πρεσβύτεροι, τὸ δὲ παιζόμενον ἦν
δίκαι καὶ κατηγορίαι καὶ ἀγωγαὶ τῶν ἁλισκο-
6 μένων. εἷς οὖν τῶν ἑαλωκότων παίδων εὐπρεπὴς
τὴν ὄψιν ὑπὸ πρεσβυτέρου παιδὸς ἀχθεὶς εἴς τι
δωμάτιον καὶ εἰρχθεὶς ἐπεκαλεῖτο τὸν Κάτωνα.
ταχὺ δὴ τὸ γινόμενον συνεὶς ἧκεν ἐπὶ τὰς θύρας
ὁ Κάτων, καὶ διωσάμενος τοὺς προεστῶτας καὶ
διακωλύοντας ἐξήγαγε τὸν παῖδα· καὶ μετ᾽ ὀργῆς

smile, but Cato made no reply and gazed fixedly and fiercely upon the strangers. Then Pompaedius said: "But thou, young man, what sayest thou to us? Canst thou not take the part of the strangers with thy uncle, like thy brother?" And when Cato said not a word, but by his silence and the look on his face seemed to refuse the request, Pompaedius lifted him up through a window, as if he would cast him out, and ordered him to consent, or he would throw him down, at the same time making the tone of his voice harsher, and frequently shaking the boy as he held his body out at the window. But when Cato had endured this treatment for a long time without showing fright or fear, Pompaedius put him down, saying quietly to his friends: "What a piece of good fortune it is for Italy that he is a boy; for if he were a man, I do not think we could get a single vote among the people."[1]

At another time a relation of his who was celebrating a birthday, invited Cato and other boys to supper, and the company were diverting themselves at play in a separate part of the house, older and younger together, their play being actions at law, accusations, and the conducting of the condemned persons to prison. Accordingly, one of those thus condemned, a boy of comely looks, was led off by an older boy and shut into a chamber, where he called upon Cato for help. Then Cato, when he understood what was going on, quickly came to the door, pushed aside the boys who stood before it and tried to stop him, led forth the prisoner, and went

---

[1] This incident must have happened, if at all, in 91 B.C., when Cato was four years old; but it need not be inferred that he had already formed an opinion on public affairs. The story is told also in Valerius Maximus, iii. 1, 2.

ἔχων ἀπῆλθεν οἴκαδε, καὶ παῖδες ἕτεροι συνη-
κολούθησαν.

III. Οὕτω δ' ἦν περιβόητος ὥστ', ἐπειδὴ Σύλλας τὴν παιδικὴν καὶ ἱερὰν ἱπποδρομίαν, ἣν
καλοῦσι Τροίαν, ἐπὶ θέα διδάσκων καὶ συναγαγὼν τοὺς εὐγενεῖς παῖδας ἀπέδειξεν ἡγεμόνας
δύο, τὸν μὲν ἕτερον οἱ παῖδες ἐδέξαντο διὰ τὴν
μητέρα (Μετέλλης γὰρ ἦν υἱός, τῆς Σύλλα
γυναικός), τὸν δὲ ἕτερον, ἀδελφιδοῦν ὄντα Πομπηίου, Σέξτον, οὐκ εἴων οὐδὲ ἐβούλοντο μελετᾶν
οὐδὲ ἕπεσθαι, πυνθανομένου δὲ τοῦ Σύλλα τίνα
βούλοιντο, πάντες ἐβόησαν "Κάτωνα," καὶ ὅ γε
Σέξτος αὐτὸς εἴξας παρῆκεν ὡς κρείττονι τὴν
φιλοτιμίαν.

2 Ἔτυχε δὲ καὶ φίλος ὢν ὁ Σύλλας πατρικὸς
αὐτοῖς, καί ποτε καὶ προσηγάγετο καὶ προσωμί-
λησεν, ὀλίγοις πάνυ νέμων τὴν τοιαύτην φιλοφροσύνην, διὰ βάρος καὶ ὄγκον ἧς εἶχεν ἀρχῆς
καὶ δυνάμεως. μέγα δὴ ποιούμενος ὁ Σαρπηδὼν
τοῦτο πρὸς τιμὴν ἅμα καὶ ἀσφάλειαν, ἦγεν
ἀσπασόμενον τὸν Κάτωνα συνεχῶς εἰς τὴν οἰκίαν τοῦ Σύλλα, μηδὲν τότε προσιδεῖν ἀσεβῶν
χώρου διαφέρουσαν, ὑπὸ πλήθους τῶν ἀγομένων
3 καὶ στρεβλουμένων. ἦν μὲν οὖν ἔτος ἐκεῖνο τῷ
Κάτωνι τεσσαρεσκαιδέκατον· ἰδὼν δὲ κεφαλὰς
ἐπιφανῶν ἀνδρῶν λεγομένων ἐκκομιζομένας, καὶ
κρύφα τοὺς παρόντας ἐπιστένοντας, ἠρώτησε τὸν
παιδαγωγὸν ὅ τι δὴ τοῦτον τὸν ἄνθρωπον οὐδεὶς
ἀποκτίννυσιν. εἰπόντος δὲ ἐκείνου, "Φοβοῦνται
γὰρ αὐτόν, ὦ παῖ, μᾶλλον, ἢ μισοῦσι," "Τί οὖν,"
εἶπεν, "οὐκ ἐμοὶ ξίφος ἔδωκας, ἵνα αὐτὸν ἀνελὼν

off home with him in a passion, followed by other boys also.

III. He was so celebrated that, when Sulla was preparing for exhibition the sacred equestrian game for boys[1] which is called "Troja," and, after assembling the boys of good birth, appointed two leaders for them, the boys accepted one of them for his mother's sake (he was a son of Metella, Sulla's wife), but would not tolerate the other (who was a nephew of Pompey, named Sextus), and refused to rehearse under him or obey him; and when Sulla asked them whom they would have, they all cried "Cato," and Sextus himself gave way and yielded the honour to a confessed superior.

Now, Sulla was friendly to Cato and his brother[2] on their father's account, and sometimes actually asked them to see him and conversed with them, a kindness which he showed to very few, by reason of the weight and majesty of his authority and power. So Sarpedon, thinking that this conduced greatly to the honour and safety of his charge, was continually bringing Cato to wait upon Sulla at his house, which, at that time, looked exactly like an Inferno, owing to the multitude of those who were brought thither and put to torture. Now, Cato was in his fourteenth year; and when he saw heads of men reputed to be eminent carried forth, and heard the smothered groans of the bystanders, he asked his tutor why no one slew this man. "Because, my child," said the tutor, "men fear him more than they hate him." "Why, then," said Cato, "didst thou not give me a

---

[1] Cf. Vergil, *Aeneid*, v. 553 ff.

[2] Both here, and in i. 1, Plutarch carelessly speaks as though Caepio were own brother, and not half-brother, of Cato.

4 ἀπήλλαξα δουλείας τὴν πατρίδα;" τοῦτον τὸν
λόγον ἀκούσας ὁ Σαρπηδών, ἅμα δὲ καὶ τὸ βλέμ-
μα καὶ τὸ πρόσωπον αὐτοῦ πιμπλάμενον ὀργῆς
καὶ μένους κατιδών, οὕτως ἔδεισεν ὥστε τὸ λοιπὸν
ἤδη προσέχειν ἀκριβῶς καὶ παραφυλάττειν, μή
τι τολμήσῃ παραβολώτερον.

5 Ἔτι μὲν οὖν παιδάριον ὢν μικρόν, ἀπεκρίνατο
τοῖς ἐρωτῶσι τίνα φιλεῖ μάλιστα, τὸν ἀδελφόν·
τίνα δεύτερον, ὁμοίως τὸν ἀδελφόν, καὶ τρίτον,
ἄχρι οὗ πολλάκις λέγοντος ἀπεῖπεν ὁ ἐρωτῶν.
γενόμενος δ' ἐν ἡλικίᾳ μᾶλλον ἐβεβαίου τὴν πρὸς
τὸν ἀδελφὸν εὔνοιαν. ἔτη γὰρ εἴκοσι γεγονὼς
χωρὶς Καιπίωνος οὐκ ἐδείπνησεν, οὐκ ἀπεδή-
6 μησεν, εἰς ἀγορὰν οὐ προῆλθε. μύρον δ' ἐκείνου
λαμβάνοντος αὐτὸς παρῃτεῖτο· καὶ τἆλλα τὰ
περὶ τὴν δίαιταν ἦν ἀκριβὴς καὶ σύντονος. ὁ
γοῦν Καιπίων ἐπὶ σωφροσύνῃ καὶ μετριότητι
θαυμαζόμενος ὡμολόγει τοιοῦτος εἶναι πρὸς τοὺς
ἄλλους ἐξεταζόμενος, "Ἀλλ' ὅταν," ἔφη, "παρὰ
τὸν Κάτωνος βίον παραβάλλω τὸν ἐμόν, οὐδὲν
ἐμαυτῷ φαίνομαι Σιππίου διαφέρειν," τῶν ἐπὶ
τρυφῇ τινα καὶ μαλακίᾳ περιβοήτων ὀνομάσας.

IV. Ὁ δὲ Κάτων ἐπειδὴ τὴν ἱερωσύνην ἔλαβε
τοῦ Ἀπόλλωνος, μετοικήσας καὶ νειμάμενος μοῖ-
ραν τῶν πατρῴων ἑκατὸν εἴκοσι ταλάντων γενομένην, τὴν μὲν δίαιταν ἔτι μᾶλλον συνέστειλεν,
Ἀντίπατρον δὲ Τύριον τῶν ἀπὸ τῆς στοᾶς φιλοσόφων προσεταιρισάμενος, τοῖς ἠθικοῖς μάλιστα
καὶ πολιτικοῖς ἐνεφύετο δόγμασι, περὶ πᾶσαν
μὲν ἀρετὴν ὥσπερ ἐπιπνοίᾳ τινὶ κατάσχετος
γεγονώς, διαφόρως δὲ τοῦ καλοῦ τὸ περὶ τὴν

sword, that I might slay him and set my country free from slavery?" When Sarpedon heard this speech, and saw also the look on the boy's face, which was full of rage and fury, he was so frightened that in future he kept him under close watch and ward, lest he should venture on some rash deed.

When he was still a little boy, and was asked whom he loved most, he answered, "My brother"; and to the question whom he loved next, likewise, "My brother"; and so a third time, until, after many such answers from him, his questioner desisted. And when he came to maturity, he maintained all the more firmly this affection for his brother. Indeed, when he was twenty years old, without Caepio he would not take supper, or make a journey, or go out into the forum. But when his brother used perfume, Cato would decline it; and in his habits generally he was severe and strict. At any rate, when Caepio was admired and praised for his discretion and moderation, he would admit that he had those qualities when tested by reference to most men; "But when," he would say, "I compare my life with that of Cato, I seem to myself no better than Sippius,"—mentioning one of those who were celebrated for luxury and effeminacy.

IV. After Cato had been made priest of Apollo, he took a house apart, accepted his share of the patrimony, which amounted to a hundred and twenty talents, and began to live yet more simply than before. He made a close companion of Antipater the Tyrian, a Stoic philosopher, and devoted himself especially to ethical and political doctrines. He was possessed, as it were, with a kind of inspiration for the pursuit of every virtue; but, above all, that

δικαιοσύνην ἀτενές, καὶ ἄκαμπτον εἰς ἐπιείκειαν
2 ἢ χάριν, ὑπερηγαπηκώς. ἤσκει δὲ καὶ τὸν
ὀργανικὸν εἰς πλήθη λόγον, ἀξιῶν ὥσπερ ἐν
πόλει μεγάλῃ τῇ πολιτικῇ φιλοσοφίᾳ καὶ μά-
χιμον εἶναί τι παρατρεφόμενον. οὐ μέντοι μεθ'
ἑτέρων ἐποιεῖτο τὰς μελέτας, οὐδ' ἠκροάσατο
λέγοντος οὐδείς, ἀλλὰ καὶ πρός τινα τῶν ἑταίρων
εἰπόντα, " Μέμφονταί σου, Κάτων, οἱ ἄνθρωποι
τὴν σιωπήν," " Μόνον," ἔφη, " μὴ τὸν βίον.
ἄρξομαι δὲ λέγειν, ὅταν μὴ μέλλω λέγειν ἄξια
σιωπῆς."

V. Ἡ δὲ καλουμένη Πορκία βασιλικὴ τιμη-
τικὸν ἦν ἀνάθημα τοῦ παλαιοῦ Κάτωνος. εἰ-
ωθότες οὖν ἐκεῖ χρηματίζειν οἱ δήμαρχοι, καὶ
κίονος τοῖς δίφροις ἐμποδὼν εἶναι δοκοῦντος,
ἔγνωσαν ὑφελεῖν αὐτὸν ἢ μεταστῆσαι. τοῦτο
Κάτωνα πρῶτον εἰς ἀγορὰν ἄκοντα προήγαγεν·
ἀντέστη γὰρ αὐτοῖς, καὶ πεῖραν ἅμα τοῦ λόγου
2 καὶ τοῦ φρονήματος δοὺς ἐθαυμάσθη. καὶ γὰρ ὁ
λόγος νεαρὸν μὲν οὐδὲν οὐδὲ κομψὸν εἶχεν, ἀλλ'
ἦν ὄρθιος καὶ περιπληθὴς καὶ τραχύς. οὐ μὴν
ἀλλὰ καὶ χάρις ἀγωγὸς ἀκοῆς ἐπέτρεχε τῇ τραχύ-
τητι τῶν νοημάτων, καὶ τὸ ἦθος αὐτοῦ καταμι-
γνύμενον ἡδονήν τινα καὶ μειδίαμα τῷ σεμνῷ
παρεῖχεν οὐκ ἀπάνθρωπον. ἡ δὲ φωνὴ μεγέθει
μὲν ἀποχρῶσα καὶ διαρκὴς εἰς τοσοῦτον ἐξικέσθαι δῆμον, ἰσχὺν δὲ καὶ τόνον ἄρρηκτον εἶχε καὶ

form of goodness which consists in rigid justice that
will not bend to clemency or favour, was his great
delight. He practised also the kind of speaking
which is effective with a multitude, deeming it right
that in political philosophy, as in a great city, a
certain warlike element should also be maintained.
However, he did not perform his exercises in
company with others, nor did any one ever hear
him rehearsing a speech. Indeed, to one of his
companions who said, "Men find fault with thee,
Cato, for thy silence," he replied: "Only let them
not blame my life. I will begin to speak when
I am not going to say what were better left
unsaid."

V. The Basilica Porcia, as it was called, had been
dedicated by the elder Cato while he was censor.[1]
Here, then, the tribunes of the people were accustomed to transact their business; and as one of
the pillars was thought to be in the way of their
seats, they determined to take it down or move it to
another place. This brought Cato for the first time,
and against his wishes, into the forum; he opposed
the tribunes, and was admired for the proof of eloquence and high character which he gave. For his
speech had nothing about it that was juvenile or
affected, but was straightforward, full of matter, and
harsh. However, a charm that captivated the ear
was diffused over the harshness of his sentiments,
and the mingling of his character with them gave
their austerity a smiling graciousness that won men's
hearts. His voice was sufficiently loud and pene-
trating to reach the ears of so large a multitude,
and it had a strength and tension which could not

---

[1] Cf. the *Cato Major*, xix. 2. This was in 182 B.C.

ἄτρυτον· ἡμέραν γὰρ ὅλην εἰπὼν πολλάκις οὐκ
ἀπηγόρευσε.

3   Τότε δ' οὖν κρατήσας τῆς δίκης πάλιν ἑαυτὸν
εἰς τὴν σιωπὴν καὶ τὴν ἄσκησιν συνέστειλε· καὶ
διεπόνει τὸ σῶμα γυμνασίοις ἐνεργοῖς, ἐθιζόμενος
ἀνέχεσθαι καὶ καύματα καὶ νιφετὸν ἀκαλύπτῳ
κεφαλῇ, καὶ βαδίζειν ἐν ταῖς ὁδοῖς πᾶσαν ὥραν
ἄτερ ὀχήματος. τῶν δὲ φίλων οἱ συνεκδημοῦντες
ἵπποις ἐχρῶντο, καὶ πολλάκις ἑκάστῳ παρέβαλλεν ὁ Κάτων ἐν μέρει προσδιαλεγόμενος, περιπατῶν αὐτὸς ὀχουμένων. θαυμαστῇ δὲ καὶ περὶ
τὰς νόσους ὑπομονῇ μετ' ἐγκρατείας ἐχρῆτο·
πυρέττων γὰρ μόνος ἐφ' ἑαυτοῦ διημέρευε μηδένα
προσιέμενος, ἄχρι οὗ βέβαιον αἴσθοιτο ῥᾳστώνην
καὶ μεταβολὴν τοῦ νοσήματος.

VI. Ἐν δὲ τοῖς δείπνοις ἐκληροῦτο περὶ τῶν
μερίδων· εἰ δὲ ἀπολάχοι, πρῶτον αἴρειν τῶν φίλων κελευόντων, ἔλεγε μὴ καλῶς ἔχειν, ἀκούσῃς
τῆς Ἀφροδίτης. καὶ κατ' ἀρχὰς μὲν ἅπαξ ἐπι-
πιὼν τὸ δεῖπνον ἀνέλυε, προϊόντι δὲ τῷ χρόνῳ
μάλιστα προσίετο τὸ πίνειν, ὥστε πολλάκις ἐν
2 οἴνῳ διάγειν εἰς ὄρθρον. αἰτίαν δὲ ἔλεγον οἱ
φίλοι τούτου τὴν πολιτείαν καὶ τὰ δημόσια
πράγματα, πρὸς οἷς ὅλας τὸν Κάτωνα τὰς ἡμέρας
ὄντα, καὶ κωλυόμενον φιλολογεῖν, νύκτωρ καὶ
παρὰ πότον συγγίνεσθαι τοῖς φιλοσόφοις. διὸ
καὶ Μεμμίου τινὸς ἐν συλλόγῳ φήσαντος ὅλας
τὸν Κάτωνα μεθύσκεσθαι τὰς νύκτας, ὑπολαβὼν
ὁ Κικέρων, "Ἐκεῖνο δὲ οὐ λέγεις," εἶπεν, "ὅτι
καὶ τὰς ἡμέρας ὅλας κυβεύει;"

3   Καθόλου δὲ τοῖς τότε βίοις καὶ τοῖς ἐπιτηδεύ-

be broken or worn out; for he often spoke all day without getting tired.

At this time, then, after winning his case, he went back again to his silence and his discipline. He built up his body by vigorous exercises, accustoming himself to endure both heat and snow with uncovered head, and to journey on foot at all seasons, without a vehicle. Those of his friends who went abroad with him used horses, and Cato would often join each of them in turn and converse with him, although he walked and they rode. In sickness, he had wonderful patience, as well as self-control; for instance, if he had an ague, he would pass the day alone by himself, admitting no visitor, until he was conscious of lasting relief and the departure of the disease.

VI. At suppers, he would throw dice for the choice of portions; and if he lost, and his friends bade him choose first, he would say it was not right, since Venus[1] was unwilling. At first, also, he would drink once after supper and then leave the table; but as time went on he would allow himself to drink very generously, so that he often tarried at his wine till early morning. His friends used to say that the cause of this was his civic and public activities; he was occupied with these all day, and so prevented from literary pursuits, wherefore he would hold intercourse with the philosophers at night and over the cups. For this reason, too, when a certain Memmius remarked in company that Cato spent his entire nights in drinking, Cicero answered him by saying: "Thou shouldst add that he spends his entire days in throwing dice."

And, in general, Cato thought he ought to take a

[1] The highest throw at dice was called the "Venus-throw."

μασιν ὁ Κάτων τὴν ἐναντίαν ὁδὸν οἰόμενος δεῖν
βαδίζειν, ὡς οὖσι φαύλοις καὶ μεγάλης δεομένοις
μεταβολῆς, ἐπεὶ πορφύραν ἑώρα τὴν κατακόρως
ἐρυθρὰν καὶ ὀξεῖαν ἀγαπωμένην, αὐτὸς ἐφόρει
τὴν μέλαιναν. πολλάκις δ᾽ ἀνυπόδητος καὶ
ἀχίτων εἰς τὸ δημόσιον προῄει μετ᾽ ἄριστον, οὐ
δόξαν ἐκ ταύτης τῆς καινότητος θηρώμενος, ἀλλὰ
ἐθίζων ἑαυτὸν ἐπὶ τοῖς αἰσχροῖς αἰσχύνεσθαι
4 μόνοις, τῶν δὲ ἄλλων ἀδόξων καταφρονεῖν. καὶ
κληρονομίαν δὲ αὐτῷ προσγενομένην ἀνεψιοῦ
Κάτωνος ἑκατὸν ταλάντων εἰς ἀργύριον συναγαγὼν παρεῖχεν ἄνευ τόκων χρῆσθαι τῷ δεομένῳ
τῶν φίλων. ἔνιοι δὲ καὶ χωρία καὶ θεράποντας
αὐτοῦ διδόντος καὶ βεβαιοῦντος ὑπέθεντο πρὸς
τὸ δημόσιον.

VII. Ἐπεὶ δὲ ὥραν ᾤετο πρὸς γάμον ἔχειν, οὐ-
δεμιᾷ γυναικὶ συνεληλυθώς, ἡρμόσατο Λεπίδαν,
πρότερον μὲν ἐγγυηθεῖσαν Σκηπίωνι Μετέλλῳ,
τότε δὲ ἀπειπαμένου τοῦ Σκηπίωνος καὶ τῆς ἐγ-
γύης λυθείσης σχολάζουσαν. οὐ μὴν ἀλλὰ πρὸ
τοῦ γάμου μεταμεληθεὶς πάλιν ὁ Σκηπίων καὶ
2 πάντα ποιήσας ἔλαβε τὴν κόρην. ὁ δὲ Κάτων
σφόδρα παροξυνθεὶς καὶ διακαεὶς ἐπεχείρησε μὲν
ἐπεξελθεῖν διὰ δίκης, ὡς δὲ οἱ φίλοι τοῦτο ἐκώλυ-
σαν, ὀργῇ καὶ νεότητι τρέψας ἑαυτὸν εἰς ἰάμβους
πολλὰ τὸν Σκηπίωνα καθύβρισε, τῷ πικρῷ προσ-
χρησάμενος τοῦ Ἀρχιλόχου, τὸ δὲ ἀκόλαστον
3 ἀφεὶς καὶ παιδαριῶδες. ἔγημε δὲ Ἀτιλίαν, Σερ-
ρανοῦ θυγατέρα, καὶ ταύτῃ πρῶτον συνῆλθεν, οὐ

course directly opposed to the life and practices of the time, feeling that these were bad and in need of great change. For instance, when he saw that a purple which was excessively red and vivid was much in vogue, he himself would wear the dark shade. Again, he would often go out into the streets after breakfast without shoes or tunic. He was not hunting for notoriety by this strange practice, but accustoming himself to be ashamed only of what was really shameful, and to ignore men's low opinion of other things. When an inheritance worth a hundred talents fell to him from his cousin Cato, he turned it into money, and allowed any friend who needed it to have the use of it without interest. And some of his friends actually pledged to the public treasury both lands and slaves which he offered for this purpose himself, and made good his offer.

VII. When he thought that he was old enough to marry,—and up to that time he had consorted with no woman,—he engaged himself to Lepida, who had formerly been betrothed to Metellus Scipio, but was now free, since Scipio had rejected her and the betrothal had been broken. However, before the marriage Scipio changed his mind again, and by dint of every effort got the maid. Cato was greatly exasperated and inflamed by this, and attempted to go to law about it; but his friends prevented this, and so, in his rage and youthful fervour, he betook himself to iambic verse, and heaped much scornful abuse upon Scipio, adopting the bitter tone of Archilochus, but avoiding his license and puerility. And he married Atilia, a daughter of Serranus. She was the first woman with whom he consorted, but not the only

μόνῃ δέ, καθάπερ Λαίλιος, ὁ Σκηπίωνος ἑταῖρος·
ἀλλ᾽ εὐτυχέστερος ἐκεῖνος, ἐν πολλοῖς οἷς ἐβίωσε
χρόνοις μίαν ἣν ἔγημεν ἐξ ἀρχῆς γνοὺς γυναῖκα.

VIII. Τοῦ δὲ δουλικοῦ πολέμου συνεστῶτος,[1]
ὃν Σπαρτάκειον ἐκάλουν, Γέλλιος[2] μὲν ἐστρατή-
γει, Κάτων δὲ τῆς στρατείας μετεῖχεν ἐθελοντής,
διὰ τὸν ἀδελφόν· ἐχιλιάρχει γὰρ ὁ ἀδελφὸς αὐτοῦ Καιπίων. καὶ χρήσασθαι μὲν εἰς ὅσον ἐβούλετο τῇ προθυμίᾳ καὶ ἀσκήσει τῆς ἀρετῆς οὐχ
ὑπῆρξεν αὐτῷ, διὰ τὸ μὴ καλῶς στρατηγεῖσθαι
τὸν πόλεμον· ἄλλως δέ, παρὰ πολλὴν μαλακίαν
καὶ τρυφὴν τῶν ἐκεῖ στρατευομένων ἐπιδεικνύμενος εὐταξίαν καὶ ἐγκράτειαν καὶ τὸ θαρραλέον
ἐν πᾶσι καὶ ξυνετόν, ἐδόκει μηθὲν ἀποδεῖν τοῦ
2 παλαιοῦ Κάτωνος. ὁ δὲ Γέλλιος ἀριστεῖα καὶ
τιμὰς αὐτῷ διαπρεπεῖς ἔγραψεν, ἃς ἐκεῖνος οὐκ
ἔλαβεν οὐδὲ προσήκατο, φήσας ἄξιον μηθὲν
εἰργάσθαι τιμῶν. ἔκ τε δὴ τούτων ἀλλόκοτος
ἐδόκει, καὶ νόμου γραφέντος ὅπως τοῖς παραγ-
γέλλουσιν εἰς ἀρχὴν ὀνοματολόγοι μὴ παρῶσι,
χιλιαρχίαν μετιὼν μόνος ἐπείθετο τῷ νόμῳ· καὶ
δι᾽ αὑτοῦ ποιησάμενος ἔργον ἀσπάζεσθαι καὶ
προσαγορεύειν τοὺς ἐντυγχάνοντας, οὐδὲ αὐτοῖς
ἀνεπαχθὴς ἦν τοῖς ἐπαινοῦσιν, ὅσον μᾶλλον ἐνό-
ουν τὸ καλὸν ὧν ἐπετήδευε, τὸ δυσμίμητον αὐτῶν
βαρυνομένοις.

763

---

[1] In 73–71 b.c. Cf. the *Crassus*, viii. ff.
[2] Lucius Gellius Publicola, consul in 72 b.c. with Cornelius Lentulus Clodianus. Both consuls were defeated by Spartacus.

one, as was true of Laelius, the friend of Scipio
Africanus; Laelius, indeed, was more fortunate, since
in the course of his long life he knew but one
woman, the wife of his youth.

VIII. When the servile war was in progress,[1]
which was called the war of Spartacus, Gellius[2] was
commander, while Cato took part in his campaign
as a volunteer, for the sake of his brother; for his
brother Caepio was a military tribune. Here he had
not the opportunity to employ as much as he wished
his zeal and discipline in virtue, because the war was
not well conducted; but notwithstanding, amidst the
great effeminacy and luxury of those who took part
in that campaign, he displayed such good discipline,
self-control, courage in all emergencies, and sagacity,
that men thought him not one whit inferior to the
elder Cato. Moreover, Gellius assigned to him prizes
of valour and distinguished honours; but Cato would
not take them nor allow them, declaring that he had
done nothing worthy of honours. And so, in consequence of this, he was thought to be a strange
creature. For instance, a law was passed forbidding
candidates for office to be attended by nomen-
clators,[3] and in his canvass for the military tribuneship he was the only one who obeyed the law. He
made it his business to salute and address without
help from others those who met him on his rounds,
but he did not avoid giving offence even to those
who praised his course; for the more clearly they
saw the rectitude of his practice, the more distressed
were they at the difficulty of imitating it.

[3] Attendants whose duty it was to tell the candidate the
names of those whom he was going to meet, that he might
appear to be acquainted with them.

IX. Ἀποδειχθεὶς δὲ χιλίαρχος εἰς Μακεδονίαν ἐπέμπετο πρὸς Ῥούβριον τὸν στρατηγόν. ἔνθα δὴ λέγεται τῆς γυναικὸς ἀχθομένης καὶ δακρυούσης ἕνα τῶν φίλων τοῦ Κάτωνος Μουνάτιον εἰπεῖν· "Ὦ Ἀτιλία, θάρσει· τοῦτον ἐγώ σοι φυλάξω." "Πάνυ μὲν οὖν," φάναι τὸν Κάτωνα, καὶ προελθόντων μιᾶς ἡμέρας ὁδόν, εὐθὺς εἰπεῖν μετὰ τὸ δεῖπνον· "Ἄγε, ὅπως, ὦ Μουνάτιε, τῇ Ἀτιλίᾳ τὴν ὑπόσχεσιν ἐμπεδώσεις,[1] μήτε ἡμέρας ἐμοῦ μήτε νυκτὸς ἀφιστάμενος." ἐκ δὲ τούτου δύο κλίνας εἰς ταὐτὸ δωμάτιον ἐκέλευε τίθεσθαι, καὶ τὸν Μουνάτιον οὕτως ἀεὶ καθεύδειν μετὰ παιδιᾶς φυλασσόμενον ὑπὸ τοῦ Κάτωνος.

Εἵποντο δὲ αὐτῷ πεντεκαίδεκα μὲν οἰκέται, δύο δὲ ἀπελεύθεροι, φίλοι δὲ τέσσαρες. ὧν ὀχουμένων ἵπποις αὐτὸς ἀεὶ περιπατῶν ἑκάστῳ παρέβαλλεν ἐν μέρει προσδιαλεγόμενος. ἐπεὶ δὲ ἧκεν εἰς τὸ στρατόπεδον, πλειόνων ταγμάτων ὄντων, ἑνὸς ἄρχων ἀποδειχθεὶς ὑπὸ τοῦ στρατηγοῦ, τῆς μὲν ἰδίας ἀρετῆς, μιᾶς οὔσης, μικρὸν ἔργον ἡγεῖτο καὶ οὐκ ἀνύσιμον[2] τὴν ἐπίδειξιν, αὑτῷ δὲ ποιῆσαι τοὺς ἀρχομένους ὁμοίους μάλιστα φιλοτιμούμενος οὐ τὸν φόβον ἀφεῖλε τῆς ἐξουσίας, ἀλλὰ προσέθηκε τὸν λόγον· ᾧ πείθων περὶ ἑκάστου καὶ διδάσκων, ἑπομένης τιμῆς καὶ κολάσεως, χαλεπὸν ἦν εἰπεῖν πότερον εἰρηνικοὺς μᾶλλον ἢ πολεμικοὺς καὶ προθυμοτέρους ἢ δικαιοτέρους παρεσκεύασε τοὺς ἄνδρας· οὕτως ἐφαίνοντο φοβεροὶ μὲν τοῖς πολεμίοις, ἥμεροι δὲ τοῖς συμμάχοις, ἄτολ-

---

[1] ἐμπεδώσεις Sintenis[2], after Cobet; ἐμπεδώσῃς Sintenis[1], Coraës, Bekker.
[2] ἀνύσιμον Sintenis' correction of the MSS. βασιλικὸν (kingly), adopted by Bekker.

IX. Appointed military tribune,[1] he was sent to Macedonia, to serve under Rubrius the praetor. At this time, we are told, his wife being full of grief and in tears, one of Cato's friends, Munatius, said to her: "Take heart, Atilia; I will watch over thy husband." "Certainly he will," cried Cato, and after they had gone a day's journey on their way, immediately after supper, he said: "Come, Munatius, see that you keep your promise to Atilia, and forsake me neither by day nor by night." Then he gave orders that two couches be placed in the same chamber for them, and thus Munatius always slept—and that was the joke—watched over by Cato.

He had in his following fifteen slaves, two freedmen, and four friends. These rode on horses, while he himself always went a-foot; and yet he would join each of them in turn and converse with him.[2] And when he reached the camp, where there were several legions, and was appointed to the command of one of them by the general, he thought it a trifling and useless task to make a display of his own virtue, which was that of a single man, but was ambitious above all things to make the men under his command like unto himself. He did not, however, divest his power of the element which inspires fear, but called in the aid of reason; with its help he persuaded and taught his men about everything, while rewards and punishments followed their acts. Consequently, it were hard to say whether he made his men more peaceful or more warlike, more zealous or more just; to such a degree did they show themselves terrible to their enemies but gentle to their allies, without

---

[1] About 67 B.C.
[2] Cf. chapter v. 3.

μοι δὲ πρὸς τὸ ἀδικεῖν, φιλότιμοι δὲ πρὸς τοὺς
4 ἐπαίνους. οὗ δὲ ἥκιστα Κάτων ἐπεμελήθη, τοῦτο
πλεῖστον ὑπῆρχεν αὐτῷ, καὶ δόξα καὶ χάρις καὶ
ὑπερβάλλουσα τιμὴ καὶ φιλοφροσύνη παρὰ τῶν
στρατιωτῶν. ἃ γὰρ ἑτέροις ἐπέταττεν ἑκουσίως
διαπονῶν, καὶ στολὴν μὲν καὶ δίαιταν καὶ πορείαν
ἐκείνοις μᾶλλον ἢ τοῖς ἄρχουσιν ὁμοιούμενος, ἤθει
δὲ καὶ φρονήματι καὶ λόγῳ πάντας ὑπεραίρων
τοὺς αὐτοκράτορας καὶ στρατηγοὺς προσαγορευο-
μένους, ἔλαθε διὰ τούτων ἅμα τὴν πρὸς αὐτὸν
5 εὔνοιαν ἐνεργασάμενος τοῖς ἀνδράσιν. ἀρετῆς γὰρ
ἀληθινὸς οὐκ ἐγγίνεται ζῆλος ἢ δι' ἄκρας τοῦ
παραδιδόντος εὐνοίας καὶ τιμῆς· οἱ δὲ ἄνευ τοῦ
φιλεῖν ἐπαινοῦντες τοὺς ἀγαθοὺς αἰδοῦνται τὴν
δόξαν αὐτῶν, οὐ θαυμάζουσι δὲ τὴν ἀρετὴν οὐδὲ
μιμοῦνται.

X. Πυθόμενος δὲ 'Αθηνόδωρον, τὸν ἐπικαλού-
μενον Κορδυλίωνα, μεγάλην ἕξιν ἐν τοῖς Στωϊκοῖς
λόγοις ἔχοντα, διατρίβειν περὶ Πέργαμον, ἤδη
γηραιὸν ὄντα καὶ πάσαις ἐρρωμενέστατα ταῖς
ἡγεμονικαῖς καὶ βασιλικαῖς συνηθείαις καὶ φιλί-
αις διαμεμαχημένον, οὐδὲν ᾤετο πέμπων καὶ γράφων περαίνειν πρὸς αὐτόν, ἀλλὰ ἔχων παρὰ τοῦ
νόμου δεδομένην ἀποδημίαν δυεῖν μηνῶν ἔπλευσεν
εἰς τὴν 'Ασίαν ἐπὶ τὸν ἄνδρα, πιστεύων τοῖς ἐν
2 αὑτῷ καλοῖς μὴ ἀτυχήσειν τῆς ἄγρας. συγγενό-
μενος δὲ καὶ καταγωνισάμενος καὶ μεταστήσας ἐκ
τῆς προαιρέσεως αὐτὸν ἧκεν ἄγων εἰς τὸ στρατόπεδον, περιχαρὴς καὶ μεγαλοφρονῶν, ὥς τι κάλ-

courage to do wrong but ambitious to win praise. Moreover, that to which Cato gave least thought was his in greatest measure, namely, esteem, favour, surpassing honour, and kindness, from his soldiers. For he willingly shared the tasks which he imposed upon others, and in his dress, way of living, and conduct on the march, made himself more like a soldier than a commander, while in character, dignity of purpose, and eloquence, he surpassed all those who bore the titles of Imperator and General. In this way, without knowing it, he produced in his men at the same time the feeling of good will towards himself. For a genuine desire to attain virtue arises only in consequence of perfect good will and respect for him who displays virtue; those, on the other hand, who praise good men without loving them may revere their reputation, but they do not admire their virtue or imitate it.

X. On learning that Athenodorus, surnamed Cordylion, who had a large acquaintance with the Stoic philosophy, was living at Pergamum, being now in his old age and having most sturdily resisted all intimacies and friendships with governors and kings, Cato thought it would be useless to send messengers or write letters to him. Instead of this, since he had a furlough of two months allowed him by law, he sailed to Asia to visit the man, relying upon his own good qualities to make him successful in the chase. He held converse with the philosopher, conquered his objections, drew him from his fixed purpose, and took him back to the camp with him. He was overjoyed and in high spirits, feeling that he had made a most noble capture, and one more

λιστον ἡρηκὼς καὶ λαμπρότερον ὧν Πομπήϊος
τότε καὶ Λεύκολλος ἐθνῶν καὶ βασιλειῶν κατε-
στρέφοντο σὺν ὅπλοις περιϊόντες.

XI. Ἔτι δὲ αὐτοῦ περὶ τὴν στρατείαν ὄντος ὁ
ἀδελφὸς εἰς τὴν Ἀσίαν βαδίζων ἐνόσησε περὶ
Θρᾴκην ἐν Αἴνῳ. καὶ γράμματα μὲν εὐθὺς ἧκε 764
πρὸς τὸν Κάτωνα· χειμῶνος δὲ πολλοῦ κατέ-
χοντος τὴν θάλατταν καὶ νεὼς ἱκανῆς μεγέθει μὴ
παρούσης, εἰς μικρὰν ὁλκάδα μόνον δύο φίλους
καὶ τρεῖς οἰκέτας ἀναλαβὼν ἐκ Θεσσαλονίκης
2 ἀνήχθη· καὶ παρ' οὐδὲν ἐλθὼν καταποντωθῆναι,
τύχῃ τινὶ παραλόγῳ σωθεὶς ἄρτι τεθνηκότος τοῦ
Καιπίωνος, ἐμπαθέστερον ἔδοξεν ἢ φιλοσοφώ-
τερον ἐνεγκεῖν τὴν συμφοράν, οὐ μόνον κλαυθμοῖς
καὶ περιπτύξεσι τοῦ νεκροῦ καὶ βαρύτητι λύπης,
ἀλλὰ καὶ δαπάνῃ περὶ τὴν ταφὴν καὶ πραγματείαις θυμιαμάτων καὶ ἱματίων πολυτελῶν
συγκατακαέντων καὶ μνήματος ξεστοῦ λίθων
Θασίων ἀπὸ ταλάντων ὀκτὼ κατασκευασθέντος
3 ἐν τῇ Αἰνίων ἀγορᾷ. ταῦτα γὰρ ἔνιοι ἐσυκοφάν-
τουν πρὸς τὴν ἄλλην ἀτυφίαν τοῦ Κάτωνος, οὐ
καθορῶντες ὅσον ἐν τῷ πρὸς ἡδονὰς καὶ φόβους
καὶ δεήσεις ἀναισχύντους ἀγνάμπτῳ καὶ στερρῷ
τοῦ ἀνδρὸς τὸ ἥμερον ἐνῆν καὶ φιλόστοργον. εἰς
δὲ ταῦτα καὶ πόλεις αὐτῷ καὶ δυνάσται πολλὰ
κατὰ τιμὴν τοῦ τεθνεῶτος ἔπεμπον, ὧν ἐκεῖνος
χρήματα μὲν παρ' οὐδενὸς ἐδέξατο, θυμιάματα δὲ
καὶ κόσμον ἐλάμβανε, τὴν τιμὴν [1] ἀποδιδοὺς τοῖς
4 πέμπουσι. τῆς δὲ κληρονομίας εἰς αὐτόν τε καὶ
θυγάτριον τοῦ Καιπίωνος ἡκούσης, οὐθὲν ὧν

---

[1] τὴν τιμὴν Bekker, after Reiske: τιμήν.

illustrious than the nations and kingdoms which Pompey and Lucullus at that time were subduing with their marching armies.

XI. While Cato was still in military service, his brother, who was on his way to Asia, fell sick at Aenus in Thrace, and a letter came at once to Cato advising him of this. A heavy storm was raging at sea and no ship of sufficient size was at hand, but nevertheless, taking only two friends and three servants with him in a small trading-vessel, he put to sea from Thessalonica. He narrowly escaped drowning, and by some unaccountable good fortune came safe to land, but Caepio had just died. In bearing this affliction Cato was thought to have shown more passion than philosophy, considering not only his lamentations, his embracings of the dead, and the heaviness of his grief, but also his expenditure upon the burial, and the pains that he took to have incense and costly raiment burned with the body, and a monument of polished Thasian marble costing eight talents constructed in the market-place of Aenus. For some people cavilled at these things as inconsistent with Cato's usual freedom from ostentation, not observing how much tenderness and affection was mingled with the man's inflexibility and firmness against pleasures, fears, and shameless entreaties. For the funeral rites, moreover, both cities and dynasts sent him many things for the honour of the dead, from none of whom would he accept money; he did, however, take incense and ornaments, and paid the value of them to the senders. Furthermore, when the inheritance fell to him and Caepio's young daughter, nothing

ἀνάλωσε περὶ τὸν τάφον ἀπήτησεν ἐν τῇ νεμήσει.
καὶ ταῦτα πράξαντος αὐτοῦ καὶ πράττοντος, ἦν ὁ
γράψας ὅτι κοσκίνῳ τὴν τέφραν τοῦ νεκροῦ μετέβαλε καὶ διήθησε, χρυσίον ζητῶν κατακεκαυ-
μένον. οὕτως οὐ τῷ ξίφει μόνον, ἀλλὰ καὶ
τῷ γραφείῳ τὸ ἀνυπεύθυνον καὶ τὸ ἀνυπόδικον
ἐπίστευσεν.

XII. Ἐπεὶ δὲ τέλος εἶχεν ἡ στρατεία τῷ
Κάτωνι, προεπέμφθη, οὐκ εὐχαῖς, ὃ κοινόν ἐστιν,
οὐδ' ἐπαίνοις, ἀλλὰ δάκρυσι καὶ περιβολαῖς
ἀπλήστοις, ὑποτιθέντων τὰ ἱμάτια τοῖς ποσὶν ᾗ
βαδίζοι καὶ καταφιλούντων τὰς χεῖρας, ἃ τῶν
αὐτοκρατόρων ὀλίγοις μόλις ἐποίουν οἱ τότε
2 Ῥωμαῖοι. βουληθεὶς δὲ πρὸ τοῦ πολιτείᾳ προσελθεῖν ἅμα μὲν πλανηθῆναι καθ' ἱστορίαν τῆς
Ἀσίας καὶ γενέσθαι θεατὴς ἠθῶν καὶ βίων καὶ
δυνάμεως τῆς περὶ ἑκάστην ἐπαρχίαν, ἅμα δὲ τῷ
Γαλάτῃ Δηϊοτάρῳ διὰ ξενίαν καὶ φιλίαν πατρῴαν
δεομένῳ πρὸς αὐτὸν ἐλθεῖν μὴ ἀχαριστῆσαι, τοῦτον τὸν τρόπον ἐποιεῖτο τὴν ἀποδημίαν. πρού-
πεμπεν ἅμ' ἡμέρᾳ τὸν ἀρτοποιὸν καὶ τὸν μάγειρον
3 ὅπου καταλύσειν ἔμελλεν. οἱ δὲ πάνυ κοσμίως
καὶ μεθ' ἡσυχίας εἰσελθόντες ἂν εἰς τὴν πόλιν,
εἰ μηδεὶς τύχοι τῷ Κάτωνι φίλος ὢν αὐτόθι
πατρῷος ἢ γνώριμος, ἐν πανδοκείῳ τὴν ὑποδοχὴν
αὐτῷ παρεσκεύαζον, ἐνοχλοῦντες οὐδενί· πανδο-
κείου δὲ μὴ ὄντος, οὕτως πρὸς τοὺς ἄρχοντας
τραπόμενοι ξενίαν ἐλάμβανον, ἀγαπῶντες τὴν
4 δοθεῖσαν. πολλάκις δὲ ἀπιστούμενοι καὶ περιορώ-

that he had expended for the funeral was asked back by him in the distribution of the property. And although such was his conduct then and afterwards, there was one [1] who wrote that he passed the ashes of the dead through a sieve, in search of the gold that had been melted down. So confidently did the writer attribute, not only to his sword, but also to his pen, freedom from accountability and punishment.

XII. When the time of Cato's military service came to an end, he was sent on his way, not with blessings, as is common, nor yet with praises, but with tears and insatiable embraces, the soldiers casting their mantles down for him to walk upon, and kissing his hands, things which the Romans of that day rarely did, and only to a few of their imperators. But before applying himself to public affairs he desired to travel about in a study of Asia, and to see with his own eyes the customs and lives and military strength of each province; at the same time he wished to gratify Deiotarus the Galatian, who had been a guest-friend of his father, and now solicited a visit from him. He therefore arranged his journey as follows. At daybreak, he would send forward his baker and his cook to the place where he intended to lodge. These would enter the city with great decorum and little stir, and if Cato had no family friend or acquaintance there, they would prepare a reception for him at an inn, without troubling anybody; or, in case there was no inn, they would apply to the magistrates for hospitality, and gladly accept what was given. But frequently they were distrusted and neglected, because they

[1] Julius Caesar, in his "Anti-Cato." See the *Caesar*, chapter liv.

μενοι διὰ τὸ μὴ θορύβῳ μηδὲ ἀπειλῇ ταῦτα
πράσσειν πρὸς τοὺς ἄρχοντας, ὑπὸ τοῦ Κάτωνος
ἄπρακτοι κατελαμβάνοντο, καὶ μᾶλλον αὐτὸς
ὀφθεὶς ὠλιγωρεῖτο, καὶ παρεῖχεν ἐπὶ τῶν φορτίων
σιωπῇ καθεζόμενος ὑπόνοιαν ἀνθρώπου ταπεινοῦ
5 καὶ περιδεοῦς. οὐ μὴν ἀλλὰ καὶ προσκαλού-
μενος αὐτοὺς εἰώθει λέγειν· "Ὦ μοχθηροί, μετα-
βάλεσθε ταύτης τῆς κακοξενίας. οὐ πάντες ὑμῖν
ἀφίξονται Κάτωνες. ἀμβλύνατε ταῖς φιλοφροσύναις τὴν ἐξουσίαν τῶν δεομένων προφάσεως, ἵνα
βίᾳ λαμβάνωσιν, ὡς παρ' ἑκόντων μὴ τυγχά-
νοντες."

XIII. Ἐν δὲ Συρίᾳ καὶ γελοῖόν τι λέγεται
παθεῖν. βαδίζων γὰρ εἰς Ἀντιόχειαν εἶδε περὶ
τὰς πύλας ἔξω πλῆθος ἀνθρώπων ἑκατέρωθεν
τῆς ὁδοῦ παρακεκριμένων, ἐν οἷς ἔφηβοι μὲν
χωρὶς ἐν χλαμύσι¹ καὶ παῖδες ἑτέρωθεν κοσμίως
εἱστήκεσαν, ἐσθῆτας δὲ καθαρὰς ἔνιοι καὶ στεφά-   765
νους εἶχον, ἱερεῖς θεῶν ὄντες ἢ ἄρχοντες. πάντων
οὖν μᾶλλον οἰηθεὶς ὁ Κάτων αὐτῷ τινα πράτ-
τεσθαι τιμὴν καὶ δεξίωσιν ὑπὸ τῆς πόλεως,
ὠργίζετο μὲν τοῖς προπεμφθεῖσι τῶν ἰδίων, ὡς μὴ
κωλύσασιν, ἐκέλευσε δὲ καταβῆναι τοὺς φίλους,
2 καὶ πεζῇ προῄει μετ' αὐτῶν. ὡς δ' ἐγγὺς ἦσαν, ὁ
πάντα διακοσμῶν ἐκεῖνα καὶ τὸν ὄχλον εἰς τάξιν
καθιστάς, ἀνὴρ πρεσβύτερος ἤδη, ῥάβδον ἐν τῇ
χειρὶ καὶ στέφανον κρατῶν, ἀπήντησε τῷ Κάτωνι
πρὸ τῶν ἄλλων, καὶ μηδὲ ἀσπασάμενος ἠρώτα
ποῦ Δημήτριον ἀπολελοίπασι καὶ πηνίκα παρέσται. Πομπηίου δὲ ἦν γεγονὼς ὁ Δημήτριος

¹ χλαμύσι MSS. and most editors: χλανίσι (mantles), after
Cobet.

raised no tumult and made no threats in their dealings with the magistrates. In such a case Cato would find their work not done when he arrived, and he himself would be more despised than his servants when men saw him, and would awaken suspicion, as he sat upon the baggage without saying a word, that he was a man of low condition and very timid. However, he would then call the magistrates to him and say : " Ye miserable wretches, lay aside this inhospitality. Not all men who come to you will be Catos. Blunt by your kind attentions the power of those who only want an excuse for taking by force what they do not get with men's consent."

XIII. In Syria, too, as we are told, he had a laughable experience. As he was walking into Antioch, he saw at the gates outside a multitude of people drawn up on either side of the road, among whom stood, in one group, young men with military cloaks, and in another, boys with gala robes, while some had white raiment and crowns, being priests or magistrates. Cato, accordingly, thinking that this could only be some honourable reception which the city was preparing for him, was angry with his servants who had been sent on in advance, because they had not prevented it; but he ordered his friends to dismount, and went forward on foot with them. When, however, they were near the gate, he who was arranging all these ceremonies and marshalling the crowd, a man now well on in years, holding a wand and a crown in his hand, advanced to meet Cato, and without even greeting him asked where they had left Demetrius and when he would be there. Now, Demetrius had once been

οἰκέτης· τότε δὲ πάντων, ὡς ἔπος εἰπεῖν, ἀνθρώπων εἰς Πομπήιον ἀποβλεπόντων, ἐθεραπεύετο
3 παρ' ἀξίαν, μέγα παρ' αὐτῷ δυνάμενος. τοῖς μὲν
οὖν φίλοις τοῦ Κάτωνος γέλως ἐνέπεσε τοσοῦτος
ὥστε ἀναλαβεῖν ἑαυτοὺς οὐκ ἐδύναντο διὰ τοῦ
πλήθους ἅμα βαδίζοντες, ὁ δὲ Κάτων τότε μὲν
ἰσχυρῶς διατραπείς, "Ὦ τῆς κακοδαίμονος,"
ἔφη, "πόλεως," ἄλλο δὲ οὐδὲν ἐφθέγξατο, χρόνῳ
δὲ ὕστερον εἰώθει γελᾶν καὶ αὐτὸς ἐπὶ τούτῳ, καὶ
διηγούμενος καὶ μνημονεύων.

XIV. Οὐ μὴν ἀλλὰ Πομπήιος αὐτὸς ἐπέστρεψε
τοὺς ἀνθρώπους οὕτω πλημμελοῦντας εἰς τὸν
Κάτωνα δι' ἄγνοιαν. ὡς γὰρ εἰς Ἔφεσον ἐλθὼν
ἐπορεύετο πρὸς αὐτὸν ἀσπασόμενος πρεσβύτερον
ὄντα, καὶ δόξῃ πολὺ προήκοντα, καὶ δυνάμεων
τότε μεγίστων ἡγούμενον, ἰδὼν ὁ Πομπήιος οὐκ
ἔμεινεν, οὐδὲ εἴασε καθεζομένῳ προσελθεῖν, ἀλλ'
ὥς τινι τῶν κρειττόνων ἀναθορὼν ἀπήντησε, καὶ
2 τὴν δεξιὰν ἐνέβαλε. καὶ πολλὰ μὲν εὐθὺς ἐν τῷ
φιλοφρονεῖσθαι καὶ ἀσπάζεσθαι παρόντα, πλείω
δὲ ἔτι μεταστάντος ἐγκώμια διῆλθεν αὐτοῦ τῆς
ἀρετῆς, ὥστε πάντας ἐπιστρεφομένους καὶ προσέ-
χοντας ἤδη τῷ Κάτωνι, θαυμάζειν ἐξ ὧν πρότερον
κατεφρονεῖτο, καὶ πραότητα καὶ μεγαλοψυχίαν
ἀναθεωρεῖν. καὶ γὰρ ἡ Πομπηίου σπουδὴ περὶ
αὐτὸν οὐκ ἐλάνθανε θεραπεύοντος οὖσα μᾶλλον ἢ
φιλοῦντος, ἀλλ' ἔγνωσαν ὅτι θαυμάζει μὲν παρ-

a slave of Pompey, but at this time, when all mankind, so to speak, had their eyes fixed upon Pompey, he was courted beyond his deserts, since he had great influence with Pompey. Cato's friends accordingly, were seized with such a fit of laughter that they could not recover themselves even when they were walking through the crowd; but Cato was greatly disturbed at the time, and said: " O the unhappy city ! " and not a word besides. In after times, however, he was wont to laugh at the incident himself also, both when he told it and when he called it to mind.[1]

XIV. However, Pompey himself put to shame the men who were thus neglectful of Cato through ignorance. For when Cato came to Ephesus and was proceeding to pay his respects to Pompey as an older man, one who was greatly his superior in reputation, and then in command of the greatest forces, Pompey caught sight of him and would not wait, nor would he suffer Cato to come to him as he sat, but sprang up as though to honour a superior, went to meet him, and gave him his hand. He also passed many encomiums upon his virtue even while he was present and receiving marks of kindness and affection, and still more after he had withdrawn. Therefore all men, being put to shame and now directing their attention to Cato, admired him for the traits which before had brought him scorn, and made a study of his mildness and magnanimity. And indeed it was no secret that Pompey's attentions to him were due to self-interest rather than to friendship; men knew that Pompey admired him when he was present, but was glad to have him go

---

[1] This story is told also in the *Pompey*, xl. 1-3.

3 ὄντα, χαίρει δὲ ἀπερχομένῳ. τοὺς γὰρ ἄλλους
νέους, ὅσοι παρ' αὐτὸν ἀφικνοῦντο, φιλοτιμούμενος κατεῖχε καὶ ποθῶν αὐτῷ συνεῖναι, τοῦ δὲ
Κάτωνος οὐδὲν ἐδεήθη τοιοῦτον, ἀλλ' ὥσπερ οὐκ
ἀνυπεύθυνος ἄρχων ἐκείνου παρόντος ἐξέπεμψεν
ἄσμενος, μόνῳ σχεδὸν ἐκείνῳ τῶν εἰς Ῥώμην
πλεόντων τὰ τέκνα καὶ τὴν γυναῖκα παρακατα-
θέμενος, ἄλλως αὐτῷ προσήκοντα καὶ διὰ συγ-
γένειαν.

Ἐκ τούτου δόξα καὶ σπουδὴ καὶ ἅμιλλα περὶ
αὐτὸν ἦν τῶν πόλεων καὶ δεῖπνα καὶ κλήσεις, ἐν
οἷς τοὺς φίλους ἐκέλευε προσέχειν αὐτῷ, μὴ λάθῃ
4 βεβαιώσας τὸν Κουρίωνος λόγον. ὁ γὰρ Κουρίων ἀχθόμενος τῷ αὐστηρῷ τοῦ Κάτωνος, φίλου
καὶ συνήθους ὄντος, ἠρώτησεν αὐτὸν εἰ πρόθυμός
ἐστι μετὰ τὴν στρατείαν γενέσθαι τῆς Ἀσίας
θεατής. τοῦ δὲ καὶ πάνυ φήσαντος, " Εὖ λέγεις,"
εἶπεν ὁ Κουρίων, " ἡδίων γὰρ ἐπανήξεις ἐκεῖθεν
καὶ μᾶλλον ἥμερος," οὕτω πως καὶ τῷ ῥήματι
χρησάμενος.

XV. Δηϊόταρος δὲ ὁ Γαλάτης μετεπέμψατο
μὲν τὸν Κάτωνα πρεσβύτερος ὢν ἤδη παραθέσθαι
τοὺς παῖδας αὐτῷ βουλόμενος καὶ τὸν οἶκον, ἐλ-
θόντι δὲ προσφέρων δῶρα παντοδαπὰ καὶ πειρῶν
καὶ δεόμενος πάντα τρόπον οὕτω παρώξυνεν ὥστε,
δείλης ἐλθόντα καὶ νυκτερεύσαντα, τῇ ὑστεραίᾳ
2 περὶ τρίτην ὥραν ἀπᾶραι. προελθὼν μέντοι μιᾶς

away. For all the other young men who came
to him were retained by Pompey, who showed an
eager longing for their companionship; of Cato, on
the contrary, he made no such request, but, as if
he must render account of his command while Cato
was there, he was glad to send him away. And yet
Cato was almost the only person among those bound
for Rome to whom Pompey commended his wife and
children, although it is true that they were relatives
of his.

As a consequence of all this, the cities eagerly
vied with one another in showing Cato honour, and
there were suppers and invitations, at which times
he would urge his friends to keep close watch upon
him, lest he should unawares confirm the saying
of Curio. For Curio, annoyed at the severity of
Cato, who was his intimate friend, had asked him
whether he was desirous of seeing Asia after his
term of service in the army. "Certainly I am,"
said Cato. "That's right," said Curio, "for you
will come back from there a more agreeable man
and more tame,"—that is about the meaning of the
word he used.[1]

XV. But Deiotarus the Galatian sent for Cato,
being now an old man, and desiring to commend to
his protection his children and his family. When
Cato arrived, however, Deiotarus offered him gifts of
every sort, and by tempting and entreating him in
every way so exasperated him that, although he had
arrived late in the day and merely spent the night,
on the next day about the third hour he set off.
However, after proceeding a day's journey, he found

---

[1] Plutarch is seeking a Greek equivalent for the Latin
"mansuetior."

ἡμέρας ὁδὸν εὗρεν ἐν Πεσσινοῦντι πλείονα τῶν
ἐκεῖ δώρων αὖθις αὐτὸν ὑπομένοντα, καὶ γράμματα τοῦ Γαλάτου δεομένου, λαβεῖν αὐτὸς εἰ
μὴ πρόθυμός ἐστιν, ἀλλὰ τοὺς φίλους ἐᾶσαι,
πάντως μὲν ἀξίους ὄντας εὖ παθεῖν δι' ἐκεῖνον,
οὐκ ὄντων δὲ τῶν ἰδίων τοῦ Κάτωνος τοσούτων.

3 ἀλλ' οὐδὲ τούτοις ἐνέδωκεν ὁ Κάτων, καίπερ 766
ἐνίους τῶν φίλων μαλασσομένους καὶ ὑπομεμφο-
μένους ὁρῶν, ἀλλὰ φήσας ὅτι πᾶσα δωροδοκία
προφάσεως ἂν εὐπορήσειεν, οἱ δὲ φίλοι μεθέξου-
σιν ὧν ἂν ἔχῃ καλῶς καὶ δικαίως κτησάμενος,
ἀπέπεμψε τὰ δῶρα πρὸς τὸν Δηΐόταρον.

4 Ἐπεὶ δὲ μέλλοντος ἀπαίρειν εἰς τὸ Βρεντέσιον
ᾤοντο δεῖν οἱ φίλοι τὰ λείψανα τοῦ Καιπίωνος
εἰς ἕτερον θέσθαι πλοῖον, εἰπὼν ὅτι τῆς ψυχῆς
μεθήσεται μᾶλλον ἢ τούτων, ἀνήχθη. καὶ μέντοι
λέγεται κατὰ τύχην ἐπισφαλέστατα περᾶσαι, τῶν
ἄλλων μετρίως κομιζομένων.

XVI. Ἐπανελθὼν δὲ εἰς Ῥώμην τὸν μὲν ἄλλον
χρόνον κατ' οἶκον Ἀθηνοδώρῳ συνών,[1] ἢ κατ'
ἀγορὰν τοῖς φίλοις παριστάμενος διετέλεσεν.
ἐπιβάλλουσαν δὲ αὐτῷ τὴν ταμιευτικὴν ἀρχὴν
οὐ πρότερον μετῆλθεν ἢ τούς τε νόμους ἀνα-
γνῶναι τοὺς ταμιευτικοὺς καὶ διαπυθέσθαι τῶν
ἐμπείρων ἕκαστα καὶ τύπῳ τινὶ τῆς ἀρχῆς τὴν
2 δύναμιν περιλαβεῖν. ὅθεν εὐθὺς εἰς τὴν ἀρχὴν
καταστὰς μεγάλην ἐποίησε μεταβολὴν τῶν περὶ

---

[1] συνὼν supplied by Sintenis².

at Pessinus more gifts again awaiting him than those he had left behind him, and a letter from the Galatian begging him, if he did not desire to take them himself, at least to permit his friends to do so, since they were in every way worthy to receive benefits on his account, and Cato's private means would not reach so far. But not even to these solicitations did Cato yield, although he saw that some of his friends were beginning to weaken and were disposed to blame him; nay, he declared that every taking of gifts could find plenty of excuse, but that his friends should share in what he had acquired honourably and justly. Then he sent his gifts back to Deiotarus.

As he was about to set sail for Brundisium, his friends thought that the ashes of Caepio should be put aboard another vessel; but Cato declared that he would rather part with his life than with those ashes, and put to sea. And verily we are told that, as chance would have it, he had a very dangerous passage, although the rest made the journey with little trouble.

XVI. After his return to Rome, he spent most of his time at home in the company of Athenodorus,[1] or in the forum assisting his friends. And though the office of quaestor was open to him, he would not become a candidate for it until he had read the laws relating to the quaestorship, learned all the details of the office from those who had had experience in it, and formed a general idea of its power and scope. Therefore, as soon as he had been instated in the office,[2] he made a great change in the assistants and

---

[1] Cf. chapter x.   [2] In 65 B.C.

τὸ ταμιεῖον ὑπηρετῶν καὶ γραμματέων, οἳ διὰ
χειρὸς ἀεὶ τὰ δημόσια γράμματα καὶ τοὺς νόμους
ἔχοντες, εἶτα νέους ἄρχοντας παραλαμβάνοντες δι᾽
ἀπειρίαν καὶ ἄγνοιαν ἀτεχνῶς διδασκάλων ἑτέρων καὶ παιδαγωγῶν δεομένους, οὐχ ὑφίεντο τῆς
ἐξουσίας ἐκείνοις, ἀλλὰ ἦσαν ἄρχοντες αὐτοί,
3 μέχρι οὗ Κάτων ἐπιστὰς τοῖς πράγμασι νεανι-
κῶς, οὐκ ὄνομα καὶ τιμὴν ἔχων ἄρχοντος, ἀλλὰ
καὶ νοῦν καὶ φρόνημα καὶ λόγον, ὑπηρέταις, ὅπερ
ἦσαν, ἠξίου χρῆσθαι τοῖς γραμματεῦσι, τὰ μὲν
ἐξελέγχων κακουργοῦντας αὐτούς, τὰ δὲ ἁμαρτά·
νοντας ἀπειρίᾳ διδάσκων. ὡς δὲ ἦσαν ἰταμοὶ καὶ
τοὺς ἄλλους ἐθώπευον ὑποτρέχοντες, ἐκείνῳ δὲ
ἐπολέμουν, τὸν μὲν πρῶτον αὐτῶν καταγνοὺς
περὶ πίστιν ἐν κληρονομίᾳ γεγονέναι πονηρὸν
ἀπήλασε τοῦ ταμιείου, δευτέρῳ δέ τινι ῥᾳδιουρ-
4 γίας προύθηκε κρίσιν. ᾧ Κάτλος Λουτάτιος ὁ
τιμητὴς ἀνέβη βοηθήσων, ἀνὴρ μέγα τὸ τῆς
ἀρχῆς ἔχων ἀξίωμα, τὸ δὲ τῆς ἀρετῆς ἔχων[1]
μέγιστον, ὡς πάντας δικαιοσύνῃ καὶ σωφροσύνῃ
Ῥωμαίων διαφέρων· ἦν δὲ καὶ τοῦ Κάτωνος
ἐπαινέτης καὶ συνήθης διὰ τὸν βίον. ὡς οὖν
ἡττώμενος τοῖς δικαίοις ἐξῃτεῖτο φανερῶς τὸν
ἄνθρωπον, οὐκ εἴα ταῦτα ποιεῖν αὐτὸν ὁ Κάτων.
5 ἔτι δὲ μᾶλλον προσλιπαροῦντος, "Αἰσχρόν,"
εἶπεν, "ὦ Κάτλε, σὲ τὸν τιμητὴν καὶ τοὺς ἡμε-
τέρους βίους ὀφείλοντα δοκιμάζειν ὑπὸ τῶν ἡμε-

---

[1] ἔχων bracketed by Bekker, after Coraës.

clerks connected with the treasury. These were fully conversant with the public accounts and the laws relative thereto, and so, when they received as their superior officers young men whose inexperience and ignorance made it really needful that others should teach and tutor them, they would not surrender any power to such superiors, but were superiors themselves. Now, however, Cato applied himself with energy to the business, not having merely the name and honour of a superior official, but also intelligence and rational judgement. He thought it best to treat the clerks as assistants, which they really were, sometimes convicting them of their evil practices, and sometimes teaching them if they erred from inexperience. But they were bold fellows, and tried to ingratiate themselves with the other quaestors, while they waged war upon Cato. Therefore the chief among them, whom he found guilty of a breach of trust in the matter of an inheritance, was expelled from the treasury by him, and a second was brought to trial for fraud. This person Catulus Lutatius the censor came forward to defend, a man who had great authority from his office, but most of all from his virtue, being thought to surpass all Romans in justice and discretion; he also commended Cato's way of living and was intimate with him. Accordingly, when Catulus had lost his case on its merits and began to beg openly for the acquittal of his client, Cato tried to stop him from doing this. And when Catulus was all the more importunate, Cato said: " It would be a shameful thing, Catulus, if thou, who art the censor, and shouldst scrutinize our lives, wert put out of

τέρων ὑπηρετῶν ἐκβάλλεσθαι." ταύτην τὴν
φωνὴν ἀφέντος τοῦ Κάτωνος, ὁ Κάτλος προσέ-
βλεψε μὲν αὐτὸν ὡς ἀμειψόμενος, εἶπε δὲ οὐδέν,
ἀλλ' εἴτε ὑπ' ὀργῆς εἴτε ὑπ' αἰσχύνης ἀπῆλθε
6 σιωπῇ διηπορημένος. οὐ μὴν ἥλω γε ὁ ἄνθρωπος,
ἀλλ' ἐπεὶ μιᾷ ψήφῳ τὰς ἀφιείσας ὑπερέβαλλον
αἱ καθαιροῦσαι, καὶ Λόλλιος Μάρκος εἷς, συνάρχων τοῦ Κάτωνος, ὑπὸ ἀσθενείας ἀπελέλειπτο
τῆς δίκης, πέμπει πρὸς τοῦτον ὁ Κάτλος δεόμενος
βοηθῆσαι τῷ ἀνθρώπῳ· κἀκεῖνος ἐν φορείῳ κομισθεὶς μετὰ τὴν δίκην ἔθετο τὴν ἀπολύουσαν. οὐ
μὴν ἐχρήσατό γε τῷ γραμματεῖ ὁ Κάτων, οὐδὲ
τὸν μισθὸν ἀπέδωκεν, οὐδὲ ὅλως ἐνάριθμον τοῦ
Λολλίου τὴν ψῆφον ἔσχεν.

XVII. Οὕτω δὲ τοὺς γραμματεῖς ταπεινώσας
καὶ ποιήσας ὑποχειρίους, καὶ τοῖς πράγμασιν ὡς
αὐτὸς ἐβούλετο χρώμενος, ὀλίγῳ χρόνῳ τὸ ταμιεῖον ἀπέδειξε τοῦ βουλευτηρίου σεμνότερον, ὡς
καὶ λέγειν καὶ φρονεῖν ἅπαντας ὅτι Κάτων ὑπα-
2 τείας ἀξίωμα τῇ ταμιείᾳ περιέθηκε. πρῶτον μὲν
γὰρ εὑρὼν χρέα παλαιὰ τῷ δημοσίῳ πολλοὺς
ὀφείλοντας καὶ πολλοῖς τὸ δημόσιον, ἅμα τὴν
πόλιν ἔπαυσεν ἀδικουμένην καὶ ἀδικοῦσαν, τοὺς
μὲν εὐτόνως καὶ ἀπαραιτήτως ἀπαιτῶν, τοῖς
δὲ ταχέως ἀποδιδοὺς καὶ προθύμως, ὥστε τὸν
δῆμον αἰδεῖσθαι τοὺς μὲν οἰομένους ἀποστερήσειν
ἐκτίνοντας ὁρῶντα, τοὺς δὲ ἃ μὴ προσεδόκων
3 ἀπολαμβάνοντας. ἔπειτα γράμματα πολλῶν οὐ
προσηκόντως ἀναφερόντων, καὶ δόγματα ψευδῆ

767

court by our bailiffs." When Cato had uttered
these words, Catulus fixed his eyes upon him as
if he would make reply; he said nothing, however,
but either from anger or from shame went off in
silence, much perplexed. However, the man was
not convicted, but when the votes for condemnation
exceeded those for acquittal by a single ballot, and
one Marcus Lollius, a colleague of Cato, was kept by
sickness from attending the trial, Catulus sent to
him and begged him to help the man. So Lollius
was brought in a litter after the trial and cast the
vote that acquitted. Notwithstanding this, Cato
would not employ the clerk, or give him his pay,
or in any way take the vote of Lollius into the
reckoning.

XVII. By thus humbling the clerks and making
them submissive, and by managing the business
as he himself desired, in a little while he brought
the quaestorship into greater respect than the senate,
so that all men said and thought that Cato had
invested the quaestorship with the dignity of the
consulship. For, in the first place, when he found
that many persons were owing debts of long standing to the public treasury and the treasury to many
persons, he made an end at the same time of the
state being wronged and wronging others; from its
debtors he rigorously and inexorably demanded
payment, and to its creditors he promptly and
readily made payment, so that the people were filled
with respect as they saw men making payments
who thought to defraud the state, and men receiving
payments which they had ceased to expect. In the
next place, though many used improper methods to
get writings filed with the quaestors, and though

παραδέχεσθαι χάριτι καὶ δεήσει τῶν προτέρων
εἰωθότων, οὐδὲν αὐτὸν ἔλαθε γινόμενον τοιοῦτον,
ἀλλ᾽ ὑπὲρ ἑνός ποτε δόγματος ἐνδοιάσας εἰ κύριον
γέγονε, πολλῶν μαρτυρούντων οὐκ ἐπίστευσεν,
οὐδὲ κατέταξε πρότερον ἢ τοὺς ὑπάτους ἐπομόσαι
4 παραγενομένους. ὄντων δὲ πολλῶν οἷς Σύλλας
ἐκεῖνος ἀποκτείνασιν ἄνδρας ἐκ προγραφῆς γέρας
ἔδωκεν ἀνὰ μυρίας δισχιλίας δραχμάς, ἅπαντες
μὲν αὐτοὺς ὡς ἐναγεῖς καὶ μιαροὺς ἐμίσουν,
ἀμύνασθαι δὲ οὐδεὶς ἐτόλμα, Κάτων δὲ προσ-
καλούμενος ἕκαστον ἔχοντα δημόσιον ἀργύριον
ἀδίκως ἐξέπραττεν, ἅμα θυμῷ καὶ λόγῳ τὸ τῆς
5 πράξεως ἀνόσιον καὶ παράνομον ἐξονειδίζων. οἱ
δὲ τοῦτο παθόντες εὐθὺς ἦσαν ἔνοχοι φόνῳ, καὶ
τρόπον τινὰ προηλωκότες ἀπήγοντο πρὸς τοὺς
δικαστὰς καὶ δίκας ἔτινον, ἡδομένων πάντων καὶ
νομιζόντων συνεξαλείφεσθαι τὴν τότε τυραννίδα
καὶ Σύλλαν αὐτὸν ἐφορᾶν κολαζόμενον.

XVIII. Ἥιρει δὲ τοὺς πολλοὺς καὶ τὸ ἐνδελεχὲς
αὐτοῦ τῆς ἐπιμελείας καὶ ἄτρυτον. οὔτε γὰρ
πρότερός τις ἀνέβη τῶν συναρχόντων εἰς τὸ
ταμιεῖον Κάτωνος οὔτε ὕστερος ἀπῆλθεν. ἐκκλησίαν δὲ καὶ βουλὴν οὐδεμίαν παρῆκε, δεδιὼς
καὶ παραφυλάττων τοὺς ἑτοίμως καὶ πρὸς χάριν
ὀφλημάτων καὶ τελῶν ἀνέσεις ἢ δόσεις οἷς ἔτυχεν
2 ἐπιψηφιζομένους. ἐπιδεικνύμενος δὲ τὸ ταμιεῖον

previous quaestors had been accustomed to receive
false decrees at the request of those whom they
wished to please, nothing of this sort could be done
now without Cato finding it out. Indeed, on one
occasion when he was doubtful whether a certain
decree had actually passed the senate, though many
testified to the fact, he would not believe them, nor
would he file the decree away until the consuls had
come and taken oath to its validity. Again, there
were many persons whom the famous Sulla had
rewarded for killing men under proscription, at the
rate of twelve thousand drachmas. All men hated
them as accursed and polluted wretches, but no one
had the courage to punish them. Cato, however,
called each one of these to account for having public
money in his possession by unjust means, and made
him give it up, at the same time rebuking him with
passionate eloquence for his illegal and unholy act.
After this experience they were at once charged
with murder, were brought before their judges condemned beforehand, one might say, and were punished. At this all men were delighted, and thought
that with their deaths the tyranny of that former
time was extinguished, and that Sulla himself was
punished before men's eyes.

XVIII. Moreover, the multitude were captivated
by his continuous and unwearied attention to his
duties. For no one of his colleagues came up to the
treasury earlier than Cato, and none left it later.
Besides, no session of assembly or senate would he
fail to attend, since he feared and kept close watch
on those who were ready to gratify people by voting
remissions of debts and taxes, or promiscuous gifts.
And so by exhibiting a treasury which was inacces-

ἄβατόν τε καὶ καθαρὸν συκοφαντῶν, πλῆρες δὲ
χρημάτων, ἐδίδασκεν ὅτι τῇ πόλει πλουτεῖν
ἔξεστι μὴ ἀδικούσῃ. κατ᾽ ἀρχὰς δὲ τῶν συναρχόντων ἐνίοις ἐπαχθὴς καὶ χαλεπὸς φανεὶς ὕστερον ἠγαπᾶτο, ταῖς ἐκ τοῦ μὴ χαρίζεσθαι τὰ
δημόσια μηδὲ κρίνειν κακῶς ἀπεχθείαις ὑποτιθεὶς
ἑαυτὸν ἀντὶ πάντων, καὶ παρέχων ἀπολογεῖσθαι
πρὸς τοὺς δεομένους καὶ βιαζομένους ἐκείνους, ὡς
ἀμήχανόν ἐστιν, ἄκοντος Κάτωνος.

3 Τῶν δὲ ἡμερῶν τῇ τελευταίᾳ σχεδὸν ὑπὸ πάντων τῶν πολιτῶν προπεμφθεὶς εἰς οἶκον, ἤκουσεν ὅτι Μαρκέλλῳ πολλοὶ συνήθεις καὶ δυνατοὶ
προσπεσόντες ἐν τῷ ταμιείῳ καὶ περιέχοντες
ἐκβιάζονται γράψαι τινὰ δόσιν χρημάτων ὀφει-
λομένων. ἦν δὲ ὁ Μάρκελλος ἐκ παίδων φίλος
τῷ Κάτωνι, καὶ σὺν ἐκείνῳ βέλτιστος ἄρχων,
αὐτὸς δὲ καθ᾽ αὑτὸν ἀγώγιμος ὑπ᾽ αἰδοῦς τοῖς
4 δεομένοις, καὶ κατάντης πρὸς πᾶσαν χάριν. εὐθὺς οὖν ὁ Κάτων ἐπιστρέψας καὶ τὸν Μάρκελλον
εὑρὼν ἐκβεβιασμένον γράψαι τὴν δόσιν, ᾔτησε
τὰς δέλτους καὶ ἀπήλειψεν, αὐτοῦ παρεστῶτος
σιωπῇ· καὶ τοῦτο πράξας κατήγαγεν αὐτὸν ἐκ
τοῦ ταμιείου καὶ κατέστησεν εἰς οἶκον, οὔτε τότε
μεμψάμενον οὔτε ὕστερον, ἀλλ᾽ ἐμμείναντα τῇ
συνηθείᾳ καὶ φιλίᾳ μέχρι παντός.

5 Οὐ μὴν οὐδὲ ἀπαλλαγεὶς τῆς ταμιείας ἀφῆκε
τῆς φρουρᾶς ἔρημον τὸ ταμιεῖον, ἀλλ᾽ οἰκέται

sible to public informers and free from their taint,
but full of money, he taught men that a state can
be rich without wronging its citizens. At first some
of his colleagues thought him obnoxious and troublesome, but afterwards they were well pleased with
him, since he took upon his own shoulders ex-
clusively the burden of the hatreds arising from
refusal to give away the public moneys or to make
unjust decisions, and furnished them with a defence
against people who tried to force requests upon
them. They would say, namely, " It is impossible ;
Cato will not consent."

On the last day of his term of office, after he had
been escorted to his house by almost the whole body of
citizens, he heard that many friends of Marcellus and
men of influence had closely beset him in the treasury,
and were trying to force him to register some remission of moneys due. Now, Marcellus had been a
friend of Cato from boyhood, and when associated
with him had been a most excellent magistrate.
When acting by himself, however, he was led by a
feeling of deference to be complaisant towards suppliants, and was inclined to grant every favour. At
once, then, Cato turned back, and when he found
that Marcellus had been forced to register the remission, he asked for the tablets and erased the
entry, while Marcellus himself stood by and said
nothing. After this had been done, Cato conducted
Marcellus away from the treasury and brought him
to his house, and Marcellus had no word of blame
for him either then or afterwards, but continued his
intimate friendship up to the end.

However, not even after he had laid down the
quaestorship did Cato leave the treasury destitute of

μὲν αὐτοῦ καθ᾽ ἡμέραν ἀπογραφόμενοι τὰς διοι-
κήσεις παρῆσαν, αὐτὸς δὲ βιβλία λόγους περιέ-
χοντα δημοσίων οἰκονομιῶν ἀπὸ τῶν Σύλλα
χρόνων εἰς τὴν ἑαυτοῦ ταμιείαν ὠνησάμενος πέντε
ταλάντων ἀεὶ διὰ χειρὸς εἶχεν.

XIX. Εἰς δὲ σύγκλητον εἰσῄει τε πρῶτος καὶ
τελευταῖος ἀπηλλάττετο· πολλάκις δὲ τῶν ἄλλων σχολῇ συναγομένων καθεζόμενος ἀνεγίνωσκεν ἡσυχῇ, τὸ ἱμάτιον τοῦ βιβλίου προϊσχόμενος. ἀπεδήμησε δὲ οὐδέποτε βουλῆς γενομένης.   76͞5
ἐπεὶ δὲ ὕστερον οἱ περὶ Πομπήϊον ἑώρων[1] αὐτὸν
ἐν οἷς ἐσπούδαζον ἀδίκως ἀμετάπειστον καὶ
δυσεκβίαστον ἀεί, διεμηχανῶντο φιλικαῖς τισι
συνηγορίαις ἢ διαίταις ἢ πραγματείαις ἔξω περι-
σπᾶν. συνεὶς οὖν ταχὺ τὴν ἐπιβουλὴν ἀπεῖπε
πᾶσι καὶ παρετάξατο βουλῆς ἀγομένης μηδὲν
2 ἄλλο πράττειν. οὔτε γὰρ δόξης χάριν οὔτε
πλεονεξίας οὔτε αὐτομάτως καὶ κατὰ τύχην,
ὥσπερ ἕτεροί τινες, ἐμπεσὼν εἰς τὸ πράττειν τὰ
τῆς πόλεως, ἀλλ᾽ ὡς ἴδιον ἔργον ἀνδρὸς ἀγαθοῦ
τὴν πολιτείαν ἑλόμενος, μᾶλλον ᾤετο δεῖν προσέχειν τοῖς κοινοῖς ἢ τῷ κηρίῳ τὴν μέλιτταν, ὅς γε
καὶ τὰ τῶν ἐπαρχιῶν πράγματα καὶ δόγματα καὶ
κρίσεις καὶ πράξεις τὰς μεγίστας ἔργον πεποίητο
διὰ τῶν ἑκασταχόθι ξένων καὶ φίλων πέμπεσθαι
πρὸς αὐτόν.
3 Ἐνστὰς δέ ποτε Κλωδίῳ τῷ δημαγωγῷ κινοῦν-
τι καὶ ταράττοντι μεγάλων ἀρχὰς νεωτερισμῶν
καὶ διαβάλλοντι πρὸς τὸν δῆμον ἱερεῖς καὶ ἱερείας,

---

[1] ἑώρων Sintenis, with one Paris MS.; Coraës and Bekker
have ὁρῶντες, with the other MSS.

his watchful care, but slaves of his were there every day copying the transactions, and he himself paid five talents for books containing accounts of the public business from the times of Sulla down to his own quaestorship, and always had them in hand.

XIX. He used to be the first to reach the senate and the last to leave it; and often, while the other senators were slowly assembling, he would sit and read quietly, holding his toga in front of the book. He never left the city when the senate was in session. But afterwards, when Pompey and his friends saw that he could never be prevailed upon or forced from his position in any unjust measures which they had at heart, they would contrive to draw him away by sundry legal advocacies for friends, or arbitrations, or business matters. Accordingly, Cato quickly perceived their design and refused all such applications, and made it a rule to have no other business on hand while the senate was in session. For it was neither for the sake of reputation, nor to gain riches, nor accidentally and by chance, like some others, that he threw himself into the management of civic affairs, but he chose a public career as the proper task for a good man, and thought that he ought to be more attentive to the common interests than the bee to its honey. And so he was careful to have the affairs of the provinces and decrees and trials and the most important measures sent to him by his connections and friends in every place.

At one time he opposed Clodius the demagogue, who was raising agitation and confusion as a prelude to great changes, and was calumniating to the people priests and priestesses, among whom Fabia, a sister of

ἐν οἷς καὶ Φαβία Τερεντίας ἀδελφή, τῆς Κικέρωνος γυναικός, ἐκινδύνευσε, τὸν μὲν Κλώδιον
αἰσχύνῃ περιβαλὼν ἠνάγκασεν ὑπεκστῆναι τῆς
πόλεως, τοῦ δὲ Κικέρωνος εὐχαριστοῦντος, τῇ
πόλει δεῖν ἔχειν ἔφη χάριν αὐτόν, ὡς ἐκείνης
4 ἕνεκα πάντα ποιῶν καὶ πολιτευόμενος. ἐκ τούτου μεγάλη δόξα περὶ αὐτὸν ἦν, ὥστε ῥήτορα
μέν, δίκῃ τινὶ μαρτυρίας μιᾶς φερομένης, εἰπεῖν
πρὸς τοὺς δικαστὰς ὡς ἑνὶ μαρτυροῦντι προσέχειν, οὐδὲ Κάτωνι, καλῶς ἔχει, πολλοὺς δὲ ἤδη
περὶ τῶν ἀπίστων καὶ παραδόξων, ὥσπερ ἐν
παροιμίᾳ τινί, λέγειν ὅτι τοῦτο μὲν οὐδὲ Κάτωνος
5 λέγοντος πιθανόν ἐστι. μοχθηροῦ δὲ ἀνθρώπου
καὶ πολυτελοῦς λόγον ἐν συγκλήτῳ διαθεμένου
πρὸς εὐτέλειαν καὶ σωφρονισμὸν ἐπαναστὰς
Ἀμναῖος, "Ὦ ἄνθρωπε," εἶπε, "τίς ἀνέξεταί
σου δειπνοῦντος μὲν ὡς Λευκόλλου, οἰκοδομοῦν-
τος δὲ ὡς Κράσσου, δημηγοροῦντος δὲ ἡμῖν ὡς
Κάτωνος;" καὶ τῶν ἄλλων δὲ τοὺς φαύλους καὶ
ἀκολάστους, τοῖς λόγοις δὲ σεμνοὺς καὶ αὐστη-
ροὺς χλενάζοντες ἐκάλουν Κάτωνας.

XX. Πολλῶν δὲ αὐτὸν ἐπὶ δημαρχίαν καλούντων οὐκ ᾤετο καλῶς ἔχειν μεγάλης ἐξουσίας καὶ
ἀρχῆς, ὥσπερ ἰσχυροῦ φαρμάκου, δύναμιν ἐν
πράγμασιν οὐκ ἀναγκαίοις ἐξαναλῶσαι. καὶ
ἅμα, σχολῆς οὔσης τῶν δημοσίων, παραλαβὼν
βιβλία καὶ φιλοσόφους ἐβάδιζεν εἰς Λευκανίαν,
ἀγροὺς αὐτόθι κεκτημένος ἔχοντας οὐκ ἀνελευ-
2 θέρους διατριβάς· εἶτα καθ᾽ ὁδὸν πολλοῖς τισιν
ὑποζυγίοις καὶ σκεύεσι καὶ ἀκολούθοις ἀπαντήσας καὶ πυθόμενος Νέπωτα Μέτελλον εἰς Ῥώμην
ἐπανέρχεσθαι δημαρχίαν μετιέναι παρεσκευα-

Cicero's wife Terentia, was in danger of conviction. But Cato put Clodius to such shame that he was forced to steal away from the city; and when Cicero thanked him, Cato told him he ought to be thankful to the city, since it was for her sake that all his public work was done. In consequence of this he was held in high repute, so that an orator, at a trial where the testimony of a single witness was introduced, told the jurors that it was not right to give heed to a single witness, not even if he were Cato; and many already, when speaking of matters that were strange and incredible, would say, as though using a proverb, "This is not to be believed even though Cato says it." Again, when a corrupt and extravagant man was expatiating in the senate on frugality and self-restraint, Amnaeus sprang to his feet and said: "Who can endure it, my man, when you sup like Lucullus, build like Crassus, and yet harangue us like Cato?"[1] And other men also who were degraded and licentious in their lives, but lofty and severe in their speech, were mockingly called Catos.

XX. Though many invited him to become a tribune of the people he did not think it right to expend the force of a great and powerful magistracy, any more than that of a strong medicine, on matters that did not require it. And at the same time, being at leisure from his public duties, he took books and philosophers with him and set out for Lucania, where he owned lands affording no mean sojourn. Then, meeting on the road many beasts of burden with baggage and attendants, and learning that Metellus Nepos was on his way back to Rome prepared to sue for the tribuneship, he stopped without a word, and

---

[1] Cf. the *Lucullus*, xl. 3.

σμένον, ἐπέστη σιωπῇ, καὶ διαλιπὼν μικρὸν ἐκέλευσεν ἀναστρέφειν ὀπίσω τοὺς ἑαυτοῦ. τῶν δὲ
φίλων θαυμασάντων, "Οὐκ ἴστε," εἶπεν, "ὅτι
καὶ καθ' αὑτὸν ὑπὸ ἐμπληξίας φοβερός ἐστι
Μέτελλος, καὶ νῦν ἐκ τῆς Πομπηΐου γνώμης
ἀφιγμένος εἰς τὴν πολιτείαν ἐμπεσεῖται δίκην
3 σκηπτοῦ πάντα πράγματα ταράττων; οὐκ οὖν
σχολῆς οὐδὲ ἀποδημίας καιρός, ἀλλὰ δεῖ κρατῆ-
σαι τοῦ ἀνδρός, ἢ καλῶς ἀποθανεῖν ὑπὲρ τῆς
ἐλευθερίας ἀγωνιζόμενον." ὅμως δὲ τῶν φίλων
παραινεσάντων ἀφίκετο πρῶτον εἰς τὰ χωρία καὶ
διέτριψεν οὐ πολὺν χρόνον, εἶτα ἐπανῆκεν εἰς
πόλιν. ἑσπέρας δὲ ἐλθὼν εὐθὺς ἕωθεν εἰς ἀγορὰν
κατέβαινε δημαρχίαν μετιών, ὡς ἀντιταξόμενος
πρὸς τὸν Μέτελλον. τὸ γὰρ ἰσχυρὸν ἡ ἀρχὴ
πρὸς τὸ κωλύειν ἔχει μᾶλλον ἢ πρὸς τὸ πράττειν·
κἂν πάντες οἱ λοιποὶ παρ' ἕνα ψηφίσωνται, τοῦ
μὴ θέλοντος μηδὲ ἐῶντος τὸ κράτος ἐστί.

XXI. Τὸ μὲν οὖν πρῶτον ὀλίγοι περὶ τὸν
Κάτωνα τῶν φίλων ἦσαν· φανερᾶς δὲ τῆς γνώμης 769
αὐτοῦ γενομένης, ὀλίγου χρόνου πάντες οἱ χρη-
στοὶ καὶ γνώριμοι συνέτρεχον καὶ παρεκάλουν
καὶ παρεθάρρυνον αὐτόν, ὡς οὐ λαμβάνοντα
χάριν, ἀλλὰ τὴν μεγίστην διδόντα τῇ πατρίδι
καὶ τοῖς ἐπιεικεστάτοις τῶν πολιτῶν, ὅτι πολλάκις ἀπραγμόνως ἄρξαι παρὸν οὐ θελήσας, νῦν
ὑπὲρ τῆς ἐλευθερίας καὶ πολιτείας ἀγωνιούμενος
2 οὐκ ἀκινδύνως κάτεισι. λέγεται δέ, πολλῶν ὑπὸ
σπουδῆς καὶ φιλοφροσύνης ὠθουμένων πρὸς αὐτόν, ἐν κινδύνῳ γενόμενος μόλις ἐξικέσθαι διὰ
πλῆθος εἰς τὴν ἀγοράν. ἀποδειχθεὶς δὲ δήμαρχος

after waiting a little while ordered his company to turn back. His friends were amazed at this, whereupon he said: "Do ye not know that even of himself Metellus is to be feared by reason of his infatuation? And now that he comes by the advice of Pompey he will fall upon the state like a thunderbolt and throw everything into confusion. It is no time, then, for a leisurely sojourn in the country, but we must overpower the man, or die honourably in a struggle for our liberties." Nevertheless, on the advice of his friends, he went first to his estates and tarried there a short time, and then returned to the city.[1] It was evening when he arrived, and as soon as day dawned he went down into the forum to sue for a tribuneship, that he might array himself against Metellus. For the strength of that office is negative rather than positive; and if all the tribunes save one should vote for a measure, the power lies with the one who will not give his consent or permission.

XXI. At first, then, Cato had only a few of his friends about him; but when his purpose became known, in a little while all the men of worth and note flocked to him with exhortations and encouragements. They felt that he was not receiving a favour, but conferring the greatest favour on his country and the most reputable of his fellow citizens; for he had often refused the office when he could have had it without trouble, and now sued for it at his peril that he might contend for the liberties of the state. It is said, moreover, that he was in peril from the many who crowded upon him in their zeal and affection, and could hardly make his way for the crowd into the forum. He was declared

---

[1] In 63 B.C.

σὺν ἑτέροις, καὶ τῷ Μετέλλῳ, τὰς ὑπατικὰς
ἀρχαιρεσίας ὁρῶν ὠνίους οὔσας, ἐπετίμησε τῷ
δήμῳ· καὶ καταπαύων τὸν λόγον ἐπώμοσε τοῦ
δόντος ἀργύριον, ὅστις ἂν ᾖ, κατηγορήσειν, ἕνα
Σιλανὸν ὑπεξελόμενος δι' οἰκειότητα. Σερβιλίαν
3 γὰρ ἀδελφὴν Κάτωνος ὁ Σιλανὸς εἶχε. διὸ τοῦτον μὲν παρῆκε, Λεύκιον δὲ Μουρήναν ἐδίωκεν
ἀργυρίῳ διαπραξάμενον ἄρχοντα μετὰ τοῦ Σιλα-
νοῦ γενέσθαι. νόμῳ δέ τινι τοῦ φεύγοντος ἀεὶ
φύλακα τῷ κατηγόρῳ διδόντος, ὥστε μὴ λαθεῖν
ἃ συνάγει καὶ παρασκευάζεται πρὸς τὴν κατηγορίαν, ὁ τῷ Κάτωνι δοθεὶς ὑπὸ τοῦ Μουρήνα
παρακολουθῶν καὶ παραφυλάττων, ὡς ἑώρα
4 μηθὲν ἐπιβούλως πράττοντα μηδὲ ἀδίκως, ἀλλὰ
γενναίως τε καὶ φιλανθρώπως ἁπλῆν τινα τῆς
κατηγορίας καὶ δικαίαν ὁδὸν πορευόμενον, οὕτως
ἐθαύμαζε τὸ φρόνημα καὶ τὸ ἦθος ὥστε κατ'
ἀγορὰν προσιὼν καὶ φοιτῶν ἐπὶ θύρας πυνθάνεσθαι τοῦ Κάτωνος εἰ μέλλει τι σήμερον πρα-
γματεύσασθαι τῶν περὶ τὴν κατηγορίαν· εἰ δὲ μὴ
φαίη, πιστεύων ἀπῄει.
5 Τῆς δὲ δίκης λεγομένης ὁ Κικέρων, ὕπατος ὢν
τότε καὶ τῷ Μουρήνᾳ συνδικῶν, πολλὰ διὰ τὸν
Κάτωνα τοὺς Στωϊκοὺς φιλοσόφους καὶ ταῦτα δὴ
τὰ παράδοξα καλούμενα δόγματα χλευάζων καὶ
παρασκώπτων γέλωτα παρεῖχε τοῖς δικασταῖς.

tribune with others [1] (including Metellus), and seeing that the consular elections were attended with
bribery, he berated the people; and in concluding
his speech he swore that he would prosecute the
briber, whoever he might be, making an exception
only of Silanus because of their relationship. For
Silanus was the husband of Cato's sister Servilia.
For this reason he let Silanus alone, but he prosecuted Lucius Murena on the charge of having
secured his election to the consulship with Silanus
by bribery.[2] Now, there was a law by which the
defendant could set a man to watch the prosecutor,
in order that there might be no secret about the
material which he was collecting and preparing for
the prosecution. Accordingly, the man appointed
by Murena to watch Cato would follow him about
and keep him under observation. When, however,
he saw that Cato was doing nothing insidiously or
unjustly, but was honourably and considerately
following a straightforward and righteous course in
the prosecution, he had such admiration for Cato's
lofty spirit and noble character that he would come
up to him in the forum or go to his house and ask
him whether he intended that day to attend to any
matters connected with the prosecution; and if
Cato said no, the man would take his word and go
away.

When the trial was held, Cicero, who was consul
at that time and one of Murena's advocates, took
advantage of Cato's fondness for the Stoics to rail
and jest at length about those philosophers and
what were called their "paradoxes," thus making

---

[1] At this time the number of the popular tribunes was ten.
[2] Silanus and Murena were consuls in 62 B.C.

τὸν οὖν Κάτωνά φασι διαμειδιάσαντα πρὸς τοὺς
παρόντας εἰπεῖν· "Ὦ ἄνδρες, ὡς γελοῖον ὕπα-
6 τον ἔχομεν." ἀποφυγὼν δὲ ὁ Μουρήνας οὐ
πονηροῦ πάθος οὐδὲ ἄφρονος ἔπαθεν ἀνθρώπου
πρὸς τὸν Κάτωνα· καὶ γὰρ ὑπατεύων ἐχρῆτο
συμβούλῳ τῶν μεγίστων, καὶ τἄλλα τιμῶν καὶ
πιστεύων διετέλεσεν. αἴτιος δὲ ἦν ὁ Κάτων αὐτός, ἐπὶ τοῦ βήματος καὶ τοῦ συνεδρίου χαλεπὸς
ὢν καὶ φοβερὸς ὑπὲρ τῶν δικαίων, εἶτα πᾶσιν
εὐνοϊκῶς καὶ φιλανθρώπως προσφερόμενος.

XXII. Πρὶν δὲ εἰς τὴν δημαρχίαν καθίστα-
σθαι, Κικέρωνος ὑπατεύοντος, ἄλλοις τε πολλοῖς
ἀγῶσι τὴν ἀρχὴν ὤρθωσεν αὐτοῦ καὶ ταῖς περὶ
Κατιλίναν πράξεσι μεγίσταις καὶ καλλίσταις
γενομέναις τέλος ἐπέθηκεν. αὐτὸς μὲν γὰρ ὁ
Κατιλίνας ὀλέθριόν τε καὶ παντελῆ μεταβολὴν
ἐπάγων τοῖς Ῥωμαίων πράγμασι καὶ στάσεις
ὁμοῦ καὶ πολέμους ταράττων ἐξελεγχθεὶς ὑπὸ
2 τοῦ Κικέρωνος ἐξέπεσε τῆς πόλεως, Λέντλος δὲ καὶ
Κέθηγος καὶ μετ᾽ αὐτῶν ἕτεροι συχνοὶ δεξάμενοι
τὴν συνωμοσίαν, καὶ τῷ Κατιλίνᾳ δειλίαν καὶ
μικρολογίαν τῶν τολμημάτων ἐπικαλοῦντες, αὐτοὶ
διενοοῦντο τὴν πόλιν ἄρδην ἀναιρεῖν πυρὶ καὶ
τὴν ἡγεμονίαν ἐθνῶν ἀποστάσεσι καὶ πολέμοις
3 ἀλλοφύλοις ἀνατρέπειν. φανερᾶς δὲ τῆς παρασκευῆς αὐτῶν γενομένης, καὶ Κικέρωνος[1] ἐν
βουλῇ γνώμην προθέντος, ὁ μὲν πρῶτος εἰπὼν
Σιλανὸς ἀπεφήνατο δοκεῖν αὐτῷ τὰ ἔσχατα
παθεῖν χρῆναι τοὺς ἄνδρας, οἱ δὲ μετ᾽ αὐτὸν ἐφε-

[1] καὶ Κικέρωνος so Sintenis[2] for the corrupt MSS. ὡς ἐν
τοῖς περὶ Κικέρωνος γέγραπται; Coraës and Bekker adopt the
early anonymous correction καὶ Κικέρωνος, ὡς ἐν τοῖς περὶ
ἐκείνου γέγραπται.

the jurors laugh. Cato, accordingly, as we are told, said with a smile to the bystanders: "My friends, what a droll fellow our consul is!" And after Murena had been acquitted, he did not feel towards Cato as a base or senseless man might have done; for during his consulship he asked his advice in the most important matters, and in other ways constantly showed him honour and trust. And Cato himself was responsible for this; on the tribunal and in the senate he was severe and terrible in his defence of justice, but afterwards his manner towards all men was benevolent and kindly.

XXII. Before he entered upon his tribuneship, and during the consulship of Cicero,[1] he maintained the authority of that magistrate in many conflicts, and above all in the measures relating to Catiline, which proved the most important and most glorious of all, he brought matters to a successful issue. Catiline himself, namely, who was trying to bring about a complete and destructive change in the Roman state, and was stirring up alike seditions and wars, was convicted by Cicero and fled the city; but Lentulus and Cethegus and many others with them took over the conspiracy, and, charging Catiline with cowardice and pettiness in his designs, were themselves planning to destroy the city utterly with fire, and to subvert the empire with revolts of nations and foreign wars. But their schemes were discovered, and Cicero brought the matter before the senate for deliberation.[2] The first speaker, Silanus, expressed the opinion that the men ought to suffer the extremest fate, and those who followed him in

[1] 63 B.C.
[2] Cf. the *Caesar*, vii. 4–v ii. 2; and the *Cicero*, x. ff.

4 ξῆς ἠκολούθησαν, ἄχρι Καίσαρος. Καῖσαρ δὲ
ἀναστάς, ἅτε δὴ καὶ δεινὸς εἰπεῖν καὶ πᾶσαν ἐν
τῇ πόλει μεταβολὴν καὶ κίνησιν ὥσπερ ὕλην
ὧν αὐτὸς διενοεῖτο βουλόμενος αὔξειν μᾶλλον
ἢ σβεννυμένην περιορᾶν, ἐπαγωγὰ πολλὰ καὶ 770
φιλάνθρωπα διαλεχθεὶς ἀποκτεῖναι μὲν ἀκρίτους
οὐκ εἴα τοὺς ἄνδρας, εἰρχθέντας δὲ τηρεῖν ἐκέ-
5 λευσεν, οὕτω δὲ τὰς γνώμας μετέστησε τῆς
βουλῆς, φοβηθείσης τὸν δῆμον, ὥστε καὶ Σιλανὸν ἔξαρνον εἶναι καὶ λέγειν ὡς οὐδ' αὐτὸς
εἴποι θάνατον, ἀλλὰ εἰργμόν· ἔσχατον γὰρ ἀνδρὶ
Ῥωμαίῳ τοῦτο κακῶν ἁπάντων.

XXIII. Γενομένης δὲ τοιαύτης τῆς τροπῆς καὶ
ἁπάντων ἐπὶ τὸ πρᾳότερον ῥυέντων καὶ φιλανθρωπότερον, ὁ Κάτων πρὸς τὴν γνώμην ἀναστὰς
εὐθὺς ἵετο τῷ λόγῳ μετ' ὀργῆς καὶ πάθους, τόν
τε Σιλανὸν κακίζων τῆς μεταβολῆς, καὶ καθα-
πτόμενος τοῦ Καίσαρος ὡς σχήματι δημοτικῷ καὶ
2 λόγῳ φιλανθρώπῳ τὴν πόλιν ἀνατρέποντος, καὶ
δεδιττομένου τὴν βουλὴν ἐφ' οἷς αὐτὸν ἔδει δεδιέναι καὶ ἀγαπᾶν εἰ τῶν γεγονότων ἀθῷος
ἀπαλλάξει καὶ ἀνύποπτος, οὕτως περιφανῶς καὶ
ἰταμῶς τοὺς κοινοὺς ἐξαρπάζων πολεμίους καὶ
τὴν παρ' οὐδὲν ἐλθοῦσαν ἀπολέσθαι πατρίδα
τοιαύτην καὶ τοσαύτην ὁμολογῶν μὴ ἐλεεῖν, ἀλλ'
οὓς ἔδει μὴ γενέσθαι μηδὲ φῦναι δακρύων καὶ
ἀνακλαιόμενος, εἰ φόνων μεγάλων καὶ κινδύνων
ἀπαλλάξουσι τὴν πόλιν ἀποθανόντες.

3 Τοῦτον μόνον ὧν Κάτων εἶπε διασώζεσθαί

turn were of the same mind, until it came to Caesar.
Caesar now rose, and since he was a powerful
speaker and wished to increase every change and
commotion in the state as so much stuff for his own
designs, rather than to allow them to be quenched,
he urged many persuasive and humane arguments.
He would not hear of the men being put to death
without a trial, but favoured their being kept in
close custody, and he wrought such a change in the
opinions of the senate, which was in fear of the
people, that even Silanus recanted and said that
he too had not meant death, but imprisonment; for
to a Roman this was the "extremest" of all evils.

XXIII. After such a change as this had been
wrought and all the senators had hastened to adopt
the milder and more humane penalty, Cato rose to
give his opinion, and launched at once into a passionate and angry speech, abusing Silanus for his
change of opinion, and assailing Caesar. Caesar, he
said, under a popular pretext and with humane
words, was trying to subvert the state; he was
seeking to frighten the senate in a case where he
himself had much to fear; and he might be well
content if he should come off guiltless of what had
been done and free from suspicion, since he was so
openly and recklessly trying to rescue the common
enemies, while for his country, which had been on
the brink of ruin, and was so good and great, he
confessed that he had no pity; and yet for men
who ought not to have lived or been born even, he
was shedding tears and lamenting, although by their
deaths they would free the state from great slaughter
and perils.

This is the only speech of Cato which has been

φασι τὸν λόγον, Κικέρωνος τοῦ ὑπάτου τοὺς διαφέροντας ὀξύτητι τῶν γραφέων σημεῖα προδιδάξαντος ἐν μικροῖς καὶ βραχέσι τύποις πολλῶν γραμμάτων ἔχοντα δύναμιν, εἶτα ἄλλον ἀλλαχόσε τοῦ βουλευτηρίου σποράδην ἐμβαλόντος. οὔπω γὰρ ἤσκουν οὐδ' ἐκέκτηντο τοὺς καλουμένους σημειογράφους, ἀλλὰ τότε πρῶτον εἰς ἴχνος τι καταστῆναι λέγουσιν. ἐκράτησε δ' οὖν ὁ Κάτων καὶ μετέστησε τὰς γνώμας, ὥστε θάνατον καταψηφίσασθαι τῶν ἀνδρῶν.

XXIV. Εἰ δὲ δεῖ μηδὲ τὰ μικρὰ τῶν ἠθῶν σημεῖα παραλιπεῖν ὥσπερ εἰκόνα ψυχῆς ὑπογραφομένους, λέγεται, τότε πολλὴν ἅμιλλαν καὶ μέγαν ἀγῶνα πρὸς τὸν Κάτωνα τοῦ Καίσαρος ἔχοντος καὶ τῆς βουλῆς εἰς ἐκείνους ἀνηρτημένης, δελτάριόν τι μικρὸν ἔξωθεν εἰσκομισθῆναι τῷ Καίσαρι. τοῦ δὲ Κάτωνος εἰς ὑποψίαν ἄγοντος τὸ πρᾶγμα καὶ διαβάλλοντος εἶναί τινας τοὺς κινουμένους, καὶ κελεύοντος ἀναγινώσκειν τὰ γεγραμμένα, τὸν Καίσαρα τῷ Κάτωνι προσδοῦναι

2 τὸ δελτάριον ἐγγὺς ἑστῶτι. τὸν δὲ ἀναγνόντα Σερβιλίας τῆς ἀδελφῆς ἐπιστόλιον ἀκόλαστον πρὸς τὸν Καίσαρα γεγραμμένον, ἐρώσης καὶ διεφθαρμένης ὑπ' αὐτοῦ, προσρῖψαί τε τῷ Καίσαρι καὶ εἰπεῖν, "Κράτει, μέθυσε," καὶ πάλιν οὕτως ἐπὶ τὸν ἐξ ἀρχῆς λόγον τραπέσθαι.

3 Φαίνεται δὲ ὅλως ἀτύχημα γενέσθαι τοῦ Κάτωνος ἡ γυναικωνῖτις. αὕτη μὲν γὰρ ἐπὶ

preserved, we are told, and its preservation was due to Cicero the consul, who had previously given to those clerks who excelled in rapid writing instruction in the use of signs, which, in small and short figures, comprised the force of many letters; these clerks he had then distributed in various parts of the senate-house. For up to that time the Romans did not employ or even possess what are called short-hand writers, but then for the first time, we are told, the first steps toward the practice were taken. Be that as it may, Cato carried the day and changed the opinions of the senators, so that they condemned the men to death.

XXIV. Now, since we must not pass over even the slight tokens of character when we are de-lineating as it were a likeness of the soul, the story goes that on this occasion, when Caesar was eagerly engaged in a great struggle with Cato and the attention of the senate was fixed upon the two men, a little note was brought in from outside to Caesar. Cato tried to fix suspicion upon the matter and alleged that it had something to do with the con-spiracy,[1] and bade him read the writing aloud. Then Caesar handed the note to Cato, who stood near him. But when Cato had read the note, which was an unchaste letter from his sister Servilia to Caesar, with whom she was passionately and guiltily in love, he threw it to Caesar, saying, "Take it, thou sot," and then resumed his speech.

But as regards the women of his household Cato appears to have been wholly unfortunate. For this

[1] Plutarch's ambiguous words here must be interpreted by comparison with the *Brutus*, v. 2 f., where the same story is told.

Καίσαρι κακῶς ἤκουσε· τὰ δὲ τῆς ἑτέρας Σερβιλίας, ἀδελφῆς δὲ Κάτωνος, ἀσχημονέστερα.
Λευκόλλῳ γὰρ γαμηθεῖσα, πρωτεύσαντι Ῥωμαίων κατὰ δόξαν ἀνδρί, καὶ τεκοῦσα παιδίον
ἐξέπεσε τοῦ οἴκου δι' ἀκολασίαν. τὸ δὲ αἴσχι-
στον, οὐδ' ἡ γυνὴ τοῦ Κάτωνος Ἀτιλία τοιούτων
ἐκαθάρευσεν ἁμαρτημάτων, ἀλλὰ καίπερ ἐξ αὐτῆς δύο παιδία πεποιημένος ἀνάγκην ἔσχεν ἐκβαλεῖν ἀσχημονοῦσαν.

XXV. Εἶτα ἔγημε θυγατέρα Φιλίππου, Μαρκίαν, ἐπιεικῆ δοκοῦσαν εἶναι γυναῖκα, περὶ ἧς ὁ
πλεῖστος λόγος· καὶ καθάπερ[1] ἐν δράματι τῷ
βίῳ τοῦτο τὸ μέρος προβληματῶδες γέγονε καὶ
ἄπορον. ἐπράχθη δὲ τοῦτον τὸν τρόπον, ὡς
ἱστορεῖ Θρασέας, εἰς Μουνάτιον, ἄνδρα Κάτωνος
ἑταῖρον καὶ συμβιωτήν, ἀναφέρων τὴν πίστιν.
2 ἐν πολλοῖς ἐρασταῖς καὶ θαυμασταῖς τοῦ Κάτωνος ἦσαν ἑτέρων ἕτεροι μᾶλλον ἔκδηλοι καὶ
διαφανεῖς, ὧν καὶ Κόϊντος Ὁρτήσιος, ἀνὴρ ἀξιώ-
ματός τε λαμπροῦ καὶ τὸν τρόπον ἐπιεικής.
ἐπιθυμῶν οὖν τῷ Κάτωνι μὴ συνήθης εἶναι μηδὲ 771
ἑταῖρος μόνον, ἀλλ' ἁμῶς γέ πως εἰς οἰκειότητα
καταμῖξαι καὶ κοινωνίαν πάντα τὸν οἶκον καὶ τὸ
γένος, ἐπεχείρησε συμπείθειν ὅπως τὴν θυγατέρα
Πορκίαν, Βύβλῳ συνοικοῦσαν καὶ πεποιημένην
ἐκείνῳ δύο παῖδας, αὐτῷ πάλιν ὥσπερ εὐγενῆ
3 χώραν ἐντεκνώσασθαι παράσχῃ. δόξῃ μὲν γὰρ
ἀνθρώπων ἄτοπον εἶναι τὸ τοιοῦτον, φύσει δὲ
καλὸν καὶ πολιτικόν, ἐν ὥρᾳ καὶ ἀκμῇ γυναῖκα
μήτε ἀργεῖν τὸ γόνιμον ἀποσβέσασαν, μήτε

---

[1] καὶ καθάπερ the καὶ is supplied by Sintenis; Bekker
has καθάπερ γάρ, after Coraës.

sister was in ill repute for her relations with Caesar;
and the conduct of the other Servilia, also a sister of
Cato, was still more unseemly. She was the wife of
Lucullus, a man of the highest repute in Rome, and
had borne him a child, and yet she was banished from
his house for unchastity.[1] And what was most disgraceful of all, even Cato's wife Atilia was not free
from such transgressions, but although he had two
children by her, he was forced to put her away because
of her unseemly behaviour.

XXV. Then he married a daughter of Philippus,
Marcia, a woman of reputed excellence, about whom
there was the most abundant talk; and this part of
Cato's life, like a drama, has given rise to dispute and
is hard to explain. However, the case was as follows,
according to Thrasea, who refers to the authority of
Munatius, Cato's companion and intimate associate.
Among the many lovers and admirers of Cato there
were some who were more conspicuous and illustrious
than others. One of these was Quintus Hortensius,
a man of splendid reputation and excellent character.
This man, then, desiring to be more than a mere
associate and companion of Cato, and in some way or
other to bring his whole family and line into community of kinship with him, attempted to persuade
Cato, whose daughter Porcia was the wife of Bibulus
and had borne him two sons, to give her in turn to him
as noble soil for the production of children. According
to the opinion of men, he argued, such a course was
absurd, but according to the law of nature it was
honourable and good for the state that a woman in
the prime of youth and beauty should neither quench
her productive power and lie idle, nor yet, by bear-

---

[1] See the *Lucullus*, xxxviii. 1.

πλείονα τῶν ἱκανῶν ἐπιτίκτουσαν, ἐνοχλεῖν καὶ
καταπτωχεύειν οὐδὲν δεόμενον,¹ κοινουμένους δὲ
τὰς διαδοχὰς ἀξίοις ἀνδράσι τήν τε ἀρετὴν ἄφθονον ποιεῖν καὶ πολύχυτον τοῖς γένεσι, καὶ τὴν
πόλιν αὐτὴν πρὸς αὑτὴν ἀνακεραννύναι ταῖς οἰ-
κειότησιν. εἰ δὲ πάντως περιέχοιτο τῆς γυναικὸς
ὁ Βύβλος, ἀποδώσειν εὐθὺς τεκοῦσαν, οἰκειότερος
αὑτῷ τε Βύβλῳ καὶ Κάτωνι κοινωνίᾳ παίδων
γενόμενος.

4 Ἀποκριναμένου δὲ τοῦ Κάτωνος ὡς Ὁρτήσιον
μὲν ἀγαπᾷ καὶ δοκιμάζει κοινωνὸν οἰκειότητος,
ἄτοπον δὲ ἡγεῖται ποιεῖσθαι λόγον περὶ γάμου
θυγατρὸς ἑτέρῳ δεδομένης, μεταβαλὼν ἐκεῖνος
οὐκ ὤκνησεν ἀποκαλυψάμενος αἰτεῖν τὴν αὐτοῦ
γυναῖκα Κάτωνος, νέαν μὲν οὖσαν ἔτι πρὸς τὸ
τίκτειν, ἔχοντος δὲ τοῦ Κάτωνος ἀποχρῶσαν
5 διαδοχήν. καὶ οὐκ ἔστιν εἰπεῖν ὡς ταῦτα ἔπραττεν εἰδὼς οὐ προσέχοντα τῇ Μαρκίᾳ τὸν Κάτωνα·
κύουσαν γὰρ αὐτὴν τότε τυγχάνειν λέγουσιν. ὁ
δ᾽ οὖν Κάτων ὁρῶν τὴν τοῦ Ὁρτησίου σπουδὴν
καὶ προθυμίαν οὐκ ἀντεῖπεν, ἀλλ᾽ ἔφη δεῖν καὶ
Φιλίππῳ ταῦτα συνδόξαι τῷ πατρὶ τῆς Μαρκίας.
ὡς οὖν ὁ Φίλιππος ἐντευχθεὶς ἔγνω τὴν συγχώ-
ρησιν, οὐκ ἄλλως ἐνεγγύησε τὴν Μαρκίαν ἢ
παρόντος τοῦ Κάτωνος αὐτοῦ καὶ συνεγγυῶντος.
ταῦτα μὲν οὖν, εἰ καὶ χρόνοις ὕστερον ἐπράχθη,
μνησθέντι μοι τὸ τῶν γυναικῶν προλαβεῖν ἔδοξε.

¹ δεόμενον Coraës supplies οἶκον.

ing more offspring than enough, burden and impoverish a husband who does not want them. Moreover, community in heirs among worthy men would make virtue abundant and widely diffused in their families, and the state would be closely cemented together by their family alliances. And if Bibulus were wholly devoted to his wife, Hortensius said he would give her back after she had borne him a child, and he would thus be more closely connected both with Bibulus himself and with Cato by a community of children.

Cato replied that he loved Hortensius and thought highly of a community of relationship with him, but considered it absurd for him to propose marriage with a daughter who had been given to another. Then Hortensius changed his tactics, threw off the mask, and boldly asked for the wife of Cato himself, since she was still young enough to bear children, and Cato had heirs enough. And it cannot be said that he did this because he knew that Cato neglected Marcia, for she was at that time with child by him, as we are told. However, seeing the earnestness and eager desire of Hortensius, Cato would not refuse, but said that Philippus also, Marcia's father, must approve of this step. Accordingly, Philippus was consulted and expressed his consent, but he would not give Marcia in marriage until Cato himself was present and joined in giving the bride away.[1] This incident occurred at a later time,[2] it is true, but since I had taken up the topic of the women of Cato's household I decided to anticipate it.

---

[1] It is plain that Cato divorced Marcia ; otherwise her father could not have given her in marriage to Hortensius.

[2] Probably in 56 B.C.

XXVI. Τῶν δὲ περὶ τὸν Λέντλον ἀναιρεθέν-
των, καὶ τοῦ Καίσαρος περὶ ὧν εἰσηγγέλθη καὶ
διεβλήθη πρὸς τὴν σύγκλητον εἰς τὸν δῆμον
καταφυγόντος καὶ τὰ πολλὰ νοσοῦντα καὶ
διεφθαρμένα τῆς πολιτείας μέρη ταράττοντος
καὶ συνάγοντος πρὸς αὐτόν, ὁ Κάτων φοβηθεὶς
ἔπεισε τὴν βουλὴν ἀναλαβεῖν τὸν ἄπορον καὶ
ἀνέμητον ὄχλον εἰς τὸ σιτηρέσιον, ἀναλώματος
μὲν ὄντος ἐνιαυσίου χιλίων καὶ διακοσίων καὶ
πεντήκοντα ταλάντων, περιφανῶς δὲ τῇ φιλαν-
θρωπίᾳ ταύτῃ καὶ χάριτι τῆς ἀπειλῆς ἐκείνης
2 διαλυθείσης. ἐντεῦθεν εἰς τὴν δημαρχίαν ἐμπεσὼν ὁ Μέτελλος ἐκκλησίας τε θορυβώδεις
συνῆγε, καὶ νόμον ἔγραψε Πομπήϊον Μάγνον
ἰέναι κατὰ τάχος μετὰ τῶν δυνάμεων εἰς Ἰταλίαν
καὶ παραλαβόντα σώζειν τὴν πόλιν, ὡς ὑπὸ
Κατιλίνα κινδυνεύουσαν. ἦν δὲ τοῦτο λόγος
εὐπρεπής, ἔργον δὲ τοῦ νόμου καὶ τέλος ἐγχειρίσαι τὰ πράγματα Πομπηΐῳ καὶ παραδοῦναι τὴν
3 ἡγεμονίαν. γενομένης δὲ βουλῆς καὶ τοῦ Κάτωνος οὐχ, ὥσπερ εἰώθει, τῷ Μετέλλῳ σφοδρῶς
ἐμπεσόντος, ἀλλ' ἐπιεικῆ πολλὰ καὶ μέτρια παρ-
αινέσαντος, τέλος δὲ καὶ πρὸς δεήσεις τραπο-
μένου καὶ τὴν Μετέλλων οἰκίαν ἀεὶ γενομένην
ἀριστοκρατικὴν ἐπαινέσαντος, ἔτι μᾶλλον ἐξαρ-
θεὶς καὶ καταφρονήσας ὁ Μέτελλος ὡς ἐνδιδόντος
αὐτοῦ καὶ πτήσσοντος εἰς ὑπερηφάνους ἀπειλὰς
καὶ λόγους θρασεῖς ἐξέπεσεν, ὡς βίᾳ πάντα τῆς
4 βουλῆς διαπραξόμενος. οὕτω δὴ μεταβαλὼν ὁ
Κάτων καὶ σχῆμα καὶ φωνὴν καὶ λόγον, ἐπειπὼν
δὲ πᾶσι τοῖς ἄλλοις διατεταμένως ὅτι ζῶντος

XXVI. Lentulus and his associates were executed, and Caesar, in view of the charges and accusations made against him to the senate, took refuge with the people and was stirring up and attaching to himself the numerous diseased and corrupted elements in the commonwealth. Cato was therefore alarmed and persuaded the senate to conciliate the poor and land-less multitude by including them in the distribution of grain, the annual expenditure for which was twelve hundred and fifty talents.[1] By this act of humanity and kindness the threatening danger was most successfully dissipated. Then Metellus, who hastened to take up the duties of his tribuneship, began to hold tumultuous assemblies of the people, and pro-posed a law that Pompey the Great should hasten with his forces to Italy[2] and undertake the preserva-tion of the city, on the ground that it was imperilled by Catiline. Now, this was a specious proposition; but the end and aim of the law was to put matters in the hands of Pompey and hand over to him the supreme power. The senate met, and Cato did not, as was his custom, attack Metellus with vehemence, but gave him much fitting and moderate advice, and finally, resorting to entreaties, actually praised the family of Metellus for having always been aristocratic in sympathy. Metellus was therefore all the more emboldened, and, despising Cato as a yielding and timorous opponent, broke out in extravagant threats and bold speeches, intending to carry everything through in spite of the senate. So, then, Cato changed his looks and voice and words, and con-cluded a vehement speech with the declaration

[1] Cf. the *Caesar*, viii. 4.
[2] Pompey had just finished his conquest of Mithridates and was on the way home from Asia (62 B.C.).

αὐτοῦ Πομπήϊος οὐ παρέσται μεθ' ὅπλων εἰς τὴν
πόλιν, ἐκεῖνο τῇ βουλῇ παρέστησεν, ὡς οὐδέτερος
μὲν καθέστηκεν οὐδὲ χρῆται λογισμοῖς ἀσφαλέ-
σιν, ἔστι δὲ ἡ μὲν Μετέλλου πολιτεία μανία δι'
ὑπερβολὴν κακίας φερομένη πρὸς ὄλεθρον καὶ
σύγχυσιν ἁπάντων, ἡ δὲ Κάτωνος ἀρετῆς ἐνθου- 772
σιασμὸς ὑπὲρ τῶν καλῶν καὶ δικαίων ἀγωνιζο-
μένης.

XXVII. Ἐπεὶ δὲ τὴν ψῆφον ὑπὲρ τοῦ νόμου
φέρειν ὁ δῆμος ἔμελλε, Μετέλλῳ μὲν ὅπλα καὶ
ξένοι καὶ μονομάχοι καὶ θεράποντες ἐπὶ τὴν
ἀγορὰν τεταγμένοι παρῆσαν, καὶ τὸ ποθοῦν
μεταβολῆς ἐλπίδι Πομπήϊον ὑπῆρχε τοῦ δήμου
μέρος οὐκ ὀλίγον, ἦν δὲ μεγάλη καὶ ἀπὸ Καί-
2 σαρος ῥώμη στρατηγοῦντος τότε, Κάτωνι δὲ οἱ
πρῶτοι τῶν πολιτῶν συνηγανάκτουν καὶ συνη-
δικοῦντο μᾶλλον ἢ συνηγωνίζοντο, πολλὴ δὲ τὴν
οἰκίαν αὐτοῦ κατήφεια καὶ φόβος εἶχεν, ὥστε
τῶν φίλων ἐνίους ἀσίτους διαγρυπνῆσαι μετ'
ἀλλήλων ἐν ἀπόροις ὄντας ὑπὲρ αὐτοῦ λογισμοῖς,
καὶ γυναῖκα καὶ ἀδελφὰς ποτνιωμένας καὶ δα-
3 κρυούσας. αὐτὸς δ' ἀδεῶς καὶ τεθαρρηκότως
ἐντυχὼν πᾶσι καὶ παρηγορήσας, καὶ γενόμενος
περὶ δεῖπνον, ὥσπερ εἰώθει, καὶ νυκτερεύσας, ὑφ'
ἑνὸς τῶν συναρχόντων, Μινυκίου Θέρμου, βαθέως
καθεύδων ἐπηγέρθη· καὶ κατέβησαν εἰς ἀγοράν,
ὀλίγων μὲν αὐτοὺς προπεμπόντων, πολλῶν δὲ
ἀπαντώντων καὶ φυλάττεσθαι παρακελευομένων.
4 ὡς οὖν ἐπιστὰς ὁ Κάτων κατεῖδε τὸν νεὼν τῶν
Διοσκούρων ὅπλοις περιεχόμενον καὶ τὰς ἀναβάσεις φρουρουμένας ὑπὸ μονομάχων, αὐτὸν δὲ
καθήμενον ἄνω μετὰ Καίσαρος τὸν Μέτελλον,

that while he lived Pompey should not enter the city with an armed force. The senate was thus led to feel that neither man was in his right mind or using safe arguments, but that the policy of Metellus was madness, which, through excess of wickedness, was leading on to the destruction and confusion of all things, while that of Cato was a wild ebullition of virtue contending in behalf of right and justice.

XXVII. When the people were about to vote on the law, in favour of Metellus there were armed strangers and gladiators and servants drawn up in the forum, and that part of the people which longed for Pompey in their hope of a change was present in large numbers, and there was strong support also from Caesar, who was at that time praetor. In the case of Cato, however, the foremost citizens shared in his displeasure and sense of wrong more than they did in his struggle to resist, and great dejection and fear reigned in his household, so that some of his friends took no food and watched all night with one another in futile discussions on his behalf, while his wife and sisters wailed and wept. He himself, however, conversed fearlessly and confidently with all and comforted them, and after taking supper as usual and passing the night, was roused from a deep sleep by one of his colleagues, Minucius Thermus; and they went down into the forum, only few persons accompanying them, but many meeting them and exhorting them to be on their guard. Accordingly, when Cato paused in the forum and saw the temple of Castor and Pollux surrounded by armed men and its steps guarded by gladiators, and Metellus himself sitting at the top with Caesar, he turned to his friends

ἐπιστρέψας πρὸς τοὺς φίλους, "'Ω θρασέος,"
εἶπεν, " ἀνθρώπου καὶ δειλοῦ, ὃς καθ᾽ ἑνὸς ἀνό-
πλου καὶ γυμνοῦ τοσούτους ἐστρατολόγησεν."
5 ἅμα δ᾽ εὐθὺς ἐβάδιζε μετὰ τοῦ Θέρμου. καὶ διέ-
στησαν αὐτοῖς [1] οἱ τὰς ἀναβάσεις κατέχοντες,
ἄλλον δὲ οὐδένα παρῆκαν, ἢ μόλις ἐπισπάσας
τῆς χειρὸς ὁ Κάτων τὸν Μουνάτιον ἀνήγαγε· καὶ
βαδίζων εὐθὺς ὡς εἶχε καθίζει μέσον ἐμβαλὼν
ἑαυτὸν τοῦ Μετέλλου καὶ τοῦ Καίσαρος, ὥστε
6 διακόψαι τὴν κοινολογίαν. κἀκεῖνοι μὲν διηπό-
ρησαν, οἱ δὲ χαρίεντες θεασάμενοι καὶ θαυμάσαντες τὸ πρόσωπον καὶ τὸ φρόνημα καὶ τὸ
θάρσος τοῦ Κάτωνος ἐγγυτέρω προσῆλθον, καὶ
βοῇ διεκελεύσαντο τῷ μὲν Κάτωνι θαρρεῖν,
μένειν δὲ ἀλλήλοις καὶ συστρέφεσθαι καὶ μὴ
προδιδόναι τὴν ἐλευθερίαν καὶ τὸν ὑπὲρ αὐτῆς
ἀγωνιζόμενον.

XXVIII. Ἔνθα δὴ τοῦ ὑπηρέτου τὸν νόμον
προχειρισαμένου, τοῦ δὲ Κάτωνος οὐκ ἐῶντος
ἀναγινώσκειν, τοῦ δὲ Μετέλλου παραλαβόντος
αὐτὸν καὶ ἀναγινώσκοντος, ὁ μὲν Κάτων ἐξήρ-
πασε τὸ βιβλίον, ὁ δὲ Θέρμος ἀπὸ στόματος τοῦ
Μετέλλου τὸν νόμον ἐπισταμένου καὶ λέγοντος
ἐπέσχε τῇ χειρὶ τὸ στόμα καὶ τὴν φωνὴν ἀπέ-
2 κλεισεν, ἄχρι οὗ, ἄμαχον ὁρῶν ἀγῶνα τοὺς
ἄνδρας ὁ Μέτελλος ἀγωνιζομένους, καὶ τὸν δῆμον
ἡττώμενον πρὸς τὸ συμφέρον καὶ τρεπόμενον,
ἐκέλευσεν ἄποθεν [2] ὁπλίτας μετὰ φόβου καὶ
κραυγῆς ἐπιτρέχειν. γενομένου δὲ τούτου καὶ
πάντων διασκεδασθέντων ὑποστάντα μόνον τὸν

---

[1] αὐτοῖς followed in the MSS. by ἐκεῖνοι, which Coraës and
Bekker delete ; Sintenis corrects to ἐκείνοις.
[2] ἄποθεν Kaltwasser: οἴκοθεν (from his house).

and said : " What a bold man, and what a coward, to levy such an army against a single unarmed and defenceless person!" At the same time he walked straight on with Thermus. Those who were occupying the steps made way for them, but would allow no one else to pass, except that Cato with difficulty drew Munatius along by the hand and brought him up ; and walking straight onwards he threw himself just as he was into a seat between Metellus and Caesar, thus cutting off their communication. Caesar and Metellus were disconcerted, but the better citizens, seeing and admiring the countenance, lofty bearing, and courage of Cato, came nearer, and with shouts exhorted him to be of good heart, while they urged one another to stay and band themselves together and not betray their liberty and the man who was striving to defend it.

XXVIII. And now the clerk produced the law, but Cato would not suffer him to read it ; and when Metellus took it and began to read it, Cato snatched the document away from him. Then Metellus, who knew the law by heart, began to recite it, but Thermus clapped a hand upon his mouth and shut off his speech. At last, seeing that the men were making a struggle which he could not resist, and that the people were giving way and turning towards the better course, Metellus ordered men-at-arms, who were standing at a distance, to come running up with terrifying shouts. This was done, and all the people dispersed, leaving Cato standing his ground alone

Κάτωνα καὶ βαλλόμενον λίθοις καὶ ξύλοις
ἄνωθεν οὐ περιεῖδε Μουρήνας ὁ τὴν δίκην φυγὼν
3 ὑπ' αὐτοῦ καὶ κατηγορηθείς, ἀλλὰ τὴν τήβεννον
προϊσχόμενος καὶ βοῶν ἀνασχεῖν τοῖς βάλλουσι,
καὶ τέλος αὐτὸν τὸν Κάτωνα πείθων καὶ περι-
πτύσσων, εἰς τὸν νεὼν τῶν Διοσκούρων ἀπήγαγεν.

Ἐπεὶ δὲ κατεῖδεν ὁ Μέτελλος ἐρημίαν περὶ τὸ
βῆμα καὶ φυγὴν δι' ἀγορᾶς τῶν ἐναντιουμένων,
παντάπασι πεισθεὶς κρατεῖν ἐκέλευσεν ἀπιέναι
πάλιν τοὺς ὁπλοφόρους, καὶ προσελθὼν κοσμίως
4 αὐτὸς ἐπεχείρει πράττειν τὰ περὶ τὸν νόμον. οἱ
δὲ ἐναντίοι ταχέως ἀναλαβόντες ἑαυτοὺς ἐκ τῆς
τροπῆς ἐπῄεσαν αὖθις ἐμβοήσαντες μέγα καὶ
θαρραλέον, ὥστε τοῖς περὶ τὸν Μέτελλον ἐμ-
πεσεῖν ταραχὴν καὶ δέος οἰομένοις ὅπλων ποθὲν
εὐπορήσαντας αὐτοὺς ἐπιφέρεσθαι, καὶ μηθένα
μένειν, ἀλλὰ φεύγειν ἅπαντας ἀπὸ τοῦ βήματος.
5 οὕτω δὴ σκεδασθέντων ἐκείνων, τοῦ δὲ Κάτωνος
προσελθόντος καὶ τὰ μὲν ἐπαινέσαντος, τὰ δ' 773
ἐπιρρώσαντος τὸν δῆμον, οἵ τε πολλοὶ παρετά-
ξαντο παντὶ τρόπῳ καταλῦσαι τὸν Μέτελλον, ἥ
τε σύγκλητος ἀθροισθεῖσα παρήγγειλεν ἀρχῆθεν
βοηθεῖν τῷ Κάτωνι καὶ διαμάχεσθαι πρὸς τὸν
νόμον, ὡς στάσιν ἐπεισάγοντα τῇ Ῥώμῃ καὶ
πόλεμον ἐμφύλιον.

XXIX. Ὁ δὲ Μέτελλος αὐτὸς μὲν ἦν ἄτρεπτος
καὶ θρασὺς ἔτι, ὁρῶν δὲ τοὺς περὶ αὐτὸν ἐκπε-
πληγμένους κομιδῇ τὸν Κάτωνα καὶ νομίζοντας

and pelted with sticks and stones from above. Here Murena, who had been denounced and brought to trial by him,[1] came to his relief, and holding his toga before him, crying to those who were pelting him to stop, and finally persuading Cato himself and folding him in his arms, he led him away into the temple of Castor and Pollux.

When, however, Metellus saw the space about the tribunal[2] empty and his opponents in flight through the forum, being altogether persuaded that he had won the day, he ordered his armed men to go away again, and coming forward himself in orderly fashion attempted to have the law enacted. But his opponents, quickly recovering from their rout, advanced again upon him with loud and confident shouts, so that his partisans were overwhelmed with confusion and terror. They supposed that their enemies had provided themselves with arms from some place or other in order to assail them, and not a man stood his ground, but all fled away from the tribunal. So, then, when these had dispersed, and when Cato had come forward with commendation and encouragement for the people, the majority of them stood prepared to put down Metellus by any and every means, and the senate in full session announced anew that it would assist Cato and fight to the end against the law, convinced that it would introduce sedition and civil war into Rome.

XXIX. Metellus himself was still unyielding and bold, but since he saw that his followers were completely terrified before Cato and thought him utterly

---

[1] Cf. chapter xxi. 3–6.
[2] The steps of the temple of Castor led down to a platform, from which the people were often addressed.

ἄμαχον καὶ δυσεκβίαστον, αἰφνίδιον ἐξεπήδησεν
εἰς τὴν ἀγοράν, καὶ συναγαγὼν τὸν δῆμον ἄλλα
τε πολλὰ περὶ τοῦ Κάτωνος ἐπίφθονα διῆλθε,
καὶ φεύγειν τὴν τυραννίδα βοῶν τὴν ἐκείνου καὶ
τὴν κατὰ Πομπηίου συνωμοσίαν, ἐφ' ᾗ μετανοή-
σειν ταχὺ τὴν πόλιν ἀτιμάζουσαν ἄνδρα τοσοῦτον, ὥρμησεν εὐθὺς εἰς Ἀσίαν, ὡς ταῦτα πρὸς
2 ἐκεῖνον κατηγορήσων. ἦν οὖν δόξα μεγάλη τοῦ
Κάτωνος ἄχθος οὐ μικρὸν ἀπεσκευασμένου τῆς
δημαρχίας, καὶ τρόπον τινὰ τὴν Πομπηίου δύναμιν ἐν Μετέλλῳ καθῃρηκότος. ἔτι δὲ μᾶλλον
εὐδοκίμησε τὴν σύγκλητον ὡρμημένην ἀτιμοῦν
καὶ ἀποψηφίζεσθαι τὸν Μέτελλον οὐκ ἐάσας,
ἀλλ' ἐναντιωθεὶς καὶ παραιτησάμενος. οἵ τε
γὰρ πολλοὶ φιλανθρωπίας ἐποιοῦντο καὶ μετριό-
τητος τὸ μὴ ἐπεμβῆναι τῷ ἐχθρῷ μηδὲ ἐνυβρίσαι
κατὰ κράτος περιγενόμενον, τοῖς τε φρονίμοις
ὀρθῶς ἐφαίνετο καὶ συμφερόντως μὴ παροξῦναι
Πομπήϊον.

3 Ἐκ τούτου Λεύκολλος ἐπανελθὼν ἐκ τῆς
στρατείας, ἧς ἔδοξε τὸ τέλος καὶ τὴν δόξαν ἀφῃ-
ρῆσθαι Πομπήϊος, εἰς κίνδυνον ἦλθε τοῦ μὴ
θριαμβεῦσαι, Γαΐου Μεμμίου καταστασιάζοντος
αὐτὸν ἐν τῷ δήμῳ καὶ δίκας ἐπάγοντος, εἰς τὴν
Πομπηίου χάριν μᾶλλον ἢ κατὰ ἔχθος ἴδιον. ὁ
δὲ Κάτων, οἰκειότητός τε πρὸς Λεύκολλον αὐτῷ
γεγενημένης, ἔχοντα Σερβιλίαν τὴν ἀδελφὴν αὐτοῦ, καὶ τὸ πρᾶγμα δεινὸν ἡγούμενος, ἀντέστη
τῷ Μεμμίῳ, καὶ πολλὰς ὑπέμεινε διαβολὰς καὶ

invincible, he suddenly rushed off into the forum, assembled the people, and made a long and invidious speech against Cato; then, crying out that he was fleeing from Cato's tyranny and the conspiracy against Pompey, for which the city would speedily repent in that it was dishonouring so great a man, he set out at once for Asia, intending to lay these accusations before Pompey. Accordingly, Cato was in high repute for having relieved the tribunate of a great burden, and for having in a manner overthrown the power of Pompey in the person of Metellus. But he won still more esteem by not allowing the senate to carry out its purpose of degrading Metellus and deposing him from his office, which course Cato opposed, and brought the senate over to his views. For the multitude considered it a token of humanity and moderation not to trample on his enemy or insult him after prevailing completely over him, and prudent men thought it right and advantageous not to irritate Pompey.

After this, Lucullus, having come back from his expedition,[1] the consummation and glory of which Pompey was thought to have taken away from him, was in danger of losing his triumph, since Caius Memmius raised a successful faction against him among the people and brought legal accusations against him, more to gratify Pompey than out of private enmity. But Cato, being related to Lucullus, who had his sister Servilia to wife, and thinking the attempt a shameful one, opposed Memmius, and thereby exposed himself to many

---

[1] He came back in 66 B.C., and had to wait three years before being allowed to celebrate a triumph. Cf. the *Lucullus*, xxxvii.

4 κατηγορίας. τέλος δέ, τῆς ἀρχῆς ἐκβαλλόμενος
ὡς τυραννίδος, τοσοῦτον ἐκράτησεν ὥστε τὸν
Μέμμιον αὐτὸν ἀναγκάσαι τῶν δικῶν ἀποστῆναι
καὶ φυγεῖν τὸν ἀγῶνα. Λεύκολλος μὲν οὖν
θριαμβεύσας ἔτι μᾶλλον ἐνεφύετο τῇ φιλίᾳ τοῦ
Κάτωνος, ἔχων ἔρυμα καὶ πρόβλημα μέγα πρὸς
τὴν Πομπηΐου δύναμιν.

XXX. Πομπήϊος δὲ μέγας ἀπὸ τῆς στρατείας
ἐπανιών, καὶ τῇ λαμπρότητι καὶ προθυμίᾳ τῆς
ὑποδοχῆς πεποιθὼς οὐδὲν ἂν δεηθεὶς ἀποτυχεῖν
τῶν πολιτῶν, προύπεμψεν ἀξιῶν τὰς ὑπατικὰς
ἀρχαιρεσίας ἀναβαλέσθαι τὴν σύγκλητον, ὡς ἂν
2 αὐτὸς παρὼν Πείσωνι συναρχαιρεσιάσῃ. τῶν
δὲ πλείστων ὑπεικόντων, οὐ τὴν ἀναβολὴν μέγιστον ὁ Κάτων ἡγούμενος, ἀλλὰ τὴν πεῖραν
ἀποκόψαι καὶ τὴν ἐλπίδα τοῦ Πομπηΐου βουλόμενος, ἀντεῖπε καὶ μετέστησε τὴν βουλήν,
ὥστε ἀποψηφίσασθαι. τοῦτο τὸν Πομπήϊον οὐχ
ἡσυχῇ διετάραξε· καὶ νομίζων οὐ μικρὰ προσ-
πταίσειν τῷ Κάτωνι μὴ φίλῳ γενομένῳ, μετεπέμψατο Μουννάτιον, ἑταῖρον αὐτοῦ· καὶ δύο τοῦ
Κάτωνος ἀδελφιδᾶς ἐπιγάμους ἔχοντος ᾔτει τὴν
μὲν πρεσβυτέραν ἑαυτῷ γυναῖκα, τὴν δὲ νεωτέραν
3 τῷ υἱῷ. τινὲς δέ φασιν οὐ τῶν ἀδελφιδῶν, ἀλλὰ
τῶν θυγατέρων τὴν μνηστείαν γενέσθαι. τοῦ δὲ
Μουννατίου ταῦτα πρὸς τὸν Κάτωνα καὶ τὴν
γυναῖκα καὶ τὰς ἀδελφὰς φράσαντος, αἱ μὲν
ὑπερηγάπησαν τὴν οἰκειότητα πρὸς τὸ μέγεθος

slanderous accusations. Finally, however, though he was on the point of being ejected from his office on the ground that he exercised tyrannical power, he so far prevailed as to compel Memmius himself to desist from his accusations and shun the contest. Lucullus, accordingly, celebrated his triumph, and therefore clung still more closely to the friendship of Cato, finding in him a great bulwark of defence against the power of Pompey.

XXX. And now Pompey returned with great prestige from his expedition,[1] and since the splendour and warmth of his reception led him to believe that he could get whatever he wanted from his fellow citizens, he sent forward a demand that the senate postpone the consular elections, in order that he might be present in person and assist Piso in making his canvass. The majority of the senators were inclined to yield. Cato, however, who did not regard the postponement as the chief matter at issue, but wished to cut short the attempt and the expectations of Pompey, opposed the measure and changed the opinions of the senators, so that they rejected it. This disturbed Pompey not a little, and considering that Cato would be a great stumbling-block in his way unless he were made a friend, he sent for Munatius, Cato's companion, and asked the elder of Cato's two marriageable nieces to wife for himself, and the younger for his son. Some say, however, that it was not for Cato's nieces, but for his daughters, that the suit was made. When Munatius brought this proposal to Cato and his wife and sisters, the women were overjoyed at thought of the alliance, in view of the greatness and high repute of

[1] In 62 B.C.

καὶ τὸ ἀξίωμα τοῦ ἀνδρός, ὁ δὲ Κάτων οὔτ᾽ ἐπι-
σχὼν οὔτε βουλευσάμενος, ἀλλὰ πληγεὶς εὐθὺς
4 εἶπε· "Βάδιζε, Μουνάτιε, βάδιζε, καὶ λέγε πρὸς
Πομπήϊον ὡς Κάτων οὐκ ἔστι διὰ τῆς γυναικω-
νίτιδος ἁλώσιμος, ἀλλὰ τὴν μὲν εὔνοιαν ἀγαπᾷ,
καὶ τὰ δίκαια ποιοῦντι φιλίαν παρέξει πάσης 77
πιστοτέραν οἰκειότητος, ὅμηρα δὲ οὐ προήσεται
τῇ Πομπηΐου δόξῃ κατὰ τῆς πατρίδος."

Ἐπὶ τούτοις ἤχθοντο μὲν αἱ γυναῖκες, ἡτιῶντο
δὲ οἱ φίλοι τοῦ Κάτωνος ὡς ἄγροικον ἅμα καὶ
5 ὑπερήφανον τὴν ἀπόκρισιν. εἶτα μέντοι πράττων τινὶ τῶν φίλων ὑπατείαν ὁ Πομπήϊος ἀργύριον εἰς τὰς φυλὰς ἔπεμπε, καὶ περιβόητος ὁ
δεκασμὸς ἦν, ἐν κήποις ἐκείνου τῶν χρημάτων
ἀριθμουμένων. εἰπόντος οὖν τοῦ Κάτωνος πρὸς
τὰς γυναῖκας ὅτι τοιούτων ἦν κοινωνεῖν καὶ ἀνα-
πίμπλασθαι πραγμάτων ἀνάγκη Πομπηΐῳ συνα-
φθέντα δι᾽ οἰκειότητος, ὡμολόγουν ἐκεῖναι κάλλιον
6 αὐτὸν βεβουλεῦσθαι διακρουσάμενον. εἰ δὲ δεῖ
πρὸς τὰ συμβάντα κρίνειν, τοῦ παντὸς ἔοικεν ὁ
Κάτων ἁμαρτεῖν τὴν οἰκειότητα μὴ δεξάμενος,
ἀλλ᾽ ἐάσας πρὸς Καίσαρα τραπέσθαι καὶ γῆμαι
γάμον ὃς τὴν Πομπηΐου δύναμιν καὶ Καίσαρος
εἰς ταὐτὸ συνενεγκὼν ὀλίγου τὰ μὲν Ῥωμαίων
ἀνέτρεψε πράγματα, τὴν δὲ πολιτείαν ἀνεῖλεν,
ὧν οὐθὲν ἂν ἴσως συνέπεσεν, εἰ μὴ Κάτων τὰ
μικρὰ τοῦ Πομπηΐου φοβηθεὶς ἁμαρτήματα τὸ
μέγιστον περιεῖδεν, αὐτὸν ἑτέρῳ δύναμιν προσ-
γενόμενον.

XXXI. Ταῦτα μὲν οὖν ἔμελλεν ἔτι. Λευκόλλου δὲ περὶ τῶν ἐν Πόντῳ διατάξεων στασιά-

Pompey; Cato, however, without pause or deliberation, but stung to the quick, said at once: " Go,
Munatius, go, and tell Pompey that Cato is not to
be captured by way of the women's apartments,
although he highly prizes Pompey's good will, and if
Pompey does justice will grant him a friendship
more to be relied upon than any marriage connection; but he will not give hostages for the glory of
Pompey to the detriment of his country."

At these words the women were vexed, and Cato's
friends blamed his answer as both rude and over-
bearing. Afterwards, however, in trying to secure
the consulship for one of his friends,[1] Pompey sent
money to the tribes, and the bribery was notorious,
since the sums for it were counted out in his gardens.
Accordingly, when Cato told the women that he
must of necessity have shared in the disgrace of such
transactions, had he been connected with Pompey by
marriage, they admitted that he had taken better
counsel in rejecting the alliance.[2] However, if we
are to judge by the results, it would seem that Cato
was wholly wrong in not accepting the marriage connection, instead of allowing Pompey to turn to Caesar
and contract a marriage which united the power of
the two men, nearly overthrew the Roman state, and
destroyed the constitution. None of these things
perhaps would have happened, had not Cato been so
afraid of the slight transgressions of Pompey as to
allow him to commit the greatest of all, and add his
power to that of another.

XXXI. These things, however, were still in the
future. Meanwhile Lucullus got into a contention

---

[1] Lucius Afranius, elected consul in 61 B.C. for the year
60 B.C. Cf. the *Pompey*, xliv. 3. [2] Cf. the *Pompey*, xliv.

σαντος πρὸς Πομπήϊον (ἠξίουν γὰρ ἰσχύειν
ἑκάτερος τὰ ὑφ' αὑτοῦ γενόμενα), καὶ Λευκόλλῳ
Κάτωνος ἀδικουμένῳ περιφανῶς προσαμύνοντος,
ἐλαττούμενος ὁ Πομπήϊος ἐν συγκλήτῳ καὶ δημαγωγῶν, ἐπὶ νομὴν χώρας ἐκάλει τὸ στρατιω-
2 τικόν. ὡς δὲ κἀνταῦθα Κάτων ἐνιστάμενος
ἐξέκρουσε τὸν νόμον, οὕτω Κλωδίῳ τε περιεί-
χετο, τοῦ τότε θρασυτάτου τῶν δημαγωγῶν, καὶ
Καίσαρα προσήγετο, τρόπον τινὰ Κάτωνος αὐτοῦ
παρασχόντος ἀρχήν. ὁ γὰρ Καῖσαρ ἀπὸ τῆς ἐν
Ἰβηρίᾳ στρατηγίας ἐπανήκων ἅμα μὲν ὑπατείαν
ἐβούλετο παραγγέλλειν, ἅμα δὲ ᾔτει θρίαμβον.
3 ἐπεὶ δὲ κατὰ νόμον ἔδει τοὺς μὲν ἀρχὴν μετιόντας
παρεῖναι, τοὺς δὲ μέλλοντας εἰσελαύνειν θρίαμβον
ἔξω τείχους ὑπομένειν, ἠξίου παρὰ τῆς βουλῆς
αὐτῷ δοθῆναι δι' ἑτέρων αἰτεῖσθαι τὴν ἀρχήν.
βουλομένων δὲ πολλῶν ἀντέλεγεν ὁ Κάτων· ὡς δὲ
ᾔσθετο χαριζομένους τῷ Καίσαρι, λέγων ὅλην
κατανάλωσε τὴν ἡμέραν καὶ τὴν βουλὴν οὕτως
4 ἐξέκρουσε. χαίρειν οὖν ἐάσας τὸν θρίαμβον ὁ
Καῖσαρ εἰσελθὼν εὐθὺς εἴχετο Πομπηΐου καὶ τῆς
ὑπατείας. ἀποδειχθεὶς δὲ ὕπατος τήν τε Ἰουλίαν
ἐνεγγύησεν αὐτῷ, καὶ συστάντες ἤδη μετ' ἀλλήλων ἐπὶ τὴν πόλιν ὁ μὲν εἰσέφερε νόμους τοῖς
πένησι κληρουχίαν καὶ νομὴν χώρας διδόντας, ὁ
5 δὲ παρῆν τοῖς νόμοις βοηθῶν. οἱ δὲ περὶ Λεύκολλον καὶ Κικέρωνα Βύβλῳ τῷ ἑτέρῳ τῶν ὑπάτων συντάξαντες ἑαυτοὺς ἀντέπραττον, μάλιστα

with Pompey over the arrangements in Pontus (each
of them, namely, demanded that his own proceedings
should be confirmed), Cato came to the aid of Lucullus,
who was manifestly wronged, and Pompey, worsted in
the senate and seeking popular favour, invited the
soldiery to a distribution of land.[1] But when Cato
opposed him in this measure also, and frustrated the
law, then Pompey attached himself to Clodius, at
that time the boldest of the popular leaders, and won
Caesar to his support, a result for which Cato himself
was in a way responsible. For Caesar, on returning
from his praetorship in Spain,[2] desired to be a candidate for the consulship, and at the same time asked
for a triumph. But since by law candidates for a
magistracy must be present in the city, while those
who are going to celebrate a triumph must remain
outside the walls, he asked permission from the
senate to solicit the office by means of others. Many
were willing to grant the request, but Cato opposed
it; and when he saw that the senators were ready to
gratify Caesar, he consumed the whole day in speaking
and thus frustrated their desires. Accordingly, Caesar
gave up his triumph, entered the city, and at once
attached himself to Pompey and sought the consulship.[3] After he had been elected consul, he gave his
daughter Julia in marriage to Pompey, and now that
the two were united with one another against the
state, the one would bring in laws offering allotment
and distribution of land to the poor, and the other
would be at hand with support for the laws. But the
party of Lucullus and Cicero, ranging themselves
with Bibulus, the other consul, opposed the measures,

[1] Cf. the *Lucullus*, xlii. 6; *Pompey*, xlvi. 3 f.
[2] In the summer of 60 B.C. [3] Cf. the *Caesar*, xiii. 1 f.

δὲ Κάτων, ἤδη μὲν ὑφορώμενος τὴν Καίσαρος καὶ
Πομπηΐου φιλίαν καὶ σύστασιν ἐπ᾽ οὐδενὶ δικαίῳ
γεγενημένην, φοβεῖσθαι δὲ φάσκων οὐ τὴν νομὴν
τῆς χώρας, ἀλλ᾽ ὃν ἀντὶ ταύτης ἀπαιτήσουσι
μισθὸν οἱ χαριζόμενοι καὶ δελεάζοντες τὸ πλῆθος.

XXXII. Ὡς δὲ ταῦτα λέγων τήν τε βουλὴν
ὁμόψηφον εἶχε, καὶ τῶν ἐκτὸς ἀνθρώπων οὐκ
ὀλίγοι παρίσταντο δυσχεραίνοντες τὴν ἀτοπίαν
τοῦ Καίσαρος· ἃ γὰρ οἱ θρασύτατοι δήμαρχοι
καὶ ὀλιγωρότατοι πρὸς χάριν ἐπολιτεύοντο τῶν
πολλῶν, ταῦτα ἀπ᾽ ἐξουσίας ὑπατικῆς, αἰσχρῶς
καὶ ταπεινῶς ὑποδυόμενος τὸν δῆμον, ἔπραττε·
2 φοβηθέντες οὖν ἐχώρουν διὰ βίας, καὶ πρῶτον
μὲν αὐτῷ τῷ Βύβλῳ καταβαίνοντι κοπρίων
ἐπεσκεδάσθη κόφινος, ἔπειτα τοῖς ῥαβδούχοις
προσπεσόντες αὐτοῦ κατέκλασαν τὰς ῥάβδους·
τέλος δὲ καὶ βελῶν φερομένων καὶ πολλῶν
συντιτρωσκομένων ἔφυγον ἐξ ἀγορᾶς δρόμῳ μὲν
οἱ λοιποὶ πάντες, ἔσχατος δὲ Κάτων ἀπῄει βάδην,
μεταστρεφόμενος καὶ μαρτυρόμενος[1] τοὺς πολίτας.
3 οὐ μόνον οὖν τὴν διανομὴν ἐκύρωσαν, ἀλλὰ καὶ 775
προσεψηφίσαντο τὴν σύγκλητον ὀμόσαι πᾶσαν
ἦ μὴν ἐπιβεβαιώσειν τὸν νόμον, καὶ βοηθήσειν
ἄν τις τἀναντία πράττῃ, μεγάλα τάξαντες ἐπιτίμια κατὰ τῶν μὴ ὀμοσάντων. ὤμνυσαν οὖν ἅπαντες ἐξ ἀνάγκης, τὸ Μετέλλου τοῦ παλαιοῦ πάθος
ἐν νῷ λαμβάνοντες, ὃν εἰς νόμον ὅμοιον ὀμόσαι
μὴ θελήσαντα περιεῖδεν ὁ δῆμος ἐκπεσόντα φυγῇ

---

[1] μαρτυρόμενος Bekker and Sintenis[2], after Emperius;
Coraës and Sintenis[1] adhere to the MSS. καταρώμενος
(cursing).

and above all Cato, who now suspected that the friendly alliance between Caesar and Pompey had been made for no just purpose, and declared that he was afraid, not of the distribution of land, but of the reward which would be paid for this to those who were enticing the people with such favours.

XXXII. By these utterances he brought the senate to unanimity, and many men outside the senate supported him out of displeasure at the strange conduct of Caesar; for whatever political schemes the boldest and most arrogant tribunes were wont to practise to win the favour of the multitude, these Caesar used with the support of consular power, in disgraceful and humiliating attempts to ingratiate himself with the people.[1] Accordingly, the opponents of Cato were alarmed and had recourse to violence. To begin with, upon Bibulus himself, as he was going down into the forum, a basket of ordure was scattered; then the crowd fell upon his lictors and broke their fasces; and finally missiles flew and many persons were wounded.[2] All the other senators fled from the forum at a run, but Cato went off last of all at a walk, turning about and protesting to the citizens. Accordingly, not only was the law for the distribution of lands passed, but also a clause was added requiring the whole senate to swear solemnly that it would uphold the law, and give its aid in case any one should act contrary to it, and heavy penalties were pronounced against such as would not take the oath.[3] All took the oath, therefore, under compulsion, bearing in mind the fate of Metellus of old, whom the people suffered to be banished from Italy because

---

[1] Cf. the *Caesar*, xiv. 1.   [2] Cf. the *Pompey*, xlviii. 1.
[3] Cf. the *Caesar*, xiv. 2 f.

4 τῆς Ἰταλίας. διὸ καὶ τὸν Κάτωνα πολλὰ μὲν
αἱ γυναῖκες οἴκοι δακρύουσαι καθικέτευον εἶξαι
καὶ ὀμόσαι, πολλὰ δὲ οἱ φίλοι καὶ συνήθεις. ὁ
δὲ μάλιστα συμπείσας καὶ ἀγαγὼν ἐπὶ τὸν ὅρκον
ἦν Κικέρων ὁ ῥήτωρ, παραινῶν καὶ διδάσκων ὡς
τάχα μὲν οὐδὲ δίκαιόν ἐστι τοῖς ἐγνωσμένοις
κοινῇ μόνον οἴεσθαι δεῖν ἀπειθεῖν, ἐν δὲ ἀδυνάτῳ
τῷ μεταστῆσαί τι τῶν γεγονότων ἀφειδεῖν ἑαυτοῦ
5 παντάπασιν ἀνόητον καὶ μανικόν· ἔσχατον δὲ
κακῶν, εἰ δι' ἣν ἅπαντα πράττει πόλιν ἀφεὶς καὶ
προέμενος τοῖς ἐπιβουλεύουσιν ὥσπερ ἄσμενος
ἀπαλλάξεται τῶν ὑπὲρ αὐτῆς ἀγώνων· καὶ γὰρ
εἰ μὴ Κάτων τῆς Ῥώμης, ἀλλ' ἡ Ῥώμη δεῖται
Κάτωνος, δέονται δὲ καὶ οἱ φίλοι πάντες· ὧν
αὐτὸν εἶναι πρῶτον ὁ Κικέρων ἔλεγεν, ἐπιβουλευόμενον ὑπὸ Κλωδίου διὰ δημαρχίας ἄντι-
6 κρυς ἐπ' αὐτὸν βαδίζοντος. ὑπὸ τούτων φασὶ
καὶ τοιούτων τὸν Κάτωνα λόγων καὶ δεήσεων
μαλασσόμενον οἴκοι καὶ κατ' ἀγορὰν ἐκβιασθῆναι
μόλις, καὶ προσελθεῖν πρὸς τὸν ὅρκον ἔσχατον
ἁπάντων πλὴν ἑνὸς Φαωνίου τῶν φίλων καὶ
συνήθων.

XXXIII. Ἐπαρθεὶς οὖν ὁ Καῖσαρ ἄλλον
εἰσέφερε νόμον, τὴν Καμπανίαν σχεδὸν ὅλην
προσκατανέμοντα τοῖς ἀπόροις καὶ πένησιν. ἀντ-
έλεγε δὲ οὐδεὶς πλὴν τοῦ Κάτωνος. καὶ τοῦτον
ἀπὸ τοῦ βήματος ὁ Καῖσαρ εἷλκεν εἰς δεσμωτήριον, οὐδέν τι μᾶλλον ὑφιέμενον τῆς παρρησίας,
ἀλλ' ἐν τῷ βαδίζειν ἅμα περὶ τοῦ νόμου δια-

he would not swear to a similar law.[1] For this reason, also, did the women of Cato's family earnestly and with tears beseech him to yield and take the oath, earnestly, too, did his friends and intimates. But the one who was most successful in persuading and inducing him to take the oath was Cicero the orator, who advised and showed him that it was possibly even a wrong thing to think himself alone in duty bound to disobey the general will; and that his desperate conduct, where it was impossible to make any change in what had been done, was altogether senseless and mad; moreover, it would be the greatest of evils if he should abandon the city in behalf of which all his efforts had been made, hand her over to her enemies, and so, apparently with pleasure, get rid of his struggles in her defence; for even if Cato did not need Rome, still, Rome needed Cato, and so did all his friends; and among these Cicero said that he himself was foremost, since he was the object of the plots of Clodius, who was openly attacking him by means of the tribuneship. By these and similar arguments and entreaties, we are told, both at home and in the forum, Cato was softened and at last prevailed upon. He came forward to take the oath last of all, except Favonius, one of his friends and intimates.

XXXIII. Elated by this success, Caesar introduced another law, which provided that almost the whole of Campania be divided among the poor and needy. No one spoke against the law except Cato, and him Caesar ordered to be dragged from the rostra to prison. Cato did not any the more remit his bold utterances, but as he walked along discoursed about

[1] In 100 B.C. Cf. the *Marius*, xxix.

315

λεγόμενον καὶ παραινοῦντα παύσασθαι τοιαῦτα
2 πολιτευομένους. ἐπηκολούθει δὲ ἡ βουλὴ μετὰ
κατηφείας, καὶ τοῦ δήμου τὸ βέλτιστον ἀγανα-
κτοῦν σιωπῇ καὶ ἀχθόμενον, ὥστε τὸν Καίσαρα
μὴ λανθάνειν βαρέως φέροντας. ἀλλὰ φιλονει-
κῶν καὶ περιμένων ὑπὸ τοῦ Κάτωνος ἐπίκλησιν
γενέσθαι καὶ δέησιν προῆγεν. ἐπεὶ δὲ ἐκεῖνος ἦν
δῆλος οὐδὲ μελλήσων τι ποιεῖν, ἡττηθεὶς ὑπὸ
αἰσχύνης καὶ ἀδοξίας ὁ Καῖσαρ αὐτός τινα τῶν
δημάρχων ὑφῆκε πείσας ἐξελέσθαι τὸν Κάτωνα.
3 τοῖς μέντοι νόμοις ἐκείνοις καὶ ταῖς χάρισι τιθα-
σεύσαντες τὸν ὄχλον, ἐψηφίσαντο Καίσαρι μὲν
Ἰλλυριῶν καὶ Γαλατίας ἀρχὴν ἁπάσης καὶ τέσ-
σαρα τάγματα στρατιᾶς εἰς πενταετίαν, προ-
λέγοντος Κάτωνος ὡς εἰς ἀκρόπολιν τὸν τύραννον
αὐτοὶ ταῖς ἑαυτῶν ψήφοις ἱδρύουσι, Πόπλιον δὲ
Κλώδιον ἐκ πατρικίων εἰς δημοτικοὺς παρανόμως
4 μεταστήσαντες ἀπέδειξαν δήμαρχον, ἐπὶ μισθῷ
τῇ Κικέρωνος ἐξελάσει πάντα πρὸς χάριν ἐκείνοις
πολιτευόμενον, ὑπάτους δὲ Πείσωνά τε Καλ-
πούρνιον, ὃς ἦν πατὴρ τῆς Καίσαρος γυναικός,
καὶ Γαβίνιον Αὖλον, ἐκ τῶν Πομπηΐου κόλπων
ἄνθρωπον, ὥς φασιν οἱ τὸν τρόπον αὐτοῦ καὶ τὸν
βίον εἰδότες.

XXXIV. Ἀλλὰ καίπερ οὕτως τὰ πράγματα
κατειληφότες ἐγκρατῶς, καὶ τὸ μὲν χάριτι τῆς
πόλεως, τὸ δὲ φόβῳ μέρος ὑφ᾽ ἑαυτοὺς ἔχοντες,
ὅμως ἐφοβοῦντο τὸν Κάτωνα. καὶ γὰρ ἐν οἷς
περιῆσαν αὐτοῦ τό γε χαλεπῶς καὶ μετὰ πόνων

the law and advised the people to put a stop to such legislation. Moreover, the senate followed him with downcast looks, as well as the best part of the people in silence, though they looked annoyed and troubled, so that Caesar could not fail to see that they were displeased ; but he was obstinate, and expected that Cato would resort to appeal or entreaty, and therefore had him led along. However, when it was clear that Cato did not so much as think of doing anything of the sort, Caesar was overcome by the shame and infamy of his course, and by his own secret persuasions induced one of the tribunes of the people to rescue Cato. Nevertheless, by these laws and by other favours Caesar's party so cajoled the people as to get a vote passed giving to Caesar the government of Illyria and all Gaul, with an army of four legions, for five years, although Cato warned the people that they themselves by their own votes were establishing a tyrant in their citadel. They also unlawfully transferred Publius Clodius from patrician to plebeian rank and got him elected tribune of the people, a man who, in order to secure Cicero's banishment as his reward, was using all his political influence for the gratification of the people. For consuls, too, they secured the election[1] of Calpurnius Piso, who was Caesar's father-in-law, and Aulus Gabinius, a man from the lap of Pompey, as those say who knew his ways of life.

XXXIV. But although they had in this way usurped the power, and although one part of the citizens was made submissive to them by gratitude and the other part by fear, nevertheless they were afraid of Cato. For even when they did prevail against him, it was with difficulty and toil and not

[1] For the year 58 B.C.

καὶ μὴ χωρὶς αἰσχύνης, ἀλλ᾽ ἐλεγχομένους βια-
2 ζεσθαι μόλις ἀνιαρὸν ἦν καὶ πρόσαντες. ὁ δὲ
Κλώδιος οὐδὲ Κικέρωνα καταλύσειν ἤλπιζε Κάτωνος παρόντος, ἀλλὰ τοῦτο διαμηχανώμενος
πρῶτον, ὡς εἰς ἀρχὴν κατέστη, μετεπέμψατο τὸν
Κάτωνα καὶ λόγους αὐτῷ προσήνεγκεν ὡς πάντων 776
ἐκεῖνον ἡγούμενος ἄνδρα Ῥωμαίων καθαρώτατον
ἔργῳ διδόναι πίστιν ἕτοιμός ἐστι· πολλῶν γὰρ
αἰτουμένων τὴν ἐπὶ Κύπρον καὶ Πτολεμαῖον
ἀρχὴν καὶ δεομένων ἀποσταλῆναι μόνον ἄξιον
ἐκεῖνον ἡγεῖσθαι καὶ διδόναι τὴν χάριν ἡδέως.
3 ἀνακραγόντος δὲ τοῦ Κάτωνος ὡς ἐνέδρα τὸ
πρᾶγμα καὶ προπηλακισμός, οὐ χάρις ἐστίν,
ὑπερηφάνως ὁ Κλώδιος καὶ ὀλιγώρως, " Οὐκοῦν,"
εἶπεν, " εἰ μὴ χάριν ἔχεις, ἀνιώμενος πλεύσῃ,"
καὶ προσελθὼν εὐθὺς εἰς τὸν δῆμον ἐκύρωσε νόμῳ
τὴν ἔκπεμψιν τοῦ Κάτωνος. ἐξιόντι δὲ οὐ ναῦν,
οὐ στρατιώτην, οὐχ ὑπηρέτην ἔδωκε πλὴν ἢ δύο
γραμματεῖς μόνον, ὧν ὁ μὲν κλέπτης καὶ παμ-
4 πόνηρος, ἅτερος δὲ Κλωδίου πελάτης. ὡς δὲ
μικρὸν ἔργον αὐτῷ Κύπρον καὶ Πτολεμαῖον
ἀναθείς, ἔτι καὶ Βυζαντίων φυγάδας κατάγειν
προσέταξε, βουλόμενος ὅτι πλεῖστον χρόνον
ἐκποδὼν ἄρχοντος αὐτοῦ γενέσθαι τὸν Κάτωνα.

XXXV. Τοιαύτῃ δὲ καταληφθεὶς ἀνάγκῃ Κικέρωνι μὲν ἐλαυνομένῳ παρῄνεσε μὴ στασιάσαι
μηδὲ εἰς ὅπλα καὶ φόνους τὴν πόλιν ἐμβαλεῖν,
ἀλλ᾽ ὑπεκστάντα τῷ καιρῷ πάλιν γενέσθαι

without the shame of exposure that they forced
their measures through at last, and this was annoying
and vexatious to them. Clodius, too, could not even
hope to overthrow Cicero while Cato was at Rome,
but since he was scheming for this above all else,
when he had come into office he sent for Cato and
made proposals to him. He said that he regarded
Cato as the purest man of all the Romans, and that
he was ready to prove this by his acts. Therefore,
though many were soliciting the commission to
Cyprus and the court of Ptolemy [1] and begging to be
sent upon it, he thought Cato alone worthy of it,
and therefore gladly offered him this favour. But
Cato cried out that the thing was a snare and an
insult, not a favour, whereupon Clodius haughtily
and contemptuously replied: "Well, then, if you
don't think it a favour, you shall make the voyage as
a punishment," and going at once before the people
he got an edict passed sending Cato on the mission.
Moreover, when Cato set out, Clodius gave him
neither ship, soldier, nor assistant, except two clerks,
of whom one was a thief and a rascal, and the other
a client of Clodius. And as if he had put a slight
task upon him in the mission to Cyprus and Ptolemy,
Clodius enjoined upon him besides the restoration of
the exiles of Byzantium, being desirous that Cato
should be out of his way as long as possible while he
was tribune.

XXXV. Subjected to such constraint as this, Cato
advised Cicero, whose enemies were trying to banish
him, not to raise a faction or plunge the city into
war and bloodshed, but to yield to the necessities of
the times, and so to become again a saviour of his

[1] A younger brother of Ptolemy Auletes the king of Egypt.

σωτῆρα τῆς πατρίδος, Κανίδιον δέ τινα τῶν
φίλων προπέμψας εἰς Κύπρον ἔπειθε τὸν Πτολεμαῖον ἄνευ μάχης εἴκειν, ὡς οὔτε χρημάτων οὔτε
τιμῆς ἐνδεᾶ βιωσόμενον· ἱερωσύνην γὰρ αὐτῷ
2 τῆς ἐν Πάφῳ θεοῦ δώσειν τὸν δῆμον. αὐτὸς δὲ
διέτριβεν ἐν Ῥόδῳ παρασκευαζόμενος ἅμα καὶ
τὰς ἀποκρίσεις ἀναμένων.

Ἐν δὲ τούτῳ Πτολεμαῖος ὁ Αἰγύπτου βασιλεὺς ὑπ' ὀργῆς τινος καὶ διαφορᾶς πρὸς τοὺς
πολίτας ἀπολελοιπὼς μὲν Ἀλεξάνδρειαν, εἰς δὲ
Ῥώμην πλέων, ὡς Πομπηΐου καὶ Καίσαρος αὖθις
αὐτὸν μετὰ δυνάμεως καταξόντων, ἐντυχεῖν τῷ
Κάτωνι βουληθεὶς προσέπεμψεν, ἐλπίζων ἐκεῖνον
3 ὡς αὐτὸν ἥξειν. ὁ δὲ Κάτων ἐτύγχανε μὲν ὢν
τότε περὶ κοιλίας κάθαρσιν, ἥκειν δὲ τὸν Πτολεμαῖον, εἰ βούλοιτο, κελεύσας πρὸς αὐτόν, ὡς δὲ
ἦλθεν, οὔτε ἀπαντήσας οὔτε ὑπεξαναστάς, ἀλλ'
ὡς ἕνα τῶν ἐπιτυχόντων ἀσπασάμενος καὶ καθί-
σαι κελεύσας, πρῶτον αὐτοῖς τούτοις διετάραξε,
θαυμάζοντα πρὸς τὸ δημοτικὸν καὶ λιτὸν αὐτοῦ
τῆς κατασκευῆς τὴν ὑπεροψίαν καὶ βαρύτητα τοῦ
4 ἤθους. ἐπεὶ δὲ καὶ διαλέγεσθαι περὶ τῶν καθ'
αὑτὸν ἀρξάμενος ἠκροάσατο λόγων νοῦν πολὺν
ἐχόντων καὶ παρρησίαν, ἐπιτιμῶντος αὐτῷ τοῦ
Κάτωνος καὶ διδάσκοντος ὅσην εὐδαιμονίαν ἀπολιπὼν ὅσαις ἑαυτὸν ὑποτίθησι λατρείαις καὶ
πόνοις καὶ δωροδοκίαις καὶ πλεονεξίαις τῶν ἐν
Ῥώμῃ δυνατῶν, οὓς μόλις ἐξαργυρισθεῖσαν ἐμ-
πλήσειν Αἴγυπτον, συμβουλεύοντος δὲ πλεῖν

country. He also sent Canidius, one of his friends, to Cyprus in advance,[1] and tried to persuade Ptolemy to yield his kingdom without fighting, promising that his future life should not be without wealth and honour, since the Romans would give him a priesthood of the goddess in Paphos. He himself, however, tarried at Rhodes, making his preparations and awaiting his answers.

Meanwhile Ptolemy the king of Egypt, who had quarrelled with the citizens of Alexandria and forsaken the city in wrath, and was now on his way to Rome in the hope that Pompey and Caesar would restore him again with an armed force, wished to have an interview with Cato, and sent a messenger to him, expecting that Cato would come to him. But Cato, as it chanced, was taking a course of medicine at the time, and bade Ptolemy come to him if he wished to see him. And when Ptolemy had come, Cato neither went to meet him nor rose from his seat, but greeted him as he would any ordinary visitor and bade him be seated. At first Ptolemy was confounded by the reception itself, and was amazed at the contrast between the haughtiness and severity of Cato's manners and the plainness and simplicity of his outfit. But after he had begun to converse with Cato about his own situation, words of great wisdom and boldness fell upon his ears. For Cato censured his course, and showed him what great happiness he had forsaken, and to how much servility and hardship he was subjecting himself in dealing with the corruption and rapacity of the chief men at Rome, whom Egypt could scarcely glut if it were all turned into money. Cato also advised him

---

[1] Cf. the *Brutus*, iii. 1.

ὀπίσω καὶ διαλλάττεσθαι τοῖς πολίταις, αὐτοῦ
δὲ καὶ συμπλεῖν καὶ συνδιαλλάττειν ἑτοίμως
5 ἔχοντος, οἷον ἐκ μανίας τινὸς ἢ παρακοπῆς ὑπὸ
τῶν λόγων ἔμφρων καθιστάμενος, καὶ κατανοῶν
τὴν ἀλήθειαν καὶ τὴν σύνεσιν τοῦ ἀνδρός, ὥρμησε
μὲν χρῆσθαι τοῖς ἐκείνου λογισμοῖς, ἀνατραπεὶς
δὲ ὑπὸ τῶν φίλων αὖθις ἅμα τῷ πρῶτον ἐν Ῥώμῃ
γενέσθαι καὶ θύραις ἑνὸς ἄρχοντος προσελθεῖν
ἔστενε τὴν αὑτοῦ κακοβουλίαν, ὡς οὐκ ἀνδρὸς
ἀγαθοῦ λόγων, θεοῦ δὲ μαντείας καταφρονήσας.

XXXVI. Ὁ δὲ ἐν Κύπρῳ Πτολεμαῖος εὐτυχίᾳ
τινὶ τοῦ Κάτωνος ἑαυτὸν φαρμάκοις ἀπέκτεινε.
πολλῶν δὲ χρημάτων ἀπολελεῖφθαι λεγομένων,
αὐτὸς μὲν ἔγνω πλεῖν εἰς Βυζαντίους, πρὸς δὲ τὴν
Κύπρον ἐξέπεμψε τὸν ἀδελφιδοῦν Βροῦτον, οὐ
πάνυ τι πιστεύων τῷ Κανιδίῳ. τοὺς δὲ φυγάδας
διαλλάξας καὶ καταλιπὼν ἐν ὁμονοίᾳ τὸ Βυζάν-
2 τιον, οὕτως εἰς Κύπρον ἔπλευσεν. οὔσης δὲ
πολλῆς καὶ βασιλικῆς ἐν ἐκπώμασι καὶ τραπέζαις
καὶ λίθοις καὶ πορφύραις κατασκευῆς, ἣν ἔδει
πραθεῖσαν ἐξαργυρισθῆναι, πάντα βουλόμενος 777
ἐξακριβοῦν καὶ πάντα κατατείνειν εἰς ἄκραν τιμὴν
καὶ πᾶσιν αὐτὸς παρεῖναι καὶ προσάγειν τὸν
ἔσχατον ἐκλογισμόν, οὐδὲ τοῖς ἔθάσι τῆς ἀγορᾶς
ἐπίστευεν, ἀλλὰ ὑπονοῶν ὁμοῦ πάντας, ὑπηρέτας,
κήρυκας, ὠνητάς, φίλους, τέλος αὐτὸς ἰδίᾳ τοῖς
ὠνουμένοις διαλεγόμενος καὶ προσβιβάζων ἕκαστον, οὕτω τὰ πλεῖστα τῶν ἀγορασμάτων ἐπώλει.
3 διὸ τοῖς τε ἄλλοις φίλοις ὡς ἀπιστῶν προσέκρουσε, καὶ τὸν συνηθέστατον ἁπάντων Μουνά-

to sail back and be reconciled with his people, holding himself ready also to sail with him and help effect the reconciliation. Then the king, as if brought to his senses by Cato's words after a fit of madness or delirium, and recognizing the sincerity and sagacity of the speaker, determined to adopt his counsels; but he was turned back to his first purpose by his friends. However, as soon as he reached Rome and was approaching the door of a magistrate, he groaned over his own evil resolve, convinced that he had slighted, not the words of a good man, but the prophetic warning of a god.

XXXVI. But the Ptolemy in Cyprus, fortunately for Cato, poisoned himself to death. And since the king was said to have left much treasure, Cato determined, while sailing himself to Byzantium, to send his nephew Brutus to Cyprus, since he did not altogether trust Canidius. Then, after reconciling the exiles and citizens of Byzantium and leaving the city in concord, he sailed to Cyprus. Now, there were many furnishings of a princely sort, such as beakers, tables, precious stones, and purple vestments, which had to be sold and turned into money. So Cato, wishing to treat everything with the greatest exactness, and to force everything up to a high price, and to attend to everything himself, and to use the utmost calculation, would not trust even those who were accustomed to the market, but, suspecting all alike, assistants, criers, buyers, and friends, and at last talking privately himself with the purchasers and encouraging each one to bid, he thus succeeded in selling most of the merchandize. For this reason he gave offence to most of his friends, who thought that he distrusted them, and Munatius, the most

τιον εἰς ὀργὴν ὀλίγου δεῖν ἀνήκεστον γενομένην
ἐνέβαλεν, ὥστε καὶ Καίσαρι γράφοντι λόγον κατὰ
τοῦ Κάτωνος πικροτάτην τοῦτο τὸ μέρος τῆς
κατηγορίας διατριβὴν παρασχεῖν.

XXXVII. Ὁ μέντοι Μουνάτιος οὐκ ἀπιστίᾳ
τοῦ Κάτωνος, ἀλλ' ἐκείνου μὲν ὀλιγωρίᾳ πρὸς
αὐτόν, αὑτοῦ δέ τινι ζηλοτυπίᾳ πρὸς τὸν Κανίδιον
ἱστορεῖ γενέσθαι τὴν ὀργήν. καὶ γὰρ αὐτὸς
σύγγραμμα περὶ τοῦ Κάτωνος ἐξέδωκεν, ᾧ μά-
2 λιστα Θρασέας ἐπηκολούθησε. λέγει δὲ ὕστερος
μὲν εἰς Κύπρον ἀφικέσθαι καὶ λαβεῖν παρημελη-
μένην ξενίαν, ἐλθὼν δὲ ἐπὶ θύρας ἀπωσθῆναι,
σκευωρουμένου τι τοῦ Κάτωνος οἴκοι σὺν τῷ
Κανιδίῳ, μεμψάμενος δὲ μετρίως οὐ μετρίας
τυχεῖν ἀποκρίσεως, ὅτι κινδυνεύει τὸ λίαν φιλεῖν,
ὥς φησι Θεόφραστος, αἴτιον τοῦ μισεῖν γίνεσθαι
πολλάκις· " Ἐπεὶ καὶ σύ," φάναι, "τῷ μάλιστα
φιλεῖν ἧττον οἰόμενος ἢ προσήκει τιμᾶσθαι χαλε-
3 παίνεις. Κανιδίῳ δὲ καὶ δι' ἐμπειρίαν χρῶμαι
καὶ διὰ πίστιν ἑτέρων μᾶλλον, ἐξ ἀρχῆς μὲν
ἀφιγμένῳ, καθαρῷ δὲ φαινομένῳ." ταῦτα μέντοι
μόνον αὐτῷ μόνῳ διαλεχθέντα τὸν Κάτωνα πρὸς
τὸν Κανίδιον ἐξενεγκεῖν. αἰσθόμενος οὖν αὐτὸς
οὔτε ἐπὶ δεῖπνον ἔτι φοιτᾶν οὔτε σύμβουλος ὑπα-
κούειν καλούμενος. ἀπειλοῦντος δὲ τοῦ Κάτωνος,
ὥσπερ εἰώθασι τῶν ἀπειθούντων, ἐνέχυρα λήψεσθαι, μηδὲν φροντίσας ἐκπλεῦσαι καὶ πολὺν

intimate of them all, he threw into a rage that was
well nigh incurable. Hence Caesar also, when he
wrote a discourse against Cato,[1] dwelt most bitterly
on this part of his denunciation.

XXXVII. Munatius, however, states that his anger
arose, not from Cato's distrust of him, but from his
inconsiderate conduct towards him, and from a certain jealousy which Munatius himself felt towards
Canidius. For Munatius himself also published a
treatise about Cato, which Thrasea chiefly followed.
Munatius says that he came to Cyprus after the
others, and found that no provision had been made
for his entertainment; he says, too, that on going to
Cato's door he was repulsed, because Cato had some
engagement inside with Canidius. He says, further,
that his measured protest met with no measured
reply, for Cato told him that excessive affection,
according to Theophrastus, was likely to become a
ground for hatred in many cases. "And so thou
too," said Cato, "by reason of thine especial affection for me, art vexed to think thyself less honoured
than is meet. Canidius I employ more than others
both because I have made trial of him, and because
I trust him; he came at the very first, and shows
himself to be incorrupt." This private conversation,
however, between himself and Cato, Munatius says
was reported by Cato to Canidius, and that therefore,
when he heard of it, he would no longer go to Cato's
table, or visit him, or share his counsels, when he
was invited. Further, Munatius says, when Cato
threatened to take security from him, as the Romans
do in the case of those who refuse to obey orders,
he paid no attention to the threat, but sailed away,

---

[1] See chapter xi. 4, and note.

4 χρόνον ἐν ὀργῇ διατελεῖν· εἶτα τῆς Μαρκίας (ἔτι
γὰρ συνῴκει τῷ Κάτωνι) διαλεχθείσης, τυχεῖν
μὲν ὑπὸ Βάρκα κεκλημένους ἐπὶ δεῖπνον, εἰσελθόντα δὲ ὕστερον τὸν Κάτωνα, τῶν ἄλλων κατα-
κειμένων, ἐρωτᾶν ὅπου κατακλιθείη. τοῦ δὲ
Βάρκα κελεύσαντος ὅπου βούλεται, περιβλεψά-
μενον εἰπεῖν ὅτι παρὰ Μουνάτιον· καὶ περιελθόντα
πλησίον αὐτοῦ κατακλιθῆναι, πλέον δὲ μηθὲν
5 φιλοφρονήσασθαι παρὰ τὸ δεῖπνον. ἀλλὰ πάλιν
τῆς Μαρκίας δεομένης τὸν μὲν Κάτωνα γράψαι
πρὸς αὐτόν, ὡς ἐντυχεῖν τι βουλόμενον, αὐτὸς δὲ
ἥκειν ἕωθεν εἰς τὴν οἰκίαν καὶ ὑπὸ τῆς Μαρκίας
κατασχεθῆναι μέχρι πάντες ἀπηλλάγησαν, οὕτω
δὲ εἰσελθόντα τὸν Κάτωνα καὶ περιβαλόντα τὰς
χεῖρας ἀμφοτέρας ἀσπάσασθαι καὶ φιλοφρονεῖσθαι. ταῦτα μὲν οὖν οὐχ ἧττον οἰόμενοι τῶν
ὑπαίθρων καὶ μεγάλων πράξεων πρὸς ἔνδειξιν
ἤθους καὶ κατανόησιν ἔχειν τινὰ σαφήνειαν ἐπὶ
πλέον διήλθομεν.

XXXVIII. Τῷ δὲ Κάτωνι συνήχθη μὲν ἀργυρίου τάλαντα μικρὸν ἑπτακισχιλίων ἀποδέοντα,
δεδιὼς δὲ τοῦ πλοῦ τὸ μῆκος ἀγγεῖα πολλὰ κατα-
σκευάσας, ὧν ἕκαστον ἐχώρει δύο τάλαντα καὶ
δραχμὰς πεντακοσίας, καλώδιον ἑκάστῳ μακρὸν
προσήρτησεν, οὗ τῇ ἀρχῇ προσείχετο φελλὸς
εὐμεγέθης, ὅπως, εἰ ῥαγείη τὸ πλοῖον, ἔχων διὰ
2 βυθοῦ τὸ ἄρτημα σημαίνοι τὸν τόπον. τὰ μὲν
οὖν χρήματα πλὴν ὀλίγων τινῶν ἀσφαλῶς διε-

and for a long time continued to be angry with Cato. Then, Munatius says, Marcia, who was still living with Cato,[1] spoke with her husband about the matter; and when it chanced that both men were invited to supper by Barca, Cato, who came late and after the others had taken their places, asked where he should recline; and when Barca told him to recline where he pleased, Cato looked about the room and said: "I will take my place by Munatius." So he went round and reclined by his side, but made no further show of friendship during the supper. Marcia, however, made a second request in the matter, Munatius says, and Cato wrote to him, saying that he wished to confer with him about something. So Munatius went to Cato's house early in the morning, and was detained there by Marcia until all the other visitors had gone away. Then Cato came in, threw both arms about him, kissed him, and lavished kindness upon him. Such incidents, now, in my opinion, quite as much as deeds of greatness and publicity, shed considerable light upon the perception and manifestation of character, and I have therefore recounted them at greater length.

XXXVIII. Cato got together nearly seven thousand talents of silver, and fearing the long voyage home, he had many coffers provided, each one of which would hold two talents and five hundred drachmas, and attached to each of them a long rope, to the end of which a huge piece of cork was fastened. This, he thought, in case the vessel were wrecked, would hold to its deep mooring and indicate the place where the treasure lay. Well, then, the money, except a very little, was safely transported;

---

[1] Cf. chapter xxv. 5.

κομίσθη, λόγους δὲ πάντων ὧν διῴκησε γεγραμ-
μένους ἐπιμελῶς ἔχων ἐν δυσὶ βιβλίοις οὐδέτερον
ἔσωσεν, ἀλλὰ τὸ μὲν ἀπελεύθερος αὐτοῦ κομίζων
ὄνομα Φιλάργυρος ἐκ Κεγχρεῶν ἀναχθεὶς ἀνε-
τράπη καὶ συναπώλεσε τοῖς φορτίοις, τὸ δὲ αὐτὸς
ἄχρι Κερκύρας φυλάξας ἐν ἀγορᾷ κατεσκήνωσε· 778
3 τῶν δὲ ναυτῶν διὰ τὸ ῥιγοῦν πυρὰ πολλὰ καιόν-
των τῆς νυκτὸς ἤφθησαν αἱ σκηναὶ καὶ τὸ
βιβλίον ἠφανίσθη. τοὺς μὲν οὖν ἐχθροὺς καὶ
συκοφάντας ἐπιστομεῖν ἤμελλον οἱ βασιλικοὶ
διοικηταὶ παρόντες, ἄλλως δὲ τῷ Κάτωνι τὸ
πρᾶγμα δηγμὸν ἤνεγκεν. οὐ γὰρ εἰς πίστιν
ὑπὲρ αὐτοῦ τοὺς λόγους, ἀλλὰ παράδειγμα τοῖς
ἄλλοις ἀκριβείας ἐξενεγκεῖν φιλοτιμούμενος ἐνε-
μεσήθη.

XXXIX. Περαιωθεὶς δὲ ταῖς ναυσὶν οὐκ ἔλαθε
τοὺς Ῥωμαίους, ἀλλὰ πάντες μὲν ἄρχοντες καὶ
ἱερεῖς, πᾶσα δὲ ἡ βουλή, πολὺ δὲ τοῦ δήμου μέρος ἀπήντων πρὸς τὸν ποταμόν, ὥστε τὰς ὄχθας
ἀμφοτέρας ἀποκεκρύφθαι καὶ θριάμβου μηδὲν
ὄψει καὶ φιλοτιμίᾳ λείπεσθαι τὸν ἀνάπλουν
2 αὐτοῦ. καίτοι σκαιὸν ἐνίοις τοῦτο ἐφαίνετο καὶ
αὔθαδες, ὅτι τῶν ὑπάτων καὶ τῶν στρατηγῶν
παρόντων οὔτε ἀπέβη πρὸς αὐτοὺς οὔτε ἐπέσχε
τὸν πλοῦν, ἀλλὰ ῥοθίῳ τὴν ὄχθην παρεξελαύνων
ἐπὶ νεὼς ἑξήρους βασιλικῆς οὐκ ἀνῆκε πρότερον
3 ἢ καθορμίσαι τὸν στόλον εἰς τὸ νεώριον. οὐ μὴν
ἀλλὰ τῶν χρημάτων παρακομιζομένων δι᾽ ἀγορᾶς
ὅ τε δῆμος ἐθαύμαζε τὸ πλῆθος, ἥ τε βουλὴ

but although he had the accounts of all his administration of the estate carefully written out in two
books, neither of these was preserved. One of them
a freedman of his, Philargyrus by name, had in
charge, but after putting to sea from Cenchreae he
was capsized and lost it, together with his cargo;
the other Cato himself had safely carried as far as
Corcyra, where he pitched his tent in the market-
place. But because it was so cold the sailors built
many fires during the night, the tents caught fire,
and the book disappeared. It is true that the royal
stewards who were at hand were ready to stop the
mouths of Cato's enemies and traducers, but nevertheless the matter gave him annoyance. For it was
not as a proof of his own integrity, but as an
example to others of scrupulous exactness that he
was eager to produce his accounts, and he was
therefore vexed.

XXXIX. The Romans did not fail to hear of his
arrival[1] with his ships, and all the magistrates and
priests, the whole senate, and a large part of the
people went to the river to meet him, so that both
banks of the stream were hidden from view, and his
voyage up to the city had all the show and splendour
of a triumph. Yet some thought it ungracious and
stubborn that, although the consuls and praetors
were at hand, he neither landed to greet them, nor
checked his course, but on a royal galley of six
banks of oars swept past the bank where they stood,
and did not stop until he had brought his fleet
to anchor in the dock-yard. However, when the
treasure was carried through the forum, the people
were amazed at the great amount of it, and the

[1] In 56 B.C.

συναχθεῖσα μετὰ τῶν πρεπόντων ἐπαίνων ἐψη-
φίσατο τῷ Κάτωνι στρατηγίαν ἐξαίρετον δοθῆναι
καὶ τὰς θέας αὐτὸν ἐν ἐσθῆτι περιπορφύρῳ θεάσασθαι. ταῦτα μὲν οὖν ὁ Κάτων παρῃτήσατο,
Νικίαν δὲ τὸν οἰκονόμον τῶν βασιλικῶν ἐλεύθερον
ἔπεισε τὴν βουλὴν ἀφεῖναι, μαρτυρήσας ἐπιμέ-
4 λειαν καὶ πίστιν. ὑπάτευε δὲ Φίλιππος ὁ
πατὴρ τῆς Μαρκίας, καὶ τρόπον τινὰ τὸ ἀξίωμα
τῆς ἀρχῆς καὶ ἡ δύναμις εἰς Κάτωνα περιῆλθεν,
οὐκ ἐλάττονα τοῦ συνάρχοντος δι' ἀρετὴν ἢ δι'
οἰκειότητα τοῦ Φιλίππου τῷ Κάτωνι τιμὴν
προστιθέντος.

XL. Ἐπεὶ δὲ Κικέρων ἐκ τῆς φυγῆς, ἣν ἔφυγεν
ὑπὸ Κλωδίου, κατελθὼν καὶ δυνάμενος μέγα τὰς
δημαρχικὰς δέλτους, ἃς ὁ Κλώδιος ἔθηκεν ἀνα-
γράψας εἰς τὸ Καπιτώλιον, ἀπέσπασε βίᾳ καὶ
καθεῖλε τοῦ Κλωδίου μὴ παρόντος, ἐπὶ τούτοις
δὲ βουλῆς ἀθροισθείσης καὶ τοῦ Κλωδίου κατη-
γοροῦντος ἔλεγε παρανόμως τῷ Κλωδίῳ τῆς
δημαρχίας γενομένης ἀτελῆ καὶ ἄκυρα δεῖν εἶναι
2 τὰ τότε πραχθέντα καὶ γραφέντα, προσέκρουσεν
ὁ Κάτων αὐτῷ λέγοντι, καὶ τέλος ἀναστὰς ἔφη
τῆς μὲν Κλωδίου πολιτείας μηδὲν ὑγιὲς μηδὲ
χρηστὸν ὅλως νομίζειν, εἰ δὲ ἀναιρεῖ τις ὅσα
δημαρχῶν ἔπραξεν, ἀναιρεῖσθαι πᾶσαν αὐτοῦ
τὴν περὶ Κύπρον πραγματείαν καὶ μὴ γεγονέναι
τὴν ἀποστολὴν νόμιμον ἄρχοντος παρανόμου

senate in special session voted, together with the
appropriate praises, that an extraordinary praetorship
should be given to Cato, and that when he witnessed
the spectacles he might wear a purple-bordered robe.
These honours, now, Cato declined, but he persuaded
the senate to bestow freedom upon Nicias, the
steward of the royal household, after bearing witness
to his care and fidelity. Philippus, the father of
Marcia, was consul at the time, and the dignity and
power of his office devolved in a manner upon Cato;
the colleague of Philippus, also, bestowed no less
honour upon Cato for his virtue than Philippus did
because of his relationship to him.

XL. But Cicero had now come back [1] from the
exile into which he was driven by Clodius, and,
relying on his great influence in the senate, had
forcibly taken away and destroyed, in the absence of
Clodius, the records of his tribuneship which Clodius
had deposited on the Capitol. When the senate was
convened to consider the matter, and Clodius made
his denunciation, Cicero made a speech in which he
said that, since Clodius had been made tribune
illegally, all that had been done or recorded during
his tribunate ought to be void and invalid. Cato
contradicted Cicero while he was speaking, and
finally rose and said that, although he was wholly
of the opinion that there was nothing sound or good
in the administration of Clodius, still, if everything
which Clodius had done while tribune were to be
rescinded, then all his own proceedings in Cyprus
would be rescinded, and his mission there had not
been legal, since an illegal magistrate had obtained it

---

[1] In 57 B.C., after an absence of sixteen months. Cf. the
Cicero, chapters xxx.–xxxiii.

ψηφισαμένου· παρανόμως μὲν οὐ δήμαρχον
αἱρεθῆναι[1] τὸν Κλώδιον ἐκ πατρικίων μετα-
στάντα νόμου διδόντος εἰς δημοτικὸν οἶκον, εἰ δὲ
μοχθηρός, ὥσπερ ἄλλοι, γέγονεν ἄρχων, αὐτὸν
εὐθύνειν τὸν ἀδικήσαντα, μὴ λύειν τὴν συναδι-
κηθεῖσαν ἀρχὴν εἶναι προσῆκον. ἐκ τούτου δι'
ὀργῆς ὁ Κικέρων ἔσχε τὸν Κάτωνα, καὶ φίλῳ
χρώμενος ἐπαύσατο χρόνον πολύν· εἶτα μέντοι
διηλλάγησαν.

XLI. Ἐκ τούτου Πομπήϊος καὶ Κράσσος
ὑπερβαλόντι τὰς Ἄλπεις Καίσαρι συγγενόμενοι
γνώμην ἐποιήσαντο κοινῇ δευτέραν ὑπατείαν
μετιέναι, καὶ καταστάντες εἰς αὐτὴν Καίσαρι μὲν
τῆς ἀρχῆς ἄλλον τοσοῦτον ἐπιψηφίζεσθαι χρόνον, αὐτοῖς δὲ τῶν ἐπαρχιῶν τὰς μεγίστας καὶ
χρήματα καὶ στρατιωτικὰς δυνάμεις. ὅπερ ἦν
ἐπὶ νεμήσει τῆς ἡγεμονίας καὶ καταλύσει τῆς
2 πολιτείας συνωμοσία. πολλῶν δὲ καὶ ἀγαθῶν
ἀνδρῶν μετιέναι τὴν ἀρχὴν τότε παρασκευαζο-
μένων, τοὺς μὲν ἄλλους ὀφθέντες ἐν ταῖς παραγ-
γελίαις ἀπέτρεψαν, μόνον δὲ Λεύκιον Δομίτιον
Πορκίᾳ συνοικοῦντα τῇ ἀδελφῇ Κάτων ἔπεισε
μὴ ἐκστῆναι μηδὲ ὑφέσθαι, τοῦ ἀγῶνος οὐ περὶ
ἀρχῆς ὄντος, ἀλλὰ περὶ τῆς Ῥωμαίων ἐλευθερίας.
3 καὶ μέντοι καὶ λόγος ἐχώρει διὰ τοῦ σωφρονοῦν- 779
τος ἔτι τῆς πόλεως μέρους, ὡς οὐ περιοπτέον, εἰς
ταὐτὸ τῆς Κράσσου καὶ Πομπηΐου δυνάμεως
συνελθούσης, παντάπασιν ὑπέρογκον καὶ βαρεῖαν
τὴν ἀρχὴν γενομένην, ἀλλ' ἀφαιρετέον αὐτῆς τὸν

---

[1] μὲν οὐ δ. αἱρεθῆναι Sintenis, after Schaefer, for the MSS.
μὲν οὖν δ. αἱρεθῆναι ; Bekker has μὲν οὖν μὴ δ. αἱρεθῆναι.

for him; but it had not been illegal, he maintained, for Clodius to be elected tribune after a transfer from patrician to plebeian rank which the law allowed,[1] and if he had been a bad magistrate, like others, it was fitting to call to an account the man who had done wrong, and not to vitiate the office which had suffered from his wrong doing. In consequence of this speech Cicero was angry with Cato, and for a long time ceased friendly intercourse with him; afterwards, however, they were reconciled.[2]

XLI. After this, Pompey and Crassus had a meeting with Caesar,[3] who had come across the Alps, in which they laid a plan to canvass jointly for a second consulship, and, after they were established in the office, to get a vote passed giving to Caesar another term in his command, of the same duration as the first, and to themselves the largest provinces, money and military forces. This was a conspiracy for the division of the supreme power and the abolition of the constitution. And although many honourable men were getting ready to canvass for the consulship at that time, they were all deterred by seeing Pompey and Crassus announce themselves as candidates, excepting only Lucius Domitius, the husband of Cato's sister Porcia. Him Cato persuaded not to withdraw from the canvass or give way, since the struggle was not for office, but for the liberty of the Romans. And indeed it was currently said among those citizens who still retained their good sense, that the consular power must not be suffered to become altogether overweening and oppressive by the union of the influence of Pompey and Crassus, but that one or the

---

[1] Cf. chapter xxxiii. 3. [2] Cf. the *Cicero*, xxxiv.
[3] At Luca, in 56 B.C. Cf. the *Pompey*, li.; the *Caesar*, xxi.

ἕτερον. καὶ συνίσταντο πρὸς τὸν Δομίτιον
παρορμῶντες καὶ παραθαρρύνοντες ἀντιλαμβά-
νεσθαι· πολλοὺς γὰρ αὐτῷ καὶ τῶν σιωπώντων
διὰ δέος ἐν ταῖς ψήφοις ὑπάρξειν.

4 Τοῦτο δὴ δείσαντες οἱ περὶ τὸν Πομπήιον
ὑφεῖσαν ἐνέδραν τῷ Δομιτίῳ καταβαίνοντι ὄρ-
θριον ὑπὸ λαμπάδων εἰς τὸ πεδίον. καὶ πρῶτος
μὲν ὁ προφαίνων ἐπιστὰς τῷ Δομιτίῳ πληγεὶς
καὶ πεσὼν ἀπέθανε· μετὰ δὲ τοῦτον ἤδη καὶ τῶν
ἄλλων συντιτρωσκομένων ἐγίνετο φυγὴ πλὴν
5 Κάτωνος καὶ Δομιτίου. κατεῖχε γὰρ αὐτὸν ὁ
Κάτων, καίπερ αὐτὸς εἰς τὸν βραχίονα τετρω-
μένος, καὶ παρεκελεύετο μένειν καὶ μὴ προλιπεῖν,
ἕως ἐμπνέωσι, τὸν ὑπὲρ τῆς ἐλευθερίας ἀγῶνα
πρὸς τοὺς τυράννους, οἳ τίνα τρόπον χρήσονται
τῇ ἀρχῇ δηλοῦσι διὰ τηλικούτων ἀδικημάτων ἐπ᾽
αὐτὴν βαδίζοντες.

XLII. Οὐχ ὑποστάντος δὲ τοῦ Δομιτίου τὸ
δεινόν, ἀλλ᾽ εἰς τὴν οἰκίαν καταφυγόντος, ἡρέ-
θησαν μὲν ὕπατοι Πομπήιος καὶ Κράσσος, οὐκ
ἀπέκαμε δὲ ὁ Κάτων, ἀλλ᾽ αὐτὸς προελθὼν
στρατηγίαν μετήει, βουλόμενος ὁρμητήριον ἔχειν
τῶν πρὸς ἐκείνους ἀγώνων καὶ πρὸς ἄρχοντας
ἀντικαθίστασθαι μὴ ἰδιώτης. οἱ δὲ καὶ τοῦτο
δείσαντες, ὡς τῆς στρατηγίας ἀξιομάχου διὰ
2 Κάτωνα πρὸς τὴν ὑπατείαν γενησομένης, πρῶτον
μὲν ἐξαίφνης καὶ τῶν πολλῶν ἀγνοούντων βουλὴν συναγαγόντες ἐψηφίσαντο τοὺς αἱρεθέντας

other of these men must be deprived of it. So they joined the party of Domitius, inciting and encouraging him to persist in his opposition; for many, they said, who now held their peace through fear, would help him when it came to voting.

This was precisely what the partisans of Pompey feared, and so they set an ambush for Domitius as he was going down at early morning by torchlight into the Campus Martius. First of all the torch-bearer who stood in front of Domitius was smitten, fell, and died; and after him the rest of the party were presently wounded, and all took to flight except Cato and Domitius. For Cato held Domitius back, although he himself had received a wound in the arm, and exhorted him to stand his ground, and not to abandon, while they had breath, the struggle in behalf of liberty which they were waging against the tyrants, who showed plainly how they would use the consular power by making their way to it through such crimes.

XLII. But Domitius would not face the peril, and fled to his house for refuge, whereupon Pompey and Crassus were elected consuls.[1] Cato, however, would not give up the fight, but came forward himself as candidate for a praetorship, wishing to have a vantage-point for his struggles against the men, and not to be a private citizen when he was opposing magistrates. But Pompey and Crassus feared this also, feeling that Cato would make the praetorship a match for the consulship. In the first place, therefore, they suddenly, and without the knowledge of the majority, got the senate together, and had a vote passed that the praetors elect should enter upon their office at

[1] For the year 55 B.C.

στρατηγοὺς εὐθὺς ἄρχειν καὶ μὴ διαλιπόντας
τὸν νόμιμον χρόνον, ἐν ᾧ δίκαι τοῖς δεκάσασι τὸν
δῆμον ἦσαν. ἔπειτα διὰ τοῦ ψηφίσματος τὸ διδόναι [1] ἀνυπεύθυνον κατασκευάσαντες ὑπηρέτας
αὑτῶν καὶ φίλους ἐπὶ τὴν στρατηγίαν προῆγον,
αὐτοὶ μὲν διδόντες ἀργύριον, αὐτοὶ δὲ ταῖς ψή-
3 φοις φερομέναις ἐφεστῶτες. ὡς δὲ καὶ τούτων ἡ
Κάτωνος ἀρετὴ καὶ δόξα περιῆν, ὑπ' αἰδοῦς τῶν
πολλῶν ἐν δεινῷ πολλῷ τιθεμένων ἀποδόσθαι
Κάτωνα ταῖς ψήφοις, ὃν καλῶς εἶχε πρίασθαι
τῇ πόλει στρατηγόν, ἥ τε πρώτη κληθεῖσα τῶν
φυλῶν ἐκεῖνον ἀπέδειξεν, ἐξαίφνης ὁ Πομπήϊος
βροντῆς ἀκηκοέναι ψευσάμενος αἴσχιστα διέλυσε
τὴν ἐκκλησίαν, εἰθισμένων ἀφοσιοῦσθαι τὰ τοιαῦτα καὶ μηδὲν ἐπικυροῦν διοσημίας γενομένης.
4 αὖθις δὲ πολλῷ χρησάμενοι τῷ δεκασμῷ, τοὺς
βελτίστους ὤσαντες ἐκ τοῦ πεδίου βίᾳ διεπρά-
ξαντο Βατίνιον ἀντὶ Κάτωνος αἱρεθῆναι στρατηγόν. ἔνθα δὴ λέγεται τοὺς μὲν οὕτω παρανόμως καὶ ἀδίκως θεμένους τὴν ψῆφον εὐθὺς ὥσπερ
ἀποδράντας οἴχεσθαι, τοῖς δὲ ἄλλοις συνιστα-
μένοις καὶ ἀγανακτοῦσι δημάρχου τινὸς αὐτόθι
παρασχόντος ἐκκλησίαν καταστάντα τὸν Κάτωνα
ἅπαντα μὲν ὥσπερ ἐκ θεῶν ἐπίπνουν τὰ μέλ-
5 λοντα τῇ πόλει προειπεῖν, παρορμῆσαι δὲ τοὺς
πολίτας ἐπὶ Πομπήϊον καὶ Κράσσον ὡς τοιαῦτα
συνειδότας αὑτοῖς, καὶ τοιαύτης ἁπτομένους
πολιτείας δι' ἣν ἔδεισαν Κάτωνα, μὴ στρατηγὸς
αὐτῶν περιγένηται. τέλος δὲ ἀπιόντα εἰς τὴν
οἰκίαν προὔπεμψε πλῆθος τοσοῦτον ὅσον οὐδὲ

---

[1] τὸ διδόναι Sintenis, after Schaefer, for the MSS. τὸ διδόναι
δίκας ; Coraës and Bekker delete also διδόναι.

once, without waiting for the time prescribed by law to elapse, during which time those who had bribed the people were liable to prosecution. In the next place, now that by this vote they had freed bribery from responsibility, they brought forward henchmen and friends of their own as candidates for the praetorship, themselves offering money for votes, and themselves standing by when the votes were cast. But even to these measures the virtue and fame of Cato were superior, since shame made most of the people think it a terrible thing to sell Cato by their votes, when the city might well buy him into the praetorship; and therefore the first tribe called upon voted for him. Then on a sudden Pompey lyingly declared that he heard thunder, and most shamefully dissolved the assembly, since it was customary to regard such things as inauspicious, and not to ratify anything after a sign from heaven had been given. Then they resorted again to extensive bribery, ejected the best citizens from the Campus Martius, and so by force got Vatinius elected praetor instead of Cato. Then, indeed, it is said, those who had thus illegally and wrongfully cast their votes went off home at once like runaways, while the rest of the citizens, who were banding together and expressing their indignation, were formed into an assembly there by a tribune, and were addressed by Cato. As if inspired from heaven he foretold to the citizens all that would happen to their city, and tried to set them against Pompey and Crassus, who, he said, were privy to such a course and engaged in such a policy as made them afraid of Cato, lest, as praetor, he should get the better of them. And finally, when he went away home, he was escorted on his way by a greater

σύμπαντας ἅμα τοὺς ἀποδεδειγμένους στρατηγούς.

XLIII. Γαΐου δὲ Τρεβωνίου γράψαντος νόμον
ὑπὲρ νομῆς ἐπαρχιῶν τοῖς ὑπάτοις, ὥστε τὸν μὲν
Ἰβηρίαν ἔχοντα καὶ Λιβύην ὑφ᾽ αὑτῷ, τὸν δὲ
Συρίαν καὶ Αἴγυπτον, οἷς βούλοιντο πολεμεῖν
καὶ καταστρέφεσθαι ναυτικαῖς καὶ πεζικαῖς δυνά-
μεσιν ἐπιόντας, οἱ μὲν ἄλλοι τὴν ἀντίπραξιν καὶ
κώλυσιν ἀπεγνωκότες ἐξέλιπον καὶ τὸ ἀντειπεῖν,
Κάτωνι δὲ ἀναβάντι πρὸ τῆς ψηφοφορίας ἐπὶ τὸ
βῆμα καὶ βουλομένῳ λέγειν μόλις ὡρῶν δυεῖν
2 λόγον ἔδωκαν. ὡς δὲ πολλὰ λέγων καὶ διδάσκων 780
καὶ προθεσπίζων κατανάλωσε τὸν χρόνον, οὐκέτι
λέγειν αὐτὸν εἴων, ἀλλ᾽ ἐπιμένοντα κατέσπασεν
ὑπηρέτης προσελθών. ὡς δὲ καὶ κάτωθεν ἱστά-
μενος ἐβόα καὶ τοὺς ἀκούοντας καὶ συναγανα-
κτοῦντας εἶχε, πάλιν ὁ ὑπηρέτης ἐπιλαβόμενος καὶ
3 ἀγαγὼν αὐτὸν ἔξω τῆς ἀγορᾶς κατέστησε. καὶ
οὐκ ἔφθη πρῶτον ἀφεθείς, καὶ πάλιν ἀναστρέψας
ἵετο πρὸς τὸ βῆμα μετὰ κραυγῆς ἐγκελευόμενος
τοῖς πολίταις ἀμύνειν. πολλάκις δὲ τούτου γενομένου περιπαθῶν ὁ Τρεβώνιος ἐκέλευσεν αὐτὸν
εἰς τὸ δεσμωτήριον ἄγεσθαι· καὶ πλῆθος ἐπηκολούθει λέγοντος ἅμα σὺν τῷ βαδίζειν ἀκροώ-
μενον, ὥστε δείσαντα τὸν Τρεβώνιον ἀφεῖναι.

4 Κἀκείνην μὲν οὕτω τὴν ἡμέραν ὁ Κάτων κατ-
ανάλωσε· ταῖς δ᾽ ἐφεξῆς οὓς μὲν δεδιξάμενοι τῶν
πολιτῶν, οὓς δὲ συσκευασάμενοι χάρισι καὶ δωροδοκίαις, ἕνα δὲ τῶν δημάρχων Ἀκύλλιον ὅπλοις
εἴρξαντες ἐκ τοῦ βουλευτηρίου προελθεῖν, αὐτὸν
δὲ τὸν Κάτωνα βροντὴν γεγονέναι βοῶντα τῆς

throng than accompanied all the elected praetors together.

XLIII. And now Caius Trebonius proposed a law for the assignment of provinces to the consuls, whereby one of them was to have Spain and Africa under him, the other Syria and Egypt, and both were to wage war on whom they pleased, and attack and subdue them with land and sea forces. The rest of the opposition were weary of their efforts to prevent such things, and forbore even to speak against the measure; but Cato mounted the rostra before the vote was taken, expressed a wish to speak, with difficulty gained permission, and spoke for two hours. After he had consumed this time in long arguments, expositions, and prophecies, he was not allowed to speak any longer, but an official went up to him as he sought to continue, and pulled him down from the rostra. But even from where he stood below the rostra he kept shouting, and found men to listen to him and share his indignation. So the official once more laid hands on him, led him away, and put him out of the forum. Then, the instant that he was released, he turned back and strove to reach the rostra, shouting, and commanding the citizens to help him. This was repeated several times, until Trebonius, in a passion, ordered him to be led to prison; but a crowd followed listening to what he said as he went along, so that Trebonius took fright and let him go.

In this manner Cato consumed that day; but during the days that followed his adversaries intimidated some of the citizens, won over others by bribes and favours, with armed men prevented one of the tribunes, Aquillius, from leaving the senate-chamber, cast Cato himself out of the forum when he cried out that there

339

ἀγορᾶς ἐκβαλόντες, οὐκ ὀλίγους δὲ τρώσαντες,
ἐνίων δὲ καὶ πεσόντων, βίᾳ τὸν νόμον ἐκύρωσαν,
ὥστε πολλοὺς συστραφέντας ὀργῇ τοὺς Πομπηΐου
5 βάλλειν ἀνδριάντας. ἀλλὰ τοῦτο μὲν ἐπελθὼν ὁ
Κάτων διεκώλυσε· τῷ δὲ Καίσαρι πάλιν νόμου
γραφομένου περὶ τῶν ἐπαρχιῶν καὶ τῶν στρατοπέδων, οὐκέτι πρὸς τὸν δῆμον ὁ Κάτων, ἀλλὰ
πρὸς αὐτὸν τραπόμενος Πομπήϊον ἐμαρτύρατο καὶ
προὔλεγεν ὡς ἐπὶ τὸν αὐτοῦ τράχηλον ἀναλαμβάνων Καίσαρα νῦν μὲν οὐκ οἶδεν, ὅταν δὲ ἄρχη-
ται βαρύνεσθαι καὶ κρατεῖσθαι μήτε ἀποθέσθαι
6 δυνάμενος μήτε φέρειν ὑπομένων, εἰς τὴν πόλιν
ἐμπεσεῖται σὺν αὐτῷ, καὶ μεμνήσεται τότε τῶν
Κάτωνος παραινέσεων, ὡς οὐδὲν ἧττον ἐν αὐταῖς
τὸ Πομπηΐου συμφέρον ἐνῆν ἢ τὸ καλὸν καὶ
δίκαιον. ταῦτα πολλάκις ἀκούων ὁ Πομπήϊος
ἠμέλει καὶ παρέπεμπεν ἀπιστίᾳ τῆς Καίσαρος
μεταβολῆς διὰ πίστιν εὐτυχίας τῆς ἑαυτοῦ καὶ
δυνάμεως.

XLIV. Εἰς δὲ τὸ ἑξῆς ἔτος αἱρεθεὶς ὁ Κάτων
στρατηγὸς οὐδὲν ἔδοξε προστιθέναι τῇ ἀρχῇ τοσοῦτον εἰς σεμνότητα καὶ μέγεθος ἄρχων καλῶς,
ὅσον ἀφαιρεῖν καὶ καταισχύνειν ἀνυπόδητος καὶ
ἀχίτων πολλάκις ἐπὶ τὸ βῆμα προερχόμενος καὶ
θανατικὰς δίκας ἐπιφανῶν ἀνδρῶν οὕτω βρα-
βεύων. ἔνιοι δέ φασι καὶ μετ' ἄριστον οἶνον
πεπωκότα χρηματίζειν· ἀλλὰ τοῦτο μὲν οὐκ ἀλη-
2 θῶς λέγεται. διαφθειρομένου δὲ τοῦ δήμου ταῖς
δωροδοκίαις ὑπὸ τῶν φιλαρχούντων καὶ χρωμέ-

340

had been thunder, and after a few of the citizens had been wounded and some actually slain, forced the passage of the law. Consequently, many banded together and wrathfully pelted the statues of Pompey. But Cato came up and stopped this. However, when once more a law was introduced concerning Caesar's provinces and armies, Cato no longer addressed himself to the people, but to Pompey himself, solemnly assuring and warning him that he was now, without knowing it, taking Caesar upon his own shoulders, and that when he began to feel the burden and to be overcome by it, he would neither have the power to put it away nor the strength to bear it longer, and would therefore precipitate himself, burden and all, upon the city; then he would call to mind the exhortations of Cato, and see that they had sought no less the interests of Pompey than honour and justice. Pompey heard these counsels repeatedly, but ignored and put them by; he did not believe that Caesar would change, because he trusted in his own good fortune and power.

XLIV. For the next year [1] Cato was elected praetor, but it was thought that he did not add so much majesty and dignity to the office by a good administration as he took away from it by disgracing it. For he would often go forth to his tribunal without shoes or tunic, and in such attire would preside over capital cases involving prominent men. Some say, too, that even after the mid-day meal and when he had drunk wine, he would transact public business; but this is untruthfully said. However, seeing that the people were corrupted by the gifts which they received from men who were fond of office and plied the bribery of

[1] 54 B.C.

νων τῷ δεκάζεσθαι καθάπερ ἐργασίᾳ συνήθει τῶν
πολλῶν, βουλόμενος ἐκκόψαι παντάπασι τὸ νόσ-
ημα τοῦτο τῆς πόλεως, ἔπεισε δόγμα θέσθαι τὴν
σύγκλητον ὅπως οἱ κατασταθέντες ἄρχοντες, εἰ
μηδένα κατήγορον ἔχοιεν, αὐτοὶ παριόντες ἐξ
ἀνάγκης εἰς ἔνορκον δικαστήριον εὐθύνας διδῶσιν.
3 ἐπὶ τούτῳ χαλεπῶς μὲν ἔσχον οἱ μετιόντες ἀρχάς,
ἔτι δὲ χαλεπώτερον ὁ μισθαρνῶν ὄχλος. ἕωθεν
οὖν ἐπὶ τὸ βῆμα τοῦ Κάτωνος προελθόντος ἀθρόοι
προσπεσόντες ἐβόων, ἐβλασφήμουν, ἔβαλλον,
ὥστε φεύγειν ἀπὸ τοῦ βήματος ἅπαντας, αὐτὸν
δὲ ἐκεῖνον ἐξωσθέντα τῷ πλήθει καὶ παραφερό-
4 μενον μόλις ἐπιλαβέσθαι τῶν ἐμβόλων. ἐντεῦθεν
ἀναστὰς τῷ μὲν ἰταμῷ καὶ θαρροῦντι τῆς ὄψεως
εὐθὺς ἐκράτησε τοῦ θορύβου καὶ τὴν κραυγὴν
ἔπαυσεν, εἰπὼν δὲ τὰ πρέποντα καὶ μεθ' ἡσυχίας
ἀκουσθεὶς παντάπασι διέλυσε τὴν ταραχήν.
ἐπαινούσης δὲ τῆς βουλῆς αὐτόν, "Ἐγὼ δέ,"
εἶπεν, "ὑμᾶς οὐκ ἐπαινῶ κινδυνεύοντα στρατηγὸν
ἐγκαταλιπόντας καὶ μὴ προσαμύναντας."
5   Τῶν δὲ μετιόντων ἀρχὴν ἕκαστος ἀπόρῳ πάθει
συνείχετο, φοβούμενος μὲν αὐτὸς δεκάζειν, φοβούμενος δὲ ἑτέρου τοῦτο πράξαντος ἐκπεσεῖν τῆς
ἀρχῆς. ἔδοξεν οὖν αὐτοῖς εἰς ταὐτὸ συνελθοῦσι 781
παραβαλέσθαι δραχμῶν ἕκαστον ἀργυρίου δεκα-
δύο ἥμισυ μυριάδας, εἶτα μετιέναι τὴν ἀρχὴν
πάντας ὀρθῶς καὶ δικαίως· τὸν δὲ παραβάντα
καὶ χρησάμενον δεκασμῷ στέρεσθαι τοῦ ἀργυ-
6 ρίου. ταῦτα ὁμολογήσαντες αἱροῦνται φύλακα
καὶ βραβευτὴν καὶ μάρτυρα τὸν Κάτωνα καὶ τὰ
χρήματα φέροντες ἐκείνῳ παρετίθεντο· καὶ τὰς
συνθήκας ἐγράψαντο πρὸς ἐκεῖνον, ἀντὶ τῶν χρη-

the masses as they would an ordinary business, he
wished to eradicate altogether this disease from the
state, and therefore persuaded the senate to make a
decree that magistrates elect, in case they had no
accuser, should be compelled of themselves to come
before a sworn court and submit accounts of their
election. At this the candidates for offices were
sorely displeased, and still more sorely the hireling
multitude. Early in the morning, therefore, when
Cato had gone forth to his tribunal, crowds assailed
him with shouts, abuse, and missiles, so that everybody fled from the tribunal, and Cato himself was
pushed away from it and borne along by the throng,
and with difficulty succeeded in laying hold of the
rostra. There, rising to his feet, by the firmness and
boldness of his demeanour he at once prevailed
over the din, stopped the shouting, and after saying
what was fitting and being listened to quietly,
brought the disturbance completely to an end. When
the senate was praising him for this, he said : " But
I cannot praise you for leaving an imperilled praetor
in the lurch and not coming to his aid."

Now, all the candidates for offices were at a loss
what to do; each one was afraid to use bribes himself, but was afraid of losing his office if another used
them. They decided, therefore, to come together
and deposit severally one hundred and twenty-five
thousand drachmas in money, and that all should
then sue for their offices in fair and just ways; the
one who transgressed and practised bribery forfeiting
his money. Having made this agreement, they chose
Cato as depositary, umpire, and witness, and bringing
their money, offered to deposit it with him; they
even drew up their agreement in his presence. Cato

μάτων ἐγγυητὰς λαβόντα, τὰ δὲ χρήματα μὴ
δεξάμενον. ὡς δὲ ἧκεν ἡ κυρία τῆς ἀναδείξεως,
παραστὰς ὁ Κάτων τῷ βραβεύοντι δημάρχῳ καὶ
παραφυλάξας τὴν ψῆφον, ἕνα τῶν παραβαλο-
μένων ἀπέφηνε κακουργοῦντα καὶ προσέταξεν
7 ἀποδοῦναι τοῖς ἄλλοις τὸ ἀργύριον. ἀλλ' ἐκεῖνοι
μὲν ἐπαινέσαντες αὐτοῦ τὴν ὀρθότητα καὶ θαυμάσαντες ἀνεῖλον τὸ πρόστιμον ὡς ἱκανὴν δίκην
ἔχοντες παρὰ τοῦ ἀδικήσαντος· τοὺς δὲ ἄλλους
ἐλύπησεν ὁ Κάτων καὶ φθόνον ἔσχεν ἀπὸ τούτου
πλεῖστον, ὡς βουλῆς καὶ δικαστηρίων καὶ ἀρχόν-
των δύναμιν αὑτῷ περιποιησάμενος.

Οὐδεμιᾶς γὰρ ἀρετῆς δόξα καὶ πίστις ἐπιφθό-
νους ποιεῖ μᾶλλον ἢ τῆς δικαιοσύνης, ὅτι καὶ
δύναμις αὐτῇ καὶ πίστις ἕπεται μάλιστα παρὰ
8 τῶν πολλῶν. οὐ γὰρ τιμῶσι μόνον, ὡς τοὺς ἀν-
δρείους, οὐδὲ θαυμάζουσιν, ὡς τοὺς φρονίμους,
ἀλλὰ καὶ φιλοῦσι τοὺς δικαίους καὶ θαρροῦσιν
αὐτοῖς καὶ πιστεύουσιν. ἐκείνων δὲ τοὺς μὲν
φοβοῦνται, τοῖς δὲ ἀπιστοῦσι· πρὸς δὲ τούτοις
ἐκείνους μὲν οἴονται φύσει μᾶλλον ἢ τῷ βούλεσθαι διαφέρειν, ἀνδρείαν καὶ φρόνησιν, τὴν μὲν
ὀξύτητά τινα, τὴν δ' εὐρωστίαν ψυχῆς τιθέμενοι,
δικαίῳ δὲ ὑπάρχοντος εὐθὺς εἶναι τῷ βουλομένῳ
μάλιστα τὴν ἀδικίαν ὡς κακίαν ἀπροφάσιστον
αἰσχύνονται.

XLV. Διὸ καὶ τῷ Κάτωνι πάντες οἱ μεγάλοι
προσεπολέμουν ὡς ἐλεγχόμενοι· Πομπήϊος δὲ καὶ
κατάλυσιν τῆς ἑαυτοῦ δυνάμεως τὴν ἐκείνου δόξαν
ἡγούμενος ἀεί τινας προσέβαλλεν αὐτῷ λοιδορη-
σομένους, ὧν καὶ Κλώδιος ἦν ὁ δημαγωγός, αὖθις
εἰς Πομπήϊον ὑπορρυεὶς καὶ καταβοῶν τοῦ Κάτω-

took pledges for their money, but would not accept the money itself. When the day appointed for the election came, Cato took his stand by the side of the presiding tribune, and after watching the vote, declared that one of the depositors was playing false, and ordered him to pay his money over to the others. But these, after admiring and praising Cato's uprightness, cancelled the penalty, feeling that they already had sufficient satisfaction from the wrong-doer. In the rest of the citizens, however, this conduct of Cato caused more vexation and odium than anything else; they felt that he was investing himself with the powers of senate, courts and magistrates.

For no virtue, by the fame and credit which it gives, creates more envy than justice, because both power and credit follow it chiefly among the common folk. These do not merely honour the just, as they do the brave, nor admire them merely, as they do the wise, but they actually love the just, and put confidence and trust in them. As for the brave and wise, however, they fear the one and distrust the other; and besides, they think that these excel by a natural gift rather than by their own volition, considering bravery to be a certain intensity, and wisdom a certain vigour, of soul, whereas any one who wishes can be just forthwith, and the greatest disgrace is visited upon injustice, as being inexcusable baseness.

XLV. For this reason all the great men were hostile to Cato, feeling that they were put to shame by him; and Pompey, who considered Cato's high repute as a dissolution of his own power, was always egging certain persons on to abuse him, among whom was Clodius the demagogue especially, who had again drifted into Pompey's following. He

νος, ὡς πολλὰ μὲν ἐκ Κύπρου χρήματα νοσφισα-
μένου, Πομπηΐῳ δὲ πολεμοῦντος ἀπαξιώσαντι
2 γάμον αὐτοῦ θυγατρός. ὁ δὲ Κάτων ἔλεγεν ὅτι
χρήματα μὲν ἐκ Κύπρου τοσαῦτα τῇ πόλει συνα-
γάγοι μήτε ἵππον ἕνα μήτε στρατιώτην λαβών,
ὅσα Πομπήϊος ἐκ πολέμων τοσούτων καὶ θριάμ-
βων τὴν οἰκουμένην κυκήσας οὐκ ἀνήνεγκε, κη-
δεστὴν δὲ μηδέποτε προελέσθαι Πομπήϊον, οὐκ
ἀνάξιον ἡγούμενος, ἀλλ' ὁρῶν τὴν ἐν τῇ πολιτείᾳ
3 διαφοράν. "Αὐτὸς μὲν γάρ," ἔφη, "διδομένης
μοι μετὰ τὴν στρατηγίαν ἐπαρχίας ἀπέστην, οὗτος δὲ τὰς μὲν ἔχει λαβών, τὰς δὲ δίδωσιν ἑτέροις·
νυνὶ δὲ καὶ τέλος ἑξακισχιλίων ὁπλιτῶν Καίσαρι
κέχρηκεν εἰς Γαλατίαν· ὃ οὔτ' ἐκεῖνος ᾔτησε παρ'
ὑμῶν οὔτε οὗτος ἔδωκε μεθ' ὑμῶν, ἀλλὰ δυνάμεις
τηλικαῦται καὶ ὅπλα καὶ ἵπποι χάριτές εἰσιν
4 ἰδιωτῶν καὶ ἀντιδόσεις. καλούμενος δὲ αὐτοκράτωρ καὶ στρατηγὸς ἄλλοις τὰ στρατεύματα
καὶ τὰς ἐπαρχίας παραδέδωκεν, αὐτὸς δὲ τῇ πόλει
παρακάθηται στάσεις ἀγωνοθετῶν ἐν ταῖς παραγ-
γελίαις καὶ θορύβους μηχανώμενος, ἐξ ὧν οὐ
λέληθε δι' ἀναρχίας μοναρχίαν ἑαυτῷ μνηστευό-
μενος."

XLVI. Οὕτως μὲν ἠμύνατο τὸν Πομπήϊον. ἦν
δὲ Μάρκος Φαώνιος ἑταῖρος αὐτοῦ καὶ ζηλωτής,
οἷος ὁ Φαληρεὺς Ἀπολλόδωρος ἱστορεῖται περὶ
Σωκράτην γενέσθαι τὸν παλαιόν, ἐμπαθὴς καὶ
παρακεκινηκὼς πρὸς τὸν λόγον, οὐ σχέδην οὐδὲ
πράως, ἀλλ' ἄκρατον αὐτοῦ καθαψάμενον ὥσπερ

loudly denounced Cato for having appropriated much treasure from Cyprus, and for being hostile to Pompey because he had declined to marry his daughter. But Cato declared that, without taking a single horse or soldier, he had got together from Cyprus more treasure for the city than Pompey had brought back from all his wars and triumphs after stirring up the habitable world; and that he never chose Pompey for a marriage connection, not because he thought him unworthy of it, but because he saw the difference in their political tenets. "I, for my part," said Cato, "when a province was offered me after my praetorship, declined it, but this Pompey took provinces, some of which he holds himself, and some he offers to others; and now he has actually lent Caesar a body of six thousand legionaries for use in Gaul. This force neither did Caesar ask from you, nor did Pompey give it with your consent, but armies of this great size and arms and horses are now the mutual gifts of private persons. And though he has the titles of general and imperator, he has handed over to others his armies and his provinces, while he himself takes up his post near the city, managing factions at the elections as though he were directing games, and contriving disturbances, from which, as we clearly see, by way of anarchy, he is seeking to win for himself a monarchy."

XLVI. With such words did Cato defend himself against Pompey. But Marcus Favonius was a companion and ardent disciple of his, just as Apollodorus of Phalerum is said to have been of Socrates in olden time. Favonius was impulsive, and easily moved by argument, which did not affect him moderately or mildly, but like unmixed wine, and to the point of

2 οἶνον καὶ μανικώτερον. οὗτος ἀγορανομίαν μετιὼν ἡττᾶτο, συμπαρὼν δὲ ὁ Κάτων προσέσχε
ταῖς δέλτοις μιᾷ χειρὶ γεγραμμέναις· καὶ τὴν 782
κακουργίαν ἐξελέγξας τότε μὲν ἐπικλήσει δημάρχων ἔλυσε τὴν ἀνάδειξιν, ὕστερον δὲ τοῦ Φαωνίου κατασταθέντος ἀγορανόμου τά τε ἄλλα τῆς
ἀρχῆς ἐπεμελεῖτο καὶ τὰς θέας διεῖπεν ἐν τῷ
θεάτρῳ, διδοὺς καὶ τοῖς θυμελικοῖς στεφάνους
3 μὲν οὐ χρυσοῦς, ἀλλ᾽ ὥσπερ ἐν Ὀλυμπίᾳ κοτί-
νων, δῶρα δὲ ἀντὶ τῶν πολυτελῶν τοῖς μὲν Ἕλλησι τεῦτλα καὶ θρίδακας καὶ ῥαφανῖδας καὶ
ἀπίους, τοῖς δὲ Ῥωμαίοις οἴνου κεράμια καὶ κρέα
ὕεια καὶ σῦκα καὶ σικύους καὶ ξύλων ἀγκαλίδας,
ὧν τὴν εὐτέλειαν οἱ μὲν ἐγέλων, οἱ δὲ ἡδοῦντο τοῦ
Κάτωνος τὸ αὐστηρὸν καὶ κατεστυμμένον ὁρῶν-
4 τες ἡσυχῇ μεταβάλλον εἰς διάχυσιν. τέλος δὲ ὁ
Φαώνιος εἰς τὸν ὄχλον ἐμβαλὼν ἑαυτὸν καὶ καθεζόμενος ἐν τοῖς θεαταῖς ἐκρότει τὸν Κάτωνα καὶ
διδόναι τοῖς εὐημεροῦσι καὶ τιμᾶν ἐβόα, καὶ
συμπαρεκάλει τοὺς θεατάς, ὡς ἐκείνῳ τὴν ἐξουσίαν παραδεδωκώς. ἐν δὲ τῷ ἑτέρῳ θεάτρῳ
Κουρίων ὁ Φαωνίου συνάρχων ἐχορήγει πολυ-
τελῶς· ἀλλ᾽ ἐκεῖνον ἀπολείποντες οἱ ἄνθρωποι
μετέβαινον ἐνταῦθα, καὶ συνέπαιζον προθύμως
ὑποκρινομένῳ τῷ Φαωνίῳ τὸν ἰδιώτην καὶ τῷ
5 Κάτωνι τὸν ἀγωνοθέτην. ἔπραττε δὲ ταῦτα δια-
σύρων τὸ πρᾶγμα, καὶ διδάσκων ὅτι παίζοντα
δεῖ τῇ παιδιᾷ χρῆσθαι καὶ χάριτι παραπέμπειν
ἀτύφῳ μᾶλλον ἢ παρασκευαῖς καὶ πολυτελείαις,
εἰς τὰ μηδενὸς ἄξια φροντίδας μεγάλας καὶ
σπουδὰς κατατιθέμενον.

frenzy. He was being defeated in a candidacy for the aedileship, but Cato, who was present, noticed that the voting tablets were all inscribed in one hand; and having exposed the foul play, at the time he stopped the election by an appeal to the tribunes. Afterwards, when Favonius had been appointed aedile, Cato both discharged the other duties of the office and managed the spectacles in the theatre. He gave to the actors crowns, not of gold, but of wild olive, as was done at Olympia, and inexpensive gifts,—to the Greeks, beets, lettuce, radishes, and pears; and to the Romans, jars of wine, pork, figs, melons, and faggots of wood. At the practical simplicity of these gifts some laughed, but others conceived respect for Cato when they saw his severe and solemn manner gradually relaxing to pleasant good-humour.[1] And at last Favonius, plunging into the crowd and taking a seat among the spectators, applauded Cato and called to him in a loud voice to give presents to the successful performers and to honour them, and helped him to exhort the spectators, as though he had delegated his powers to Cato. Now, in the other theatre, Curio, the colleague of Favonius, was managing things with a lavish hand; but the people left him and went over to the other place, and readily shared in a sport where Favonius was playing the part of a private citizen and Cato that of master of the games. But Cato did all this in disparagement of the usual practice, and with an effort to show that in sport one must adopt a sportive manner and conduct matters with unostentatious gladness rather than with elaborate and costly preparations, where one bestows upon trifling things great care and effort.

[1] Cf. chapter i. 2.

XLVII. Ἐπεὶ δέ, Σκηπίωνος καὶ Ὑψαίου καὶ
Μίλωνος ὑπατείαν μετερχομένων οὐ μόνον ἐκείνοις
τοῖς συντρόφοις ἤδη καὶ συμπολιτευομένοις ἀδική-
μασι, δωροδοκίαις καὶ δεκασμοῖς, ἀλλ' ἄντικρυς
δι' ὅπλων καὶ φόνων εἰς ἐμφύλιον πόλεμον ὠθουμένων τόλμῃ καὶ ἀπονοίᾳ, Πομπήϊόν τινες ἠξίουν
ἐπιστῆναι ταῖς ἀρχαιρεσίαις, τὸ μὲν πρῶτον ἀντεῖπεν ὁ Κάτων, οὐ τοῖς νόμοις ἐκ Πομπηΐου
φάμενος, ἀλλ' ἐκ τῶν νόμων Πομπηΐῳ δεῖν ὑπάρ-
2 χειν τὴν ἀσφάλειαν, ὡς δὲ πολὺν χρόνον ἀναρχίας οὔσης καὶ τριῶν στρατοπέδων τὴν ἀγορὰν
ὁσημέραι περιεχόντων ὀλίγον ἀπέλιπεν ἀνεπί-
σχετον γεγονέναι τὸ κακόν, ἔγνω τὰ πράγματα
πρὸ τῆς ἐσχάτης ἀνάγκης εἰς Πομπήϊον ἑκουσίῳ
χάριτι τῆς βουλῆς περιστῆσαι, καὶ τῷ μετριω-
τάτῳ τῶν παρανομημάτων χρησάμενος ἰάματι
τῆς τῶν μεγίστων καταστάσεως τὴν μοναρχίαν
ἐπαγαγέσθαι μᾶλλον ἢ περιϊδεῖν τὴν στάσιν εἰς
3 μοναρχίαν[1] τελευτῶσαν. εἶπεν οὖν ἐν τῇ βουλῇ
γνώμην Βύβλος οἰκεῖος ὢν Κάτωνος, ὡς χρὴ
μόνον ἑλέσθαι Πομπήϊον ὕπατον· ἢ γὰρ ἕξειν
καλῶς τὰ πράγματα ἐκείνου καταστήσαντος, ἢ
τῷ κρατίστῳ δουλεύσειν τὴν πόλιν. ἀναστὰς
δὲ ὁ Κάτων οὐδενὸς ἂν προσδοκήσαντος ἐπῄνεσε
τὴν γνώμην καὶ συνεβούλευσε πᾶσαν ἀρχὴν ὡς
ἀναρχίας κρείττονα, Πομπήϊον δὲ καὶ προσδοκᾶν
ἄριστα τοῖς παροῦσι χρήσεσθαι πράγμασι καὶ
φυλάξειν διαπιστευθέντα τὴν πόλιν.

XLVIII. Οὕτω δ' ἀποδειχθεὶς ὕπατος ὁ Πομπήϊος ἐδεήθη τοῦ Κάτωνος ἐλθεῖν πρὸς αὐτὸν

---

[1] μοναρχίαν Sintenis[1] and Coraës, with the MSS.; Sintenis[2]
and Bekker adopt the ἀναρχίαν of Emperius.

XLVII. But presently Scipio, Hypsaeus, and Milo sought the consulship.[1] They not only used those illegal means which were now a familiar feature in political life, namely, the giving of gifts and bribes, but were openly pressing on, by the use of arms and murder, into civil war, with daring and madness. Some therefore demanded that Pompey should preside over the elections. Cato opposed this at first, saying that the laws ought not to derive their security from Pompey, but Pompey from the laws. However, when there had been no regular government for a long time,[1] and three armies were occupying the forum daily, and the evil had well-nigh become past checking, he decided that matters ought to be put into the hands of Pompey by the voluntary gift of the senate, before the extreme necessity for it came, and that by employing the most moderate of unconstitutional measures as a healing remedy for the conservation of the greatest interests, they should themselves introduce the monarchy, rather than allow faction to issue in monarchy. Accordingly, Bibulus, a kinsman of Cato, moved in the senate that Pompey should be chosen sole consul; for either matters would be rectified by his settlement of them, or the state would be in subjection to its most powerful citizen. Then Cato rose up and, to everyone's surprise, approved the measure, advising any government as better than no government at all, and saying that he expected Pompey would handle the present situation in the best manner possible, and would guard the state when it was entrusted to him.

XLVIII. After Pompey had in this way been appointed consul, he begged Cato to come to him in the

[1] For the year 52 B.C. Riots in Rome prevented any election. Cf. the *Pompey*, chapter liv.

εἰς τὸ προάστειον. ἐλθόντα δὲ δεξάμενος φιλοφρόνως ἀσπασμοῖς καὶ δεξιώσεσι καὶ χάριν
ὁμολογήσας παρεκάλει σύμβουλον αὐτῷ καὶ
2 πάρεδρον εἶναι τῆς ἀρχῆς. ὁ δὲ Κάτων ἀπεκρίνατο μήτε τὰ πρῶτα πρὸς ἀπέχθειαν εἰπεῖν
Πομπηΐου μήτε ταῦτα πρὸς χάριν, ἀλλ᾽ ἐπὶ
συμφέροντι πάντα τῆς πόλεως· ἰδίᾳ μὲν οὖν
αὐτῷ παρακαλοῦντι σύμβουλος ἔσεσθαι, δημοσίᾳ
δέ, κἂν μὴ παρακαλῆται, πάντως ἐρεῖν τὸ φαινό-
3 μενον. καὶ ταῦτα ἔπραττεν ὡς εἶπε. πρῶτον
μὲν γὰρ ἐπὶ τοὺς δεκάσαντας ἤδη τὸν δῆμον
ἐπιτίμια καινὰ καὶ δίκας μεγάλας τοῦ Πομπηΐου
νομοθετοῦντος ἀμελεῖν ἐκέλευσε τῶν γεγονότων
καὶ προσέχειν τοῖς μέλλουσιν· οὔτε γὰρ ὅπου
στήσεται τὸ τὰ προημαρτημένα ζητεῖν ὁρίσαι
ῥᾴδιον, ἐάν τε νεώτερα γράφηται τῶν ἀδικημάτων
ἐπιτίμια, δεινὰ πείσεσθαι τούς, ὃν οὐ παρέβαινον
ὅτ᾽ ἠδίκουν νόμον, κατὰ τοῦτον κολαζομένους.
4 ἔπειτα πολλῶν κρινομένων ἐπιφανῶν ἀνδρῶν,
ἐνίων δὲ καὶ φίλων τοῦ Πομπηΐου καὶ οἰκείων,
ὁρῶν αὐτὸν ἐνδιδόντα ἐν[1] πολλοῖς καὶ καμπτό-
μενον ἐπετίμα σφοδρῶς καὶ διήγειρεν. ἐπεὶ δὲ
νόμῳ τοὺς εἰωθότας λέγεσθαι περὶ τῶν κρινομένων ἐπαίνους αὐτὸς ἀφελών, Μουνατίῳ Πλάγκῳ
συγγράψας ἔπαινον ἐπὶ τῆς δίκης ἔδωκεν, ἐπι-
σχόμενος ὁ Κάτων τὰ ὦτα ταῖς χερσίν (ἔτυχε
γὰρ δικάζων) ἐκώλυεν ἀναγινώσκεσθαι τὴν μαρ-
5 τυρίαν. ὁ δὲ Πλάγκος ἀπέλεξεν αὐτὸν ἐκ τῶν

783

---

[1] ἐν Coraës and Bekker, with most MSS.: τοῖς, with M.

suburbs. And when Cato was come, Pompey gave him a friendly welcome with salutations and hand-clasps, acknowledged his obligations to him, and invited him to be his counsellor and associate in the government. But Cato replied that he had neither spoken as he did at first out of enmity to Pompey, nor as he afterwards did to win his favour, but in every case in the interests of the state; in private, therefore, upon his invitation, he would be his counsellor, but in public, even without his invitation, he would certainly say what he thought was best. And he did this, as he said he would. In the first place, for instance, when Pompey was proposing to fix by law fresh penalties and heavy punishments for those who had already bribed the people, Cato urged him to ignore the past and give his attention to the future; for, he said, it would not be easy to fix the point at which the investigation of past transgressions should stop, and if penalties should be fixed subsequent to the crimes, those would be outrageously dealt with who were punished in conformity with a law which they were not transgressing when they committed their crime. In the second place, when many prominent men were on trial, some of whom were friends and relations of Pompey, Cato saw that Pompey was giving in and yielding in many cases, and therefore rebuked him sharply and tried to spur him on. Moreover, though Pompey himself had made illegal the customary panegyrics upon men under trial, he wrote a panegyric upon Munatius Plancus and handed it in at his trial; but Cato (who chanced to be one of the jurors) stopped his ears with his hands and prevented the reading of the testimony.[1] Plancus got

---

[1] Cf. the *Pompey*, lv. 5.

δικαστῶν μετὰ τοὺς λόγους, καὶ οὐδὲν ἧττον ἧλω.
καὶ ὅλως ἄπορον ἧν πρᾶγμα καὶ δυσμεταχείρι-
στον ὁ Κάτων τοῖς φεύγουσι, μήτε βουλομένοις
αὐτὸν ἀπολιπεῖν δικαστὴν μήτε ἀπολέγειν τολ-
μῶσιν. ἥλωσαν γὰρ οὐκ ὀλίγοι τῷ Κάτωνα
φεύγειν δόξαντες οὐ θαρρεῖν τοῖς δικαίοις· ἐνίοις
δὲ καὶ προὔφερον οἱ λοιδοροῦντες ὡς ὄνειδος μέγα
τὸ μὴ δέξασθαι κριτὴν Κάτωνα προτεινόμενον.

XLIX. Ἐπεὶ δὲ Καίσαρος αὐτοῦ μὲν ἐμπεφυ-
κότος τοῖς στρατεύμασιν ἐν Γαλατίᾳ καὶ τῶν ὅπλων ἐχομένου, δώροις δὲ καὶ χρήμασι καὶ φίλοις
μάλιστα πρὸς τὴν ἐν τῇ πόλει χρωμένου δύναμιν,
ἤδη μὲν αἱ Κάτωνος προαγορεύσεις ἀνέφερον τὸν
Πομπήϊον ἐκ πολλῆς ἤδη τῆς πρόσθεν ἀπιστίας
ὀνειροπολοῦντα τὸ δεινόν, ἔτι δὲ ἧν ὄκνου καὶ
μελλήσεως ἀτόλμου πρὸς τὸ κωλύειν καὶ ἐπιχειρεῖν ὑπόπλεως, ὥρμησεν ὁ Κάτων ὑπατείαν παραγγέλλειν ὡς ἀφαιρησόμενος εὐθὺς τὰ ὅπλα τοῦ
2 Καίσαρος ἢ τὴν ἐπιβουλὴν ἐξελέγξων. οἱ δ'
ἀντιπαραγγέλλοντες αὐτῷ χαρίεντες μὲν ἧσαν
ἀμφότεροι, Σουλπίκιος δὲ καὶ πολλὰ τῆς τοῦ
Κάτωνος ἐν τῇ πόλει δόξης τε καὶ δυνάμεως ἀπο-
λελαυκώς· οὐ μέτριον οὖν ἐδόκει πρᾶγμα ποιεῖν
οὐδ' εὐχάριστον· οὐ μὴν ὅ γε Κάτων ἐνεκάλει·
"Τί γάρ," ἔφη, "θαυμαστὸν εἰ ὅ τις νομίζει τῶν
3 ἀγαθῶν μέγιστον ἑτέρῳ μὴ παρίησι;" πείσας δὲ
τὴν βουλὴν ψηφίσασθαι τοὺς μετιόντας τὴν ἀρχὴν αὐτοὺς δεξιοῦσθαι τὸν δῆμον, δι' ἑτέρου δὲ μὴ
δεῖσθαι μηδὲ ἐντυγχάνειν ὑπὲρ αὐτῶν περιόντος,

him removed from the jury after the speeches were over, and was convicted none the less. And altogether Cato was a perplexing and unmanageable quantity for defendants; they neither wished to allow him to be a juror in their cases nor had the courage to challenge him. For not a few of them were convicted because their attempted rejection of Cato made it appear that they had no confidence in the justice of their cases; and some were bitterly assailed by their revilers for not accepting Cato as juror when he was proposed.

XLIX. But Caesar, though he devoted himself to his armies in Gaul and was busy with arms, nevertheless employed gifts, money, and above all friends, to increase his power in the city. Presently, therefore, the admonitions of Cato roused Pompey from the great incredulity which he had indulged in up to this time, so that he had forebodings of his peril. However, he was still given to hesitation and spiritless delay in checking or attacking the threatening evil, and therefore Cato determined to stand for the consulship, that he might at once deprive Caesar of his armed forces, or convict him of his hostile designs. But his competitors were both acceptable men, and Sulpicius had actually derived much benefit from Cato's repute and power in the city, and was therefore thought to be acting in an improper and even thankless manner. But Cato had no fault to find with him. "Pray, what wonder is it," said he, "if a man will not surrender to another what he regards as the greatest of all good things?" However, by persuading the senate to pass a decree that candidates for office should canvass the people in person, and not solicit nor confer with the citizens through the

ἔτι μᾶλλον ἐξηγρίανε τοὺς ἀνθρώπους, εἰ μὴ μόνον τὸ λαβεῖν μισθόν, ἀλλὰ καὶ τὸ διδόναι χάριν
αὐτοὺς ἀφῃρημένος ἄπορον καὶ ἄτιμον ὁμοῦ τὸν
4 δῆμον πεποίηκε. πρὸς δὲ τούτῳ μήτε αὐτὸς ἐντυχεῖν ὑπὲρ αὑτοῦ πιθανὸς ὤν, ἀλλ᾽ ἐν ἤθει τὸ τοῦ
βίου μᾶλλον ἀξίωμα βουλόμενος φυλάσσειν ἢ
προσλαβεῖν τὸ τῆς ἀρχῆς ποιούμενος τὰς δεξιώ-
σεις, μήτε τοὺς φίλους ἐάσας οἷς ὄχλος ἁλίσκεται
καὶ θεραπεύεται ποιεῖν, ἀπέτυχε τῆς ἀρχῆς.

L. Φέροντος δὲ τοῦ πράγματος οὐκ αὐτοῖς μόνοις τοῖς ἀποτυχοῦσιν, ἀλλὰ καὶ φίλοις αὐτῶν
καὶ οἰκείοις σὺν αἰσχύνῃ τινὶ κατήφειαν καὶ πέν-
θος ἐφ᾽ ἡμέρας πολλάς, οὕτως ἤνεγκε ῥᾳθύμως τὸ
συμβεβηκὸς ὥστε ἀλειψάμενος μὲν ἐν τῷ πεδίῳ
σφαιρίσαι, μετ᾽ ἄριστον δὲ πάλιν, ὥσπερ εἴθιστο,
καταβὰς εἰς ἀγορὰν ἀνυπόδητος καὶ ἀχίτων περι-
2 πατῆσαι μετὰ τῶν συνήθων. αἰτιᾶται δὲ Κικέρων
ὅτι, τῶν πραγμάτων ἄρχοντος τοιούτου δεομένων,
οὐκ ἐποιήσατο σπουδὴν οὐδὲ ὑπῆλθεν ὁμιλίᾳ
φιλανθρώπῳ τὸν δῆμον, ἀλλὰ καὶ πρὸς τὸ λοιπὸν
ἐξέκαμε καὶ ἀπηγόρευσε, καίτοι τὴν στρατηγίαν
3 αὖθις ἐξ ὑπαρχῆς μετελθών. ἔλεγεν οὖν ὁ Κάτων
ὅτι τῆς μὲν στρατηγίας οὐ κατὰ γνώμην ἐξέπεσε
τῶν πολλῶν, ἀλλὰ βιασθέντων ἢ διαφθαρέντων,
ἐν δὲ ταῖς ὑπατικαῖς ψήφοις μηδεμιᾶς κακουργίας
γενομένης ἔγνω καὶ τῷ δήμῳ προσκεκρουκὼς διὰ
τὸν αὑτοῦ τρόπον, ὃν οὔτε μεταθέσθαι πρὸς ἑτέρων χάριν οὔτε χρώμενον ὁμοίῳ πάλιν ὅμοια 784
παθεῖν νοῦν ἔχοντος ἀνδρός ἐστι.

agency of another going about in their behalf, Cato
still more exasperated the common folk, in that he
deprived them, not only of getting money, but also of
bestowing favour, and so made them at once poor and
without honour. And besides this, he was not persuasive himself in canvassing for himself, but wished
to preserve in his manners the dignity of his life,
rather than to acquire that of the consulship by
making the customary salutations; neither would
he permit his friends to do the things by which the
multitude is courted and captivated. He therefore
failed to obtain the office.

L. Though the matter brought, not only to the
unsuccessful candidates themselves, but also to their
friends and relatives, dejection and sorrow tinged
with considerable shame for many days, Cato bore
so easily what had happened that he anointed himself and practised ball in the Campus Martius, and
after the mid-day meal, again, as was his wont, went
down into the forum without shoes or tunic and
walked about there with his intimates. But Cicero
finds fault with him because, when affairs demanded
a man like him for office, he would not exert himself
nor try to win the people by kindly intercourse with
them, but for the future also ceased to make any
effort and gave up the contest, although he had re-
newed his candidacy for the praetorship. Cato replied,
accordingly, that he had lost the praetorship, not
because the majority wished it to be so, but because
they were constrained or corrupted; whereas, since
there had been no foul play in the consular elections,
he saw clearly that he had given offence to the people
by his manners. These, he said, no man of sense
would change to please others, nor, keeping them
unchanged, would he again suffer a like disaster.

357

LI. Τοῦ δὲ Καίσαρος ἐμβαλόντος εἰς ἔθνη μά-
χιμα καὶ παραβόλως κρατήσαντος, Γερμανοῖς δὲ
καὶ σπονδῶν γενομένων δοκοῦντος ἐπιθέσθαι καὶ
καταβαλεῖν τριάκοντα μυριάδας, οἱ μὲν ἄλλοι τὸν
δῆμον ἠξίουν εὐαγγέλια θύειν, ὁ δὲ Κάτων ἐκέλευεν ἐκδιδόναι τὸν Καίσαρα τοῖς παρανομηθεῖσι
καὶ μὴ τρέπειν εἰς αὐτοὺς μηδὲ ἀναδέχεσθαι τὸ
2 ἄγος εἰς τὴν πόλιν. "Οὐ μὴν ἀλλὰ καὶ τοῖς
θεοῖς," ἔφη, "θύωμεν, ὅτι τῆς τοῦ στρατηγοῦ
μανίας καὶ ἀπονοίας τὴν δίκην εἰς τοὺς στρατιώτας οὐ τρέπουσιν, ἀλλὰ φείδονται τῆς πόλεως."
ἐκ τούτου Καῖσαρ ἐπιστολὴν γράψας ἀπέστειλεν
εἰς τὴν σύγκλητον· ὡς δὲ ἀνεγνώσθη βλασφημίας
πολλὰς ἔχουσα καὶ κατηγορίας τοῦ Κάτωνος,
3 ἀναστὰς ἐκεῖνος οὐχ ὑπ' ὀργῆς οὐδὲ φιλονεικίας,
ἀλλ' ὥσπερ ἐκ λογισμοῦ καὶ παρασκευῆς τὰ μὲν
εἰς ἑαυτὸν ἐγκλήματα λοιδορίαις καὶ σκώμμασιν
ὅμοια καὶ παιδιάν τινα καὶ βωμολοχίαν τοῦ Καίσαρος ἀπέδειξεν, ἁψάμενος δὲ τῶν ἐκείνου βου-
λευμάτων ἀπ' ἀρχῆς καὶ πᾶσαν αὐτοῦ τὴν διάνοιαν, ὥσπερ οὐκ ἐχθρός, ἀλλὰ συνωμότης καὶ
κοινωνός, ἐκκαλύψας, καὶ διδάξας ὡς οὐ Γερμα-
4 νῶν οὐδὲ Κελτῶν παῖδας, ἀλλ' ἐκεῖνον αὐτόν, εἰ
σωφρονοῦσι, φοβητέον ἐστὶν αὐτοῖς, οὕτως ἐπέστρεψε καὶ παρώξυνεν ὡς τοὺς φίλους τοῦ Καίσαρος μετανοεῖν, ὅτι τὴν ἐπιστολὴν ἀναγνόντες ἐν
τῇ βουλῇ καιρὸν τῷ Κάτωνι λόγων δικαίων καὶ
κατηγοριῶν ἀληθῶν παρέσχον. ἐκυρώθη μὲν οὖν
οὐδέν, ἀλλ' ἐλέχθη μόνον ὅτι καλῶς ἔχει διάδοχον
5 Καίσαρι δοθῆναι. τῶν δὲ φίλων ἀξιούντων καὶ
Πομπήιον ἐξ ἴσου τὰ ὅπλα καταθέσθαι καὶ ἀπο-

LI. After Caesar had fallen upon warlike nations and at great hazards conquered them, and when it was believed that he had attacked the Germans even during a truce[1] and slain three hundred thousand of them, there was a general demand at Rome that the people should offer sacrifices of good tidings, but Cato urged them to surrender Caesar to those whom he had wronged, and not to turn upon themselves, or allow to fall upon their city, the pollution of his crime. "However," said he, "let us also sacrifice to the gods, because they do not turn the punishment for the general's folly and madness upon his soldiers, but spare the city." After this, Caesar wrote a letter and sent it to the senate; and when it was read, with its abundant insults and denunciations of Cato, Cato rose to his feet and showed, not in anger or contentiousness, but as if from calculation and due preparation, that the accusations against him bore the marks of abuse and scoffing, and were childishness and vulgarity on Caesar's part. Then, assailing Caesar's plans from the outset and revealing clearly all his purpose, as if he were his fellow conspirator and partner and not his enemy, he declared that it was not the sons of Germans or Celts whom they must fear, but Caesar himself, if they were in their right minds, and so moved and incited his hearers that the friends of Caesar were sorry that by having the letter read in the senate they had given Cato an opportunity for just arguments and true denunciations. However, nothing was done, but it was merely said that it were well to give Caesar a successor.[2] And when Caesar's friends demanded that Pompey also, as well as Caesar, should lay down his arms and give up his provinces,

[1] Cf. Caesar, *Bell. Gall.* iv. 12-15; Plutarch, *Caesar*, xxii.
[2] Cf. the *Caesar*, xxx.; the *Pompey*, lviii.

δοῦναι τὰς ἐπαρχίας ἢ μηδὲ Καίσαρα, νῦν ἐκεῖνα
βοῶν ὁ Κάτων ἃ προύλεγεν αὐτοῖς ἥκειν, καὶ
βιάζεσθαι τὸν ἄνθρωπον ἀναφανδὸν ἤδη τῇ δυνάμει χρώμενον ἣν ἔσχεν ἐξαπατῶν καὶ φενακίζων
τὴν πόλιν, ἔξω μὲν οὐδὲν ἐπέραινε, τοῦ δήμου
θέλοντος ἀεὶ τὸν Καίσαρα μέγιστον εἶναι, τὴν δὲ
σύγκλητον εἶχε πειθομένην καὶ φοβουμένην τὸν
δῆμον.

LII. Ὡς δὲ Ἀρίμινον κατείληπτο καὶ Καῖσαρ
κατηγγέλλετο μετὰ στρατιᾶς ἐλαύνειν ἐπὶ τὴν
πόλιν, ἐνταῦθα δὴ πάντες ἐπ᾽ ἐκεῖνον ἀφεώρων, οἵ
τε πολλοὶ καὶ Πομπήϊος, ὡς μόνον μὲν ἐξ ἀρχῆς
προαισθόμενον, πρῶτον δὲ φανερῶς προειπόντα
2 τὴν Καίσαρος γνώμην. εἶπεν οὖν ὁ Κάτων·
"Ἀλλὰ εἴ γε οἷς ἐγὼ προύλεγον ἀεὶ καὶ συνεβούλευον ἐπείσθη τις ὑμῶν, ἄνδρες, οὔτ᾽ ἂν ἕνα
ἐφοβεῖσθε νῦν οὔτε ἐν ἑνὶ τὰς ἐλπίδας εἴχετε."
Πομπηΐου δὲ εἰπόντος μαντικώτερα μὲν εἰρῆσθαι
Κάτωνι, φιλικώτερα δὲ αὐτῷ πεπρᾶχθαι, συνεβούλευεν ὁ Κάτων ἑνὶ Πομπηΐῳ τὰ πράγματα
τὴν σύγκλητον ἐγχειρίσαι· τῶν γὰρ αὐτῶν εἶναι
3 καὶ ποιεῖν τὰ μεγάλα κακὰ καὶ παύειν. ὁ μὲν
οὖν Πομπήϊος οὔτε δύναμιν ἔχων ἑτοίμην οὔτε οὓς
κατέλεγε τότε προθύμους ὁρῶν ἐξέλιπε τὴν Ῥώμην, ὁ δὲ Κάτων ἕπεσθαι καὶ συμφεύγειν ἐγνωκὼς
τὸν μὲν νεώτερον υἱὸν εἰς Βρεττίους ὑπεξέθετο
πρὸς Μουνάτιον, τὸν δὲ πρεσβύτερον εἶχε σὺν
ἑαυτῷ. τῆς δὲ οἰκίας καὶ τῶν θυγατέρων κηδε-

or else that Caesar should not do so either, "Now" shouted Cato, "those things are come to pass which I foretold to you, and the man is at last resorting to open compulsion, using the forces which he got by deceiving and cheating the state." Outside the senate-house, however, Cato could accomplish nothing, since the people wished all along that Caesar should have the chief power; and although Cato had the senate under his influence, it was afraid of the people.

LII. But when Ariminum was occupied[1] and Caesar was reported to be marching against the city with an army, then all eyes were turned upon Cato, both those of the common people and those of Pompey as well; they realised that he alone had from the outset foreseen, and first openly foretold, the designs of Caesar. Cato therefore said: "Nay, men, if any of you had heeded what I was ever foretelling and advising, ye would now neither be fearing a single man nor putting your hopes in a single man." Pompey acknowledged that Cato had spoken more like a prophet, while he himself had acted too much like a friend. Cato then advised the senate to put affairs into the hands of Pompey alone; for the same men who caused great evils, he said, should put a stop to them. Pompey, however, who had no forces in readiness, and saw that those which he was then enrolling were without zeal, forsook Rome; and Cato, who had determined to follow him and share his exile, sent his younger son to Munatius in Bruttium for safe keeping, but kept his elder son with himself. And since his household and his daughters needed someone to

[1] In 49 B.C. Cf. the *Caesar*, xxxii. *fin.*; the *Pompey*, lx. 1.

μόνος δεομένων ἀνέλαβε πάλιν τὴν Μαρκίαν
χηρεύουσαν ἐπὶ χρήμασι πολλοῖς· ὁ γὰρ Ὁρτή-
4 σιος θνήσκων ἐκείνην ἀπέλιπε κληρονόμον. εἰς ὃ
δὴ μάλιστα λοιδορούμενος ὁ Καῖσαρ τῷ Κάτωνι
φιλοπλουτίαν προφέρει καὶ μισθαρνίαν ἐπὶ τῷ
γάμῳ. τί γὰρ ἔδει παραχωρεῖν δεόμενον γυναικὸς ἢ τί μὴ δεόμενον αὖθις ἀναλαμβάνειν, εἰ μὴ
δέλεαρ ἐξ ἀρχῆς ὑφείθη τὸ γύναιον Ὁρτησίῳ καὶ
νέαν ἔχρησεν, ἵνα πλουσίαν ἀπολάβῃ; πρὸς μὲν
οὖν ταῦτα μετρίως ἔχει τὸ Εὐριπίδειον ἐκεῖνο·

> πρῶτον μὲν οὖν τἄρρητ'· ἐν ἀρρήτοισι γὰρ   785
> τὴν σὴν νομίζω δειλίαν, ὦ Ἡράκλεις·

5 ὅμοιον γάρ ἐστι τῷ Ἡρακλεῖ μαλακίαν ὀνειδίζειν
καὶ κατηγορεῖν αἰσχροκέρδειαν Κάτωνος. εἰ δὲ
ἄλλη πη μὴ καλῶς πέπρακται τὰ περὶ τὸν γάμον,
ἐπισκεπτέον. ἐγγυησάμενος γὰρ τὴν Μαρκίαν ὁ
Κάτων, καὶ τὸν οἶκον ἐπιτρέψας ἐκείνῃ καὶ τὰς
θυγατέρας, αὐτὸς ἐδίωκε Πομπήιον.

LIII. Ἀπ' ἐκείνης δὲ λέγεται τῆς ἡμέρας μήτε
κεφαλὴν ἔτι κείρασθαι μήτε γένεια μήτε στέφανον
ἐπιθέσθαι, πένθους δὲ καὶ κατηφείας καὶ βαρύτη-
τος ἐπὶ ταῖς συμφοραῖς τῆς πατρίδος ἐν σχῆμα
νικώντων ὁμοίως καὶ νικωμένων ἄχρι τελευτῆς
διαφυλάξαι. τότε δὲ κλήρῳ λαχὼν Σικελίαν
διέβη μὲν εἰς Συρακούσας, πυθόμενος δὲ Ἀσίννιον Πολλίωνα παρὰ τῶν πολεμίων ἀφῖχθαι μετὰ

look after them, he took to wife again Marcia, now a widow with great wealth; for Hortensius, on his death,[1] had left her his heir It was with reference to this that Caesar heaped most abuse upon Cato,[2] charging him with avarice and with trafficking in marriage. "For why," said Caesar, "should Cato give up his wife if he wanted her, or why, if he did not want her, should he take her back again? Unless it was true that the woman was at the first set as a bait for Hortensius, and lent by Cato when she was young that he might take her back when she was rich." To these charges, however, the well-known verses of Euripides[3] apply very well :—

"First, then, the things not to be named; for in that class
  I reckon, Heracles, all cowardice in thee;"

for to charge Cato with a sordid love of gain is like reproaching Heracles with cowardice. But whether on other grounds, perhaps, the marriage was improper, were matter for investigation. For no sooner had Cato espoused Marcia than he committed to her care his household and his daughters, and set out himself in pursuit of Pompey.

LIII. But from that day, as we are told, Cato neither cut his hair nor trimmed his beard nor put on a garland, but maintained the same mien of sorrow, dejection, and heaviness of spirit in view of the calamities of his country, alike in victory and in defeat, until the end. At the time, however, having had Sicily allotted to him as a province, he crossed over to Syracuse, and on learning that Asinius Pollio had come

[1] In 50 B.C. Cf. chapter xxv.
[2] In his treatise entitled "Anti-Cato." Cf. chapter xi. 4.
[3] *Hercules Furens*, 173 f. (Kirchhoff).

δυνάμεως εἰς Μεσσήνην ἔπεμψε, λόγον ἀπαιτῶν
2 παρ' αὐτοῦ τῆς διαβάσεως. ἀνταπαιτηθεὶς δὲ
λόγον ὑπ' ἐκείνου τῆς τῶν πραγμάτων μεταβολῆς,
καὶ Πομπήιον ἀκούσας ἐκλελοιπότα παντελῶς
Ἰταλίαν ἐν Δυρραχίῳ στρατοπεδεύειν, πολὺν ἔφη
περὶ τὰ θεῖα πλάνον εἶναι καὶ ἀσάφειαν, εἰ Πομπήιον ἐν οἷς ὑγιὲς οὐδὲν οὐδὲ δίκαιον ἔπραττεν
ἀήττητον γενόμενον νῦν, ὅτε τὴν πατρίδα βούλεται σώζειν καὶ τῆς ἐλευθερίας ὑπερμάχεται,
3 προλέλοιπε τὸ εὐτυχεῖν. Ἀσίννιον μὲν οὖν ἔφη
δυνατὸς εἶναι Σικελίας ἐκβαλεῖν, ἄλλης δὲ μείζονος ἐπερχομένης δυνάμεως οὐ βούλεσθαι τὴν
νῆσον ἐμπολεμῶν ἀπολέσαι, χωρεῖν δὲ πρὸς τὸ
κρατοῦν καὶ σώζεσθαι παραινέσας Συρακουσίοις
ἐξέπλευσεν.

Ἀφικόμενος δὲ πρὸς Πομπήιον ἀεὶ μὲν εἴχετο
μιᾶς γνώμης, χρονοτριβεῖν τὸν πόλεμον, ἐλπίζων
διαλύσεις καὶ μὴ βουλόμενος ἐν ἀγῶνι χείρω
γενομένην τὴν πόλιν αὐτὴν ὑφ' αὑτῆς παθεῖν τὰ
4 ἔσχατα, σιδήρῳ διακριθεῖσαν. ἄλλα δὲ τούτων
ἀδελφὰ Πομπήιον ἔπεισε καὶ τοὺς συνέδρους ψηφίσασθαι, μήτε πόλιν ὑπήκοον Ῥωμαίων διαρ-
πάζειν μήτε ἄνδρα Ῥωμαῖον ἔξω παρατάξεως
ἀναιρεῖν· ἃ καὶ δόξαν ἤνεγκε καὶ προσηγάγετο
πολλοὺς τῇ Πομπηίου μερίδι, τὴν ἐπιείκειαν
αὐτοῦ καὶ τὸ ἥμερον ἀσπασαμένους.

LIV. Ἐκπεμφθεὶς δὲ εἰς Ἀσίαν, ὡς τοῖς ἐκεῖ
συνάγουσι πλοῖα καὶ στρατιὰν ὠφέλιμος γένοιτο,
Σερβιλίαν ἐπηγάγετο τὴν ἀδελφὴν καὶ τὸ Λευ-
κούλλου παιδίον ἐξ ἐκείνης γεγονός. ἠκολούθησε

to Messana with a force from the enemy, he sent and demanded a reason for his coming. But having been asked by Pollio in turn a reason for the convulsion in the state, and hearing that Pompey had abandoned Italy altogether, and was encamped at Dyrrhachium, he remarked that there was much inconsistency and obscurity in the divine government, since Pompey had been invincible while his course was neither sound nor just, but now, when he wished to save his country and was fighting in defence of liberty, he had been deserted by his good fortune. As for Asinius, indeed, Cato said he was able to drive him out of Sicily; but since another and a larger force was coming to his aid, he did not wish to ruin the island by involving it in war, and therefore, after advising the Syracusans to seek safety by joining the victorious party, he sailed away.

After he had come to Pompey, he was ever of one mind, namely, to protract the war; for he looked with hope to a settlement of the controversy, and did not wish that the state should be worsted in a struggle and suffer at its own hands the extreme of disaster, in having its fate decided by the sword. Other measures, too, akin to this, he persuaded Pompey and his council to adopt, namely, not to plunder a city that was subject to Rome, and not to put a Roman to death except on the field of battle. This brought to the party of Pompey a good repute, and induced many to join it; they were delighted with his reasonableness and mildness.

LIV. When Cato was dispatched to Asia, that he might help those who were collecting transports and soldiers there, he took with him Servilia his sister and her young child by Lucullus. For Servilia had

γὰρ αὐτῷ χηρεύουσα, καὶ πολὺ τῶν εἰς τὸ ἀκόλαστον αὐτῆς διαβολῶν ἀφεῖλεν ὑποδῦσα τὴν
ὑπὸ Κάτωνι φρουρὰν καὶ πλάνην καὶ δίαιταν
2 ἑκουσίως. ἀλλ᾽ ὅ γε Καῖσαρ οὐδὲ τῶν ἐπ᾽ ἐκείνῃ
βλασφημιῶν τοῦ Κάτωνος ἐφείσατο.

Πρὸς μὲν οὖν τἆλλα τοῦ Κάτωνος οὐδέν, ὡς
ἔοικεν, ἐδεήθησαν οἱ Πομπηΐου στρατηγοί, Ῥοδίους δὲ πειθοῖ προσαγαγόμενος καὶ τὴν Σερβιλίαν αὐτόθι καὶ τὸ παιδίον ἀπολιπὼν ἐπανῆλθε
πρὸς Πομπήϊον, ἤδη πεζικῆς τε λαμπρᾶς καὶ
3 ναυτικῆς δυνάμεως περὶ αὐτὸν οὔσης. ἔνθα δὴ
καὶ μάλιστα τῆς γνώμης κατάφωρος ἔδοξε γεγονέναι Πομπήϊος. ὥρμησε μὲν γὰρ ἐγχειρίσαι τῷ
Κάτωνι τὴν τῶν νεῶν ἡγεμονίαν· ἦσαν δὲ πεντακοσίων μὲν οὐκ ἐλάττους αἱ μάχιμοι, λιβυρνικὰ
δὲ καὶ κατασκοπικὰ καὶ ἄφρακτα παμπληθῆ·
4 ταχὺ δὲ ἐννοήσας ἢ διδαχθεὶς ὑπὸ τῶν φίλων
ὡς ἕν ἐστι κεφάλαιον Κάτωνι πάσης πολιτείας
ἐλευθερῶσαι τὴν πατρίδα, κἂν γένηται κύριος
τηλικαύτης δυνάμεως, ἧς ἂν ἡμέρας καταγωνί-
σωνται Καίσαρα, τῆς αὐτῆς ἐκείνης ἀξιώσει καὶ
Πομπήϊον τὰ ὅπλα καταθέσθαι καὶ τοῖς νόμοις
ἕπεσθαι, μετέγνω, καίπερ ἤδη διειλεγμένος αὐτῷ,
5 καὶ Βύβλον ἀπέδειξε ναύαρχον. οὐ μὴν ᾔσθετό
γε παρὰ τοῦτο τῆς προθυμίας τοῦ Κάτωνος ἀμ-
βλυτέρας· ἀλλὰ καὶ λέγεται πρός τινα μάχην
πρὸ τοῦ Δυρραχίου αὐτοῦ τε Πομπηΐου παρορ-   786
μῶντος τὴν δύναμιν, καὶ τῶν ἄλλων ἕκαστον
ἡγεμόνων εἰπεῖν τι καὶ προτρέψασθαι κελεύοντος,
ἀργῶς καὶ σιωπῇ τοὺς στρατιώτας ἀκούειν, Κά-

followed Cato, now that she was a widow, and had put an end to much of the evil report about her dissolute conduct [1] by submitting to Cato's guardianship and sharing his wanderings and his ways of life of her own accord. But Caesar [2] did not spare abuse of Cato even on the score of his relations with Servilia.

Now, in other ways, as it would seem, Pompey's commanders in Asia had no need of Cato, and therefore, after persuading Rhodes into allegiance, he left Servilia and her child there, and returned to Pompey, who now had a splendid naval and military force assembled. Here, indeed, and most clearly, Pompey was thought to have made his opinion of Cato manifest. For he determined to put the command of his fleet into the hands of Cato, and there were no less than five hundred fighting ships, besides Liburnian craft, look-out ships, and open boats in great numbers. But he soon perceived, or was shown by his friends, that the one chief object of Cato's public services was the liberty of his country, and that if he should be made master of so large a force, the very day of Caesar's defeat would find Cato demanding that Pompey also lay down his arms and obey the laws. Pompey therefore changed his mind, although he had already conferred with Cato about the matter, and appointed Bibulus admiral. Notwithstanding, he did not find that in consequence of this the zeal of Cato was blunted; nay, it is even said that when Pompey himself was trying to incite his forces to a battle before Dyrrhachium, and bidding each of the other commanders to say something to inspire the men, the soldiers listened to them sluggishly and in silence;

[1] Cf. chapter xxiv. 3.
[2] In his "Anti-Cato." Cf. chapter xi. 4.

τωνος δὲ μετὰ πάντας ὅσα καιρὸν εἶχε τῶν ἀπὸ
φιλοσοφίας ἀκούειν λεγομένων περὶ ἐλευθερίας
καὶ ἀρετῆς καὶ θανάτου καὶ δόξης διελθόντος
6 αὐτοπαθῶς, καὶ τελευτῶντα τρέψαντος τὸν λόγον
εἰς θεῶν ἀνάκλησιν, ὡς παρόντων καὶ ἐφορώντων
τὸν ὑπὲρ τῆς πατρίδος ἀγῶνα, τηλικοῦτον ἀλα-
λαγμὸν γενέσθαι καὶ τοσοῦτον κίνημα τῆς στρατιᾶς ἐπαρθείσης ὥστε πάντας ἐλπίδων μεστοὺς
ἐπὶ τὸν κίνδυνον ὁρμῆσαι τοὺς ἡγεμόνας. τρεψα-
μένων δὲ καὶ κρατησάντων ἀφείλετο τὴν παντελῆ
νίκην ὁ Καίσαρος δαίμων, τῇ Πομπηΐου χρησάμενος εὐλαβείᾳ καὶ ἀπιστίᾳ περὶ τὸ εὐτύχημα.
7 ταῦτα μὲν οὖν ἐν τοῖς περὶ Πομπηΐου γέγραπται.
χαιρόντων δὲ πάντων καὶ μεγαλυνόντων τὸ
ἔργον ὁ Κάτων ἀπεδάκρυε τὴν πατρίδα, καὶ τὴν
ὀλέθριον καὶ κακοδαίμονα φιλαρχίαν ὠδύρετο,
πολλοὺς καὶ ἀγαθοὺς ὁρῶν πολίτας ὑπ' ἀλλήλων
πεπτωκότας.

LV. Ἐπεὶ δὲ Καίσαρα διώκων Πομπήϊος εἰς
Θεσσαλίαν ἀνεζεύγνυε πολλὰ καταλιπὼν περὶ
Δυρράχιον ὅπλα καὶ χρήματα καὶ σώματα συγ-
γενῆ καὶ οἰκεῖα, πάντων ἀπέδειξεν ἡγεμόνα καὶ
φύλακα τὸν Κάτωνα πεντεκαίδεκα σπείρας ἔχοντα
στρατιωτῶν διὰ πίστιν ἅμα καὶ φόβον τοῦ ἀνδρός. ἡττωμένῳ μὲν γὰρ πάντων εἶναι βεβαιό-
τατον ἐνόμιζεν, εἰ δὲ νικῴη, μὴ ἐπιτρέψειν παρόντα χρήσασθαι τοῖς πράγμασιν ὡς προῄρηται.
2 πολλοὶ δὲ καὶ τῶν ἐπιφανῶν ἀνδρῶν ἀπερρίφη-
σαν ἐν Δυρραχίῳ μετὰ Κάτωνος.

Γενομένης δὲ τῆς κατὰ Φάρσαλον ἥττης οὕτως
ἔστη τοῖς λογισμοῖς ὁ Κάτων ὥς, εἰ μὲν τεθνήκοι

but that when Cato, after all the other speakers, had rehearsed with genuine emotion all the appropriate sentiments to be drawn from philosophy concerning freedom, virtue, death and fame, and finally passed into an invocation of the gods as eye-witnesses of their struggle in behalf of their country, there was such a shouting and so great a stir among the soldiers thus aroused that all the commanders were full of hope as they hastened to confront the peril. They overcame and routed their enemies, but were robbed of a complete and perfect victory by the good genius of Caesar, which took advantage of Pompey's caution and distrust of his good fortune. These details, however, have been given in the Life of Pompey.[1] But while all the rest were rejoicing and magnifying their achievement, Cato was weeping for his country, and bewailing the love of power that had brought such misfortune and destruction, as he saw that many brave citizens had fallen by one another's hands.

LV. When Pompey, in pursuit of Caesar, was breaking camp to march into Thessaly, he left behind him at Dyrrhachium a great quantity of arms and stores, and many kindred and friends, and over all these he appointed Cato commander and guardian, with fifteen cohorts of soldiers, because he both trusted and feared him. For in case of defeat, he thought that Cato would be his surest support, but in case of a victory, that he would not, if present, permit him to manage matters as he chose. Many prominent men were also ignored by Pompey and left behind at Dyrrhachium with Cato.

When the defeat at Pharsalus came, Cato resolved that, if Pompey were dead, he would take over to

---

[1] Chapter lxv. Cf. the *Caesar*, xxxix.

Πομπήϊος, εἰς Ἰταλίαν τοὺς σὺν αὐτῷ περαιώ-
σων, αὐτὸς δὲ πορρωτάτω τῆς τυραννίδος ἐπὶ
φυγῇ βιωσόμενος· εἰ δὲ σώζοιτο, πάντως ἐκείνῳ
3 διαφυλάξων τὴν δύναμιν. οὕτω δὴ διαβαλὼν εἰς
Κέρκυραν, ὅπου τὸ ναυτικὸν ἦν, ἐξίστατο μὲν
Κικέρωνι τῆς ἀρχῆς ὡς ὑπατικῷ στρατηγικός,
οὐ δεξαμένου δὲ Κικέρωνος, ἀλλ' ἀπαίροντος εἰς
Ἰταλίαν, ἰδὼν τὸν Πομπήϊον ὑπ' αὐθαδείας καὶ
φρονήματος ἀκαίρου βουλόμενον κολάζειν τοὺς
ἀποπλέοντας, πρώτῳ δὲ μέλλοντα τῷ Κικέρωνι
προσφέρειν τὰς χεῖρας, ἐνουθέτησεν ἰδίᾳ καὶ κατεπράϋνεν, ὥστε τὸν Κικέρωνα περισῶσαι σαφῶς
ἐκ θανάτου καὶ τοῖς ἄλλοις ἄδειαν παρασχεῖν.

LVI. Τεκμαιρόμενος δὲ Πομπήϊον Μάγνον εἰς
Αἴγυπτον ἢ Λιβύην διεκπεσεῖσθαι καὶ σπεύδων
πρὸς ἐκεῖνον ἀνήχθη μὲν ἔχων ἅπαντας, ἔπλει δὲ
πρῶτον ἀπιέναι διδοὺς καὶ ὑπολείπεσθαι τοὺς οὐ
προθύμως συστρατευομένους. ἁψάμενος δὲ Λιβύης καὶ παραπλέων ἐντυγχάνει Σέξτῳ τῷ νεω-
τέρῳ τῶν Πομπήϊου παίδων ἀγγέλλοντι τὴν ἐπ'
2 Αἰγύπτου τοῦ πατρὸς τελευτήν. πάντες μὲν οὖν
βαρέως ἤνεγκαν, οὐδεὶς δὲ μετὰ Πομπήϊον ἠξίου
Κάτωνος παρόντος οὐδὲ ἀκούειν ἄλλον ἡγεμόνα.
διὸ καὶ Κάτων αἰδούμενος καὶ οἰκτείρων ἄνδρας
ἀγαθοὺς καὶ πίστεως δεδωκότας πεῖραν ἐπὶ ξένης
ἐρήμους καὶ ἀπόρους ἀπολιπεῖν, ὑπέστη τε τὴν
ἀρχὴν καὶ παρῆλθεν εἰς Κυρήνην· ἐδέξαντο γὰρ

Italy those who were with him, but would himself live in exile as far as possible from the tyranny of Caesar; if, on the contrary, Pompey were alive, he would by all means keep his forces intact for him. Accordingly, having crossed over to Corcyra, where the fleet was, he offered to give up the command to Cicero, who was of consular rank, while he himself had been only a praetor. But Cicero would not accept the command, and set out for Italy. Then Cato, seeing that the younger Pompey[1] was led by his obstinacy and unseasonable pride into a desire to punish all those who were about to sail away, and was going to lay violent hands on Cicero first of all, admonished him in private and calmed him down, thus manifestly saving Cicero from death and procuring immunity for the rest.

LVI. Conjecturing, now, that Pompey the Great would make his escape into Egypt or Libya, and being eager to join him, Cato put to sea with all his company and sailed away, after first giving those who had no eagerness for the expedition leave to depart and remain behind. After reaching Libya, and while sailing along its coast, he fell in with Sextus, the younger son of Pompey, who told him of his father's death in Egypt. All, of course, were deeply distressed, but no one, now that Pompey was gone, would even listen to any other commander while Cato was at hand. For this reason also Cato, who had compassion on men who were brave and had given proof of fidelity, and was ashamed to leave them helpless and destitute in a foreign land, undertook the command, and went along the coast to Cyrene, the people of which received him kindly,

[1] Gnaeus Pompey, the elder son of Pompey the Great. Cf. chapter lix. 5.

ἐκεῖνον, ὀλίγαις ἡμέραις ἔμπροσθεν ἀποκλείσαν-
3 τες Λαβιηνόν. ἐνταῦθα πυνθανόμενος Σκηπίωνα
τὸν Πομπηίου πενθερὸν ὑπὸ Ἰόβα τοῦ βασιλέως
ἀνειλῆφθαι, καὶ Οὔαρον Ἄττιον, ὃς ἦν ὑπὸ Πομπηίου Λιβύης ἀποδεδειγμένος ἡγεμών, εἶναι σὺν
αὐτοῖς μετὰ δυνάμεως, ἐξώρμησε πεζῇ χειμῶνος
ὥρᾳ, πολλοὺς μὲν ὄνους ὕδωρ κομίζοντας συναγα-   787
γών, πολλὴν δὲ λείαν ἐλαύνων, ἔτι δὲ ἅρματα καὶ
τοὺς καλουμένους Ψύλλους ἐπαγόμενος, οἳ τά τε
δήγματα τῶν θηρίων ἰῶνται τοῖς στόμασιν ἕλκοντες τὸν ἰόν, αὐτά τε τὰ θηρία κατεπᾴδοντες
4 ἀμβλύνουσι καὶ κηλοῦσιν. ἡμέρας δὲ συνεχῶς
ἑπτὰ τῆς πορείας γενομένης πρῶτος ἡγήσατο
μήτε ἵππῳ μήτε ὑποζυγίῳ χρησάμενος. ἐδείπνει
δὲ καθήμενος ἀφ᾽ ἧς ἡμέρας τὴν κατὰ Φάρσαλον
ἧτταν ἔγνω· καὶ τοῦτο τῷ λοιπῷ προσέθηκε πέν-
θει, τὸ μὴ κατακλιθῆναι πλὴν καθεύδων. ἐν δὲ
Λιβύῃ διαγαγὼν τοῦ χειμῶνος ἐξήγαγε τὴν στρα-
τιάν· ἦσαν δὲ μυρίων ὀλίγον ἀποδέοντες.

LVII. Τὰ δὲ πράγματα κακῶς εἶχε τοῖς περὶ
Σκηπίωνα καὶ Οὔαρον, ἐκ διαφορᾶς καὶ στάσεως
ὑποδυομένοις καὶ θεραπεύουσι τὸν Ἰόβαν, οὐκ
ἀνεκτὸν ὄντα βαρύτητι φρονήματος καὶ ὄγκῳ διὰ
πλοῦτον καὶ δύναμιν· ὅς γε Κάτωνι πρῶτον ἐντυγχάνειν μέλλων μέσον ἔθηκε τὸν ἑαυτοῦ θρόνον
2 τοῦ Σκηπίωνος καὶ τοῦ Κάτωνος. ὁ μέντοι Κάτων

---

[1] Now a partisan of Pompey, and a fugitive from Pharsalus.
Cf. the *Caesar*, xxxiv. 2.   [2] Cf. Herodotus, iv. 173.

although a few days before they had closed their
gates against Labienus.[1] There he learned that
Scipio, the father-in-law of Pompey, had been well
received by Juba the king, and that Attius Varus,
who had been appointed governor of Libya by Pompey, was with them at the head of an army. Cato
therefore set out thither by land in the winter season,
having got together a great number of asses to carry
water, and driving along with him many cattle. Besides, he took with him chariots, and the people called
Psylli.[2] These cure the bites of serpents by sucking
out the venom, and charm and deaden the serpents
themselves by means of incantations. Though the
march lasted for seven days consecutively, Cato led
at the head of his force, without using either horse
or beast of burden. Moreover, he used to sup in a
sitting posture from the day when he learned of the
defeat at Pharsalus; yes, this token of sorrow he
added to others, and would not lie down except
when sleeping. After finishing the winter in Libya,
he led forth his army;[3] and it numbered nearly ten
thousand.

LVII. But matters were in a bad way with Scipio
and Varus. Their dissension and quarrelling led them
to pay court to Juba in efforts to win his favour, and
the king was unendurable for the severity of his
temper and for the arrogance which his wealth and
power gave him. When he was going to have an
interview with Cato for the first time, he placed his
own seat between that of Scipio and that of Cato.
Cato, however, when he saw the arrangement, took

---

[3] The text of this sentence is uncertain: Sintenis and
Bekker assume a lacuna. Libya means here the Roman
province of Africa.

ὡς εἶδεν, ἄρας τὸν ἑαυτοῦ μετέθηκεν ἐπὶ θάτερα,
μέσον λαμβάνων τὸν Σκηπίωνα, καίπερ ἐχθρὸν
ὄντα καί τι καὶ βιβλίον ἐκδεδωκότα βλασφημίας
ἔχον τοῦ Κάτωνος. εἶτα τοῦτο μὲν εἰς οὐδένα
τίθενται λόγον, εἰ δὲ Φιλόστρατον ἐν Σικελίᾳ
μέσον εἶχε περιπατῶν ἐπὶ τιμῇ φιλοσοφίας,
ἐγκαλοῦσι. τότε δ' οὖν καὶ τὸν Ἰόβαν ἔπαυσε
μονονουχὶ σατράπας πεποιημένον ἑαυτοῦ τοὺς
3 περὶ τὸν Σκηπίωνα, κἀκείνους διήλλαξεν. ἀξιούντων δὲ πάντων ἄρχειν αὐτόν, καὶ πρώτων τῶν
περὶ Σκηπίωνα καὶ Οὔαρον ἐξισταμένων καὶ
παραδιδόντων τὴν ἡγεμονίαν, οὐκ ἔφη καταλύσειν
τοὺς νόμους περὶ ὧν τῷ καταλύοντι πολεμοῦσιν,
οὐδὲ ἑαυτὸν ἀντιστράτηγον ὄντα παρόντος ἀνθυ-
πάτου προτάξειν. ἀνθύπατος γὰρ ὁ Σκηπίων
ἀπεδέδεικτο, καὶ θάρσος εἶχον οἱ πολλοὶ διὰ τοὔ-
νομα, κατορθώσειν ἄρχοντος ἐν Λιβύῃ Σκηπίωνος.

LVIII. Ἐπεὶ μέντοι τὴν ἀρχὴν ὁ Σκηπίων
παραλαβὼν εὐθὺς ἐβούλετο Ἰόβᾳ χαριζόμενος
Ἰτυκαίους ἡβηδὸν ἀποκτεῖναι καὶ κατασκάψαι
τὴν πόλιν ὡς τὰ Καίσαρος φρονοῦσαν, οὐχ ὑπέμεινεν ὁ Κάτων, ἀλλὰ μαρτυρόμενος καὶ κεκραγὼς
ἐν τῷ συνεδρίῳ καὶ θεοκλυτῶν μόλις ἐξείλετο τῆς
2 ὠμότητος αὐτῶν τοὺς ἀνθρώπους· καὶ τὰ μὲν
αὐτῶν δεηθέντων, τὰ δὲ τοῦ Σκηπίωνος ἀξιοῦντος,
ἀνεδέξατο φρουρήσειν τὴν πόλιν, ὡς μήτε ἄκουσα
μήτε ἑκοῦσα Καίσαρι προσγένοιτο. καὶ γὰρ ἦν
εἰς ἅπαντα τὸ χωρίον ὠφέλιμον καὶ διαρκὲς

374

up his own seat and moved it over to the other side, thus placing Scipio in the middle, although Scipio was an enemy, and had published a book which contained abuse of Cato. And yet there are those who give Cato no credit for this, although they censure him because, in Sicily, as he was walking about with Philostratus, he placed him in the middle, to show his respect for philosophy. But at the time of which I speak, Cato actually put a check upon Juba, who had all but made Scipio and Varus his satraps, and reconciled the two Romans. And though all thought it meet that he should have the command, especially Scipio and Varus, who resigned and tendered to him the leadership, he refused to break the laws to support which they were waging war with one who broke them, nor, when a pro-consul was present, would he put himself, who was only a propraetor, above him. For Scipio had been made proconsul, and the greater part of the army were emboldened by his name; they thought that they would be successful if a Scipio had command in Africa.

LVIII. When Scipio, however, after assuming the command, straightway desired to gratify Juba by putting all the people of Utica to death and demolishing their city, on the ground that it favoured the cause of Caesar, Cato would not suffer it, but by adjurations and loud outcries in the council, and by invoking the gods, with difficulty rescued the people from this cruelty; and partly at the request of the people, and partly at the instance of Scipio, he undertook to watch over the city, that it might not, either willingly or unwillingly, attach itself to Caesar. For the place was in every way advantageous for

τοῖς ἔχουσιν· ἔτι δὲ μᾶλλον ὑπὸ τοῦ Κάτωνος
ἐρρώσθη. καὶ γὰρ σῖτον εἰσήγαγεν ὑπερβάλλοντα
πλήθει καὶ κατεσκεύαζε τὰ τείχη πύργους ἐπαιρό-
μενος καὶ τάφρους ὀχυρὰς καὶ χαρακώματα πρὸ
3 τῆς πόλεως βαλλόμενος. Ἰτυκαίων δὲ τοὺς μὲν
ἡβῶντας ἐν τοῖς χαρακώμασιν ἔταξεν οἰκεῖν, τὰ
ὅπλα παραδόντας αὐτῷ, τοὺς δὲ ἄλλους ἐν τῇ
πόλει συνεῖχεν, ἰσχυρῶς ἐπιμελόμενος μὴ ἀδι-
κεῖσθαι μηδὲ πάσχειν κακῶς ὑπὸ τῶν Ῥωμαίων.
ὅπλα δὲ πολλὰ καὶ χρήματα καὶ σῖτον ἐξέπεμψε
τοῖς ἐπὶ στρατοπέδου, καὶ ὅλως εἶχε τοῦ πολέμου
4 τὴν πόλιν ταμιεῖον. ἃ δὲ Πομπηΐῳ συνεβούλευε
πρότερον καὶ τότε Σκηπίωνι, μὴ μάχεσθαι πρὸς
ἄνδρα πολεμιστὴν καὶ δεινόν, ἀλλὰ τῷ χρόνῳ
χρῆσθαι πᾶσαν ἀκμὴν ᾗ τυραννὶς ἰσχύει μαραί-
νοντι, τούτων ὁ Σκηπίων ὑπὸ αὐθαδείας κατε-
φρόνει· καί ποτε τῷ Κάτωνι δειλίαν ὀνειδίζων
ἔγραψεν, εἰ μὴ μόνον αὐτὸς ἀγαπᾷ καθήμενος ἐν
πόλει καὶ τείχεσιν, ἀλλὰ μηδὲ ἑτέρους ἐᾷ πρὸς
τὸν καιρὸν εὐθαρσῶς χρῆσθαι τοῖς λογισμοῖς.
5 πρὸς ταῦτα ὁ Κάτων ἀντέγραψεν ὡς ἕτοιμός
ἐστιν οὓς ἤγαγεν αὐτὸς εἰς Λιβύην ὁπλίτας καὶ
ἱππεῖς παραλαβὼν εἰς Ἰταλίαν περαιοῦν, καὶ
Καίσαρα μεθιστάναι καὶ τρέπειν ἀπ' ἐκείνων 788
πρὸς αὑτόν. ὡς δὲ καὶ τούτων ὁ Σκηπίων κατε-
γέλα, πάνυ δῆλος ἦν ἀχθόμενος ὁ Κάτων τῇ
παραχωρήσει τῆς ἀρχῆς, ὡς οὔτε τῷ πολέμῳ
καλῶς τὸν Σκηπίωνα χρησόμενον, οὔτε, ἂν παραλόγως εὐτυχήσῃ, μέτριον ἐν τῷ κρατεῖν πρὸς τοὺς

those who held it, and fully capable of defence; and it was still further strengthened by Cato. For he brought in a great abundance of grain, and perfected the walls by building towers and by running formidable trenches and palisades in front of the city. To the men of Utica who were of military age he assigned the palisades for quarters, and made them give up their arms to him; the rest he kept together in the city, taking great pains that they should not be wronged or suffer harm at the hands of the Romans. Moreover, he sent out great quantities of arms and stores and grain to the Romans in their camp, and, in a word, made the city a store-house for the war. But as for the advice which he had given Pompey before and now gave Scipio, namely, not to give battle to a man who was versed in war and of formidable ability, but to trust to time, which withers away all the vigour which is the strength of tyranny, —this advice Scipio, out of obstinate self-will, despised. And once he wrote to Cato reproaching him with cowardice, seeing that he was not only well content to sit quietly in a walled city himself, but would not even allow others to carry out their plans with boldness as opportunity offered. To this Cato wrote in reply that he was ready to take the legionaries and the horsemen whom he himself had brought to Libya and cross the sea with them to Italy, thus forcing Caesar to change his plan of campaign, and turning him away from Scipio and Varus against himself. When Scipio mocked at this also, it was very clear that Cato was distressed at having declined the command, being convinced that Scipio would neither conduct the war well, nor, in case he should have unexpected good fortune behave with moder-

6 πολίτας ἐσόμενον. διὸ καὶ γνώμην εἶχεν ὁ Κάτων,
καὶ πρὸς τοὺς συνήθεις ἔλεγεν, οὐ χρηστὰς μὲν
ἐλπίδας ἔχειν ὑπὲρ τοῦ πολέμου δι' ἀπειρίαν καὶ
θρασύτητα τῶν ἡγεμόνων, εἰ δ' οὖν εὐτυχία τις
γένοιτο καὶ καταλυθείη Καῖσαρ, οὐ μενεῖν ἐν
Ῥώμῃ, φεύξεσθαι δὲ τὴν χαλεπότητα καὶ πικρίαν
τοῦ Σκηπίωνος, ἤδη τότε δεινὰς καὶ ὑπερηφάνους
ποιουμένου κατὰ πολλῶν ἀπειλάς.

7 Ἀπέβη δὲ μᾶλλον ἢ προσεδόκα· καὶ περὶ
ἑσπέραν βαθεῖαν ἧκέ τις ἀπὸ στρατοπέδου τρι-
ταῖος ἀγγέλλων ὅτι μάχης μεγάλης πρὸς Θάψῳ
γενομένης διέφθαρται παντάπασι τὰ πράγματα
καὶ κρατεῖ Καῖσαρ τῶν στρατοπέδων, Σκηπίων
δὲ καὶ Ἰόβας σὺν ὀλίγοις ἐκπεφεύγασιν, ἡ δὲ
ἄλλη δύναμις ἀπόλωλε.

LIX. Τούτων προσπεσόντων ἡ μὲν πόλις, οἷον
εἰκὸς ἐν νυκτὶ καὶ πολέμῳ, πρὸς τοιοῦτον ἄγγελμα
μικροῦ δεῖν ἔκφρων γενομένη μόλις ἑαυτὴν ἐντὸς
τειχῶν κατεῖχεν, ὁ δὲ Κάτων προελθὼν τότε μέν,
ὡς ἑκάστοις ἀπήντα διαθέουσι καὶ βοῶσιν, ἐπι-
λαμβανόμενος καὶ παραμυθούμενος ἀφῄρει τοῦ
δέους τὸ περιθαμβὲς καὶ ταραχῶδες, ὡς οὐ τηλικούτων ἴσως γεγονότων, ἀλλὰ ἐπὶ μεῖζον αἰρο-
μένων τῷ λόγῳ, καὶ κατέστησε τὸν θόρυβον·

2 ἅμα δ' ἡμέρᾳ τοὺς τριακοσίους οἷς ἐχρῆτο βουλῇ,
Ῥωμαίους μὲν ὄντας, ἐν δὲ Λιβύῃ πραγματευομέ-

ation towards his fellow citizens in the hour of victory. Therefore Cato made up his mind, and said to his intimate friends, that there were no good hopes for the war owing to the inexperience and rashness of the commanders; but that if, then, by any good fortune, Caesar should be overthrown, he himself would not remain in Rome, but would fly from the harshness and cruelty of Scipio, who was even then making extravagant and dreadful threats against many.

But his fears were realized more fully than he expected; for late one evening there came a messenger from the camp who had been three days on the road, announcing that there had been a great battle at Thapsus, that their cause was utterly ruined, that Caesar was in possession of their camps,[1] that Scipio and Juba had escaped with a few followers, and that the rest of the force had perished.

LIX. These things coming suddenly upon the city, the people, as was natural at night and in time of war, were almost beside themselves at such tidings, and could with difficulty keep themselves within the walls. But Cato came forth, and for the present, whenever he met people running about and shouting, would lay hold of them one by one, and with encouraging words would take away the excessive wildness and confusion of their fear, saying that perhaps the defeat was not so bad as reported, but had been magnified in the telling, and thus he allayed the tumult; but as soon as it was day, he issued proclamation that the three hundred who made up his senate (they were Romans, and were doing business

---

[1] Scipio had separated from his allies and was encamped apart. Cf. the *Caesar*, liii.

νους ἀπὸ ἐμπορίας καὶ δανεισμῶν, εἰς ἱερὸν Διὸς
ἐκήρυττε συνιέναι, καὶ ὅσοι παρῆσαν ἀπὸ συγ-
κλήτου, καὶ παῖδας αὐτῶν. ἔτι δὲ συλλεγομένων
ἐκείνων προσελθὼν ἀθορύβως καὶ μετὰ εὐστα-
θείας, ὥσπερ οὐδενὸς καινοῦ γεγονότος, βιβλίον
ἔχων ἐν ταῖς χερσὶν ἀνεγίνωσκεν. ἦν δὲ ἀνα-
γραφὴ τῶν πρὸς τὸν πόλεμον ὀργάνων, ὅπλων,
3 σίτου, τόξων, ὁπλιτῶν.¹ ἐπεὶ δὲ συνῆλθον,
ἀρξάμενος ἀπὸ τῶν τριακοσίων καὶ διελθὼν πολὺν ἔπαινον τῆς προθυμίας αὐτῶν καὶ τῆς πίστεως,
ἣν ἐπεδείξαντο καὶ χρήμασι καὶ σώμασι καὶ
βουλαῖς ὠφελιμώτατοι γενόμενοι, παρεκάλει μὴ
διαλυθῆναι ταῖς ἐλπίσιν ἕκαστον αὐτῷ φυγὴν
ἰδίαν ἢ ἀπόδρασίν τινα ποριζόμενον. ἂν γὰρ ἐν
ταὐτῷ συμμένωσι, καὶ πολεμούντων ἧττον κατα-
φρονήσειν Καίσαρα, καὶ φείσεσθαι μᾶλλον δεο-
4 μένων. βουλεύεσθαι δ' ἐκέλευεν αὐτοὺς ὑπὲρ
αὑτῶν, οὐδέτερα μεμψόμενος, ἀλλ' εἰ μὲν τρέ-
ποιντο τῇ γνώμῃ πρὸς τὴν τύχην, τῆς ἀνάγκης
θησόμενος τὴν μεταβολήν· ἱσταμένων δὲ πρὸς τὰ
δεινὰ καὶ δεχομένων τὸν ὑπὲρ τῆς ἐλευθερίας
κίνδυνον, οὐκ ἐπαινεσόμενος μόνον, ἀλλὰ καὶ
θαυμασόμενος τὴν ἀρετήν, καὶ παρέξων ἑαυτὸν
5 ἄρχοντα καὶ συναγωνιζόμενον, ἄχρι οὗ τὴν ἐσχάτην τύχην τῆς πατρίδος ἐξελέγξωσιν, ἣν οὐκ
Ἰτύκην οὐδὲ Ἀδρούμητον οὖσαν, ἀλλὰ Ῥώμην,
πολλάκις ἐκ χαλεπωτέρων σφαλμάτων ὑπὸ μεγέ-
θους ἀναφέρεσθαι. πολλῶν δ' αὐτοῖς εἰς σωτηρίαν καὶ ἀσφάλειαν ὑποκειμένων, καὶ μεγίστου
πρὸς ἄνδρα πολεμεῖν ἐπὶ πολλὰ τοῖς καιροῖς

---

¹ ὁπλιτῶν bracketed by Bekker.

in Libya as merchants and money-lenders) should assemble in the temple of Jupiter, as well as all the senators from Rome who were present, with their children. And while they were still coming together, he advanced quietly and with a composed countenance, and as if nothing unusual had happened, with a book in his hands from which he was reading. This was a register of his military engines, arms, grain, and men-at-arms. After they had come together, beginning with the three hundred and commending at great length their zeal and fidelity, which they had manifested by making themselves most helpful with their means and persons and advice, he exhorted them not to ruin their good prospects by trying to procure for themselves severally some separate flight or escape. For if they should hold together, he said, Caesar would despise them less as foes, and show them more mercy as suppliants. Moreover, he urged them to deliberate upon their future course, declaring that he would have no fault to find with either decision which they might make. If they should turn their allegiance to the fortunate side, he would attribute their change to necessity; but if they should face the threatening evil and accept danger in defence of liberty, he would not only praise them, but would admire their valour and make himself their leader and fellow combatant, until they had fully tested the ultimate fortunes of their country; and this country was not Utica, nor Adrumetum, but Rome, and had many times by her greatness recovered from more grievous disasters. Besides, he said, many things favoured their salvation and security, and chiefly the fact that they were waging war against a man who was drawn in many opposing

ἀνθελκόμενον, Ἰβηρίας τε πρὸς Πομπήϊον ἀφε-
6 στώσης τὸν νέον, αὐτῆς τε τῆς Ῥώμης οὔπω δι'
ἀήθειαν παντάπασι δεδεγμένης τὸν χαλινόν, ἀλλ'
ἀναξιοπαθούσης καὶ συνεξανισταμένης πρὸς πᾶσαν μεταβολήν, οὐδὲ τὸν κίνδυνον εἶναι φευκτέον,
ἀλλὰ ἔχειν διδάσκαλον τὸν πολέμιον ἀφειδοῦντα
τῆς ψυχῆς ἐπὶ ταῖς μεγίσταις ἀδικίαις, οὐχ
ὥσπερ ἑαυτοῖς εἰς τὸν εὐτυχέστατον βίον κατ-
ορθοῦσιν ἢ πταίουσιν εἰς τὸν εὐκλεέστατον
θάνατον τὴν ἀδηλότητα τοῦ πολέμου τελευτᾶν.
7 οὐ μὴν ἀλλ' ἐκείνους γε δεῖν ἔφη βουλεύεσθαι 789
καθ' ἑαυτούς, συνευχόμενος ἀντὶ τῆς πρόσθεν
ἀρετῆς καὶ προθυμίας αὐτοῖς τὰ δόξαντα συνε-
νεγκεῖν.

LX. Τοιαῦτα τοῦ Κάτωνος εἰπόντος, ἦσαν μὲν
οἱ καὶ τοῖς λόγοις ἀγόμενοι πρὸς τὸ θαρρεῖν, οἱ
δὲ πλεῖστοι πρὸς τὸ ἀδεὲς καὶ γενναῖον αὐτοῦ
καὶ φιλάνθρωπον ὀλίγου δεῖν ἐκλαθόμενοι τῶν
παρόντων, ὡς μόνον ὄντα τοῦτον ἀήττητον ἡγεμόνα καὶ πάσης κρείττονα τύχης, ἐδέοντο χρῆσθαι καὶ σώμασιν αὐτῶν καὶ χρήμασι καὶ ὅπλοις, ὅπως αὐτὸς ἔγνωκε· κρεῖττον γὰρ ἐκείνῳ
πειθομένους ἀποθανεῖν ἢ σώζεσθαι προδόντας
ἀρετὴν τοσαύτην.
2 Εἰπόντος δέ τινος ὡς χρὴ ψηφίσασθαι δούλοις
ἐλευθερίαν, καὶ τῶν πλείστων συνεπαινεσάντων,
οὐκ ἔφη τοῦτο ποιήσειν ὁ Κάτων· οὐ γὰρ εἶναι
νόμιμον οὐδὲ δίκαιον, αὐτῶν μέντοι τῶν δεσποτῶν
ἀφιέντων τοὺς ἐν ἡλικίᾳ δέχεσθαι. γενομένων
δὲ πολλῶν ὑποσχέσεων κελεύσας ἀπογράφεσθαι
3 τὸν βουλόμενον ἀπηλλάττετο. καὶ μετὰ μικρὸν

directions by the exigencies of the times. For Spain had gone over to the younger Pompey, and Rome herself had not yet altogether accepted the bit to which she was so unaccustomed, but was impatient of her lot and ready to rise up unitedly at any change in the situation. Nor, he assured them, was danger a thing to be shunned, but they must learn a lesson from their enemy, who spared not his life in perpetrating the greatest wrongs, while in their own case, so different from his, the uncertainties of war would end in a most happy life, if they were successful, or in a most glorious death, if they failed. However, it was for them to deliberate by themselves, he said, and in return for their former bravery and zeal he joined them in praying that what they decided might be for their advantage.

LX. When Cato had thus spoken, there were some whom his words merely restored to confidence, but the majority, in view of his fearlessness, nobility, and generosity, almost forgot their present troubles in the conviction that he alone was an invincible leader and superior to every fortune, and they begged him to use their lives and property and arms as he himself judged best; for it was better to die as his willing followers than to save their lives by betraying such virtue as his.

And now someone proposed that they should pass a vote giving freedom to the slaves, and the majority approved; but Cato said he would not do this, since it was not lawful or right; if, however, the masters of their own accord gave up their slaves, those slaves who were of military age should be accepted. Many promises to do this were made, and after ordering a list to be made of all who were willing, Cato with-

ἧκεν αὐτῷ γράμματα παρὰ Ἰόβα καὶ Σκηπίωνος,
Ἰόβα μὲν ἐν ὄρει κεκρυμμένου μετ᾽ ὀλίγων ἐρω-
τῶντος ὅ τι πράττειν δέδοκται τῷ Κάτωνι· καὶ
γὰρ περιμενεῖν Ἰτύκην ἐκλιπόντα καὶ πολιορκου-
μένῳ μετὰ στρατιᾶς ἐπιβοηθήσειν, Σκηπίωνος δὲ
πρὸς ἄκρᾳ τινὶ ναυλοχοῦντος οὐ πόρρω τῆς Ἰτύκης ἐπὶ τοῖς αὐτοῖς καραδοκοῦντος.

LXI. Ἔδοξεν οὖν τῷ Κάτωνι τοὺς γραμματοφόρους ἐπισχεῖν, ἄχρι οὗ βεβαιώσῃ τὰ παρὰ τῶν
τριακοσίων. οἱ μὲν γὰρ ἀπὸ βουλῆς ἦσαν πρό-
θυμοι, καὶ τοὺς οἰκέτας εὐθὺς ἀφιέντες ἐλευθέρους
ὥπλιζον· τῶν δὲ τριακοσίων, ἅτε δὴ πλωτικῶν
καὶ δανειστικῶν ἀνθρώπων καὶ τὸ πλεῖστον ἐν
τοῖς οἰκέταις τῆς οὐσίας ἐχόντων, οὐ πολὺν οἱ
Κάτωνος λόγοι χρόνον ἐμμείναντες ἐξερρύησαν·
2 καθάπερ γὰρ τῶν σωμάτων τὰ μανὰ δέχεται
ῥᾳδίως τὴν θερμότητα καὶ πάλιν μεθίησι, τοῦ
πυρὸς ἀπαχθέντος ψυχόμενα, παραπλησίως
ἐκείνους ὁ μὲν Κάτων ὁρώμενος ἀνεζωπύρει καὶ
διεθέρμαινεν, αὐτοὺς δὲ ἑαυτοῖς λόγον διδόντας
ὁ Καίσαρος φόβος ἐξέκρουσε τῆς πρὸς Κάτωνα
καὶ τὸ καλὸν αἰδοῦς. "Τίνες γάρ," ἔφασαν,
"ὄντες, τίνι τὸ προστασσόμενον ποιεῖν ἀπαξιοῦ-
3 μεν; οὐχὶ Καῖσαρ μὲν οὗτος εἰς ὃν ἡ Ῥωμαίων
ἅπασα περιέστηκεν ἰσχύς; ἡμῶν δὲ Σκηπίων
οὐδεὶς οὐδὲ Πομπήιος οὐδὲ Κάτων. ἀλλὰ ἐν οἷς
καιροῖς πάντες ἄνθρωποι ταπεινότερα τῶν προσηκόντων διὰ φόβον φρονοῦσιν, ἐν τούτοις ἡμεῖς
ὑπερμαχοῦντες τῆς Ῥωμαίων ἐλευθερίας πολε-
μοῦμεν ἐξ Ἰτύκης ᾧ Κάτων μετὰ Πομπηίου
Μάγνου φεύγων ὑφεῖτο τῆς Ἰταλίας; καὶ δού-

drew. After a little while there came to him letters
from Juba and Scipio. Juba, who was hidden on a
mountain with a few men, asked what Cato had decided to do; for if he abandoned Utica, Juba would
wait for him, and if he underwent a siege, Juba
would come to his aid with an army. Scipio, who
was stationed with his fleet off a certain headland not
far from Utica, awaited Cato's decision in the same
way.

LXI. Accordingly, Cato decided to detain the
bearers of the letters until he felt sure of the attitude of the three hundred. For the Romans of
senatorial rank were eager in his cause, and after
promptly manumitting their slaves, were arming
them; but as for the three hundred, since they were
men engaged in navigation and money-lending and
had the greater part of their property in slaves, the
words of Cato did not long abide in their minds, but
lapsed away. For just as porous bodies readily receive heat and as readily yield it up again and grow
cold when the fire is removed, in like manner these
men, when they saw Cato, were filled with warmth
and kindled into flame; but when they came to think
matters over by themselves, their fear of Caesar drove
away their regard for Cato and for honour. "Who,
pray, are we," they said, "and who is he whose
commands we are refusing to obey? Is he not Caesar,
upon whom the whole power of Rome has devolved?
And not one of us is a Scipio, or a Pompey, or a Cato.
But at a time when all men are led by fear to think
more humbly than they ought to think, at such a time
shall we fight in defence of the liberty of Rome, and
wage war in Utica against a man before whom Cato,
with Pompey the Great, fled and gave up Italy? And

385

λους ἐλευθεροῦμεν κατὰ Καίσαρος, οἷς αὐτοῖς
ἐλευθερίας, ὅσον ἂν ἐκεῖνος θέλῃ, μέτεστιν; ἀλλ᾽
ἔτι νῦν, ὦ μοχθηροί, γνόντες ἑαυτοὺς παραιτώ-
μεθα τὸν κρατοῦντα καὶ πέμψωμεν τοὺς δεη-
σομένους."

4   Ταῦτα οἱ μετριώτατοι τῶν τριακοσίων παρή-
νουν· οἱ δὲ πλεῖστοι τοῖς συγκλητικοῖς ἐπε-
βούλευον, ὡς, εἰ τούτους συλλάβοιεν, ἱλασόμενοι
τὴν πρὸς αὐτοὺς ὀργὴν τοῦ Καίσαρος.

LXII. Ὁ δὲ Κάτων ὑπονοῶν τὴν μεταβολὴν
οὐκ ἤλεγχε, τῷ μέντοι Σκηπίωνι καὶ τῷ Ἰόβᾳ
γράψας ἀπέχεσθαι τῆς Ἰτύκης ἀπιστίᾳ τῶν
τριακοσίων ἐξέπεμψε τοὺς γραμματοφόρους. τῶν
δὲ ἱππέων οἱ διαφυγόντες ἀπὸ τῆς μάχης, ἀριθμὸς
οὐκ εὐκαταφρόνητος, προσελάσαντες τῇ Ἰτύκῃ
πέμπουσι πρὸς τὸν Κάτωνα τρεῖς ἄνδρας οὐ τὴν
2   αὐτὴν γνώμην ἀπὸ πάντων ἔχοντας. οἱ μὲν γὰρ
ἀπιέναι πρὸς Ἰόβαν, οἱ δὲ τῷ Κάτωνι προσχω-
ρεῖν ὥρμηντο, τοὺς δὲ καὶ δέος εἶχεν εἰς Ἰτύκην
παριέναι. ταῦτα ὁ Κάτων ἀκούσας τοῖς μὲν
τριακοσίοις ἐκέλευσε προσέχειν Μάρκον Ῥού- 790
βριον, ἀτρέμα τὰς ἀπογραφὰς τῶν ἐλευθερούντων
3   δεχόμενον καὶ μὴ προσβιαζόμενον, αὐτὸς δὲ τοὺς
συγκλητικοὺς ἀναλαβὼν προῆλθεν ἔξω τῆς Ἰτύκης, καὶ τοῖς ἱππάρχοις ἐνέτυχε δεόμενος μὴ
προέσθαι Ῥωμαίων ἄνδρας ἀπὸ βουλῆς τοσούτους μηδὲ Ἰόβαν ἑλέσθαι στρατηγὸν ἀντὶ Κάτωνος, ἀλλὰ σώζεσθαι κοινῇ καὶ σώζειν, παρελθόν-
τας εἰς πόλιν οὔτε κατὰ κράτος ἁλώσιμον εἰς

shall we give our slaves freedom in opposition to Caesar, we who ourselves have only as much freedom as he may wish to give us? Nay, before it is too late, poor wretches, let us know ourselves, crave the conqueror's grace, and send men to entreat him."

This was the course which the more moderate of the three hundred advised; but the majority of them were laying a plot against the men of senatorial rank, in the hope that by seizing these they might mitigate Caesar's wrath against themselves.

LXII. Cato suspected their change of heart, but would not tax them with it. However, he wrote to Scipio and Juba advising them to keep away from Utica, because the three hundred were not to be trusted, and sent away the letter-bearers. And now the horsemen who had escaped from the battle, in numbers quite considerable, rode up to Utica and sent three of their number to Cato. These men, however, did not bring the same proposition from the whole body. For one party among them was bent on going off to Juba, another wanted to join Cato, while a third was prevented by fear from entering Utica. On hearing their views, Cato ordered Marcus Rubrius to attend to the three hundred; he was to accept quietly the lists of those who gave freedom to their slaves, and was to use no compulsion. But Cato himself took the men of senatorial rank and went forth outside of Utica. Here he conferred with the leaders of the horsemen, entreating them not to abandon so great a number of Roman senators, and not to choose Juba as their commander instead of Cato, but to save others as well as save themselves by coming into a city which could not be taken by storm,

ἔτη τε πάμπολλα σῖτον καὶ τὴν ἄλλην παρα-
4 σκευὴν ἔχουσαν. ταῦτα δὲ καὶ τῶν συγκλητικῶν
δεομένων καὶ δακρυόντων οἱ μὲν ἵππαρχοι διελέ-
γοντο τοῖς ἱππεῦσιν, ὁ δὲ Κάτων ἐπὶ χώματός
τινος καθίσας μετὰ τῶν συγκλητικῶν ἀνέμεινε
τὰς ἀποκρίσεις.

LXIII. Ἐν δὲ τούτῳ παρῆν ὁ Ῥούβριος σὺν
ὀργῇ κατηγορῶν τῶν τριακοσίων ἀκοσμίαν πολλὴν καὶ θόρυβον, ὡς ἀφισταμένων καὶ διατα-
ραττόντων τὴν πόλιν. ἐφ᾽ οἷς οἱ μὲν ἄλλοι
παντάπασιν ἀπογνόντες ἑαυτῶν εἰς δάκρυα καὶ
ὀδυρμοὺς ἐξέπεσον, ὁ δὲ Κάτων ἐκείνους τε θαρ-
σύνειν ἐπειρᾶτο καὶ πρὸς τοὺς τριακοσίους ἔπεμψεν
2 ἀναμεῖναι κελεύων. οἱ δὲ ἀπὸ τῶν ἱππέων ἧκον
οὐ μέτρια προστάττοντες· ἔφασαν γὰρ οὔτε Ἰόβα
δεῖσθαι μισθοδοτοῦντος οὔτε Καίσαρα φοβεῖσθαι
Κάτωνος αὐτῶν ἄρχοντος, Ἰτυκαίοις δέ, Φοίνιξιν
ἀνθρώποις εὐμεταβόλοις, συγκαθείργνυσθαι δεινὸν εἶναι· καὶ γὰρ εἰ νῦν ἀτρεμοῦσιν, ὅταν
Καῖσαρ ἐπίῃ, συνεπιθήσεσθαι καὶ προδώσειν.
3 εἴπερ οὖν δεῖταί τις αὐτῶν συμπολεμούντων καὶ
συμπαρόντων, ἐκβαλὼν ἅπαντας Ἰτυκαίους ἢ
διαφθείρας, οὕτως εἰς πόλιν καθαρὰν πολεμίων
καὶ βαρβάρων καλείτω. ταῦτα ὁ Κάτων ἄγρια
μὲν δεινῶς ἡγεῖτο καὶ βάρβαρα, πρᾴως δὲ ἀπεκρίνατο βουλεύσεσθαι μετὰ τῶν τριακοσίων.

4 Καὶ παρελθὼν αὖθις εἰς τὴν πόλιν ἐνετύγχανε
τοῖς ἀνδράσιν οὐκέτι σκήψεις οὐδὲ παραγωγὰς
πλασσομένοις ὑπ᾽ αἰδοῦς πρὸς αὐτόν, ἄντικρυς δὲ
χαλεπαίνουσιν εἴ τις αὐτοὺς βιάζοιτο πολεμεῖν
Καίσαρι μὴ δυναμένους μηδὲ βουλομένους. ἔνιοι

and had grain and other requisite provision for very many years. In these entreaties the senators also joined, and with tears; whereupon the leaders of the horsemen discussed the matter with the horsemen, while Cato sat down on a mound with the senators and awaited the answers.

LXIII. At this juncture Rubrius came up, wrathfully denouncing the three hundred for great disorder and tumult, inasmuch as they were falling away and throwing the city into confusion. Thereupon the other Romans altogether despaired of their case and burst into tears and lamentations; but Cato tried to encourage them, and sent to the three hundred bidding them await his coming. And now the spokesmen of the horsemen came with immoderate demands. They said they neither wanted Juba for a paymaster, nor feared Caesar if Cato were their leader, but that to be shut up with the people of Utica, a fickle Phoenician folk, was a fearful thing; for even though they were quiet now, whenever Caesar came up against them they would play the traitor and aid him in his attacks. If, therefore, any one wanted their aid in war and their presence, he must first drive out or destroy all the people of Utica, and then invite the horsemen into a city that was free from Barbarians and enemies. This proposal Cato regarded as excessively barbarous and cruel, but he returned a mild answer, saying that he would advise with the three hundred.

So he went back into the city, where he found the men no longer manufacturing pretexts or evasions out of regard for him, but downright angry that any one should try to force them to war with Caesar when they were neither able nor willing. And some of

δὲ καὶ παρεφθέγγοντο περὶ τῶν συγκλητικῶν, ὡς
καθεκτέον ἐν τῇ πόλει Καίσαρος προσιόντος.
5 ἀλλὰ τοῦτο μὲν ὡς οὐκ ἀκούσας ὁ Κάτων παρ-
ῆκε· καὶ γὰρ ἦν ὑποκωφότερος· ὡς δέ τις αὐτῷ
προσελθὼν ἀπήγγειλε τοὺς μὲν¹ ἱππεῖς ἀπιέναι,
φοβηθεὶς μὴ παντάπασιν οἱ τριακόσιοι κατὰ τῶν
συγκλητικῶν ἀπονοηθῶσιν, ἐβάδιζε μετὰ τῶν
φίλων ἐξαναστάς· καὶ θεασάμενος ἤδη προκεχω-
6 ρηκότας ἵππον λαβὼν ἐδίωκε πρὸς αὐτούς. οἱ δὲ
ἰδόντες ἄσμενοι προσελαύνοντα καὶ ἐδέξαντο καὶ
παρεκάλουν σώζεσθαι μετ᾽ αὐτῶν. τότε καὶ δα-
κρῦσαι τὸν Κάτωνά φασιν ὑπὲρ τῶν συγκλητικῶν
δεόμενον καὶ προτείνοντα τὰς χεῖρας, ἐνίων δὲ καὶ
τοὺς ἵππους ἀναστρέφοντα καὶ τῶν ὅπλων ἀντι-
λαμβανόμενον, μέχρι οὗ κατειργάσατο τὴν γοῦν
ἡμέραν ἐκείνην ἐπιμείναντας ἀσφαλῆ τοῖς ἀνδράσι φυγὴν παρασχεῖν.

LXIV. Ὡς οὖν ἔχων αὐτοὺς ἀφίκετο καὶ τοὺς
μὲν ἐπὶ τὰς πύλας κατέστησε, τοῖς δὲ τὴν ἄκραν
φυλάττειν παρέδωκεν, ἔδεισαν οἱ τριακόσιοι μὴ
δίκην δῶσι τῆς μεταβολῆς· καὶ πρὸς τὸν Κάτωνα
πέμποντες ἐδέοντο πάντως ἀφικέσθαι πρὸς αὐτούς. οἱ δὲ συγκλητικοὶ περιχυθέντες οὐκ εἴων,
οὐδὲ ἔφασαν προήσεσθαι τὸν κηδεμόνα καὶ σω-
2 τῆρα τοῖς ἀπίστοις καὶ προδόταις. σαφεστάτη
γάρ, ὡς ἔοικεν, αἴσθησις τότε παρέστη καὶ πόθος
καὶ θαῦμα τῆς τοῦ Κάτωνος ἀρετῆς πᾶσιν ὁμαλῶς τοῖς ἐν τῇ Ἰτύκῃ γενομένοις, ὡς οὐδὲν ἄρα
κίβδηλον οὐδὲ ἀπατηλὸν ἐμέμικτο τοῖς πραττο-
μένοις ὑπ᾽ αὐτοῦ.

Πάλαι δὲ ἄνθρωπος ἑαυτὸν ἐγνωκὼς ἀνελεῖν

¹ μὲν bracketed by Coraës and Bekker.

them actually muttered that the men of senatorial rank ought to be detained in the city while Caesar was approaching. But this Cato let pass, as though he had not heard it (and indeed he was somewhat deaf); when, however, men came to him with tidings that the horsemen were going away, he was afraid that the three hundred might become altogether desperate in their hostility to the senators, and therefore rose up and set out on foot with his friends; and when he perceived that the horsemen had already gone on, he took a horse and hastened after them. The horsemen were glad when they saw him riding up, and greeted him, and exhorted him to save himself with them. Then, it is said, Cato actually burst into tears as he begged with outstretched hands in behalf of the senators, even trying to turn back the horses of some of the horsemen and laying hold of their arms, until he prevailed upon them to remain there that day at least, and to make the flight of the senators safe.

LXIV. Accordingly, when he came to the city with them, stationed some of them at the gates, and committed the citadel to others to guard, the three hundred were afraid they might be punished for their change of allegiance, and sending to Cato they begged him by all means to come to them. But the senators crowded about him and would not let him go, declaring that they would not give up their saviour and guardian to treacherous and faithless men. For by that time all the inhabitants of Utica alike most clearly perceived and fondly admired the virtuous qualities of Cato, convinced that nothing deceitful or spurious entered into what he did.

But for a long time the man had determined to

δεινοὺς πόνους ἐπόνει καὶ φροντίδας καὶ ὠδῖνας
εἶχεν ὑπὲρ ἄλλων, ὅπως εἰς ἀσφαλὲς καταστήσας
3 ἅπαντας ἀπαλλάξαιτο τοῦ ζῆν. οὐ γὰρ ἦν ἄδη- 791
λος ἡ πρὸς τὸν θάνατον αὐτοῦ φορά, καίπερ οὐ
φάσκοντος. ὑπήκουσεν οὖν τότε τοῖς τριακοσίοις
παραμυθησάμενος τοὺς συγκλητικούς· καὶ μόνος
ἧκε πρὸς αὐτοὺς χάριν ἔχειν ὁμολογοῦντας καὶ
δεομένους τὰ μὲν ἄλλα χρῆσθαι καὶ πιστεύειν, εἰ
δὲ Κάτωνες οὐκ εἰσὶν οὐδὲ τὸ Κάτωνος φρόνημα
4 χωροῦσιν, οἰκτείρειν τὴν ἀσθένειαν αὐτῶν· ἐγνω-
κότες δ᾽ οὖν Καίσαρος δεῖσθαι καὶ πέμπειν πρὸς
αὐτόν, ὑπὲρ ἐκείνου μάλιστα καὶ πρώτου ποιήσε-
σθαι δέησιν· εἰ δὲ μὴ πείθοιεν, οὐδ᾽ αὐτοῖς διδο-
μένην δέξεσθαι τὴν χάριν, ἀλλ᾽ ἄχρι ἂν ἐμπνέωσι
πολεμήσειν ὑπὲρ ἐκείνου.

Πρὸς ταῦτα ὁ Κάτων ἐπαινέσας τὴν εὔνοιαν
ἔφη χρῆναι τῆς αὐτῶν σωτηρίας ἕνεκα πέμπειν
5 κατὰ τάχος, ὑπὲρ αὐτοῦ δὲ μὴ δεῖσθαι· κεκρατη-
μένων γὰρ εἶναι δέησιν καὶ ἀδικούντων παραί-
τησιν· αὐτὸς δὲ οὐ μόνον ἀήττητος γεγονέναι
παρὰ πάντα τὸν βίον, ἀλλὰ καὶ νικᾶν ἐφ᾽ ὅσον
ἐβούλετο καὶ κρατεῖν Καίσαρος τοῖς καλοῖς καὶ
δικαίοις· ἐκεῖνον δ᾽ εἶναι τὸν ἑαλωκότα καὶ νενι-
κημένον· ἃ γὰρ ἠρνεῖτο πράττων κατὰ τῆς πατρίδος πάλαι, νῦν ἐξηλέγχθαι καὶ πεφωρᾶσθαι.

LXV. Τοιαῦτα διαλεχθεὶς τοῖς τριακοσίοις
ἀπηλλάττετο· καὶ πυθόμενος Καίσαρα πᾶσαν
ἄγοντα τὴν στρατιὰν ἤδη καθ᾽ ὁδὸν εἶναι, "Πα-
παί," εἶπεν, "ὡς ἐπ᾽ ἄνδρας ἡμᾶς ἐκεῖνος." καὶ
τραπόμενος πρὸς τοὺς συγκλητικοὺς ἐκέλευε μὴ
μέλλειν, ἀλλ᾽ ἕως παραμένουσιν οἱ ἱππεῖς σώζε-

destroy himself, and he was undergoing dreadful toils
and suffering anxiety and pain in behalf of others,
that he might put them all in the way of safety before he took his leave of life. Indeed, there was no
secret about his resolution to die, although he said
nothing about it. Accordingly, after comforting the
senators, he obeyed the call of the three hundred. He
came alone to them, and they thanked him, and
begged him in all other ways to trust and make use
of them, but if they were not Catos and could not
carry the large thoughts of Cato, to have pity on
their weakness; and now that they had determined
to send to Caesar and pray for his mercy, for Cato
first of all they would make their prayers; and if
they could not prevail with Caesar, they would not
accept the grace which he might offer to them, but
as long as they had breath would fight for Cato.

In reply to this, after praising their good will, Cato
said that to secure their own safety they ought to
send to Caesar with all speed, but they must make no
prayer for him; prayer belonged to the conquered,
and the craving of grace to those who had done
wrong; but for his part he had not only been unvanquished all his life, but was actually a victor now as
far as he chose to be, and a conqueror of Caesar in all
that was honourable and just; Caesar was the one who
was vanquished and taken; for the hostile acts against
his country which he had long denied, were now
detected and proven.

LXV. After this discourse to the three hundred,
he withdrew; and on learning that Caesar with all
his army was already on the march, "Aha!" he
said, "he thinks we are men!" Then turning to the
senators he bade them not delay, but save themselves

σθαι. καὶ τὰς μὲν ἄλλας ἀπέκλεισε θύρας, μιᾷ
δὲ τῇ πρὸς θάλασσαν φερούσῃ[1] τά τε πλοῖα τοῖς
ὑφ' ἑαυτὸν διένειμε καὶ τάξεως ἐπεμελεῖτο, παύων
τὰς ἀδικίας καὶ διαλύων τοὺς θορύβους, καὶ τοὺς
2 ἀπόρως ἔχοντας ἐφοδιάζων. ἐπεὶ δὲ Μάρκος
Ὀκτάβιος ἄγων δύο τάγματα πλησίον κατεστρα-
τοπέδευσε καὶ πέμπων ἠξίου τὸν Κάτωνα περὶ
ἀρχῆς διορίσασθαι πρὸς αὐτόν, ἐκείνῳ μὲν οὐθὲν
ἀπεκρίνατο, πρὸς δὲ τοὺς φίλους εἶπεν· "Εἶτα
θαυμάζομεν ὅπως ἀπόλωλε τὰ πράγματα, τὴν
φιλαρχίαν ὁρῶντες ἡμῖν ἐν αὐτῷ τῷ ὀλέθρῳ
βεβηκόσι παραμένουσαν;"

3 Ἐν τούτῳ δὲ τοὺς ἱππεῖς ἀκούσας ἀπιόντας
ἤδη φέρειν καὶ ἄγειν τὰ τῶν Ἰτυκαίων ὥσπερ
λάφυρα, δρόμῳ συνέτεινε πρὸς αὐτοὺς καὶ τοῖς
πρώτοις ἐντυχὼν ἀφῃρεῖτο, τῶν δὲ ἄλλων ἕκαστος ἔφθανε ῥίπτων καὶ κατατιθέμενος, πάντες
δὲ ὑπ' αἰσχύνης σιωπῇ καὶ κάτω βλέποντες
ἀπῄεσαν. ὁ δὲ Κάτων εἰς τὴν πόλιν τοὺς Ἰτυκαίους συναγαγὼν ἐδεῖτο περὶ τῶν τριακοσίων,
μὴ παροξῦναι Καίσαρα κατ' αὐτῶν, ἀλλὰ καὶ
4 κοινῇ τὴν σωτηρίαν πράττειν ἀλλήλοις. εἶτα
πάλιν τραπόμενος πρὸς τὴν θάλατταν ἐπεσκόπει
τοὺς ἐμβαίνοντας, καὶ τῶν φίλων καὶ ξένων ὅσους
ἔπεισεν ἠσπάζετο καὶ προὔπεμπε. τὸν δὲ υἱὸν
οὐκ ἔπεισε λαβεῖν πλοῖον, οὐδὲ ᾤετο δεῖν ἀποτρέπειν περιεχόμενον τοῦ πατρός. ἦν δέ τις Στατύλλιος, ἀνὴρ τῇ μὲν ἡλικίᾳ νέος, ἰσχυρὸς δὲ τῇ

---

[1] φερούσῃ after this word one Paris MS. (C) has ἐχρῆτο
πρὸς ἔξοδον (he used as an exit). Bekker adopts what other
editors regard as a gloss, adding also καί; Sintenis[2] assumes
a lacuna.

while the horsemen were still there. He also closed
the other gates of the city, and stationing himself
at the one leading to the sea, he assigned transports
to those under his command, and tried to keep things
in order, stopping deeds of wrong, quelling tumults,
and supplying stores to those who were destitute.
And when Marcus Octavius with two legions encamped near by and sent to Cato demanding that
he come to terms with him about the command in
the province, Cato would make no reply to him, but
said to his friends: "Can we then wonder that our
cause is lost, when we see that the love of command
abides with us though we are standing on the brink
of destruction?"

At this juncture, hearing that the horsemen, as
they went away, were already plundering the people
of Utica as though their property was booty, he ran
to them as fast as he could; from the first whom he
met he took away their plunder, but the rest, every
man of them, made haste to lay down or throw away
what they had, and all felt so ashamed that they went
off in silence and with downcast looks. Then Cato,
after calling the people of Utica together into the city,
begged them not to embitter Caesar against the three
hundred, but to unite with one another in securing
safety for all. Next, he betook himself again to the sea
and superintended the embarcation there, embracing
and escorting on their way all the friends and acquaint-
ances whom he could persuade to go. His son, however, he could not persuade to take ship, nor did he
think it his duty to try to turn the young man from his
purpose of clinging to his father. But there was one
Statyllius, a man who was young in years, but minded

γνώμῃ βουλόμενος εἶναι καὶ τοῦ Κάτωνος ἀπομι-
5 μεῖσθαι τὴν ἀπάθειαν. τοῦτον ἠξίου πλεῖν·
καὶ γὰρ ἦν καταφανὴς μισοκαῖσαρ· ὡς δὲ οὐκ
ἤθελεν, Ἀπολλωνίδῃ τῷ Στωϊκῷ καὶ Δημητρίῳ τῷ Περιπατητικῷ προσβλέψας ὁ Κάτων,
" Ὑμέτερον," εἶπεν, " ἔργον οἰδοῦντα τοῦτον
μαλάξαι καὶ καταρτίσαι πρὸς τὸ συμφέρον."
αὐτὸς δὲ τοὺς λοιποὺς συνεκπέμπων καὶ χρημα-
τίζων τοῖς δεομένοις τήν τε νύκτα διέτριβε περὶ
ταῦτα καὶ τῆς ἐπιούσης ἡμέρας τὸ πλεῖστον
μέρος.

LXVI. Ἐπεὶ δὲ Λεύκιος Καῖσαρ, οἰκεῖος μὲν
ὢν Καίσαρος ἐκείνου, μέλλων δὲ πρεσβεύειν ὑπὲρ
τῶν τριακοσίων, παρεκάλει τὸν Κάτωνα λόγον
αὐτῷ συνυποθέσθαι πιθανὸν ᾧ χρήσεται περὶ
ἐκείνων, " ὑπὲρ σοῦ μὲν γὰρ αὐτοῦ καὶ χειρῶν
ἐμοὶ καλὸν ἅψασθαι καὶ γόνασι προσπεσεῖν
Καίσαρος," οὐκ εἴα ταῦτα ποιεῖν ὁ Κάτων αὐτόν. 792
2 " Ἐμοὶ γάρ," εἶπεν, " εἰ σώζεσθαι χάριτι Καίσαρος ἐβουλόμην, αὐτῷ βαδιστέον ἦν πρὸς ἐκεῖνον μόνον. οὐ βούλομαι δὲ τῷ τυράννῳ χάριν
ἔχειν ὑπὲρ ὧν παρανομεῖ. παρανομεῖ δὲ σώζων
ὡς κύριος ὢν αὐτῷ δεσπόζειν οὐδὲν προσῆκεν.
ὅπως μέντοι παραιτήσῃ τοὺς τριακοσίους κοινῇ
3 σκοπῶμεν, εἰ βούλει." γενόμενος δὲ πρὸς τούτῳ
μετὰ τοῦ Λευκίου τὸν υἱὸν αὐτῷ συνέστησε καὶ
τοὺς ἑταίρους ἀπιόντι· καὶ προπέμψας ἐκεῖνον
καὶ δεξιωσάμενος ἐπανῆλθεν οἴκαδε, καὶ τὸν υἱὸν
καὶ τοὺς φίλους συναγαγὼν ἄλλα τε πολλὰ διε-
λέχθη καὶ πολιτείας ἀπεῖπεν ἅψασθαι τῷ μειρα-
κίῳ· τὸ μὲν γὰρ ἀξίως Κάτωνος οὐκέτι τὰ πρά-

to be strong in purpose and to imitate Cato's calmness. This man Cato insisted should take ship ; for he was a notorious hater of Caesar. But when Statyllius would not consent, Cato turned his eyes upon Apollonides the Stoic and Demetrius the Peripatetic, saying : " It is your task to reduce this man's swollen pride and restore him to conformity with his best interests." He himself, however, continued to assist the rest in getting off, and to supply the needy with ways and means, and was thus engaged all through the night and the greater part of the following day.

LXVI. Lucius Caesar, a kinsman of the great Caesar, was about to go on an embassy to him in behalf of the three hundred, and requested Cato to suggest to him a convincing speech which he might employ in the case ; " for," said he, " in thine own behalf it were well for me to fall down at Caesar's knees and clasp his hands." But Cato would not suffer him to do this. " For if," said he, " I were willing to be saved by grace of Caesar, I ought to go to him in person and see him alone ; but I am unwilling to be under obligations to the tyrant for his illegal acts. And he acts illegally in saving, as if their master, those over whom he has no right at all to be the lord. However, if it is thy wish, let us consider jointly how thou mayest obtain mercy for the three hundred." After his conference with Lucius on this matter, he presented his son and his companions to him as he was going away ; and after escorting him on his way and bidding him farewell, he came back home, called together his son and his friends, and discoursed with them on many subjects. In particular, he forbade the young man to engage in political matters ; for to do so worthily of a Cato was no longer possible, as

γματα δέξασθαι, τὸ δὲ ἄλλως αἰσχρὸν εἶναι. καὶ περὶ ἑσπέραν ἤδη τρέπεται πρὸς τὸ βαλανεῖον.

4 Ἐν δὲ τῷ λούεσθαι τοῦ Στατυλλίου μνησθεὶς καὶ μέγα φθεγξάμενος, "Ἐξέπεμψας," εἶπεν, "ὦ Ἀπολλωνίδη, τὸν Στατύλλιον ἀπὸ τοῦ φρονήματος ἐκείνου καθελών; καὶ πέπλευκεν ὁ ἀνὴρ μηδὲ ἀσπασάμενος ἡμᾶς;" "Πόθεν;" εἶπεν ὁ Ἀπολλωνίδης· "καίτοι πολλὰ διελέχθημεν· ἀλλὰ ὑψηλός ἐστι καὶ ἄτρεπτος, καὶ μένειν φησὶ καὶ πράττειν ὅ τι ἂν σὺ πράττῃς." πρὸς ταῦτά φασι τὸν Κάτωνα μειδιᾶσαι καὶ εἰπεῖν· "Ἀλλὰ τοῦτο μὲν αὐτίκα φανεῖται."

LXVII. Λουσάμενος δὲ μετὰ πολλῶν ἐδείπνει καθήμενος, ὥσπερ εἰώθει μετὰ τὴν μάχην· οὐ γὰρ κατεκλίθη πλὴν καθεύδων· συνεδείπνουν δὲ πάντες οἱ ἑταῖροι καὶ τῶν Ἰτυκαίων οἱ ἄρχοντες. καὶ μετὰ τὸ δεῖπνον ὁ πότος ἔσχε μοῦσαν πολλὴν καὶ χάριν, ἄλλων ἐπ' ἄλλοις λόγων φιλοσόφων κυκλούντων, ἄχρι οὗ περιῆλθεν ἡ ζήτησις εἰς ταῦτα δὴ τὰ παράδοξα καλούμενα τῶν Στωϊκῶν, τὸ μόνον εἶναι τὸν ἀγαθὸν ἐλεύθερον, δούλους δὲ 2 τοὺς φαύλους ἅπαντας. ἐνταῦθα δή, ὡς εἰκός, ἀντιβάντος τοῦ Περιπατητικοῦ, σφοδρὸς ἐμπεσὼν ὁ Κάτων καὶ τόνον προσθεὶς καὶ τραχύτητα φωνῆς ἀπέτεινε πορρωτάτω τὸν λόγον, ἀγῶνι θαυμαστῷ χρησάμενος, ὥστε μηδένα λαθεῖν ὅτι τῷ βίῳ πέρας ἔγνωκεν ἐπιθεὶς ἀπαλλάττεσθαι τῶν παρόντων. διὸ καὶ μετὰ τὸν λόγον σιωπῆς καὶ κατηφείας γενομένης ἐν πᾶσιν, ἀναλαμβάνων αὐτοὺς καὶ ἀπάγων τῆς ὑποψίας ὁ Κάτων αὖθις ὑπὲρ τῶν παρόντων ἐνέβαλλεν ἐρωτήματα καὶ

things were going, and to do so otherwise would be disgraceful. And presently, towards evening, he betook himself to the bath.

But while he was bathing he bethought himself of Statyllius, and called out in loud tones, saying: "Apollonides, didst thou send off Statyllius? And didst thou bring him down from that lofty purpose of his? And has the man set sail without even bidding me good-bye?" "By no means," said Apollonides; "although we reasoned much with him; but he is lofty and unbending, and says he will remain and do whatever thou doest." At this, we are told, Cato smiled, and said: "Well, we shall see about that presently."

LXVII. After his bath, he took supper with a large company, sitting at table, as was his wont after Pharsalus; indeed, he lay down only when he slept;[1] and there were at supper with him all his companions, and the magistrates of Utica. After supper, there was much literary and genial discourse over the wine, and one philosophical tenet after another made the rounds, until there came up the enquiry into what were called the "paradoxes" of the Stoics, namely, that the good man alone is free, and that the bad are all slaves. Here, as was to be expected, the Peripatetic made objections, whereupon Cato broke in with vehemence, and in loud and harsh tones maintained his argument at greatest length and with astonishing earnestness, so that everyone perceived that he had made up his mind to put an end to his life and free himself from his present troubles. Therefore, as all were dejected and silent after his discourse, Cato tried to revive their spirits and remove their suspicions by once more putting questions and expressing anxiety about what was going on, implying that he feared for those

1 Cf. chapter lvi. 4.

φροντίδας, ὡς δεδιὼς μὲν ὑπὲρ τῶν πλεόντων,
δεδιὼς δὲ ὑπὲρ τῶν ὀδευόντων ἐρημίαν ἄνυδρον
καὶ βάρβαρον.

LXVIII. Οὕτω δὲ διαλύσας τὸ σύνδειπνον,
καὶ περιπατήσας μετὰ τῶν φίλων τὸν συνήθη
μετὰ τὸ δεῖπνον περίπατον, καὶ τοῖς ἄρχουσι τῶν
φυλάκων ἃ καιρὸς ἦν προστάξας, ἀπιὼν εἰς τὸ
δωμάτιον ἤδη, τόν τε παῖδα καὶ τῶν φίλων
ἕκαστον μᾶλλον ἢ πρότερον εἰώθει προσαγαγόμενος καὶ φιλοφρονηθείς, πάλιν ὑποψίαν παρέσχε
2 τοῦ μέλλοντος. εἰσελθὼν δὲ καὶ κατακλιθεὶς
ἔλαβεν εἰς χεῖρας τῶν Πλάτωνος διαλόγων τὸν
περὶ ψυχῆς· καὶ διελθὼν τοῦ βιβλίου τὸ πλεῖστον
καὶ ἀναβλέψας ὑπὲρ κεφαλῆς, ὡς οὐκ εἶδε κρεμά-
μενον τὸ ξίφος (ὑφῄρητο γὰρ ὁ παῖς ἔτι δειπνοῦντος αὐτοῦ), καλέσας οἰκέτην ἠρώτησεν ὅστις
λάβοι τὸ ἐγχειρίδιον. σιωπῶντος δὲ ἐκείνου
πάλιν ἦν πρὸς τῷ βιβλίῳ· καὶ μικρὸν διαλιπών,
ὥσπερ οὐ σπεύδων οὐδὲ ἐπειγόμενος, ἄλλως δὲ
3 τὸ ξίφος ἐπιζητῶν, ἐκέλευσε κομίσαι. διατριβῆς
δὲ γινομένης καὶ μηδενὸς κομίζοντος, ἐξαναγνοὺς
τὸ βιβλίον αὖθις ἐκάλει καθ᾽ ἕνα τῶν οἰκετῶν
καὶ μᾶλλον ἐνέτεινε τὴν φωνὴν τὸ ξίφος ἀπαιτῶν·
ἑνὸς δὲ καὶ πὺξ τὸ στόμα πατάξας ἥμαξε τὴν
αὐτοῦ χεῖρα, χαλεπαίνων καὶ βοῶν ἤδη μέγα
παραδίδοσθαι τῷ πολεμίῳ γυμνὸς ὑπὸ τοῦ παιδὸς
αὐτοῦ καὶ τῶν οἰκετῶν, ἄχρι οὗ κλαίων ὁ υἱὸς
εἰσέδραμε μετὰ τῶν φίλων καὶ περιπεσὼν ὠδύρετο 793
4 καὶ καθικέτευεν. ὁ δὲ Κάτων ἐξαναστὰς ἐνέ-
βλεψέ τε δεινὸν καὶ "Πότε," εἶπεν, "ἐγὼ καὶ
ποῦ λέληθα παρανοίας ἡλωκώς, ὅτι διδάσκει μὲν

who were going away by sea, and feared, too, for those whose path lay through a barbarous and waterless desert.

LXVIII. Thus the supper came to an end, and after walking about with his friends as he usually did after supper, he gave the officers of the watch the proper orders, and then retired to his chamber, but not until he had embraced his son and each of his friends with more than his wonted kindness, and thus awakened anew their suspicions of what was to come. After entering his chamber and lying down, he took up Plato's dialogue "On the Soul," [1] and when he had gone through the greater part of the treatise, he looked up above his head, and not seeing his sword hanging there (for his son had taken it away while Cato was still at supper), called a servant and asked him who had taken the weapon. The servant made no answer, and Cato returned to his book; and a little while after, as if in no haste or hurry, but merely looking for his sword, he bade the servant fetch it. But as there was some delay, and no one brought the weapon, he finished reading his book, and this time called his servants one by one and in louder tones demanded his sword. One of them he smote on the mouth with his fist, and bruised his own hand, angrily crying now in loud tones that his son and his servants were betraying him into the hands of the enemy without arms. At last his son ran in weeping, together with his friends, and after embracing him, betook himself to lamentations and entreaties. But Cato, rising to his feet, took on a solemn look, and said: "When and where, without my knowledge, have I been adjudged a madman, that no

[1] The *Phaedo.*

οὐδεὶς οὐδὲ μεταπείθει περὶ ὧν δοκῶ κακῶς βεβουλεῦσθαι, κωλύομαι δὲ χρῆσθαι τοῖς ἐμαυτοῦ
λογισμοῖς καὶ παροπλίζομαι; τί δ' οὐχὶ καὶ
συνδεῖς, ὦ γενναῖε, τὸν πατέρα καὶ τὰς χεῖρας
ἀποστρέφεις, μέχρι ἂν ἐλθὼν Καῖσαρ εὕρῃ με
5 μηδὲ ἀμύνασθαι δυνάμενον; οὐ γὰρ ἐπ' ἐμαυτόν
γε δέομαι ξίφους, ὅπου καὶ τὸ πνεῦμα βραχὺν
χρόνον ἐπισχόντα καὶ τὴν κεφαλὴν ἅπαξ πατά-
ξαντα πρὸς τὸν τοῖχον ἀποθανεῖν ἔνεστι."

LXIX. Ταῦτα λέγοντος αὐτοῦ τὸ μὲν μειράκιον
ἐξῆλθε μετὰ κλαυθμοῦ καὶ πάντες οἱ λοιποί· τῷ
δὲ Δημητρίῳ καὶ τῷ Ἀπολλωνίδῃ μόνοις ὑπο-
λειφθεῖσι πρᾳότερον ἤδη λαλῶν, "Ἦ που καὶ
ὑμῖν," ἔφη, "δέδοκται βίᾳ κατέχειν ἄνδρα τοσοῦτον ἡλικίας ἐν τῷ βίῳ καὶ καθημένους αὐτοῦ
σιωπῇ παραφυλάσσειν, ἢ λόγον ἥκετε κομίζοντες
ὡς οὐ δεινὸν οὐδὲ αἰσχρόν ἐστιν ἀποροῦντα
σωτηρίας ἑτέρας Κάτωνα τὴν ἀπὸ τοῦ πολεμίου
2 περιμένειν; τί οὖν οὐ λέγετε πείθοντες ἡμᾶς
ταῦτα καὶ μεταδιδάσκοντες, ἵνα τὰς προτέρας
δόξας ἐκείνας καὶ λόγους, οἷς συμβεβιώκαμεν,
ἐκβαλόντες καὶ γενόμενοι διὰ Καίσαρα σοφώτεροι
μείζονα χάριν εἰδῶμεν αὐτῷ; καίτοι βεβούλευμαι
μὲν οὐθὲν ἔγωγε περὶ ἐμαυτοῦ· δεῖ δέ με βουλευ-
3 σάμενον εἶναι κύριον οἷς ἔγνωκα χρῆσθαι. βου-
λεύσομαι δὲ τρόπον τινὰ μεθ' ὑμῶν, βουλευόμενος
μετὰ τῶν λόγων οἷς καὶ ὑμεῖς φιλοσοφοῦντες
χρῆσθε. θαρροῦντες οὖν ἄπιτε, καὶ κελεύετε τὸν
υἱὸν ἃ μὴ δύναται τὸν πατέρα πείθειν μὴ βιάζεσθαι."

LXX. Πρὸς ταῦτα μηθὲν ἀντειπόντες οἱ περὶ
τὸν Δημήτριον, ἀλλὰ δακρύσαντες ὑπεξῆλθον.

one instructs or tries to convert me in matters wherein I am thought to have made bad decisions, but I am prevented from using my own judgement, and have my arms taken from me? Why, generous boy, dost thou not also tie thy father's hands behind his back, that Caesar may find me unable to defend myself when he comes? Surely, to kill myself I have no need of a sword, when I have only to hold my breath a little while, or dash my head against the wall, and death will come."

LXIX. As Cato said these words the young man went out sobbing, and all the rest also, except Demetrius and Apollonides. These alone remained, and with these Cato began to talk, now in gentler tones. "I suppose," said he, "that ye also have decided to detain in life by force a man as old as I am, and to sit by him in silence and keep watch of him: or are ye come with the plea that it is neither shameful nor dreadful for Cato, when he has no other way of salvation, to await salvation at the hands of his enemy? Why, then, do ye not speak persuasively and convert me to this doctrine, that we may cast away those good old opinions and arguments which have been part of our very lives, be made wiser through Caesar's efforts, and therefore be more grateful to him? And yet I, certainly, have come to no resolve about myself; but when I have come to a resolve, I must be master of the course which I decide to take. And I shall come to a resolve with your aid, as I might say, since I shall reach it with the aid of those doctrines which ye also adopt as philosophers. So go away with a good courage, and bid my son not to try force with his father when he cannot persuade him."

LXX. Without making any reply to this, but bursting into tears, Demetrius and Apollonides slowly

εἰσπέμπεται δὲ διὰ παιδίου μικροῦ τὸ ἐγχειρίδιον·
καὶ λαβὼν ἐσπάσατο καὶ κατενόησεν. ὡς δὲ
εἶδεν ἑστῶτα τὸν ἀθέρα καὶ τὴν ἀκμὴν διαμένου-
σαν, εἰπών, "Νῦν ἐμός εἰμι," τὸ μὲν ξίφος ἔθηκε,
τὸ δὲ βιβλίον αὖθις ἀνεγίνωσκε, καὶ λέγεται δὶς
2 ὅλον διεξελθεῖν. εἶτα κοιμηθεὶς ὕπνον βαθύν,
ὥστε τοὺς ἐκτὸς αἰσθέσθαι, περὶ μέσας νύκτας
ἐκάλει τῶν ἀπελευθέρων Κλεάνθην τὸν ἰατρὸν
καὶ Βούταν, ᾧ μάλιστα πρὸς τὰς πολιτικὰς
πράξεις ἐχρῆτο. καὶ τοῦτον μὲν ἐπὶ θάλατταν
ἔπεμψεν, ὅπως σκεψάμενος εἰ πάντες ἀνηγμένοι
τυγχάνουσι, φράσοι πρὸς αὐτόν· τῷ δὲ ἰατρῷ τὴν
χεῖρα φλεγμαίνουσαν ὑπὸ τῆς πληγῆς ἣν ἔπληξε
3 τὸν οἰκέτην, ἐπιδῆσαι παρέσχε. καὶ τοῦτ᾽ ἐποίησεν ἡδίους ἅπαντας, ὡς ζωτικῶς ἔχοντος αὐτοῦ.
μετ᾽ ὀλίγον δὲ παρῆν ὁ Βούτας ἀπαγγέλλων τοὺς
μὲν ἄλλους ἀνῆχθαι, Κράσσον δὲ λείπεσθαι ὑπὸ
ἀσχολίας τινός, ὅσον δὲ οὔπω καὶ τοῦτον ἐμβαί-
νειν, πολὺν δὲ χειμῶνα καὶ μέγα πνεῦμα κατέχειν
τὴν θάλατταν. τοῦτο ἀκούσας ὁ Κάτων ἐστέναξεν
οἴκτῳ τῶν πλεόντων, καὶ πάλιν ἔπεμψε τὸν
Βούταν ἐπὶ θάλατταν, εἴ τις ἄρα παλινδρομήσας
δέοιτό τινος τῶν ἀναγκαίων, ἀπαγγελοῦντα πρὸς
αὐτόν.
4 Ἤδη δὲ ὄρνιθες ᾖδον, καὶ μικρὸν αὖθις κατη-
νέχθη πρὸς ὕπνον. ἐπανελθόντος δὲ τοῦ Βούτα
καὶ φράσαντος πολλὴν ἡσυχίαν περὶ τοὺς λιμένας εἶναι, προσέταξεν αὐτῷ τὴν θύραν κλεῖσαι,
καὶ καθῆκεν ἑαυτὸν εἰς τὸ κλινίδιον ὡς τὸ λοιπὸν
5 ἔτι τῆς νυκτὸς ἀναπαυσόμενος. ἐξελθόντος δὲ
τοῦ Βούτα σπασάμενος τὸ ξίφος ἔωσε μὲν ὑπὸ τὸ

withdrew. Then the sword was sent in, carried by a little child, and Cato took it, drew it from its sheath, and examined it. And when he saw that its point was keen and its edge still sharp, he said: "Now I am my own master." Then he laid down the sword and resumed his book, and he is said to have read it through twice. Afterwards he fell into so deep a sleep that those outside the chamber heard him. But about midnight he called two of his freedmen, Cleanthes the physician, and Butas, who was his chief agent in public matters. Butas he sent down to the sea, to find out whether all had set sail successfully, and bring him word; while to the physician he gave his hand to bandage, since it was inflamed by the blow that he had given the slave. This made everybody more cheerful, since they thought he had a mind to live. In a little while Butas came with tidings that all had set sail except Crassus, who was detained by some business or other, and he too was on the point of embarking; Butas reported also that a heavy storm and a high wind prevailed at sea. On hearing this, Cato groaned with pity for those in peril on the sea, and sent Butas down again, to find out whether anyone had been driven back by the storm and wanted any necessaries, and to report to him.

And now the birds were already beginning to sing, when he fell asleep again for a little while. And when Butas came and told him that the harbours were very quiet, he ordered him to close the door, throwing himself down upon his couch as if he were going to rest there for what still remained of the night. But when Butas had gone out, Cato drew his sword from its sheath and stabbed himself below

στῆθος, τῇ δὲ χειρὶ κουφότερον διὰ τὴν φλεγμονὴν
χρησάμενος οὐκ εὐθὺς ἀπήλλαξεν ἑαυτόν, ἀλλὰ
δυσθανατῶν ἐξέπεσε τῆς κλίνης καὶ ψόφον ἐποίησε, καταβαλὼν ἀβάκιόν τι τῶν γεωμετρικῶν
παρακείμενον, ὥστε τοὺς θεράποντας αἰσθομένους
ἀναβοῆσαι καὶ τὸν υἱὸν αὐτίκα καὶ τοὺς φίλους 794
6 ἐπεισελθεῖν. ἰδόντες δὲ πεφυρμένον αἵματι καὶ
τῶν ἐντέρων τὰ πολλὰ προπεπτωκότα, ζῶντα δ'
αὐτὸν ἔτι καὶ βλέποντα, δεινῶς μὲν ἅπαντες
ἔσχον, ὁ δὲ ἰατρὸς προσελθὼν ἐπειρᾶτο τῶν ἐντέρων ἀτρώτων διαμεινάντων ταῦτά τε καθιστάναι
καὶ τὸ τραῦμα διαρράπτειν. ὡς οὖν ἀνήνεγκεν ὁ
Κάτων καὶ συνεφρόνησε, τὸν μὲν ἰατρὸν ἀπεώ-
σατο, ταῖς χερσὶ δὲ τὰ ἔντερα σπαράξας καὶ τὸ
τραῦμα ἐπαναρρήξας ἀπέθανεν.

LXXI. Ἐν ᾧ δὲ οὐκ ἄν τις ᾤετο χρόνῳ τοὺς
κατὰ τὴν οἰκίαν πάντας ᾐσθῆσθαι τὸ πάθος, ἐπὶ
ταῖς θύραις ἦσαν οἱ τριακόσιοι, καὶ μικρὸν ὕστερον ὁ δῆμος ἤθροιστο τῶν Ἰτυκαίων, μιᾷ φωνῇ
τὸν εὐεργέτην καὶ σωτῆρα καὶ μόνον ἐλεύθερον
2 καὶ μόνον ἀήττητον καλούντων. καὶ ταῦτα ἔπραττον ἀγγελλομένου προσιέναι Καίσαρος· ἀλλ' οὔτε
φόβος αὐτοὺς οὔτε κολακεία τοῦ κρατοῦντος οὔτε
ἡ πρὸς ἀλλήλους διαφορὰ καὶ στάσις ἀμβλυτέ-
ρους ἐποίησε τῆς πρὸς Κάτωνα τιμῆς. κοσμή-
σαντες δὲ τὸ σῶμα λαμπρῶς καὶ πομπὴν ἐπιφανῆ
παρασχόντες καὶ θάψαντες παρὰ τὴν θάλασσαν,
οὗ νῦν ἀνδριὰς ἐφέστηκεν αὐτοῦ ξιφήρης, οὕτως
ἐτράποντο πρὸς τὸ σώζειν ἑαυτοὺς καὶ τὴν πόλιν.

LXXII. Καῖσαρ δὲ πυνθανόμενος παρὰ τῶν
ἀφικνουμένων ὑπομένειν ἐν Ἰτύκῃ τὸν Κάτωνα
μηδὲ φεύγειν, ἀλλὰ τοὺς ἄλλους προπέμπειν,

the breast. His thrust, however, was somewhat feeble, owing to the inflammation in his hand, and so he did not at once dispatch himself, but in his death struggle fell from the couch and made a loud noise by overturning a geometrical abacus that stood near. His servants heard the noise and cried out, and his son at once ran in, together with his friends. They saw that he was smeared with blood, and that most of his bowels were protruding, but that he still had his eyes open and was alive; and they were terribly shocked. But the physician went to him and tried to replace his bowels, which remained uninjured, and to sew up the wound. Accordingly, when Cato recovered and became aware of this, he pushed the physician away, tore his bowels with his hands, rent the wound still more, and so died.

LXXI. Before one would have thought that all in the house could learn of the event, the three hundred were at the door, and a little later the people of Utica had assembled. With one voice they called Cato their saviour and benefactor, the only man who was free, the only one unvanquished. And this they continued to do even when word was brought that Caesar was approaching. But neither fear of the conqueror, nor a desire to flatter him, nor their mutual strife and dissension, could blunt their desire to honour Cato. They decked his body in splendid fashion, gave it an illustrious escort, and buried it near the sea, where a statue of him now stands, sword in hand. Then they turned their thoughts to their own salvation and that of their city.

LXXII. When Caesar learned from people who came to him that Cato was remaining in Utica and not trying to escape, but that he was sending off the

αὐτὸν δὲ καὶ τοὺς ἑταίρους καὶ τὸν υἱὸν ἀδεῶς
ἀναστρέφεσθαι, δυστέκμαρτον ἡγεῖτο τὴν γνώμην
τοῦ ἀνδρός, ἅτε δὲ τὸν πλεῖστον λόγον ἔχων
ἐκείνου προσῆγε μετὰ τῆς δυνάμεως ἐπειγόμενος.
2 ὡς δὲ ἤκουσε τὸν θάνατον αὐτοῦ, λέγεται τοσοῦτον εἰπεῖν· "Ὦ Κάτων, φθονῶ σοι τοῦ θανάτου·
καὶ γὰρ ἐμοὶ σὺ τῆς σαυτοῦ σωτηρίας ἐφθόνησας."
τῷ γὰρ ὄντι σωθῆναι Κάτων ἀνασχόμενος ὑπὸ
Καίσαρος οὐκ ἂν οὕτω δοκεῖ καταισχῦναι τὴν
αὐτοῦ δόξαν, ὡς κοσμῆσαι τὴν ἐκείνου. τὸ δὲ
πραχθὲν ἂν ἄδηλον· εἰκάζεται δὲ τὰ χρηστότερα
παρὰ Καίσαρος.

LXXIII. Ἐτελεύτησε δὲ Κάτων ἔτη δυεῖν δέ-
οντα πεντήκοντα βεβιωκώς. ὁ δὲ υἱὸς αὐτοῦ
ὑπὸ Καίσαρος μὲν οὐδὲν ἠδικήθη· λέγεται δὲ
ῥᾴθυμος γενέσθαι καὶ περὶ γυναῖκας οὐκ ἀνεπί-
ληπτος. ἐν δὲ Καππαδοκίᾳ ξένῳ τινὶ χρησάμενος Μαρφαδάτῃ τῶν βασιλικῶν ἔχοντι γύναιον
εὐπρεπές, καὶ πλείονα παρ' αὐτοῖς ἢ καλῶς εἶχε
2 διατρίβων χρόνον, ἐσκώπτετο τοιαῦτα γραφόντων
εἰς αὐτόν·

αὔριον Κάτων βαδίζει μετὰ τριάκονθ' ἡμέρας·

καί,

Πόρκιος καὶ Μαρφαδάτης, δύο φίλοι, ψυχὴ μία.

Ψυχὴ γὰρ ἐκαλεῖτο τοῦ Μαρφαδάτου τὸ γύναιον.
καὶ ἔτι,

εὐγενὴς καὶ λαμπρὸς ὁ Κάτων· βασιλικὴν
ψυχὴν ἔχει.

rest, while he himself, his companions, and his son, were fearlessly going up and down, he thought it difficult to discern the purpose of the man, but since he made the greatest account of him, he came on with his army in all haste. When, however, he heard of his death, he said thus much only, as we are told : " O Cato, I begrudge thee thy death ; for thou didst begrudge me the sparing of thy life." For, in reality, if Cato could have consented to have his life spared by Caesar, he would not be thought to have defiled his own fair fame, but rather to have adorned that of Caesar. However, what would have happened is uncertain ; though the milder course is to be conjectured on the part of Caesar.

LXXIII. When Cato died,[1] he was forty-eight years old. His son received no harm at the hands of Caesar, but he was of an easy disposition, as we are told, and in his relations with women not blameless. In Cappadocia he enjoyed the hospitality of Marphadates, one of the royal family, who had a comely wife ; and since young Cato spent more time with them than was seemly, he was satirized in such writings as these :

" On the morrow Cato journeys,—after a good
    round thirty days;"

and,

" Marphadates and Porcius, two friends with but a
    single Soul."

For the wife of Marphadates was named Psyche (*soul*). And again :

" Nobly born, illustrious, our Cato hath a royal
    Soul."

[1] In 46 b.c. A single letter of his to Cicero is extant (*ad div.* xv. 5) : cf. chapter xxiii. 3.

3 ἀλλὰ πᾶσάν γε τὴν τοιαύτην ἐξήλειψε καὶ
ἠφάνισε τῷ θανάτῳ δύσκλειαν. ἀγωνιζόμενος
γὰρ ἐν Φιλίπποις πρὸς Καίσαρα καὶ ᾿Αντώνιον
ὑπὲρ τῆς ἐλευθερίας, καὶ κλινομένης τῆς φάλαγγος οὔτε φυγεῖν οὔτε λαθεῖν ἀξιώσας, ἀλλὰ προ-
καλούμενος τοὺς πολεμίους ἔμπροσθεν ἑαυτὸν ἐμ-
φανίζων καὶ συνεξορμῶν τοὺς συμμένοντας ἔπεσε,
θαῦμα τῆς ἀρετῆς τοῖς ἐναντίοις παρασχών.

4 Ἔτι δὲ μᾶλλον ἡ θυγάτηρ τοῦ Κάτωνος οὔτε
σωφροσύνης οὔτε ἀνδρείας ἀπολειφθεῖσα (Βρούτῳ
γὰρ συνῴκει τῷ κτείναντι Καίσαρα) αὐτῆς τε
τῆς συνωμοσίας μετέσχε, καὶ προήκατο τὸν βίον
ἀξίως τῆς εὐγενείας καὶ ἀρετῆς, ὡς ἐν τοῖς περὶ
Βρούτου γέγραπται. Στατύλλιος δὲ φήσας μι-
μεῖσθαι Κάτωνα τότε μὲν ὑπὸ τῶν φιλοσόφων
ἐκωλύθη βουλόμενος ἑαυτὸν ἀνελεῖν, ὕστερον δὲ
τῷ Βρούτῳ πιστότατον ἑαυτὸν παρασχὼν καὶ
χρησιμώτατον ἐν Φιλίπποις ἀπέθανεν.

But all such ill-report was blotted out and removed by the manner of his death. For he fought at Philippi against Caesar and Antony, in behalf of liberty; and when his line of battle was giving way, he deigned not either to fly or to hide himself, but challenged the enemy, displayed himself in front of them, cheered on those who held their ground with him, and so fell, after amazing his foes by his valour.

And still more true is it that the daughter of Cato was deficient neither in prudence nor courage. She was the wife of the Brutus who slew Caesar, was privy to the conspiracy itself, and gave up her life in a manner worthy of her noble birth and her lofty character, as is told in the Life of Brutus.[1] Statyllius, too, who declared that he would follow Cato's example,[2] was prevented at the time by the philosophers from destroying himself, as he wished to do, but afterwards gave most faithful and efficient service to Brutus, and died at Philippi.[3]

---

[1] Chapters xiii. and liii.   [2] Cf. above, chapter lxvi. 4.
[3] Cf. the *Brutus*, li. 4.

A PARTIAL DICTIONARY OF
PROPER NAMES

A PARTIAL DICTIONARY OF
PROPER NAMES

A

Adrumetum (or Hadrumetum), 381, a Phoenician sea-port on the coast of northern Africa, a few miles south of Carthage.

Afranius, 53, Lucius A., a warm partisan of Pompey, and one of his legates in Spain during the war with Sertorius, as well as in Asia during the Mithridatic war. In 55 B.C. he was sent by Pompey with Petreius, to hold Spain for him. He was killed after the battle of Thapsus (46 B.C.).

Annius, 19, Caius A. Luscus, had served under Metellus Numidicus in the Jugurthine war (108 B.C.).

Antaeus, 25, a fabled Libyan giant and wrestler, son of Poseidon, whose strength was invincible as long as he remained in contact with his mother Earth. Heracles discovered his secret and slew him.

Antigonus, 5, 85, 211, 215, surnamed the One-eyed, a general of Alexander who received the provinces of Phrygia, Lycia and Pamphylia in the division of Alexander's empire, and succeeded in making himself king of all Asia. He fell in the battle of Ipsus (301 B.C.).

Antipater the Tyrian, 245, died shortly before 44 B.C. according to Cicero (de off. ii. 86).

Antipater, 87, 91–95, 145, 185, 197, 201–217, regent of Macedonia during Alexander's absence in the East, and of Alexander's empire after the murder of Perdiccas in 321 B.C. He died in 319.

Antiphilus, 199, 201, an Athenian general known only from these events of the Lamian war.

Antonius, 73, known only from this incident.

Apollonides the Stoic, 397, 399, 403, known only from these incidents.

Aquinus, 37, known only from these incidents.

Archilochus, 161, 251, of Paros, one of the earliest Ionian lyric poets, flourishing in 650 B.C.

Ariminum, 361, an important city of Umbria, on the sea-coast, about nine miles south of the Rubicon.

Aristophon, 161, of the Athenian deme Colyttus, a prominent orator and politician contemporary with Demosthenes.

Athenodorus (1), of Imbros, 187, an Athenian of Imbrian family, and a mercenary captain in the East, who attained political power in Thrace in 359 B.C. He was a supporter of Persia against Alexander, by whom he was captured at Sardis in 334.

Athenodorus (2), surnamed Cordylion, 257, 269, a Stoic philosopher, born at Tarsus. He was keeper of the library at Pergamum, whence he removed to Rome in 70 B.C., and lived there with Cato.

B

Baetica, 21, 31, the southern district of Spain, traversed by the great river Baetis.

Barca, 327 not otherwise known.

Bibulus, 293, 295, 311, 313, 351, 367, Lucius Calpurnius B., aedile in 65 B.C., praetor in 62, and consul in 59, in each case a colleague of Julius Caesar. He died in 48.

Boëdromion, 207, the Attic month corresponding to parts of our September and October.

Butas, 405, known also as an author from the *Romulus*, xxi. 6.

C

Caepio (1), 7, Quintus Servilius C., consul in 106 B.C., and pro-consul in Gallia Narbonensis for the following year. Ten years after his defeat by the Cimbri (*Camillus*, xix. 7) he was brought to trial for misconduct of the war, condemned, and thrown into prison.

Caepio (2), 237, 239, 243, 245, 253, Quintus Servilius C., half-brother of Cato.

Caesar, 397, Lucius, not otherwise known.

Callimedon, 221, 227, 229, surnamed the Crab, one of the Athenian orators who favoured the Macedonian interest.

Canidius, 321–325, not otherwise known.

Carbo, 15, 19, 61, Gnaeus Papirius C., one of the leaders of the Marian party. After his flight to Libya (*Sulla*, xxix. 8) he was taken prisoner by Pompey and cruelly put to death (*Pompey*, chapter x.).

Cardia, 79, 85, 87, one of the chief towns of the Thracian Chersonese.

Cassander, 215, 217, a son of Antipater the regent of Macedonia, to whom his father refused the succession. He was master of Athens from 318 to 307 B.C., and died in 297.

Castulo, 7, an important city in the southern part of Hispania Tarraconensis, on the upper waters of the Baetis.

Catiline, 287, Lucius Sergius, the famous conspirator in the consulship of Cicero (63 B.C.). See the *Cicero*, chapters x.-xxii.

Catulus, 271, 273, Quintus Lutatius C., a leading aristocrat of the nobler sort, consul in 78 B.C., censor in 65, died in 60.

Cenchraeae, 329, the eastern harbour-town of Corinth.

Cephisodotus, 189, a celebrated Athenian sculptor. In 371 B.C. he executed for the Athenians a group of Peace holding Plutus the god of riches in her arms.

Ceraunian Mountains, 211, sometimes called Acroceraunian, a range in the northern part of Epirus.

Chabrias, 157–161, an able and successful Athenian general, prominent from 392 B.C. till his gallant death at the siege of Chios in 357.

Chaeroneia, 181, a town commanding the entrance from Phocis into Boeotia, celebrated for the number of important battles fought in its neighbourhood. Here Philip of Macedon defeated the allied Greeks in 338 B.C.

Chares (1), 155, 175, a famous Athenian general, prominent from 367 to 334 B.C.

Chares (2), 185, of Mitylene, court chamberlain of Alexander, and author of an anecdotical history of Alexander's campaigns.

Charicles, 193, 195, 221, 229, known only from these incidents.

Charidemus, 5, 179, 183, an Athenian general and a roving soldier of fortune, prominent from 367 to 349 B.C.

Cinna, 11–15, Lucius Cornelius C., leader of the Marian party during Sulla's absence in the East (87–84 B.C.). He was consul in 87, 86, 85, and 84. He was slain in a mutiny of his soldiers at Brundisium, where he hoped to prevent the landing of Sulla. See the *Pompey*, v. 1.

Cleanthes, 405, known only from this passage.

DICTIONARY OF PROPER NAMES

Cleitus, 225, 227, successfully commanded the fleet of Antipater in the Lamian war (323 B.C.), and later (318) that of Polysperchon at Byzantium, but was surprised by Antigonus, defeated, and slain.

Clodius, 279, 281, 311, 315–319, 331, 333, 345. Publius Claudius (Clodius) Pulcher, youngest son of the Appius Claudius mentioned in the *Sulla*, xxix. 3. He helped to demoralise the soldiers of Lucullus (*Lucullus*, xxxiv.), and became a venomous foe of Cicero.

Corcyra, 329, 371, an island in the Ionian sea, opposite Epirus; the modern Corfu.

Cotta, 31, possibly the Marcus Aurelius Cotta who became consul with Lucullus in 74 B.C. now a legate under Caius Annius (pp. 19 f.).

Crassus, 405, not otherwise known.

Craterus, 91–95, 187, 201, 203, one of the ablest of Alexander's officers, and a man of noble character. He fell in battle against Eumenes in 321 B.C. See the *Eumenes*, v. ff.

Ctesippus, 159, not otherwise known.

Curio, 267, 349, probably the Caius Scribonius Curio who was consul in 76 B.C. He was a steadfast opponent of Julius Caesar, and a friend of Cicero and Cato. He was pontifex maximus in 57, and died in 53.

Cyrene, 371, the most important Greek colony on the northern coast of Africa, almost directly south of Crete. It was founded in 631 B.C.

D

Deiotarus the Galatian, 261, 267, 269, tetrarch of Galatia in Asia Minor, and an old man in 54 B.C. (*Crassus*, xvii. 1 f.). He was a faithful friend of the Romans in their Asiatic wars, and in 63 was rewarded by the senate with the title of King. Caesar could never be brought to pardon him for siding with Pompey.

Demades, 145, 181, 191, 195, 213, 215, an Athenian politician and orator of Macedonian sympathies, and bitterly hostile to Demosthenes.

Demetrius the Peripatetic, 397, 403, not definitely known.

Demetrius of Phalerum, a celebrated rhetorician and orator (346–283 B.C.). He was regent of Athens for Cassander from 318 to 307.

Demophilus, 233, not otherwise known.

Didius, 7, Titus Didius, consul in 98 B.C. He fell in battle during the Marsic war (89 B.C.).

Diopeithes, 161, an Athenian general, father of the poet Menander. He was arraigned by the Macedonian party at Athens, and was defended by Demosthenes in the extant oration " On the Chersonese."

Dodona, 209, a town in Epirus, famous in earlier times for its oracle of Zeus, the influence of which among the Greek states was later assumed by the oracle of Apollo at Delphi.

Domitius (1), 31, Lucius Domitius Ahenobarbus, known only from this defeat, in which he was killed.

Domitius (2), 333, 335, Lucius Domitius Ahenobarbus, consul in 54 B.C. He was one of the ablest supporters of the aristocratic party. He opposed both Pompey and Caesar until their quarrel, then sided with Pompey. He met his death at Pharsalus.

Drusus, 237, 239, ·Marcus Livius D., at first an able and ardent supporter of the aristocratic party and the senate, but afterwards an agitator like the Gracchi. He was assassinated in 91 B.C.

Duris, 79, 153, 185, the Samian, a

pupil of Theophrastus, historian and, for a time, tyrant of Samos, lived *circa* 350–280 B.C.

Dyrrhachium, 365–369, a city on the coast of Illyricum, opposite to Brundisium, known in Greek history as Epidamnus. It was a free state, and sided with the Romans consistently.

E

Ebro (Iberus), 41, a large river the basin of which forms the north-eastern part of the peninsula of Spain.

Echecratides the sophist, 187, not otherwise known.

Elateia, 223, a city of Phocis in a plain commanding passes into southern Greece.

Epicurus, 233, not otherwise known.

Eubulus, 161, a leading Athenian orator and statesman, highly successful as a minister of finance. He was of the party opposed to Demosthenes.

F

Favonius, 315, 347, 349, Marcus F., called the "Ape of Cato," was aedile in 52 B.C. and praetor in 49. He joined Pompey in the East, notwithstanding personal enmity towards him, and accompanied him in his flight from Pharsalus (cf. the *Pompey*, lxxiii. 6 f.). He was put to death by order of Octavius Caesar after the battle of Philippi (42 B.C.).

Fimbria, 65, Caius Flavius F., a partisan of Marius. He won important successes against Mithridates in 85 B.C., but was defeated and brought to death by Sulla in 84. See the *Sulla*, xxiii.-xxv.

Fufidius, 31, a creature of Sulla, mentioned also in the *Sulla*, xxxi. 3.

G

Gabinius, 317, Aulus G., tribune of the people in 66 B.C., praetor in 61, consul with Piso in 58, the year during which Cicero was in exile. He was recalled from his province of Syria in 55, prosecuted for taking bribes, and exiled. He died in 48.

Glaucippus, 153, not otherwise known.

Gracinus, 69, not otherwise known.

H

Hagnonides (or Agnonides), 211, 221, 223, 227, 233, an Athenian sycophant and demagogue, whose career is known mostly from this *Life*.

Harpalus, 191–195, the faithless treasurer of Alexander. Antipater demanded his surrender by the Athenians, who put him in prison. Thence he escaped and went to Crete, where he was assassinated.

Hegemon, 225, 229, a minor Athenian orator of the time of Demosthenes, who supported the interests of Macedon.

Hephaestion, 29, 81, 83, officer and beloved friend of Alexander.

Hortensius, 293, 295, 363, the great oratorical rival of Cicero, a man of high character, brilliant parts, and great wealth. He died in 50 B.C.

Hypereides, 153, 161, 169, 183, 197, 203, 205, 211, a great Athenian orator, who stood with Demosthenes at the head of the anti-Macedonian party.

Hypsaeus, 351, Publius Plautius H., tribune of the people in 54 B.C., and candidate for the consulship two years later. He was accused of corrupt practices, tried, and convicted. Pompey, whom he had devotedly served, forsook him in the hour of need.

DICTIONARY OF PROPER NAMES

I

Iberians, 69 and *passim*, a general name for the original peoples of the Spanish peninsula.

Ios, 5, an island in the eastern Aegean sea, one of the Sporades, south of Naxos.

J

Juba (1), 373–379, 385–389, Juba I., king of Numidia, and a supporter of Pompey, to whom he owed his throne. He followed Cato's example and put an end to his own life.

Juba (2), 25, Juba II., king of Mauretania, son of the preceding. After his father's death in 46 B.C., he was taken as a child to Rome by Caesar, where he was educated. He became a learned and voluminous writer, and among his works was a History of Rome.

L

Labienus, 373, though a trusted officer of Caesar in Gaul, he went over to Pompey in the Civil War, fled to Africa after the battle of Pharsalus, and after the battle of Thapsus (46 B.C.) to Spain, where he was the immediate cause of the defeat of the Pompeians at Munda, and was slain (45 B.C.).

Laelius, 253, Caius L., a brilliant commander and statesman, whose deeds are inseparably interwoven with those of his friend and companion, the elder Scipio. He died about 170 B.C.

Laomedon, 3, a mythical king of Troy, the father of Priam.

Lauron, 49, a small town in the S.E. part of Spain, south of Valentia, near the sea.

Leonnatus, 85, 187, 201, one of Alexander's most distinguished officers.

Leosthenes, 161, 195–203, an Athenian, general of the league for expelling the Macedonians from Greece after the death of Alexander.

Lollius, 273, Marcus L., not further known.

Lusitanians, 25–31, 69, the people of the western district or province of Spain.

Lycurgus (1), 191, the great Spartan lawgiver.

Lycurgus (2), 161, 167, 183, an able Athenian orator and a highly successful minister of finance (396–323 B.C.), one of the noblest specimens of old Attic integrity and virtue in a degenerate age.

M

Manlius (1), 33, Lucius M., proconsul in Narbonese Gaul in 78 B.C. He was badly defeated by one of the generals of Sertorius.

Manlius (2), 69, 71, 75, not otherwise known.

Marcellus, 277, perhaps the Caius Claudius Marcellus who was consul in 50 B.C., a friend of Cicero and Pompey, and an uncompromising foe of Caesar.

Marius, 15, an adopted son of the elder Marius. He became consul at the age of twenty-seven, and was as merciless and cruel as his father. His death by his own hands is noted in the *Sulla*, xxxii. 1.

Mellaria, 31, a small town on the southern coast of Spain.

Memmius (1), 55, Caius M., a brother-in-law of Pompey, and his quaestor in Spain. Cf. the *Pompey*, xi. 2.

Memmius (2), 305, 307, Caius M. Gemellus, tribune of the people at this time (66 B.C.), and two years later an unsuccessful candidate for the consulship. He left Rome under impeachment for

corrupt practices, and spent the rest of his life in Mitylene.

Menestheus, 161, a son of the famous Athenian general Iphicrates by a Thracian princess. He was distinguished for his military skill, and was prominent with his father in the Social War (356 B.C.). Nothing is heard of him after 325 B.C.

Menon the Thessalian, 201, a citizen of Pharsalus, and a man of great influence and reputation. His cavalry bore themselves well in the battle of Crannon. In 321 he was defeated and slain by Polysperchon.

Mentor, 81, not further known.

Menyllus, 207, 209, 213, 217, known only from these passages.

Metellus (1), 5, 31–61, 73, Quintus Caecilius M. Pius, consul with Sulla in 80 B.C., and one of his most successful generals. After Sulla's death in 78 Metellus was sent to Spain as pro-consul to prosecute the war against Sertorius. He died about 63.

Metellus (2), 281–285, 297–305, Quintus M. Nepos, a partisan of Pompey, and for a time a violent opponent of Cicero. As consul, however, in 57 B.C., he did not oppose the recall of Cicero from exile. He died in 55.

Metellus (3), 313, Quintus Caecilius M. Numidicus, victor over Jugurtha in 109 B.C., but supplanted by Marius. He was censor n 102, was unjustly expelled from the senate, and went into exile, from which he was recalled in 99 B.C., largely through the efforts of his son, Metellus Pius.

Micion, 201, known only from this passage.

Milo, 351, Titus Annius Papianus, a ruffian and swashbuckler, tribune of the people in 57 B.C., and from that time on involved in a fierce quarrel with Clodius, which ended with the murder of Clodius. Milo was impeached for the crime, defended by Cicero in an extant oration, condemned, and

sent into exile. Attempting to return by force in 48, he was slain.

Mithridates, 11, 63–67, the sixth king of Pontus bearing this name, commonly called the Great, 120–63 B.C., the most formidable enemy of the Romans in the East.

Molossus, 175, not otherwise known.

Munatius, 255, 293, 301, 307, 309, 323–327, 361, the bosom friend of Cato.

Murena, 285, 287, 303, Lucius Licinius M., had served under Lucullus (*Lucullus*, xix. 7). On his trial he was defended by Hortensius and Cicero (in an extant oration), and acquitted.

N

Nearchus, 81, the able and trusted admiral of Alexander.

Neoptolemus, 79, 89–101, an officer of Alexander.

New Carthage, 19, a famous colony of Carthage on the southeastern coast of Spain.

Nicanor, 217–221, held the Peiraeus for Cassander, and afterwards served him successfully as naval commander in the Hellespont, but awakened his jealousy and was put to death by him.

Nicocles, 183, 229, 231, not otherwise known.

Norbanus, 15, Caius N., consul in 83 B.C. After his defeats by Sulla and Metellus, he fled to Rhodes, where he put an end to his own life.

O

Octavius (1), 11, 13, Gnaeus O., consul with Cinna in 87 B.C. His death is described in the *Marius*, xlii.

DICTIONARY OF PROPER NAMES

Octavius (2), 395, Marcus O., consul in 54 B.C., and a supporter of Pompey in the Civil War. He fled to Africa in 47. He is last heard of as serving under Antony at the battle of Actium in 31.

Osca, 37, 69, a Roman colony in north-eastern Spain.

P

Paccianus, 23, not otherwise known.

Pella, 87, the capital city of Macedonia.

Perdiccas, 79, 85, 89–93, the officer to whom the dying Alexander is said to have given his signet-ring, and regent for the royal successors of Alexander till 321 B.C.

Perpenna, 39, 41, 67–75, Marcus P. Vento, a leading partisan of Marius. On the death of Sulla (78 B.C.) he joined Lepidus in his attempt to win the supreme power, and failing here, retired to Spain and served under Sertorius.

Pessinus, 269, an important town in the west of Galatia, famous for its cult of Cybele.

Pharsalus, 369, 373, an ancient town in southern Thessaly, near which Caesar finally defeated Pompey.

Philip, 5, 79, Philip of Macedon, father of Alexander.

Philippi, 411, a city of Macedonia on the river Strymon, formerly called Crenides, but renamed by Philip II.

Philippus, 293, 295, 331, Lucius Marcius P., consul in 56 B.C., and step-father of Octavius Caesar. He remained neutral in the civil wars, and lived to see his step-son master of the world.

Philostratus, 375, the Aegyptian, a professed but degenerate follower of the Academy, afterwards associated with Antony and Cleopatra (*Antony*, lxxx. 2).

Phocus, 189, 191, 213, 229, 233, the son of Phocion, not otherwise known.

Pigres, 95, an officer not otherwise known.

Piso, 307, 317, Lucius Calpurnius P., father-in-law of Julius Caesar. He plundered his province of Macedonia shamelessly, and was recalled in 55 B.C. He is covered with invective in Cicero's oration *de Provinc. Cons.* He took no part in the Civil War.

Pityussa, 19, the name of two islands (often spoken of as one) lying off the southern coast of Spain.

Plancus, 353, Titus Munatius P. Bursa, tribune of the people in 52 B.C. and largely responsible for the riots of that year, for complicity in which he was tried and condemned. He was restored to civil rights by Julius Caesar, and served under Antony.

Plutarch the Eretrian, 171, 173, sought the aid of the Athenians against his rival, the tyrant of Chalcis, who had allied himself with Philip of Macedon.

Pollio, 363, 365, Caius Asinius P., a famous orator, poet, and historian, 76 B.C.–4 A.D. He was an intimate friend of Julius Caesar, fought under him in Africa and Spain, and after Caesar's death supported Octavius Caesar. After 29, he devoted himself entirely to literature, and was a patron of Vergil and Horace. None of his works are extant.

Polyeuctus the Sphettian, 165, an Athenian of the deme Sphettus, a political friend of Demosthenes, and an orator of some note.

Polysperchon, 217, 221–225, a distinguished officer of Alexander, appointed by Antipater to succeed him in the regency. He connived at some of the worst crimes of Cassander.

Pompeius (1), 371 (" the younger Pompey "), Gnaeus P., the elder son of the triumvir by his third

421

wife, put to death by the troops of Caesar after the battle of Munda in Spain (45 B.C.).

Pompeius (2), 371, 383, Sextus P., the younger son of the triumvir by his third wife, escaped after the battle of Munda and was active against the triumvirate until his death in 35 B.C.

Porcia (1), 333, Cato's own sister, died in 46 B.C., ten years after her husband.

Porcia (2), 293, 411, Cato's daughter, married first to Bibulus, Caesar's consular colleague, in 59 B.C. Bibulus died in 48, and in 45 Porcia married Brutus the conspirator.

Ptolemy (1), 81, 91, Ptolemy Lagus, the most far-sighted and successful of the officers of Alexander, afterwards Ptolemy I. of Egypt.

Ptolemy (2), 321, Ptolemy XI. of Egypt, commonly known as Ptolemy Auletes. After many disappointments he was at last restored to his throne in 55 B.C., through the influence of Pompey, but never regained the goodwill of his people.

Ptolemy (3), 319, 321, younger brother of Ptolemy Auletes, and king of Cyprus. He incurred the enmity of Clodius, who, as tribune of the Roman people, brought in a decree depriving him of his kingdom.

Pytheas, 191, an Athenian orator chiefly known for his unreasoning hatred of Demosthenes. He was a man of no fixed character, and in the Lamian War became a renegade from Athens. See the *Demosthenes*, xxxii.

Pythocles, 229, not otherwise known.

R

Rubrius (1), 255, known only from this allusion.

Rubrius (2), Marcus R., not otherwise known.

S

Saguntum, 55, a rich commercial city on the east coast of Spain, near the sea.

Salinator, 19, Julius, not otherwise known.

Scipio (1), 3, 253, Publius Cornelius S. Africanus Major (234–183 B.C.), the conqueror of Hannibal.

Scipio (2), 3, Publius Cornelius S. Aemilianus Africanus Minor (185–129 B.C.), the destroyer of Carthage.

Scipio (3), 15, 17, Lucius Cornelius S. Asiaticus, belonged to the Marian party in the civil wars, and was consul in 83 B.C., the year when Sulla returned from the East (cf. the *Sulla*, xxviii. 1–3). He was proscribed in 82, and fled to Massilia, where he died.

Scipio (4), 251, 351, 375–379, 385, 387, Publius Cornelius S. Nasica, adopted by Metellus Pius and therefore called Metellus Scipio, was made Pompey's colleague in the consulship late in the year 52 B.C., and became a determined foe of Caesar. He commanded Pompey's centre at Pharsalus, fled to Africa, and killed himself after the battle of Thapsus (46 B.C.). Though a Scipio by birth, a Metellus by adoption, and the father-in-law of Pompey, he was rapacious and profligate.

Serranus, 251, probably the Sextus Atilius S. Gavianus, who was quaestor in 63 B.C. and favoured by Cicero, but as tribune of the people in 57 opposed the recall of Cicero from exile.

Servilia (1), 285, 291, half-sister of Cato, and faithless wife of Silanus.

Servilia (2), 293, 305, 365 f., another half-sister of Cato, the faithless wife of Lucullus.

Silanus, 285–289, Decimus Junius S., consul in 64 and 62 B.C.

Silo, 239, 241, Pompaedius S., leader of the Marsi in the Social

War, and confederate with Drusus. He displayed great military ability in the war, but was finally defeated by Metellus Pius in 88 B.C., and died in battle.

Statyllius, 395–399, 411, known only from these passages.

Sucro, 51, a river in south-eastern Spain, between Valentia and Lauron.

Sulpicius, 355, Servius S. Lemonia Rufus, a friend and fellow-student of Cato, and a successful competitor against him for the consulship in 51 B.C. He supported the cause of Caesar, and died in 43.

Thrasea, 293, 325, Publius T. Paetus, a noble Roman who fell a victim to the hatred of Nero in 66 A.D. In his youth he was devoted to the Stoic philosophy, and wrote a study of the life of Cato the Younger.

Thudippus, 229, not otherwise known.

Trebonius, 339, Caius T., tribune of the people in 55 B.C., and an instrument of the triumvirs. He was afterwards legate of Caesar in Gaul, and was loaded with favours by him, but was one of the conspirators against his life.

Turia, 51, a small town near the upper waters of the Sucro, in south-eastern Spain.

T

Taenarum, 211, the promontory at the extreme south of Laconia.

Tagonius, 43, a tributary of the river Tagus, in south-western Spain.

Thapsus, 379, a maritime city of northern Africa, south of Carthage.

Theodorus the Atheist, 233, a philosopher of the Cyrenaic school, banished from his native city of Cyrene, and resident at Athens during the regency of Demetrius the Phalerian (318–307 B.C.).

Theophrastus, 35, 325, the most famous pupil of Aristotle, and his successor as head of the Peripatetic school at Athens. He was born at Eresos in Lesbos, and died at Athens in 287 B.C., at the age of eighty-five.

Thermus, 299, 301, Minucius, not otherwise definitely known.

Thessalonica, 259, the capital of the Roman province of Macedonia, situated at the head of the Thermaic gulf.

Thoranius, 31, not otherwise known.

U

Utica, 375–407, a Phoenician colony from Tyre, older than Carthage, on the northern coast of Africa twenty-seven miles north-west of Carthage.

V

Vaccaei, 59, an important people in the interior of Hispania Tarraconensis, or north-eastern Spain.

Varus, 373–377, Publius Attius V., a zealous partisan of Pompey. When Pompey forsook Italy in 49 B.C., Varus took possession of Africa, where he had formerly been pro-praetor. In conjunction with King Juba he crushed Curio, the legate of Caesar. He fell in the battle of Munda (45).

Vatinius, 337, Publius V., a leading partisan of Caesar, praetor in 55 B.C., after which he served Caesar as legate in Gaul, and in important commands during the Civil War. He is last heard of in 43.

DICTIONARY OF PROPER NAMES

X

Xenocrates, the philosopher, 205, 213, a native of Chalcedon in Bithynia, and a disciple at Athens of Aeschines the Socratic. He lived 396–314 B.C.

Z

Zeno, 155, probably the Stoic philosopher is meant, who taught at Athens in the third century B.C., and wrote on law and government.

THE LOEB CLASSICAL LIBRARY

1

CICERO: DE SENECTUTE, DE AMICITIA, DE DIVINATIONE. W. A. Falconer.

CICERO: IN CATILINAM, PRO FLACCO, PRO MURENA, PRO SULLA. New version by C. Macdonald.

CICERO: LETTERS TO ATTICUS. E. O. Winstedt. 3 Vols.

CICERO: LETTERS TO HIS FRIENDS. W. Glynn Williams, M. Cary, M. Henderson. 4 Vols.

CICERO: PHILIPPICS. W. C. A. Ker.

CICERO: PRO ARCHIA, POST REDITUM, DE DOMO, DE HARUSPICUM RESPONSIS, PRO PLANCIO. N. H. Watts.

CICERO: PRO CAECINA, PRO LEGE MANILIA, PRO CLUENTIO, PRO RABIRIO. H. Grose Hodge.

CICERO: PRO CAELIO, DE PROVINCIIS CONSULARIBUS, PRO BALBO. R. Gardner.

CICERO: PRO MILONE, IN PISONEM, PRO SCAURO, PRO FONTEIO, PRO RABIRIO POSTUMO, PRO MARCELLO, PRO LIGARIO, PRO REGE DEIOTARO. N. H. Watts.

CICERO: PRO QUINCTIO, PRO ROSCIO AMERINO, PRO ROSCIO COMOEDO, CONTRA RULLUM. J. H. Freese.

CICERO: PRO SESTIO, IN VATINIUM. R. Gardner.

CICERO: TUSCULAN DISPUTATIONS. J. E. King.

CICERO: VERRINE ORATIONS. L. H. G. Greenwood. 2 Vols.

CLAUDIAN. M. Platnauer. 2 Vols.

COLUMELLA: DE RE RUSTICA. DE ARBORIBUS. H. B. Ash, E. S. Forster and E. Heffner. 3 Vols.

CURTIUS, Q.: HISTORY OF ALEXANDER. J. C. Rolfe. 2 Vols.

FLORUS. E. S. Forster.

FRONTINUS: STRATAGEMS and AQUEDUCTS. C. E. Bennett and M. B. McElwain.

FRONTO: CORRESPONDENCE. C. R. Haines. 2 Vols.

GELLIUS. J. C. Rolfe. 3 Vols.

HORACE: ODES and EPODES. C. E. Bennett.

HORACE: SATIRES, EPISTLES, ARS POETICA. H. R. Fairclough.

JEROME: SELECTED LETTERS. F. A. Wright.

JUVENAL and PERSIUS. G. G. Ramsay.

LIVY. B. O. Foster, F. G. Moore, Evan T. Sage, and A. C. Schlesinger and R. M. Geer (General Index). 14 Vols.

LUCAN. J. D. Duff.

LUCRETIUS. W. H. D. Rouse. Revised by M. F. Smith.

MANILIUS. G. P. Goold.

MARTIAL. W. C. A. Ker. 2 Vols. Revised by E. H. Warmington

MINOR LATIN POETS: from PUBLILIUS SYRUS to RUTILIUS NAMATIANUS, including GRATTIUS, CALPURNIUS SICULUS, NEMESIANUS, AVIANUS and others, with "Aetna" and the "Phoenix." J. Wight Duff and Arnold M. Duff. 2 Vols.

MINUCIUS FELIX. Cf. TERTULLIAN.

2

NEPOS, CORNELIUS. J. C. Rolfe.

OVID: THE ART OF LOVE and OTHER POEMS. J. H. Mozley. Revised by G. P. Goold.

OVID: FASTI. Sir James G. Frazer. Revised by G. P. Goold.

OVID: HEROIDES and AMORES. Grant Showerman. Revised by G. P. Goold.

OVID: METAMORPHOSES. F. J. Miller. 2 Vols. Revised by G. P. Goold.

OVID: TRISTIA and EX PONTO. A. L. Wheeler. Revised by G. P. Goold.

PERSIUS. Cf. JUVENAL.

PERVIGILIUM VENERIS. Cf. CATULLUS.

PETRONIUS. M. Heseltine. SENECA: APOCOLOCYNTOSIS. W. H. D. Rouse. Revised by E. H. Warmington.

PHAEDRUS and BABRIUS (Greek). B. E. Perry.

PLAUTUS. Paul Nixon. 5 Vols.

PLINY: LETTERS, PANEGYRICUS. Betty Radice. 2 Vols.

PLINY: NATURAL HISTORY. 10 Vols. Vols. I.–V. and IX. H. Rackham. VI.–VIII. W. H. S. Jones. X. D. E. Eichholz.

PROPERTIUS. H. E. Butler.

PRUDENTIUS. H. J. Thomson. 2 Vols.

QUINTILIAN. H. E. Butler. 4 Vols.

REMAINS OF OLD LATIN. E. H. Warmington. 4 Vols. Vol. I. (ENNIUS AND CAECILIUS) Vol. II. (LIVIUS, NAEVIUS PACUVIUS, ACCIUS) Vol. III. (LUCILIUS and LAWS OF XII TABLES) Vol. IV. (ARCHAIC INSCRIPTIONS).

RES GESTAE DIVI AUGUSTI. Cf. VELLEIUS PATERCULUS.

SALLUST. J. C. Rolfe.

SCRIPTORES HISTORIAE AUGUSTAE. D. Magie. 3 Vols.

SENECA, THE ELDER: CONTROVERSIAE, SUASORIAE. M. Winterbottom. 2 Vols.

SENECA: APOCOLOCYNTOSIS. Cf. PETRONIUS.

SENECA: EPISTULAE MORALES. R. M. Gummere. 3 Vols.

SENECA: MORAL ESSAYS. J. W. Basore. 3 Vols.

SENECA: TRAGEDIES. F. J. Miller. 2 Vols.

SENECA: NATURALES QUAESTIONES. T. H. Corcoran. 2 Vols.

SIDONIUS: POEMS and LETTERS. W. B. Anderson. 2 Vols.

SILIUS ITALICUS. J. D. Duff. 2 Vols.

STATIUS. J. H. Mozley. 2 Vols.

SUETONIUS. J. C. Rolfe. 2 Vols.

TACITUS: DIALOGUS. Sir Wm. Peterson. AGRICOLA and GERMANIA. Maurice Hutton. Revised by M. Winterbottom, R. M. Ogilvie, E. H. Warmington.

TACITUS: HISTORIES and ANNALS. C. H. Moore and J. Jackson. 4 Vols.

TERENCE. John Sargeaunt. 2 Vols.

TERTULLIAN: APOLOGIA and DE SPECTACULIS. T. R. Glover. MINUCIUS FELIX. G. H. Rendall.

TIBULLUS. Cf. CATULLUS.
VALERIUS FLACCUS. J. H. Mozley.
VARRO: DE LINGUA LATINA. R. G. Kent. 2 Vols.
VELLEIUS PATERCULUS and RES GESTAE DIVI AUGUSTI. F. W. SHIPLEY.
VIRGIL. H. R. Fairclough. 2 Vols.
VITRUVIUS: DE ARCHITECTURA. F. Granger. 2 Vols.

Greek Authors

ACHILLES TATIUS. S. Gaselee.
AELIAN: ON THE NATURE OF ANIMALS. A. F. Scholfield. 3 Vols.
AENEAS TACTICUS. ASCLEPIODOTUS and ONASANDER. The Illinois Greek
    Club.
AESCHINES. C. D. Adams.
AESCHYLUS. H. Weir Smyth. 2 Vols.
ALCIPHRON, AELIAN, PHILOSTRATUS: LETTERS. A. R. Benner and F. H.
    Fobes.
ANDOCIDES, ANTIPHON. Cf. MINOR ATTIC ORATORS Vol. I.
APOLLODORUS. Sir James G. Frazer. 2 Vols.
APOLLONIUS RHODIUS. R. C. Seaton.
APOSTOLIC FATHERS. Kirsopp Lake. 2 Vols.
APPIAN: ROMAN HISTORY. Horace White. 4 Vols.
ARATUS. Cf. CALLIMACHUS.
ARISTIDES: ORATIONS. C. A. Behr.
ARISTOPHANES. Benjamin Bickley Rogers. 3 Vols. Verse trans.
ARISTOTLE: ART OF RHETORIC. J. H. Freese.
ARISTOTLE: ATHENIAN CONSTITUTION, EUDEMIAN ETHICS, VICES AND
    VIRTUES. H. Rackham.
ARISTOTLE: GENERATION OF ANIMALS. A. L. Peck.
ARISTOTLE: HISTORIA ANIMALIUM. A. L. Peck. Vols. I.–II.
ARISTOTLE: METAPHYSICS. H. Tredennick. 2 Vols.
ARISTOTLE: METEOROLOGICA. H. D. P. Lee.
ARISTOTLE: MINOR WORKS. W. S. Hett. On Colours, On Things
    Heard, On Physiognomies, On Plants, On Marvellous Things
    Heard, Mechanical Problems, On Indivisible Lines, On Situations
    and Names of Winds, On Melissus, Xenophanes, and Gorgias.
ARISTOTLE: NICOMACHEAN ETHICS. H. Rackham.
ARISTOTLE: OECONOMICA and MAGNA MORALIA. G. C. Armstrong (with
    METAPHYSICS, Vol. II).
ARISTOTLE: ON THE HEAVENS. W. K. C. Guthrie.
ARISTOTLE: ON THE SOUL, PARVA NATURALIA, ON BREATH. W. S. Hett.
ARISTOTLE: CATEGORIES, ON INTERPRETATION, PRIOR ANALYTICS. H. P.
    Cooke and H. Tredennick.

4

5

DIONYSIUS OF HALICARNASSUS: CRITICAL ESSAYS. S. Usher. 2 Vols.
EPICTETUS. W. A. Oldfather. 2 Vols.
EURIPIDES. A. S. Way. 4 Vols. Verse trans.
EUSEBIUS: ECCLESIASTICAL HISTORY. Kirsopp Lake and J. E. L. Oulton. 2 Vols.
GALEN: ON THE NATURAL FACULTIES. A. J. Brock.
GREEK ANTHOLOGY. W. R. Paton. 5 Vols.
GREEK BUCOLIC POETS (THEOCRITUS, BION, MOSCHUS). J. M. Edmonds.
GREEK ELEGY AND IAMBUS with the ANACREONTEA. J. M. Edmonds. 2 Vols.
GREEK LYRIC. D. A. Campbell. 4 Vols. Vols. I. and II.
GREEK MATHEMATICAL WORKS. Ivor Thomas. 2 Vols.
HERODAS. Cf. THEOPHRASTUS: CHARACTERS.
HERODIAN. C. R. Whittaker. 2 Vols.
HERODOTUS. A. D. Godley. 4 Vols.
HESIOD AND THE HOMERIC HYMNS. H. G. Evelyn White.
HIPPOCRATES and the FRAGMENTS OF HERACLEITUS. W. H. S. Jones and E. T. Withington. 7 Vols. Vols. I.–VI.
HOMER: ILIAD. A. T. Murray. 2 Vols.
HOMER: ODYSSEY. A. T. Murray. 2 Vols.
ISAEUS. E. W. Forster.
ISOCRATES. George Norlin and LaRue Van Hook. 3 Vols.
[ST. JOHN DAMASCENE]: BARLAAM AND IOASAPH. Rev. G. R. Woodward, Harold Mattingly and D. M. Lang.
JOSEPHUS. 10 Vols. Vols. I.–IV. H. Thackeray. Vol. V. H. Thackeray and R. Marcus. Vols. VI.–VII. R. Marcus. Vol. VIII. R. Marcus and Allen Wikgren. Vols. IX.–X. L. H. Feldman.
JULIAN. Wilmer Cave Wright. 3 Vols.
LIBANIUS. A. F. Norman. 2 Vols..
LUCIAN. 8 Vols. Vols. I.–V. A. M. Harmon. Vol. VI. K. Kilburn. Vols. VII.–VIII. M. D. Macleod.
LYCOPHRON. Cf. CALLIMACHUS.
LYRA GRAECA, III. J. M. Edmonds. (Vols. I.and II. have been replaced by GREEK LYRIC I. and II.)
LYSIAS. W. R. M. Lamb.
MANETHO. W. G. Waddell.
MARCUS AURELIUS. C. R. Haines.
MENANDER. W. G. Arnott. 3 Vols. Vol. I.
MINOR ATTIC ORATORS (ANTIPHON, ANDOCIDES, LYCURGUS, DEMADES, DINARCHUS, HYPERIDES). K. J. Maidment and J. O. Burtt. 2 Vols.
MUSAEUS: HERO AND LEANDER. Cf. CALLIMACHUS.
NONNOS: DIONYSIACA. W. H. D. Rouse. 3 Vols.
OPPIAN, COLLUTHUS, TRYPHIODORUS. A. W. Mair.
PAPYRI. NON-LITERARY SELECTIONS. A. S. Hunt and C. C. Edgar. 2 Vols. LITERARY SELECTIONS (Poetry). D. L. Page.

PARTHENIUS. Cf. DAPHNIS AND CHLOE.

PAUSANIAS: DESCRIPTION OF GREECE. W. H. S. Jones. 4 Vols. and Companion Vol. arranged by R. E. Wycherley.

PHILO. 10 Vols. Vols. I.–V. F. H. Colson and Rev. G. H. Whitaker. Vols. VI.–IX. F. H. Colson. Vol. X. F. H. Colson and the Rev. J. W. Earp.

PHILO: two supplementary Vols. (*Translation only.*) Ralph Marcus.

PHILOSTRATUS: THE LIFE OF APOLLONIUS OF TYANA. F. C. Conybeare. 2 Vols.

PHILOSTRATUS: IMAGINES; CALLISTRATUS: DESCRIPTIONS. A. Fairbanks.

PHILOSTRATUS and EUNAPIUS: LIVES OF THE SOPHISTS. Wilmer Cave Wright.

PINDAR. Sir J. E. Sandys.

PLATO: CHARMIDES, ALCIBIADES, HIPPARCHUS, THE LOVERS, THEAGES, MINOS and EPINOMIS. W. R. M. Lamb.

PLATO: CRATYLUS, PARMENIDES, GREATER HIPPIAS, LESSER HIPPIAS. H. N. Fowler.

PLATO: EUTHYPHRO, APOLOGY, CRITO, PHAEDO, PHAEDRUS. H. N. Fowler.

PLATO: LACHES, PROTAGORAS, MENO, EUTHYDEMUS. W. R. M. Lamb.

PLATO: LAWS. Rev. R. G. Bury. 2 Vols.

PLATO: LYSIS, SYMPOSIUM, GORGIAS. W. R. M. Lamb.

PLATO: REPUBLIC. Paul Shorey. 2 Vols.

PLATO: STATESMAN, PHILEBUS. H. N. Fowler; ION. W. R. M. Lamb.

PLATO: THEAETETUS and SOPHIST. H. N. Fowler.

PLATO: TIMAEUS, CRITIAS, CLEITOPHON, MENEXENUS, EPISTULAE. Rev. R. G. Bury.

PLOTINUS: A. H. Armstrong. 7 Vols.

PLUTARCH: MORALIA. 16 Vols. Vols. I.–V. F. C. Babbitt. Vol. VI. W. C. Helmbold. Vols. VII. and XIV. P. H. De Lacy and B. Einarson. Vol. VIII. P. A. Clement and H. B. Hoffleit. Vol. IX. E. L. Minar, Jr., F. H. Sandbach, W. C. Helmbold. Vol. X. H. N. Fowler. Vol. XI. L. Pearson and F. H. Sandbach. Vol. XII. H. Cherniss and W. C. Helmbold. Vol. XIII. 1–2. H. Cherniss. Vol. XV. F. H. Sandbach.

PLUTARCH: THE PARALLEL LIVES. B. Perrin. 11 Vols.

POLYBIUS. W. R. Paton. 6 Vols.

PROCOPIUS. H. B. Dewing. 7 Vols.

PTOLEMY: TETRABIBLOS. F. E. Robbins.

QUINTUS SMYRNAEUS. A. S. Way. Verse trans.

SEXTUS EMPIRICUS. Rev. R. G. Bury. 4 Vols.

SOPHOCLES. F. Storr. 2 Vols. Verse trans.

STRABO: GEOGRAPHY. Horace L. Jones. 8 Vols.

THEOCRITUS. Cf. GREEK BUCOLIC POETS.

THEOPHRASTUS: CHARACTERS. J. M. Edmonds. HERODAS, etc. A. D. Knox.